The IRA

Tim Pat Coogan, Ireland's most prominent journalist, is also well known as a historian, broadcaster and writer. He has appeared on television in most English-speaking countries and throughout Europe, and has written for a number of Irish, European and American publications including the *Sunday Times* and the *New York Times*. He was appointed Editor of the *Irish Press* in 1968. His first book, *Ireland Since the Rising* (1966), was the first history of that period. The original edition of *The IRA* followed in 1970 and *The Irish: a Personal View* in 1975. Tim Pat Coogan and his wife have six children and five grandchildren.

TIM PAT COOGAN

The IRA

St. Martin's Griffin
New York

THE IRA. Copyright © 1970, 1980, 1987, 1995, 2000 by Tim Pat Coogan. All rights reserved. Printed in the United States of America. For information, address St. Martin's Press, 175 Fifth Avenue, New York, N.Y. 10010.

www.stmartins.com

Library of Congress Cataloging-in-Publication Data

Coogan, Tim Pat.
  The IRA / Tim Pat Coogan.
    p.   cm.
  Includes bibliographical references and indexes.
  ISBN 978-0-312-29416-8 (trade paperback)
  1. Irish Republican Army—History. 2. Political violence—Northern Ireland. 3. Political Violence—Ireland. 4. Ireland—Politics and government—20th century. 5. Northern Ireland—Politics and government. I. Title.
  DA959 .C68   2002
  941'60824—dc23

2002279675

Our books may be purchased in bulk for promotional, educational, or business use. Please contact your local bookseller or the Macmillan Corporate and Premium Sales Department at (800) 221-7945, extension 5442, or by e-mail at MacmillanSpecialMarkets@macmillan.com.

First published in Great Britain by HarperCollins Paperbacks

Previously published by Palgrave Macmillan, a division of St. Martin's Press LLC

First St. Martin's Griffin Edition: January 2002

D 20 19 18

Dedicated to the memory of my Aunt Josephine Toal and to the friendship of John Taylor and Barbara Mullen

CONTENTS

ACKNOWLEDGEMENTS

I am under a heavy debt to a great many people for the assistance I have received in writing this book. Some, because of the nature of the subject matter, must remain anonymous; in the case of others it is inadvisable to be too explicit about who told me what. I shall, therefore, for the most part merely name them, with my sincerest gratitude for their help.

Anthony Heade, Frank Carty, Michael Traynor, Brian O'Neill, Frank Edwards, Seamus Byrne, Dan Breen, Laurence de Lacy, 'Pa' Murray, W. Roe, Pat Clare, Con Lehane, Sean MacBride, Mick Fitzpatrick, Seamus G. O'Kelly, Colonel Roger McCorley, Frank Driver, Pearse Kelly, Eoin MacNamee, the late Hugh McAteer, Paddy MacNeela, Tearlach O'Huid, Joseph Deighan, Sean O'Broin, Rory Brugha, General Sean MacEoin, Eamon MacThomas, Joseph Clarke, Charles Murphy, Eamon Boyce, Tom Mitchell, Donal Murphy, Pat O'Reegan, Myles Shevlin, Joseph Christle, Danny Donnelly, Terry O'Toole, Gerry Higganbotham, Lord and Lady Brookeborough, Noel Kavanagh, Harry Short, Stephen Hayes, Harry White, J. P. MacGuinness, Jimmy Steele, Jack Mulvenna, Roddy Connolly, J. F. Reegan, 'Micksey' Conway, Mrs Carmel O'Boyle, Lieutenant General M. J. Costello, General Michael Brennan, Jim Killeen, Jack Brady, Seamus Sorahan, Senator Gerald Boland, the late Peter Kearney, Detective Inspector James Fanning, Francis Stuart, Colonel Dan Breen, Ambrose Martin, Sean Dowling, Sammy McVicker, William McMullen, Miceal O'hAodh, Charles Gilmore, Anthony Butler, Pat Shanahan. (As Lord and Lady Brookeborough are included in this list it is probably superfluous to point out that not all the foregoing are connected with the IRA. Sadly I must also note that many, indeed most, have died. The twenty-five years since this book was first published have taken their toll.)

I am particularly indebted to the late Commandant General Tom Barry for his lengthy, handwritten reminiscence of the Civil War; to An tAthair Columcille for much research on sources and, in particular, for a long dossier on the Civil War in Co. Tipperary; to Eamon Timmoney and Seamus Ramsey for their long assessment of the border campaign; and to the family of Fergal O'Hanlon for letting me examine his diaries. If I did not always quote from the material these (and others mentioned above) supplied me with, it was invaluable as background.

For American source material, I am indebted to Joseph McGarrity's daughter, the late Mrs Elizabeth de Feo of Philadelphia; to Sister Bernard

Mary Tarpey, who has written a thesis on McGarrity; and again to the late
Eoin MacNamee and the late Harry Short. For checking references and
carrying out research, I must thank Professor Samuel Fanning and his col-
leagues at St John's University, New York, Professors Hogan and Griffith.
Attorney Charles T. Rice of New York was helpful in checking information.
My thanks are also due to Jim Ballance for much research and checking
and to the late Sean Nunan for information on the role of the Clann na Gael
in 1919–21. The late Professor Robert Stewart of the Fletcher School of
Diplomacy, Tufts University, Boston, guided my hand through the State
Department's volumes on American foreign relations that deal with war-
time Ireland. To Dr Alan J. Ward my thanks for giving me his fine paper,
'America and the Irish Problem 1899–1921' (reprinted from *Irish Historical
Studies*, March, 1968).

In London I must thank the British Museum for providing photostats of
material not available in Dublin and my friend Denis Lynch for being such a
diligent and uncomplaining consulter of files and reference works.

In Belfast the late Jack Mulvenna and Andrew Boyd were unfailingly
helpful in providing introductions or looking up information for me. The
former editor of the *Belfast Telegraph*, the late Jack Sayers, his librarian Mr
Gilbert and Mr Gilbert's successor also deserve my thanks for providing
photos and cuttings.

In Dublin I must thank my many journalistic colleagues who covered IRA
trials or inquests for giving me their impressions and, for helping me with
material and photographs, the staffs of the libraries of the *Irish Press* and the
Irish Times. For providing me with other sources and reference books the
staffs of the National Library and, in particular, of Dun Laoghaire Public
Library are entitled to my gratitude.

And particular thanks are due to Ciaran Mac An Ali, Matt Russell and
Maurice Manning for the time and care they devoted to checking the manu-
script and proofs.

The opinions expressed in the book are, of course, entirely my own responsibility.

T.P.C.

INTRODUCTION

Had anyone told me, as I came to the end of the first UK edition of this book towards the end of 1969, that it was but the first of many editions, and that a quarter of a century later, the book would be bigger than *War and Peace*, with the war more strongly in evidence than the peace, I would have replied to the effect that I had been shown the future and it did not work. Such a prospect was utterly inconceivable.

Yet, as the world knows, though the future did not work, it happened all the same. The reader will, I hope, have fathomed why by the time he or she has digested this relentlessly swelling tome of blood and violence, gallantry and squalor, cruelty and courage. To understand the IRA is to understand Ireland and the Irish; their past, and regrettably, their present.

And by Irish I do not mean merely the Irish in Ireland. The Irish diaspora is so huge that at census time in America alone, some 43 million give their ethnic origins as Irish. Readers will see for themselves what the involvement of but a fraction of the Irish-American population has meant to the story of the IRA. I believe that if a larger percentage took a constructive, constitutional interest, the resultant political pressure could bring that story to a happy ending.

I do not believe that it is the karma of the Irish and the English to forever torture each other, acting out an ancient blood feud that should long ago have ended. However, my researches have driven me to the conclusion that until an outside force helps to fill the vacuum in constitutional progress which has existed for decades within six of Ireland's North-eastern counties, that the vacuum will continue to be filled by the IRA and their mirror image Protestant paramilitary organizations.

I had come to believe that the only hope of peace was a UN presence backed by the US and EC, but the League of Nations-like cowardice and self-seeking shown over Bosnia by the international community weakened that vision. Perhaps however, the future holds a fruitful outcome to what was begun between the Irish Taoiseach, Albert Reynolds and the British Prime Minister John Major, in the shape of a far-reaching Anglo-Irish Accord that would provide a blueprint for a new and peaceful Ireland. But, pending such a blueprint, I can at least make this claim on behalf of my judgement: no other writer has devoted so much time and energy as I have to studying the IRA, and the reasons that young men and women join that organization. It is a painful story, especially painful for an Irish author.

Embattled, controversial countries like Ireland or Israel or Poland have developed a peculiar intensity of their own. They are not only nation states, but states of mind.

Unless one has allowed oneself to develop a writer's necessary detachment to the point of becoming de-sensitized, interviewing people who have been through trauma of some sort is a harrowing experience. But it is as nothing to finding that 'contacts' cease to be merely one's normal sources of information, and become the names and faces of people you have recently talked with and who have suddenly been done to death.

In the world of the IRA, its membership and its victims, such incidents may become frequent, but never commonplace. Hatred, prejudice, and their all too frequent outcome, grief and bereavement, are not lightly encountered. Even the 'lesser' traumas of the Six Counties have a searing effect; finding someone, or some family you have known, suddenly implicated in a shooting, a jailing, a knee-capping, a robbery or an arms smuggling. The pitch of intensity is far higher; the sense of personal involvement is incomparably greater.

Let me give an example of what I mean exactly as I experienced it. Early on in the troubles, shortly after the first, relatively slim edition of this book had appeared, I made contact with a Catholic West Belfast family. I normally stay in Clonard Monastery, that strategically situated oasis of kindness and hospitality between the Protestant Sandy Row and the Catholic Falls Road, run by the Redemptorist Fathers. The monastery is one of the best listening posts in Ireland.

Things were getting bad on the ground and I could see trouble ahead. I asked if Father Superior could use the monastery's contacts to arrange for me to spend a weekend with a typical Republican-minded family so that I could judge for myself what sort of people supported the IRA. Father Superior, a grave and courteous monk, acceded to my request and arranged that I be guided to Andersonstown where I would meet my hostess for the weekend. 'She was,' he informed me, 'a good lady whose uncle was a member of the Monastery Community.'

Knowing the piety of Belfast Catholics at the time, this last detail made me uneasy. As I followed the monk in the car ahead of me, I calculated that, unlike the broad-minded atmosphere of the Monastery, the 'good lady's' household would certainly expect me to go to Mass. I could, in fact, find myself in disfavour for not going to Holy Communion. I might even have to join in the family rosary that night, and a drink seemed out of the question. All of a sudden my research project did not seem such a good idea. But I resigned myself to seeing the thing through and as my guide rang the bell composed my features in what I hoped was a combination of courtesy and piety.

And then it happened: the door was opened by the 'good lady' with the uncle in the monastery. She turned out to be a beautiful blonde in her late twenties wearing a mini-skirt and halter top. While I was going through a spasm of mental readjustment that rendered me temporarily inarticulate, she bade goodnight to my guide, led me to a sofa, and inquired warmly: 'Would you like a wee go at my bush, or would you prefer something more exotic?'

Mood swing is, I understand, the correct term to describe the sensations induced by her use of the Belfast language. However it emerged that all she wanted to know was would I have a glass of the Bushmills 'Black Bush' Whiskey she was drinking, or would I prefer white rum, tequila or somesuch.

I poured a second tumbler full of 'Bush' over what remained of my shortlived hopes a little later when her husband arrived home with their three children. All girls, all favouring their mother; beautiful little blonde 'steps of stairs' aged four, three and two. They were still 'tryin' for the boy', the parents informed me. I offered to assist in this laudable endeavour. The jest and the husband's bawdy riposte, embroidering the theme that he was 'up for Sinn Fein' which he translated as 'ourselves alone', set the tone for the night of ribaldry and hospitality that followed. They had arranged a party for me. There was so much laughter and singing that I could not accept that one tall, rather shy young man, their babysitter, was also the 'OC of the Third Battalion, a real good lad. You wouldn't believe some of the things he's done.' Nor could I accept that another innocuous young chap who was pointed out as being 'dead on' had 'done in two of them'.

While I was discussing Spanish holidays with a couple who worked as spare-time marriage counsellors, a jolly, well-dressed woman was persuaded to sing. 'Her son's away,' said the marriage-counselling wife, nodding towards the singer. She meant not Spain, but Long Kesh prison. I had come to try to understand the mindset of such people, but the comfortable, semi-detached, house-proud normalcy of the surroundings militated against a grasp of the dark, brooding Belfast reality that existed outside the party – just outside it.

Next morning, as the 'good lady' prepared breakfast, the husband brought me into the garden to air our hangovers and to show me something. In the flower beds all round the house were large clear boot-prints. 'The BA,' exclaimed my host. He told me that the British Army (BA in slang) often lay under windows, listening to gain information. 'The patrol would have seen the big Southern car outside the house, heard the party, wondered what's up.'

I subsequently found out that my host was telling the truth. Lying under windows was a primitive British Army intelligence tactic in those early days of conflict. As the IRA's terror campaign intensified, things changed. The army's techniques grew more sophisticated. Electronic surveillance gadgets, a network of spies, 'supergrasses', blackmail, 'shoot-to-kill' policies, torture; all the black, unacknowledged arts of counter-insurgency were deployed.

Things changed for my hosts also. For a time their lives moved out of synch with the troubles. As the overall situation got worse theirs got better. A new house, a new business. The boy they were 'tryin' for' arrived. But for a family in West Belfast to remain unscathed by the troubles would be more remarkable than for one in the West Bank to remain untouched by the *Intifada* and what gave rise to it. Slowly, but inexorably, the situation began to engulf them. Did their Sinn Fein sympathies broaden to include some kind of IRA supportive action? The police suspected that they did, and at different times both of them were locked up and interrogated for long periods.

I played some small part in helping to secure their releases, and did what little I could to assist when new jobs and locations were called for, as various stresses, largely generated by the troubles, began to affect the family.

One undoubted bright spot on the family horizon was Sean, the boy. He had his mother's blond hair, was six feet, two inches tall and, though more gentle than either, possessing much of his parents' personalities as I remembered them when we first met: cheerful, fun-loving, hard-working, and with a good sense of humour. While he supported Sinn Fein, the political arm of the IRA, by a miracle, his temperament kept him clear of the troubles.

I was once visiting the family on a Sunday morning. The day was fine and we sat in the front garden drinking beer while lunch was being prepared. An army patrol came by, seven soldiers guarding one community policeman wearing a flak jacket. His mission was to win the minds and hearts of the people. But the Royal Ulster Constabulary are so hated in the area that he would have been killed within seconds were it not for the army escort. It reminded me of a similar doomed effort by the Americans which I had witnessed in Vietnam, the *Chieu Hoi* programme. The officer in charge of the patrol came into the garden, both ignoring us as individuals, and at the same time, sweeping the group with his rifle. After standing in the garden for five minutes, sighting his weapon at a non-existent target on the road, he left, still without saying anything. But the point was made: 'We have the guns. You can only sit out here, even if it is your own garden, because we let you.' And of course he had had a good look at the person driving the southern registered car. A commonplace, unremarkable Andersonstown incident.

It left me feeling rather angry, but Sean just smiled. Unlike most of the lads around the district, he had no knee-jerk reaction against the soldiers. Once, an uncle of his had been one of the two men in a car who blessed themselves passing a Catholic church. Two Loyalist paramilitaries who had been waiting for the Catholic passengers to identify themselves, immediately shot both men dead. Sean went to their funerals and mourned his uncle. The killings strengthened his support for Sinn Fein, but he did not join the IRA to get even.

Then, nearly three years ago, approaching his twenty-first birthday, Sean came to see me in Dublin. By then he had acquired a pretty girlfriend and a steady job driving a van. There was talk of his taking up night classes. The family troubles had not brought him down at least. He said he had something to tell me. He thought I should be the first to know because, though I had not realized it, I meant a lot to the family. I smiled deprecatingly and prepared to congratulate him on his engagement. It was not that. His news was that he was 'joinin' the 'RA'.

His decision had been triggered by the fatal shooting of a teenager, with a rubber bullet, by a member of the security forces. To me, and to most people outside Northern Ireland, it was another statistic; just one of the 3,000 death roll created since the beginning of the troubles when I had first met Sean's family. But obviously events had been carrying him towards his decision for years, as I found out when I tried to remonstrate with him.

We were alone in my 'bunker' where I write and I had plenty of time to develop my arguments. But it was point, counter-point all the way. He had no faith whatever in any events which might bring about change. 'Sure what else can you do,' he kept saying. To him the rubber bullet shooting was not an aberration, merely a continuation of conduct on the part of the security forces. Even though charges had been brought against the man responsible, he was convinced by the evidence of similar cases in the past that the culprit would beat the rap and would be emulated by his colleagues when the heat died down.

So far as he was concerned, the British were responsible for shoring up a rotten situation and would have to be forcibly driven out so that a fresh start could be made. And if the driving process involved him in killing people?

'Sure what else can you do? It's a war isn't it? People get killed in war.'

Did he realize that he might very easily be killed himself or at best get a long jail sentence?

'Sure what else can you do?'

Did he realize what effect his decision might have on his family and girlfriend?

'Ah sure they understand – they'll get over it. They know in their hearts nothin' else'll do any good.'

He seemed to regard the IRA as omnipotent. When I asked him had he thought about the career he was probably throwing away his answer was: 'Sure the 'RA'll get me a job, drivin' a black taxi or somethin'.' (Public transport did not run in the West Belfast area at that time because so many buses had been destroyed. Instead London taxis plied frequently and cheaply. The situation has changed lately with a few bus lines now running through the area.) I put it to him that he could conceivably face the worst case scenario of being captured, breaking under interrogation and then being shot by the IRA as a result.

He replied: 'Ah sure what can them ones do to you? Sure the 'RA torture you before they let you in.' (He was referring to the IRA's counter-interrogation techniques.)

By this stage he had proved himself so steadfast that I almost felt I was in some way violating his integrity. But I tried one final objection. I pointed out that though up to then he had not been 'connected' he had attended several Republican funerals and demonstrations. As a result, particularly given his family background, he must have appeared on a myriad of Special Branch videos. I told him bluntly: 'You're all wrong for a guerrilla. With your hair and your height you'll stick out like a spare prick.'

He replied: 'Ah sure the 'RA disguise you.'

And sure enough, when he called on me unexpectedly a year later, he did look different. His hair was much shorter, no longer curly, and appreciably darker. He had never been overweight, but now he seemed leaner, fitter. Instead of his normal denims he was wearing an olive-tinted khaki safari outfit and lightweight laced boots. His girlfriend was with him. If anything, she looked even prettier.

'I done that, Tim Pat,' he said.

'You don't have to tell me,' I replied, 'you're obviously an off-duty soldier. Some fucking guerrilla you are!'

We talked for a while, joking, keeping it light. But he obviously knew that I was upset. As we said goodbye he held my hand for a moment and said: 'Cheer up, Tim Pat. One of these days we'll have a pint in Belfast in . . .' He paused for a moment thinking of a suitable pub. And then this gentle young man, whom I had literally known since he was a twinkle in his mother's eye, said something that underlined the unconscious brutalization of Belfast which had brought us to this parting.

He thought of a good place. 'We'll see each other in the Corporal's Rest.' He was referring to the Belfast club so cruelly nicknamed following the lynching of two British corporals outside it. (They had been set upon by a mob after accidentally driving into a crowd attending a Republican funeral.) As he drove off, with his girlfriend gazing adoringly at him, I consoled myself with the thought that at least he had been right about one thing. His girlfriend did get over his joining the IRA. But I had been correct in my forecast about the risks he was running. A few months later I received a 'comm'.

A 'comm' is a communication from a prisoner, inscribed in block letters on cigarette papers, stuck together, folded into a tiny square, sealed in cling-film and smuggled out at visiting time. As the 'comms' are not submitted to the censor, they have to be composed when the warder is not around; and hence, apart from the materials and methodology involved, even a small one takes quite a long time to prepare. This one was above average length, four cigarette papers. It was from Sean – he and a group of other young men had been arrested on explosives charges. It began like any other letter, 'Dear Tim', and continued:

Big Sean here, reporting here from the Crum [Crumlin Road, Belfast]. Just thought I would drop you a line as things at my end are quiet at the moment . . .

He described his arrest and went on:

. . . Tim, Mary [his girlfriend] and I were only two days away from seeing you as we had planned to go to the Michael Jackson concert and call in on you. Well that's the way it goes, so if I can't talk to you face to face I will have a go at the writing . . . I was hoping to read Michael Collins, but they won't let it in in hardback. I should have read it on the outside, well I'll have plenty of time now, ha ha ha!

Things aren't too bad. I'm doubled up with a young lad from Ballymurphy. He's one of six lads that got lifted after an attack on the Brits. They are all between seventeen and twenty and all totally innocent, just like a lot of lads in here. He is eighteen and he's here a year now. His trial will come up in about ten months. When it does he'll probably walk. It's all just another form of internment.

Tim, things isn't great here. There's thirty six men on our landing. Twenty five republicans and the rest are prods, so you can picture the problems that brings. We are locked up twenty hours a day and some days we don't get out at all. Not even to empty our pots. So on those days you can get very down. We have a good structure [an IRA command structure] when we get out, but things are still very hard in here. The cells are cold, the food is bad, but our spirits are high and that's what keeps us going.

Tim, I'm up for bail next week, my ma has her hopes up, but the way the courts work here I have no chance. The RUC can get up and say whatever they want about you without any evidence, so I'm not expecting it. If the worst happens Mary and my ma will be wrecked. That's the hard thing, everybody gets effected [sic]. That's all that worries me. What a country we live in . . .

That was 1992. Sean did not get bail and is in jail at the time of writing (August 1994). It is unlikely that he will be able to pay me another visit for at least five more years. There is nothing very unusual about his case. There are thousands of young men like him in the jails of Northern Ireland. They see themselves as having been sent to a smaller prison from the larger one that formed them. Sent because they tried to change the rules by which the larger prison is run.

I do not condone the methods by which they seek to bring about change, but I understand why they try. If the Six Counties were not a sick society, Sean and his like would be sending people like me postcards from holiday resorts, or invitations to a christening – not 'comms'. My hope for the publication of this book is that it will help bring about change by peaceful means. I concluded the first edition in 1969 by quoting a letter from a defiantly cheerful young prisoner, Conor Lynch. Almost a quarter of a century later I am commencing this edition by quoting from yet another young prisoner's jail correspondence. This is not progress. 'Comms' are definitely one form of Irish literary creativity that I want to see ended.

There is no possibility of lasting peace coming to Northern Ireland while the British link remains fixed and immovable. Britain has had to pass the greatest vote of no confidence in a vassal state recorded in Western Europe since World War II ended: the abolition of its parliament because it had proved itself to be unfit to govern. Stormont, the former Belfast seat of the Protestant and Unionist dominated regime, fell in 1972, not long after I first met Sean's family. Britain has since presided over a political vacuum. There is no more stark indication that a society has failed than the presence of combat troops on the streets.

The full history of how Stormont came to be set up in the first place and how and why it went, is told in this book. In brief, however, it may be said that the Unionist regime in Northern Ireland closely resembled that of the old Boer oligarchy in South Africa. There was the same fundamentalist form of Protestantism, the same apartheid culture in which Catholics got the sanctions of the law, but not its protections. It was this denial of civil rights that finally drove young Catholics into the arms of the IRA, as it drove many young blacks into the military wing of the ANC. Unlike South Africa, however, the recognition of the need for change in Northern Ireland has not been followed by a sustained move towards sharing power and guaranteeing the position of the former Unionists within the majority culture of Catholic Ireland.

The British, after removing the Northern Ireland parliament and imposing direct rule from London, continued to assure the Unionists that they had a veto on change. So long as Protestants do not wish it, they are free to regard the rest of Ireland, in the words of one of their principal leaders, Ian Paisley, as a 'foreign country'. But a desire to remain united to Britain depends on the British people remaining united with Paisley and his like. The average Englishman wants nothing to do with 'Ulster', as they mistakenly call the Six Counties. It is inertia, combined with the political clout, and prejudice, of old blood and old money, that keeps Britain in Ireland. A combination of the

House of Lords element, many of them possessing Irish titles, and the 'Shire Tories' or 'Euro Sceptics', who not alone mistrust Dublin, but Europe into the bargain.

The tragedy is that while there is no widespread enthusiasm for staying in Ireland, lack of affection takes a long time to build into a positive policy. Meanwhile, the British Government is distracted by internal economic problems and, externally, the country's continual decline in world standing. A Ministry of Defence so strapped for cash that it has had to disband that treasured centrepiece of British military pageantry, the Coldstream Guards, cannot afford either to keep half its dwindling army in Northern Ireland, or to endure the heart being blown out of its financial district in the City of London.

Nevertheless, bereft of any leap of the political imagination, the British continue to make sporadic attempts to cobble together a short term political solution within the confines of the Six Counties. This is like trying to mend a broken leg with bandaids. Firstly, the Unionists resent being told by London that they will remain in the United Kingdom for as long as they wish while at the same time being pushed towards Dublin. Secondly, they can resist that push simply by invoking the veto which London has given them. Then, as if this Catch-22 situation were not bad enough, the motor force of the entire process (albeit a destructive one), the Republicans, the IRA and Sinn Fein, are not fully included in the peace process at the time of writing.

Dependent on the Unionists' votes in the House of Commons for survival, and influenced by the hawks in the British military estab-lishment, the Tories are hindering rather than helping the doves in Sinn Fein who brought about the IRA ceasefire of 1994. As readers will see within, when the IRA have had truces with the British before now, the interludes were not used for meaningful political dialogue (in their terms), but as an opportunity for intelligence gathering by the British, another Catch-22 situation. Sinn Fein want an end to the Unionist veto, and progress towards a post-British withdrawal Ireland. In other words, self-determination. The President of Sinn Fein, Gerry Adams, spells out how he sees this being achieved in the concluding chapter of this book. But his goals are, publicly at least, anathema to the British and not on the agenda.

This is the position at the time of writing. The hope is that, in the wake of the Downing St Declaration of December 1993 (described on page 640) that the two Prime Ministers involved, Ireland's John Bruton and Britain's John Major, may be able to overcome the obstacles and come up with a blueprint for a new Ireland which will bring Sinn Fein to the negotiating table. Although the two men are friendly the negotiations between them, which went on throughout 1994, were tough, and came close to breaking point on several occasions. Reynolds has been the one urging change, Major at times resisting because of the situation within his party.

Meanwhile, as the heads of the two sovereign governments involved cautiously edge towards an uncertain future, there is no doubt that in certain Westminster circles one will encounter a general view, based on the demographics of Northern Ireland, which can be summed up as: 'Oh Lord, make me good, but not yet. For You know that the Catholic birth rate will inevitably bring change by the year 2000 plus.' And in Dublin Irish diplomats articulate the obverse opinion, which is also widely met with in the Six Counties: 'The Brits are letting the air out of the tyres gently.' This is unquestionably the long term scenario, but it is not as optimistic or desirable as might at first appear.

Firstly, it naturally puts up Protestant paramilitary blood pressures. Secondly, the Protestants' hates and fears are also being added to by the demographic shifts within the Six Counties. Last year's census figures show that the traditional population balance has altered sharply. The seemingly permanent two thirds Protestant to one third Catholic ratio has given way to 53 per cent Protestant, 41.5 per cent Catholic, with the remainder prudently styling themselves 'others'.

These changes have encouraged the Protestant paramilitaries to go in for some pre-pre-emptive 'ethnic cleansing' before the tyres go flat. During the years 1991–3, Protestant paramilitary groups have killed more people than the IRA. There are suspicions, which for the first time, as readers will see later, I have been able to give a disquietingly authentic colouration to, that the security forces have been grooming Protestant undercover squads. The process is part of the 'Ulsteriza-tion' policy, the British equivalent of the American 'Vietnamization' policy towards the end of the war. In plain language: get the natives to do the fighting and the dirty work while the tyres slowly subside.

Too slowly, that way leads to too many deaths, too many Seans. The IRA has a practically inexhaustible source of recruitment in the high birth rate of the unemployment ravaged ghetto Catholics. And their recruitment is far from being confined to ghettos. As I write, after the longest continuous period of warfare in the Western World, the IRA is better armed, better organized and stronger than ever before. Britain is not part of the solution, it is part of the problem. Nor, as Britain claims, is the matter 'solely domestic to the UK', thus frustrating any US backed or EC backed intervention. If it is solely domestic to the UK, why do so many British politicians spend so much time trying to influence American decision takers? Why, for example, are British decision makers so hostile to President Clinton's admirable proposal to send a peace envoy to Northern Ireland? What are they afraid he or she will find there? Why was there so much British anger at Gerry Adams being granted a visa to the US? The truth is that the final push which brought the Downing St Declaration into being came from President Clinton, following intense Dublin-backed Irish-American lobbying. I share the widespread hope that the Downing St Declaration will prove to be the foundation on which a new Ireland comes into being. But if it does Britain and Ireland will need American help in bringing about peaceful change just as much as it is needed in other areas where the US has helped to broker peace settlements, notably in Jordan and the West Bank.

The Anglo-Irish problem was already old when Columbus discovered America. In so doing, he blazed a trail that millions of Irish have long since followed. It is time that we ended this quarrel, this relic of a retreating colonial glacier. Ireland is not Bosnia or Croatia. Neither the problem nor the terrain raise the same spectre of huge commitments of manpower and long term involvements. Given American support, Ireland, and England, could be at peace. Ireland and England are both mother countries. There is a time in life when parents look to their children for support. That time is now.

Tim Pat Coogan,
Dublin, August 1994

Ireland

Border ---·---·

County boundaries ----------

0 10 20 30 40 50
miles

Donegal

Derry

Derry

Antrim

Tyrone

Belfast

Fermanagh

Armagh

Down

Sligo

Monaghan

Mayo

Leitrim

Cavan

Roscommon

Louth

Longford

Galway

Meath

Galway

Westmeath

Dublin

Dublin

Offaly

Kildare

Clare

Leix

Wicklow

Carlow

Tipperary

Kilkenny

Limerick

Wexford

Kerry

Cork

Waterford

Cork

PART I

Beginnings to 1969

1

The Origins of the IRA

What is Ireland? To many people it is a green and misty isle far out in the western Atlantic. A nation of saints and scholars, of drunkards and blasphemers, of priests and publicans, of piety and machine-minded politicians. A land where Christ and Caesar are hand in glove so that churches are full, and homes empty into the migrant ships, leaving behind saddened mothers consoling themselves on the diaspora of their vast families with the three great reassurances of a peasant people – mystery, miracle and religious authority.

All of these stereotypes reflect an Ireland that can still be seen behind the facade of Cathleen Ní Houlihan's latest expression – the neon Ireland of office blocks and traffic jams, the fashionable eating places and the tourist trade. You can still find the Ireland of your choice in the pinking masses of cumuli that shift and melt into purples and greys under a blue sky over the Sugar Loaf, in the shy smile of the mantillaed girl who, unhappy in a love affair, joins the thronged congregation in Whitefriars Street Carmelite Church in Dublin to hear the priest read her petition 'that a friendship may be restored', along with other petitions seeking God's mercy on a mother suffering from an incurable illness, His help for a wife who is a dipsomaniac, or a pregnant wife's prayer that her first child be a red-haired boy. All these form a pattern forged many years ago from great issues involving conquest, land, religion and politics.

In the North Christ and Caesar are commonly – though not inevitably – honoured in roars of bigotry and defiance to the rattle of the Lambeg Drum as preachers such as the Rev. Ian Paisley call down contumely on the head of Pope and Papist whom they see as working to overthrow the constitution of Ulster and the Protestant religion, aided by a constantly cited organization known as the IRA. It is an organization which more than any other shows us what the real Ireland is like.

Why should God elicit such a different response from a congregation in Whitefriars Street Church in Dublin, the capital of Southern Ireland, and from a congregation in the Rev. Ian Paisley's
church on the Ravenhill Road in Belfast, the capital of Northern
Ireland?

To understand it is necessary to turn to Irish history and to look
particularly at the Irish Home Rule movement, the formation of the
Ulster Volunteers and the 1916 Rebellion. As taught in the South,
Irish history has tended to portray Irish revolutionary movements as
occurring in cycles which always ended in disaster until the triumphant self-immolation of the 1916 leaders, whose sacrifice and
courageous example put new heart into the Irish people, and gave
rise to an independence movement from which came liberation and
prosperity. This oversimplified view is true to a certain extent in so
far as liberation goes, but it overlooks the central fact that the 1916
Rebellion by the Irish Volunteers was in fact an armed gesture by a
body which came into being only *in reply* to an earlier gesture by the
Protestants of Northern Ireland – the formation of the Ulster
Volunteer Force to frustrate the British Liberal government's plans
to introduce Home Rule to all Ireland. Had the Protestants of the
North not acted thus Home Rule would have been passed, and it is
difficult to see what force would have existed to stage the 1916
Rebellion. It seems certain however that there would have been no
Irish Republican Army; no IRA.

The partition issue that helped to keep the IRA alive for fifty
years after 1916 dates back to the 'Plantations' begun under
James I, in which six Ulster counties in north-eastern Ireland were
handed over to 'Undertakers' to be colonized by Protestants, mainly
Scots Presbyterians. In other parts of Ireland land was also given
over to 'Planters' but in the North tenants as well as landlords were
dispossessed and the plantation was therefore most complete.

The ensuing centuries of rebellion and massacre, when Protestant
fought Catholic, were as much an effort by the native Catholic
landowners to win back their land from the usurping English and
Scots as they were religious wars, but they imparted to Irish affairs
an all-pervasive tint of religion. The most notable Protestant victory
was that of the Battle of the Boyne, 12 July 1690 (1 July in the
Julian calendar of the day), which is commemorated annually and
vigorously in Ireland today. 'Good King Billy', William of Orange,
routed James of England and enthroned in power in Ireland a

Protestant ascendancy. For long this was Anglican in character regarding Presbyterianism with only a little less disfavour than Roman Catholicism.

By the last generation of the eighteenth century a situation similar to that with which we are now familiar in Rhodesia prevailed in Ireland. There was a parliament of planters largely independent of England and equally largely indifferent to the sufferings of the Catholic peasantry whom they ruled and exploited. (This is not to say, however, that had an independent parliament ruled it might have evolved into a more democratic and equitable form of government.) Then in September 1791 a young Trinity graduate from Kildare named Theobald Wolfe Tone attempted to change the existing situation by issuing a pamphlet, *An Argument on Behalf of the Catholics in Ireland*. Tone was himself a Protestant and the pamphlet met with an immediate success. Within a month of its appearance societies of 'United Irishmen' were formed in Dublin and Belfast.

In 1795 Wolfe Tone and his fellow United Irishmen – Russell, Neilson, Simms and McCracken – stood on Cave Hill overlooking the present Stormont parliament and swore 'never to desist in our efforts until we have subverted the authority of England over our country and asserted our independence'. The United Irishmen hoped to form a 'brotherhood of affection, a communion of rites and union of power among Irishmen of every religious persuasion, and thereby to obtain a complete reform of the legislature founded on principles of political and religious liberty.'

Wolfe Tone was a gay, ardent, outgoing spirit, clearheaded and far-seeing in his political thinking. The failure of his movement was to be a tragedy for Ireland. His effort at revolt in 1798 cost him his life and set in train many consequences which have their effect on Ireland yet. First there was the Act of Union in 1800 whereby Pitt and Castlereagh linked Ireland with England, greatly to Ireland's detriment. Ireland could no longer legislate for herself under the British crown, and the hundred or so members that she sent to Westminster were able to make very little impression on an assembly of 670 when it came to matters affecting Irish interests. Irish trade and industry were discriminated against in favour of British interests throughout the nineteenth century and several evils flowed from this. The Irish system of land tenure resulted in the parcelling out of land into minute, badly worked holdings and to rack-renting by landlords, many of them absentees who did nothing to improve their lands.

Then, in the 1840s an ignorant population, grossly inflated beyond what the economy could support by the Catholic birthrate, was struck by famine and a new chapter of horror in Irish history was written.

Between 1841 and 1951 the population fell by two million people; approximately one million died, and another million emigrated. Many of these died on the way to England, Scotland or America, but enough survived to give rise to a tradition of emigration which continues to this day, and created in America the political force of the Irish Americans which subsequently provided much of the impetus and finance for Irish revolutions against England.

The Act of Union was to have three major effects. One was that by its very presence it generated a current in Irish affairs dedicated to the destruction of the act by armed force. It was this current which gave rise to Robert Emmet's rebellion in 1803, that of the Young Irelanders in 1848, and of the Fenians in 1867 whose lineal descendants, the Irish Republican Brotherhood, blossomed forth again in 1916.

The second great development was the growth of a constitutional movement for the repeal of the Union and for Home Rule. First Daniel O'Connell, then Isaac Butt, and finally Charles Stewart Parnell made repeal of the Union and Home Rule for Ireland their political platform. It was under Parnell that the constitutional and revolutionary movements began to coalesce. In 1879 he launched, through the initiative of John Devoy and Michael Davitt, a new departure whereby the revolutionary and constitutional movements met and mingled with the third force in nationalist Catholic Irish affairs, the Land League. This was begun under the ex-Fenian Michael Davitt at Irishtown, Co. Mayo, on 20 April 1879, and although it immediately fell foul of the Church – its first success was to get a parish priest, Canon Burke, to reduce his rents – the League prospered, and was a principal force in introducing the Land Acts through which by the opening of the twentieth century Irish farmers had won the 'three Fs': Fixity of Tenure, Fair Rents, and the rights of Free Sale.

This largely settled the land issue in Southern Ireland and as there were fewer Protestants than in the North conflict between Catholic and Protestant was also rare. Thus despite the fact that Parnell's fall after the O'Shea divorce scandal left the Home Rule issue in the doldrums, the South became relatively peaceful. The North, however, was less peaceful. O'Connell's Catholic agitation in the South and his conjuring up and utilization of Catholic power accelerated the drift of Protestant wealth and interest from the South to the North – the third effect of the Act of Union. Industrialists moved North, although landowners retained their holdings in the South. As the industrialists moved North, bringing with them knowledge, drive and initiative, they created jobs in the linen, shipbuilding, and rope-spinning industries which they founded. Catholics flocked to Belfast in pursuit of these jobs and sectarian feeling was aroused by their arrival.

Beginning principally with the activities of the Rev Henry Cooke, who died in 1868 and whose statue stands in Belfast today, there arose a line of Protestant clergymen agitators which stretches from Cooke to the Rev Ian Paisley in a line of unbroken turbulence. From Cooke's day on, one can date no less than seven occasions between 1857 and 1912 when Belfast was the scene of fullscale sectarian rioting resulting in tragedy, loss of innocent lives, evictions, destruction of property and an embittering of relationships between the Catholic and Protestant sects. As Emrys Jones says, in his *Social Geography of Belfast*: 'the support which was given to the extreme anti-Papist attitude of Henry Cooke was probably an expression of Protestant dismay at the great increase in the numbers of the other sect. Tensions certainly rose as their numbers increased.'

These tensions focused upon an Orange Order founded by the Protestant privileged classes 'to maintain the laws and peace of the country and the Protestant constitution' as a reply to Wolfe Tone's United Irishmen.

The Order became such a force in Northern life that its influence in jobs, politics and religion is commonly held to be all-pervasive, and at all times its intent is to divide Catholic from Protestant so that the working classes of either sect will never unite to overthrow the Protestant ascendancy. In times of peace, the Order may only be used to ensure that Catholics do not get houses or to see that the Orange Brethren circulate through the lodges such choice items of anti-Catholic propaganda as the more incautious utterances of some Southern Irish Catholic bishops.

In peacetime one only becomes publicly aware of the Orangemen when they stage their annual picturesque march on 12 July, the anniversary of the Battle of the Boyne, to commemorate 'Good King Billy' and Orange triumphs such as the routing of Catholics at the 'Battle of the Diamond' in Co. Armagh in 1795, after which the

Orangemen were encouraged to take over Catholic land. But at times of civil disturbance the Order becomes an instrument of savagery, and burnings, lootings and shootings bestrew its unlovely history.

It was to this history and this Order that the English Conservatives under Lord Randolph Churchill turned in 1886 when they seized on the issue of Home Rule for Ireland to smash Gladstone's Liberal government. Lord Randolph summed up the Conservative policy in the historic letter he wrote to his friend James Fitzgibbon: 'I have decided some time ago that if GOM [i.e. Gladstone] went for Home Rule, the Orange card would be the one to play.'

He played it in Belfast, giving to the Orangemen their still emotive slogan: 'Ulster will fight, Ulster will be right.' Gladstone, under pressure from Parnell, took up the issue and foundered under the weight of Tory opportunism and Ulster bigotry in the 1886 elections. The fall of Parnell in 1890 wrecked his Irish Parliamentary Party and years of painstaking reconciliation and manoeuvring lay ahead before the party, under John Redmond, again brought Home Rule to the edge of realization.

Herbert Asquith, the British Liberal prime minister, became dependent on the Irish Party for support against the Conservatives and attempted to implement his Home Rule pledge with such determination that the House of Lords' veto, an habitual stumbling block for Home Rule proposals emanating from the House of Commons, was removed in 1911. Once again, however, the Orange card was played.

As a result of religio-economic clashes, and the rantings of political priests the average Protestants of Ulster were conditioned to believe that Home Rule was Rome Rule, which would deliver them into the power of the Papacy, the bishops, the priests.* (To further incite these fears *circa* 1910–12 there was a controversy involving the *Ne Temere* decree promulgated in 1908, which declared that marriages between Catholics and Protestants were null and void if the children were not brought up in the Catholic religion.)

---

* The actual measure of Home Rule to be granted was quite minute. Ireland was really only to have been granted local government powers under the Crown with severe limitations to her autonomy in the spheres of law, education and finance. The king was still to rule and Westminster to control the British troops who would defend the country in time of war and the Royal Irish Constabulary would police it in time of peace, although after six years this control was to be ceded to Dublin and in peace time the Irish parliament was to make its own laws relating to law and order.

George Bernard Shaw correctly summed up the feelings of the Protestant rank and file in Ulster when he wrote:

> ... political opinion in Ulster is not a matter of tact and bluff as it is in England. No English Home Ruler has the faintest intention, in any event, of throwing actual paving stones at any English Unionist ... the Ulsterman is not like that. He is inured to violence. He has thrown stones and been hit by them. He has battered his political Opponent with fist and stick, and been battered himself in the same manner ... he has to avenge not only the massacre of St Bartholomew and the wrongs of Maria Monk, but personal insults, injuries and blood lettings of quite recent date and considerable frequency. Consequently, when he sings 'Oh God Our Help in Ages Past', he means business. And there is a strength in his rancour which lifts it above rancour.

Bonar Law, the Conservative leader, was unquestionably largely motivated by political expediency in his espousal of the Unionist cause, but he was also the son of an Ulster Presbyterian clergyman, the Rev James Law, born in Coleraine in 1822, and he was a frequent visitor to Ulster. He was not altogether indulging in mere rhetoric, when at a Unionist rally at Blenheim Palace in July 1912 he said 'I can imagine no length of resistance to which Ulster can go in which I would not be prepared to support them, and in which, in my belief, they would not be supported by the overwhelming majority of the British people.' And though the leader of the Unionists may have been a Dublin man, Edward Carson, one of the two members returned to the House of Commons for Trinity College, Dublin, he was also totally convinced that Ireland's future lay in union with England, and he advocated this view with all the forensic skill which had destroyed Oscar Wilde, and remade Archer-Shee.

It was Carson who, in 1912 standing on the steps of Craigavon, read the Ulster Covenant:

> Being convinced in our consciences that Home Rule would be disastrous to the mental well-being of Ulster as well as the whole of Ireland, subversive of our civil and religious freedom, destructive of our citizenship, and perilous to the unity of the Empire, we, whose names are under written, men of Ulster, loyal subjects of His Gracious Majesty King George V, humbly relying on the God whom our fathers in days of stress and trial confidently trusted, do hereby pledge ourselves in solemn covenant throughout this our time threatened by

calamity to stand by one another in defending for ourselves and our children our cherished position of equal citizenship in the United Kingdom, and in using all means which may be found necessary to defeat the present conspiracy to set up a Home Rule Parliament in Ireland. And in the event of such a Parliament being forced upon us we further solemnly and mutually pledge ourselves to refuse to recognize its authority. In sure confidence that God will defend the right we hereto subscribe our names. And further, we individually declare that we have not already signed this Covenant. God Save the King.

This document owed as much to memories of the Reformation and the Scottish Covenanters as it did to any loyalty to the King. Imbued with this spirit during 1912 some 471,414 people are said to have signed this Covenant, some of them with their own blood. This was the origin of the Ulster Volunteer Force.

The Unionist lawyers were not long in discovering that an anomaly in the law allowed two justices of the peace to authorize drilling and other military operations within the area of their jurisdiction, provided that the object was 'to render citizens efficient in military arts for the defence of the United Kingdom Constitution and protecting their rights and liberties under this Constitution'. Ulster justices granted licences so enthusiastically that it was possible for the Unionists to recruit, arm and drill upwards of 100,000 men. Behind them was a network of sympathizers who provided contingency plans, transportation, an army of nurses in case of war, and sufficient manpower to immobilize every bridge, road and canal in the Province. A fund of over one million pounds was set up – Rudyard Kipling sent £30,000 and the Unionists were able to call on powerful support in high places in England also, men such as F. E. Smith, Lord Charles Beresford, Lord Salisbury, James Campbell, Lord Hugh Cecil and Lord Willoughby de Broke.

Moreover the army signified its sympathy with the Ulstermen during the celebrated 'Curragh Mutiny' affair of March 1914, when a group of cavalry officers stationed at the Curragh, Co. Kildare, the largest British garrison in the south of Ireland, decided they would not engage in hostilities against the Ulster Volunteers. In fact, the Unionists had a staunch if devious champion in the very highest echelons of the army command in Sir Henry Wilson, the Director of Military Operations. Wilson was the archetype of those many senior British officers who felt that it was shocking to throw the loyalist Ulstermen to the Southern Papist wolves with their history of disrespect for the Crown and perhaps more important to the military mind, disrespect for British uniforms. Wilson openly connived with Bonar Law and supplied him with military intelligence and guidance.

Behind the Ulster Volunteer Force there was an Ulster provisional government set up by the Ulster Union Council, and this government gained some teeth by the Larne gun-running of April 1914, in which the Unionist Volunteers landed 35,000 rifles at Larne, Co. Antrim, unloaded them, distributed them and secreted them without the loss of a rifle or a single arrest. The Home Rule movement was visibly grinding to a halt.

In so far as the Liberal vacillation was concerned, Asquith was afraid that an attempt to put down the Ulster Volunteers by force might provoke a civil war in England as much as a war between the Crown and its Ulster subjects. Also he doubted, possibly with good reason, whether he had sufficient backing in English public opinion to invoke the Crown against a minority of the King's subjects whose crime was that they wished to remain under the Crown. A poem by Rudyard Kipling in the *Morning Post* articulated the sentiments of those who felt that to drive Ulster out would be wrong:

> The blood our fathers spilt
> Our love our toils our pains,
> Are counted us for guilt,
> And only bind our chains.
> Before an Empire's eyes,
> The traitor claims his price.
> What need of further lies?
> We are the sacrifice.
>
> We know the war prepared
> On every peaceful home,
> We know the hells declared
> For such as serve not Rome –
> The terror, threats, and dread
> In market, hearth, and field –
> We know, when all is said,
> We perish if we yield.
>
> Believe, we dare not boast,
> Believe, we do not fear –

> We stand to pay the cost
> In all that men hold dear.
> What answer from the North?
> One law, one land, one throne.
> If England drive us forth
> We shall not fall alone.

However it was not England that drove the Home Rule issue forth, but Germany and the onset of the First World War. John Redmond, leader of the Nationalist Party, agreed to postpone the implementation of the Home Rule Bill until after the war and there the matter rested until 1916. By then a number of things were established concerning the Irish question. One was the form Home Rule was intended to take. Another was the extent of Northern Irish resistance to it, which prior to 1916 had the important effect of raising though not defining the question of partition.

On 11 June 1912 when the Home Rule Bill discussions had reached the committee stage a Liberal MP, Agar-Robartes, had moved an amendment to exclude Antrim, Armagh, Down and Londonderry from the Bill because he said he didn't think that 'Orange bitters will mix with Irish whiskey'. The Unionists supported the amendment which was ultimately defeated, but it brought home to the Unionists the fact that effective resistance to Home Rule could only be carried on in certain Ulster counties: in fact in the six ultimately decided on, the four mentioned above, with the addition of Fermanagh and Tyrone although they have large Catholic populations.

Most importantly it also convinced a group of young men in Southern Ireland that if they wanted independence they would be better off fighting for it rather than waiting for the constitutionalists at Westminster to decide how little and how late would be the amount of Home Rule which they could enforce upon the alliance of the Orangemen and Conservatives.

These young men, and one Thomas Clarke who was not so young, were our Fenians or members of the Irish Republican Brotherhood. Padraig Pearse, Sean MacDiarmada, Joseph Plunkett and many others were to give their lives in a tradition of revolutionary activity which had flickered sporadically and unsuccessfully since Wolfe Tone's rebellion in 1798; during Robert Emmet's insurrection of 1803; the Young Irelanders' outbreak of 1848; and the abortive

Fenian uprising of 1867. The latter degenerated into a debauch of floggings and firing squads as the British scotched plans for what was intended to be a year of destiny for Ireland with an efficiency made easy by equal parts of Irish bungling and British spies.

The Fenian tradition still persists in Ireland in the form of the IRA and it merits examination. The movement was originally founded in Ireland on St Patrick's Day, 1858, by James Stephens and Thomas Clarke Luby, following the suppression of an earlier revolutionary group, the Phoenix National and Literary Society. The Phoenix Society had been set up by Jeremiah O'Donovan, better known in Irish history as O'Donovan Rossa after his birthplace at Rosscarbery, Co. Cork. Stephens and Luby called their organization the Irish Republican Brotherhood, or IRB. The American wing became known as the Clann na Gael. (In Ireland it was sometimes called 'the Organization' and sometimes the IRB.) Both wings came under the blanket description of 'Fenians' because John O'Mahony, the Clann's principal leader in America, was a man of literary tastes, who saw in the Fianna of Irish legend (who were something of a cross between the knights of the Round Table and Japanese Samurai) an appropriate title for an Irish republican organization. Stephens saw the Fenians as being part of the same revolutionary movement which had shaken the Continent but in Ireland the Fenians depended for their support on the Catholics. In America and in England, their propagandists and financial supporters were also Catholic emigrants.

The IRB's organizational plan was as follows. In each parish there was a circle of nine men, one known as the centre or leader. The county centres were elected from the parish centres and the idea was that only the centres knew each other or knew who the members of each circle were – how far in fact this was true could only be judged by having recourse to the files of the British Intelligence Corps of the time! Membership of the IRB was confined to Irishmen who were sworn to accept the organization's constitution and who were prohibited from joining any other oathbound society without its permission.

The following are key extracts from its constitution:

1. The Supreme Council of the IRB is declared to be the sole Government of the Irish Republic.
2. The President of the IRB shall be in law and in fact the President of the Irish Republic.

3. The Supreme Council being the sole Government of the Irish Republic retains the right to make treaties and declare war, and negotiate terms of peace.

Penalties for breaches of these stipulations were to be 'in accordance with the nature of offence'. These penalties were framed to include death, banishment, or lesser punishments. Sentence of death could only be carried out for treason, and then only with the permission of the Supreme Council. (Treason was defined as being disloyal to the objectives of the IRB – not to the Republic.)

In so far as the social philosophy of the Fenians' founders was concerned, it was arguably international and beyond mere separatism. Writing in his recollections of Fenians and Fenianism John O'Leary, himself a Fenian, said of O'Mahony that he was 'an advanced democrat of socialist opinions'. *The Flag of Ireland*, published in London following the suppression of the Fenians' own organ the *Irish People* in Dublin, 1865, said of the Fenians: 'It took its rise in the Latin quarter of this city when John O'Mahony, Michael Doheny and James Stephens were here in exile after 1848.' (The paper was quoting from a Paris correspondent.)

The ranks of the Catholic laity were keenly defended against Fenian recruitment by the upper echelons of the Irish Church. Some clerics went to extreme lengths in their condemnations. Bishop Moriarty of Kerry said that 'Hell was not hot enough nor Eternity long enough to punish such miscreants'. Others such as the ultra-montane Cardinal Cullen, archbishop of Dublin, saw Fenianism as a kind of Irish manifestation of Mazzini's views and opposed it by more subtle, but no less effective, methods, a pattern which continues to this day. However, in another pattern which also still exists, the Fenians found many supporters among the younger clergy, who returning for their holidays to their home towns from seminaries in which they were acquiring a Jansenistic brand of theology, found that these horned Fenians were, in fact, no more startling personages than their younger brothers, cousins and friends.

The Fenian Brotherhood displayed all the characteristics of Irishmen throughout the ages. The Fenians had colossal energy, daring, flair, suspicion, illogicality, a tendency to disunity and splits, lack of organization, courage, naivety and sometimes a high degree of shrewd commonsense coupled with an extraordinary tenacity that did occasionally bring spectacular consequences. Despite the damp squib at home Fenians were active abroad. The Fenian invasion of Canada in 1867 was a full-scale affair involving some thousands of men (predictably estimates of the numbers differ). The sailing ship *Catalpa* was chartered to sail around the world to western Australia in 1876 to rescue a group of Fenian prisoners. And it was the Fenians who commissioned the first American submarine, the *Fenian Ram*, designed by John P. Holland and launched in 1881.

The Fenian movement or off-shoots of it, such as the 'Invincibles', or members of the Clann na Gael, known as the 'Triangle', were also associated with some darker activities. To the Invincibles may be ascribed the murder of T. H. Burke and Lord Frederick Cavendish, the newly appointed chief secretary for Ireland, on 6 May 1882. It was a terrible deed and a great setback for the Irish Home Rule movement because of its effect on British public attitude. In America members of the Triangle were eventually sentenced for the murder of Dr Henry Cronin, a fellow-member of Clann na Gael who had been asking awkward questions about the misappropriation of Clann funds.

But there were other incidents which served to give both heroes and a folk memory to the movement, such as the execution of the 'Manchester Martyrs', Allen, Larkin and O'Brien, hanged in Manchester Jail for the death of a constable who was accidentally shot as a group of Fenians attempted to rescue a prisoner from a police van. (It was their deaths which inspired the ballad 'The Smashing of The Van', which I first heard sung by Brendan Behan, who had himself walked in the footsteps of the Fenians.)

On the heroic side also the Fenian movement gave tradition such figures as that of O'Donovan Rossa. Arrested in 1865 on the suppression of the *Irish People*, of which he was business manager, he was sentenced to life imprisonment on 13 December 1865. He was released on 5 January 1871 after experiences in various British prisons that were authenticated by the Devon Commission. These included having had his hands handcuffed behind his back for thirty-five days in Chatham Jail, and being kept naked day and night on a punishment diet of bread and water, in solitary confinement in a darkened cell, because of his intransigent attitude towards his jailers – an attitude which many Republican prisoners afterwards attempted to emulate.

After his release Rossa went to America and became a prominent member of the Clann na Gael, and one of the prime movers behind the 'dynamite campaign', a series of dynamitings carried out by young Irishmen throughout England for approximately two years beginning in 1883. Like its later offshoot, the IRA bombing campaign in England of 1939, the dynamiting campaign seemed to end with small loss of life, the alienation of English public opinion, and the imprisonment of a number of patriotic young Irishmen, with no other effect than to embitter them and deprive their friends and families of their company and support.

But when an amnesty was granted to the Fenian prisoners in 1898 one such young man emerged from jail determined that this would not be the full story. Following the amnesty Thomas Clarke went to New York, but he returned to Ireland in 1907 because foreseeing a European war he decided that a time was coming when John Mitchel's doctrine 'that Ireland's opportunity would come when England was in difficulty' might have a chance to prove itself.*

In the colonial Ireland to which Clarke returned opportunities for revolution were few. Free primary school education was widespread throughout the country, County Councils and Urban District Councils were controlled by members elected by the Irish themselves by democratic franchise and generally supported the Irish Party. Tenant farmers were buying back their holdings from the landlords by a system of annuities payable to the British government which had compensated the landlords in the first place. Granted, slum conditions in Dublin were appalling – twenty thousand families were living in one room each according to a survey in 1910, and the infant mortality was 142 per thousand as compared with 103 in London – but the bulk of the country was peaceful. Men of Clarke's generation in the IRB did little for the movement beyond talk of the old days which grew more heroic with each telling.

However a group of young men – Denis MacCullagh, P. S. O'Hegarty and Bulmer Hobson – had been active in the north in setting up Dungannon Clubs, called after the town in Co. Tyrone where the Irish Volunteers were founded in 1782. These literary and debating clubs were a cloak for IRB activities which consisted of little more than preaching separatism and republicanism and introducing new recruits to the writing of other authors of either a revolutionary or nationalistic nature – the Republican and separatist Wolfe Tone,

---

* John Mitchel, the leading polemicist of the 1848 militants, had outlined his theory in his paper the *United Irishman*. The idea of striking at England while she was preoccupied with war was used again in 1939 when Sean Russell master-minded the IRA's bombing campaign against England.

John Mitchel, nationalists Charles Kickham, who had edited the Fenian newspaper the *Irish People* and Thomas Davis the leader of the Young Irelanders of the 1840s. The poetry of Eithne Carbery and Alice Milligan and James Fintan Lalor's writings on the land issue all helped towards creating a body of opinion, however small, in favour of staging a rising against the British.

This opinion was shared by very few people outside IRB circles, and though they had a newspaper, *Irish Freedom*, Clarke and the young IRB men cannot have had more than a handful of active members spread throughout the country at the onset of the Ulster crisis. None the less using the Communist tactic of infiltration they had manipulated themselves into positions of influence in a number of what might be termed 'Irish Ireland Societies' – notably the Gaelic League and the Gaelic Athletic Association, both of which had a nation-wide following by 1912. They were non-sectarian (the Gaelic League in fact was founded by a Protestant, Douglas Hyde) and in the period of relative peace and prosperity that followed Parnell's death these associations combined with the influence of the Abbey Theatre and W. B. Yeats to arouse a very definite awareness among young people of a distinctively Irish culture and identity.

The IRB seized its chance to capitalize on this sense of identity when Eoin MacNeill, vice-president of the Gaelic League, wrote an article in the organ of the Gaelic League, *An Claidheamh Soluis* in October 1913, proposing that a body of Southern Volunteers be formed on the same line as the Ulster Volunteers. Using the respected name of MacNeill as a front, the IRB organized a meeting to which all parties were invited, at the Rotunda Hall, Dublin, on 25 November. At the meeting MacNeill said: '. . . the more genuine and successful the local Volunteer Movement in Ulster becomes, the more completely does it establish the principle that Irishmen have the right to decide and govern their own national affairs. We have nothing to fear from the existing Volunteers in Ulster nor they from us. We gladly acknowledge the evident truth that they have opened the way for a National Volunteer Movement . . .'

It was put to the meeting that the formation of the Southern Volunteers was a reply to the course of action 'deliberately adopted by one of the great English Parties . . . to make a display of military force, and a menace of armed violence the determining factor in the future relations between this country and Great Britain'.

Unlike the Ulster Force which was unified in a single aim under the discipline of regular British army officers the Volunteers suffered from conflicting motives behind their creation and different views as to who should control them.

MacNeill and the vast bulk of those who joined believed, until the 1916 Rising, that the Volunteers would only be used to fight if by some chance the Conservatives and Orangemen were to use the UVF to attempt to frustrate the introduction of Home Rule. Redmond insisted that the Volunteers should be controlled, at least in part, by himself, not wishing an armed force to spring up in Ireland, and thus jeopardize the prospect of Home Rule. The Volunteers split after he made a recruiting speech in favour of the British army at Woodenbridge in September 1914 leaving the Republican element in control of approximately 10,000 men against Redmond's estimated 170,000. Next, on the very eve of the 1916 Rising itself there were splits, postponements and the capture of arms being sent from Germany at the instigation of Clann na Gael and Sir Roger Casement, who paid with his life on the scaffold for his enterprise. These setbacks nearly doomed the movement to failure and Eoin MacNeill, learning at the last moment of the IRB's plans for rebellion, countermanded their orders for a mobilization of Volunteers on Easter Sunday. Consequently when the Volunteers marched out to challenge the might of the British Empire on Easter Monday, 24 April 1916, under the leadership of Padraig H. Pearse, poet, schoolteacher and principal source of inspiration of Republicans thereafter, the total force comprised roughly 1,200 Volunteers and members of James Connolly's Citizen Army.

This army had been founded by Captain Jack White, a son of White of Ladysmith fame, to defend the workers in the great 1913 lockout in which the strikers were finally defeated, forcing their leader James Larkin to emigrate to America. However, Connolly stayed, having succeeded Larkin as head of the Irish Transport and General Workers Union, and having himself founded in 1896 the Irish Socialist Republican Party. (In 1903, while living in America he was to become a co-founder of the International Workers League.)

However Connolly himself would never have got much widespread support had the revolution of 1916 been confined to his followers only. In a small-farmer economy, strongly influenced by the Church, the emasculated Labour Party which succeeded him had to expend so much of its time assuring the hierarchy that it wasn't Communist that it never even gave the appearance of being likely to form a government until, after Pope John, its leaders felt it safe to declare that the Labour Party was in favour of socialism and a workers' republic and as a result was beaten badly in the elections of June 1969. Nevertheless by 1916 Connolly's continual incitements to riot and rebellion were such an embarrassment to the IRB's plans that it co-opted him onto the Supreme Council, and he, with Joseph Plunkett, worked out the plans for the Rising of 24 April.

There is no need to go into the oft-told story of the events of that week. The insurgents fought with a typical Irish gallantry, attacked by soldiers using artillery and outnumbering them twenty to one. Cut off from all possible support from the country, or from reinforcement of any kind, they held out for almost a week, during which Dublin was badly damaged and over three thousand people died. The leaders knew their rising was bound to fail, but they were prepared to barter their lives against the possibilities of their various dreams coming true after their deaths.

Some, such as Pearse, Plunkett and MacDiarmada wanted to set up an Ireland that would be 'not merely free but Gaelic as well, not merely Gaelic but free as well'. In so far as his anti-British separatist feelings went Clarke was still the same young man who had gone to jail nearly thirty years earlier. Connolly, a long-time exponent of force, also hoped for the dawning of a socialist republic that would guarantee equality of opportunity to every citizen. Other activists, such as sixteen-year-old Sean Lemass, a strange mixture of idealist and ruth-less political opportunist, who later became a successful Irish prime minister and principal architect of Southern Ireland's industrial drive, merely wanted to carry on the tradition of a rising in every generation, a tradition which had lapsed in their parents' generation because of the Conservative policy of 'killing Home Rule by kindness', a carrot and stick policy of ameliorative and coercive legislation.

All found their aspirations expressed in large measure in the 'Dec-laration of the Republic' drawn up by Pearse and Connolly and read outside the General Post Office on the morning that the Rising began.

Poblacht na h-Eireann

The Provincial Government
of the
IRISH REPUBLIC
TO THE PEOPLE OF IRELAND

Irishmen and Irishwomen: In the name of God and of the dead genera-tions from which she receives her old tradition of nationhood, Ireland, through us, summons her children to her flag and strikes for her freedom.

Having organized and trained her manhood through her secret revolutionary organization, the Irish Republican Brotherhood, and through her open military organizations, the Irish Volunteers and the Irish Citizen Army, having patiently perfected her discipline, having resolutely waited for the right moment to reveal itself, she now seizes that moment and, supported by her exiled children in America and by gallant allies in Europe, but relying in the first on her own strength, she strikes in full confidence of victory.

We declare the right of the people of Ireland to the ownership of Ireland and to the unfettered control of Irish destinies, to be sovereign and indefeasible. The long usurpation of that right by a foreign people and government has not extinguished the right, nor can it ever be extinguished except by the destruction of the Irish people. In every generation the Irish people have asserted their right to national freedom and sovereignty: six times during the past three hundred years they have asserted it in arms. Standing on that fundamental right and again asserting it in arms in the face of the world, we hereby proclaim the Irish Republic as a Sovereign Independent State, and we pledge our lives and the lives of our comrades-in-arms to the cause of its freedom, of its welfare and of its exaltation among the nations.

The Irish Republic is entitled to, and hereby claims, the allegiance of every Irishman and Irishwoman. The Republic guarantees religious and civil liberty, equal rights and equal opportunities to all its citizens, and declares its resolve to pursue the happiness and prosperity of the whole nation and of all its parts, cherishing all the children of the nation equally, and oblivious of the differences, carefully fostered by an alien government, which have divided a minority from the majority in the past.

Until our arms have brought the opportune moment for the establishing of a permanent national Government, representative of the whole people of Ireland, and elected by the suffrages of all her men and women, the Provisional Government, hereby constituted, will administer the civil and military affairs of the Republic in trust for the people. We place the cause of the Irish Republic under the protection of the Most High God, Whose blessing we invoke upon our arms, and we pray that no one who serves that cause will dishonour it by cowardice, inhumanity or rapine. In this supreme hour the Irish nation must, by its valour and discipline, and by the readiness of its children to sacrifice themselves for the common good, prove itself worthy of the august destiny to which it is called.

Signed on Behalf of the Provisional Government,

Thomas J. Clarke

Sean MacDiarmada	Thomas MacDonagh
P. H. Pearse	Eamonn Ceannt
James Connolly	Joseph Plunkett

It will be seen that this document, which has subsequently become the Magna Carta of all Irish Republicans, North or South, whether constitutionalists or not, was irreconcilably opposed to the claims of the signatories of the Ulster Covenant. The proclamation of 1916 expressed a distillation of the traditions and hopes of Catholic Ireland, leavened by Connolly's socialism, and asserted independence from England, equality of opportunity, and sovereignty over the whole country. The Ulster Covenant of 1912 spoke for Protestant Ireland, descendants of English and Scottish settlers. Its signatories wished to maintain their link with the Crown with all its consequent liberties and safeguards. To the Northerners 'equality of opportunity' in the Southern document meant putting the Catholics in a position from which they could overthrow Protestant hegemony. And in fact, revolution, time and the Catholic birth rate did do just this. In the North the Protestants circumvented the Catholic birth rate by gerrymandering the electoral system, and a policy of discrimination in employment whereby the Catholic and Protestant ratios remained almost static from the time the northern state was set up in 1920 to the time of writing. To the Northerner the proposed Irish Republic was a cloak for 'Catholic authoritarianism'. To the Catholic 'Protestant liberties' meant Catholic enslavement. It is an interpretation of terminology on which the Irish are still far from agreement.

After the 1916 Rising events took their predictable course. Great roaring fires of patriotism banked up as the British executed the principal leaders of the revolt, imprisoned others, imposed martial law, and hanged Sir Roger Casement in August, long after any danger of another Easter Rising had passed.

British efforts to arrest the development of events were swept aside. An attempt, shortly after the Rising, to forge an agreement between Carson and Redmond on the introduction of Home Rule, with the exclusion of the northern counties until after the war, broke down.

In this new atmosphere public opinion began to focus on the prisoners in English jails. The uncommon-sounding name de Valera, elected leader of the prisoners in Dartmoor, and the last commandant to surrender in Easter Week, became familiar. In Ireland people began to turn their eyes away from Westminster and to examine the doctrines of Sinn Fein, founded in 1905 by Arthur Griffith, who was neither Republican nor a revolutionary. In social and economic matters he was inclined to capitalism, believing in protection and condemning strikes. He was influenced by the writings of Deak, a Hungarian patriot, and saw a link between Hungary and Austria and Ireland and Britain. Griffith proposed that the Irish members withdraw from Westminster, rejecting that parliament's claim to legislate for internal Irish affairs. He advocated a dual monarchy similar to that of Austro-Hungary, in which the British monarch would act as king of Ireland and England, with separate parliaments in both countries – in effect restoring the pre-Act of Union position in Ireland.

In February 1917 a by-election fell due in Co. Roscommon and Count Plunkett, father of the executed Rising leader Joseph Plunkett, was elected on a platform of non-recognition of the British parliament. Using the banner of a monarchist he inspired the party to press a demand for the implementation of the 1916 declaration of an all Ireland republic. In May Sinn Fein won another seat when a prisoner in Lewes Jail, Joseph McGuinness, was elected in a campaign during which the Sinn Fein supporters largely based their appeal on 'putting him in to get him out', and overruled the appeals of the Irish Parliamentary Party veteran Joseph Devlin, a Belfast man who could see the difficulties of implementing the Sinn Fein policy and warned the electorate that Sinn Fein stood for 'a hopeless fight for an Irish Republic'. In June and August the two men who were to lead the political struggle on opposite sides of the fence in post-Civil War Ireland, William T. Cosgrave and Eamon de Valera, were elected for Kilkenny and Clare.

Behind the scenes IRB organizers, principally Michael Collins and Thomas Ashe, both of whom had taken part in the 1916 Rising, were directing this activity as they went about the country reorganizing the IRB and enlisting more and more young Irishmen in a volunteer army sworn to fight for an Irish republic. Ashe was arrested and died of forcible feeding while on hunger strike. Collins, a guerrilla chieftain of Mao-like stature, escaped the net, and day by day the Volunteers grew stronger, drilling more openly and waving tricolours. The clang of prison doors on the ever increasing numbers of young rebels picked up under the Defence of the Realm Act (DORA) failed to drown the defiantly swelling chorus of 'Up the Republic'.

A Lloyd George-inspired Irish convention set up to frame proposals for Irish self-government within the British Empire on 25 July 1917 was boycotted by both Sinn Fein and Labour on the grounds that its membership was representative neither of Sinn Fein nor of post-revolutionary Irish sentiment. Sinn Fein held its own convention (known in Irish as an 'Ard-Fheis') at the Mansion House in Dublin on 25 October, and de Valera was elected president of Sinn Fein. Then on 16 April 1918, the British delivered the initiative to the Sinn Feiners by passing the Conscription Act. The Irish Party immediately withdrew in protest. The party then joined Sinn Fein and Labour in drawing up a joint anti-conscription pledge which was signed, with a solidarity like that accorded to the Ulster Covenant, at church doors following Sunday Masses. Even the Catholic hierarchy denounced conscription, a major shift in authoritative opinion as prior to the 1916 Rising Cardinal Logue's name had appeared on recruiting posters urging young Southern Irishmen to join the British army. To compound this error of judgement on 19 May the British authorities cooked up 'a German plot' and used it as an excuse to arrest Griffith, de Valera and many other prominent Sinn Fein leaders.

The election of 14 December 1918 completely discredited parliamentarianism on the old British model. Redmond's party won only six seats, and over a hundred years of Irish political development disappeared, taking with it Redmond's health, happiness, and, most unfairly, his reputation, which deserves to stand high with Irishmen. The newly elected Sinn Fein deputies held their first Dail (parliament) on 21 January 1919 in Dublin. This revolutionary parliament was not, of course, recognized by the British. Thirty-six of its seventy-three members were in jail, including de Valera, but it appointed delegates to the peace conference in Versailles and it adopted a 'Democratic Programme' based on the proclamation of Easter Week, watering down James Connolly's socialistic principles, but retaining the 1916 proclamation's demand for an all-Ireland republic. (To some members of the IRB its constitution meant that the Irish republic was in fact established before 1916 and had existed *de jure* if not *de facto* since James Stephens had set up a provisional government in February 1867 to take command of the revolution which failed to take place the following March.)

The IRB had joined Sinn Fein seeing it only as another nationalist society that might help its aims. But at the Sinn Fein convention of October 1917, working towards an Irish republic within a political party which advocated setting up a king in Ireland, the IRB agreed to frame an article in the Sinn Fein convention declaring the movement's aim to be the securing of international recognition of Ireland as an independent Irish republic. The Irish people would then 'by Referendum freely choose their own form of Government'.

Constitutionally therefore the party kept its options open on the form of settlement it was prepared to make with England. In character however it was becoming a markedly republican organization. Parallel to the rebirth of Sinn Fein after 1916 there occurred the reorganization of the Volunteers, formed to defend Home Rule but now directed by IRB men such as Collins and Richard Mulcahy. By 1918 the August issue of *An tOglach*, the Volunteer organ, could declare that 'The Irish Volunteers are the Army of the Irish Republic'.

The Volunteers however had their own executive and constitution, and though there was some overlapping of membership between individual volunteers and other national organizations they had a largely autonomous existence from Sinn Fein and the Dail. The first shooting of policemen, for instance, was not sanctioned by the Dail. It took place at Soloheadbeag, Co. Tipperary, on the day the first Dail met. A number of volunteers, led by Sean Treacy and Dan Breen, decided to strike a blow for Ireland and shot two policemen dead in a hold-up for gelignite.

The attitude of many rural volunteers, who subsequently took action like that of Breen and Treacy, was summarized in a remark made to me by one of the most famous guerrilla leaders – Tom Barry – who said of the Volunteers' relationship with headquarters, 'if we pulled off some action that worked they sanctioned it'.

However, this fairly typical reaction of the man in the field to a GHQ anywhere does not minimize the fact that GHQ did co-ordinate policies which emerged from leaders in the field, such as Liam Lynch who advocated the mass destruction of RUC barracks, or Dick McKee who thought up the flying columns, small highly mobile groups of guerrillas, or Collins himself who originated the most effective weapon of all, the destruction of the network of spies which the British used as their eyes and ears in keeping control of the country.

Throughout the course of the Anglo-Irish War the Volunteers and the Sinn Fein party pursued separate though complementary courses of action. Sinn Fein gradually took juridical control of the many county councils, setting up courts and settling land disputes, and the Volunteers sought to achieve military supremacy where they could.

During all this period the question of the Dail's control of the Volunteers remained one of some doubt and even controversy, partially through the antipathy which some members of the cabinet,

notably Cathal Brugha and Austin Stack, felt towards Collins in particular, and the idea of secret societies generally. Brugha had left the
IRB after the 1916 Rising, as had the 'Priomh Aire' or First Minister
of Dail Eireann, Eamon de Valera, and after his election as minister
for defence in the First Dail Brugha sought to bring the Volunteers
under Dail control. Collins rejected the idea of trying to run an army
under a civilian council. (Michael Collins was president of the IRB,
the Dail's minister for finance, the Volunteers' director of intelligence
and adjutant-general.) The clearest statement of the position, which
de Valera felt free to make a few months after the setting up of the
Dail, was a statement to the Dail on 10 April that the 'Minister for
Defence is of course in close association with the Voluntary military
forces which are the foundation of the National Army' – 'in close
association with' only, not 'in control of'.

Brugha, who disliked and mistrusted Collins, tried again on
20 August when he proposed to the Dail that Volunteers and Dail
deputies alike should take an oath 'to support and defend the Irish
Republic and the Government of the Irish Republic, which is Dail
Eireann against all enemies, foreign and domestic, and I will bear
true faith and allegiance to the same'. Arthur Griffith, acting in place
of de Valera, who had gone to America on a publicity tour, backed
the proposal and the Dail approved the oath. However under pressure of the military situation the Volunteers never made a similar
formal acceptance of the oath. The individual commanders were left
to discuss it with their troops, most of whom, in the light of their
subsequent alignments during the Civil War, seem to have decided in
favour of the oath.

The IRB in secret session amended its constitution to delete its
claim that the president of the IRB was also president of the Irish
Republic, and to recognize that the Dail set up as a result of IRB
policy was a 'duly elected public authority competent to declare the
will of the Irish people'.

But still the issue of autonomy of the Volunteers persisted. It was
not until March 1921, only a few months before the truce which
ended the Anglo-Irish hostilities, that the Dail agreed with de Valera
that the Dail should take public responsibility for the Volunteers'
military actions, and formally accept the fact that a state of war
existed. It was left to him to issue a statement to this effect saying
that the Volunteers were 'under the Civil Control of elected representatives, and that their officers held their commissions from these

representatives. The Government therefore is responsible for the actions of this army.'

During the course of the war, backed by a sympathetic population, the IRA, as the Volunteers became known after the first Dail, carried out a campaign of ambushing, raiding police barracks, and inflicting casualties which were estimated, between the time of the sitting of the first Dail and the truce, at 600 killed, and 1,200 wounded on the British side, and 752 IRA men killed and 866 wounded. In the South these incidents were coupled with midnight police searches, martial law and a fear and tension which were grim enough, but as nothing compared to the situation in the North. There the IRA, being fewer in number and relying almost exclusively on Catholics for recruits, was unable to make much progress. The sectarian question continually threw itself across the path of the conflict in the north-east. Derry was the scene of a fierce Protestant onslaught on the Catholic quarter on 19 July 1920 after Carson made a speech at an Orange celebration on the 12th, during which he said, 'I am sick of words without action'. The rioters carried the Union Jack and were not halted by the military over the five-day period during which looting and street fighting went on unabated. When the military did intervene, it was to fire on IRA men who were standing guard on Catholic property.

Other Ulster towns had a similar story. In Belfast, after prominent Unionists had addressed Protestant workers in the Belfast shipyards on 12 July, calling for a 'show of revolvers' to drive the 'Fenians' out, an orgy of looting, shooting and petrol bombing broke out. Catholic workers were driven out of the shipyards, homes were burned and, again, the military did not offer protection to the beleaguered Catholics. Commenting on these incidents in a report to the *Westminster Gazette* in London on 24 July 1920, a correspondent wrote: 'It is common knowledge in Belfast and had frequently been admitted by individual Unionists, that plans were matured at least two months ago to drive all the Home Rule workers in the shipyards out of their employment.'

The steps towards the truce were initiated in a conciliatory speech which King George V made at the Stormont parliament which he opened on the coming into force of the Government of Ireland Act on 3 May 1920. What this act did in real terms was to recognize that there was in Ireland a large Protestant element in the North who did not want to be governed by the South and, in fact, it effectively partitioned the country from that time on. Under the act, by which Northern Ireland is still governed, the South was to send thirty-three members to Westminster and to have 128 members in a Dublin parliament. The North was to send representatives to Westminster and to have its own parliament. Both Irish parliaments were to have senates. However, the Dail refused to recognize the elections for the Southern senate because the act entitled the Crown to nominate some of the members. It regarded the elections for the lower house as being held for the second Dail, not for the Dublin parliament. In the South, the 124 Sinn Fein candidates were returned unopposed, the only non-nationalist candidates being the four senate members for Trinity who were unopposed. When the Dublin parliament opened, on 28 June, only the Trinity representatives and the Crown-nominated senators turned up. This 'parliament' sat for fifteen minutes and was adjourned *sine die*.

This act was both a tragedy and a triumph for the Unionists, a triumph because it prevented them from being placed under any Dublin government in the future, a tragedy because the North wanted Ireland partitioned no more than the South. However, partitioned it was and the treaty which the Irish negotiators signed with the British on 6 December 1921 accepted this fact.

How strongly extremist Republican feeling ran against the treaty may be gauged from Brugha's speech against it on the day he left the Dail, never to return:

> If instead of being so strong, our last cartridge had been spent and our last man was lying on the ground and his enemies howling round him and their bayonets raised, ready to plunge them into his body, that man should say – true to the traditions handed down – if they said to him: 'Now will you come into the Empire?' – he should say, and he would say: 'No, I will not.' That is the spirit which has lasted all through the centuries and you people in favour of the Treaty know that the British Government and the British Empire will have gone down before that spirit dies out in Ireland.

The treaty set up an Irish Free State, as a self-governing dominion of the British Empire, with the same constitutional status as Canada, Australia, New Zealand and South Africa.

A representative of the Crown was to be appointed in the same way as a dominion governor-general and the members of the Irish parliament were to take an oath of allegiance to the constitution of the Irish

Free State which pledged them to 'be faithful to His Majesty King George V, his heirs and successors'. The Free State was to assume responsibility for part of the United Kingdom's public debt, yield certain defence facilities to the British forces and in time of war give whatever assurance might be required by the British.

Furthermore, the treaty granted to Northern Ireland the right to withdraw from the jurisdiction of the Dublin parliament. Of these provisions, the oath, partition and the office of the governor-general were clearly incompatible with the republican aspiration of the nationalist movement and the affection with which Collins regarded it may be seen from his prophetic statement that he was signing his own death warrant. He felt, however, that it was the best 'stepping stone' as he put it, that could be got for the time being towards a full republic.

Moreover, while to the public mind the IRA seemed all-powerful the guerrillas were in fact almost at the end of their tether. Losses had been heavy and arms were running dangerously short; the nearest landmass to the Irish was that of their enemy, England, and all military and other supplies had to run the gauntlet of British ships. Once the truce was signed and the IRA lost the momentum and anonymity which had been among its greatest assets in the struggle, any attempt to restart the war would have been disastrous.

The treaty was ratified by the Dail on 7 January 1922, by sixty-four votes to fifty-seven, and an administration was formed three days later led by Arthur Griffith. The constitutional opponents of the treaty, including de Valera, Austin Stack, Cathal Brugha, Robert Barton and Erskine Childers, left the Dail in protest. Outside the Dail the Church, big business, labour and a large proportion of the general public supported the treaty and peace. Opposed to it were the deputies who had left the Dail under de Valera, a high proportion of the IRA and the women's organization Cumann na mBan, an auxiliary of the IRA.

The great polemicist on the Republican side was Erskine Childers, and his influence coupled with that of the women deputies led to those who supported de Valera becoming derisively tagged as 'The Women and Childers Party'. He was not as influential on the Republican side as the pro-treaties supposed as they winced under his barbs,* but in addition to his polemics they blamed him for using his

---

* Childers' high-pitched polemical style continued to be emulated by Republican controversialists down the years and even today the style of the *United Irishman* is evocative of that employed by Childers in the broadsheets which he turned out against the treaty and its upholders.

influence with his cousin Barton who had signed the treaty later to reject it, and for having much to do with influencing de Valera's attitude also. Consequently when he was captured during the Civil War he was executed on a trumped-up charge of being in possession of arms – a revolver given to him by Michael Collins.

But it was not the de Valera faction or the constitutional group which now proceeded to make the running against the wealthy. This opposition came mostly from the advocates of physical force – young men who had sworn an oath to an Irish Republic. Their leaders were men such as Liam Lynch (the only member of the Supreme Council of the IRB to vote against the treaty), Tom Barry, Rory O'Connor, Liam Mellows, Sean Deasy, Joseph McKelvey, Eaman O'Malley, Sean Moylan, Sean Dowling, Peadar O'Donnell, George Gilmore, Maurice Twomey, Sean Russell, Sean MacBride and many others.

Though the Irish Civil War like any civil war was a terrible business it was not an unmitigated evil. At first sight it might appear difficult to see how this might be. Reports of deaths and damage so fill the columns of contemporary newspapers that little space remains for other news. The bill in money for the cost of the war was probably £20 million, in deaths approximately 700 and in long-term effect the embittering of Southern political life has still not entirely run its course. But at the same time a democratic two-party system did emerge from the Civil War as first the victorious and then the vanquished formed political parties, and above all the Civil War, centring as it did on the refusal of young men who had taken an oath to an Irish Republic to accept anything else, diverted Southern energies from the possibility of a North-South, Orange against Catholic conflict which would have been much greater in scale and horror, and which would also have inevitably brought in the British again on the side of the North. (As matters turned out the Conservative-Unionist section of the British cabinet so disliked the treaty that everyone who signed it was out of office in four years.)

Inevitably, also, given the Northern background, sectarian strife did break out in places and neither police nor army did very much to help the Catholics. Sir Henry Wilson was so active in his unofficial post as military adviser to the Northern Irish government that Collins had him shot dead in June 1922 on the steps of his London home by two former British servicemen named Dunne and Sullivan. This shooting was held by Republicans to be the precipitating factor of the Civil War, but in fact a state of virtual civil war had existed for some time earlier. From February and March of 1922 groups of Republicans, most notably those in the South who gave, nominally at any rate, allegiance to Liam Lynch, and those in Dublin who followed Rory O'Connor, were conducting operations of a paramilitary nature to obtain funds either to maintain the troops or the republic – the staffs of the various post offices and banks which involuntarily provided the money were never quite clear which.

Attempts to bring the IRA into line with the Dail failed when the cabinet refused to sanction an army convention timed for 15 March lest it lead to the setting up of an army dictatorship. General Mulcahy suggested on 20 March that a joint council be set up 'to frame definite proposals for associating the IRA with the government elected by the Irish people'. The militants' acceptance of this proposal was conditional on a provision which the cabinet found totally unacceptable: that recruiting for the new Irish police force, an unarmed body known as the Civic Guard, be suspended.

Following this the militants made a clean break with the cabinet section. And on 23 March a manifesto signed by leading anti-treaty IRA men appeared in the public press summoning the convention for 26 March in defiance of the cabinet's order. At a press conference on 23 March, Rory O'Connor said 'that the Army would not obey President Griffith' because 'he had violated his oath'. He said that there was no government in Ireland to which the army gave allegiance, that the holding of the convention meant that 'we repudiate the Dail' and he announced the setting-up of an executive which would issue orders to the IRA all over the country. In response to a question as to whether this betokened a military dictatorship he said, 'You can take it that way if you like'.

The convention was duly held at the Mansion House in Dublin on 26 March. Only anti-treaty men attended, and the meeting unanimously reaffirmed allegiance to the republic, and placed its forces under the supreme control of an executive to be appointed by the convention. It adjourned when a new constitution was drawn up stipulating that:

The Army shall be known as the Irish Republican Army. It shall be on a purely volunteer Army basis. Its objects shall be:
1. To safeguard the honour and maintain the independence of the Irish Republic.

2. To protect the rights and liberties common to the people of Ireland.
3. To place its services at the disposal of an established Republican Government which faithfully upholds the above objects.

A sixteen-man executive was chosen and it was to this body that the anti-treaty Volunteers were to subsequently hold themselves responsible. The executive established an Army Council, composed of Liam Lynch, chief of staff of the Irish Republican Army; Joseph McKelvey, deputy chief of staff; F. O'Donoghue, adjutant general; Eamon O'Malley, director of organization; Joseph Griffin, director of intelligence; Liam Mellows, quartermaster-general; Rory O'Connor, Seamus O'Donovan and Sean Russell, directors of engineering, chemicals and ammunitions.

On 13 April this council decided to occupy a number of strong points in Dublin, the principal one of which was the Four Courts, the seat of juridical control in Ireland. There ensued a confused dangerous period with barracks being seized around the country, banks being raided, people being shot, and in the South an effort by the Four Courts garrison to countermand the authority of the constitutional authorities. These derived their authority as follows: as required by the treaty the Southern parliament met on 14 January 1922. This parliament was composed of the sixty-four pro-treaty members of the second Dail who were elected in May 1921 in the elections called for by the Government of Ireland Act. There were also the four representatives of Trinity College. This parliament elected a provisional government for the twenty-six counties and declared itself in favour of the provision in the treaty whereby the provisional government was to evolve into the government of the Irish Free State the year after the signing of the treaty. That much was settled although not of course in the minds of the dissident Republicans. The second Dail never met as the Republican deputies never returned to it, but it was to this 'second Dail' that a number of Republicans subsequently looked for legality – not the meetings which stemmed from the provisional government.

The shades gathered around their aspirations during what was to prove to be all too literally a flaming month of June. Collins had kept in touch with a section of the dissidents, those led by Liam Lynch who was nominally the commander-in-chief of all the Republican forces, to the extent that with Lynch he arranged the planning and armament for a campaign in the North in support of the beleaguered

Catholics. This was in March. In May he concluded a pact with de Valera, both sides agreeing to go into the elections of 10 June under a shared Sinn Fein banner calling on the electorate to vote only for pro- or anti-treaty candidates and to forget about such light considerations as the interests of farmers, labour, Unionists, etc. The pact also provided for the enactment of a republican constitution after the election, although the day before the Four Courts was seized Winston Churchill had declared in the House of Commons that: 'If a Republic was set up, that is a form of Government in Ireland which the British Empire in no circumstances whatever can tolerate or agree to.'

Understandably therefore the pact displeased the British who exerted pressure to have it abrogated – which Collins did on the eve of the election, in a speech in which he urged the electorate to vote for anyone it fancied, thus ending the prospect of a coalition government about which his colleagues had been unenthusiastic anyway.

Three days before the elections were held Sir Henry Wilson was shot and on the same day the Four Courts prison arranged for the kidnapping of General O'Connell, the Free State army chief of staff. Either happening would have provided a catalyst for momentous events. Together they were irresistible and, on 28 June, field pieces borrowed from the British loomed across the Liffey and blasted the Four Courts garrison from their fortress. The bombardment brought the issue of the treaty from the debating table to the sterner tests of ambush, reprisal, military action and execution.

It was a war of young men. Kevin O'Higgins, the strong man of the Free State government, said that: 'The Provisional Government was simply eight young men in the City Hall standing amidst the ruins of one administration, with the foundations of another not yet laid and with wild men screaming through the key hole.' The Republican leaders were young men also, in their late teens or early twenties. They hadn't the cohesion and resources of their opponents, nor did they have the backing of a sympathetic population. Houses that were friendly to the IRA during the Anglo-Irish war were closed to them during the war of brothers. The worst of them contributed to the statistics of death and crime of the period and all the best of them had to fight a war were the qualities exhibited in these extracts from his last letter to his mother, written by Liam Mellows:

> Mountjoy Prison, Dublin
> Dec. 8th 1922
> 5 a.m.

My dear Mother,

The time is short and much I would like to say must go unsaid but you will understand in such moments heart speaks to heart. At 3.30 a.m. this morning, we (Dick Barrett, Rory O'Connor, Joe McKelvey and I) were informed that we were to be executed as a reprisal. Welcome be the will of God, for Ireland is in His keeping despite foreign monarchs and treaties. Though unworthy of the greatest human honour that can be paid an Irishman or woman, I go to join Tone and Emmet, the Fenians, Tom Clarke, Connolly, Pearse, Kevin Barry and Childers. My last thoughts will be on God, and Ireland and on you.

You must not grieve Mother Darling. Once before you thought you had given me to Ireland. The reality has now come. You will bear this as you have borne all the afflictions the cause of Ireland brought you – nobly and bravely. It is a sore trial for you, but that great courageous soul of yours will rejoice for I die for the truth – life is only for a little while, and we shall be returned hereafter.

Through you I also send another message: it is this, let no thought of reprisal or revenge dominate Republicans because of our deaths. We die for the truth, vindication will come, the mist will be cleared away, and brothers in blood will before long be brothers in arms, against the oppression of our country and imperialist England . . . in this belief I die happy forgiving all, as I hope myself to be forgiven. The path the people of Ireland must tread is straight and hard and true, though narrow; only by following it can they be men. It is a hard road, but it's the road our Saviour followed – the road of Sacrifice. The Republic lives, our deaths make that a certainty.

I have had the Chaplain to see me. It is sad but I cannot agree to accept the Bishops' Pastoral, my conscience is quite clear, Thank God, with the old Gaels. I believe that those who die for Ireland have no need for prayer.

> God Bless and Protect you,
> Your Loving Son Willie

Mellows' reference to the bishops' pastoral concerned the issuing by the hierarchy on 10 October of a joint pastoral letter condemning the Republicans' war effort as 'morally only a system of murder and assassination of the National forces.' The bishops wrote of the Republicans' oath that 'No oath can bind any man to carry on a warfare against his own Country in circumstances forbidden by the law of

God.' Following the publication of this pastoral many priests began to refuse confession to Republicans who would not repent of their ways. As a result men under sentence of death sometimes could not receive communion and died without the Viaticum, although as in Fenian times there were always some priests who defied the ban and heard Republican confessions.*

This was and is a continuing trait of sane Irish priests, best exemplified by an anecdote from the period of preparation (1938) for Sean Russell's bombing campaign against England.

At the time a reservoir was being built at Poulaphoucca, Co. Wicklow, and upwards of thirty young IRA men were in the habit of stealing gelignite and angle irons (for testing the strength of the charges) from the site. One of the lads went to confession:

'I stole Father.' 'What did you steal my son?' 'Explosives Father.' 'For use in Ireland?' 'No Father – in England.' 'That's all right my son,' said the priest, who gave the young bomber absolution, told him to send along his colleagues to be absolved also and wound up by getting the OC of the group to carry the Eucharistic flag at the head of a procession held to mark the closing of a mission.

However, the Civil War period was a rougher era and the bishops' pastoral took note of another grim factor then entering the war and urged the Republicans to take advantage of an amnesty which the government offered on 3 October – because military courts were due to come into operation on 15 October.

When the courts did begin functioning on 17 November, they condemned seventy-seven men, including Childers and four leading members of the Courts' garrison who were executed as a reprisal after two pro-treaty deputies who had voted for the military courts were shot, one fatally. The executed men were Rory O'Connor, Liam Mellows, Richard Barrett and Joseph McKelvey. The executions of

---

* It is still not clear whether or not he did receive the sacraments but a letter to the press in Dublin on 24 April 1968, from Captain Ignatius O'Rourke who was present at the execution, seems to indicate that he may have. According to the letter, a few minutes before Mellows was executed he sent for the prison chaplain, Father McMahon, and O'Rourke describes how, 'A few minutes later' he saw Father McMahon leaving the room 'accompanied by Liam Mellows with his right arm around Liam's shoulders and they walked along together leading the group as we all walked to the sandbags. Liam and Father McMahon appeared to be in deep, friendly conversation, with no sign of discord, disagreement or argument, just like two men discussing some point in a friendly fashion. They continued to talk until Father McMahon left Liam in the number one position at the sandbags . . .'

those leaders on 8 December, two days after the Free State by the terms of the treaty officially came into existence, initiated a policy of reprisals whereby men who were already imprisoned were liable to execution if an IRA operation took place in the district in which they were held.

It was against this background of religious and military pressures that an executive meeting was held in the remote Nier Valley in Co. Waterford on 10 March, which de Valera attended as the political leader of the Republican side. He voted for peace, but Liam Lynch stood out for a continuation of the struggle. Further meetings were held in April on the run near Mullinahone, Co. Tipperary, and in Dublin between which Liam Lynch was killed and Austin Stack captured.

At the Dublin meeting a special Army Council formed from the depleted executive and consisting of Barry, Liam Pilkington, Sean Hyde and Frank Aiken agreed with de Valera and the three members of the Republican cabinet who were not in prison (P. J. Ruthledge, M. P. Colivet and Donal O'Callaghan) to issue a proclamation calling a halt to hostilities. Frank Aiken succeeded Lynch and on 30 April issued an order calling on the IRA to suspend 'all offensive operations' and on 24 May the Civil War came finally to an end with a 'cease fire and dump arms' order also signed by Aiken.

As far as the ending of partition was, or is, concerned, the Civil War was a total irrelevance – as even the briefest of chats with any Northern Unionist would show. The point is vividly demonstrated by my talk with Viscount Brookeborough, from 1943 until his retirement in 1963 the prime minister of that strange political entity that the Government of Ireland Act created in the north-east, like a political leftover from the Reformation.

Coincidentally, the day before I went north to see Brookeborough I was in Dublin for the funeral of Dunne and Sullivan, the killers of Sir Henry Wilson, whose remains were brought back to Ireland on 6 July 1967. A guard of honour of the contemporary IRA marched openly on either side of the two coffins through the streets of Dublin. The guards were set-face, stern young men, moving to military commands and dressed in a strange 'uniform' of ordinary peaked caps and gloves. Police kept the crowds back, guarding men who had been under sentence of death by the state as they honoured their dead, some praying openly.

The Brookeboroughs lived on a huge estate, Colebrook, near Brookeborough, in Co. Fermanagh. Outside the door stood two howitzers in memory of two relations of Brookeborough who were awarded posthumous Victoria Crosses in the First World War for gallantry at Ypres and at Givrenchy.

The relations and admirers of Dunne and Sullivan also remember Ypres. It was there that Sullivan lost a leg so that he could not flee after the shooting of Wilson, and Dunne stayed with him to save him from the enraged London mob, thereby ensuring his own execution also. At his trial, which was of course only a legal halt on the way to an inevitable execution, Dunne prepared a statement which said that they had 'fought for small nationalities ... The same principles which led us to shed our blood on the battlefield of Europe led us to commit the act we are charged with.'

Lord Brookeborough and his wife said frankly that they considered Dunne and Sullivan to be murderers. Brookeborough had lost several relations in war for England, including two sons in the Second World War. 'I'm a Britisher,' he said, but he reminded me of the French General Massu of the OAS, both facially and physically and indeed in other ways too. He lived in almost feudal style at Brookeborough, pottering around in corduroys with a large clasp-knife dangling from his belt. In the wooded grounds around his mansion deer stalked through the trees, fat cattle grazed, and yards, barns and clusters of agricultural equipment, tended with nonchalant competence by innumerable workmen, combined to give a picture of a typical English demesne set down in an Irish countryside.

Lady Brookeborough, a woman of character rather than beauty, made me welcome, offered me coffee and then gave up a chance to watch Wimbledon on television to sit down and attempt to put me right about loyal Ulster. The contrast between the Brookeboroughs and the IRA men whom I had seen in Dublin the previous night could not have been more striking.

Lord Brookeborough told me that he first heard of the 1916 Rising in his family pew at the local church. Just back on leave from the war, his first reaction was shame. He felt embarrassed for the country, for his regiment and for those who had died in the war. At the time of the Rising his wife was having a baby in the Rotunda Hospital in Dublin and both were impressed at the manner in which the rebels paralysed the city. This made them determined to withstand any such rising in the North.

When Brookeborough returned in 1918 he decided that nothing serious was being done to put down the menace of Sinn Fein. The IRA was becoming active locally and by the end of 1919 he had lost his faith in the efficacy of the RIC as a police force. Demoralized RIC men were being sent north as Sinn Fein and the IRA took control of the South. Brookeborough felt that something had to be done. At Dublin Castle he saw Sir John Anderson and General McCreedy who told him that a force was to be established in the North, issued with whistles. Brookeborough believed that even more should be done and decided to form his own force and issue them with something more lethal than whistles.

Thus began the celebrated B-Special Corps. He organized it first in Brookeborough, from men who had been Ulster Volunteers and from former members of the British army, then moved throughout the six north-eastern counties building the force to the strength of the pre-First World War Ulster Volunteer Force. He and his men regarded Catholics as potential traitors and Sinn Feiners. The B-Specials were the rock on which any mass movement by the IRA in the North inevitably foundered.

2

Dilemmas of Violence and Politics

From the end of the Civil War until the present day a debate on the use of force has continued within the IRA and the Republican movement generally. At some stages in the IRA's development the debate takes the form of Force *v.* Six Cos., or Force *v.* Free State; at other times it is Force *v.* England or Force *v.* Six Cos.; and sometimes it is Force *v.* a concentration on economic and social issues.

The use of force is a dilemma which the movement can never solve. The guns, the excitement and the secrecy attract new members thirsting for adventure. The guns go off and the authorities act. Take away the guns and the excitement and how do you offer a credible possibility of achieving the IRA's objectives and so attract new members? Even in 1970 when the movement had, for some years, rejected the ending of partition as its main objective (speech by Cathal Goulding, reported in *United Irishman*, July 1967) and committed itself instead to a radical social and economic policy somewhat to the left of Albania, it still found it necessary, for recruiting purposes, to hold out the lure of the use of force to 'disrupt the existing state'. The ploy cut it away from the significantly large Republican socialist element in the country who would have supported a constitutional movement, no matter how radical its policies. Thus it was in 1970, and thus it was in 1924 when Eamon de Valera emerged from the jail where he had spent the year following the end of the Civil War.

The best illustration of de Valera's attitude towards the treaty is contained in a letter of 10 September 1922 to Joseph McGarrity in which he said, 'If the Republicans stand aside and let the Treaty come into force acquiescence in it means the abandonment of National sovereignty [for which of course he had fought in 1916] ... if the Republicans do not stand aside ... resistance means armed opposition to what is undoubtedly the decision of the majority of the people ...'

It was a circle that could not be squared. On the one hand his speeches and actions were, to the pro-treaty side, at the worst outright incitements to bloodshed and violence and at the best were designed to wreck their efforts to make the treaty work. On the other hand to the militant Republicans these speeches and attitudes, while they showed that his heart lay in the right place, gave no indication of where his head lay. Politically his concept of 'external association' – an Irish Republic externally associated with England in the same way as later led to Indian independence – was ahead of his time and found little acceptance. The treaty was signed and he was forced to live with a *fait accompli*.

De Valera, coming out to freedom under the tattered banner of Sinn Fein, saw in the confused landscape confronting him little hope of implementing his own kind of policies. On the other hand, having spent the Civil War somewhat outside the military councils which had made the running throughout the conflict (he had stipulated that while he honoured his responsibility to stand by his comrades he was not to be regarded as a leader of the armed wing) he was the most popular political leader on the Republican side if not in the country. The war had claimed the lives of Collins, Liam Lynch, Childers, Rory O'Connor, Liam Mellows, Arthur Griffith and many others and despite their military defeat Republicans had done remarkably well in the general elections of August 1923.

Roughly 15,000 Sinn Fein and IRA prisoners had been released from internment camps all over the country by 16 July 1924, when the three most important Republican prisoners, de Valera, Austin Stack and Liam Deasy, were set free. In the six north-eastern counties, now beginning to settle down to the idea of partition, the IRA were smashed. The remnants that had survived the brutalities of the preceding years had to content with the B-Specials, a large and well armed Royal Ulster Constabulary, the British army and the full force of the Protestant ascendancy controlling business and industry.

At Stormont, the Nationalist MPs were still boycotting that institution. In the South, the Republicans emerging from jail and internment camps had to face a largely hostile population also. Many people agreed with the bishops' pastorals condemning the Republicans, or at least Republican militants, which stated:

They have wrecked Ireland from end to end, burning and destroying national property of enormous value, breaking roads, bridges and railways, seeking by an incessant blockade to starve the people or bury them in social stagnation. They have caused more damage to Ireland in three months than could be laid to the charge of British rule in so many decades . . .

Formerly friendly houses shut their doors on IRA men seeking shelter. Such jobs as were available were being swallowed up by demobilized Free State soldiers, and throughout the ranks of the IRA there was much confusion and bitterness at their leaders, and particularly at their political leaders in Sinn Fein whom they felt had let them down, by opposing the treaty but offering no viable alternative. They could not understand how the pro-treatyites were able to defeat an IRA which, prior to the truce, had been in control of the greater part of the country. Increasingly in the IRA also there was a feeling that the political leaders had not been as intent on directing the struggle as they had been in making political capital out of their opponents. Many of the young men were simply waiting for the call, believing that the 'dump arms' order by Frank Aiken was a bluff, that the war was going to start again any moment and that this time they would win.

Part of their determination was based on the bitter experiences of the Civil War. In Kerry, in particular, terrible things were done. Men were chained to mined barricades and blown to pieces, interrogations were conducted with the aid of a hammer and men went mad or were found to be castrated. Bitter Civil War memories are one reason why to this day Kerry is a fertile breeding ground for the IRA.

To the Free State side any Republican killing was an atrocity, no matter how justified such action may have seemed to the Republicans. The pro-treaty side regarded the anti-treaty forces as irregulars who had murderously turned on their fellow Irishmen in defiance of the lawfully constituted state for which they had successfully and with great sacrifice fought. Some Free State soldiers reacted against the Republicans with a rigour born of this attitude.

The Free State army intelligence department was believed to have been implicated in many of the killings. On 26 August 1922, shortly after Collins was killed in an ambush, three teenage youths were taken out of a lorry and shot dead near Clondalkin; a week later a prominent IRA man called Banfield was killed in the same area, and there were sufficient other such deaths as to embitter the young IRA men and make them wish for revenge. Michael Fitzpatrick, who in the 1930s was to be one of the most prominent members of the IRA, told me that while being interrogated after capture in the Civil War at Oriel House in Westland Row, the headquarters of the Criminal Investigation Department, he was forced to walk up and down a downstairs cell while shots were fired from a .45 pistol at either side of his head. He had become so desperate that he had decided to turn his head into the path of a bullet, when the interrogation ceased. Another life-long Republican, Joseph Clarke, a vice-president of Sinn Fein, told me how his moustache was ripped off during an interrogation, and that while he was waiting to enter the room where this happened he saw another prisoner being taken out with his entrails hanging out through his anus after a kicking.

Whether all these stories are true or not one can hardly vouch but the important thing is that they were believed, and used extensively for propaganda.

However, it is worth noting that unlike either the Russian or Spanish Civil Wars, the Irish affair differed in the degree of magnanimity shown by the victors towards the losers. There was no seizure of land or possessions for instance, and the losing side was left free to form political parties and to pursue professional or business interests uninterruptedly. On the IRA side those who preferred to struggle on towards the Republic on leaving the jails or internment camps had first to answer the question – why had they left the jails or internment camps! All intending recruits were presented with a document in the name of Oglaigh na hEireann in which they were asked to state as follows:

1. Did you sign on any undertaking in order to obtain your release from Free State custody?
2. If so, give reasons why.

Those who signed out were either not allowed into the army, of if let in court-martialled and then rejected once they were found out. Selectivity was also enjoined in general order No. 21 issued by the chief of staff, Frank Aiken, on 14 July 1923, on the matter of recruits. This made three points:

1. No man would be permitted to join the ranks who was over 19 years of age on 12 July 1923.
2. No recruit would be accepted without the express sanction of the battalion OC to whom full particulars must be forwarded.

3. Recruits when sanctioned by the battalion OC would be sworn in
   by the company OC.

The IRA was trying to exclude both faint hearts who might have been
old enough to take part in the Civil War or War of Independence and
had not, would-be spies and of course those who had committed the
heinous crime of 'signing-out'. And despite the setbacks of the Civil
War, jailings, internments and loss of life, the IRA had sufficient
strength by July 1923 to hold a two-day meeting in the Elliot Hotel
in Harcourt Street, Dublin. Here organizational plans were drawn
up, and a draft constitution and rules agreed upon. At this meeting
also it was decided to have nothing more to do with the IRB.

At this time the principal IRA leaders were Frank Aiken, Andy
Cooney, Maurice Twomey, Micky Carolan, Sean Russell, Jim
Donovan, Sean Moylan, Sean Lemass, Tom Daly, Sean MacBride,
Michael Price and Jim Killeen, who constituted the headquarters
staff. Next in importance were prominent figures such as Peadar
O'Donnell, George Gilmore, David Fitzgerald, Tom Maguire in
Mayo, Ben Maguire (no relation) in Leitrim and Michael Fitzpatrick,
all of whom were Civil War veterans. And there were other districts
in the country that also provided recruiting grounds and sources of
strength for the IRA.

I found in my interviewing that it was always safer to ascribe IRA
strength or influence to a particular leader, or to a local tradition,
than to the formal organizational title held by a member of the organization. The organizational blueprint that emanated from the 12 July
executive meeting contained twenty-five closely typed pages, but in
my experience the elaborate provisions it made for scouting, signal-
ling, captains of right-half companies, captains of the left-half companies etc., existed only on paper, partially to impress young men.
Whatever work was done in any given district depended on one good
man.

As far as a social or economic policy was concerned the IRA
organization at this stage was blank and provided only for a military
organization. The following extracts from the constitution are the
most important ones:

(3) Its object shall be:
    (a) To guard the honour, and maintain the independence of the
        Irish Republic.

(b) To protect the rights and liberties common to the people of IRELAND.

(c) To place its service at the disposal of an established Republican Government whcih faithfully upholds the above objects.

(4) CONTROL OF THE ARMY

The army shall be controlled by an Executive of 16, which shall be appointed by a Committee of twenty-five elected as follows:–

Each Province elects five delegates.
Each Province nominates five further delegates, from whom the whole Convention will elect the remaining five. Any serving Volunteer to be eligible to act on the Executive.

This Executive shall have supreme control of the Army, and the Executive shall not itself, directly or indirectly, be subordinate to, or be controlled by any other body, subject to any alterations necessary to put into operation Section 3, subsection (c) above.

Such proposed alterations to be sanctioned by a General Convention.

(5) DUTIES AND POWERS OF EXECUTIVE

The duties of the Executive shall be to define policy for the Army. It shall have supreme control over the Army Council, and General Headquarters Staff. It shall not, however, have power to interfere with General Headquarters Staff in respect of purely Army matters such as Organization, Training, method of conducting operations etc.

Ten shall form a quorum of meetings of the Executive.

(6) FINANCIAL POWERS

The Executive shall be responsible for the raising and safeguarding of funds for Army purposes.

(8) ARMY COUNCIL

The Executive shall appoint an Army Council of seven, of which four shall be chosen from members of the Executive, and the remaining three may be appointed from outside the Executive. Four shall form a quorum at meetings of the Army Council. In the event of a vacancy occurring on the council, it shall be filled by co-option, to be approved by the Executive.

(9) GENERAL HEADQUARTERS STAFF

The Executive shall appoint a Chief of Staff, who will appoint his Staff.

(10) GENERAL CONVENTION
A General Convention, representative of the whole Army, shall meet at least once in each twelve months, and shall elect a Committee to appoint an Executive as in Section 4, who shall hold office until the next General Convention. It shall also receive a report from the Chief of Staff, and a Financial statement from the Executive.

(14) GENERAL CONVENTION
The constitution of the General Convention shall be as follows:

(a) All members of the Executive.
(b) All members of the Army Council.
(c) A member of the General Headquarters Staff.
(d) All Divisional Commandants, and two other members of the Divisional Staff as elected by that Staff.
(e) The delegates elected at the Brigade Convention.

(20) OATH
The oath of Allegiance to be taken by every member of the Army shall be as follows:
I .... do solemnly swear that to the best of my knowledge and ability I will support and defend the Irish Republic against all enemies, foreign and domestic, that I will bear true faith and allegiance to the same. I do further swear that I do not and shall not yield a voluntary support to any pretended Government, Authority, or Power within Ireland hostile or inimical to that Republic.

I take this obligation freely without any mental reservation or purpose of evasion – so help me God.[*]

The principal organizers of the IRA chosen at the July meeting were Patrick McLogan, David Fitzgerald and James Killeen.

By April 1924 the IRA felt strong enough to express itself politically at least, and it was decided to support the Sinn Fein party. On 28 April, a memo to this effect was issued to all volunteers urging 'every officer' to see 'that the men of his Unit not only join Sinn Fein Clubs, but that they work the clubs with the proper spirit of enthusiasm and along the straight lines of Republicanism. It is necessary to have a sympathetic civilian population. We must begin to

---

[*] Over the years the Church's opposition to the IRA's being an oath-bound society led to the recruit being asked not to 'solemnly swear' but to make only a 'declaration' of loyalty to the IRA. This is the position at the time of writing.

develop it immediately and our starting off point is the Sinn Fein Clubs. We must join Sinn Fein Clubs.'

The sort of activity which the IRA reorganization and planning led to in the subsequent decade was not calculated to win a 'sympathetic civilian population'. Here it is important to recognize the two ways in which IRA activity has to be assessed: how the IRA judged itself and how the public judged it. The IRA did contain many a laughing cavalier, such as Frank Ryan, who saw nothing wrong in either a drink or a pretty face. But officially the organization took itself with deadly seriousness, laying great emphasis on conventions, the holding of meetings, the keeping of records and on styles and titles. Was a man properly appointed or not? Was this the adjutant general's job or should the instruction come from the chief of staff? These questions mattered and IRA policy was viewed as something sacrosanct.

Individual deviations from policy, or interpretations of it, were regarded by the many and implacable purists with the same severity shown by the Roman Curia to errant theologians. And what IRA policy came down to is evident in an agreement between the IRA and the American Clann na Gael of 15 September 1926. Luke Dillon, secretary of the Clann, pledged to Dr Andrew Cooney, chief of staff of the IRA, that the Clann would give 'its undivided support, physically, morally and financially to Oglaigh na hEireann [Irish Volunteers] to secure by force of arms the absolute independence of Ireland'. This policy was, of course, easier to state than to implement. And even though the whole IRA ethos was antipathetic to politicians, circumstances continually forced political debates upon the organization and even sometimes forced it into positive attempts at political action.

The public was not aware of the time and energy which the IRA devoted to planning and manoeuvring. But it was very much aware of the army's overt activities which followed from its policy of using physical force.

Some of these activities were directed by IRA headquarters; others were not. One of these latter was the shooting of a British private, who with a party of other soldiers, women and children, was coming ashore on a tender from Spike Island, at Cobh, Co. Cork. This was motivated simply by anti-British feeling and was carried out by four IRA men who had been on the IRA side during the Civil War. Like many another incident it was their association with the old IRA and access to guns rather than a deliberate policy decision which led to the killing.

There were other shootings too in 1924 such as that on 6 May, when two guards were fired on by an IRA man at Creag, Co. Tipperary, as he was about to be arrested. One of the guards died five months later, but the IRA man escaped unscathed to America. The following year there were incidents such as the shooting of a man, Stephen Joyce, in Claremorris (as he was coming home from a dance) by armed men, presumably members of the IRA. Other incidents can be attributed to the IRA with more certainty. On 6 November the Hill of Down railway station, Co. Westmeath, was taken over by a party of IRA men under George Plunkett (a brother of the executed 1916 leader) to rescue Jim Killeen when the train arrived at the station. But the train had left five minutes earlier and Killeen went to court and to jail (he had been arrested for organizing the IRA). With eighteen other prisoners, he was rescued by an IRA party under the leadership of George Gilmore on 27 November.

An IRA policy directive of 1925 concerned the showing of 'British Propaganda Films'. In Dublin, the Masterpiece Cinema was blown up after the film *Ypres* was shown, and in Galway the film *Zeebrugge* was seized and burned. Cinema managers were warned by the IRA that if such films were shown they would be 'drastically dealt with'. And the year closed with a garda, Thomas Dowling, being 'drastically dealt with' by armed men who shot him dead at a graveyard in Fanore, Co. Clare, as he was coming home after patrol duty. As far as can be determined the shooting was in line with the general IRA policy not to interfere with guards who did not take any particular interest in the IRA, but to discourage, and if necessary to shoot, those who did. (Surveillance of the IRA was normally carried out by the armed Criminal Investigation Department.)

The IRA paid dearly for issuing voluminous reports and directives. On 30 July 1925, police raided 68, Adelaide Road, Dublin, and in a secret room captured Michael Carolan and his secretary Margaret Clancy, and seized a vast pile of documents, publication of which as the trial proceeded (it opened on 22 November) gave the public an embarrassing insight into the workings of the IRA. This fondness for paperwork often amazed me as I attempted to research the subject. On the one hand I frequently met with evasions or refusals to give any information on the grounds that the IRA was an oathbound, secret organization, or that somebody might be incriminated, yet this same organization churned out mimeographed documents in vast and incriminating quantities, inevitably to be found or seized by the authorities.

This urge to conceal and at the same time express oneself is a very Irish characteristic, and on 20 June 1925 it found a noble expression in the launching of an IRA newspaper *An Phoblacht* under the editorship of Maurice Twomey. An article on its front page entitled 'Wolfe Tone and Ireland Today' was written by Frank Gallagher (who was later to become the first editor of the *Irish Press*). One would imagine that no secret society would dare sponsor a newspaper, which, when analysed by trained scrutineers in the secret service, would certainly yield important information as to changes in policy or personnel, but the IRA apparently found this disadvantage outweighed by the tremendous influence, not only on Republicans, but also on left-wing young people, which the paper very shortly began to enjoy.

In 1926 the following, among other incidents, occurred:

2 June – Raid on sheriff's office, Dublin, by armed men. The jury list was seized, intimidation of jurors being a favourite IRA tactic.

20 August – John Doyle, Seatown Place, Dundalk, was shot dead by a party of armed men.

14 November – A number of Garda stations were raided by IRA men. A Sergeant Fitzsimons was killed in the course of a raid in Cork, and a guard was killed as a result of a raid on Hollyfort Station, Co. Tipperary. These raids resulted in considerable controversy when, following a number of arrests, allegations were made that the police had maltreated some of the prisoners. A sworn inquiry resulted in a number of police being severely reprimanded.

20 November – Crumlin Barracks in Dublin was attacked. A guard was wounded and the attackers driven off.

24 November – Knockanore Garda Barracks, Co. Waterford, was raided by armed men, who, after locking the guards in a cell, took away station records.

The same night Guard Hanly, Ballinakill, Leix, was badly wounded by two cyclists whom he stopped because they had no lights.

A touch of anti-Semitism also showed in a series of armed raids on money lenders in Dublin, Limerick and other centres from July to October. The parties concerned, who were mainly Jewish, were threatened and all their books and records seized, the raiders in each case producing official authority from the IRA. Cars were stolen to carry out operations which were, to be fair, at least as much motivated by a desire to stamp out the practice of money-lending as to strike at Jews.

In 1927 there were the following incidents:

10 July – Murder of Kevin O'Higgins.

27 August – Detective Officer O'Donnell of Mallow was fired on by a wanted member of the IRA, named Con Healy (known as the 'One Eyed Gunner'). Healy was subsequently sentenced to five years' penal servitude for this offence.

There were innumerable arrests for IRA activities during the year, illegal drilling being the most common offence.

In 1928 there were the following activities:

23 January – Three IRA men fired on Robert Grace, the principal warder, Mountjoy Prison, North Circular Road, Dublin, after complaints had circulated in IRA circles about ill-treatment of prisoners.

28 January – When Mr Sean Harling was entering his home, Woodpark Lodge, Dartry, Dublin, he was fired on by two men. He returned the fire and after an exchange of shots one of the attackers, a man named Coughlan, was wounded and died later. On 15 February the government appointed a tribunal which was satisfied that Harling did not fire until he had been fired at by Coughlan.

10 April – During a police search of a Sinn Fein office in Dawson Street, documents were found which led to a search of the home of Miss Florence McCarthy. Further documents were found which included a jury panel for the February sitting of the Central Criminal Court, and a circular addressed to each member of the jury panel signed 'Ghosts'. She was subsequently sentenced to six months' imprisonment.

The rest of this year was characterized by an increase in the number of attempts to intimidate jurors, and by incidents of a markedly anti-British character. The Grafton Street, Dawson Street, Dame Street part of Dublin, a predominantly Protestant area of fashionable business premises, customarily displayed Union Jacks in shop windows around Armistice Day or on occasions such as royal birthdays. Throughout the year these were torn down and destroyed by young IRA men. The subsequent prosecutions frequently failed when an intimidated jury feared to convict. British Legion and scouting halls were also burned down throughout the year.

The pace of violence really stepped up in 1929 when intimidation of jurors took the form of shooting them.

23 January – John White was shot in the stomach as he stood at the doorway of his home at Terenure in Dublin. He had served on the jury that tried Con Healy.

2 February – Albert Armstrong, an insurance inspector, was shot dead while he was putting his car in his garage. He had given evidence against IRA men accused of removing a Union Jack from his insurance company.

11 June – Detective Officer T. O'Sullivan was killed by a trap mine at Tullycrine, Co. Clare. Detective O'Driscoll of Knock Station had received an anonymous letter: 'I found a box of ammunition and papers in a butt of hay in the haggard. The times are so dangerous I was afraid to keep it near the place. I threw it inside the ditch at Lahiff Cross in Ardil's Meadow yesterday. I want you to take it away. I do not want to get into trouble with people around here. [Signed] Farmer.'

O'Driscoll found the box and carried it to Tullycrine. There he met O'Sullivan and another guard. While O'Sullivan was attempting to open the box it blew up killing him outright and badly wounding O'Driscoll.

8 November – The roof of the British ex-Servicemen's Hall, Inchicore, was blown off by an explosion which shattered glass in several adjoining houses. This hall had previously been blown up on 10 November 1927.

11 December – Arms and an ammunition dump were found at the home of Sean Russell at Spring Garden Street, North Strand, Dublin. Russell was arrested and sentenced to three months' imprisonment.

Attacks on the police continued the following year though not on the same scale. The three following incidents in 1930 are worth mentioning:

27 July – A warder of Mountjoy Prison was chained to the railings of the 'Black Church', off Mountjoy Street, with a placard alleging ill-treatment of prisoners in Mountjoy pinned to him.

20 September – A member of the Garda Siochana was chained to railings in Drumcondra with an inscription: 'Informer Farrell arrests Republicans.'

23 November – Sergeant O'Regan, while on protection duty at the residence of the Ceann Comhairle (chairman of the Dail), Rathgar, Co. Dublin, was shot in the leg.

The year 1931 was notable for a tremendous upsurge in IRA activity, for killings, shootings and for continual seizures of arms and explosives by the police, and by October it was obvious that the normal process of the law could no longer deal with the IRA and a military tribunal was instituted. The shootings of jurymen and police witnesses made it almost impossible to get a verdict in an ordinary court, and the IRA paper, *An Phoblacht*, was continually stoking the fires of revolt with statements such as the following for 20 June: '*An Phoblacht* states that members of the CID should be treated as "social Pariahs" . . . that treatment must be extended to . . . Judges and District Justices, to uniformed police – to every individual who is a willing part of the machine by which our Irish patriots are being tortured.'

After a month in which several ammunition dumps were discovered by the police, Patrick Carroll of Inchicore, Dublin, was shot in Dublin by the IRA as a police spy and the *coup de grâce* administered by a hand grenade which blew part of his head off. This occurred on 30 January. A police superintendent named Curtin was shot dead in Tipperary, 21 March, as he entered his house late at night.

5 April – a hundred members of the IRA were found drilling openly at Daingean, Offaly, under Sean McGuinness.

15 April – A campaign to boycott British goods began in Dublin and shopkeepers were intimidated.

23 April – While an IRA party was drilling at Killakee, Co. Dublin, two students chanced by and were fired on by an IRA man who thought they were policemen. Fortunately his cartridge was defective and the bullet merely wounded one student.

10 June – A large IRA dump at Killakee, constructed by the Gilmores, was discovered. It contained twenty-nine rifles, thirteen revolvers, four automatic pistols, one Lewis machine gun, three shotguns, three Very light pistols, bombs, explosives, 3,137 rounds of assorted ammunition, spare parts for firearms, documents, the head of King William of Orange whose statue had been blown up sometime earlier, and ironically in such surroundings the original of the Sinn Fein document addressed to the Versailles peace conference in 1919.

20 July – Killing of John Ryan at Oyle, Co. Tipperary. His body was found with a placard around his neck reading: 'Spies and Informers Beware. IRA.' Ryan had given evidence in a prosecution for illegal drilling. He received a threatening letter on 29 April purporting to come from the adjutant, South Tipperary brigade, IRA, stating that he

had been found guilty of treachery and warning him that if he were found in the country after 17 May his life would be forfeited.

12 September – New and unoccupied Garda barracks at Kilreekle, Co. Galway, blown up.

13 September – Attempted murder of William McInerney, Kilrush. He was seriously wounded by revolver fire while examining a notice, 'Spies Beware', that had been posted on his hall door. McInerney had been very outspoken in his denunciation of the IRA and of Republican activity generally.

Very early on in this appalling sequence of events it became clear to de Valera and other pragmatists such as Sean Lemass that militarily the Republican movement had neither arms nor the organization to attempt a rising. They also saw that Sinn Fein, to which the IRA gave allegiance, by its policy of refusing to recognize this Dublin parliament, was clearly isolating itself from the mainstream of Irish political life despite the grandiloquent directives in the name of the Republican government from the Sinn Fein headquarters in Suffolk Street, Dublin.

Nevertheless, to the hard-core IRA militants any other course was a betrayal of the Republic. When it became publicly known at an IRA convention on 17 November 1925 that discussions had taken place among leading Republican figures to find a more fruitful political and constitutional role, uproar broke out. Peadar O'Donnell secured an overwhelming majority for a resolution cutting away 'the army' from Sinn Fein, which more or less disappeared into a world of political make-believe. Subsequently the IRA was to be a purely military organization, thus frustrating the basic intention O'Donnell had had in proposing his resolution – an attempt not merely to cut away from Sinn Fein but to shake off the organization's preoccupation with partition, the oath, and the second Dail, and to direct its energies into a leftward path of socialist Republicanism inspired equally by O'Donnell and Karl Marx. This was to aid in the formation of three other political organizations from within the womb of Republicanism: Saor Eire which lapsed without greatly influencing the movement one way or another; the Republican Congress which split the 'army' in half; and Fianna Fail which became the dominating political movement of Southern Ireland.

Three days after the IRA convention passed O'Donnell's resolution the Ard Fheis of Sinn Fein itself was held. In private session a resolution opposing the discussions that were taking place within Sinn Fein, along the lines advocated by Lemass and others, was discussed. The resolution was:

> Owing to the insidious rumours that Republicans will enter the Free State Parliament if the oath be removed, we call on Sinn Fein to get a definite statement from the Government [The 'Government' of the non-existent second Dail] that they will adhere to the policy of Cathal Brugha, Erskine Childers, and their fellow martyrs and enter only an Irish Republican Parliament, for all Ireland.

De Valera, as president of Sinn Fein, held that no declaration should be made which would appear to prevent the consideration of 'any honourable line of policy, or to hamper any tendency towards the unification of the Irish people'.

Finally the following resolution in the names of Countess Markievicz and Sean Lemass was passed by a majority:

> That no change be made in the policy of Sinn Fein at this Ard Fheis, but it is agreed that no subject of discussion is barred from the whole organization, or any part of it, with the exception of the questions of the accepting of allegiance to a foreign king and the partition of Ireland, and if at any stage a change of policy is proposed an Ard Fheis must be summoned to deal with the proposal.

But it was soon clear that major political developments could not be influenced from outside the Dail. On 23 November the *Morning Post* published the findings of the Boundary Commission showing that the border was to remain as it had been since the treaty was signed.

This report, which caused a sensation in Ireland, requires some explanation. Following the royal signature of the constitution of the Irish Free State Act on 5 December 1922, the North, by provisions in the treaty, availed itself of its powers to opt out from under the rule of the Irish Free State by presenting an address to the king from both houses of the Northern parliament. The treaty provisions however had called for the setting up of a boundary commission, with a representative from each of the Irish governments under a British-nominated chairman. But the North refused to nominate a representative and the British nominated J. R. Fisher under the chairmanship of Judge Feetham of South Africa to negotiate with Dr Eoin

McNeill, the South's minister of education, who immediately resigned his portfolio on publication of the *Morning Post*'s report. The South seethed with rage at the loss of expected portions of the Catholic areas of Tyrone and Fermanagh. Even those who were hostile to the Republicans in the Civil War for a moment contemplated renewing the struggle to get back the six north-eastern counties and Sir James Craig, the Northern prime minister, sternly warned that Ulster was prepared to fight against anyone who would take away 'the loved soil of Ulster from any of the loyalists who want to remain there'.

It had been wishful thinking on the part of supporters of the treaty to imagine that any such commission could have, or would have, altered the border in favour of the South and in the circumstances the Free State government had no option but to sign an agreement, on 3 December, whereby the border stayed as it was. The Free State was freed from making various contributions to the United Kingdom's public debt and the payment of pensions to former members of the Royal Irish Constabulary. However it was not a popular settlement and told against Cumann na nGaedheal (the government) long afterwards.

The Ard Comhairle of the Sinn Fein executive agreed to call the extraordinary Ard Fheis provided for in the Markievicz-Lemass resolution on 9 March. At this meeting de Valera asked Sinn Fein to accept the proposition that 'Once the admission oaths of the twenty-six and six county assemblies are removed, it becomes a question not of principle but of policy whether or not republican representatives should attend these assemblies.' It was also suggested that in the next general election candidates should be put forward who would 'assert their right to enter any assembly where the other electorate representatives meet for public business'. These proposals were rejected and de Valera resigned as president of Sinn Fein.

On 16 May in the La Scala Theatre, Dublin, he founded his own party Fianna Fail (the 'Warriors of Destiny'). The Fianna Fail attitude was that while the Free State Dail was not the legitimate parliament of the Republic, it would use it to achieve such a parliament. Members would assert their right to represent their constituents without being forced to take the oath. If the oath were to continue in being they would attempt to create a majority of representatives in the Republican interest, to meet outside the Dail and take over the administration of the country.

The IRA met the new situation with a meeting at Peadar O'Donnell's house, in 39, Marlborough Road, Donnybrook, and decided on a programme for uniting Sinn Fein, the IRA and Fianna Fail. There was to be a three-party delegate conference with a panel of candidates to go forward at the forthcoming election with IRA support. These candidates were to 'win a majority'. With this majority secured, they would meet outside the Free State parliament, agree on a government and 'restore the Republic peacefully'. The Republicans were to enter the Free State parliament and take over all the instruments of state. Restoring the Republic peacefully would entail repudiation of the treaty, of the boundary settlement, and all agreements with Great Britain. The IRA was to get control of all arms in the Free State, and all enemy forces (that is the Free State Army) were to be withdrawn from Dublin, disarmed and demobilized 'to prevent clashing and overlapping'.

Sinn Fein agreed to this conference but stipulated that Fianna Fail must not 'enter any foreign controlled Parliament as a minority or majority, with or without an oath, or other formal declaration'. The national executive of Fianna Fail turned down these proposals unanimously.

Elections were held on 23 June 1927 and Fianna Fail won forty-four seats, but when the deputies presented themselves at the Dail they were met by the clerk of the Dail who told them that first they must comply with what he called a 'little formality' – the taking of the oath prescribed by Article 17 of the constitution. That blocked the line of approach to Dail Eireann, but de Valera announced that he was going to try another, also provided for by the constitution, which stipulated that a national referendum could be held on the oath question provided that 75,000 signatures were collected. Legal proceedings to test the constitutionality of Fianna Fail's being debarred from the Dail were also instituted but before either of these manoeuvres had a chance of succeeding a political murder occurred which changed the whole tenor of Irish politics.

Kevin O'Higgins, vice-president of the Executive Council, the cabinet formed by Cumann na nGaedheal, was murdered on his way to Mass on 10 July. O'Higgins was the most able man in Irish parliamentary politics at the time. Apart from the reconstruction work which the Dail undertook after the Civil War, he had sustained the government throughout the war itself, and through many crises afterwards. He was a principal architect of the Statute of Westminster which came into being two years after his death and which de Valera was able to use to get rid of the oath. As often happens when a man of that calibre is killed, the shooting was not the result of a deep-laid plot, but the impetuous act of two young IRA men acting unofficially and without authority from the movement. One of them had been chosen to play in a football match in the south-east of the country, and they escaped the police dragnet by driving to the game as though nothing had happened. They were never brought to justice although one of them was killed in cross-fire years afterwards when the IRA unsuccessfully tried to execute one of its opponents.

The government replied to O'Higgins's murder by introducing three bills designed to bring stability to the country and Fianna Fail into the Dail. The public safety bill gave the authorities the most drastic powers; another required candidates at all future elections to make an oath-bound declaration, that if elected they would sit in the Dail and take the oath of allegiance. The third bill would have disqualified the election and vacated the seats of the Fianna Fail deputies who failed to take the oath. The bills did not have to become law. The day after they were introduced on 11 August de Valera and the Fianna Fail deputies took their seats.

De Valera addressed the clerk of the chamber in Irish as follows: 'I am not prepared to take the oath, I am not going to take an oath, I am prepared to put my name down on this book in order to get permission to go into the Dail, but it has no other significance.' Putting aside a Bible which lay on the table he said, 'You must remember I am taking no oath.'

Fianna Fail had lost for both political and emotional reasons by sounding militantly Republican. Speaking in the Dail on 12 March 1928 Sean Lemass, who had been 'minister for defence' in the underground Republican government in his Sinn Fein days, said: 'Fianna Fail is a *slightly* constitutional party. We are open to the definition of a constitutional party, but before anything we are a Republican party. We have adopted the method of political agitation to achieve our end because we believe, in the present circumstances, that method is best in the interests of the nation and of the Republican movement, and for no other reason. Five years ago the methods we adopted were not the methods we have adopted now. Five years ago we were on the defensive, and perhaps in time we may recoup our strength sufficiently to go on the offensive. Our object is to establish a Republican government in Ireland. If that can be done by the present methods we have, we will be very pleased, but if not, we would not confine ourselves to them.'

The following year on 27 February, Sean T. O'Kelly referred to the Cumann na nGaedheal minister for defence as the 'so-called minister for defence', when speaking in the Dail, and on 14 March de Valera made one of the most important statements of all on the legitimacy of the state: He said:

I still hold that our right to be regarded as the legitimate Government of this country is faulty, that this House itself is faulty. You have secured a *de facto* position. Very well. There must be some body in charge to keep order in the community, and by virtue of your *de facto* position you are the only people who are in a position to do it. But as to whether you have come by that position legitimately or not, I say you have not come by that position legitimately. You brought off a *coup d'état* in the summer of 1922 . . .

If you are not getting the support from all sections of the community that is necessary for any executive if it is going to dispense with a large police force, it is because there is a moral handicap in your case. We are all morally handicapped because of the circumstances in which the whole thing came about. The setting up of this State put a moral handicap on everyone of us here. We came in here because we thought that a practical rule could be evolved in which order could be maintained; and we said that it was necessary to have some assembly in which the representatives of the people by a majority vote should be able to decide national policy. As we were not able to get a majority to meet outside this House, we had to come here if there was to be a majority at all of the people's representatives in any one assembly . . .

As a practical rule, and not because there is anything sacred in it, I am prepared to accept majority rule as settling matters of national policy, and therefore as deciding who it is that shall be in charge of order . . .

I for one, when the flag of the Republic was run up against an Executive that was bringing off a *coup d'etat*, stood by the flag of the Republic, and I will do it again. As long as there was a hope of maintaining that Republic, either by force against those who were bringing off that *coup d'etat* or afterwards, as long as there was an opportunity of getting the people of this country to vote again for the Republic, I stood for it.

My proposition that the representatives of the people should come in here and unify control so that we would have one Government and one Army was defeated, and for that reason I resigned. Those who continued on in that organization which we have left can claim exactly the same continuity that we claimed up to 1925. They can do it . . .

You have achieved a certain *de facto* position, and the proper thing for you to do with those who do not agree. that this State was established legitimately, and who believe that as a matter of fact there was a definite betrayal of everything that was aimed at from 1916 to 1922, is to give those people the opportunity of working, and without in any way forswearing their views, to get the Irish people as a whole again behind them. They have the right to do it. You have no right to debar them from going to the Irish people and asking them to support the re-establishment, or if they so wish to put it, to support the continuance of the Republic.

The Executive have been trying to use force, and have been using it all the time. If they are going to meet force by force, then they cannot expect the co-operation of citizens who wish that there should not be force.

Of all this, the most important point is de Valera's proposal that those who continued in the IRA could claim the same continuity that Fianna Fail had been claiming up to 1925. New IRA men I spoke to from this period said that this statement gave it, the IRA, a particular standing of responsibility in their eyes. Thus when President Cosgrave finally introduced the constitutional amendments setting up the Military Tribunal on 14 October 1931, de Valera replied to him the following day saying: 'These men are misguided, if you will, but they were brave men, anyhow, let us at least have for them the decent respect that we have for the brave.'

This sort of Fianna Fail utterance, of course, was given much wider circulation within the IRA than were appeals to moderation like that of de Valera at the Fianna Fail convention on 9 November 1933, when he expressed disappointment at the Republican continuation in militancy despite the fact that he had abolished the oath.

However, though the broad mass of IRA supporters remained sympathetic to Fianna Fail while infuriating Cumann na nGaedheal constitutionalists they buttered no parsnips for the socialist-minded members of the IRA. Some, in particular, Peadar O'Donnell, David Fitzgerald and Michael Price, tried to harness the mutually antipathetic currents of force and constitutional socialism within the organization after a great deal of debate with those who wanted to concentrate mainly on building the movement as a purely military organization. And this of course says in a sense all that needs to be known of the strength and weakness of the movement, for although the organization grew to the point of being a dangerous nuisance to law and order and of contributing significantly to the overthrow of the Cumann na nGaedheal government, it remained an organization whose hour had passed and which refused to recognize this. Its espousal of physical force wrecked its political chances and it was so weak that when the crunch came and the constitutional government really exerted strength against the movement it did not have the broad-based national support to withstand the setback, even though the government itself was shortly to be defeated by Fianna Fail.

The IRA's 'politicals' however scored a temporary victory when an organization of workers and working farmers was set up in May 1931, following a decision of the IRA convention of February 1931. The chief organizers were David Fitzgerald, Peadar O'Donnell, Michael Price, Sean Russell and Michael Fitzpatrick. At a parade of the Dublin brigade, IRA, on 7 June, Peadar O'Donnell said that the days of active service were over for the present and that the need for a Republican Workers' Party, working for a 'Peasants' Republic' and controlled jointly by peasants and workers, was very pressing.

The first congress was held in Dublin on 26 and 27 September 1931, with about 150 delegates present. The draft constitution contained the following proposals:

> To abolish, without compensation, landlordism in lands, fisheries and minerals.
> To establish a State monopoly in banking and credits.
> To create a State monopoly in export and import services and to promote co-operative distribution.
> To make the national wealth and credit available for the creation and fullest development of essential industries and mineral resources, through Industrial Workers' Co-operatives, under State direction and management, workers to regulate internal working conditions.

The names of the national executive of Saor Eire, as the party was called, were as follows: Sean McGuinness† (Mountjoy), (substitute, Fionan Walsh, Kerry), Sean Hayes (Clare), May Laverty† (Belfast), Helena Moloney, Sheila Dowling, Sheila Humphries†, D. McGinley, M. Fitzpatrick, Sean MacBride, M. Price†, Peadar O'Donnell†,

David Fitzgerald (Dublin), M. Hallissey (Kerry), M. O'Donnell (Offaly), Patrick McCormack (Antrim), Tom Kenny (Galway), L. Brady (Leix), Nicholas Boran (Kilkenny), John Mulgrew† (Mayo), and Tom Maguire† (Westmeath). (The daggers denote those who also signed the manifesto of the Republican Congress.)

But there was a strong body of opinion which was unenthusiastic about the new movement. Maurice Twomey in particular was cautious, not only about entering constitutional politics but also about the possibly damaging effects of any taint of Communism attaching to the movement. Twomey, a Corkman who became the outstanding influence on the IRA after the resignation of Frank Aiken (whom he eventually succeeded as chief of staff)* remained a formative influence on the IRA until the outbreak of the Second World War. A dedicated, right-wing Fenian, scrupulous in his religious observance, it is generally agreed in political circles that had he abandoned his republicanism to join Fianna Fail a cabinet post would have automatically been bestowed upon him. (Although often condemned by bishops and clergy, most IRA men shared Twomey's strong Catholicism. Jack Brady, who became an organizer with Jim Killeen, told me that one of the hazards that he and others like him regularly encountered was identification by local police, who would immediately notice their strange faces when they attended Mass in some small country village. Yet Brady would never think of not going to Mass because of this.)

The 1932 army convention's support for Saor Eire was restricted to a not very enthusiastic resolution: 'That we approve of Saor Eire. That the activities of Saor Eire be confined to an effort to educate the people in the principles of Saor Eire without publicly organizing it as Saor Eire.'

The caution of this wording also was vindicated in an incident which may be seen as a microcosm for the failure of Saor Eire. David Fitzgerald addressed a meeting in Co. Louth to explain Saor Eire policy to a farming audience – all of them sympathetic towards Republicanism. He was describing how Saor Eire would break up the landlords' holdings and distribute them to the landless when he was interrupted:

'Be Jasus then,' said the proud owner of 200 acres sitting in the front row, 'an you'll not take my land.'

---

* Aiken was succeeded for a period by Dr Andy Cooney.

Saor Eire received its national quietus when it was declared an unlawful association on 20 October 1931, along with the IRA itself, Fianna Eireann, Cumann na mBan, Friends of Soviet Russia and a group of other Communist-sounding organizations. On the same day the Special Powers Tribunal was set up consisting of five military officers. Introducing the bill which made this possible (Constitution Amendment No. 17) President Cosgrave said: 'The powers and machinery provided by this Bill are necessary not merely for this Government, but for any Government that may be in power if the will of the majority is to prevail.' (The will of the majority was shortly to prevail against Cosgrave, at least partially through the influence of the IRA at whom his statement was aimed.)

The IRA's involvement in Fianna Fail's defeat of Cumann na nGaedheal took place in three ways: by working enthusiastically for Fianna Fail candidates at grass-root level, in the land annuities affair, and in the 'Release the Prisoners' campaign. Fianna Fail party campaigning was carried out by rank and file IRA men. For the most part these men were united in outlook and social background with Fianna Fail supporters: small farmers, labouring men, tradesmen, people who in another country would be associated with a Labour Party. Though the scale and membership of the IRA support (the best estimates place its membership on paper at this time as around 30,000) was considerably less than that of Fianna Fail it was an extremely valuable asset in an election campaign, being both energetic and vocal.

The IRA seems to have extracted almost no concessions from Fianna Fail in return. Some prominent members grumbled at the policy of support. One, Michael Conway, told me how he had warned his colleagues against de Valera, saying: 'I'm telling ye that fella will be as bad as Cosgrave, he'll hang ye when he gets in, mark my words he'll hang ye.' Conway was close to being a true prophet: de Valera very nearly did have him hanged.

The second great IRA-based issue from which Fianna Fail benefited was the 'Release the Prisoners Campaign', a loose-knit movement centring upon a number of Republican women: Madame Maude Gonne MacBride, Helena Moloney, Mrs Sheehey Skeffington and Madame Despard.

Madame MacBride was the widow of Major John MacBride, the executed 1916 leader; Helena Moloney was a life-long socialist and trade unionist, sympathetic always to underdogs. Mrs Skeffington's husband had been murdered by a British officer in 1916, and Madame Despard, a friend of Stafford Cripps and other British socialist leaders, donated a house in Eccles Street, Dublin to be used as a workers' college, only to have it set fire to by a right-wing mob.

These ladies organized a 'Republican Prisoners' Dependents Fund' to alleviate hardships caused by the jailing of IRA men. 'Release the Prisoners' is always an emotive cry in Ireland and public opinion was easily stirred by rules of prison hardships endured by idealistic Republicans. Some were genuine, the traditional Fenian defiance of prison regulations often bringing warders and Republicans into abrasive contact; some were self-inflicted, such as those of George Gilmore who refused to wear prison clothes because of his political status, and spent from October 1931 to February 1932 naked in a windowless cell. (By contrast his brother Charlie, who wanted to see for himself how poor George was getting along, told me that he spent the best part of an afternoon walking up and down outside Rathfarnham police station with blankets under his arm. Supposedly badly wanted by the police, he was trying to get himself arrested. He was, finally, after threatening to put a brick through the station window.) The issue of the prisoners played a considerable part in Fianna Fail's win. Actually it should have rebounded to the IRA's advantage but the movement failed to realize how sorely it was trying Cumann na nGaedheal. The setting up of the Military Tribunal had been a last desperate throw on the part of the administration, at its wits' end to know how to combat the IRA.

Generally speaking the IRA, not recognizing the state which set them up, did not recognize the courts. Any IRA man, or woman, charged before a normal court generally refused to plead and announced that he 'refused to recognize the court'. However, the police, in order to place some curb on known IRA men's activities, resorted to a tactic, known as the 'cat and mouse', of picking up suspects, holding them for a few days, releasing them and picking them up again shortly afterwards. But apart from the damaging publicity which this practice engendered, some members of the IRA shook Cumann na nGaedheal badly by retaliating in March 1930, by claiming damages for wrongful arrest and false imprisonment.

The four men concerned, Patrick McKee, Charles O'Neill, John Sugrue and Donal O'Donoghue succeeded in the circuit court in winning damages of £100, £80, £40 and £100, respectively. We need not discuss the merits of the cases of the first three plaintiffs, but

O'Donoghue was at the time on the IRA Army Council, so his legal victory had considerable implications for the police and the Department of Justice. The success of these four was followed up in the courts by eight other IRA suspects who if they did not recover anything worth having in the way of damages (£5 to £10 each) further underlined the government's almost complete inability to deal with the IRA. But curiously enough the IRA did not appear to be aware of this near immunity and did not push its activities to the extent it might have.

Some members of the executive, however, either through natural bellicosity or an appreciation of the true situation, did push their luck pretty far. Frank Ryan, for instance, gave an interview to the *Daily Express* (published 24 August 1931) in which he not only justified the killings of Ryan, Carroll and Curtin, but claimed that the IRA could act on an even wider scale. It was this speech, I understand, which led the Department of Justice to advise President Cosgrave to reinstate the Tribunal. Peadar O'Donnell addressed a parade of IRA men (which the police had tried and failed to prevent) from nineteen counties on 20 June in which he said of the government: 'All the powers in their hands we must take into ours, and in the final phase we must meet force with force.'

In the event whatever 'powers' lay in the hands of the IRA were allowed to slip into the grasp of Fianna Fail. There was friendly personal contact between some IRA men and Fianna Fail ministers such as Sean Moylan and Oscar Traynor, but no formal alliance. The IRA let the political initiative drift away from it, apparently because, in Peadar O'Donnell's phrase, the IRA felt that its cause would be best advanced by 'nipping at the heels of Fianna Fail' to push the party along paths favoured by the IRA. However, the heels of one Eamon de Valera were not for nipping at and he gratefully accepted the present of the final weapon presented to him by the IRA – the land annuities campaign.

The land annuities dispute had its origin in a campaign sponsored by Peadar O'Donnell, in his native Donegal. He describes in his book, *There Will Be Another Day*, how 'in late 1925 or early 1926' on the run from the police he discovered that neighbours of his were being served with summonses for non-payment of land annuities which had accrued in the trouble times (roughly from 1916 onwards) and decided to help them. With the aid of Colonel Maurice Moore, brother of George Moore the novelist, O'Donnell organized a campaign to help people hide their cattle so that they couldn't be seized by bailiffs, and urging more people not to pay either arrears or any annuities at all. The annuities were the sums which the farmers paid to the Irish Land Commission, which in turn passed the money over to the government for payment to the British national debt commissioners to meet the loans raised for the purpose of buying out the landlords in the 1891–1909 period. After the treaty these payments were made pursuant to the financial agreement of 12 February 1923, which was signed by W. T. Cosgrave and Major John W. Hills, the financial secretary to the British Treasury, and to the Ultimate Financial Settlement, as it was called, of 19 March 1926, which was signed by Ernest Blythe for Ireland and Winston Churchill for England. Between these payments and others covered by the two agreements specified for payments of pensions to former members of the Royal Irish Constabulary the total amount involved per year came to £5 million.

O'Donnell's Donegal agitation, which later spread to adjoining counties west of the Shannon, eventually petered out, but it generated sufficient support for Fianna Fail to take it up and make the retention of the land annuities by the Irish government seem a very attractive idea to small farmers in the 1932 election campaign.

All these factors and the fact that Cumann na nGaedheal had been in power for ten years ending in a period of economic slump helped to win the February election for Fianna Fail, and a sense of relief went through the IRA when Cumann na nGaedheal was defeated. One man, a prominent Dublin lawyer, said to me, 'I felt a tremendous release. It was a marvellous thing, we really hated those buggers, it was great to see them out.'

3

The Triumph of Fianna Fail

The defeat of Cumann na nGaedheal was not, however, to herald a new dawn for the IRA. In power de Valera immediately began taking steps to abolish the oath, and he released the prisoners from Arbour Hill Barracks on 10 March, after he had formed his cabinet, amid scenes of great rejoicing in the streets of Dublin. Two days later *An Phoblacht*, which had been banned for the previous three months, appeared with an article by Maurice Twomey which said: 'Fianna Fail declares its intention to chop off some of the imperial tentacles; every such achievement is of value and will be welcomed. Notwithstanding such concessions, the Irish Republican Army must continue its work, and cannot escape its role as the vanguard of the freedom movement.'

Six days later on 18 March the Military Tribunal was suspended, and the orders which had declared the IRA and Saor Eire to be unlawful were revoked. On 19 June the IRA marched in strength to Wolfe Tone's grave at Bodenstown where an oration was delivered by Sean Russell to a gathering estimated at over 15,000 members of the IRA. At a big demonstration to welcome the prisoners, held in College Green, Dublin, a few days after their release, one of the freed prisoners, Sean McGuinness, was reported as believing that 'The members of the defunct Executive Council were ... a menace to society and the independence of Ireland, and it behoved all Republicans to unite and wipe out that menace at all costs.' (*Irish Times*, 14 March.)

On 15 and 22 October *An Phoblacht* announced in successive issues that 'Free speech and the freedom of the press must be denied to traitors and treason mongers.' Speaking in Dublin at a public meeting two of the most prominent members of the IRA, Frank Ryan and Peadar O'Donnell, both spoke against allowing Cumann na nGaedheal speakers to be heard. Ryan said, 'No matter what anyone says to the contrary, while we have fists, hands and boots to use, and guns if necessary, we will not allow free speech to traitors.' O'Donnell said, 'The policeman who puts his head between Mr Cosgrave's head, and the hands of angry Irishmen, might as well keep his head at home.'

These were not cheering words for Cosgrave's supporters. Three days after McGuinness made his statement a convention of the Army Comrades Association was held to appoint a national executive. This body drew its membership from members of the army who had fought on the Free State side in the Civil War. Its aims were claimed to be benevolent, such as securing jobs in County Councils for out-of-work former Free State soldiers and its committee contained figures such as General Richard Mulcahy, and Dr Tom O'Higgins, a brother of the murdered Kevin O'Higgins.

Prior to Fianna Fail's taking office, rumours were rife that sections of the army and of the police would not allow this to happen. The rumours made the pre-election formation of the Army Comrades Association a highly suspect move to some Fianna Fail and IRA supporters. This suspicion deepened after some Fianna Fail followers began to apply the IRA policy of denying Cumann na nGaedheal speakers, in particular W. T. Cosgrave and Richard Mulcahy, a hearing at public meetings. The Army Comrades Association started to provide bodyguards to put down the bully-boys.

The IRA and the Army Comrades Association also came into conflict when the idea of boycotting British goods, which was always flickering at the edges of IRA planning, arose. A senior executive of Bass, the English brewing firm, made disparaging remarks about Ireland and a lorry load of Bass was destroyed in Dublin on 14 December 1932. Following this, the Dublin vintners appealed to the ACA for protection and shipments of Bass were guarded by bodyguards of ACA without further incident.

But the IRA became involved with the ACA most damagingly over the backlash of the land annuities campaign. On 1 July 1932, following its election pledges, the Fianna Fail government defaulted on the annuities due that day, and the British retaliated with a bill of 11 July allowing the government of the United Kingdom to recoup itself by imposing extra duties on imports from Ireland. The Irish struck again on 23 July with a similar bill, and what was known as the 'economic war' began. As Fianna Fail both reduced the amount of land annuities payable by the tenants, and at the same time funded arrears for three years, and sometimes longer, this was a highly popular policy with the small farmers.

The larger farmers, however, whose products were excluded from England by the tariff wall raised by the economic war, were incensed. A custom sprang up among the larger farmers of refusing to pay their land annuities, so that the Land Commission had to take legal proceedings in separate cases, involving thousands of defaulters, thereby clogging the courts. The government countered this move by passing the Land Act 1933 under which a warrant issued by the Land Commission took the place of legal proceedings, and over 400,000 of these warrants were lodged in twelve half-yearly periods, beginning in November/December 1933 and ending in May/June 1939, as a result of which a sum of over £2.5 million was levied or collected by the end of 1939.[*]

In the midst of this uproar a new complication arose on 22 February 1933. General O'Duffy had been dismissed from his post as commissioner of police by Fianna Fail. As Cumann na nGaedheal had been unable to hold meetings unscathed under a friendly police chief his going led many people on the Cumann na nGaedheal side to believe that they were in for an IRA-Fianna Fail onslaught.

But although the Cumann na nGaedheal was not to allow this the leadership of the IRA and of Fianna Fail had already come to a parting of the ways. Only four days before O'Duffy was dismissed the following directive was issued by the Army Council to the 'Commander of Each Independent Unit':

OGLAIGH NA hEIREANN
(Irish Republican Army)

ROINN; A/G   ARD OIFIG,
UIMHIR: BB 74   ATH CLIATH
                                                  18adh Febhra, 1933

To:
The Commander of
Each Independent Unit

GENERAL ARMY CONVENTION, 1993

A chara,
    The following statement from the Army Council will be read at each

---

[*] It would be impossible to chronicle all the deeds of violence and acts of sabotage, which the 'no annuities' campaign inspired – in east Cork alone there were hundreds of such incidents.

parade and Battalion Staff meeting called for the purpose of electing delegates to the Battalion Convention. Copies of the Army constitution are herewith enclosed.

1. In accordance with the constitution the Army Council had decided to convene the annual General Army Convention.

Briefly, the aim of the volunteer organization is to assert the sovereignty and unity of the Republic of Ireland in which the ownership of the means of production, distribution and exchange will be vested in the Irish people. It will be the function of the forthcoming General Army Convention to consider how the task of achieving this object can be faced and to decide upon the policy of the Army.

2. The position of the Irish Republican Army from a military stand-point is dealt with in the Adjutant General's report which will be submitted to the General Army Convention. From this report it will be seen that the strength, training and discipline of the organization have improved since the last convention. Whilst the strength of the organization has shown a marked increase every year since 1925, the Army Council is of the opinion that the wide field for recruiting at the disposal of our forces has not been availed of.

In considering the policy of the Army, the General Army Convention will have to decide how the changes in the political situation, North and South, can best be utilized.

3. THE TWENTY-SIX COUNTIES: At the last Convention it was decided not to take any action which would actively impede the newly established Fianna Fail 'Government'. This decision governed to a great extent the policy of the Army Council, and every effort was made by the Council to avoid clashes. On the other hand, to put it mildly, not much assistance was given by the Fianna Fail 'Government' in carrying out this policy; the police and CID tried in many instances to provoke conflict. The Coercion legislation passed under the Cosgrave regime was not repealed – on the contrary in many cases it was actually used against Republicans, and thus we have witnessed the jailing of many of our comrades.

In dealing with England, the Fianna Fail 'Government' agreed to submit the question of the payment of tribute to arbitration. The payment of any tribute to England is an encroachment on the sovereignty of Ireland, which sovereignty is, and must remain, non-judicial. The oath of allegiance has been abolished, but the over-lordship of Britain was recognized by the appointment of a Governor General.

In its economic policy the Fianna Fail 'Government' has upheld and bolstered the capitalist system so that the economic war with England is being used for the advancement of both British and Irish capitalism within our shores.

Thus, these facts bring us to the realization that the policy of the

Fianna Fail Government is not directed towards the achievement of our aims.

4. It is the opinion of the Army Council that the policy of the Fianna Fail 'Government' is bound to lead to widespread disillusionment amongst a great proportion of its Republican supporters, and of the workers and working farmers. One of the principal tasks of the convention will be to decide whether such disillusionment can be availed of to assist in the achievement of the aims of the Irish Republican Army.

If it is considered that the title of Republicanism arising from the disillusionment in the Fianna Fail policy can, and should be harnessed, the next consideration will be the means by which this should be done. Four means present themselves:

1. Through the medium of the Irish Republican Army alone.
2. By the re-organization of Saor.
3. Through the medium of existing political organizations.
4. By the creation of a new organization.

5. The next problem for consideration will be the policy of the Volunteer Organization towards the Free State 'Government'. Since the last General Army Convention there has been no change in the attitude of the 'Government'. It claims that it is the legitimate government of the Twenty-six Counties, and that the Irish Republican Army is usurping its powers. In brief, it makes the same claims as regards the control of arms, and as regards its legitimacy as the previous 'Government'.

6. The proposed creation of a Volunteer Force* as an auxiliary to the Free State Army will also require the attention of the convention. It is the opinion of the Army Council that the creation of this new appendage to the Free State Army is aimed at diverting the activities of the manhood of Ireland from the Revolutionary Movement, and that its ultimate purpose will be to uphold the Treaty and Constitution of the Free State. The Convention will have to consider how best the threat of the creation of this force can be met.

7. Since the last convention the Army Council has approved of the initiation of the Boycott British Campaign. It is to be regretted that this campaign has not received the support that might have been expected

---

* This was a kind of territorial army which Fianna Fail was setting up at this time. Recruiting opened on 20 February 1934, and the volunteers were a frequent target for assaults by the IRA afterwards, particularly in Kerry. No loss of life was ever involved, although volunteers were sometimes raided in their homes, and their uniforms stolen. The uniforms were modelled on those designed by Sir Roger Casement for the brigade which he unsuccessfully attempted to raise among Irish prisoners of war captured while fighting for England during the First World War.

from the volunteer organization. It will be for the Convention to advise whether this campaign shall be intensified or discontinued . . .

10. The Army Council must again draw the attention of all ranks to the absolute importance of training, both in a military and economic sense. It is vital that every member of the Organization has an intelligent conception of the task to which the Army has pledged itself.

The influx of recruits to the Army further intensifies the necessity for renewed efforts by unit commanders to raise the standard of training and discipline to the highest possible point.

The last General Army Convention decided:

THAT THE ARMY COUNCIL BE INSTRUCTED TO ESTABLISH AN OFFICERS' TRAINING CAMP FOR THREE MONTHS, JUNE, JULY AND AUGUST: THAT EACH UNIT BE COMPELLED TO SEND AT LEAST TWO OFFICERS TO THE CAMP FOR ONE WEEK

The Adjutant General's report shows how it was found almost impossible by General Headquarters to get units to provide suitable venues for these camps. The Army Council must express its regret at the lack of co-operation given by unit commanders to the General Headquarters Staff on this important matter.

11. The absolute necessity for the provision by units of financial support for the maintenance and equipment of the Army must again be emphasized. It is for that which some units are worthy of every commendation, many others have made no efforts to fulfil the obligations undertaken by them in this respect.

————————————

Do chara
D
Adjutant General

The conditions of the time prevented Cummun na nGaedheal from trusting to Shakespeare's dictum that 'Two stars keep not their motion in the one orb', which in fact had begun to assert itself and continued to do so to the detriment of the stars of the IRA. Out of these conditions there arose a movement for whose creation the IRA was largely responsible – the Blueshirts.

On 20 July 1933 an organization known as the National Guard was formed from the Army Comrades Association to safeguard 'National interests and National culture'. Its director-general was General Eoin O'Duffy. At the suggestion of the secretary of the Army Comrades Association, Commandant Ned Cronin, it had adopted a blue shirt as uniform in April.

Its philosophy was militant from the start. The *United Irishman* of 12 July 1933 said, 'If a comrade is subjected because of his membership of the Association to gross abuse his reply should be a swift blow or series of blows.' (The *United Irishman* was, at this time, the organ of Cumann na nGaedheal, edited by Ernest Blythe, a former minister. The present day IRA paper is also called the *United Irishman*.) By this time, *An Phoblacht* was coming out in successive issues with demands for the nationalization of the banks and the breaking up of the larger farms but Professor M. Tierney, one of the secretaries of the ACA, wrote in the *United Ireland* on 13 December 1933: 'The corporate state must come in the end to Ireland as elsewhere', and the other secretary Professor James Hogan, wrote a powerful series of articles attacking the IRA which were later reprinted in a widely sold pamphlet, 'Could Ireland Go Communist?'

Another correspondent in *United Ireland*, 'Oghnach', suggested that the Blueshirt audiences should imitate the Nazis when greeting their leaders and 'give three sudden staccato bursts of mass cheering, each burst consisting of one sharply ejected syllable ... the word may be Heil (Hail) pronounced sharply or it may be Hoch (Up)'. This sort of thinking was like a red rag to a bull to the leftists of the IRA. The spectacle of the bigger farmers, who had not helped very greatly in the struggle for independence and were tainted with the brush of 'land-lordism', particularly in the Cork area, joining the rates campaign was also highly distasteful. These conflicting ideologies coupled with Civil War memories were enough to set the IRA against the Blueshirts in a weakening and disastrous interlude for the IRA.

O'Duffy's first major effort as director-general of the National Guard was timed for Sunday 13 August 1933 – a march of the National Guard to government buildings to revive a ceremony of laying wreaths on the graves of O'Higgins and Collins. Inside the Dail the idea of thousands of blue-shirted O'Duffy supporters bearing down even on Sunday aroused Fianna Fail reactions. The government hastily set up what was known as the S-Branch, or 'Broy Harriers', called after Colonel Broy, the commissioner of police who had re-placed O'Duffy. The S-Branch was drawn from members of the Republican armed forces during the Civil War and must have been the most hastily organized police force in the world's history. One man, Sergeant Willie Rowe, told me that he was asleep at midnight one Saturday evening and a knock came to his door. Somewhat fearfully he looked out the window – in those days midnight knocks could mean anything – to find not a hostile figure but a man who wanted him to come down immediately to Dublin Castle to be enrolled in a 'new police force they were founding'. One senior officer of the ordinary police force told me that he was on duty at a meeting of Cosgrave's in Dublin which was attacked by a number of Fianna Fail supporters and four IRA companies who marched to the meeting in open formation. Many a head was broken and many a backside kicked at that meeting before Cosgrave was given a hearing through the efforts of the police and his own supporters. But to the officer's consternation a number of the IRA attacking party were among the recruits who were admitted to the new force.

The Army Council of the IRA decided to attack O'Duffy's marchers when they got as far as the Ballast Office at O'Connell Bridge, Dublin, a point where high buildings on either side make an ideal ambush site, and a headquarters to mastermind this operation was set up in Kevin Barry's old house in Fleet Street.[*] The IRA also arranged to have armed men near every railway station and government building in Dublin. In addition, individual members of Fianna Fail armed themselves with a view to fighting off what seemed to all concerned like an attempt at a Mussolini-type coup. However, on the very eve of the march the government revived the stringent public safety measures of the Cosgrave regime, which it had repealed on taking office, banned the parade and revived the Military Tribunal. O'Duffy called off the parade and changed the name of his now proscribed organization to that of the Young Ireland Association.

For the moment O'Duffy's personality added a new and significant dimension to Irish politics. On 8 September 1933 Cumann na nGaedheal and a farming party known as the Centre Party united to form a new party, Fine Gael (Tribe of Gaels), under the leadership of William T. Cosgrave, and of James Dillon and Frank MacDermot of the Centre Party. These men were to be its parliamentary leaders, but its national organizer and leader was O'Duffy. Cosgrave, to the architects of the new merger, though a man of supreme integrity, did not appear to have the flamboyance and panache necessary to combat that of de Valera.

The Young Ireland Association was banned on 8 December following clashes between it and the IRA. The bulk of the IRA leadership, Maurice Twomey and Sean MacBride in particular, deplored these

---

[*] Barry, one of the youthful heroes hanged by the British during the Anglo-Irish struggle, gave his name to the ballad 'Kevin Barry' which is a favourite with nationalist Irish men and women of all shades of public opinion today.

futile fights. On 17 January 1934, a document was issued as a directive
to IRA company commanders stating that 'The present policy of the
Army Council is that clashes between Volunteers and Imperialists are
forbidden, and that conflicts are to be avoided.' This was largely
ignored. Nor indeed did the government's actions during this time do
a great deal to assuage opposition fears that Fianna Fail and the IRA
were closer than the public knew and that therefore Blueshirt militancy
was necessary and justified.

The historic incident in particular caused a great deal of uneasiness.
Mrs McGrory was fatally injured on the night of 11 February 1934,
when the house of Joseph McGrory, Chapel Street, Dundalk, was
blown up by a mine thrown through the front window. Two children
also received serious injuries. Very little satisfaction was granted to
either the public or the McGrory family over this outrage, which was in
fact carried out by members of the local IRA as an act of revenge.
Joseph McGrory had given evidence against two members of the IRA
who were released by the Military Tribunal after the armed hold-up of
a Blueshirt collector in Dundalk on 9 January.

Thomas Lynch of Dunleer, Thomas Greene of Dundalk, and four
other members of the IRA in the Dundalk area were brought before
the Military Tribunal on 19 March on charges of refusing to account
for their movements. Lynch was convicted of this and an additional
charge of unlawful possession of ammunition, and was sentenced to six
months, three months not to be enforced if he entered into recognizances (he was granted a 'free pardon' on 27 September 1935). On 23
March, Richard Goss, James Finnigan and Matt McCrystal were
sentenced to three months' imprisonment in default of entry into
recognizances, and on 3 May, Thomas Greene and Bernard Murphy
were sentenced to six months' imprisonment, three months not to be
enforced if they entered into recognizances. After release Finnigan left
the IRA and joined the Republican Congress group. Later he abandoned this organization and operated on his own – as a battalion
quartermaster in the IRA he had had control of arms and ammunition
and after leaving he refused to give them up to the IRA. On 14
October the IRA kidnapped him and held him prisoner for a week
before he escaped. Arms were discovered in Finnigan's possession on
10 November and he was arrested and brought before the Military
Tribunal. On 26 November he was sent to prison for fifteen months.
In July 1935, while still serving this sentence, he was charged jointly
with Richard Goss, Eamon Coffey, Thomas Walsh and Bernard

Murphy, all of Dundalk, with the murder of Mrs McGrory. McCrystal was a state witness. This was the first murder trial before the Military Tribunal. On 20 July, after a five-day hearing, all the accused were acquitted. (Goss was later executed in connection with a shooting incident in 1940.)

Before this, however, the country was swept with rumours concerning IRA and Fianna Fail links when on 16 February, speaking in the Dail, W. T. Cosgrave stated that a meeting of the IRA had been held in 44, Parnell Square on 11 February. On the same date he said police officers entered 5, Parnell Square, which was closed by order of the Military Tribunal. From here, he said, police officers kept number 44 under observation with field glasses. The meeting, he alleged, was to give instruction in the use and construction of a land mine to be exploded the following day. But the only explosion which took place the following day was in Dundalk, resulting in the death of Mrs McGrory. On 21 February the Minister for Justice, replying, said that all he was prepared to state to the house or to the people outside at that stage was that the police were satisfied that there was no relation between what happened in Dundalk and anything that took place in Dublin on the previous day.

Following the banning of the Young Ireland Association O'Duffy retaliated by founding the League of Youth six days later. Immediately an application was lodged in the high court seeking a declaration that the League was a lawful association, the object being to prevent the government's banning it. The hearing of this case dragged on for a number of years during which the Blueshirt movement wore itself out in a series of unconstitutional activities.

Whether the Blueshirts' shirt was a gesture of solidarity with shirted Fascist movements on the Continent, as the IRA and Fianna Fail claimed, or whether it was adopted merely, as its originator claimed, to keep members from hitting each other in mistake for IRA men at meetings, is a moot point. Certainly the movement was associated with the idea of the corporate state, then so fashionable with right-wing commentators. Certainly also its membership and support tended to be drawn from among the larger farmers and bigger businessmen, whereas that of the IRA and Fianna Fail tended to come from the smaller farmers and the working classes.

Equally certainly however there had been a civil war and the IRA and Fianna Fail members were breaking up Cumann na nGaedheal meetings. Both circumstances contributed to the speedy rise and fall of

Blueshirtism. O'Duffy's personality was not suited to politics. His tactics included paying young lads to turn up in their blue shirts to rallies. As they also got their meals and free transport he both ensured large meetings and a correspondingly large strain on the organization's resources. (The fee varied but some ex-Blueshirts told me they got ten shillings a meeting, a lot of money in those days.) He also boasted that the local government elections of July 1934 would give Fine Gael a sweeping victory – Fianna Fail swept the boards. In August, he backed a motion at the Blueshirt congress which called on farmers to refuse to pay their rates until the economic war ended. He followed this up by declaring that Britain was fortifying her outposts in the six counties and the Free State, and if this meant war he, O'Duffy, would be in along with 'ninety-five per cent' of the Blueshirts. 'The other five per cent should give up their shirts.'

That was the end for the constitutionalists of the movement. Professor Hogan resigned from the Fine Gael on 31 August as a protest against 'the generally destructive leadership of its president'. On 21 September O'Duffy was pushed out of Fine Gael under pressure from its central council. He set up another League of Youth and subsequently a National Corporate Party, both unsuccessful. W. T. Cosgrave was elected president of Fine Gael and by the following September the League of Youth was amending its constitution 'to alter the dictatorial status which had been given to the office of Director-General'. By the following September the general was in Spain leading a group of ex-Blueshirts in Franco's army.

Tactically, it would have been far better for the IRA either to have stayed aloof from the Blueshirts *versus* Fianna Fail struggle or else to join in on the side of the Blueshirts and Cumann na nGaedheal and attempt to disrupt the government, but the rank and file of the IRA, particularly in Cork under the leadership of Tom Barry, threw itself enthusiastically into the struggle. The table opposite gives an idea of the volume of incidents which the police were able to bring before the Tribunal.

Of the IRA men and Blueshirts it is the Blueshirts who were sentenced to any lengthy period who are more to be pitied – the IRA members at least emerged to find some sort of an organization still in existence as a reminder of their sacrifice, but the speedy end of the Blueshirt movement meant that politically its members became nobody's children.

The elimination of the rightist Blueshirt movement should have

Year	No. of days on which the Military Tribunal sat	No. of persons convicted by the Military Tribunal			
		IRA	Blueshirts	Others	Total
1931	23	28	Nil	3	31
1932	23	17	Nil	2	19
1933	28	34	11	–	45
1934	110	102	349	–	451
1935	107	112	74	–	186
1936	43	129	Nil	–	129
1937	5	12	Nil	–	12
Total	339	434	434	5	873

led to a strengthening of the left. In fact the IRA's continuing and bedevilling debate on the use of force against some or all of three enemies – the Free State authorities, the Stormont government and the British – erupted again in such a way as to split the movement and leave Fianna Fail undisputedly the strongest force in Irish politics.

In a sense the Blueshirt upheaval and the IRA's preoccupation with economic issues brought about the rupture, because in allying itself against the right the IRA allowed itself to be driven further to the left than many of its members, Maurice Twomey in particular, thought either appropriate or prudent. Two incidents in particular alarmed the conservative element and brought matters to a head. These were the Gralton case and the Connolly House burning.

James Gralton of Effernagh, Co. Leitrim, a naturalized American citizen, had emigrated from Ireland to America in 1909. He returned in 1932 an avowed atheist and Communist, and became very active in propagating Communist doctrines. He was the owner of a dance hall in which he ran free dances to entice workers and young people to listen to his views. As the local clergy frowned on dances of any sort he drew large crowds and provoked corresponding resentment in clerical rightist circles. His dance hall was attacked and shots were fired into it. On 9 February 1933 he was served with a deportation order. He gave a personal undertaking to leave the country before 4 March, but in the meantime he went on the run. As soon as he was caught he was arrested and deported.

The matter was taken up by the Revolutionary Workers Groups, as the Communist Party then styled itself, and by left-wing notabilities such as Mrs Sheehey Skeffington and Captain Jack White who had founded Connolly's Citizen Army, and a public campaign to 'Keep Gralton here' was launched.

In so far as the IRA was concerned if Gralton had not existed Peadar O'Donnell and Frank Ryan would have been delighted to invent him, and *An Phoblacht* almost drowned out the *Workers Voice*, the Communist organ, in demanding the retention of Gralton. At a mass meeting in the Mansion House, Dublin, on 27 February to protest his expulsion a statement from the IRA adjutant general was read saying that the army had already 'taken up the matter with the Army Unit in Leitrim and urged that everything possible be done to organize protests against the expulsion of James Gralton from his native land . . .'

What the statement did not say was that the Leitrim IRA commandant, Sean O'Farrell, had advised against becoming involved with Gralton and allowed his men to stand neutral in the affair. Moreover Peadar O'Donnell had been pelted with mud and stones when he attempted to address a meeting in Drumsna, Co. Leitrim, and in fact while prominent left-wing IRA men did attend the meeting the Army Council did not permit the adjutant general to deliver his statement in person and Michael Price and Frank Ryan were ordered not to speak either.

Gralton was caught and deported a few days later, but before the IRA had had time to expunge the red hue he had imparted to their colours the Connolly House fracas blew up. As mentioned above Madame Despard's house in Eccles Street was used as a workers' college by the left-wing IRA. It was also the headquarters of the Irish section of the Friends of Soviet Russia. Connolly House in Great Strand Street was the headquarters of the Irish Revolutionary Workers' Party. Both premises came under public scrutiny during February and March of 1933, largely because the Lenten lectures took note of the Gralton affair and the dangers of Communism generally. The preacher in the Jesuit church in Gardiner Street, not far from Eccles Street, was particularly strong on the issue.

Then a group of socialists formed an organization known as the St Patrick's Young Men's League which at first merely marched in the streets, occasionally stopping pedestrians in O'Connell Street to ask if they were wearing their scapulars! However on 27 March either this organization or a like-minded group attacked the houses in Eccles Street and Strand Street, causing some damage to fittings. Two nights later the mob looted and wrecked Connolly House before setting it on fire.

Charlie Gilmore, who had attempted to defend the place with a revolver, was arrested, charged with illegal possession of firearms and the attempted murder of a police officer. He conducted his own defence and was acquitted but the IRA was deeply riven by the incident. He stated in court that he had had authority from the IRA to bear arms in the defence of the Communist building. This was denied in an IRA communique to the *Independent* on 30 March. On 1 April however, the man who had given him permission to carry a weapon, his brother Harry, wrote contradicting this statement.

Harry was court-martialled on Sunday 9 April, but was acquitted on all counts even though he refused to sign a prepared letter to the press exonerating the IRA of having dealings with Communists.

These two incidents imposed a severe strain on the IRA. To the right the movement was in danger of being ground between Communism and Fianna Fail. To the left the army soldiered to no purpose. In March 1932 a 'Constitution and Government Programme for the Republic of Ireland' had been issued and the Army Council's manifesto for Easter 1933 said the IRA believed that 'the reorganization of Irish life demands the public ownership of the means of production, distribution and control' but neither 'constitution' nor 'programme' nor 'reorganization' seemed to make any progress amid the welter of Blueshirtism, drilling and fisticuffs. What was needed, said the left, was a new political party. On 17 and 18 March 1934, a convention was held in Dublin to resolve the issue. It voted against the creation of a new political party. The margin was only one vote, that of Maurice Twomey, but Ryan, Price, Gilmore, O'Donnell, Fitzgerald and some of their supporters walked out of the convention and immediately set about trying to form a new movement without trying to win over their opponents. Offices were taken at 202, Pearse Street, later at 112, Marlborough Street, and on 8 April a conference was held at Athlone at which the new Republican Congress Party was launched, proclaiming itself 'So revolutionary that its achievement means the overthrow of all the existing political and economic machinery which at present holds this country and our people in subjection. Therefore our call is: Workers and working farmers unite on to the Workers' Republic.'

The manifesto from which this extract is taken was printed in the national press and drew an immediate rejoinder from the Army Council, published in part in the national press, and in full in *An Phoblacht* on 4 April. This said that 'in so far as the statement referred to is an attack on the present social and economic system, and an indictment of the policies of the Governments of the Six and Twenty-Six Counties, the Army Council is in complete agreement with it . . . this statement is merely repeating what has been stated over and over by the Army Council in its public pronouncements and through the columns of *An Phoblacht*.' But the Army Council went on to disown O'Donnell and Gilmore and said that 'This attack by Republicans can only assist the campaign of the Capitalist and Imperialist elements.'

The Army Council statement contained a passage which illustrates the very core of the hard-line, Fenian-cum-IRA attitude towards constitutionalism: 'This Party will, in course of time, contest elections and enter the Free State Parliament. Inevitably it will follow the road which has been travelled by other constitutional Parties which, though setting out with good intentions, ended in failure. It is not very long ago since Fianna Fail leaders told us that they wanted to go into the Free State Parliament only for the purpose of smashing it up, but they now hold this institution and the whole Free State machine as sacred.'

The Army Council did not content itself with issuing this document, but continued to exert less public pressure on the Congress movement. Price, O'Donnell, Gilmore and Ryan were court-martialled *in absentia*, and expelled with ignominy – O'Donnell sending back word on hearing of the verdict that 'as he had been court-martialled in his absence, the sentence could be carried out in his absence also'.

However, Sheila Humphries, a prominent member of Cumann na mBan, and Eithne Coyle, another signatory, withdrew from the new movement on 18 July 1934 because of the feuding which the new departure generated between the two organizations. Three well-known members, Charles Reynolds, Seamus de Burca and George Leonard, publicly recanted and reaffirmed their allegiance to GHQ in a letter which appeared in *An Phoblacht* on 21 April 1934. 'We are satisfied,' they said, 'with the Army Council's expression of agreement with the [Athlone] statement in reference to the attack on the present social and economic system.' The Army Council forbade IRA men to have anything to do with the new movement under threat of dismissal and a few who disobeyed were in fact dismissed, but a much greater number – mostly in Dublin* – voluntarily resigned and went over to the Congress. Liam Kelly and Joseph Doyle were recruited in this way. Other active recruits were Norah Connolly O'Brien, a signatory of the Athlone manifesto; her brother, Roddy Connolly – both children of the executed 1916 leader James Connolly; Cora Hughes; and Frank Edwards, a Waterford schoolteacher who was later involved in a public controversy with his bishop following his dismissal, at the Bishop's instigation, for joining the Congress. All in all the effect of the Congress was to split the IRA down the middle.

The Congress inaugurated its public campaign at a meeting in Rathfarnham on 23 April, presided over by Liam Kelly, and on 5 May a newspaper, the *Republican Congress*, 'Organ of the Committees of Workers and Small Farmers working for the United Front against Fascism and for the Workers' Republic' made its first appearance.

Differences, however, built up within the Congress and came to light at a convention in Rathmines Town Hall on 29 and 30 September. Michael Price differed from the majority of delegates on methodology and consequently was not elected to the executive. Price wanted the organization to concentrate on strikes, resisting evictions, and the creation of a political organization to contest municipal and Dail elections. O'Donnell, Ryan, Gilmore and others did not consider the time opportune for such a programme. They wished first to establish 'cells' in trade unions and to place their men in key positions in political organizations. Subsequently Price broke away from the Republican Congress and joined the 'Citizen Army' (a sort of hangover from Connolly's 1916 army, which still kept itself within the Republican ethos, dimly hoping someday to achieve Connolly's goals). Here again he opposed the majority, and in a short time he left that body. By 1936 his views had carried him on the platforms of the Irish Labour Party advocating the cause of the constitutional Labour Party.

At the end of 1934 the Republican Congress movement was in debt. George Gilmore had been sent to America to look for funds

---

* I was persistently given a figure of 4,000 for this defection, but I cannot estimate exactly either this or most other numerical claims for the IRA. Numbers of names on roll books did not in themselves give an exact picture of the numbers available to fight. However, it can be safely assumed that the IRA, in the South alone, had upwards of 30,000 in its ranks at this time.

and meantime the Congress weekly was forced to suspend publication, flickering into life for an occasional issue as did the movement itself at times such as strikes when members came into conflict with police. There were activities such as those of January, 1935, when the Dublin chain, Bacon Shops Ltd, was strike-hit by Michael Fitzpatrick, a trade unionist who was also on the IRA Army Council. The strike of the Dublin tram and bus workers in March 1935 provided another basis for a united front with the IRA, as did agitations for the release of political prisoners, or events such as the IRA Easter Week commemoration during which there were special contingents from the tramway strikers, the Workers' Union of Ireland, the Republican Congress, the Communist Party and the Unemployed Workers' Movement. At a May Day demonstration in College Green, the Republican Congress, the Communist Party of Ireland and the Unemployed Workers' Movement were represented. But relationships with the IRA ruptured again at Bodenstown in June. The attitude of the IRA was criticized in a leader in the 29 June issue of the *Republican Congress* which said:

From 1932 on it was clear the IRA should rouse the Republican population of Ireland into the new national advance.

Instead, Volunteers were sent out on silly attacks on neighbour lads of the same home circumstances who, in the absence of any lead from the IRA, were joining the Fianna Fail Reserve in the belief that it was to be used against the Fascists.

Instead of raising the economic war into an assertion of the nation's sovereignty, IRA Leaders tried to develop it into a squabble over Bass bottles in public-houses.

Instead of opening the road for afterwards movement, the IRA leaders, to the cheers of such men as Professor Hogan, opened an attack on their own left-wing elements.

They took the same attitude as the Irish Hierarchy and the *Independent*[*] towards the revolutionary workers within their ranks.

IRA leaders refused to permit Northern workers to carry banners in 1934, and actually tore the banner – 'United Irishmen of 1934' – carried by the Shankhill contingent.

And in 1935 IRA leaders ordered country units to attempt to smash up Republican Congress marchers.

[*] Which after the 1916 Rising carried a leading article calling for the punishment of the leaders.

But the shades were drawing in on the Republican Congress Movement.

Peadar O'Donnell announced the formation of an 'Active Service Unit' one hundred strong, on 3 January 1936. His proposals were:

> The active service unit will meet once a week; full strength. It will be in four sections:
>
> First Section will take on the task of penetrating the Fianna Fail Cumainn, IRA units and Trade Union branches with a view to developing demonstrations to reveal the strength of Republican feeling and to accelerate the independence ferment.
>
> Second Section will organize the housing struggles and extend Tenant Leagues throughout the City.
>
> Third Section will co-operate with the unemployed workers' movements, and also bring to general notice and support those small strikes that have become a feature of Dublin in these days when an injury to one is no longer the concern of all, and it will co-operate generally with strike committees.
>
> Fourth Section will cater for the social, financial and educational side of the movement; will organize outings, collections and classes.

The 'Independence ferment' was far less than O'Donnell hoped. Early in 1936 the *Republican Congress* weekly was forced to suspend publication, and by the end of the year the Congress offices at 57, Middle Abbey Street had to be vacated, as there was no money to pay the rent. An attempt was made to revive the paper under the name of the *Irish People* (the name of the first Fenian paper edited by Charles Kickham in the 1860s). Like its predecessor, it was printed by Frank Ryan, at the Co-operative Press, St Anthony's Place, but only one number seems to have appeared, on 29 February 1936.

O'Donnell, Gilmore, Ryan, Roddy Connolly and Cora Hughes gamely continued their efforts, co-operating with the Communists, then under the leadership of Sean Murray, in connection with the visit to Dublin of the Scottish Communist, William Gallacher MP, in April 1936. Gallacher attended the IRA Easter Commemoration on 12 April as one of the Communist and Republican Congress contingent. The presence of this group – whose members displayed a red button in their coats – provoked a good deal of public hostility and the marchers were stoned by one section of the crowd. The next day a large crowd assembled in College Green and prevented the holding of a public meeting at which Gallacher had been announced as a speaker. Peadar O'Donnell had to be rescued from the mob by the police. The crowd, on breaking up, marched through the streets and demonstrated outside the headquarters of the Communist Party. Subsequently the Congress group had to abandon a number of other proposed meetings through fear of attack.

By November 1936 the Republican Congress had pathetically ceased to exist, and the same may almost be said of the Communist Party of Ireland which was also in such financial difficulties that its organ, the *Workers' Voice*, ceased publication.

Meanwhile on the right the IRA proper attempted to give itself a semi-constitutional role such as that of the Republican Congress. These efforts were not successful. In fact, its role in a bitter transport strike, which began in Dublin on 3 March 1935, led to widespread arrests. The government had placed army lorries on the streets to alleviate the distress caused by the strike, and on 25 March the Army Council issued the following manifesto:

> Oglaigh na hEireann,
> Ard Aifig, Atha Cliath,
> 22 March 1935

Roinn: Army Council,
Uimhir: XD/61.

To the Joint Strike Committee,
Dublin Tram and Bus Workers.

A Chairde,
    The Army Council has had under consideration the dispute between the Dublin transport workers and the Dublin United Tramways Company.
    In the opinion of the Army Council, the situation is one in which more than the immediate causes of the dispute is involved. The action of the Free State Government in using the Free State Army for strike-breaking purposes, in the interest of a company to which the Government has given a monopoly, constitutes a definite challenge to all workers. That the complete transport system of Dublin should be at the mercy of a private monopoly is a matter affecting the welfare of all Dublin citizens.
    The Army Council takes the view that the matters at issue call for the

intervention of all Republicans who stand by the proclamation of Easter Week, wherein equal rights and opportunities are guaranteed to all citizens.

The Army Council, realizing the importance of the principles involved, feels that the joint efforts of the Free State Government and of the combine must be defeated. To meet this attack, the organized support of all those who stand for decent working and social conditions is necessary. For these reasons, the Army Council hereby expresses its willingness to assist the workers in their struggle.

Further, the Army Council is interested, as the governmental programme of the Irish Republican Army on the question of transport provides:–

'Railways, canals, air and waterways, and all forms of public inland transport shall be operated by a body set up by the National Economic Council'

The Army Council offers the services of the Army to assist in mobilizing the maximum support for the Dublin transport workers in their struggle, and is prepared to send representatives to meet the Strike Committee for this purpose.

le Sinne,
The Army Council,
Per..........Secretary

This statement alerted the government and on the following day, the houses of prominent members of the IRA and of the Republican Congress were raided by the police and forty-four men were taken into custody. Some of them, including Peadar O'Donnell, were released after interrogation, but on 24–29 April the Military Tribunal imposed the following sentences: eighteen months' imprisonment on Con Lehane, solicitor (a member of the Army Council at the time) for sedition, membership of an unlawful association and refusing to give an account of his movements; six months' imprisonment on Claude O'Loughlin, Richard Batterbury, Leo Burdock, Thomas Farrington, Patrick McElroy, Thomas Merrigan, Donal O'Donoghue, James Hannigan, Andrew Walsh, John Farrington, Joseph Hendley, Sean Brunswick, James Cole, Michael Neary and Laurence Carwood, on charges of membership of unlawful associations, etc.; one month's imprisonment on John Nalty, William Scott and Michael Kelly for membership of an unlawful association, etc.

Sean MacBride, Maurice Twomey, Michael Fitzpatrick and Sean

Russell went on the run, but Tom Barry, who had been arrested in Cork on 26 March on charges of seditious utterances at Tralee on 6 January, was caught and got six months.

These setbacks promoted the growth of another burst of activity in favour of 'constitutional' advance, and at a convention held in Dublin on 17 August the agenda included proposals for contesting future elections and, in certain cases, recognizing the courts. As usual those who believed in force objected strongly and there were threats of resignation. Nevertheless, another convention was held on 21 September and those present voted four to one to contest the next general election.

At a meeting at Barry's Hotel, Dublin on 7 March 1936 a new political party, Cumann Poblachta na hEireann, was formed. It was decided to try to have it both ways, by contesting parliamentary elections in the North and the South but stipulating that successful candidates would not take their seats. Maurice Twomey, who was lukewarm about the proposal, and Sean MacBride who was strongly for it, represented the IRA, and Republicans who abhorred Fianna Fail and Fine Gael and could see no sign of advancement in the nearly moribund Sinn Fein movement, also attended. Chief among these was the former chief of staff, Dr Andrew Cooney, who had been particularly active in the IRA in the 1920s; Dr James P. Brennan who was later to become active in Clann na Poblachta, a party Sean MacBride would lead; the Misses Fiona Plunkett, a sister of the executed 1916 leader; Florence McCarthy; Madge Daly of Limerick, sister of the widow of the executed 1916 leader Thomas Clarke, and Patrick MacLogan, the IRA organizer who was at the time Nationalist MP for South Armagh. He was subsequently elected chairman of the new party.

However, the opposition, particularly in the Dublin brigade, to the proposal that the IRA should have a political wing continued to be strong. A special convention was surrounded in Dublin on 19 May at which the two most prominent IRA men were again Sean MacBride and Maurice Twomey. MacBride proposed that Cumann Poblachta na hEireann should receive the active support of the IRA but Twomey objected and pointed out that there was no difference between this proposal and the first Fianna Fail proposal. The discussion was heated and finally Twomey walked out of the meeting followed by the more prominent Dublin Brigade officers: Claude O'Loughlin, James Coulton and Kevin Lawless.

The meeting revealed both the typical IRA man's Fenian distrust of constitutional politics, and his native belief that once he entered politics power was his for the taking. This view was not shared by the public as is shown by a table giving the votes secured by Republican Congress and Clan na Poblachta. The Communists put forward no candidates in this election but worked for the Republican Congress candidates. (The elections were held on 30 June.)

Republican Congress

Name	Area	Votes	Total Poll
Frank Ryan	No. 2	418	32,517
George Gilmore	No. 3	730	32,617
Cumann Poblachta na hEireann			
J. McGrath	No. 1	675	21,519
A. Lynn	No. 2	482	32,517
M. Fitzpatrick	No. 3	720	32,617
S. Malin	No. 4	630	21,556
Madame Maude Gonne MacBride	No. 5	689	29,733

For a personal assessment of how people generally felt about the movement I turned to my friend and colleague Anthony Butler, author, art critic, raconteur and television personality, who was both involved and at the same time sufficiently detached to be authoritative. He gave me the following characteristically humorous reminiscence:

'The first idea I had of the existence of the IRA came in 1927 when police invaded my school to arrest one of the teachers in connection with the shooting of Kevin O'Higgins. I was in a low primary grade and since we all hated the teacher involved – a sadistic brute – we were all on the side of law and order. Rumour spread that the arrest was only a fake to get him for his use of the cane. Mixed with this report was some mention of the IRAs which we assumed was just a higher class than the ABCs. From that moment until the late 1940s the IRA was a background to any thinking I might do on politics. It was the Mafia; it was truth; it was cruelty; it was justice – you didn't know what and this shifting assessment of their place in Irish life was one which most people shared.

'You couldn't escape the shadow of Republicanism and the IRA in Dublin of the late 1930s. They weighed heavily on the nation; they were powerful and whatever the reality – menacing.

'The ebbing tide of revolution which was dying on the beaches of the new state had received some fresh impetus from the discontent generated by depressed economic conditions and the IRA overlapped many other organizations in the labour field.

'In the great building strike of 1936 it played a large part even though the activities of its members were unofficial – this meant no more than an implied hand-washing by the Army: "Don't blame us if you're caught."

'While I was too cowardly – rather than too prudent – to involve myself with the IRA I was like many others delighted to sniff the powder and vicariously enjoy the actions of others who were deeply involved, delighted to hang about the fringes of the movement and know people who were involved. One of my friends kept his private armoury in his cushions which didn't make for comfort or a peaceful mind, but he was an exciting person for a boy to know.

'The building strike went on for a long time and my father was involved in it so I, with little else to do at sixteen, took part as well. One feature of these days was the hunger march – the suffering artisans exposing their agonies to the people of Dublin. I marched with them but didn't last long.

'Plump, fresh-skinned and most definitely outside the classification of deprived citizen at least in appearance, I was poor propaganda material. But the whole thing introduced me to Paddy.

'Paddy was an IRA hatchetman and executioner who, it was reputed, would shoot his own mother if the organization demanded. Since she was faster on the draw than he was the reputation was purely theoretical. Through Paddy I was drawn into the Sunday morning discussion groups around the Nelson Pillar. Here a million plots were hatched although not one per cent ever reached fruition.

'Paddy would vanish now and then for a few days as the police made it a habit to pick him up no matter what happened through Republican activism. They always arrested him away from his home as it required siege tactics to take him in the bosom of his family and his mother was a deadly shot with a saucepan. Indeed until they learned to arrest him away from his home the political police tried as far as possible to take him on Fridays. It was much less dangerous to be hit by a fried kipper than to risk the scalding downpour of a stew outside the flesh-eating abstinence of that day.

'There was a vehicle builders strike on with the building strike and a number of "blackleg" workers were imported from England. Since this combined the national enemy with social justice Paddy offered himself and his "Peter the Painter" to the vehicle builders.

'Whether they accepted his offer or not I don't know but the decision was made to shoot the scabs. Knowing nothing of this I drifted into Paddy's small group one Sunday morning before the leader himself arrived. One of the faithful asked me if I was going to help Paddy the following morning and I said I was without being too sure what it was all about.

'When Paddy arrived I was an integrated if ignorant conspirator. The guarded language of the group, which stated nothing directly or concretely, contributed to keeping me in the dark.

'As arranged I turned up the next day outside the Northern Star Hotel in Amiens Street at 12.30. It was a hot steaming summer's day but Paddy and his two companions were ear-deep in trench coats that bulged in unexpected places as if they were carrying massive loads of scrap-iron. I wore an open-necked shirt, a sports coat and flannels and was the coolest man in every way amongst them. Paddy shook my hand and almost choked with emotion.

'"I didn't think you had the guts."

'Slightly puzzled I sat quietly on my bright new bicycle and discussed the weather, trying at the same time to work out what was involved. They didn't seem interested in chit-chat and kept looking up Amiens Street with fierce restlessness.

'An hour went by while I waited and talked and they displayed even greater apprehension and impatience. Finally we dispersed with Paddy thanking me profusely. I cycled away.

'It was a week or two before I found out Paddy's plans for that morning. A report in an evening newspaper told of the shooting in the leg of a British vehicle builder outside the Northern Star Hotel in Amiens Street. Paddy read it with a grin and nudged me.

'"Sorry, I couldn't ask you along for this one. Two of us was enough."

'He seemed a little ashamed of his neglect.

'"But don't worry, oul son. The next action is on I'll see you're in on it."

'The full horror of the event didn't strike me immediately but when it did I erupted in goose pimples. From that time on I kept clear of Paddy and put an end to my revolutionary career as an assassin.'

The year, 1936, that Butler abandoned his revolutionary career coincided with the government's coming to conclusions similar to his concerning the IRA and for very similar reasons.

On 29 April and 21 May large-scale swoops on IRA men in Cork and Dublin resulted in Twomey, most of the Dublin brigade and all the principal Cork IRA men with the exception of Tom Barry (commanding officer Cork County), Tadgh Lynch (battalion adjutant), and Denis Griffin (County intelligence officer) being arrested. Sean Russell and Sean MacBride escaped the net but Donal O'Donoghue, who was then editing *An Phoblacht*, was arrested on 8 July in Co. Kerry. He went on hunger strike in Arbour Hill prison on 11 July, remaining without food until 7 August when he was released.

The incidents that directed the government's attention to the IRA varied from idiotic episodes like that which occurred on 25 January in the Masonic Hall at Tuckey Street, Cork, where a party of IRA men struck a blow for Ireland by holding up the diners in the midst of a convivial occasion and smashing up plates and furniture, to incidents in which three lives were lost. The three deaths were those of Roderick More O'Farrell, who was fatally wounded on 9 February 1935; Vice-Admiral Henry Boyle Townsend Somerville, who was shot dead at 9.30 p.m. on 24 March 1936 as he stood at the door of his home at Castle-Townsend, Co. Cork; and John Egan, who on 26 April 1936 was shot dead in full view of everyone in Mitchell Street, Dungarvan, Co. Waterford.

The first two killings were not sanctioned by the Army Council but the death of Egan was as a result of an IRA court-martial. It was probably never intended to kill More O'Farrell at all. This tragedy arose out of a rent agitation on the Sanderson estate in Co. Longford. Tenants were demanding a 50 per cent reduction in rent and the English agent, Captain Montague, was unable to collect any rents while the dispute continued. More O'Farrell, Senior, was appointed in his stead and the dispute simmered throughout 1934. On 2 December, at a public meeting at Edgeworthstown, Co. Longford, official IRA speakers, who had been formally invited by the Tenants Association to join in the agitation, made inflammatory speeches on the lines of: 'there must be plenty of pitchforks and boughs on the trees around

Edgeworthstown but one strong bough should be left on a tree convenient to More O'Farrell's in case of need.' On 9 February 1935, a party of armed men raided the More O'Farrell house, outside Edgeworthstown, during a dinner party. More O'Farrell and his son strongly resisted the raiders' attempts to take away More O'Farrell* and several shots were fired, one of them striking young More O'Farrell who later died. Seven members of the IRA were arrested and charged with murder at the Central Criminal Court in Dublin, but on 10 December 1935, before the evidence for the defence was taken, the jury brought in a verdict of not guilty.

When Frank MacDermot, speaking in the Dail on 16 June 1936, asked Minister for Justice Gerald Boland why the case had not been heard before the Military Tribunal, the minister replied that a certificate was not issued empowering the Tribunal to hear the case as the minister 'could not conscientiously state that the crime was committed for the purpose of interfering with the machinery of government, or the administration of justice'.

MacDermot was reflecting an opposition view that the Fianna Fail government and the IRA were still in some form of collusion. This unease spread to the public, so that when IRA trigger-happiness claimed two more lives Fianna Fail was driven, both by the necessity of upholding governmental authority and the need to show people where the government stood, to act forcefully against its former friends.

Admiral Somerville was shot dead because the Cork IRA, strongly anti-British and anti-Protestant, took violent exception to his giving references to young local men who wished to join the British navy. The shooting of an elderly man who had come unsuspectingly to the door of his home to answer a knock did more to alienate popular sympathy from the IRA than any single act since the shooting of Kevin O'Higgins.

Then on 26 April came the Egan killing. Egan was an ordinary country lad, and his death horrified the countryside. He had been one of a party of five IRA men arrested on 12 July 1935, for illegal drilling in Co. Waterford. On 18 July the commander of the West Waterford battalion of the IRA, William O'Donoghue, was arrested, and on 30 July received three months' imprisonment. He had been in charge of

---

* I am informed that tarring and feathering, rather than shooting or hanging, was intended.

the drill sessions for which Egan and the others were arrested. At O'Donoghue's hearing Egan and two others were released, but the IRA believed that Egan had earned their *nolle prosequi* by turning state's evidence, and that the other two men released with him were set free only as a sort of smoke screen. He was shot from a motor car (stolen earlier in the evening from the home of a district justice) and on 14 May four members of the IRA – William O'Donoghue, John Tobin, Edmund Carraigan and Michael Conway – were arrested and charged with his murder.

Conway was sentenced to death but was released on 4 May 1938, his case having become in the meantime a *cause célèbre*. First, his counsel, Albert Wood and Art O'Connor, refused to appear before the Military Tribunal, saying that they would not act for him because they would not appear in any case before the Military Tribunal. Then his solicitors Messrs Hogan & Lehane – Con Lehane being a former member of the Army Council, who had by then severed his connection with the army – sent the correspondence to the press. Only one paper, the *Mayo News*, printed it on 18 July. After this, Conway's case proved a rallying point for IRA publicists. 'Micksey', as he was called, was one of the best-known IRA men in Ireland at the time, and a classical example of a figure of menace to those outside the movement, and the epitome of decency, kindness, and sincerity to those within it. (He later became a monk.)

Twomey got three years from the Military Tribunal for membership of an unlawful organization, on 19 June, a day after the IRA had been outlawed by an order from the executive council, after a two-day debate in the Dail. In the course of the debate the acting Minister for Justice, Gerald Boland, made the following significant statement concerning future government policy towards the IRA: '. . . the fact that these murders have occurred . . . makes it clear that stern action must be taken against any organization which claims to have the power of life and death over its members, or ex-members, or other citizens, or which claims that it is entitled to use force upon the community to compel obedience to its will. I now give definite notice to all concerned that the so-called Irish Republican Army, or any organization which promotes or advocates the use of arms for the attainments of its object will not be tolerated . . .'

The next day he followed this up by saying, '. . . we smashed them [Blueshirts] and we are going to smash the others [the IRA] . . . if there are people who know where arms are, and their sense of civic duty will not encourage them to tell where they are, then if any form of reward is necessary to induce them to do so, we will give it . . .'

The government also banned the Bodenstown meeting, fixed for 21 June. Trains and buses heading for the meeting were stopped, an aeroplane hovered overhead, and on the ground armed cars and police were grouped. One band of young Limerick IRA men seized a lorry and attempted to make their way to Bodenstown but were arrested and sentenced to nine months by the Military Tribunal. And a young man, Sean Glynn, committed suicide in Arbour Hill prison on 13 September. A subsequent commission of inquiry investigating his death found that imprisonment had so worked on his mind that he became depressed and took his own life.

4

The IRA's Foreign Links

The IRA did not make any great impact on the outside world after the end of the Anglo-Irish war, and the outside world has never impinged very greatly on the IRA. There were some peripheral contacts with European countries, and improbably enough with Russia, but the only country to which the IRA looked for assistance in any sustained manner was America, where large-scale emigration from Ireland following the great famine of the 1840s had created a powerful source of strength. Embittered Irishmen in America were approached by Irish leaders as diverse in their policies and appeal as Parnell, Redmond, de Valera and Sean Russell.

The IRA's contact with Europe was, on the other hand, principally through its left-wing members, such as David Fitzgerald or Peadar O'Donnell. Fitzgerald was a frequent visitor to Russia during the 1920s and the IRA was officially represented at the World Congress of the Anti-Imperialist League in Brussels in 1927 by Frank Ryan and O'Donnell, and by Sean MacBride and Donal O'Donoghue at Frankfurt on Main in 1929. As a result of IRA representations the Frankfurt congress (which met 20–31 July) passed a resolution calling on 'the organized workers of Great Britain to withdraw the threat of war against Ireland and allow Ireland freely to organize her own life in accordance with working class ideals'.

The congress also pledged that the 'revolutionary organizations in Ireland' would receive the 'whole-hearted backing of the Congress' for their 'next attempt' to set up the desired state and elected an IRA man called Magennis, who had been given two years' hard labour for the possession of a revolver, as a member of the honorary praesidium of the congress. This was the most tangible result the IRA deputation achieved.

Peadar O'Donnell and Sean Hayes introduced to Ireland an offshoot of the Third International with the formation of a branch of the

European Peasants Committee which O'Donnell represented at the international congress of the movement in Berlin during March 1930. However, neither the IRA nor the Communists thought much of each other. Police records of the 1930s show that two members of the British Communist Party who were deputed to visit Ireland during 1930 to study conditions on behalf of the Communist International reported that the Irish were 'too Mexican' to make good Communist revolutionaries. Presumably this means too volatile and unamenable to discipline. The Irish Catholic Republicans were certainly unmoved by appeals such as that of Peadar O'Donnell to 'think of the Army as the armed members of the toiling and working masses. The leadership must be that of a revolutionary working-class party whose membership may be all IRA, though the Army will be larger than the Party.'

First Saor Eire and then the Republican Congress failed to marry the class struggle to the IRA's efforts. In Irish circumstances such an outcome was inevitable as Stalin himself recognized when he had dealings with the IRA not long after it had reorganized itself following the Civil War.

In the spring of 1925 IRA headquarters considered seeking aid from Russia through 'Pa' Murray, a formidable figure during the war of independence and with extensive contacts in Russian circles in London. Through these he arranged for an IRA delegation to be received in Moscow. The other militant Republican in the pay was Sean Russell, with Gerald Boland sent by de Valera to hold a watching brief on behalf of the more constitutionally minded section of the movement. The trio reached Germany and left Hamburg on 27 June with forged passports. (Ironically the outbreak of the Second World War would see Russell dying on a German submarine and Boland, as Minister of Justice in a government led by de Valera, distinguishing himself by the rigour with which he dealt with men who were still following Russell's leadership.)

At Leningrad the men were shown a variety of weapons – but 'Pa' was the only one who could use them! He has told me that his impression at the time was that the Russians simply did not have very much armament to give anyone, though this was not the reason which the Communists gave for refusing to help. After Leningrad they went to Moscow where Murray met Stalin. Stalin asked him what precautions he could guarantee against any weapons they might be given being seized by the Free Staters. He rocked Murray by producing a complete list of the amount of guns the government authorities had seized in Ireland to that date. In addition he wanted to know how many trained men the IRA could guarantee to use the weapons. The interview lasted for about half an hour during which Stalin made it clear that he was worried that any weapons he might give to the IRA would be discovered and used by Russia's enemies as a pretext for invasion. He thought that such a gift might particularly inflame the British.

All in all the interview and the visit were not successes. Stalin told Murray that, aboard the liner from Hamburg, the others had talked too much and that several people knew of their mission. Checking on this episode with Boland, he told me how they had met a friendly woman Communist 'who knew all about the Irish problem. She knew all about the Church and about our agricultural economy.' Whether or not the lady was a Cheka agent, the Russians do not seem to have been too impressed with the Irish revolutionaries. Boland told me that the first question he was asked on arrival was, 'How many bishops did you hang?' When he answered, 'None', his interrogator replied, 'Ah you people are not serious at all.'

This trip ended the IRA's chances, though not their hopes, of getting a large supply of armament from abroad. A trickle of Thompson guns with a significant history did continue to straggle in from New York. The guns were part of a consignment of 500 Thompson guns ordered from the Auto Ordnance Company, set up by Colonel Thompson in New York, on 5 April 1921. They were stored in a warehouse in the Bronx on La Fontaine Avenue, under the supervision of Lawrence DeLacy. DeLacy arranged to have them smuggled aboard the ship *East Side* for transhipment to Ireland on 17 June. However, on 16 June the consignment was discovered and seized as the *East Side* lay in her berth in Hoboken. The US customs held on to the guns until 14 September 1925, when an order of discontinuance was issued allowing them to pass into the hands of Joseph McGarrity. This of course precluded their use in the Anglo-Irish war, but the IRA did manage to smuggle some Thompson guns into Ireland during the war. On 16 June 1921, two of them were used to ambush a troop-train moving from Amiens Street to Kingsbridge – the first time Thompsons were used in warfare. (The ambush was carried out by a twelve-man party, led by Oscar Traynor, between Drumcondra Road and Botanic Road. The British admitted to three casualties, one of them serious.)

Eventually some of the American weapons found their way to Ireland, some in the personal luggage of a famous Kerry All-Ireland football team which visited America in 1927. Tom Barry told me that he had taken more ashore at Cork Harbour where he was an executive with the Port and Docks board. And Jim Killeen and Frank Driver recalled taking a lorry to Galway to pick up a consignment with Sean Russell. Killeen remembers the Galway episode vividly because two days after he and Russell had driven across Ireland with a lorry-load of illicit Thompsons he discovered that Russell had not taxed the lorry and that at any moment a vigilant policeman could have had them arrested.

The Russian episode convinced Murray, as it helped to convince other, more constitutional Republicans, that the IRA had little future and he dropped out of the movement shortly after his return. By the end of 1925 the paths of the militants and of de Valera's followers had also diverged.

In America however the ground for Republican propaganda, though it shrank enormously after the end of the Anglo-Irish war, still continued fruitful as Murray could attest. Murray, who died at the end of 1968, was already an old man, interested in literature and history, when I first interviewed him in 1964. He told me of other incidents which he had taken part in during the War of Independence before going on to talk of America.

For instance at one stage during the war while the conscription crisis was raging Cathal Brugha took him along with a party of volunteers who, if conscription had been introduced, were going to machine-gun the British government benches from the visitors gallery of the House of Commons. As the debate wore on member after member of the group lost his nerve, but Murray, whose special task was the assassination of Balfour, stayed on in London, although the delay was telling on him too. One day he learned that Balfour was to preside at Oxford at a university function that afternoon and to test his nerve he went to Oxford and accosted Balfour on the street under the pretext of seeking directions. Balfour courteously walked with him for about a hundred yards, during which Murray satisfied himself that he could have carried out his mission if he had to.

When we spoke of America we were sitting in his house in Terenure waiting for a priest to call to hear his confession, because he had been unable to leave the house for some months following a car accident. He said to me that he had been in America and then said no more. I thought that his mind was dwelling on the priest's visit, and after a few moments' silence ventured to prod him again.

'What were you doing there?'

There was a moment's silence and his kindly blue eyes flickered as though they had focused on something distasteful. Then he replied, 'Shootin' a poor divill.'

The man had been condemned to death as a traitor by the IRA after a party of Volunteers was betrayed to Crown forces at Clonmult, Co. Cork. After they had surrendered they were tortured and then shot out of hand. The man had gone to America and it was not until after the signing of the truce that Collins got word of his whereabouts in New York. Murray and two comrades were sent to carry out the sentence, but when they got to New York they found that their quarry had changed his address. However, by extraordinary ill-luck the unfortunate man turned up to watch the St Patrick's Day parade down Fifth Avenue, across the street from where Murray and his confederates were standing. With the aid of an Irish-American policeman who was on duty at the parade they traced him to his new lodgings at 483 Columbus Avenue. Murray shot him with a revolver borrowed from a New York policeman on 13 April 1922. Somehow the victim, Patrick Connor, a 29-year-old Corkman, who worked as a book-keeper at Altman's department store, survived the attack. Four bullets were removed from his body at the Reconstruction Hospital at Central Park West and 100th St.

Sitting in his red-bricked respectability in suburban Dublin nearly fifty years later Murray sighed and said, 'I was sorry after. We heard later that the poor devil had been tortured to make him talk. We didn't know that at the time.'

Even today it is conceivable that a modern IRA party might receive similar assistance in New York, but it was not at all to be wondered at in the 1916–22 period. Current American statistics of the Irish population in America estimate that there are more than forty million people born in Ireland or of Irish descent, living there. The generation which lived around the time of the Anglo-Irish war had comparatively recent memories of crowding in ghettoes; persecutions by nativist groups such as the Know Nothings; of grinding poverty and hostility from the white Anglo-Saxon Protestants who denied them employment; of discrimination in boarding houses and sometimes in jobs with signs saying 'No Irish or colored need apply'; and of an anguished parting from the country they loved followed by a smelly, dangerous and often deadly voyage to the States in conditions which have branded the phrase 'coffin ships' into Irish folklore. Probably as many Irish died aboard these badly ventilated, over-crowded ships and were buried at sea as were claimed by every revolution from the time of Wolfe Tone to the signing of the treaty with England in 1921.

The Irish relied heavily on the consolation of relation, and took with them their own brand of ultramontane Jansenistic Roman Catholicism. To many a hungry immigrant Irishman or woman the Church was the only lifebuoy in a sea of hostility. Thus today in America while some Irish are organized in the service of the Democratic Party almost all Irish are organized in the service of the American Catholic Church. An annual display such as the St Patrick's Day Parade down Fifth Avenue is not organized by Irishmen to draw attention to Ireland, or to gain scholarships or industries for their native land, but as a predominantly Catholic festival which is organized under the direction of the archdiocese of New York by the Ancient Order of Hibernians.

Before 1922 the British were still in Ireland and it was relatively easy to canalize both religious fervour and patriotic anti-British nationalism into organizations of some power and significance. The combination of these emotions is caught exactly in an appeal which Joseph McGarrity issued in Philadelphia on 4 June 1914. Two days earlier the Clann na Gael executive had met in New York and set up a committee, headed by McGarrity, to attempt to organize and equip a volunteer force for Ireland. In his appeal McGarrity implored nationalist-minded Irishmen to attend a meeting at 726, Spruce Street, on 7 June: 'In the name of God, in the name of Tone's bleeding throat, in the name of Emmet's severed head, in the name of Fr Murphy of '98, and in the countless dead, who died for Ireland, we ask you to be there.'

These emotions may seem quaint today but they helped to create the 1916 Rising and change the course of Irish history. And earlier John Redmond with his constitutional United Irish League of America, founded in 1901, used these emotions to get contributions which paid for the Irish Parliamentary Party's expenses in the elections of 1906 and 1910 and, until salaries were introduced for MPs, a large part of the ordinary living expenses of the Irish MPs.

In America as in Ireland the constitutional movement for Irish independence had to contend with the influence of the revolutionary movement of the IRB's American offshoot, Clann na Gael. It was the army which in 1907 sent Thomas Clarke back from New York to help revivify the IRB in Ireland. Through men like John Devoy and Joseph McGarrity Clann money and policies passed into Ireland, and in 1916 helped to destroy the influence of Redmond in America as in Ireland. McGarrity also played an influential part in saving de Valera's life after the 1916 Rising. After de Valera's baptismal certificate was procured from St Agnes Church, New York, thus demonstrating his American birth, McGarrity got a lawyer friend, Francis Doyle, a prominent Irish American, to use it to bring pressure to bear on President Wilson (through Joseph Tumulty) who in turn contacted the American ambassador in London who successfully entreated with the British cabinet not to execute de Valera.

The Irish in America, like the Irish at home, were a fractious lot and there was an obvious conflict of interest between the United Ireland League – the constitutionalists – and the Clann na Gael, the revolutionaries. John Devoy founded a paper, the *Gaelic American*, in 1903 to combat the influence of Patrick Ford's *Irish World* which supported Redmond and parliamentarianism. The principal leaders of the Clann at this time were John Devoy, the old Fenian, Judge Daniel Cohalan, a Democratic politician of standing, and Joseph McGarrity. The Clann operated on a principle which was outlined by Cohalan that 'Ireland's true interest will be best served by a steady, resolute and progressive policy of organization among our own people the world over and the cultivation of alliances with English enemies'.

The success of Clann propaganda may be gauged from the comment of the Irish-American *Chicago Citizen* of July 1908 – 'There is not an Irishman in America today, in whose veins good red blood is flowing, who would not rejoice to hear that a German army was marching in triumph across England from Yarmouth to Milford Haven.' The 1916 Rising put the final seal on the decline of the United Ireland League which had been speedily going downhill since Redmond had pledged support to Britain in 1914.

The German ambassador to America, von Bernstorff, co-operated with the Clann through John Devoy in assisting Sir Roger Casement in his attempt to organize an Irish brigade from captured prisoners of war. Through Devoy again, Germany supplied arms for use in the Rising, but due to muddling over dates they did not arrive in time, and were scuttled off Cobh.

Following the Rising the Clann rode high in Irish-American affairs and attempted to force President Wilson to include Irish independence in the post-war peace settlement, for Wilson had made the point that the war was being fought for the freedom of small nations. Wilson, however, though not antipathetic towards the Irish as such, was bitterly at odds with Cohalan and also hesitated to offend Britain, needing England's support in launching the League of Nations. He held out against the Irish claim despite strong Irish-American pressure but on 4 March 1919, the House of Representatives in response to this influence voted 216 to 45 that the peace conference should favourably consider Ireland's claim to self-determination, and on 6 June the Senate voted 60 to 1 in favour of de Valera, Griffith and Count Plunkett being allowed to appear before the conference.

The Clann na Gael leaders, through the 'Friends of Irish Freedom', founded in 1916, had set up an Irish society fund which by the end of 1920 had collected almost $900,000. Only $115,000 found its way to Ireland, but $750,000 was spent in attacking the League of Nations – 'Britain's League'. Cohalan and Devoy joined forces with prominent domestic opponents of the League such as Henry Cabot Lodge and William Borah and they organized huge protest meetings against Wilson during his speaking tour in September 1919, taking full-page advertisements in the newspapers along his route.

This was the position when de Valera arrived in the States in June 1919. He stayed first at McGarrity's home in Philadelphia, and formed a strong personal friendship with him. Indeed the *Irish Republic*, produced in New York by a group of McGarrity associates, in September 1940 was correct in stating that it was McGarrity who persuaded de Valera to use the title 'President of the Irish Republic' instead of 'Priomh Aire', thus committing de Valera irrevocably to that title. Clann propagandists also allege that the title was one of the reasons why he split with Cohalan and Devoy. They, as IRB supporters, recognized Collins, the head of the IRB, as automatically 'President of the Republic'.

But there were more cogent reasons for this disagreement. Devoy, an old man, was very much under the influence of the dynamic Cohalan, who, while passionately devoted to the cause of Irish freedom, felt that it was subordinate to the interests of America. Cohalan felt there inevitably could be a war between America and England, whose sponsorship of the League of Nations he saw as part of a plot to overthrow America. De Valera felt he was entitled to control the Irish in America and set out to destroy Cohalan's leadership. He was ultimately successful, but the damaging split which ensued greatly weakened the 'clout' of the Irish Americans.

In January 1920 an Irish bond drive was launched, with Irish bond certificates sold on a guarantee of exchange for Irish Republican bonds after the Irish Republic was recognized. It is estimated that $5.5 million were subscribed. De Valera prevented approximately half of this money from going to Ireland. It lay for years in American banks. Part of it was ultimately returned to the original subscribers, but de Valera also succeeded in getting control of sufficient funds from the bond drive to enable him to set up the Irish Press newspaper group in Dublin which became a de Valera family enterprise. By November 1920 de Valera was able to set up his own Irish-American Association, popularly known as 'Growl' because of the sound of the acronym AARI – for American Association for the Recognition of the Irish Republic. This organization soon became dominant in Irish-American affairs. Out of it arose a self-appointed commission, the American Commission on Conditions in Ireland, which reported the sufferings imposed on the Irish by the British (for the purposes of the report these sufferings, though basically genuine enough, were somewhat overdrawn) and an American Committee for Relief in Ireland was formed. This collected an additional $5 million to alleviate conditions in Ireland.

De Valera, however, also aroused considerable controversy in Irish-American circles by attacking Cohalan and the *Gaelic American* and by appearing at the Republican Party's national convention against the wishes of Cohalan who also led a delegation there. The two groups made a bad impression with their quarrelling. Most of all he offended by an interview published in the *Westminster Gazette* on 6 February 1920 (after his return) in which he proposed a solution for the Irish question similar to the association between Cuba and America.

Yet by the time de Valera slipped back to Ireland for Christmas of 1920 he had so mobilized American public opinion on the side of the Irish struggle that it became clear to the British that American funds and public opinion could continue to support the Irish for an indefinite period. There was also a very considerable body of sympathy for the Irish cause in England itself and both facts weighed heavily with the British cabinet when it called for a truce and entered the negotiations which culminated in the signing of the treaty and the British departure from the South of Ireland.

In America the withdrawal of the British was hailed as a great Irish victory. The subtleties of Home Rule, self-determination, dominion status, partition, government by devolution and all the rest of it largely

escaped the vast bulk of those who supported the Irish independence movement. From 1921 it is true to say that the Americans as
a nation switched off the Irish problem. She had got her independence, the British were gone. What more remained to be done?

For the Irish-American politicians most involved in the struggle
the issue was not immediately clear either. For instance, McGarrity
who was to spend nearly twenty years trying to wreck the treaty in
fact welcomed it with an editorial in his *Irish Press* on 10 December
1920. He said, under the heading 'Irish Republic Triumphs': 'Ireland's sovereign Independence is acknowledged by the British
Cabinet and their action is approved by Britain's King. This much
is certain . . .' After castigating sections of the American press for
their 'despicable' attempts to 'make it appear that the citizens of the
Republic of Ireland are to give allegiance to King George', he went
on to show that the 'supposed Oath' was merely a 'very clever
juggling with words' to give as little hurt to the British ministers and
'the King's pride as possible'.

The difficult hurdle of the new state's title he took without a
blink:

> Many people will say that the name Republic has been dropped. No
> such thing has happened. Ireland is to be a Gaelic not an English
> nation, and at the first sitting of Dail Erin the Gaelic name for the
> recreated nation was adopted. That name is Saor-stat, pronounced
> Seer Sthath. If England prefers the correct English translation of the
> Gaelic term, which is Free State, instead of the Latin word Republic,
> Ireland should be quite happy that England has made such a choice.

He wound up by saying that 'putting aside all meaningless phrases if
the Treaty made is approved and carried into effect, Ireland again
becomes an independent sovereign nation among the nations'. The
British, he said, would move out and the Irish take possession of
their rightful heritage, boons for which he asked that 'every Irish
heart be lifted up to his maker in gratitude'.

Michael Collins didn't go so far. He saw the treaty as not confer-
ring full freedom, but 'freedom to achieve freedom', a 'stepping
stone to the Republic'. Certainly de Valera didn't share McGarrity's
view. He greeted the treaty's signing with a letter to the *Dublin
Press*, co-signed by Brugha and Austin Stack, saying that the treaty
was 'in violent conflict with the wishes of the Irish people'.

McGarrity soon swung back into line behind de Valera and a split paralleling the split in Ireland built up in the Clann. McGarrity sided completely with de Valera, Devoy with the upholders of the treaty (who gave him a state funeral through Dublin when he died in 1927). Clann na Gael split into two bodies: Clann na Gael, under Devoy, and the Clann na Gael Reorganized, or Clann na Gael and IRA as it is better known, under McGarrity and Luke Dillon. This grouping remained imbued with the same sentiments as the IRA in Ireland but McGarrity, though he became particularly bitter against Devoy, did not cool in his friendship with de Valera until the middle 1930s when de Valera began to jail IRA men. (Once, however, de Valera entered the Dail in 1927 the Clann decided officially no longer to support Fianna Fail.)

After the Civil War Irish-American activities were mainly confined to the Clann. Broadly speaking New York City went to the Cohalan-Devoy section (as did a number of lesser centres throughout the country) but the principal Irish centres of Boston, Chicago, Cleveland, San Francisco, Philadelphia, Detroit and, in Canada, Ontario, all sided with McGarrity and his chief lieutenants, Luke Dillon, Connie Neenan, John Ryan and Major Enright.

McGarrity was born in 1874 near the village of Carrickmore in Co. Tyrone. He attended the local national school and worked on the family holding but at fourteen, during his parents' absence at Mass one Sunday morning, he ran away to Liverpool. About a year later a man in his lodgings who had bought a ticket to America had to return to Ireland on his mother's death. McGarrity, who had spent the previous nights praying to the Blessed Virgin for some way of getting to America himself, was able to buy the docket from him for £2. He travelled in a black jersey and corduroy pants without any luggage. After about a day at sea a ship's officer began questioning him about his lack of luggage, but an American overhearing him asked, 'Has that boy got a ticket?' The officer replied, 'Yes,' 'Well then,' said the American, 'why don't you mind your own business? What right have you got to question him?' He and a group of Indians befriended the young McGarrity for the rest of the passage. The incident never left McGarrity's mind and confirmed him in his belief that America was a wonderful country.

He must have had extraordinary personality because another passenger, who arrived with him in New York, discovering that McGarrity had no money, gave him the fare to Philadelphia where McGarrity had a sister working in a hotel. Her first gesture of initiation into American society was to place a Derby hat on his head – which may have been why McGarrity always affected this type of headgear. He worked at the usual diversity of jobs which a young immigrant from Ireland at that period found himself lucky to get but, being a teetotaller and enormously able and energetic, by the time he was twenty he owned a saloon in Philadelphia.

He brought his family to America and throughout his life continued the pattern of generosity he experienced on the boat. To give an example: at the time of the Irish independence controversy, McGarrity was driving a huge open touring car. Stopping one day at a street light he was surprised to find a passerby getting into the seat behind him without saying a word, and then after ten blocks tapping him on the shoulder and handing him a dime, thinking the car was a bus! Years later, during the Wall Street crash, McGarrity happened to meet this same man weeping in the small hours of the morning in Philadelphia station. He had lost his money, his wife was very ill and suicide seemed to be the only outlet. McGarrity gave him some thousands of dollars on the spot. No one knew of this until after McGarrity's funeral when the man turned up with almost three thousand dollars and told the story as he handed the money over to the relatives.

No one can say how much time, energy and money McGarrity expended on the Irish cause. *The Irish Press*, which he founded in Philadelphia in March 1918 because the American government was inhibiting the circulation of the *Gaelic American* and the *Irish World* (the two existing Irish-American organs), is estimated to have cost him about two hundred thousand dollars, and his subsequent support for other independence groups must have cost at least as much.

It is a measure of the calibre of the man and of his friends that people were prepared to act on an equally generous scale with him. During 1920 the Clann na Gael leader, Major Michael Enright, hearing that McGarrity was in difficulties gave him his entire savings and had to go to work as a clerk in city hall, Chicago, as a result. Connie Neenan, another prominent Clann figure, who had mentioned McGarrity's difficulties to Enright, said, 'I'm awful sorry that I came and asked you to get money for Joe.' Enright's reply was, 'Joe McGarrity wanted it and if it was ten times as much and I knew I was going to lose it I would still give it to him.' When the Irish Hospitals Sweepstakes began to prosper in America about 1934 McGarrity was appointed an agent, and he became relatively well-off again.

He had a literary bent as well, publishing three books of poetry and contributing to Irish culture and literature whenever he could. His concept of what constituted art was, however, strongly influenced by his political beliefs. During the 1911–12 tour of America by the Abbey Players the Clann's Anglophobia caused it to regard Yeats and the players as 'fellow agents of England' because they considered the Abbey's work 'stage Irish' and so of benefit to English propaganda about Ireland. McGarrity was very active in the attempts to get the company prosecuted in Philadelphia and after causing a disturbance at *The Playboy of the Western World*, wrote to his friend Patrick McCartan in Ireland: 'There was nothing in the play that would cause anyone who would witness it to have love or admiration for the people and the country represented in it. If the *Playboy* is art, to hell with art and those who create it.'

Luke Dillon, son of Co. Sligo parents who had emigrated to America from Leeds when he was six, was an Old Testament figure, stern, scrupulously honest, and undying in his hatred of England. Men went mad or died in prison conditions which he endured, to emerge in good physical and mental health. In prison he had refused the entreaties of Clann leaders such as McGarrity that he acknowledge his guilt and petition for mercy, sending out a letter that such a course would mean that, 'The rest of my life would not be worth such a surrender of principle.' He had been jailed for an attempt to blow up the locks of the Welland canal to prevent the Canadians sending troops to aid the British in the Boer War.

Dan Breen told me that he visited Dillon on his death bed, and that the dying man said to him, 'Dan, I've bombed the bastards and I'd bomb them again, but you have tasted their blood.' He had been active in dynamite plots in England during the winter of 1883–84, being responsible for, among other explosions, those at the Carlton Club and the House of Commons. Cornelius Neenan, who had emigrated to America from Cork, and who succeeded him as secretary of Clann na Gael after his death in 1929, took part in these also. Breen told me that when a beggar set up a pitch outside the rebuilt Carlton Club with a placard on his chest saying 'blinded by the Fenian outrages' Dillon asked that all Clann sympathizers passing through London give the man a halfcrown. 'That's the way I'd like to see all the so-and-sos,' he said, according to Breen.

Other prominent Irish-Americans who continued in the Clann after the rifts and upheavals of 1921–23 were John Sullivan of Boston, Tom

Pearse of Cincinnati, John Stanton of Cleveland, Jimmy McGee in New York and Harry McCarney in Philadelphia.

As with the IRA in Ireland the same names recur over a period of decades. Those I have mentioned were men of above average ability, but they were deprived of strong public sympathy for getting the British out of Ireland and had many factors militating against the slightest chance of success. Moreover, the strong streak of sentimentality in Irish-American affairs tended to promote a situation in which Irish-Americans were swayed by what they would like to be true. They rarely applied themselves to finding out what the present situation was and how it differed from the land and problems of their youth. And if they were too young to remember Ireland or were born of Irish parents in America, they were subject both to parental memories and Irish-American education which, like that at home, had until very recently a strong anti-intellectual bias and an emphasis on inculcating devotion to the Roman Catholic Church.

The confusion, uncertainty and lack of initiative produced by this type of training predisposed most of those exposed to it towards accepting the *status quo* and the strong, simple certainties propounded on any issue from pulpit or platform. The day to day shifts in domestic Irish politics, the new allegiances, fresh groupings and new faces were a mystery to those in America who continued to send money and militant advice home to 'the boys'. They grew increasingly baffled and pained when the Irish refused their seemingly manifest duty of rising in wrath to drive the British out of 'Occupied Ireland'. McGarrity, for example, was so out of touch with the shifts in Irish politics that when Frank Aiken came to America in 1926 after the formation of Fianna Fail he was unaware that Aiken was no longer chief of staff of the IRA and was shaken when Neenan, who had been back to Ireland, informed him. McGarrity complained in a letter to Aiken that 'America has been asked to give its support for the past three or four years to the Republicans at home, but I have failed to learn up to the present time just what the platform or the policy of the party is.' Americans would always be in the position of never knowing clearly what the 'platform or policy' was back in Ireland.

At the end of the Civil War on 4 June 1923 McGarrity had been receiving letters from de Válera, co-signed by Aiken as chief of staff, asking that McGarrity co-operate with 'Commandant General

Moylan' whom Aiken and de Valera sent to America to build up support for the defeated Republicans. McGarrity does not seem to have appreciated the implications of another letter from de Valera, received a month later saying, ' . . . the only hope for the future that I can now see is by *political* action. It would be a great mistake to imagine that the people were really in love with the Free State. With proper organization we should be able to secure revision of the "Treaty" within four or five years. The main thing is not to let any time slip by in inactivity. If we could contest one seat in each constituency, we would have laid a solid foundation for the future. The trouble is the old one – money. Until we have made arrangements for the wounded and the army, we cannot use any of the money on hand for political purposes, even though the purpose is fundamental.' In the letter de Valera mentions that about $100,000 would be needed for the elections. This transfer of emphasis from physical force to political activity seems to have been lost on McGarrity who had rapturously accepted the now-to-be-revised treaty.

In a personal diary entitled 'Partial Records by Joseph McGarrity' (in the home of his daughter, Mrs Elizabeth Defoe of Philadelphia who kindly allowed me to see it) one can trace a growing disillusionment with Fianna Fail. He could not understand why de Valera should jail IRA men and other prominent Irish-American figures were similarly bewildered. In June 1935 the leaders of all the most prominent Irish-American organizations issued an appeal to coincide with the Bodenstown procession, asking Fianna Fail and the IRA to unite. The pamphlet, called 'Republicans Must Unite', is addressed to 'Members of Fianna Fail and of the IRA'.

Extracts from it show the lack of understanding among Irish-Americans about domestic Irish politics. Under the heading 'Who Wants More Civil War', the appeal says:

This year there are again rival pilgrimages to the grave of Tone – Tone who died for a United Irish Republic.

The rival processions occur because the Fianna Fail Government and the IRA are practically at war. So serious is the danger of Civil War that LEADING SUPPORTERS OF FIANNA FAIL AND OF THE IRA IN USA HAVE COME TOGETHER AND HAVE ISSUED AN APPEAL FOR UNITY AMONG ALL IRISH REPUBLICANS.

TO UNITE THE IRISH PEOPLE WAS THE AIM OF TONE. WHY CANNOT WE UNITE TODAY? OUR COMRADES IN THE USA HAVE SET US AN EXAMPLE; LET US FOLLOW IT!

Irish Republicans in America view with grave concern the present developments which, if allowed to continue, will lead to hostility between Republican sections in Ireland. We believe that Ireland has reached the critical stage when the Republican enthusiasm of the people can be used to re-establish the Republic or may be dissipated in civil strife.

In this serious situation, we urge the Irish people to insist that representatives of all Republican thought in Ireland must meet in conference to find a means of reconciling their various differences, uniting on unswerving principle, presenting a solid front to the common enemy and re-establish the independence of the country as a Republic. Signed:

JOHN J. REILLY, National Chairman, American Association for the Recognition of the Irish Republic.
JOE MCGARRITY, representing Clann na Gael of America.
JAMES BRADY, Sec., Federation of Societies for Irish Independence.
SEAN HAYES, Chairman, Associated Irish Societies of New York.
JOHN STAUNTON, Chairman, Irish Societies of State of Ohio.
CON MOUNIHAN, Chairman, Irish Societies, Boston, Mass.
PAT HEGARTY, Chairman, United Irishmen of Springfield, Mass.
M. J. MULLANE, Chairman, Irishmen of Butte, Montana.
M. J. MCGING, Chairman, Associated Irish Societies of Chicago.
M. H. ENRIGHT, Colonel, Clann na Gael Guards of Chicago.
ROBERT MONTEITH, Captain, Casement Brigade.
GERALD O'REILLY, representing Congress Supporting Groups of US.

This appeal completely misjudges the tone and temper of the Irish electorate at the time. There was no danger of civil war. But the signatures on the appeal show how widespread was the feeling among Irish-Americans that the IRA and Fianna Fail were somehow the same organization having a family quarrel. In fact, they were two mutually antipathetic political organizations with different goals, or rather very different views about how to achieve the same goals of getting the British out and reuniting the country.

The constitution of the VC (the Clann na Gael is known to its members by the code name of VC!) adopted at a Clann convention in Philadelphia at which the nearly moribund body was revived in 1946, contains the following:

ARTICLE I
Section 1

This organization shall be known as the VC, it shall be non-sectarian and shall not interfere in American Party politics.

Section 2

Its objects are: *First* – To aid the people of Ireland in maintaining their complete national independence under a republican form of government with full civil and religious liberty guaranteed to all its inhabitants. *Second* – To foster and encourage a study of the language, literature, history, music, laws and traditions of Ireland at home and abroad. The Gaelic language shall be used at all public and private functions whenever feasible. *Third* – To foster a spirit of friendship between the Republicans of the US and Ireland.

But the real flavour of the organization comes across in the initiation ceremonies, a mixture of cloak-and-dagger IRB–IRA, Masons and Elks type ritual appealing both to the conspiratorial-minded and to those who like the mystery, miracle and authority of the Church.

The initiation ceremonies are laid down as follows:

Perfect silence should prevail during initiation. Nothing else should occupy the attention of the meeting.

The Warden will see that the Camp is not disturbed during the ceremony, and that every member shall avoid any needless movement or word. At such time a whisper may disturb a candidate or an officer, and mar the impressiveness of the ceremony. Each member shall endeavour to make the ceremony what it is designed to be – solemn and impressive.

SG [Senior Guard] – 'Conductor, proceed to the ante-room and ascertain if there are any candidates in waiting.'

When the Conductor reports the names, addresses, etc., of the candidates, the SG asks:

SG – 'Recording Secretary, have these candidates been duly elected?'

The Recording Secretary reports, giving data of election in each case.

SG – 'Conductor, proceed to the ante-room and interrogate the candidates.'

The Conductor then retires and asks the candidates the following questions in their proper order:

Conductor – 'State your name, age, birth-place and occupation.'

Conductor – 'Do you believe in Ireland's right to be a separate and independent nation?'

Conductor – 'As the Irish Republic is established, are you willing to sustain it by all means?'

Conductor – 'Understanding, as you do, that the object of this Organization is the freedom of Ireland and the elevation of the Irish race, are you willing to bind yourself by a solemn obligation to aid in carrying out the object and to obey the laws of this Order?'

Conductor – 'Are you now, or have you ever been, a member of an organization having for its object the freedom of Ireland?'

The Conductor having ascertained that the candidate has answered all questions satisfactorily to the Camp will return to the ante-room and collect the initiation fee. If any candidate admits being now, or having ever been a member of this or any similar organization or if any of the answers should be unsatisfactory, or should call for special action, the Camp may act as may be required by the Constitution. If the answers are satisfactory, the SG will say:

SG – 'Conductor, prepare the candidates and present them for initiation.'

The SG will detail a sufficient number of brothers to act as escort to the candidates. The Conductor will then take his sword and retire to the ante-room. The Conductor will then give three knocks at the door as a signal for his assistants to retire, one assistant conductor being selected for each candidate, who shall take a position on the right of the candidate. The Conductor will direct the march and place himself at the head of the escort. At the entrance door he will give three distinct knocks with his sword. The Sentinel will at once open the door and the escort will pass inside with the candidates, after which the Sentinel will close the door. When the escort has advanced three paces into the room the Sentinel will abruptly and in a clear voice say to the Conductor:

Sentinel – 'Halt! Who comes there?'

(Escort halts.)

Conductor – 'Friends who desire to unite with us in the cause of Ireland.'

Sentinel (to SG) – 'Shall I permit these friends to proceed?'

SG – 'Advance.'

Conductor – 'Forward, march.'

The Conductor will lead the escort and candidates to within three paces of the SG, making a circuit of the centre table and will command:

Conductor – 'Halt.'

The candidates will be aligned by the assistants facing the SG.

Conductor (to SG) – 'Sir, I present these candidates for final examination.'

SG – 'Friends, you have come to us seeking the privilege of membership. That privilege is denied to unworthy men and granted only to those who can stand the test of a strict examination as to character and patriotism. We are engaged in a holy cause that can be served only by men of courage, devotion and loyalty. We are banded together to free the land of our fathers from English rule and to sustain the Republic of Ireland as now established. We admit no man to our ranks who is not fully in sympathy with this object. Every man in our Order has taken a solemn oath binding himself to aid in accomplishing it. It is an oath which does not conflict with any duty you owe to God, to your country, your neighbour or yourself and which no true Irishman can condemn. It must be taken before you can be admitted to our Order. You have already signified your willingness to take our obligation, but we give you, even now, the privilege of withdrawing if you so desire. Answer honestly and freely, are you willing to take this oath?'

If the answer be satisfactory the SG will say:

SG – 'Conduct the candidates to the proper office for obligation.'

The Conductor and his assistants will then march the candidates to the JG [Junior Guard] and align them facing the JG's chair.

Conductor – 'Hold up your right hands.'

(SG gives two raps.)

The JG then administers the obligation, speaking clearly and distinctly, dividing the sentences into short clauses, so that the candidates may have no difficulty in repeating the words after him. He will not tell the candidates to kiss the book, the Ritual not being for that purpose, and the uplifted right hand being sufficient.

OBLIGATION

I (name), do solemnly swear that I will labour while life is left me to put an end to English rule in Ireland and to sustain the Republic now established on Irish soil and to elevate the position of the Irish race everywhere.

That I will obey and respect the Constitution and Laws of the VC and all orders coming from the proper authority.

That I will never reveal its secrets to anyone not entitled to know them, even if my connection with the Organization should cease from any cause whatever.

That I will foster a spirit of Unity and Brotherly Love among Irish Nationalists.

That I do not now belong, and never will belong, to any organization opposed to the principles or policy of the VC.

And finally I swear that I take this oath without any mental reservation whatever, and that I will keep it in letter and spirit until death. So Help Me, God.

All Present – 'We are all witnesses to the obligation you have taken.'

Conductor – 'Keep it as you love Ireland and value your honor as a man.'

JG – 'Conduct the brothers to the SG.'

(One rap.)

On arriving at the SG's chair the Conductor will align the new brothers and say:

Conductor – 'SG, I present these brothers for final instructions.'

SG (Shaking hands with each of the new brothers) – 'Brothers, I greet you and welcome you to our ranks in the name of Ireland.'

The name of the Organization is the VC. Its local subdivisions, or branches, are styled Camps, and each Camp is known by a number.

The Republican Congress breakaway in Ireland was reflected in a similar split in America under Gerald O'Reilly who took most of the left-wing support with him. Then de Valera introduced a pension scheme for IRA men who had taken part in the Civil War, and as many of these had emigrated to America after the war (where they supported the Clann) their acceptance of the pension cut them off from revolutionary activity against the government that was paying the money, and further weakened the Clann. And there were natural American disunities. For instance during 1930 the Clann split down the middle over the opening of a speak-easy to raise funds. One club, the James Connolly Club, led by James O'Mahoney, opposed the scheme and both the club and some individual members of other clubs broke away.

The greatest single weakening factor, however, was the spread of the Irish Sweepstakes movement to America. This took some of the ablest executive brains, as well as rank and file, out of the Clann organization. Joe McGrath, principal founder of the sweep, was astute enough to see the possibility of the old IRA arms and letter smuggling network as a machine for smuggling illegal lottery tickets back to Dublin, and many Clann na Gaelite members devoted themselves more to ticket-pushing than to revolution. Other Irish Americans also supported the sweepstake enthusiastically, distributing tickets throughout the United States, sending counterfoils and money to the counterfeit addresses in Ireland or on the Continent, to be passed on to the sweep headquarters in Dublin. They behaved with that enterprising abandon that the Irish display when they can defy authority and make money at the same time.

Both the vigilance of the postal services and the enterprise of the Irish were well demonstrated on one occasion when a sweep agent, called Irwin, a steward on a Cunard liner, was arrested at Pier 16 and taken with his counterfoils and remittances to a neighbouring precinct station for the night before facing fines and confiscations in the morning. The fine was not serious, heavy though it was, because the sweep would remit this money to him, but the loss of the counterfoils meant that there could be a lack of trust on the part of subscribers. However, the following morning after being fined and losing his counterfoils and the money he had collected, Irwin walked out of the court whistling. All through the night while he was in custody the entire precinct staff, most of whom were Irish (and those who were not knew better than to protest) had laboured to fill in duplicate counterfoils made out on police stationery. These were duly sent to Dublin and accepted by the sweep authorities as being valid counterfoils under the circumstances.

All this meant of course that there was very little time left in Clann circles for fomenting revolution in Ireland.

Harry Short, who was present at the hall on 125th Street when Sean Russell announced, for the first time in America, his scheme for a bombing campaign in England, reckoned there were only forty people present.

5

The Bombing Campaign

Sean Russell's path to New York apparently began when he met Joseph McGarrity in Ireland in 1929. McGarrity's business had temporarily collapsed. He had been expelled from the New York Stock Exchange but a subsequent inquiry cleared his name, fixing the responsibility on his partner, a man named Kenny, and restoring McGarrity to his seat. McGarrity had gone to Bolivia but returned to New York within months, full of plans for development in South America. When these met with no response from his associates he went to Ireland and there became friendly with Russell.

McGarrity's visit helped to create further dissension within the movement. On what might be called the 'physical force wing' there were two plans for action. One was Tom Barry's scheme for seizing a northern town, as the Dublin post office was seized in 1916, holding out for as long as possible and then falling back on the border at, say, Armagh, to rouse the people behind them. The scheme, known as the 'Barry Plan', was widely discussed but never became official army policy.

Unfortunately Russell's plan did. McGarrity had a friend approach a young German chemist in Cleveland who was an expert on explosives, and after talking to the chemist, became convinced that small, easily concealed and easily disposed of explosives with a high destructive content if let off in busy English cities would be the best method of freeing 'occupied Ireland'. Russell had seen too much of civil war in Ireland to want to embroil North against South on the lines of the Barry Plan and, moreover, he did not want to destroy Irish property or to take Irish lives if he could help it. To Russell, as Britain was, in his view, maintaining partition, Britain was the logical place to carry on the war.

The scheme was of course impracticable with the weakened IRA and its position following the governmental crack-down, but it was the

very weakness of the IRA which enabled Russell to come to the top. The
Blueshirt-IRA struggle took itself off to Spain at the end of 1936. Frank
Ryan left from Dun Laoghaire (a borough of Dublin) on 11 November
with a group of Republican Congress supporters, notably Frank
Edwards and Christie Walsh, and O'Duffy's men began setting off two
days later from Dublin. For the IRA this meant a renewal of internal
controversy as MacBride, Fitzpatrick and MacLogan tried to persuade
their followers from going after Ryan, who was appealing to both
socialist inclinations and the desire for 'action'. Russell was offering a
possibility of 'action' nearer home and against a more familiar enemy
than the forces in Spain. Moreover McGarrity continued to lend him
moral and financial support. Probably as much as 80 per cent of the
money required for the campaign was supplied by him and he grew
more determined in his support as de Valera took an increasingly stiff
line with the IRA.

In McGarrity's diary for August 1936 are references to meetings
with Russell, by then quartermaster-general of the IRA; to Maurice
Twomey's arrest by de Valera's 'Free State' police; to Micksey Conway's being charged with murder, and to reports of 'brutalities' against
IRA prisoners. He describes with sadness the sentences meted out to
IRA men who came from Republican families prominent in the time of
the Anglo-Irish struggle. (Sean McSwiney, a brother of Terence
McSwiney who died on hunger strike, and Sean Og MacCurtain, a son
of the murdered mayor of Cork, were at that time before the Military
Tribunal.) After noting that in the North the Craigavon government was
also cracking down on the IRA McGarrity writes, 'Craigavon and de
Valera at least agree on one thing and that is that all those known to be
Republicans must be jailed or hanged.' McGarrity was unimpressed
with de Valera's constitutional attempts to give the Free State a more
Republican appearance. These included removing the governor general, on 11 December 1936: enacting a new constitution by referendum
on 1 June 1937, abolishing the senate's power of veto and altering its
nature in an attempt to give it a 'vocational' character – which failed as
the electoral colleges which put forward the senatorial nominees do so
on party lines; and changing the name of the state from the Irish Free
State to Ireland, or, in Irish, Eire. The changes were of course internal
to the twenty-six county State and had no effect on partition.

In the midst of these changes de Valera set up a cabinet committee, on
15 December 1936, to make recommendations concerning the release
of prisoners sentenced by the Military Tribunal. On the day this

committee was announced an IRA convention in Dublin, meeting not altogether in secret as police records of the time show, proposed that battalion commanders be given greater powers to deal with 'deserters' and those showing hostility to the IRA. This was the sort of thing which caused young Egan's death, for which Micksey Conway had been sentenced, but despite this Conway was one of those whom the Dail committee freed.

The case of the young Limerick man, Sean Glynn, who committed suicide in Arbour Hill prison after the proscribing of the Bodenstown procession, affected McGarrity powerfully. He describes the IRA prisoners being 'so unmercifully treated in prison that young Glynn was found hanging dead in a cell in Arbour Hill Prison, Dublin . . . This was the last straw for me. I had already spoken at a public meeting of the Clann in the Town Hall, New York, in protest at the jailings and prison tortures.' He went on to note that he had given an interview to the *Philadelphia Ledger* protesting the 'Free State Government policy and that of the Craig Government'.

Although he was still in touch with de Valera and growing increasingly friendly with Russell, McGarrity laboured under the old American difficulty of being out of touch. He was surprised to find that Sean Russell had had an inteview with de Valera, in April 1935, to talk over the possibilities of cooperation', as McGarrity termed it, between the IRA and de Valera. De Valera's version of this 'cooperation' was that Russell and the IRA would turn in their arms and disband. According to McGarrity's diary, Russell reminded de Valera of his statement after the Civil War about Republicans hiding arms and munitions – not to part with them 'until the country was independent'. This Russell said the IRA was willing to do. According to the diary: 'Russell asked, or rather promised cooperation with the Fianna Fail party in every way for a period of five years from that date if Dev would promise to declare a Republic for all Ireland at the end of the final year period. Dev refused to agree to that, saying "You want it both ways".'

McGarrity notes that he had been in Dublin during December 1935 and on a visit to de Valera's house had a long talk about changes de Valera was proposing in the Free State constitution. But he had not been aware that de Valera had been in contact with the IRA. McGarrity wrote that 'Russell believes Dev has taken orders from Anthony Eden to suppress the IRA in anticipation of some promised concession being fulfilled by England; there is no proof of this.'

An entry in the McGarrity diary for 31 October 1936 gives evidence of his naïvety in Irish affairs. He had arranged to send J. O'Hara Harte of the Society of Friends to Ireland to seek peace between the IRA and the Free State Government, and the IRA and the Craig regime in the six counties. McGarrity wrote: 'Have arranged a plan. $1,000 already provided for expense of the mission, balance of 1,000 will be ready by the time the mission is ready to sail – God grant it success.' McGarrity adds, 'de Valera has according to reports published his long looked for constitution for his Free State. Not a word about United and Independent Ireland, Six Counties forgotten – shame on Dev and his party.'

O'Hara Harte sailed from New York for Ireland on 18 November, and a month later a baffled O'Hara Harte sent a cable from London recounting his interview with de Valera. He had told de Valera that the IRA had signed a statement that they were willing to negotiate outstanding differences. Harte was amazed, McGarrity wrote, when the president said, 'he would not enter into any negotiations. Not only would he not meet the IRA as a body or as individual persons but he would not accept my service as a mediator.'

So, mad though the British bombing campaign may seem to us, it must have appeared logical to men in Ireland in 1936 who thought it possible that de Valera, Craigavon and the IRA (illegal on both sides of the border) should sit down together to arrange for the unification of the country under the chairmanship of an unknown Irish-American Quaker.

In America Russell first publicly announced his plan in early August 1936 to a handful of Clann supporters. In an interview with the *Daily Mirror* on 14 August, Russell made a number of amazing claims:

> You know, of course, that de Valera has betrayed the trust of the Irish nation by becoming the tool of Great Britain.
> Instead of fighting, as he promised, for the Republic of Ireland, he has been content to allow her to be a nation subject to a foreign King.
> Republican forces are awaiting an opportune moment to fight with all their might for the nation's freedom.

When the moment will come I do not know. It may come when the British become embroiled in a European conflict. But our plan of campaign is ready.

As de Valera knows only too well, we have splendid military forces in Ireland, with cleverly hidden arsenals.

Then, over in England, where we shall also take the offensive, we have another secret army of Irishmen, who meet quietly, for drill and target practice.

We have also quantities of ammunition and other war material in England.

Our Air Force may be small, but it is reasonably efficient.

When hostilities start we shall certainly send planes to bomb England.

It is a very definite plan in our scheme for an offensive.

Admiral Somerville was recruiting for the British Navy, and we won't tolerate a foreign Power recruiting for its navy or army.

I plainly warn the British people not to interfere with Ireland.

Russell's statement was pure propaganda. (There was a scheme in New York Clann na Gael circles at the time to fly an aeroplane across the Atlantic, bomb the British House of Commons, and then crash land on the coast of France, because there would not be enough petrol left to recross the Atlantic. There was not the slightest hope of laying hands on such an aeroplane, and the scheme never got beyond the level of discussion.) It is doubtful if Russell even had any title to make propaganda for the IRA at home. Tom Barry wanted to have Russell court-martialled over the loss of two Thompson machine guns. He had no faith in Russell's plans nor had Sean MacBride who took particular exception to his involvement with the O'Hara Harte mission. But Russell directed his appeal at the younger men and with their help carried the day.

Some time during March 1938 the die was cast at a meeting in Dublin. (Eoin MacNamee, a principal spokesman on Russell's behalf, Michael Fitzpatrick, then chief of staff and who presided at the meeting, and Sean O'Broin who stood guard at the door taking credentials were unable to tell me the exact date and place of the meeting.) Earlier on the morning of the meeting an unofficial convention was held in the home of Mairtin O'Cadain to plan strategy. MacNamee went to this meeting with the names of twelve Russell supporters from whom an Executive was to be picked.

These were Jack McNeela, Tony D'Arcy (both of whom were to die on hunger strike), Victor Fagg, who, interestingly enough, was a

Protestant from Westmeath, Charlie Dolan, John Tully, Jimmie Traynor, John James Kelly, George Plunkett, Ted Moore, Ned Kerrigan, Johnny O'Connor and Larry Grogan. Grogan was one of those who later signed the declaration of war on England, served on Lord Halifax. MacNamee also had a letter from Russell explaining his position. This was read by Maurice Twomey. The convention was a tense affair, run on military lines, each man giving his name and rank to Sean O'Broin who called it out from the entrance while the applicant stood to attention before being admitted.

The anti-Russell section was armed – one of the few times at which arms were carried at an army convention. Joseph McGarrity was present although he was a member of the Clann, not of the IRA. Russell himself was not present. In his opponents' view he was no longer in the IRA through his refusal to take direction from the then executive. Barry proposed that as there were sufficient arms in Dublin to arm the Dublin brigade the IRA should march on the North that very night, but the Russell scheme was carried at the end of an all-night sitting. Russell sensed the difficulties that had arisen and felt they should strike a blow at the earliest moment.

The fatal result was that the bombing party chosen to go to England was only half-trained in the use of explosives and hence some of the fatalities to the bombers and to innocent English bystanders. The destruction of property was all Russell aimed at, but badly made bombs in inexperienced hands went off at the wrong times with disastrous results. Russell possibly thought that more efficient explosives would be coming from America. MacNamee remembers passing Park Lane Hotel with him one afternoon and being asked by Russell, 'would he like to be able to blow that up with a pen?' MacNamee said, 'Certainly, but how?', pointing out that it was made of reinforced concrete. Russell smiled and went on to impess MacNamee with the sort of advanced methods of warfare to be placed at their disposal. (These were apparently pen bombs, mentioned to me by members of Clann na Gael as being talked about in America during the 1930s but they either proved impractical or could not be got out of the country for they never figured in the campaign.)

The campaign was appallingly ill-conceived. MacNamee told me that there was, as far as he was aware, only one Thompson gun and possibly six revolvers doing the rounds of the London units of the IRA at the time. There was an Irish Republican Defence Committee, an open organization which raised funds and carried out propaganda and Cumann na mBan, the women's auxiliary group which did somewhat similar work, but in terms of military power the IRA scarcely functioned. In August 1937 MacNamee, intelligence officer of the London battalion, returned to Ireland for a holiday and learned of the projected bombing campaign and of the differences concerning its merits. MacNamee, a Co. Tyrone man, supported the idea because he understood that it was to be accompanied by an attack on the North.

At the time, apart from its military weaknesses, the London IRA was split into various factions. Jack Lynch, the officer commanding Britain, was arrested during MacNamee's visit to Ireland and Jimmy Joe Reynolds was appointed in his place. Reynolds, later to be blown up in a faulty mine explosion at Clady, Co. Donegal, made one of his first steps on being appointed OC the dismissal of all the battalion staff. The result was that officers from GHQ in Dublin came over to set up the inevitable courts of inquiries. The row, a foolish affair involving Cumann na mBan women's gossip, was patched up and on MacNamee's recommendation London in 1938 was split into various companies with defined spheres of influence. During this period prominent Dublin IRA officers such as Seamus Malin, Mairtin O'Cadain, Maurice Twomey and Thomas MacCurtain spoke in London.

From October on groups of handpicked IRA men were brought back from England to be trained in Dublin and to return and spread their knowledge. The classes consisted largely of instruction in bomb-making and were held mainly in a hall known as The Green Lounge in St Stephen's Green. Other venues were also used around Dublin, one of the most important being Killiney Castle in Killiney. (Today in the summer amiable English tourists visit it unaware of the castle's history. Occasionally the words 'Up the IRA' appear in large whitewash letters on the gates but these are speedily obliterated before they arouse any questions among the English visitors. In the 1938–49 period the castle was owned by a Dublin civil servant who was violently anti-British and, when the castle was commandeered on the outbreak of the Second World War by the military for use as a billet, he used to emerge from the basement which he retained for his own use, to run up the tricolour on the flag pole whenever a German victory was announced!)

The principal instructors in bomb-making were Patrick McGrath, who was later executed for the shooting of a policeman in Dublin, and Jim O'Donovan, Russell's former colleague in the war against the British. O'Donovan had come out of retirement at Russell's request to train a new generation of young Irishmen, a decision which was to cause him considerable loss. He was a member of a semi-state body, the Electricity Supply Board, in a comfortable position at the time, and when the campaign misfired he lost his job and spent the war years interned in the Curragh. It was O'Donovan who drew up the 'S-plan', the official blueprint for the campaign, which called for the destruction of obvious military targets such as communications centres, BBC transmitters, aerodromes, bridges and military installations.

Twelve handpicked volunteers crossed over to England during Christmas week 1938 and went to five centres: Walsh and O'Kennedy to Glasgow; Eoin MacNamee, Charlie Casey and S. McGuinness to London; Rory Campbell and Patrick Fleming to Manchester; Joe Deighan, G. Quigley, and M. Cleary to Liverpool; and Jackie Kearns and J. Fuller to Birmingham.

On 8 December Russell announced an event that he hoped would give respectability and authority to the campaign. This was the taking over by the IRA of the authority of the 'Government of the Republic of Ireland' from the 'Executive Council of Dail Eireann'. This meant that those who had recognized the second Dail as the *de jure* government of Ireland now recognized the Army Council (and Sean Russell as its head) as the legitimate rulers of Ireland. The announcement was printed on page one of the *Wolfe Tone Weekly*.

The people of Ireland were largely unaware of this transfer, but after it Russell could claim, as de Valera had said, that the authority of the Dail lay outside that assembly, that he now had this authority for his actions. Yet on the day the notice was published, an abortive effort was made, without his authority, to blow up the Nelson Pillar. Peadar O'Flaherty, believed to be Russell's right-hand man, planned the explosion for a Saturday evening, when the street would normally be full of people. To avoid fatalities, he planned to set the explosives, withdraw and notify the police, giving them time to cordon off the area. Joseph Deighan told me that he and the other members of the group actually walked down through O'Connell Street (from An Stad in Upper Frederick Street where most IRA men stayed) with wads of gelignite on them, liable to be blown up at any moment by a jostling passer-by, but quite prepared to carry out the task. Arriving at the pillar they found that O'Flaherty had forgotten that it closed earlier on Saturdays in winter. When Russell heard of this harebrained scheme, he was furious and sacked O'Flaherty on the spot, but his control of the organization was so loose that he could not prevent O'Flaherty signing the declaration of war on England which the IRA issued a month later.

When the chosen twelve arrived in England they found organization so lax that they had great difficulty in finding dumps for the explosives. Russell had excellent contacts in the customs service and in shipping circles and he managed to get the stuff into England. But once there it was no easy matter for young Irishmen living in 'digs' to find dumps for hundredweights of potassium chloride, sulphuric acid and iron oxide. Some willing friends who stored material knowing nothing about the campaign itself or what they were storing found their business gone, their families broken up and themselves behind prison bars after the campaign began and Scotland Yard began to round up suspects. One man who stored some stuff for Eoin MacNamee knew so little about him that he told the police that his name was McKenna. When the bombs started to go off he realized the position and in his desperation dug holes in the garden and covered them in. However, the police raided him before he had properly obliterated all traces and he got seven years' hard labour.

A fact which cannot be too strongly stressed is the innocence, or if one wishes the ignorance, of the volunteers with whom the 'operations officers' in the various cities worked. Most were young men who, having left school around the age of twelve, emigrated to labouring jobs and had not the slightest resentment against England.

Paddy McNeela was a typical recruit. His brother Jack was to die on hunger strike and was at the time the principal IRA officer in England. Paddy came from Ballycroy, Co. Mayo, where his memories were of the fiddler coming into the village, playing in one or two houses for a fortnight and taking up a collection at the end of the week, maybe getting thirty shillings in twopences for his work. Some overriding laws governed upbringing in Paddy's day. The Rosary was said every night; Mass was attended in all weathers though it meant a four-mile walk. At Christmas the average stipend to a priest was ten shillings, almost a week's wages. A wedding cost perhaps thirty or forty pounds but it was one great day out in everyone's lives and the money had to be found.

The priest's authority was near absolute.* Paddy remembers a parish priest going to a house and burning what he called 'bad books'. In nearby Spiddal a cross was erected to poteen stills which were publicly burned by the famous Redemptorist priest, Father Conneally. Sermons were of the order 'two men will die in this parish' if mixed dancing or poteen drinking were not given up immediately. Growing up, Paddy and his companions firmly believed that the priest could, if he wished, 'put horns on you'.

Understandably, coming from this background, Paddy was far from mechanically minded. He remembers one drill session at which a hand grenade was thrown and failed to explode. Another young man picked it up, tested it with his teeth and said, 'Hm, it's alright, it should have gone off.' They tossed it around for some moments until their horrified instructor took it from them and threw it away, whereupon it duly exploded. When Paddy emigrated to England he was completely lost in London, but in a village in one of the Home Counties he found a life more like the one he had left and got on famously with the people. He remembers he found them very backward and simple.

'They'd listen to everything I'd tell them and take it in, jokes and all.'

When he was asked to take part in the bombing campaign, he no more associated those simple villagers with going to war for the Republic and the end of partition, than he claimed to have any knowledge of the rights or wrongs of the issues involved.

Paddy was lucky enough to escape detection but a more experienced colleague, J. F. Reegan from Cork, back from the Spanish Civil War and its hardship (the common diet was a few drops of olive oil in water, and a handful of grapes; with bread, meat, milk or coffee almost unknown) crossed to England and was captured, probably through an informer, and sentenced to twelve years' hard labour.

A leading contemporary Irish journalist, then just a homesick boy from Derry, was recruited when he went into Mooneys in the Strand in

---

* A 'station' in Kerry was the following anecdote to the nation. A 'station' consists of Mass and communion followed by a large breakfast in a house, not a church. The custom, which dates from the penal days, is now dying out in Ireland except in the more remote areas, but at Paddy's time it flourished. A priest, who arrived at the house on a fine hunter, placed his umbrella in the kitchen, still open as he wished to dry it. Two of the menfolk of the place, not having seen him arrive, were trying unsuccessfully to push it out the narrow doorway when the priest returned for it. They watched in amazement as he folded it with a flick of his thumb, and then Pat turned to Mick as the priest galloped off and said, 'Dey has de Power. Didn't I tell you dey has de Power?'

London where he hoped to pick up some Irish company. A man he knew slightly from his boyhood came up to him at the bar and spoke. Learning that the bombing campaign was being planned, he offered his services, was enrolled and began mixing 'Paxo', as the explosive was known, in his landlady's saucepans. The National Gallery in Trafalgar Square was to be his first target but his superior officer, a plumber, decided that there were too many tiles in it and that it wouldn't burn. Meanwhile his landlady, discovering the white substance, very sensibly flushed it down the lavatory.

MacNamee, who lived in Roseken Road, Fulham, used to test balloons in his fireplace, timing how long it would take for the acid to eat through the rubber and ignite the iron oxide. Once he went out while waiting for the acid to take effect, and came back to find that the landlady had cleared out the fireplace, balloons, iron oxide and all. She warned him that two yardsmen in a local scrapdealing business, whom he had prosecuted for stealing his bicycle, knew him to be an IRA man and were going to get him locked up. MacNamee immediately quit the digs. The police called to pick him up that night.

Michael McInerney, former political correspondent of the *Irish Times*, disposed of some half ton of explosives down his landlady's lavatory after he learned what his Irish friends intended to do with the stuff that they had asked him to store.

Not all landladies were sympathetic although most of the young IRA men of course stayed with established Republicans who had been in Britain for some years which, however, made it easy for the police to pick them up. Then the IRA habit of keeping documents, writing out receipts, and leaving incriminating evidence lying around terminated many a promising arsonist's career. There was also the problem of accents. A group of young IRA men from west Cork or Mayo going into a shop for an alarm clock, to be used as a timing device for a bomb, would give a cheery greeting to the assistant such as, 'Tell us, daughter, would ye be after havin' a few alarm clocks there?' They would be told, 'Certainly sir, do you mind waiting for a moment?' and would obligingly stay on the premises while the assistant went to telephone Scotland Yard.

Nevertheless some of the operation officers in the campaign did show considerable expertise in eluding the police. Joe Deighan told me that even though he was well-known in Liverpool as an IRA suspect at least, if not something more active, and was continually shadowed, he was nevertheless able to set off a number of successful detonations –

carrying his bombs in what looked like a lunch box on his knee in crowded public transport! (Public transport was frequently used by the IRA. Where a taxi driver might remember one fare, a bus conductor would not. It is a miracle that this did not lead to some really ghastly accidents. A jolting tram or bus is not the best conveyance for gelignite.)

It should also be pointed out that had the IRA made more use of women it might have done better because women were less likely to be seized by the police. I met one lady who had emptied several cinemas on different occasions by letting off tear-gas bombs. She could have easily destroyed substantial installations.

The bombing campaign began formally on 12 January 1939, with an ultimatum to the British prime minister, the government in Northern Ireland, the British foreign secretary, Hitler, Mussolini, and anyone else whom the IRA thought would be moved by such a document. It said:

> I have the honour to inform you that the Government of the Irish Republic, having as its first duty towards the people the establishment and maintenance of peace and order, herewith demand the withdrawal of all British armed forces stationed in Ireland. These forces are an active incitement to turmoil and civil strife not only in being a symbol of hostile occupation but in their effect and potentialities as an invading army.
>
> It is secondly the duty of the Government to establish relations of friendship between the Irish and all other people. We must insist on the withdrawal of British troops from our country and a declaration from your Government renouncing all claims to interfere in our domestic policy.

The letter declared that neither the government of the Irish Republic nor the Irish people were actuated by any feelings of hostility towards England but warned:

> We shall regret if this fundamental feeling is ignored and we are compelled to intervene actively in the military and commercial life of your country as your Government are now intervening in ours.
>
> The Government of the Irish Republic believe that a period of four days is sufficient for your Government to signify its intention in the matter of the military evacuation and for the issue of your declaration of abdication in respect of our country. Our Government reserve the right

of appropriate action without further notice if on the expiration of the period of grace these conditions remain unfulfilled.

(Signed) Patrick Fleming

Four days later on finding that neither the British nor the Orangemen seemed disposed to meet its wishes the IRA issued another declaration. It was written by McGarrity* and said:

On the twenty-third day of April in the year 1916 in the city of Dublin, seven men, who were representative in spirit and outlook and purpose of the Irish nation that had never yielded to nor accepted the British conquest, set their humble and almost unknown names to the foregoing document that has passed into history, making the names of the seven signatories immortal.

Those signatures were sealed with the blood of the immortal seven, and of many others who followed them into one of the most gallant fights in the history of the world; and the Irish nation rose from shame to honour, from humiliation to pride, from slavery to freedom.

Three years later (on 21 January 1919), the Republic proclaimed in Easter week 1916 was ratified and formally established by the elected representatives of all Ireland and a solemn declaration of independence sent out to the nations of the world.

To combat that declaration and to prevent the proclamation of the Republic of Ireland from becoming effective, the Armed Forces of the English enemy made war upon the people of this country. They were met by the Irish Republican Army, and challenged and resisted so stubbornly that after five years of bloody warfare the English were forced to ask for a truce with a view to settlement by negotiation.

Unfortunately, because men were foolish enough to treat with an armed enemy within their gates, the English won the peace. Weakness and treachery caused a resumption of the war and the old English tactics of 'Divide and Conquer' were exploited to the fullest extent. Partition was introduced, the country divided into two parts with two separate parliaments subject to and controlled by the British Government from London. The Armed Forces of England still occupy six of our counties in the North and reserve the right 'in time of war or strained relations' to re-occupy the ports which they have just evacuated in the Southern part of Ireland. Ireland is still tied, as she has been for centuries past, to take part in England's wars. In the Six Counties, a large number

---

* McGarrity died in the 1940s but IRA documents were still signed with his name as late as the 1970s, showing the continuation of his influence.

of Republican soldiers are held prisoners by England. Further weakness on the part of some of our people, broken faith and make believe have postponed the enthronement of the living Republic, but the proclamation of Easter week and the Declaration of Independence stand and must stand forever. No man, no matter how far he has fallen away from his national faith, has dared to repudiate them. They constitute the rallying centre for the unsought manhood of Ireland in the fight that must be made to make them effective and to redeem the nation's self-respect that was abandoned by a section of our people in 1922.

The time has come to make that fight. There is no need to re-declare the Republic of Ireland, now or in the future. There is no need to re-declare the Declaration of Irish Independence. But the hour has come for the supreme effort to make both effective. So in the name of the unconquered dead and of the faithful living, we pledge ourselves to that task.

We call upon England to withdraw her armed forces, her civilian officials and institutions, and representatives of all kinds from every part of Ireland, as an essential preliminary to arrangements for peace and friendship between the two countries; and we call upon the people of all Ireland, at home and in exile, to assist us in the effort we are about to make in God's name, to compel that evacuation and to enthrone the Republic of Ireland.

Signed on behalf of
The Republican Government and the Army
Council of Oglaigh na hEireann
(Irish Republican Army)

Stephen Hayes   Patrick Fleming
Peadar O'Flaherty   George Plunkett
Laurence Grogan   Sean Russell

The ultimatum had been greeted with derision or disbelief, but the declaration of war was followed by explosions one of which immediately showed the futility of Russell's aim of conducting such a campaign without losing any life. A twenty-seven-year-old fish porter, Albert Ross, was killed on his way to work in Manchester when a bomb went off in a street main.

In London there were three explosions at electricity plants and throughout the north and the midlands other power units, gas and

. electricity mains, were damaged. On 26 July a young Scotsman, standing in the left-luggage office at King's Cross station, was killed in an explosion that severely injured his wife and fourteen other people.

On Friday 25 August the worst incident of all occurred. Five people were killed, including an old man of eighty-one, and a schoolboy of fifteen, twelve very badly injured and forty more less seriously hurt in an explosion at 2.30 p.m. in the thoroughfare of Broadgate in Coventry. Two IRA men were executed for this, one of them, Peter Barnes, being at least morally innocent. He had been involved in buying flour bags for the mixing and carrying of explosives (though he didn't know where these were to go off). The man who actually cycled into the street with a bomb in the carrier and parked the bicycle outside Astky's Shop was a psychopath, who later received extensive treatment.

During the next fifteen months bombs went off in letter boxes, lavatories, telephone boxes, railway cloakrooms, cinemas, post offices and business premises of all sorts. Sometimes cinemas were emptied by tear gas.

Curiously enough it was the Irish government that first passed laws directed at the IRA. The British had of course been rounding up IRA agents by the score but it was in Dublin that the Offences against the State Act was passed on 14 June, setting up military tribunals (special criminal courts composed of army officers) and stating:

> Every person who usurps or unlawfully exercises any function of Government whether by setting up, maintaining or taking part in any way in a body of persons purporting to be a Government or by any other action or conduct whatsoever shall be guilty of felony and shall be liable in a conviction thereof to suffer penal servitude for a term not exceeding ten years or to imprisonment for a term not exceeding two years.

The act also gave the government power to issue a suppression order against anybody who 'raises or maintains a military or armed force'. The following day the IRA was declared an unlawful organization and police and military clashed with the Republicans in a riot when the IRA tried to make the annual pilgrimage to Bodenstown. Incredibly enough, in London after several explosions the previous day, some two hundred Irishmen marched through the centre of the city in honour of Wolfe Tone, carrying banners demanding the release of IRA prisoners in the custody of Scotland Yard – their procession guarded by British police.

This tolerance wore thin. On 24 July when Home Secretary Sir Samuel Hoare introduced the Prevention of Violence (Temporary Provisions) Bill in the House of Commons, he told the House that sixty-six members of the IRA had been convicted, and that 1,500 sticks of gelignite, 1,000 detonators, tons of potassium chlorate, a quantity of ferrous oxide, seven gallons of sulphuric acid, and four hundredweight of aluminium powder had been seized. By then there had been 127 terrorist attacks, fifty-seven in London.

Sir Samuel said the government had been informed that the IRA campaign was 'being closely watched and actively stimulated by foreign organizations'. With the darkening face of Europe the House was not disposed to question whether the foreign organizations meant Clann na Gael or Nazis. Four days later the bill became law. It gave the Home Secretary powers to issue expulsion orders against suspected persons living in England and to issue prohibition orders against suspects wishing to enter the country. In emergencies, search warrants were to be issued by police officers not below the rank of superintendent and the police could arrest and detain suspects for five days without warrants. There might have been some opposition to these drastic provisions for Arthur Greenwood, the Labour MP, said that while the opposition recognized the need for stronger powers, it regretted that the government should have quite so much authority. But on 26 July further explosions occurred at the left-luggage offices at King's Cross and Victoria stations. At King's Cross the Scottish doctor, Dr Campbell, lost both his legs in the explosion.

Speaking in the Seanad on the same day de Valera said, 'No one can have any doubt as to the result of the campaign in England, and no one can think that this government has any sympathy with it.' He appealed to those carrying on the campaign, asking them how they could hope to reach a decision by these means. He believed that a number of them were animated by high ideals, but that they were misreading Irish history and making no allowance for changed circumstances.

Although the horror of Coventry had not yet come there was by then no hope of the IRA's 'having a decision' from the campaign. Failure and disorganization had done their work. Thus, after his near escape in London Eoin MacNamee had gone to the Leamington Spa and Stratford areas. With only a bicycle he could transport very little explosive and he asked for a car, but there was no money to spare.

During mid-Lent in Coventry, MacNamee was told to report to GHQ in Dublin. Here he found Sean Fuller, one of the Birmingham operations officers, who said that opinion within the movement was now swinging against Russell. Mairtin O'Cadain, in whose house the plot to install Russell was given its final polish, was by now very anti-Russell. Nor was there any sign of the promised campaign against the North. This depressed MacNamee, now that most of his friends in London were captured.

He attended a meeting of GHQ staff with Larry Grogan, Stephen Hayes, Micksey Conway, Sean Russell, Michael Traynor and Sean Fuller. Russell, depressed and waspish, asked MacNamee what he was doing there and wanted to know why he had not told the people in London where the dumps were. Confusion on the whereabouts of the explosives had led to MacNamee's recall to Dublin. He explained that he had told IRA officers in authority where the dumps were, but that these men were now all behind bars, and that in any case he would always restrict the spread of such knowledge because he believed in secrecy. To which Russell replied, rather oddly for a conspirator, 'you're trying to create an air of mystery'.

Russell next criticized Fuller's handling of operations, and Fuller, as chagrined as MacNamee, did not return to the campaign. He dropped out of the IRA after his arrest later in a round-up by the Irish police. MacNamee went back to England with Michael Traynor via Rosslare. Keeping apart on the boat, they separated on docking to give MacNamee an opportunity of checking on the ammunition dumps.

When MacNamee met Leo Duigan, now officer commanding London, he found most of the 'stuff' had been disposed of. Checking a yard owned by a Jack Healy he learned that the explosive materials had been seized by Scotland Yard, and that Healy had been given ten years' penal servitude at the Central Criminal Court. Meeting his contact with Russell at Regent's Park he told him what had happened and advised against any intensification of the campaign because during that month (March) the cases of captured IRA men were being heard at the Old Bailey and he felt it would prejudice them to have any further bombings for the time being. The contact disregarded this and said that continuation of the campaign would show the IRA meant business. MacNamee knew how some of the prisoners were being treated and asked Russell to see that at least their dependents were cared for as cases of near starvation occurred when breadwinners were suddenly hurled into jail for storing a sack of white powder in a closet.

Ill-treatment of IRA men in jail was by no means infrequent: Sometimes it occurred through the defiant attitude of the prisoner. Sometimes an episode such as the Coventry explosion prejudiced warders and police against the IRA. One big row in Dartmoor broke out after the Coventry explosion and eleven IRA men were so badly beaten up that they had to be treated in hospital. After this, the IRA prisoners in Dartmoor had to drill and work separately from the other prisoners. However, neither MacNamee's counselling, nor that of like-minded members of the movement had any effect.

When MacNamee returned to Dublin after checking on the dumps in London, he found that Russell, though depressed, had no intention of calling off the campaign. In fact he set out for America on 8 April, shortly after receiving MacNamee's report, to publicize the campaign there and raise funds for it. But though he attracted enormous publicity in America, by the end of 1939 the campaign was dead. Only about a dozen incidents occurred in 1940, the last recorded one being in March when an unexploded bomb was found in a litter bin at Grosvenor Place. Another bomb that was not found went off at a Westminster City Council refuse depot after the bin had been tipped into the heap. The most serious explosion of 1940, on 22 February, was in a bus litter bin in Oxford Street, which seriously injured seven people. This can be seen as a kind of futile postscript to the hanging of Barnes and Frank Richards (alias McCormick) on 7 February for their part in the Coventry explosion.

This hanging aroused a wave of bitterness against England in Ireland. Emotional scenes recalled the height of the 'troubles' and every public body and the legislature itself pleaded for clemency for the condemned men. They have since passed into an only slightly lesser place in the martyrology of Ireland as have Dunne and Sullivan, the men who shot Sir Henry Wilson.

In English law, both Barnes and McCormick were guilty under the rule of 'Common Purpose' whereby if two or more persons agree to commit a dangerous felony, resulting in a death, all the persons in the combination or conspiracy are guilty of murder. Before being sentenced Richards said to the judge, 'My Lord, before you pass sentence of death, I wish to thank sincerely the gentlemen who have defended me during my trial and I wish to state that the part I took in these explosions since I came to England I have done for a just cause. As a soldier of the Irish Republican Army I am not afraid to die, as I am doing it for a just cause. I say in conclusion, God bless Ireland and God bless the men who have fought and died for it. Thank you, my lord.' Barnes said, 'I would like to say as I am going before my God, as I am condemned to death, I am innocent, and later I am sure it will all come out that I had neither hand, act, nor part in it. That is all I have to say.'

By English law Barnes's possession of a receipt for a flour bag and suitcases used in the incident, and a letter to a friend in the Republican movement in Dublin, made him an accessory. So far as intent to kill or complicity in the actual deed is concerned, Peter Barnes was innocent. Barnes was not in Coventry while the bomb was being prepared, and not there when it went off. The tragedy of Peter Barnes typifies the tragedy of all the confused, well-meaning, idealistic, uneducated young men who joined the IRA without realizing what they were letting themselves in for.

At thirty-two he gave up his job with Offaly County Council and went to an industrial England in 1939, while England was on the verge of a war with Germany, to free his country of 'British domination'. He probably never visited the North in his life, and had no inkling of the complexity of the Protestant-Catholic relationships. He paid for his idealism with his life on an English scaffold.

6

Years of Disaster

In Ireland the effect of the bombing campaign on the IRA and on public opinion was to make a bad situation worse. The Offences Against the State Act, which allowed for imprisonment and detention without trial, became law on 14 June 1939. A few days later the IRA was declared an unlawful organization and the Bodenstown march was proscribed. The army was called out and the IRA made no effort to defy the ban. Then on 22 August the special military court* for which the Offences Against the State Act allowed was proclaimed and from then until the end of the war the operation of the court was to cast a gloomy shadow over the IRA.

The international situation resulted in a declaration of emergency on 2 September, whereby the government, both Dail and Seanad, resolved 'that arising out of the armed conflict now taking place in Europe, a national emergency exists affecting the vital interests of the State'. The Emergency Powers Bill was enacted the following day. From then on the government had control of supplies, tillage, transport, censorship, military matters and, of course, all measures to be taken against the IRA. To emphasize this hard line Gerald Boland became Minister for Justice on 8 September.

The government also reorganized the Special Branch, although it was hardly the instrument upon which a government might depend for its internal security during wartime. The reorganized branch was headed by Chief-Superintendent Patrick Carroll, Chief-Superintendent Sean Gantly and Chief-Superintendent Michael Weymes. Its most colourful member, one Michael Gill, a sergeant at the outbreak of the war, was speedily promoted to chief-superintendent, through his talent for catching IRA members. More than any other figure of the

---

* The court's members were Colonel Bennett, Colonel McKenna, Major Joyce, Major Whelan, Major Tuite.

war, he was regarded as Nemesis by the IRA and was feared and hated.

On the military side, the Director of Military Intelligence at the outbreak of the war was Colonel Liam Archer. He was succeeded by Colonel Dan Bryan with a formidable team, Lieutenant Colonel Joe Guilfoyle and Major Florrie O'Donoghue (who had both gained experience against the British under Collins) and Dr Richard Hayes, who later became director of the National Library. He was a cipher expert who trained himself to master every German code.

Junior officers who served under these men all later distinguished themselves in civilian life. Norman Hewitt became a top travel agent, Con McGovern an airline manager for an American company, and Douglas Gageby, one of Ireland's best journalists, founded the *Evening Press* and later became editor of the *Irish Times*. This team, with more experience, education, energy and resources than the IRA, soon proved itself more than a match for both the IRA and the spies whom the Nazis sent to Ireland. (They were sent, in part, to take advantage of the existence of the IRA.) The poor resources of the IRA had been demonstrated the previous year when in November at Clady, Co. Tyrone, three IRA men were killed when a faulty mine went off.

The three were James Joseph 'Jimmy Joe' Reynolds, one of the six men charged with the murder of Roderick More O'Farrell in Longford in 1935 (he was acquitted after the second trial) and also one of the prime movers in the British bombing campaign, John J. Kelly from Donegal, and Charlie McCaffrey from Tyrone. They had been making a mine to destroy some customs posts along the border. Blowing up customs huts had always been a favourite IRA tactic and a number had gone up in 1937 in protest against a visit by King George VI and Queen Elizabeth. (This gave rise to the IRA ballad 'A Bonfire on the Border'.) The 1938 explosions were intended to start Russell's northern campaign, to reproduce in Ireland the kind of onslaught made in England.

Tarlach O'hUid, who visited Charlie McCaffrey in hospital where he lingered for two days before dying of his injuries, remembers that McCaffrey, who never fully recovered consciousness, kept repeating over and over again, 'Stand back John Joe there's a wee thing wrong.' Clearly the bomb was inexpertly made. Children sleeping in the house where it was made had to be dug out from the debris, mercifully unhurt. Patrick Kelly, a brother of the dead man who was not in the IRA, had allowed his brother to use his cottage. He, his wife and daughter were flung across an adjoining room but escaped serious injury. A neighbour who had been saying the Rosary at the time of the blast said that it was her prayers that saved the family.

A number of customs huts that did go up were destroyed by bombs placed in attaché cases handed to bus conductors, carriage paid, with addresses to non-existent people. The cases were then deposited in the customs hut awaiting 'callers'. It was intended that the cases should explode after the customs' officials had gone home. One time, a driver, Peter Lony of the Erne Bus Company, was given a case addressed to a Miss Eileen Douglas, Lisnascigh, c/o Clontivran Customs House. Like any rural bus driver in Ireland he made it his business to see that Miss Douglas got her case and took it on the bus from the customs hut where he found there was no Miss Eileen Douglas there for it. After inquiries for the non-existent lady he and his conductor took the case in the front of a crowded bus back to the Clontivran post and left it there to await Miss Douglas's arrival. Happily, the hut was still open. (When it was shut the normal procedure was for the driver to take the case home with him and deliver it again in the morning.) A few hours later the case exploded and parts of the hut were found a mile away.

Police activity in the North naturally increased after these explosions and deaths, and on 22 December the RUC made a big swoop in Belfast, putting thirty-four IRA men behind bars. Their arrest, which ruined any chance of a northern campaign getting off the ground, was accompanied by a statement from Sir Dawson Bates, the Northern Ireland Minister for Home Affairs, saying, 'The fact having come to the knowledge of the police that plans have been prepared by the Irish Republican Army for attacks upon persons occupying prominent positions and upon Government and other property during that Christmas and New Year period, the Government decided ... there was no alternative other than to arrest and intern well-known leaders and prominent members of this illegal organization.'

In the South imprisonments after the English campaign had brought less established figures to the top of the IRA, in particular Stephen Hayes. Hayes, from Co. Wexford, an amiable ex-footballer, fond of a drink, and an official in the County Council, had been appointed adjutant-general by Russell in October 1938. Before leaving for America in April 1939, Russell had him promoted to chief of staff during his own absence. This appointment was never ratified in the normal fashion by an Army Council meeting. Hayes did not insist on regular meetings of the Army Council, and there were differences of opinion as to the proper course in the disasters which were occurring. Cork and Kerry IRA split from the main body, and from each other, and the North began to look more to Belfast than Dublin for direction. In the South, Michael Traynor, Tony D'Arcy, Jack McNeela and Dom Adams, all new faces on the Army Council, were thinking of guerrilla raids on the North from southern bases. All were disillusioned with the routine of parades and confusion which existed in the South and realized that there was very little hope of overthrowing the southern state. Then sometime before Christmas 1939, Tom Doyle, a civil servant in the Department of Defence, presented an audacious scheme for raiding the Magazine Fort in Phoenix Park, Dublin, where the bulk of the Irish army's ammunition was stored. This idea appealed to Traynor and the others because, while they had a considerable number of guns stored around the country,* ammunition was in very short supply. Prior to Doyle's approach, Traynor had switched his emphasis from bomb making to guerrilla warfare, so the raid, although it involved fantastic risks, fell into their general scheme. An Army Council meeting, in the unlikely setting of the home of a Radio Eireann musician in Booterstown, Co. Dublin, decided to go ahead with the raid.

It began about half-past eight in the evening of 23 December 1939, and continued for two hours. The IRA immobilized the entire garrison (an officer, two NCOs and ten men armed with rifles and a Lewis gun) and got away with 1,084,000 rounds of ammunition in thirteen lorries. Entrance to the inner gate of the fort was gained when a military policeman left this open to answer a ring at the outer gate. There he met a man in civilian clothes who said he had a parcel for the officer in charge. The military policeman opened the gate for him and was promptly held up.

In a way, conditions in the Fort symbolized the attitude of the country as a whole to the threat of war. According to standing orders the inner gate should have been locked behind the military policeman, but in practice this was never done and Doyle knew of the laxity prevailing throughout the Fort. The policeman and the sentry on duty were captured with equal ease; the rest of the garrison was sitting around a fire in the guardroom when the IRA burst in. Heads

---

* Ballykinlar army camp in the North of Ireland was raided so often and so many Tommies stationed there were convicted of selling rifles to the IRA that it became known in IRA circles as 'the Stores'.

rolled in the upper echelons of the army for the unpreparedness that left the country virtually defenceless.

Stung by the IRA's audacity the government reacted with a ruthless speed and efficiency which showed results almost immediately. All army and police leave was cancelled, roads were blocked, cars and lorries had to pass checkpoints and money was liberally spent by intelligence agents. Beginning on St Stephen's Day, the ammunition was gradually recovered. Only about one lorry load got away to the Cooley mountain district of Co. Louth, where some incredible feats of endurance were performed by a farmer who made repeated journeys up the side of a precipitous mountain, carrying bucket loads of bullets.

'The arms were almost dragged out of me,' he told me years later.

On 4 January the Dail met in emergency sessions and by eighty-two votes to nine passed a measure allowing the government to set up detention camps at the Curragh headquarters of the regular army. Henceforward the IRA men knew that, if captured, they might be thrown into the Curragh and left there until the government felt it was safe to let them out. This disturbed more people than those in the IRA.

Apart from the nose-twitching of the Magazine Fort raid, the government faced an ever growing number of unconstitutional activities by the IRA, legal challenges, and constitutional threats on its political front.

On 22 October 1939, a gelignite bomb had been exploded at the outer wall of Mountjoy Jail in an unsuccessful attempt to release four IRA prisoners: Paddy McGrath, Willy McGuinness, Peadar O'Flaherty and Laurence Grogan. About the same time, the Killiney Castle bomb-making factory was discovered and machine guns, revolvers and large quantities of Paxo were seized. On 18 November, Amiens Street post office, in Dublin, was held up and £5,000 taken. Five days later the National Bank in Clonliffe Road was raided and £200 taken. In the wake of these doings the legal difficulty presented itself.

On 1 December, Mr Justice Gavan Duffy, in the case of a *habeas corpus* application for Seamus Burke of Mayo, who was interned in Arbour Hill Jail, held that part six of the Offences Against the State Act 1939 was in conflict with the constitution and therefore invalid. He found that the minister's power, under the act, to order the detention of a person when he was 'satisfied' that it was necessary to do so was the assumption by a minister of the executive branch of powers reserved by the constitution to the judiciary. He consequently ordered Burke released. While an appeal to the Supreme Court was immediately entered this decision raised the question whether the other IRA prisoners in Arbour Hill should be set free. After a private debate to decide whether new legislation should be introduced, or whether the prisoners should be freed, the government released fifty-three IRA men from Arbour Hill on 2 December. On the same day a bread van was held up on the North Strand in Dublin, and nearly £500 was taken. The driver was badly beaten up.

December saw the sentencing of Barnes and McCormick, which had a powerful effect on Republican sentiment in Ireland, and the issuing of a circular from the Irish Republican Publicity Bureau to users of the Northern and Ulster Banks advising them to transfer their accounts to southern based banks, because 'those banks with headquarters in Belfast are considered to be operating against the best interests of national economic freedom'. Then came the Magazine Fort raid itself, the seizure on 29 December of an IRA pirate radio station in a Dublin suburb and the fatal shooting of a policeman in Cork on 3 January as he attempted to arrest an IRA man Thomas MacCurtain.

The government took parliamentary action following Mr Justice Duffy's decision. On 5 January the Emergency Powers (Amendment) Act, 1940 was passed, giving the government the right to intern Irish citizens without trial, in the same way as aliens could be interned without trial during the war which then existed. Because the emergency powers acts were passed pursuant to the resolution relating to the Second World War their constitutionality could not be challenged; the Offences Against the State Act, having been passed before the war began, was subject to judicial review. When part six of this act was declared repugnant to the constitution the government decided to carry out future internments under the Emergency Powers Act of 1939, as amended by the act of 5 January enabling it to intern Irish citizens. Such internments could not be challenged in the courts as the acts were not subject to judicial review.

All this legal manoeuvring aroused some shrewd misgivings on the part of responsible people. President Douglas Hyde, for the first time since the constitution came into force on 29 December 1937, convened a meeting of the Council of State[*] to advise him whether the act

---

[*] It consisted of the prime minister, the deputy prime minister, the chief justice, the president of the High Court, the chairman of Dail Eireann, the chairman of the Seanad, the attorney general, Deputy William T. Cosgrave, Deputy James M. Dillon, Senator Robert P. Farnan, Senator John Keane, Deputy General Richard Mulcahy, Deputy William Norton, Senator Michael Tierney.

should be referred to the Supreme Court (under article 26 of the constitution) for a decision as to its constitutionality. After consultation he decided to do so. Even though both houses of parliament had passed the bill it could not become law until he signed it, and this he would not do until he heard the court's decision. On 9 February the court declared the bill to be valid in relation to the constitution and it was duly signed and became law.

The next day the IRA again raided the Ballykinlar camp and got away with 100 rifles. This was an irrelevant episode as the IRA did not have bullets of the calibre required for the stolen rifles. The raid was inspired by a false idea within the IRA as to the strength of republican sympathy throughout the country. This false idea developed partially from reasons which have already been suggested and partially from what seemed to be tangible evidence that the public was swinging towards republicanism – albeit of a constitutional sort.

In Dublin at this time there was much talk of a new political movement which was believed to be a challenge to the government and was popularly reported to be ready to take over the government on some form of corporative basis. This movement, which came to be known as Coras na Poblachta (System of Republicans), did in fact contain the nucleus of a party. Eight years later it formed the core of a coalition which introduced some new ideas into Irish politics and which took power from Fianna Fail. In the early months of 1940, however, its leaders were not capable of such a feat nor were the times right for a change.

The principal figures in Coras na Poblachta were Simon Donnelly, who had fought in Boland's Mill under de Valera in 1916, Sean Fitzpatrick, another War of Independence man, Con Lehane, who had lately left the IRA, Sean Gibbons, Tom O'Rourke, Sean Dowling, one of Rory O'Connor's principal lieutenants in the Civil War days, Colonel Roger McCorley, one of the principal IRA leaders in Belfast who during the Anglo-Irish war had taken the Free State side in the Civil War, Frank Thornton, one of Michael Collins's top intelligence officers, Roger McHugh, a lecturer in English at University College, Dublin, Captain Martin Bell and Peter O'Connor.

Coras na Poblachta sought the formal declaration of a republic. Though it realized that its writ would run only in the twenty-six counties, it would claim that the jurisdiction extended over the six counties. Nobody bothered too much about how this writ could be enforced, either on a wartime England, or a wartime North of Ireland.

In fact this declaration of a Republic was made eight years later by the coalition which ousted Fianna Fail. Its language policy required the use of the Irish learned at school, with Irish street signs, shop signs and government documents and bank notes. This policy was followed by successive governments. Coras na Poblachta also proposed to introduce national service, for educational purposes, to ensure that everyone understood his responsibilities.

The basic economic principle of the Coras na Poblachta founders was the statutory right to employment and a living wage. In other economic fields the party's thinking was strictly republican in the IRA sense. It proposed breaking the link with British currency, the nationalization of banks and the making of people employed in banks into civil servants.

Free education for all children over primary age was proposed as a right, as was a university education when feasible. This last proposal has become Irish governmental policy only since the mid-1960s, although another of the party's ideas, the introduction of children's allowances, was taken up by Fianna Fail three years after Coras na Poblachta was dissolved. Dissolution occurred because people tended to discuss the party rather than join it. Indeed some of the Coras leaders themselves, notably Frank Thornton, felt that duty lay in joining some of the forces then springing up to defend the country.

The IRA, meanwhile, elated with its upsurge, the psychological effects of the Magazine Fort raid and an undue reliance on the sympathy during the Barnes-McCormick hangings, persevered with plans for an attack on the North and a meeting was arranged in the Meath Hotel in Parnell Square, Dublin. The normal procedure for such a meeting was for delegates to visit a nearby hotel for directions, making their way unobtrusively in ones and twos to the chosen venue. But in this case each person was told to go direct to the hotel, and vigilant Special Branch men on duty at railway stations and bus depots realized that prominent IRA men from Mayo, Donegal, Tyrone, Sligo, Galway, Belfast, Roscommon, Leitrim and other parts of the country were in Dublin, converging on the Meath. In a police raid everyone was captured. Knowing nothing of Traynor's, Dom Adams' and Paddy McNeela's plans the authorities thought the meeting was merely a gathering of IRA men and sentences ranged only from three to six months.

Even so, these imprisonments began a grim chapter in the history of the IRA. In Mountjoy, prisoners were treated as ordinary criminals and there was continual agitation for political treatment. After the influx of new prisoners it was decided in February to back these demands by hunger striking. On 1 March, Jack McNeela and Jack Plunkett, both of whom had been seized with the ill-fated pirate transmitter in December, were due to appear before the Special Criminal Court in Collins Barrack, Dublin. It was decided to prevent their being taken to the court. The prisoners barricaded themselves in D-wing (which also contained the execution chamber), using their beds, tables and any-thing else they could get, and armed themselves with the legs of tables and chairs. Some very savage fighting broke out when the warders, augmented by members of the Special Branch, stormed the barricades.

Cornered, the prisoners fought fiercely and the police were not too particular how they subdued them. Traynor remembers seeing D'Arcy standing with his hands up after surrendering when a policeman brought down his baton across his head. On the other hand, Seamus Byrne, who had also been arrested in the transmitter swoop, recalls how a big sergeant approached him with a baton in one hand, and stuck out his hand to say, 'Musha is that yourself Mr Byrne?' He remembered him from his appearances as a solicitor in court. The two of them retired to an empty cell and smoked until things quietened down – after hoses had been turned on the prisoners. (Hosing is an effective form of riot control. It not only knocks down the protester but takes his breath away, leaving him chilled, shaken and unfit for further activity. With men who had been on hunger strike for four days this was a harrowing ordeal.)

Hunger-striking is a double-edged weapon. It damages the striker physically almost as much as it increases his moral stature among his sympathizers. Until February, 1940 IRA hunger strikers had generally carried the day against the government, understandably in a country that had won its independence partly from deaths on hunger strikes during 1916–21 of men such as Terence McSwiney and Thomas Ashe. Fianna Fail had come under considerable pressure afterwards – both from those who wanted the prisoners let out, and from those who wished to have them kept in.

Within the six-month period before the Mountjoy strike, an IRA internee in Arbour Hill Military Jail, Charles McCarthy of Cork (on hunger strike from 16 September to 12 October) was released. On the same day Con Lehane* went on a hunger and thirst strike. His case

* He had left the IRA and was furious at being caught in one of the many IRA sweeps of the time.

was raised in the Dail on 19 October by the Labour leader Deputy William Norton. Lehane abandoned the strike two days later and was subsequently released.

The government had also been pressed into showing clemency towards a group of other Cork men, Jeremiah Daly, Richard McCarthy and John Lynch, who had gone on strike despite the government statement of 31 October '. . . that as arrest and detention in accordance with the powers conferred by Parliament are the only means available for the maintenance of public order and security they cannot permit the State authorities to be deprived of these means through the policy of hunger strike. The prisoners on hunger strike will, accordingly, not be released.'

Each of the strikers was told of this decision formally and individually. But on 8 November the Labour Party called on the government to release all prisoners on hunger strike. The next day de Valera defended the government's action but when Jeremiah Daly abandoned his hunger strike on the 11th he was released three days later, and Lynch and McCarthy, who had been removed to St Bricin's Military Hospital, were also released after treatment.

Above all there had been the case of Patrick McGrath, the chief operations officer who had been severely wounded in the fight against the British, during which he had been an outstanding figure. His case was considered to be sufficiently important for the Government Information Bureau to issue a statement to the effect that a government order had been obtained for his removal on 15 November to Jervis Street Hospital from Mountjoy Prison, where he had been on hunger strike from 23 October. He left hospital on 4 December and a *nolle prosequi* was entered in his case before the Special Criminal Court on 7 December; his spell at liberty was not to be very long – he was executed the following year for shooting two policemen.

The sort of dilemma that these cases had presented to the government is well illustrated by the following passage from the debate in the Seanad on the Offences Against the State (Amendment) Bill, 1940.

> Mr MacDermot: Might I ask the Minister one question? He said that he intended to intern these people. Does he intend to continue to hold them if they go on hunger-strike?
> Mr Boland: I certainly hope so.
> Mr Fitzgerald: Say 'Yes' or 'No'.

Mr Boland: The intention certainly is to hold them, hunger-strike or no hunger-strike because things have gone too far altogether.

Mr Fitzgerald: The last Senator who spoke here mentioned that the Taoiseach said: 'All Parties now know where they are', and he commends the action of the Government in releasing the hunger-strikers. How does the statement of the Taoiseach yesterday, that all Parties now know where they are, fit in? He went into the Dail and he stopped the operations of the Dail, departed from the whole procedure there, to give a public assurance that there would be no release for the hunger-strikers, and then he released them. Yesterday he gave us an assurance that the Government are going to take their responsibilities seriously and see that any means that may be necessary will be used to put down this criminal organization. He may tomorrow change his mind, just as he did with regard to the hunger-strikers. How are we to know where we stand, and how are any Parties to know where they stand.

Mr Boland: As regards the question of vacillation and letting out the hunger-strikers, I do not want to run away from that either. I admit that, on the surface, it looks bad. It looks like weakness and it may be very hard to justify making a statement and going back on it. But there are all sorts of considerations. We have got to deal with a very delicate problem and members of a Government have to listen to cases made by responsible members of the Oireachtas who come to them and put up propositions. These propositions were not made in public, but I may mention a matter that was put to me. I am breaking no confidence because I shall mention no names.

A prominent member of the Opposition said to me in private – I mention no names and I hope I am breaking no confidence; this was a man who had taken very strong action against these people – that, in his view, we were not entitled to let these people die on hunger-strike because, due to our attitude and general policy towards these people in the past, they were entitled to believe that if they went on hunger-strike, we would let them out. He said:

'You did not make this announcement before they went on hunger-strike and I believe you are bound not to let them die.' Things like that had to be borne in mind, but I can assure this House that we are not going to let people take the law into their own hands and that we shall not be prevented from detaining them if we are satisfied they must be detained. Our patience has certainly been tried. Our policy of conciliation has got perhaps an over-trial; I think that is on the credit side, and I wish to pay a tribute to Senator Tierney for having said so much – that it was well worth while to have tried it. We tried that *ad nauseam*. We may have gone too far, but that has got to stop. There is no question of ruthlessness or rigour, but I am sure that there is going to be insistence that everybody in this country will obey the law.

A hunger strike begun shortly after Boland's declaration was obviously coming at a moment of peak determination on the government's part to resist such pressure and the seven men who rejected their food on 25 February realized this but were determined to die if necessary in order to achieve their aim.

The strikers were Thomas MacCurtain, Thomas Grogan, John Lyons, Michael Traynor, Tony D'Arcy, John McNeela and John Plunkett. Their principal demand was that they be allowed to walk around the jail freely without being confined to their cells at four o'clock each evening. They also sought to have John Dwyer and Nicholas Doherty, each serving five years' penal servitude in Mountjoy, transferred to military custody.

Doherty was convicted of being in possession of a rifle and ammunition taken from the Magazine Fort. He and Lyons went on hunger strike on 25 February but took food on 6 March. Dwyer had been sentenced for having attempted to induce members of the defence forces to disclose information concerning Baldonnell Aerodrome. On 1 March, John McNeela was sentenced to two years' imprisonment and John Plunkett to eighteen months' imprisonment on a charge of 'conspiracy to usurp a function of Government' (running a pirate radio). They were transferred to Arbour Hill and were removed to St Bricin's Hospital on 7 March. Tony D'Arcy and Michael Traynor were sentenced to three months' imprisonment on 5 March for refusing to answer questions about the Meath Hotel case. They were transferred to Arbour Hill and were removed to St Bricin's Hospital on 27 March. D'Arcy died on 16 April and McNeela on 19 April.

Thomas MacCurtain, a son of a lord mayor of Cork who had been killed by the Black and Tans, had been in the IRA since boyhood and was continually involved in its activities. He was awaiting trial for the murder of Detective Officer Roche and was removed from Mountjoy to St Bricin's on 6 April. Thomas Grogan, awaiting trial in connection with the raid on Magazine Fort, was removed on 1 April from Mountjoy to St Bricin's suffering from pleurisy. On 19 April, the day of McNeela's death, the hunger strike at St Bricin's was abandoned.

Michael Traynor recalled the strike for me without horror or bitterness.

'There were two nice doctors in the ward, one was Fianna Fail and one was Fine Gael. The Fianna Fail man was very embarrassed but the Fine Gael man was all in favour of us. Each evening we'd take it in turn to tell each other in great detail about the best meals we'd ever had or what the best meal we could ever hope to have would be like.

'The old bedboard had been done away with by Fianna Fail and our beds were fibre mattresses with a spring upon an iron bed. After a while, we had to have all our joints bandaged because they were only skin and bone and bedsores or gangrene would have set in easily.

'After a bit, I remember, I couldn't even turn in the bed without help. We had to be rubbed down each day with olive oil to prevent the bedsores. I could smell death off myself, a sickly nauseating stench. We would have died except that we drank a great deal of water each day.

'But our other appetites went, and we concentrated on saving our energies and our lives to beat the strike. I'd been on two hunger strikes before in Crumlin Road [Belfast's jail] but these were only canter strikes – this was a real galloping strike. Tony D'Arcy died first, he called out, "Jack, Jack, Jack McNeela, I'm dying." McNeela was in the bed opposite to D'Arcy and he insisted on getting out to go to his friend. I pleaded with him not to. There was no one in the ward at the time. The armed guard was outside a locked door. After the orderlies got the door open they lifted McNeela back to bed but he died two days later. Then we got word from Stephen Hayes telling us that all we had struck for was granted and that we were to call off the strike.'

Their first meal was two poached eggs on toast, tea, milk and sugar, followed by a dose of hydrochloric acid to replace their lost digestive juices. The acid treatment continued for a week and after every meal the prisoners could see the blankets rising round their distended stomachs.

The prisoners' euphoria after the strike was short-lived because they did not get what they had struck for, and they were served either with internment orders or with notification of their prison sentences. This was stunning for Grogan who got fourteen years for his part in the Magazine Fort raid.

MacCurtain was one who survived to become a leader of the IRA campaign of 1956–62. The Roche case, for which he was to be tried, began when in the course of a scuffle a shot was fired as Roche and detectives tried to take MacCurtain into custody in Cork on 3 January 1940. Roche was fatally wounded, dying the next morning.

This case aroused tremendous interest in Ireland because of Mac-Curtain's background. He was sentenced to death by the special Criminal Court on 13 June, and the execution was fixed for 5 July. But after an application for *habeas corpus* the execution was postponed for a week. The Supreme Court dismissed the appeal and the country seethed with controversy. MacCurtain's father had fought alongside many members of the present Fianna Fail for a thirty-two-county Republic and while everyone accepted that the IRA and Fianna Fail travelled on parallel lines up to the point where the use of force was sanctioned, MacCurtain's case was seen as a test to whether Fianna Fail was prepared to kill to prevent force being used. It seemed certain that MacCurtain would die, but on 10 July a government statement declared: 'The President, acting on the advice of the government, has commuted the sentence of death on Thomas MacCurtain to penal servitude for life.' No one in Ireland outside the small circle from the government of that day knows the truth of what happened, but it is authoritatively supposed that a sister of Cathal Brugha's widow, the Reverend Mother of a convent in Armagh, interceded with Cardinal MacRory to have a last talk with de Valera, and that this final appeal decided him.

The hunger strikers' ordeal naturally excited much controversy throughout the country but government censorship restricted newspaper comment and coverage of the event. D'Arcy's death for instance was recorded in a short single column story on page eight of the *Irish Independent*. It was wartime and most people realized that episodes such as the Magazine Fort raid would jeopardize Ireland's claim to neutrality during the war. At the inquests on the dead men only relatives were allowed to attend. Sean MacBride appeared for the next of kin in both cases.

The verdict on D'Arcy was 'died of inanition, secondary to cardiac failure while on hunger strike'. This was the first time a coroner's jury had sat on a hunger-strike case since the death of Thomas Ashe, and the jury ordered a rider that, 'Immediate action should be taken with regard to the five men at present on hunger strike and in a serious condition. We desire to express our sincerest sympathy with the widow, relatives and friends of the late Anthony D'Arcy in their bereavement.' Most people in the country would have had sympathy with that rider but when McNeela died and the hunger strike was called off, the death of a bishop, Dr Hugh McSharry at the age of eighty-nine, was the main-page lead in the *Irish Independent* with a hundred and four lines of type. The end of the strike and the death of Jack McNeela rated only twenty-five. The *Irish Times* gave it a slightly bigger show but on a left-hand, inside page, and the *Irish Press* also played it down.

The inquest on McNeela on 22 April aroused some controversy because a Carmelite priest, the Rev. John J. O'Hare gave evidence that he had seen the prisoners on the day of McNeela's death, and that as a result of his conveying instructions to them from IRA headquarters, the strike was called off. He said the strike could have been called off three weeks earlier and both lives saved, if de Valera and Boland had allowed him to visit the prisoners. He gave evidence of meeting with the prisoners to substantiate his claims. As he had already spoken at the D'Arcy inquest, making somewhat similar statements, Boland felt constrained to go into the box during the McNeela hearing and make a statement which in effect denied the allegations. This exposed him to a scorching cross-examination from Sean MacBride.

However, any sympathy the IRA might have hoped to gain by the martyrdom of D'Arcy and McNeela was speedily dissipated by the tottering organization's subsequent tactics. In retaliation for the deaths, a mine was exploded in the laneway off the Lower Castle Yard in Dublin Castle, headquarters of the Special Branch, injuring a number of guards and the castle's housekeeper (part of the castle and the Chapel Royal are open to the public) and two policemen were shot at in the streets of Dublin. Public sympathy for the IRA dwindled.

The two detective officers who were taking mails from Pearse Street sorting depot to the Department of External Affairs were attacked in Holles Street by a group of IRA men, armed with Thompson guns. The mails were thought to contain dispatches for Sir John Maffey, the British representative. Both policemen, Detective Officers McSweeney and Shanahan were immediately promoted to the rank of sergeant and government offered rewards of up to £5,000 for information leading to the arrest and conviction of the persons who took part in the attack. (These were never claimed.)

The following day, after visiting the wounded men in hospital, de Valera, who had hitherto allowed Boland to make most of the stern public utterances concerning the IRA, went on the air from Radio Eireann to personally issue a statement:

'This moment, when small nations throughout Europe are devoting all their effort to strengthening national unity in order the better to defend their independence, is a moment that a group in this country has chosen to attempt to destroy our organized life.'

He referred to the 'dastardly attack made on two gallant police-men and the exploding of the time bomb in the headquarters of Dublin Castle'. He said, 'Were these deeds allowed to continue, Civil War would be the inevitable consequence and such a weaken-ing of our strength as to make our country an easy prey to any invader.' He warned that no such situation would be permitted to develop and said to those 'now planning new crimes against the nation that they would not be allowed to continue their policy of sabotage. They have set the law at defiance, the law will be enforced against them. If the present law is not sufficient, it will be strengthened; and in the last resort, if no other law will suffice, then the Government will invoke the ultimate law – the safety of the people.'

He was backed up the next day by the leader of the Fine Gael party, W. T. Cosgrave, who speaking on a motion to issue a writ for a by-election in West Galway, announced that having heard the de Valera broadcast his party would not contest the Galway by-election. This election was for a seat formerly held by a government deputy, but Cosgrave went further and announced that neither would Fine Gael move a writ for a by-election in Co. Kilkenny where a seat formerly held by a Fine Gael deputy* was now vacant. He said that Fine Gael had decided that a contest 'would not be in the interest of the country . . . if by any chance there was a marked reduction in the support accorded to the Government, it might be interpreted that that lack of support was due to the action which the Govern-ment, in recent months, had taken in connection with order in the State.' Fine Gael was 'particularly anxious that those engaged in unlawful activities . . . should realize that their activities should cease definitely once and for all and that there should be at least this much unanimity in the country that every citizen who respected his country would do his utmost to ensure that that sort of activity would cease.'

This inter-party co-operation was taken a step further and almost completely ruled out any prospects of IRA recruitment of new members for the war years. An all-party defence conference was

---

* This seat was later won by my father.

formed on 28 May and this body organized and propagandized to such effect that the prevailing spirit of patriotism was canalized within six months into the setting up of a Local Security Force of 133,000 men, drawn from towns, villages and baronies throughout the country.

Nevertheless between May and the following August upward of twenty incidents involving IRA men with the police occurred. Arms dumps were seized; German spies hoping to make contact with the IRA were captured; an IRA man died after shots were fired at men digging a tunnel from Lapp's private asylum in College Road, Cork, in the direction of the Cork Jail which had recently been converted into a military detention centre.

Micksey Conway came into the news again. He had been on the run for some months and was captured at Harold's Cross Greyhound Track, after resisting arrest and being shot in the leg. Then on the morning of 16 August three detectives raiding No. 98a, Rathgar Road, Dublin, were fired on. Detective Officer Hyland was killed instantly, the other two detectives, McKeown and Brady being so severely wounded that McKeown died the following day in the Meath Hospital. On learning of the shootings the government immediately deleted from the Emergency Powers Act the right of appeal from findings of the Military Tribunal. That court was given a new brief under legislation which came into force on 16 August. It was charged with the 'imposition and the carrying out of the sentence of death, and no appeal shall lie in respect of such conviction or sentence.'

Patrick McGrath and Thomas Harte, who were captured in the raid, were brought before the Military Court the following day. They were remanded until 20 August when they were found guilty of the murder of Hyland and sentenced to death by shooting. Sean MacBride defended them and appealed to the High Court and then to the Supreme Court, where after a three-day hearing (2, 3, 4 September) the appeal was again rejected. McGrath and Harte were duly executed by shooting in Mountjoy Prison at 6.45 p.m. on 6 September.

It might be noted here that the trigger happiness of both police and IRA should be examined in the light of the prevailing circumstances. Nerves were strained to breaking point as a programme of searches and raids was carried out in the most intensive fashion at all hours of the day and night on the homes and haunts of suspected IRA men. Members of the Special Branch and of the IRA frequently came into verbal conflict and both sides began to develop personal grudges and fears as to what might happen if one should fall into the hands of the other. Public opinion had also swung away from the IRA and behind the government so that when on 8 September a communication similar to that circulated by the Cork IRA on the execution of Barnes and McCormick was issued to cinema managers ordering them to close their cinemas as a mark of respect 'to the memory of Major-General Patrick McGrath and Thomas Harte, officers of the Irish Republican Army, who were murdered in Mountjoy on Friday', none of the cinemas closed – although all had shut for Barnes and McCormick. No incidents occurred, but to be on the safe side the police rounded up some forty-four IRA suspects. Then on 5 November an event took place which stiffened the government's resolve to resist all pressures whether internal or external.

Speaking in the House of Commons on the U-boat sinkings in the Atlantic approaches to Britain, Churchill referred to Britain's being barred from using the south and west of Ireland to refuel her aircraft and flotillas. This, he said, was 'a heavy and invidious burden which Britain should never have to shoulder'. He suggested that if Britain could use Lough Swilly and Berehaven the whole situation could be changed.

De Valera replied two days later saying, 'There can be no question of handing over these ports so long as this State remains neutral.' He added that any attempt to bring pressure on the Irish government by any of the belligerents could only lead to bloodshed, and that so long as his government stayed in power it intended to defend its rights to the ports and to every other part of Irish territory. The following day two IRA men were arrested in Dublin, after an exchange of shots, and given fourteen years each. On 14 November, the police scotched a plan to raid a number of Dublin banks when they made a series of arrests which uncovered the plans of the banks.

As a result of the continuing decline of IRA fortunes the belief became current in IRA circles that the growing toll of arrests and set-backs was not so much a result of either bad IRA planning or good police work, but of treachery within the movement. Where the IRA was able to establish to its satisfaction that its code of honour had been infringed the punishment was drastic. For instance, on 20 November John Quinn, a lorry driver from Dundalk who had given evidence for the state after he had been arrested collecting ammunition for the IRA, was shot in the right thigh and in the left arm in reprisal.

To a group of IRA men in Belfast, whom death and jailings had now brought to the top of the movement, it appeared that something more sinister lay behind the happenings in the South. Sean McCaughey, Liam Rice, Charles MacGlade, Liam Burke and later Pearse Kelly and Eoin MacNamee in particular, began to believe that there was a traitor at the very top of the organization – Chief of Staff Stephen Hayes. The idea apparently originated with McCaughey who, like the other young men, was reared in the North and had very little contact with, or knowledge of, the South. Whatever reasons he had for becoming suspicious of Hayes in the first place died with him but investigations over a period of months led his colleagues to the conclusion that McCaughey was right. They decided that Hayes should be arrested, charged with high 'treason' and, if and when he admitted his treachery, executed.

Hayes knew nothing of their suspicions and arriving in Dublin for a routine meeting on 30 June 1941 he was immediately kidnapped. Then began a nightmare lasting almost two months during which, in Hayes's own words, he was both 'thunderstruck and gunstruck'. His captors took him and his brother-in-law, Lawrence De Lacy, also of Enniscorthy, Co. Wexford (the man who had been instrumental in smuggling arms in conjunction with Joe McGarrity during the Troubles), to an isolated cottage in the Wicklow Mountains owned by Roger McHugh, a Coras na Poblachta founder and a Republican sympathizer though not a member of the IRA or a party to the Hayes kidnapping. Prior to being taken to this cottage, Hayes was taken to the Cooley Mountains in Co. Louth, and then, after De Lacy had escaped from the Wicklow cottage, he was force marched to the Wicklow hills and down through Templeogue and Terenure to a house at Castlewood Avenue, owned by a friend of Pearse Kelly's aunt, a Mrs MacEoin, again a Republican sympathizer though not a member of the IRA.

There are two versions of what occurred during this period, that of Hayes and that of the IRA. It is not possible to say which is correct at this stage, without access to closely guarded Department of Justice files if, indeed, even these contain any information. It is possible to say, however, that the episode almost certainly caused two deaths and quite certainly wrecked the IRA for the time being.

The IRA version of the sequence of events is as follows. Immediately following Hayes's arrest a provisional Army Council was formed. Eoin MacNamee was brought down from Belfast to serve on it with

McCaughey, MacGlade, Sean Harrington, who later served for a month or two as chief of staff, Jack Lynch, Tom Mullally, Stephen Rynne, Andy Skelton and Joe Atkinson. It was an unusually large council because of the importance of the affair and the necessity of getting a broad measure of agreement within the organization on a course of action. The IRA says that Hayes was continually interrogated but not tortured or harmed in any way. Pearse Kelly told me that a light dog-chain was fixed to his legs but that he was not otherwise harmed and that it was arranged that after his court-martial Hayes would be examined by a doctor, a member of a well-known Dublin family, who could then testify that Hayes had not been ill-treated.

Hayes was court-martialled on 23 July. The court-martial consisted, according to his recollection, of McCaughey, Pearse Kelly and two IRA men called McCarthy and Farrell, from Cork and Galway respectively. Also present were MacGlade, Liam Rice and Liam Burke. Pearse Kelly acted as official note-taker and procedural expert (because he had worked in a solicitor's office and as a reporter).

Sean McCaughey as prosecutor put the following two charges to Hayes:

1. That you, Stephen Hayes, conspired with 'The Irish Free State Government' to obstruct the policy and impede the progress of the Irish Republican Army.
2. That you, Stephen Hayes, are guilty of treachery for having deliberately forwarded information of a secret and confidential nature concerning the activities of the Irish Republican Army to a hostile body, to wit, the 'Irish Free State Government'.

The court-martial, which lasted from 9.00 p.m. to 7.00 a.m., found Hayes guilty on both counts and sentenced him to death for being, as an official IRA 'Special Communique' stated, 'a party to the most heinous conspiracy of crime in Irish history'. The IRA version adds that Hayes, after the verdict was announced, expressed a wish to write a confession.

The 'Special Communique' says that Hayes did this 'with the hope that it will undo some of the harm and injury I did to Oglaigh na hEireann [Irish Republican Army] through my co-operation with them [Free State government personnel].

'I decided on making this confession after I was made aware of the verdict of the court-martial. I further affirm that this confession of facts is the truth, the whole truth, and nothing but the truth, and has been made voluntarily by me.'

Pearse Kelly's recollection is that he and McCaughey were in a house rented by the IRA in Gaeltacht Park, Whitehall and used as a temporary headquarters, when Liam Rice arrived and said, 'He's prepared to talk.' McCaughey and Kelly were surprised as they had been trying to collect additional evidence with which to confront Hayes, with a view to clearing up unexplained mysteries about some recent arrests.

McCaughey, Kelly, Rice and MacGlade then went to Castlewood Avenue and asked Hayes if he was prepared to talk. According to Kelly he replied, 'I might as well.' The next problem was, what form would his confession take, a question and answer or a straight handwritten account from Hayes himself? The latter course was agreed to and Kelly got rolls of the type of parchment used in solicitors' offices for Hayes to use. The writing took until 8 September.

It had been decided to shoot Hayes on the morning of the all-Ireland football final later in the month. However, on the morning of 8 September, Wright had gone to bed leaving Burke writing a letter in the same room as Hayes. Burke was called to the door by Mrs MacEoin and Hayes noticed that Burke had left his revolver and holster hanging on the mantelpiece. He grabbed the revolver, flung himself out of the window and shuffled down Castlewood Avenue, his legs still shackled, into the busy suburban shopping centre of Rathmines and through the bewildered shoppers to the Rathmines Garda station where he gave himself up.

Hayes's versions of what happened are quite different from that of the IRA. One is contained in a statement he wrote with the aid of a barrister, Eoin O'Mahony, on 18 March 1949, in which he gives a point by point refutation of the statements in the confession and describes how he was tortured and starved. This written statement amplifies the evidence he gave during the trial of McCaughey before the Special Criminal Court.

Both statements say that he was captured at gun-point and taken to various places of detention where he was beaten, starved, continually urged to admit that he was a traitor and forced to write a confession admitting the allegations put to him. In court he stated that he had partially met their demands by admitting some of the charges after beatings, threats of being shot or of being tied up and beaten to death. He said that he had finally decided to write a full confession when, after his court-martial, McCaughey threatened to hang him from a hook on a wall and to leave him there to die if he refused to meet their demands completely. He was prevented from sleeping for twenty-four hours and in this state of terror and fatigue, he finally gave in and began to write a confession of over 150 pages.

In the handwritten statement which he gave me, Hayes says that he purposely dragged out the confession to gain time. This statement says that the confession 'took over a month to write during which time I was being subjected to torture ... Starvation diet, head beaten. All left side. Chained to bed at night. Tied to bed. Rope and chain fetters day and night. The substance of the confession was dictated by McCaughey.'

Hayes told me that he was beaten with a rifle butt all along the left arm so that it swelled up horribly. A broom handle was also used. His right side, he said, was spared so that he could write. He claimed that he never offered to write any confession and that the partial ones which he was forced to make before the trial were used in evidence against him. These, he said, were dictated by McCaughey and others. He denied completely that he was a traitor.

Hayes blamed the whole episode on the atmosphere of suspicion at the time. 'A man called Murphy by one group would be known as Smith to another, which could make his doing suspect if he were found out by the first group. That sort of thing.

'The Irish are rebels not revolutionaries,' he said. 'After the Magazine Fort raid, there was great debate about what we should do next. I favoured a coup, taking over the Dail, capturing the heads of the Government. There was no hope at all during the war of getting a man, let alone a bomb, across to England so the campaign there was finished. The atmosphere was very tense. George Plunkett had an idea that he would take four or five fellows down O'Connell Street, and if anyone stopped them they'd pull on them.

'The Army couldn't march anywhere. Our strength was overrated, we'd no arms. In my county of Wexford, for instance, there were about twenty rifles and two Thompson guns. The recruiting grounds of the ordinary young fellows growing up in the country were closed to us because of the Local Defence Forces organized by the Government which took all the manpower. So the "Army" was back to the pre-bombing campaign stage of trying to build itself up to a point where we could "talk as equals" to Germany when they won the war. The main thing, as I saw it, was to try and keep the organization intact and we were sending fellows round the country to try and organize things.

'We had a good bit of support at the time. Even though people would vote Fianna Fail they would keep stuff in the house for us or do a run for us. But we obviously hadn't a hope of doing very much. I only took over from Russell when he went to America because there was no one else and Russell begged me to do it. I remember, before he went away, he took me up to George Plunkett's house to try to get him to persuade Peadar O'Flaherty not to sign the Declaration of War on England because everyone was annoyed with him for trying to blow up the pillar. But we had to let him sign it in the end.

'That shows you how things were even then, and you can imagine what they were like when the Free Staters started to round us up and everybody got jittery. Russell had been saying that the people would fall in behind the IRA when the campaign broke out and that the Government wouldn't take any action against us. He put too much faith into an organization that wasn't there. You can imagine how everyone got more and more suspicious and nervy. McGrath had no authority to carry a gun, for instance, but with the executions and deaths and hunger strike, no one was too eager to check before they fired on someone. Everything was going wrong and I suppose these fellows wanted a scape-goat. I don't think that McCaughey was the full shilling anyway.'

Hayes's own written statement was drawn up to circulate among Republicans to exonerate him but this plan fell through. The statement ends:

> I am prepared to swear an oath that I never entered into any conspiracy with the Free State Government, through Dr James Ryan, TD, Minister for Agriculture, Thomas Deirg, TD, Minister for Education, Senator Chris Byrne or Lawrence De Lacy, to wreck the Irish Republican Army. Further, I would like to affirm an oath, that I made no confession voluntarily.
>
> Stephen Hayes

This comes at the end of a lengthy refutation of the IRA's 'Special Communique'. In all, it deals with fifty-one points made in the communique. Checking Hayes's statement against that of the IRA, any informed Irish person can see at a glance that, if one must make a choice, Hayes's document is much more likely to be accurate. Hayes, according to his confession, was supposed to have acted for the government so that Russell would be confined in America and the British bombing campaign go off half-cock. The Coventry bomb explosion was supposed to have been done to discredit the IRA. Hayes is supposed to have carried out the Magazine Fort raid at the suggestion of the government; to have deliberately timed useless explosions in England at the time of the Barnes and McCormick appeals so that the two men would be condemned in the outbreak of public indignation; to have connived at the assassination of Sean Russell by British secret agents in Gibraltar; to have arranged the murder of an innocent victim, Michael Devereaux of Wexford, for which an IRA man, George Plant, was subsequently executed; to have carried out the Dublin Castle explosion at the express wishes of the government and to have further attempted to discredit the IRA by arranging a number of bank raids as a result of which a young man called Richard Goss was arrested on 18 July 1941, and executed in Portlaoise Prison on 9 August.

These allegations do not merit a detailed serious consideration. On the Magazine Fort raid charge, for instance, it is only necessary to remember the period when it took place, and to ask what government in the world would allow an underground organization deliberately to come and make off with all its ammunition. Such analysis shows that the statements in the IRA communique are false and were obtained by force. It does not shed any light on whether Hayes was a traitor but if he was the government took a very strange method of rewarding him. On 19 June 1942, the Special Criminal Court gave him five years' penal servitude for 'maintenance of an illegal force'. A similar sentence was handed out to a member of the Special Branch, James Crofton, who had been mentioned in the confession as being a link with Hayes through whom the government passed instructions.

Crofton was arrested for trying to get a Nazi spy, Herman Goertz, out of Kerry in a fishing boat from Fenit on the Dingle Peninsula.

During the time Hayes was being held, McCaughey was approached to say that the life of Richard Goss, an IRA man accused of shooting at military and police, might be saved if Hayes were set free. McCaughey refused this plea. Goss was executed at Portlaoise Prison.

Hayes's escape upset the IRA. It came at a time of great tribulation. McCaughey had been arrested a few days earlier as he sat on a train en route to the house where Hayes was writing his 'confession'. Immediately after the escape Burke left Castlewood Avenue to tell Kelly what had happened and Rice stayed behind to warn any IRA men who might call to make themselves scarce. Rice was standing on the footpath watching for Kelly when a police car from Rathmines drew up. He fired on Detective Officer Dinny O'Brien. O'Brien and his colleagues fired back and Rice was badly wounded in the lung.

In this atmosphere, a meeting was held in Mountjoy Square to decide what to do next, and by whatever yardstick one judges the matter, an incredibly bad decision was taken. It was decided to publish Hayes's confession and Dr Lombard Murphy, chairman of the board of directors of the Irish Independent Newspapers Ltd, was contacted and asked if he would publish the Hayes confessions.

The idea was ludicrous. The policy of the *Independent* was right-wing, pro-clerical and anti-IRA. It was war-time and all papers were subject to censorship. Dr Murphy turned down the proposal at once and the IRA decided to issue the document itself. Pearse Kelly and a number of helpers used a copy of *Thom's Directory*, which gave the addresses of Dail deputies, senators, bishops and other dignatories among whom they circulated the 'Special Communique' with disastrous results.

The vast majority of IRA members had been quite unaware of Hayes's kidnapping, and this confession of deceit and treachery dismayed them. Tarlach O'hUid summed up the general reaction saying: 'As far as I was concerned the confession meant the end of the IRA for me. There I was in Derry Jail, already fed up to the back teeth with my comrades, and with the circumstances which had led me there, and this thing came. To me it meant that though Hayes was a traitor, in which case the IRA was a lousy organization for having such a man at the top, or else he was innocent, in which case the IRA was a doubly lousy organization to extract such a document from him. Either way I was finished.' (Incidentally O'hUid, despite this, refused to sign out of Derry Jail, and stayed there for the remainder of the war, being in fact one of the very last prisoners to be released.)

Apart from all this, the publication of Hayes's 'confession' brought tragedy. It described how Michael Devereaux of Wexford, a battalion officer, was allegedly framed on government instructions. The IRA, believing he had given away dumps and information leading to the capture of some of his colleagues, had him court-martialled *in absentia*, found him guilty and ordered him to be shot. The IRA communique said that the sentence was carried out by the divisional OC of the Wexford area. Within forty-eight hours of the communique being issued detectives were on their way to the area. Masquerading as IRA emissaries from GHQ they persuaded a local IRA man, who could not read and accepted their credentials, to lead them to a cave on the Knockmealdown Mountains where Devereaux had been shot and his body buried. Whether Devereaux was framed and shot in error, or whether he was innocent but shot through misunderstandings, or whether he was, indeed, a traitor, the publication of his fate was more than indiscreet. It was clear that the man's former colleagues might be in jeopardy.

The finding of Devereaux's body opened one of the most distressing chapters in Irish legal history. After widespread police inquiries two IRA men, Joseph O'Connor and George Plant, were charged with Devereaux's murder. Two former IRA men, Patrick Davern and Michael Walshe, gave evidence against them. However, during the trial they withdrew their statements and the prosecution case collapsed. It was an open secret that IRA pressure had been put on the two witnesses. Pearse Kelly told me that he met the two in jail and found them greatly disturbed. Being simple men, they had not realized their statements could incriminate former comrades. He advised them that they could retract their statements and destroy the prosecution's case. One may guess at what other pressures were brought to bear.

The government met this situation with a manipulation of the legal code, counteracting the IRA's tactics by issuing an Emergency Powers Order on 30 December 1941. This order dealt with the law relating to the admissibility of evidence before the Special Military Court. It provided that whether the offence was committed before the making of the order or not, 'It was proved that a statement relevant to the charge was made by any person including the accused and that such statement . . . was made voluntarily, lawfully . . . taken down in writing and was acknowledged by the person who made it, then at any stage of the trial the prosecution may read such a statement as evidence and may cross-examine the person who made it.'

The power of the court concerning such a statement was that it could act on the statement against the accused and that an application to read a statement could be made even though the person who made it was not present at the trial, or was dead, or was present at the trial even though he did not give evidence. The order further provided that if a military court considered it proper on any occasion during a trial that it should not be bound by any rule of evidence, whether of military or common law, then the court should not be bound by such rule.

Under this order Plant was put on trial again with the two IRA men who had rescinded their confessions, Davern and Walshe. All three were sentenced to death. The last two sentences were commuted but Plant was executed in Portlaoise Prison on 5 March 1942.

Plant bore his sentence philosophically. He told one of the prison orderlies that 'those who live by the gun die by the gun.' Sean MacBride told me that of all the trials in which he took part during the war, he found that of Plant the most harrowing.

'He was a particularly nice fellow and seemed to have no fear. The night before his execution he sat up reading, completely composed all night, and went to his death wearing his best suit.'

After the Hayes affair, the IRA in the South was smashed although it refused to admit it. Pearse Kelly became chief of staff after MacGlade was picked up within days of McCaughey being caught, and tried to resuscitate the movement. The Brugha family, Helena Molony, the businessman Lucas and Brian O'hUiginn worked with him to draw up a social and economic programme on which the IRA could work.

In addition to all the setbacks the IRA had little money. At the beginning of the war, police who were investigating the possible consequences of a visit to Ireland by Joseph McGarrity (he left on 14 August) swooped on a house, 16 Rathmines Park, Dublin, on 9 September, arrested the four IRA men in the house and seized a quantity of ammunition, some IRA documents and $8,265. Both Eoin MacNamee and Hugh McAteer told me that during the war bank raids were necessary to pay IRA debts and to get enough money to continue operations. And certainly the treatment of the deportees who were sent from England as a result of the IRA bombing campaign points to an acute lack of funds.

Clearing centres were set up to help the flood of deportees who arrived from England. But a letter from the deportees' committee shows how little money was available.

DEPORTEES' COMMITTEE
41 Parnell Square, Dublin

14/8/1940

A chara,

We enclose PO for ten shillings. We regret to state that this Fund is now completely exhausted, and except money is forthcoming from an unexpected source you cannot expect any remittance next week, or will you, we're afraid, any further remittance from this committee.

We extremely regret the necessity for sending this notice to you, but we have exhausted every source known to us. If, in the future, we see any prospect of getting further help for you, we shall communicate with you.

Yours sincerely,

L. Kearns MacWhinney	Agnes McCullough
Una de Staic	Helena Molony

No further help was forthcoming although Kelly pressed on and spoke to Eoin O'Duffy to see what help could be expected from the Italians or Germans. These activities succeeded only in placing him behind bars when he called on Herman Goertz, the German spy living in Dublin, to warn him that the police were looking for him. They were looking for Kelly too, and after arresting Goertz a few hours before Kelly's call, seized Kelly himself when he knocked on the door of Goertz's hide-out in Clontarf.

7

The IRA in the North

Whether Hayes was a traitor ot not, it is certain that the IRA men who went to the South to assess his guilt or innocence were from backgrounds so different from his (and those of the average Southern IRA man) as to make understanding between the two groups a very difficult business at the best of times, and almost an impossibility in the tension and suspicion of war. These differences in tone and background are basic not only to an understanding of the IRA but to the whole partition issue. First, most prominent IRA men in the North are Catholics and thus they are in an inferior social, political and economic position. Catholics drifted into the IRA in great numbers. Protestants if they were militantly minded (and in the North in the 1920s and 1930s it was difficult not to be so), joined the B-Specials. So there was an armed 'them and us' situation. The Royal Ulster Constabulary was of course open to Catholics, but Catholics never showed much enthusiasm for it. Though one-third of the force was expected to be Catholic at its inception only about 12 per cent ever became so, and if one looks at the careers of some IRA men one can understand why.

One of the most prominent IRA men in Belfast after the end of the Civil War was Jimmy Steele, a baker's roundsman. Jimmy, who spent most of his life in prison, literally devoted his life to the IRA. He and his wife had only one week's holiday together before the end of the 1956–62 campaign in twenty-five years of marriage. Steele was reared in the famous Queen Street area of Belfast. Queen Street runs parallel to York Street, adjoining the dockland area. Queen Street is Catholic, York Street, Protestant, and between these two main arteries run a series of smaller intersections with names like Frederick Street, Lancaster Street, Great George's Street, Little George's Street, Henry Street, Cecil Street, Grove Street and Earl Street. At times of civil commotion, notably in 1932 and 1935, these were little more than shooting ranges. When disorder began anyone crossing those intersecting streets took the risk of being hit by a Catholic bullet coming down or a Protestant one coming up. So began the tunnelling through garden walls, and through the actual houses themselves, so that shoppers wanting to pass along one of these little death traps could walk the entire street without being fired on. But it meant little comfort or privacy in the lives of those who occupied these houses. In those circumstances, one did not have to ask, 'Why did you become an IRA man?' of Steele. For a lad with his spirit and courage, there were few other courses open.

Much the same applied in the case of Michael Traynor, a man with a national reputation in the movement since the 1930s. He grew up in a mixed area of Protestants and Catholics and remembers regular bombings and shootings in the early 1920s. He recalled how as a small boy during the Anglo-Irish war in 1920 he and two friends went to see the naked bodies of three IRA men found with crosses cut into their foreheads and insteps.

'There were small black holes in their heads,' he said. 'I remember they were found in Dan O'Neill's loanin [a Belfast term for a boreen or lane] in the Whiterock Road area. They had been shot as a reprisal for the deaths of three auxiliaries. I remember the MacMahon murder,[*] we didn't think that especially brutal for the time. I remember we thought that throwing hand grenades into the bedroom of two elderly sisters on St Patrick's night in Thompson Street was far worse because there was an awful job cleaning up afterwards with feathers and bits of bedding and pieces of flesh all splashed around the room. That was done by the B-Specials.'

The youthful Traynor and his family regarded the B-Specials as being outside the law. They seemed able to shoot anyone they wished and to get away with it. During the Anglo-Irish war there were sound reasons for Traynor's opinion of this group's immunity, and very sound reasons also for fearing another organization known as the 'Murder Gang'. This flourished in Belfast during the period, carrying out assassinations and reprisal raids on Catholic strongholds. The gang was composed of former British soldiers, members of the UVF,

---

[*] This was committed by the 'Murder Gang' which, on 23 March 1922, broke into the home and shot male members of the MacMahon family and a man employed by them. The reprisal came on 19 May. IRA men went to a cooperage in Little Patrick Street, Belfast, and asked the coopers, 'Who are the Mickies here?' The Protestants pointed out the 'Mickies' (as the Catholics were known) whereupon the Protestants were lined up against a wall and five of them shot, three fatally.

and some sprinkling of RIC men and B-Specials. Its members would set out from their cars and tenders in stockinged feet, with blacking on their faces to raid Catholic areas after dark. In the poor Belfast street lighting these marauders created terror among Catholics, as they loomed up out of the darkness to shoot a passer-by dead on the street or to hurl a hand grenade through a window, escaping like phantoms. Their tactics were eventually met by a simple strategy worked out between the civilian population and the IRA.

A custom known as the 'murder yell' sprang up. Anyone seeing a member of the gang gave a long, drawn-out, high-pitched, keening yell of 'M – u – r – derr – eh' which was taken up by the entire district. Colonel Roger McCorley told me that this sound, with the banging of dustbin lids, pots and pails, was the most eerie he had ever heard. On hearing it, McCorley and his IRA patrols would hasten to the spot, guiding each other with red-tinted flashlights. When the shooting stopped and the invaders were driven off, the keening died away. The flashlights would be switched to green for 'all clear'. The custom of banging bin lids to warn of either loyalist or British army incursions into nationalist areas was revived when the 'Troubles' recommenced in 1968 and the memory of those terrible days also survives today in a street ballad:

> Oh, she got up and rattled her bin,
> For the Specials were a-coming in,
> Tiddy-fal-la, Tiddy-fal-la.
> Oh, she got up and rattled her bin,
> For the Specials were a-coming in,
> Tiddy-fa-la, Tiddy-fa-la.

Such a legacy of fear and hatred can still erupt. Two Protestant gunmen marched out one night in 1966, so moved by the songs and ceremonies with which the South was commemorating the 1916 Rebellion that they determined to kill IRA men. They didn't find any, but they shot up some Catholic barmen, killing one of them. Such bigotry and tension lay behind the rioting and destruction which the world learned of during the fearful days of August 1969.

The principal IRA Leader to emerge from Derry, the second city of the North, after the 'Troubles' was Hugh McAteer, who became chief of staff in 1941 for a time. His family had been nationalists for generations. One of his great-grandfathers was a 'reader' – a man who read *The Nation*, Thomas Davis's paper of the 1840s, to neighbours at Ceili houses. *The Nation* cost sixpence, which in 1845–48 was a day's pay, and the fact that it should be so readily bought shows the strength of the nationalist tradition in the Derry area. Derry is, of course, a classical example of gerrymandering and discrimination. Today not even the most bigoted Unionist could deny that a Catholic majority in this city was unjustly denied its civil rights by a Protestant minority. That is why the civil rights movement had such a success in the area, making the world's headlines after an RUC baton charge on 5 October 1968. Led by a Protestant, Ivan Cooper, and a Catholic, John Hume, it cut across sectarian barriers to the tune of 'We Shall Overcome' and demanded, not Catholic power, but civil rights and justice for all in the name of the city's noble traditions.

All the boys in McAteer's area joined the Fianna, the boy Republican's scout movement, as children in happier areas would join the. Cubs, to become scouts later. McAteer remembers police surrounding them in a field as they drilled in 1928 and firing over their heads. Experiences like these, schooling by the Christian Brothers, attendance at Gaelic League classes (then controlled by the IRA), readership of *An Phoblacht*, inevitably turned him to the IRA. Such social philosophy as he and his friends felt was expressed in trade unionism, or in discussions about the land war. To the young men of McAteer's youth it was a toss-up whether they joined the IRA or became missionaries. Religious fervour and Republicanism were completely entwined.

'Independence was nearly as strong in our minds as religion,' said McAteer.

'We would go out unthinkingly after Mass at 11.00 a.m. and we'd walk fourteen miles for our copy of *An Phoblacht*.'

He was a member of the St Vincent de Paul charitable organization at this time, but it did not occur to him or his friends to apply St Vincent de Paul's social principle to his Republicanism. Independence, separatism, getting the British out, these were their goals. Success in these objectives would end the conditions they saw around them. The average house had concrete floors downstairs and there was little furniture or firing. But everywhere were numbers of children turning green with malnutrition. Were it not for the Christian Brothers, who dosed the children with cod liver oil daily, many of these children would not have survived the hungry 1930s. Some of them were known as 'half timers', being half-time at school and half-time at work, generally four-hour stints at each, and all under the age of twelve. McAteer formally joined the IRA at Easter 1933. He remembers celebrating Fianna Fail's election victory that year by smashing windows. He and his friends had worked in Donegal as Fianna Fail election supporters.

In the countryside, for a young Catholic the differences were of degree rather than kind. Joe Deighan came from South Armagh outside Newry, a predominantly Catholic centre, not far from the border, and close to the Gap of the North through which (from the days of the Fianna legends) the men of Ulster sallied forth to attack the tribes of Leinster. It is a small farming area where memories of the 'Troubles' were much in mind. No Catholic in that area would join the British army although relationships between Catholic and Protestant were good. There was little hardship though in nearby Newry hunger was common among the Catholics, particularly in the 1920s and 1930s. Growing up, however, young Deighan realized there were more differences between him and the Protestants than the blue gates and blue cartwheels with which the Protestants adorned their property.

The sons of Protestant neighbours could get jobs in their own country but he couldn't. And in 1931, this fact, coupled with the songs about Emmet, Parnell and the stories of Fenians that he heard as a child, drove him to join the local IRA at seventeen. They met in the mountains to drill in barrack-ground style unsuited to guerrilla warfare. There were a few revolvers, an occasional rifle, but anything larger, such as a Thompson gun, was as rare as plum cake in Oliver Twist's orphanage. Local people turned a blind eye to their activities and would hide them in times of trouble. At election times the young IRA lads would back the Nationalist candidates in whatever way they could.

Deighan's first sentence was six months in Crumlin Road for 'promoting sedition'. In those years, constitutional politics in Northern Ireland for a nationalist-minded Catholic, like young Deighan, offered only frustration and disillusionment, or, if caught trying to lick the system by unconstitutional methods, jail. The Council for Civil Liberties issued a report on the Northern situation in 1936 which said:

> *Firstly*, that through the operation of the Special Powers Act contempt has been begotten for the representative institutions of government.

Secondly, that through the use of Special Powers, individual liberty is no longer protected by law, but is at the disposition of the Executive. This abrogation of the rule of law has been so practised as to bring the freedom of the subject into contempt.

Thirdly, that the Northern Government has used Special Powers towards securing the domination of one particular political faction and, at the same time, towards curtailing the lawful activities of its opponents ... The Government's policy is thus driving its opponents into the way of extremists.

Fourthly, that the Northern Irish Government, despite its assurances that Special Powers are intended for use only against law-breakers, has frequently employed them against innocent and law-abiding people, often in humble circumstances, whose injuries, inflicted without cause or justification, have gone unrecompensed and disregarded.

This report was issued after the 1935 riots when there had been eleven murders, two attempted murders, 574 cases of criminal injuries, 133 cases of arson and 367 cases of malicious damage. Westminster had refused an official inquiry saying 'the matter was one which came solely within the jurisdiction of the Northern Ireland Government', when pressed by Catholic spokesmen such as T. J. Campbell, Cardinal MacRory and Bishop Mageean.

From the start, Stormont did not seem to be a seat of either justice or permanence to Catholic nationalists, who were split themselves between Sinn Fein and the Irish Parliamentary Party. In the early days of the Northern parliament the parliamentary faction, led by 'Wee Joe' Devlin, was paramount, but both sides boycotted the new institution, expecting the Boundary Commission to carve up Ulster and so make the new state unworkable.

After the commission's findings, 'Wee Joe' realized that the border was there to stay and took his seat. By 1927 he was the leader of a ten-man opposition, but unable to influence Northern affairs to any extent. One of the Unionists' first actions had been to abolish proportional representation in local government elections and to rearrange constituencies to give control to Unionists. In 1929 proportional representation was abolished in parliamentary elections also, wiping out independents and leaving a Protestant government finally entrenched by a majority of three to one over a Catholic opposition. Schooling was also firmly established on a denominational basis (by the Education Act of 1923 and subsequent amendments to it in 1925 and 1930) thus perpetuating the ghetto mentality on both sides.

The IRA began to make inroads into the opposition support after the 1933 election, when de Valera was elected for South Down. He did not take his seat but his victory gave the Republicans an idea for an election strategy. They put up candidates for the 1935 Westminster elections, and to avoid splitting the vote the Nationalists stood down. The Sinn Fein philosophy overcame the traditions of the old Irish Parliamentary Party, but not that of the Unionists, and the ill conceived strategy cost the Nationalists seats in West Belfast, Armagh and Down. It also reintroduced abstentionism to the Northern political scene, and by the outbreak of war in 1939 only T. J. Campbell, who had succeeded Devlin as leader of the opposition, attended Stormont with any regularity. Catholic mistrust of Stormont was such that when Campbell accepted a judgeship from the government, this champion of the Catholic cause was dubbed 'Judas' Campbell by those he had striven to serve.

These were bad, bitter times. The rank-and-file of Protestant and Catholic followers heard declarations from Sir Basil Brooke that Catholics were disloyal and should not be employed, and from Cardinal MacRory that the Protestant Church was not part of the true Church of Christ.

It was their Northern Catholic birth which inevitably turned two of the most prominent IRA men of the Hayes era towards Republicanism. Eoin MacNamee and Pearse Kelly were born in Co. Tyrone, Kelly in the town of Dungannon and MacNamee in the district of Broughdearg.

MacNamee's wild, mountainous, poverty stricken area had turned against the IRA by the time he reached his teens, because around Tyrone and south Derry, the IRA had lent themselves to a clerically-inspired anti-poteen campaign, smashing stills and pouring away the liquid which had been an impoverished people's only means of keeping out cold and reality. That the IRA had survived at all was attributable to the traditions of the county, the home of the O'Neills and also the birthplace of Joseph McGarrity, and the fact that the Catholic majority was discriminated against by the Protestants through control of political power at Stormont and of local government bodies allocating houses and state jobs throughout the province.

MacNamee remembers being confused in his early days in the IRA because the local IRA were all Catholic whereas in his early reading about the freedom movements of 1798 and 1805 there were copious references to Protestants. He could not grasp what had happened in the meantime. Nor could he reconcile the fact that local IRA men saw no difficulty in shouting 'Up Dev' and 'Up the IRA' in the same breath. Even as a boy of sixteen this slogan struck MacNamee as containing within it a certain paradox. However, the rebel streak was strong in him and he overcame these confusions and his distaste of the local IRA who were rowdy and given to drink. He moved out of his own parish to the neighbouring Greencastle parish and joined a more orderly and responsible company. At that time, in 1934–35, little was happening. After six or nine months he, like the young Deighan, emigrated to England and found his way to London where, at the age of seventeen, he became interested in socialism. He found his way into the Republican Congress, which was then active in London, principally under Michael Kelly, Charlie Donnelly (who was killed in Spain fighting for the Republicans), Sean Mulgrew and Tommy Paton. Eventually after the bombing campaign he returned to become ultimately head of the IRA in the North.

. Pearse Kelly joined the IRA in Dungannon in late 1939 or early 1940. He was one of a group who had been to school together, attended Irish classes and shared a common Catholic nationalist 'Irish Ireland' outlook. War's outbreak saw troops billeted in the town, and the thoughts of fighting the British became more immediate. Kelly remembers, 'We thought the movement had reached very sad days when the people we saw in it locally were IRA men.' They considered starting a movement of their own, but because of its tradition they decided to join the IRA *en bloc*. They formed a company and absorbed those present. It was a good example of how the IRA exists as a tradition rather than as a cohesive movement. Shortly before joining, Kelly, who was a junior reporter at the time, attended a court at which he saw Eoin MacNamee for the first time. He remembers him as being 'a solid indestructible man who seemed to have a rock-like tenacity'. MacNamee got six months after a hearing which apparently interested him as much as it did the flies on the wall.

It was after this case that Kelly joined the IRA. Kelly's area was apparently better armed than MacNamee's because he remembers Thompsons and rifles being used for training around Esker Lough and at his father's and grandfather's farms around the Dungannon area. His first active engagement was against the British when it was proposed that a hall in the Catholic part of the town be used as a billet. The local population regarded this as a slight because an Orange Hall in the Protestant part would have done just as well. Accordingly Kelly and his friends burned down the hall and ended the attempt to billet troops in the Catholic area.

Kelly, a very rigid and upright man, also established a Republican police in the Dungannon area, with a view to keeping the some fifty or so IRA men under his command busy, and at the same time curbing a spate of petty hooliganism and larceny which had broken out in the area. Kelly's police rounded up those concerned in the hooliganism and took them to Edendork outside Dungannon and beat them up. The hooliganism stopped and the IRA stock soared.

As a result of these activities Kelly was brought to Belfast where the principal leaders, Sean McCaughey, Liam Rice and Charlie MacGlade, were just beginning to get suspicious about events in the South and Stephen Hayes. They began to pay frequent visits to the South, thereby paving the way for MacNamee, McCaughey and Kelly to rise in the movement.

In Belfast Kelly was involved in a major IRA coup. An IRA sympathizer, Fergus Kelly, who worked for a chemist in Armagh, had been standing behind his counter when a group of, as he described them, 'British brass hats' came in, made some purchases and went off leaving a long, official-looking envelope on the counter. Opening it he found that it contained various documents which turned out to be the new code, complete with key, for British troops in Northern Ireland. It was due to come into operation in seven days.

Fergus Kelly immediately made an exact copy of everything in the envelope, and then called on Pearse Kelly with the result. They restored the envelope, and when the officers returned the next day they were met in the shop with courtesy, blandness and duplicity. 'Had they found anything?' the officers asked. 'Well what?' asked Fergus. 'An envelope?' 'Ah yes. There was an envelope somewhere.' Then after much searching, 'Would this be it?' and the envelope was taken down from a shelf where it had been shoved casually between two jars of medicine. Some very relieved British officers went off not knowing that the code had been cracked. It duly went into operation and was frequently broken by the IRA, although this did not add much to IRA effectiveness. Shortly after Kelly's arrival in Belfast two IRA men got drunk and raced up the Falls Road in a stolen car firing shots, one of which wounded a girl. Two innocent IRA men were pulled in by the RUC. Kelly ordered an investigation of IRA men and issued a statement. After describing the events this ended:

At a Courtmartial, James Murphy, ('Spotter') 7, Garnet St, was found guilty of (1) having taken part in the stealing of the car, (2) being in illegal possession of a Revolver the property of the QMG, Oglaigh na hEireann, (3) endangering the life of Mary Teer by indiscriminate use of Revolver, while under the influence of drink. Accused was dismissed from the Army with ignominy and deported from Belfast.

Terence Donegan, 30, Milan St, was also ordered to leave Belfast, and the remaining three defendants [passengers in the car], were also punished by order of the Courtmartial. The sentences on all five have now been carried out.

Following the pronunciation of the Sentences by the Courtmartial the Northern Command Staff made the appended announcement:–

'In view of the alarming frequency of incidents of this nature, and the fact that they are popularly attributed to Oglaigh na hEireann, we desire to issue a stern warning of our determination in future to take drastic measures to stamp out ruthlessly all such attempts to bring Oglaigh na hEireann into disrepute, and we are confident that we shall have the earnest support and co-operation of every loyal citizen of the Republic in our efforts to ensure the efficient administration of justice.'

Signed for and on behalf of the
Northern Command Staff.

Dated this 5th day of July, 1941.

This statement was accepted by the RUC and the two IRA men who had been arrested were released. Had a similar statement been issued by Protestant extremists in the Shankill Road area the RUC would probably have accepted it also. In both areas it was the Protestants and the Catholics who reigned supreme, never the RUC or the government of Northern Ireland.

This denominational solidarity dated back to the days of the famine, when a census in Belfast showed that the population of the city was 35 per cent Catholic, the majority living along the line of today's Falls Road in western Belfast. Unfortunately, in the near vicinity, attracted by the same hopes of getting work that had brought in the Catholics, were the working-class Protestants who lived along the Shankill Road parallel to the Falls. The two sections were frequently in savage conflict because of economics, religion and political allegiances. Around 12 July each year the Shankill people come out in a blaze of bunting to honour King Billy, commemorate the Battle of the Boyne and swear fealty to the union with Britain. Lady's Day, 15 August, was traditionally a time of Catholic fervour, though it was not so extreme.

While Catholic sympathy with the IRA was heartening to its leaders, they knew that the influences that drove Catholics into the IRA were also driving Protestant and Catholic apart to such an extent that the IRA must inevitably be lost between them. To present themselves as armed Catholics on the Northern scene would gain no Protestant support, and without this a thirty-two county republic was impossible.

Accordingly the IRA made two major efforts during the 1930s to bridge the religious divide. One attempt was defeated by the Protestants, the other by internal dissension in the IRA itself. The opportunity for the first attempt came during the outdoor relief riots which disfigured Belfast in 1932. These arose over a governmental proposal to cut the rate of outdoor relief as an austerity measure, and it temporarily united both the Protestant and Catholic poor in common outrage.

The Army Council tried to take advantage of this feeling by issuing an 'address from the Army Council of the Irish Republican Army' to the 'men and women of the Orange Order' to coincide with the July celebrations:

Fellow Countrymen and Women,

It is a long call from the ranks of the Irish Republican Army to the marching throngs that hold the 12th July Celebrations in North East Ulster. Across the space we have sometimes exchanged shots, or missiles or hard words, but never forgetting that on occasions our ancestors have stood shoulder to shoulder. Some day we will again exchange ideas and then the distance which now separates us will shorten. For we of the Irish Republican Army believe that inevitably the small farmers and wage-earners in the Six County area will make common cause with those of the rest of Ireland, for the common good of the mass of the people in a Free United Irish Republic. Such a conviction is forming itself in an ever increasing number of minds in North East Ulster.

Working-farmers and wage-earners of North East Ulster! You surely must see that your future is bound up with the mass of the people in the remainder of Ireland. To preserve yourselves from extinction, you and they must combine and go forward to the attainment of A Free Irish Nation within which life and living will be organized and controlled by you to serve your needs and thus end the present economic and social injustices for ever. *The industrial capacity, and training of you industrial workers, of North East Ulster ensure for you a leading influence and place in the economy and life of a Free Irish Nation.*

EXPLOITATION OF RELIGIOUS PREJUDICES

To prejudice you it is emphasized that we of the Irish Republican Army and the mass of Republicans are mainly Catholic, and that your religious beliefs would not be respected in a free Ireland! It is quite true we are mainly Catholics, but in Southern Ireland the same political and economical interests and voices that tell you we are Catholics, tell the Catholic population of the South that we are Anti-God fanatics, and yearning for an opportunity to make war on the religion to which the majority of us belong!

The fact is we are quite unaware of religious distinctions within our Movement. *We guarantee you, you will guarantee us, and we will both guarantee all full freedom of conscience and religious worship in the Ireland we are to set free.* This is the simple truth, and just now when Imperial interests are attempting to conceal themselves behind the mad fury of religious strife, you and we should combine to make certain that no such escape should be provided them.

Do you not see yourselves queued shoulder to shoulder outside the Unemployment Exchanges waiting for the 'Dole', that crumb which the exploiters throw to the exploited of different religions? In these vital matters your religion or your membership of the Orange Order counts for little, nor does Catholicism to the unemployed and starving Catholics in Southern Ireland.

The fact is that the religious feelings of the masses of both Orangemen and Catholics are played on and exploited by the Imperialists and Capitalists the more surely to enslave them.

THE VICTORY OF THE BOYNE!

You celebrate the victory of the Boyne. This battle was a victory for the alliance of the then Pope and William of Orange; strange alliance for you to celebrate; strange victory for Catholics to resist. History has been muddled to hide the occasions when your forefathers and ours made common cause, and passions are stirred to manufacture antagonisms. If Wiliam of Orange and His Holiness could achieve an alliance, there is hope that 'No Surrender' may come from a throng which also roars 'Up the Republic'.

Your stock was the founders and inspiration, and North East Ulster the cradle, of the modern Revolutionary Movement for National Independence and Economic Freedom. Your illustrious ancestors and

co-religionists, The United Irishmen, by their gallant struggle in 1798
set aflame the ideals of Republicanism which never since have been
extinguished. We ask that you should join us to achieve their ideals –
National Freedom and religious toleration.

The offer of friendship went further than that appeal according to
rumours surviving from the period. One member of the Army
Council told me flatly that these were not rumours – 'We put guns
into the hands of Orangemen for use against the B-Specials,' he
averred. When I attempted to check the truth of this story with Lord
Brookeborough he was thunderstruck. 'You shatter me,' he said and
his wife and he shook their heads in disbelief.

But the old sectarianism of Belfast reasserted itself during rioting
throughout October 1932. Republicans said that this was deliberately
fomented by some members of the RUC in baton charging and firing
on Catholics. This is not impossible. In those bad times there was
strong Protestant feeling on which the IRA with its emotional appeals
could never get a purchase.

The Ulster Protestant League, founded in 1931, adjured its members 'neither to talk nor walk with, neither to buy nor sell, borrow nor
lend, take nor give, or have any dealings at all with them, nor for
employers to employ them, nor employees to work with them'. The
'them' of course were Catholics and the League habitually paraded
through Belfast with bands and banners flying, lambasting the government for being 'soft' on Roman Catholics, just as Paisley's followers did prior to the 1969 riot, calling for the resignation of the
minister of home affairs. All this began to have an effect on Protestant support for the government and government spokesmen were
driven to show their reliability to the Unionist cause by extremist
replies. In his July address, Lord Craigavon made the first of his
statements about Protestantism and government in the North – still
quoted by long-memoried Nationalists. He said, 'Ours is a Protestant
government and I am an Orangeman' and by July 1934 he had
escalated this to 'we are a Protestant parliament and a Protestant
State . . . I am an Orangeman first and a member of parliament
afterwards.'

Efforts to create unity still, however, continued. The *Republican
Congress*, organ of the breakaway IRA section led by Gilmore, Ryan
and O'Donnell, had carried in its issue for 2 June 1934 a triumphant
page-one headline proclaiming a 'United front between Orange and

Green' following the formation of *one* James Connolly Club for unemployed Protestant and Catholic workers.

Small though this beginning was, it was nevertheless a highly significant step forward, and it was arranged that a sizeable contingent from the Shankill Road would march later on 17 June to Bodenstown with banners bearing inscriptions such as 'Wolfe Tone Commemoration, 1934, Shankill Rd, Belfast Branch. Break the connection with capitalism', 'Connolly's message our ideal', 'James Connolly Club, Belfast, United Irishmen of 1934'. However, when the United Irishmen of the North reached the assembly field at Sallins en route to the graveyard of the founder of the United Irishmen of all Ireland they found the disunited Irishmen of the South waiting for them. A group of Tipperary IRA men, led by a redoubtable figure called Matty Ryan, attacked the Congress group in an attempt to seize the Congress banners which had been proscribed by the Twomey-Fitzpatrick section of the IRA. The attempt failed as the two groups clashed to the accompaniment of 'Up Tipp' and 'Come on the Shankill Road'. Eventually the battered Belfast men marched on to Wolfe Tone's grave where further scuffles broke out in which the only lasting damage was to the United Orange-Green front.

Such were the efforts which the Catholic IRA made to woo the Protestants. On the Protestant side another tradition existed which, properly cultivated, should have been more promising. This was the liberal Presbyterian strain of Wolfe Tone exemplified by Rev W. Montgomery who, though worsted by Cooke, helped to give Northern Protestantism that more attractive vein which never quite dies out, even at moments of extreme religio-politico fervour. Thus during the Home Rule crisis of 1912 one of the sponsors of the plan which brought Winston Churchill to speak in favour of Home Rule in Belfast on 8 February of that year, was the Rev James Armour of Ballymoney, a man whose memory is justifiably revered in the annals of Northern liberalism. There were Protestant subscribers to this tradition active on the Republican side during the Anglo-Irish war and it was still alive in 1939–40 both in constitutional and unconstitutional politics.

Constitutionally there was the Irish Union Movement, founded by Denis Ireland, a Presbyterian who later became a senator in the Dublin parliament through Sean MacBride's influence. This movement also attracted a considerable amount of liberal Protestant support in the North because of its programme of better relationship with the South, a programme which stemmed from Wolfe Tone's writings.

However, on 10 September 1942, it was discovered during an RUC raid on IRA men that some of them, in particular one John S. Graham, had been active in the movement. As the Orangemen had always regarded Denis Ireland as a traitor and renegade because of his all-Ireland view, the IRA men's arrest afforded an opportunity to detain and interrogate members of the Irish Union. This spread the suspicion that it was an IRA hot-bed. Not surprisingly the movement collapsed. (Graham and some of the other liberal Protestants, who constituted one of the best IRA companies in Belfast, had joined the Union, not for purposes of infiltration but through the same tradition that brought them into the IRA: an interest in socialism, Wolfe Tone's writings, the Irish language and the Gaelic League. This group figured in a major crisis within the Belfast IRA).

Despite all the speeches and slogans, the martyrs, commemorations and appeals to tradition the average young IRA man's existence consisted largely of shooting around fields or back streets, holding drill sessions with obsolete weapons in disused halls and talking about 'action' that practically never came. The action that did occur was usually disastrous. In particular there were the two raids on the armoury at Campbell's College which resulted in the celebrated Crown Entry* raid by the RUC in the midst of an IRA court-martial. The RUC swoop settled some very big IRA fish, including Jim Killeen, Michael Traynor and Tony MacLaverty, OC of the Belfast battalion, who was being court-martialled at the time. This was not for any misdemeanour but because he had issued instructions to some of the IRA men who were caught in the armoury raids, allowing them to recognize the courts so that they had a chance of making a defence.

Increased wartime pressures on the IRA made communication between Dublin and Belfast more difficult, and some Northerners began to think that a self-contained Northern unit was desirable. The principal architect of this idea was Charles MacGlade, a Belfast printer, and so 'Northern Command' came into being. The command in fact embraced seven counties, the six counties of Ulster proper and Co. Donegal. Eoin MacNamee, who later became its head, first heard of this unit in June 1939, after his return from the bombing campaign in England. The formation of this command meant that the IRA in the

---

* An 'entry' in Belfast is a narrow lane for passers-by from one street to another.

South was led from Dublin, in the North from Belfast, in England from God knows where and that each group carried on more or less independently of each other.[*]

Although it was widely discussed in IRA circles, Northern Command's level of organization may be judged from the fact that there were supposed to be two battalions in Co. Tyrone, Eoin MacNamee's native county, but when he began to organize there weren't twenty members in the whole county. But such was the spirit of the volunteers and MacNamee's expertise in training, that he remembers being able to set up fairly good battalions in both east and west Tyrone within six weeks. Their armaments, however, consisted only of a few weapons left over from 1922.

It is worth following MacNamee's career as it impinged on most aspects of IRA activity. He was captured on 11 June 1939, charged with being a member of the IRA and sentenced to six months in Crumlin Road Jail. After serving his time he told the authorities that he was going to Newry to give them the impression he was going to cross the border. He was issued with a Newry ticket, but on leaving the prison he was met by a girl, and placed in a 'pound loney' area of the Falls Road used as an IRA barracks. He remembers young men with guns and batons setting out on all sorts of military excursions. Everyone in the house was courteous to him but he soon discovered that he was under a form of house arrest! The Command had apparently decided to suspend him for illegal organizing in Tyrone. When this news leaked out a mutiny took place in Tyrone. Then a communication arrived ordering MacNamee to return home. Part of this silly row lay in the fact that there is a traditional Tyrone versus Belfast animus somewhat akin to that existing between Cork and Dublin. However, since he was to be reinstated without trouble, the row blew over and Eoin returned to find himself a hero in Co. Tyrone.

He also found that there was little a hero could do apart from organizing parades and training camps, but he was then appointed Adjutant General in West Tyrone and about April 1940 he went on the run. He remembers that four or five other prominent Tyrone men had to do the same, so there were a number of full-time organizers

---

[*] This picture of a lack of communication is not exaggerated. Pearse Kelly, one of the first people I interviewed for this book, compared my lack of knowledge on starting my research to his incomprehension about Dublin's affairs when the Hayes investigation first took him to the South.

working throughout Tyrone. (The adjoining Donegal, though partially in the Free State area, was much more difficult to organize
because it did not have the abrasive reality of Union Jacks, British
uniforms, gerrymandering and discrimination before it.) About this
time he met Sean McCaughey for the first time. McCaughey was OC
of the Northern Command, which had a headquarters in Carrickmore, near Joe McGarrity's old homestead. All seemed to be going
well now, but the course of IRA ways never runs smooth. With the
exception of MacNamee all the fulltime organizers in Tyrone were
captured in a gun battle with the RUC at Carrickmore.*

Eoin then moved up to become brigade OC, reorganizing the
brigade staff to cover gaps left by the arrests, and despite these had
the brigade whipped into a pretty effective unit by the autumn of
1940. It was at this stage that the issue of the Belfast battalion
courts-martial blew up. For some time past volunteers had complained that battalion officers had been beating them up. There was
at the time a strong Fascist influence in Belfast IRA circles. An
occasional IRA man affected the Bersaglieri cap of Mussolini's crack
troops and Fascist techniques, such as beatings with batons and
doses of castor oil, were frequently employed by what was known as
the 'belt and boot brigade'.

Looking at newspapers of the time one will sometimes come across
small paragraphs about young men being beaten up by unidentified
passers-by. These incidents were the ones that came to the surface;
others did not, and some were pretty savage. A favourite IRA punishment of the time for serious dereliction of duty was wounding a man
in the leg, or in both legs for more serious cases, with a revolver shot.
Frank Morris of Convoy, Co. Donegal, one of the few reliable men
whom Eoin had been able to recruit to the IRA in the county, told
me that his first noteworthy IRA action was to attend a court-martial
at which the sentence on a suspected informer was wounding in both
legs. This was later reduced to wounding in one leg only, but the
sentence was duly carried out.

---

* They were Arthur Kearney, Jim Brogan, Pat McCallan and Jim Kirk. Another
prominent IRA man, Dan McMahon, was captured and left in his own home on the
night of the raid under the guard of an RUC man while the rest of the party went to
surround the men at Carrickmore. However, when the RUC man guarding McMahon
heard the shooting at nearby Carrickmore he went to the door to see what was
happening. What he couldn't see happening was Dan McMahon making his escape
through the back door!

Those who sanctioned these punishments felt that volunteers needed fear to keep them in line, whereas other prominent leaders, in particular Jimmy Steele, disagreed violently. To Steele, membership of the IRA was an honour and privilege, and this fact alone enjoined a high standard of conduct. He first heard of these activities in Crumlin Road Jail, and began taking statements from incoming volunteers so that on his release he had a complete dossier. With this he had the entire battalion staff court-martialled in a little hall in a 'loney' off the Falls. It was a strange business and while it was being held Belfast was like an armed camp, with armoured cars, ordinary police cars and foot patrols four and five strong on every side of the street in the area. Evidently the RUC had word of some impending IRA activity, but didn't know what it was to be.

The outcome of the court-martial was that a number of officers were reduced to the ranks. This curbed the 'belt and boot' faction for some time, but the issue arose again when the command staff was arrested in the Hayes affair.

All that prevented serious trouble then was the fact that McCaughey's case was before the courts in Dublin. Everyone felt that any outbreak of shooting would prejudice a verdict. McCaughey was sentenced to death but was reprieved and sent to Portlaoise Jail. It is thought that his reprieve came through the intercession of Cardinal MacRory. The IRA did make overtures to the Church on his behalf; MacNamee went to see the Bishop of Down and Connor, Dr Mageean, who was generally regarded in Nationalist circles as a Republican sympathizer, but he offered no encouragement. But perhaps the bishop took another line in private with the cardinal because McCaughey's reprieve was quite unexpected. On the other hand, although the government was incensed at the Hayes confession and the embarrassment it caused, McCaughey had not been captured bearing arms, or as a result of any affray that had cost life. So, even in wartime, his execution would have aroused violent reaction. (The IRA had made preparations so that if he had been executed, a prominent intelligence officer from the Gardai who had been decoyed to Belfast, ostensibly to meet Eoin MacNamee, would have been ambushed and shot.)

After the reprieve, MacNamee and Hugh McAteer found that in the wake of the Hayes affair the activities of the 'belt and boot' brigade resumed and their own leadership was challenged. So, one night in November 1941, MacNamee mobilized the Protestant company, led by John Graham. They drafted in a squad of men from county brigades and left a man on the Falls Road to tell Graham that, if they did not return very shortly, he and McAteer were to be followed into a house on the Falls Road where the battalion was meeting – with guns blazing if necessary.

MacNamee and McAteer were both armed and their appearance at the battalion meeting caused alarm. Eoin told the senior officer present that if the battalion failed to co-operate with the command, he would be shot. In a tense atmosphere, a member of the battalion staff, Patsy Hicks, one of its strongest figures, stammered out, 'I've seen these things before. I'm taking orders from the command OC.' Hicks was known to have seen some stern affairs, so his reaction deflated the balloon of defiance at once. The atmosphere grew more cordial as allegiance was reaffirmed and everybody settled down to discuss future plans. Meantime, the Protestant squad, whom MacNamee had forgotten, rushed into the room prepared to shoot. Seeing MacNamee unharmed, they too calmed down and the incident ended peaceably.

After the Hayes affair it was clear that the IRA had no immediate role in the South and a series of provincial conventions were set in train to decide future policy. MacNamee took over the one in Connacht; Sean McCool, who had succeeded Pearse Kelly as chief of staff, that of Munster; Hugh McAteer that of Ulster, and Frank Driver the Leinster gathering. Out of these conventions some degree of reorganization took place with a view to transferring activities across the border and beginning a campaign exclusively in the North. About 20,000 rounds of the Magazine Fort ammunition, .303 calibre bullets for rifles, had found its way into MacNamee's custody in Tyrone, and between this and a quantity of arms still existing in various dumps throughout the South, it was felt that the IRA was still relatively well-organized in the North. Against a backdrop of strong Catholic support, it could strike a reasonably effective blow against the administration.

But as with the English campaign the first blows were stuck by the Southern authorities against the IRA. MacNamee, who was attending Skerry's College in St Stephen's Green, Dublin, under the name of Diamond, ostensibly to learn Morse code, but in reality to provide a cover for his presence in Dublin, was picked up in Brandon Road as he walked towards a dump in the Drimnagh area of Dublin. Within a few weeks Sean McCool joined him in the Curragh.

However, the defiant and resilient Northerners pressed ahead with their plans for a campaign which was finally agreed to at a Northern Command convention held on 25 March 1942, in Belfast. The funds for the campaign were obtained by a raid on the Academy Street Civil Defence Headquarters, which netted about £4,200 of payroll for civil defence workers throughout the North. The IRA was in debt at the time to landladies who had put up men on the run and part of the Academy Street money went to paying these bills. The rest went on buying information* from police sources, on the provision of medical attention for wounded men, for printing Tarlach O'hUid's newspaper, the *Republican News*, running radio transmitters and buying ammunition or guns from British soldiers. It would have been better if no guns had been obtained for the campaign. Three IRA men died as a result, one by hanging, two by shooting on the streets of Belfast, and five members of the RUC and of the special constabulary lost their lives.

Constable Thomas James Forbes, a married man with four children, was the first policeman to be shot in the North for ten years when he and a group of other police were fired on in Dungarmon on 4 April 1942. Constable William Mackey survived with fractured ribs because a bullet, aimed at his heart, struck a button in his coat. The following day Constable Patrick Murphy was shot dead in Cashmere Road, Belfast. A group of young IRA men involved in this shooting, all of them under nineteen, retreated to Cawnpore Street, where they made their way into a house. Here they were arrested by four of Murphy's comrades, whom they could easily have killed as they came up the stairs, but did not. All six were sentenced to death for the murder of the policeman, and this sparked off the greatest agitation initiated by IRA action during the whole of the war.

In Dublin Sean MacBride set up a reprieve committee and acted as its secretary. No fewer than 207,000 signatures were collected, and huge meetings were addressed by such diverse speakers as Denis Ireland of the Irish Union, Jim Larkin, the trade unionist, and past and present Republicans of every shade and hue, including members of Fianna Fail. The agitation spread outside Ireland. Secretary of State Cordell Hall took up the matter after being pressed by the Irish

---

* Before being picked up MacNamee had established contacts with intelligence personnel in the Southern army who, he told me, showed him their reports before passing them on to their superiors.

minister in Washington, Robert Brennan. The execution of six IRA men for the death of one would have jeopardized Fianna Fail's effort to keep order, to say nothing of the effect in the North.

Hull also saw Anthony Eden in Washington and put pressure on Lord Halifax, the British ambassador. In London the American ambassador, John Winant, made representations. In Dublin the American ambassador, David Gray, said that 'some measure of clemency is probably expedient. The British and Canadian representatives here hold the same opinion. Hanging six for one would shock public opinion.' However, Gray took a poor view of all the pressure for reprieves, and in a letter dated 27 August 1942 to de Valera wrote:

> Those of us who like yourself have attempted and are attempting by diplomatic means to procure a measure of clemency for these young men, find ourselves embarrassed by the pressure exerted here upon the Northern Government. As you know, governments, especially in war time, do not like to be coerced and fear that clemency used under pressure will be interpreted as weakness.
>
> I am afraid that if we fail, the originators of the pressure campaign will have a heavy responsibility. I appreciate your sincere desire to help this agitation within reasonable bounds and your considerable success in this direction, but repeat what I said in our recent talk – that, except for yourself and a few others, Ireland does not come to appreciate what the war means, the gravity of the situation and the danger of rocking the boat at such a time.
>
> Yours sincerely
David Gray.

Irish sentiment in America was less sensitive than Gray's and influential congressmen such as the majority leader Senator McCormick, and many others urged the State Department to intervene.

The agitation was largely successful. Five of the six were reprieved, only Thomas Williams being hanged on 2 September. It is believed in Belfast that the British cabinet favoured hanging all six, to deter the IRA from activity for the rest of the war, but that Cardinal MacRory from Armagh approached Cardinal Hinsley, who was friendly with Brendan Bracken, Churchill's wartime minister for information. Bracken, an Irishman himself, could claim superior local knowledge and his word probably carried exceptional weight.

Williams's hanging was a frightful business that could have

occurred only in Belfast. On the night before his death, Catholics kept vigil outside the jail saying the Rosary, while an Orange mob jeered them, shouting obscenities about Williams and singing Orange ballads.

Before his execution Williams wrote the following letter to McAteer:

Hugh, a Cara,

Just a note to let you know how my comrades and I are getting along. I do not expect an answer as your answer to Joe serves us all in that respect.

I am proud to know that you are our leader. My comrades and I are sure that you will use your utmost powers to free our dear, beloved country. And bring about the reestablishment of the Republic and its constitution.

It is beyond the powers of my humble intellect to describe the pride of my comrades, in knowing that they are going to follow in the footsteps of those who have given their lives to Ireland and the Republic. To describe the courage and coolness shown when sentenced to death. As Joe has previously stated to you. Our sorrow is not being able to attack the court and the 'Northern' Junta. But now you know the reason.

My God, can we tell you and our comrades who will carry on the fight, can we tell you of the gladness and joy that is in our hearts. To know that the Irish people are again united, aye, and well may England quake, Irelands awake, Irelands awake. After 20 years of slumber our nation will once again strike, Please God, at the despoilers who have infringed the nation's liberty, freedom and murdered her sons, her daughters, who have given us a foreign tongue; shall please God, strike and strike hard and make the tyrants go on their knees for mercy and forgiveness.

But shall we make the mistake of '21, no, no, tis men like you and your staff will see to it. That no farcical so-called Treaty shall in anyway be signed by a bunch of weak-kneed and willed Irishmen. Better that the waves of the mighty oceans sweep over Erin than take and divide our nation, murder her true sons again. Better would be that heavens would open and send fire to destroy Erin, than to accept another Treaty like it.

In writing this, dear Hugh, do not think that I am saying it to you or the gallant soldiers of Oglaigh na hEireann, it is from my heart that it comes to the weak-willed and ignorant Irish men who may put any trust in England. My only regret is now I will not be with you in the fight and last stand of Ireland's battle for freedom. But with the help of God and His Blessed Mother we may be in heaven looking down upon our dear, beloved, tortured, crucified Erin, and look with pride on the men and women who will carry on the battle until victory.

Well dear Hugh I'll close with the message to Oglaidh na hEireann, 'To carry on, no matter what odds are against you, to carry on no matter what torments are inflicted on you. The road to freedom is paved with suffering, hardships and torture, carry on my gallant and brave comrades until that certain day.'

Your comrade in Ireland's cause,
Lieut. Tom Williams,
'C' Coy. Belfast Brigade,
Oglaigh na hEireann.

For days before and after Williams's execution, tension hung over Belfast, particularly in Nationalist quarters. Two days before Williams was hanged, one of Hugh McAteer's principal lieutenants, Gerry O'Callaghan, was shot dead when the RUC raided a dump at Harmanstown outside Belfast. O'Callaghan was moving arms to a safer place, for use in avenging Williams's death. Demonstrations took place in Dublin against business premises that refused to close and riots broke out throughout the city. In the North the reaction was grimmer – although the condemned man himself had sent a letter to his comrades asking that no reprisals be taken for his death. Within an hour of his execution police patrols were being fired on. At Clady, Co. Tyrone, Constable James Laird and Special Constable Samuel Hamilton were shot dead on 5 September. In Belfast on the same day a shooting took place in Abercorn Street, when an RUC man and a boy of sixteen were wounded. And of four IRA men arrested under arms in Belfast on the same day, two were sixteen and one seventeen years old.

The wave of bombing and shootings finally led to a curfew in Nationalist areas of west Belfast. From 10 October no movement was permitted on the streets between 8.30 p.m. and 6.00 a.m. On the first day of the curfew a battle broke out outside Donegal Pass police barracks after a bomb was thrown there. Special Constable James Lyons was fatally wounded and a number of other police and passers-by received lesser injuries. All these incidents affected the nerves of Belfast people, but the campaign petered out with the enforcement of the curfew, although a shooting on 1 October 1943 claimed the life of Constable Patrick McCarthy, shot dead during a payroll raid on Clonard Mill at Odessa Street off the Falls Road.

The IRA had intended to bring a number of other police officials and warders to their Maker but these plans misfired. One of the most celebrated policemen Northern Ireland has ever produced is District Inspector James Fanning, who was a particular scourge of the IRA. He was cycling to work one morning when a car passed him and a Chicago-style assassination was attempted. He was shot off his bicycle, and he described to me how he lay on the pavement with 'a feeling of cold and surprise. I felt the sting of the bullets, but no pain, just terrible cold.' The car carrying his would-be killers passed so close that he could see the men in it, handkerchiefs round their faces, as they fired through the windows at him. The bullets struck the pavement near his head and around his body. His wounds were so bad that when he was picked up blood ran out through the eyelets of his shoes, but he recovered after a lengthy stay in hospital and returned to duty.

He was not long back at work when one of those responsible for shooting at him (both IRA and RUC very often had a shrewd idea of what transpired in the enemy's camp without always being in a position to do anything about it) sought a permit to go to England. Fanning duly issued one, but could not resist asking the man if 'he was not ashamed of what he had done'. His assailant replied, 'Oh now Mr Fanning I don't want to talk about that at all.' In the circumstances, Fanning regarded his attitude as being entirely understandable, if reprehensible, and there the exchange closed.

All these incidents made the IRA seem a formidable force to the public, but in fact, as in the South, the reality was quite otherwise. A week after the hanging of Williams, on 10 September, the publicity headquarters of Northern Command was raided and the owner of the house, Sean Dynan, John Graham, the OC of the Belfast battalion, and David Fleming from Kerry were captured along with a complete issue of the IRA paper the *Republican News*. This last loss was remedied by the efforts of McAteer, Gerry O'Reilly and others who sat up during the night producing a further 6,000 copies which duly were distributed.

Then on 6 October McAteer and O'Reilly were themselves captured. They had been decoyed to the home of a boyhood friend of McAteer's who was then a member of the RUC and who had, by chance, bumped into McAteer earlier in the week and promised him some worthwhile information if McAteer would call to his home. The life of this young man hung by a very slender thread thereafter, but McAteer refused to have him executed as he could easily have done either later in the war or after it. (However, the man's father's undertaking business fell off and he went bankrupt as a result of an unofficial boycott against him.) After his capture McAteer received a fifteen-year sentence and was sent to Crumlin Road Jail, from which he immediately planned to escape.

The walls of the jail are more than three feet thick, the windows are barred and thick glass is set into steel frames. A twenty-foot wall surrounds the front garden overlooked by warders' quarters and the administrative offices and, during the war, this wall was patrolled by armed guards. If a prisoner did succeed in getting so far he then had to run past the windows of the warders' cottages outside the walls. Normally there was also a police patrol on Crumlin Road itself, a busy artery in the heart of Belfast. However, a trapdoor was discovered in the ceiling of the lavatory which led to an attic under the slates of the jail roof. McAteer, Paddy Donnelly, the prisoners' leader, Jimmy Steele and Edward Maguire decided to escape together. Ladders were made from sheets torn lengthwise in halves and the halves then sewn together end to end and bound with waxen cords. A hook was made from a brass bed end to catch the top of the wall and bandages were wrapped around it so that it would catch in the barbed wire with which the wall was protected.

On the morning of 15 January 1943, the four received permission to go to the lavatory and, standing on a table which was later removed by their friends, hauled themselves up into the attic, replacing the trapdoor underneath them. Once in the attic, they smashed their way out on to the roof. Incredibly, no one heard the noise of the breaking slates. They reached the wall without mishap, here to discover that the jointed stick which they had made to hoist the hook on to the wall was too short. Maguire stood on McAteer's shoulders in an attempt to hoist the hook on, but fell off. He and McAteer began squabbling as to whose fault this was when Donnelly intervened to say specifically, 'I think, lads, ye should finish this conversation on the other side of the wall!'

They eventually got over the wall safely, McAteer alone being injured with torn ligaments in his ankle and a badly reefed hand from the barbed wire. In the gloom of the January morning no one noticed them mingling with the crowds and, despite the fact that they were wearing prison clothes, Belfast's wartime shabbiness afforded them protection in this regard also. A £3,000 reward was immediately posted for the capture of any or all of the four, but Maguire and Donnelly stayed free to the end of the war, Steele lasted until May, and McAteer was not picked up until the following November.

The escape gave the IRA a brief injection of life and McAteer and Steele figured in two spectacular exploits during their freedom. The first of these was the Derry Jail escape which was being prepared before McAteer's and Steele's exploit. The ground floor cells of Derry Jail were floored with wood, beneath which was nothing but clay. A group of prisoners – Liam Graham, Eddie Steele, John McGreevy and James O'Hagan – began to tunnel under the floor of Liam Graham's cell and, working for over five months, they and their prison comrades managed to sink a shaft extending twenty feet straight down and turning sharply to extend out under the roadway outside the jail and up into the coal hole of the Logue family in Harding Street. The clay was dumped into lavatories and twice the sewers clogged as a result, but although the sewers were laid bare and the clay discovered, the authorities apparently never connected its presence with an escape bid. The larger boulders which the diggers encountered were hidden under the floorboards of other ground floor cells. Once the escape nearly ended in tragedy when a tunnel collapse buried Graham, but he was dug out before he suffocated.

The escape was timed for 21 March and the day before this Steele hired a truck in Belfast and drove to Derry. En route the driver stopped at an RUC barracks to deliver a message which gave Steele a nasty scare. While the driver was inside, for all Steele knew giving the game away, he had the unnerving experience of sitting on a level with a poster announcing a £3,000 reward for the capture of Hugh McAteer, James Steele, Paddy Donnelly or Edward Maguire who had feloniously broken out of Crumlin Road Jail. Nobody in the barracks connected the driver's helper with the photograph on the poster and the driver went on blithely to Derry where, to his horror, Steele produced a revolver and informed him of what lay ahead.

Twenty-one prisoners made their escape through Graham's tunnel, while outside the door one of the inmates played the bagpipes to cover the noise of their departure. The last prisoner to shoulder his way to escape was Brendan O'Boyle (who got clean away and remained at liberty throughout the war in Dublin only to die tragically later). Fifteen prisoners piled into the truck and made their way over the border where they were picked up by the Southern army and lodged in the Curragh for the duration of the war. Unknown to the army patrol which held up the truck, a woman with a camera was standing behind a hedge when this happened and took a photograph of the incident.

This escape created a fantastic impact on Nationalist sentiment, coming on top of the Crumlin Road breakout. The IRA leaders began casting round for some similar exploit to impress public opinion and raise morale within the IRA without, at the same time, endangering life. A young volunteer suggested holding up either a picture house or a dance hall for the purpose of making a demonstration while volunteers guarded the doorways. Steele and McAteer were highly enthusiastic, but to avoid loose talk they told the volunteer that his idea was impractical. They themselves decided that the following Easter they would take over a place of public amusement. The Broadway Cinema not far from the Falls Road was selected as the target and on Holy Saturday afternoon, sixteen volunteers set off, two at a time, to converge on the cinema. The manager and projectionist were held up while armed volunteers guarded every exit and entrance. A slide was then flashed on the screen:

> This cinema has been commandeered by the Irish Republican Army for the purpose of holding the Easter Commemoration for the dead who died for Ireland.

Jimmy Steele then read the 1916 Proclamation from the stage and Hugh McAteer read a statement of IRA policy for the coming year. The proceedings closed with the observance of a one minute's silence for the dead and the raiders got away safely. Statements were issued to all the newspapers and Lord Haw-Haw included the incident in his broadcast from Berlin that evening.

While these exploits raised the stock of the IRA enormously among its sympathizers they had the opposite effect on their enemies, particularly among prison warders. Up to the time when the war began to swing against the Germans, warders in Belfast generally treated the IRA prisoners with some deference, but when it became apparent that the allies were likely to win, the IRA came in for sterner treatment, and jail escapes marked a turning point in warder-IRA relationships. Hitherto, the hundred or so Republican prisoners in Belfast Jail had tried various methods to secure political treatment. These included not doing the prescribed prison work and going on hunger strike, and though they failed to gain their objective a kind of unofficial political status was accorded the prisoners. After the Crumlin Road escape, however, prison regulations were sternly enforced, and cell searches and bread-and-water diets became commonplace. One result of these antics was that the prisoners sent out word asking their comrades to shoot a particularly bullying warder, but the most popular warder in the prison was killed by mistake.

The prisoners then resorted to the 'strip strike'. John Graham and David Fleming had argued against a hunger strike, because it either weakened prisoners irretrievably or had to be carried through to the death. So a strip strike started in mid June, 1943. Twenty-two prisoners* in Belfast Jail took off their prison clothes and the authorities retaliated by taking every other article from their cells, including their handkerchiefs. Bedding and blankets were not restored until 8.30 each evening. Towels were taken after the morning wash and no reading material was permitted other than religious books. Cells were then left empty apart from the prisoner himself, the frame of his iron bed, his sanitary vessel and a carafe of water for the whole day.

An account of what the strip strike was like was written by Seamus Steele in a journal he produced in 1954, *Resurgent Ulster*:

> The prison bell goes at 7 o'clock. You awaken with a start. No nice slow leisurely wakening here but before the last clang you are wide awake. The cold bare walls stare back at you and you realize that you have another long day to spend naked. You ponder how long it is until you will see that bed again – 13 hours – 780 minutes – 46,800 seconds and you have to live thru' every second. But you have a half hour yet for the warders do not come until 7.30. How you treasure that last half hour. The old lumpy fibre mattress, the army blankets, and the hard worsted sheets feel like down. For soon you hear the clang of the keys and the rush of feet. The warders have arrived. They are laughing and joking and full of the ordinary joys of life. You wonder if the fight is really worth while. But this passes very quickly and you get the courage to at least last another day. The slops are removed and the door is banged in your face again. You still have another minute or two and you get back

* James Brogan, Tyrone; Frank Morris, Tyrone; David Fleming, Kerry; John McMahon, Portadown; Ned Tennyson, Portadown; Sean Gallagher, Derry; P. Heggarty, Derry; John Graham, Belfast; Joe Cahill, Belfast; Dan McAlister, Belfast; Gerry Adams, Belfast; James Hannon, Belfast; Joe Myles, Belfast; R. Dempsey, Belfast; H. O'Hara, Belfast; S. McParland, Belfast; P. Corrigan, Belfast; Charles McCotter, Belfast; T. Morley, Belfast; W. Doyle, Belfast; J. McCusker, and Seamus 'Jimmy' Steele, Belfast.

into bed again. When the bed is moved you stand naked in your cold bare cell.

At eight o'clock the breakfast arrives. This consists of one pint of tea, eight ounces of bread, and half an ounce of margarine. Your table and chair have been removed so you take your treasure to the old bedstead. You try to eat it slowly as you know it will do you more good and it will last longer, but the hunger is so great that you eat it very quickly. Any stray crumbs are quickly retrieved. You drink the tea and all is finished and you are nearly as hungry as ever. It will be four and a half hours before you get any more.

Now the day has really begun. You hear the prisoners going out to work. How you envy them their warm clothes. They are happy people. Nevertheless the fight must go on. The day must be spent. You begin the parade again. Eight paces up, one at the turn, and eight paces back again. You begin this parade and people wonder what is the matter with you. Perhaps you make a football out of an old pair of socks and try to get the blood to circulate. You think on how cold it is even though it is the month of June. What will it be like in January? You put this out of your head at once. The sun is shining outside but this does not reach your cell. What is that? A knock on the wall and then a knock on the pipes. It is the signal that your next door neighbour wants to speak to you. You listen at the door and all is quiet. You get your enamel mug and use it as a kind of telephone on the pipes. Perhaps there is some news. But no! Your pal is finding it hard also and you try to encourage him. Stick it a little longer and there is no knowing what will happen. Suddenly the spy-hole is opened and an unfriendly eye looks in and gives a sharp order to get off the pipes. Even this small luxury is denied us. Well, on it must go. You begin the parade again or perhaps read a few pages of the Bible. You read but you do not take anything in. There is such a vast difference between what you read and the position you are in. Perhaps if you read the part on Job you get a little comfort. He has done his suffering for God, you are suffering for a principle. It helps a lot if you offer it to God too.

It is usual for them to search your cell. What do they expect to get in your empty tomb? Perhaps a small butt of a cigarette that you managed to get. At any rate everything is gone through, even at times your hair and beard. You will have a beard by this time for you are not allowed a razor. Perhaps if they did the death of Tone could be reenacted. You cannot see this beard for your mirror has also been removed.

The dinner arrives and you are just ravenous. This consists of one pint of soup, two ounces meat, one ounce vegetables and about three small potatoes. If one potato is bad it is a calamity. There is no use asking for another one for you will in all probability get another bad one and draw down the enmity of a warder on your defenceless shoulders. Well, you eat everything – potatoes, skins – every scrap, no matter how unpalatable it is it fills an empty space. It is now only twelve o'clock and you think it is only four and a half hours from the morning, that is another eight and a half hours to go until you get into that bed again. You lie on the cold bedstead and try to rest for you have been on the constant move since the morning trying to keep warmth in your body. You are so cold that you begin the whole parade again. Perhaps you have a visit from the prison chaplain. You are delighted to see him and at the same time feel embarrassed and ashamed. You do not like to detain him too long as he has to visit all the other fighters and perhaps some of the other prisoners as well. He has a very difficult job. You can see the light of sympathy in his eyes and at the same time he gives you to understand that he thinks you are striking your head against a stone wall. Perhaps you are too. You are in the grip of a mighty machine. What is the use? Others fought against it for years. Some went to an early grave, while others went mad. What was to be your fate? Nevertheless you must not let your comrades down. We are all in this to the end.

At two o'clock the noise starts again. The other prisoners go out to work and you have simply nothing to do. In these circumstances a man realizes how incomplete he is on his own and how much a social creature he really is. How content you would be doing anything. Even the hateful monotonous task of sewing mail bags that you were doing before the strike began. Perhaps you climb on the back of your bed and look out of your window. There is very little to be seen. Perhaps some hapless creatures marching around a ring in the courtyard awaiting trial. Perhaps some of your own comrades who will get the same kind of a trial that you got and a savage sentence. If you are caught it will almost certainly mean a report followed by a sentence of 'bread and water'. They cannot confine you any closer but your diet will be reduced to a total of eight ounces of bread and one pound of potatoes per day. These morsels make you feel more hungry than if you get nothing at all.

At four o'clock the prisoners return from the shops and the tea arrives which consists of the same as the morning with one pint of porridge and half a pint of milk. This has to keep you going till eight o'clock the next morning. You could eat it at once and still be hungry but you must keep a little for later in the evening. Even though there is still four hours left you have the day's back broken. You have done nine hours and every hour you do leaves one more down and one less to do. If you get a chance now you try to get something from the prisoner next to you. This is done by using a string, which you had concealed, and a weight. Perhaps you have a few booklets to exchange that will while away the monotony of the evening. If you are caught it will mean punishment but it is worth the risk. Look at the satisfaction you get if you succeed. Even if it is only a small thing you have a feeling that you have beaten them.

Perhaps the prisoner below you who is in sympathy with your ideals sends you some of his food on the line. His own food is little enough and if he is caught it will mean punishment for him but he knows you are fighting his fight too. The time is passing but will 8.30 never come? At long last you hear the rattle of the keys. How welcome is that sound now. They start at the top. Will they never reach your length? The door opens and you get your bed. You are under the clothes in a few minutes. You are asleep in a few more. It does seem a pity to go to sleep as you don't find the time until that awful bell goes again.

Conditions seem to have been even colder than they would have been in winter for in prison the heating is switched off during the summer and the stone cells had no way of heating up. The strike was called off after about three months to allow John Graham to get treatment for a badly swollen knee.

McAteer was recaptured on 21 November as he was coming out of St Paul's Church, and with his capture the era of the IRA as a significant fighting force in Belfast came to an end. In jail, prisoners still asserted their demands for political treatment by going on hunger strike, but outside, police pressure and the war itself combined to destroy the organization. Protestants and Catholics who huddled together in air raid shelters during the Belfast bombings never had quite the same bitter animosity towards each other after the war. And the introduction by the British Labour government of the welfare state to the North (despite the votes of twelve Tory candidates from the North against these innovations) damped down rebellious feelings. Henceforward, Northern Catholics began to seek an end to gerrymandering and discrimination in housing and jobs, rather than a reunion of the country under a Dublin parliament. When the IRA campaign broke out in 1956, it was obvious even to IRA leaders in Dublin, who had grown up in the meantime, that Belfast was not a suitable theatre for operations. The city remained calm despite events along the border.

8

The Years of the Curragh

Ground between the Military Court and the Curragh, the IRA men in the South shared similar experiences to those of the North with street shootings, individual acts of heroism, executions and defiance of prison regulations. While the provincial conferences were being held and the Northern campaign plans were being laid, it became obvious that the prime need to carry out such plans was the provision of some reliable men. Sean McCool sent word from the Curragh for a number of selected personnel to 'sign out' – that is, to give undertakings of good behaviour for the future.

Two of these were Seamus 'Rocky' Burns and Harry White. Burns was killed in a gun battle with the RUC in Belfast on 2 June 1944. Even though he had 'signed out' under orders, such was the rigidity of the traditional Republican sentiment to 'signing out', or recognizing courts, that several Belfast Republicans refused to attend his funeral because he had 'signed out'.

White, a plumber by trade, had been active in the bombing campaign in England before his internment. After his release he went on the run and escaped police surveillance until one evening in November, 1942, when he and a comrade, Maurice O'Neill from Kerry, were holed up in a house in Donnycarney, Dublin, and a party of Special Branch men made a lightning raid.

Shooting followed and Detective Officer Mordant was killed. White made a break and succeeded in getting out the back, across a number of adjoining gardens and walls until finally, hurling himself over a wall leading to a railway embankment, he fell sixteen feet into a dense thicket of briars. He lay there for two days with a gunshot wound in the leg while around him the police combed the area. Eventually, covered in mud and blood, he made his way to a bus-stop, boarded a bus, dismounted in crowded O'Connell Street in the heart of Dublin, and walked to a refuge in the Summerhill area of Dublin, where he learned that there was a price of £5,000 on the head of one Harry White, alias Anderson.

A few days later, Maurice O'Neill was executed in Mountjoy Prison for Mordant's murder. His execution provoked particularly widespread protests as he was a popular figure in his native Kerry, but the government, desperately trying to preserve its neutrality, was adamant. An iron-gloved approach to the IRA was the order of the day with vigorous raids and interrogations. As a result relations between individual IRA men and the Special Branch became understandably strained, and the IRA, in its shattered and disorganized condition, came to regard the Special Branch as a greater enemy than the British Crown.

On 9 September 1942, Detective Sergeant Denis O'Brien, one of the most prominent Special Branch detectives and a brother of Sean Lemass's secretary, was shot dead as he left his home in Ballyboden, Rathfarnham, Co. Dublin to go to work. The shooting greatly increased public feeling against the IRA, particularly as the murder was carried out almost in view of his wife. As she held her dying husband she watched his assailants cycling past.

A number of IRA men were charged at various times in connection with this killing, but only one was executed for it – Charles Kerins, twenty-six, of Kerry, on 1 December 1944. At the end of his trial the president of the Military Court delayed sentence until later in the day to allow Kerins, if he wished, to make an application whereby he might have avoided the capital sentence. When the court resumed Kerins said:

'You could have adjourned it for six years as far as I'm concerned, as my attitude towards this Court will always be the same.'

He thus deprived himself of the right to give evidence, to face cross-examination or to call witnesses.

The Special Branch was equally tense when dealing with IRA men, and in such an atmosphere guns blazed on both sides in cases where a prisoner would normally have gone quietly. The best one can say of a shooting on 4 July 1943 in Mount Street when a young IRA man, Jacky Griffith, was machine-gunned off his bicycle by the Special Branch, is that it was the last fatal shooting in the South of Ireland between police and IRA for over twenty years.

Through all this period, Harry White managed to stay free, remaining on the run for five years and surviving some remarkable adventures. Once he had the audacity to attend a public meeting in O'Connell Street, Dublin, to protest the hanging of Thomas Williams. Mrs Kathleen Clarke, widow of the 1916 leader Thomas Clarke, made a fiery speech threatening that if it took place, there would be a march on the border. As Mrs Clarke was a Fianna Fail senator and a former lord mayor of Dublin, White became enraged at what he considered hypocritical rabble-rousing and he called out, 'What about George Plant?' He was nearly lynched by Fianna Fail supporters but managed to get away. He later took a lorry-load of men in full daylight across the border, hoping to capture a British officer, any British officer, in reprisal for Williams's death.

Later that month he was attending a wedding in Ballyjamesduff, Co. Cavan, when police surrounded the house, shots were fired and the bride's brother, Patrick Dermody, was shot dead in a gun battle which also took the life of a guard. This affray provoked great bitterness, from police and public, at the death of the policeman and, in IRA circles, over Dermody's death. Dermody was so powerful in border areas that he held regular courts at which he settled land disputes and other squabbles. White managed to shoot his way out of this trap also and did not see the inside of a jail again until 1946 when he was picked up in Derry and handed over to the Gardai by the RUC.

IRA apologists say that White was handed over because the RUC hoped that the Southern 'death court' would condemn him to death. However Sean MacBride persuaded the court of the fact that while the bullet which killed Detective Officer Mordant was fired from White's gun he was entitled to defend himself as the raiding police had not identified themselves before opening fire. The court held that this was not murder, but excessive use of force by White when resisting unlawful arrest and it found him guilty of manslaughter. O'Neill had been tried and executed on the charge that he had murdered Mordant on the date in question. But it is clear from the evidence that White and O'Neill were separated at the time the fatal shot was fired and it is at least arguable that O'Neill knew nothing about it.

The years in the Curragh left their mark on those who remained in the camp after White and Burns. Most men, on leaving the internment camp, were so unable to deal with ordinary life that it took upwards of six months before any of them could screw up their courage to do normal things such as signing on at the Labour Exchange to draw unemployment benefit or applying for jobs. Even to cross the road was a terrible effort, the traffic, thin enough after the war, seemed fantastic after the years in the Curragh. The difference in women's fashion frightened them and added to the general air of unfamiliarity. After years in confinement with adult men, children seemed fragile and small-scale. Most remained Republican in sympathy but had no means of solving the border problem. Some were broken and turned to drink or developed nervous breakdowns.

Strangely enough, only one case of homosexuality in the Curragh has ever been mentioned to me. There was a great deal of horseplay. Sometimes the clothes were stripped off an internee by his friends, and he was left to run naked through the camp on a winter's day, but the overwhelming majority of prisoners made a deliberate effort not to allow sex to unbalance them. Between almost frenzied bouts of football or other athletic activity and hours spent making medals, baskets, leather-work and so on, sexual frustration was largely exercised. But dissension, the principal bugbear of Republicans, remained.

Pearse Kelly, who was camp OC during the greater part of his five years internment, described his first impressions of the Curragh in a prison record which he was kind enough to give me:

It was December with the usual dismal rain. The car stopped at a big, barricaded gate just above the camp and one of my escorts remarked 'well, you'll have plenty of time to hibernate down here. This isn't a health resort at any time, but it's at its worst now so you know what's in store for you.'

From my elevated position I had a panoramic view of the camp, a conglomeration of long low wooden huts erected in military lines, behind a quadruple fence of barbed wire and completely surrounded by a deep trench, evidently designed to prevent tunnelling. I was conscious of a slight shiver of apprehension as I took in the dead, drab look of the place.

After being searched and stripped. I was given a dilapidated mattress and a pillow with four old army blankets. The compound gate was unlocked to allow me in and I entered to find no sign of life apart from a Military Policeman who directed me to Hut 314.

When I entered the hut, I stood aghast. For a moment I couldn't make out what was happening. The rise and fall of the babble of voices that filled the turbulent air stilled momentarily as attention centred on the newcomer. Almost at once the din broke out again with men shouting at each other across the hut with voices raised to be heard above the general bedlam. A scene of apparent disorder met my eyes, all I could discern was a litter of beds with lines of discarded clothing hanging from the rafters and men, some squatting in silence on their beds, others huddled up in their blankets. Thirty men lived and slept in this hut and out of the forty in the compound there were sixteen similarly occupied, almost 500 internees.

Heating was supplied by small turf stoves and the walls and window-frames were of such inferior quality that, in bad weather, rain seeped through.

Before Kelly's arrival, the camp had been going through a particularly bad phase. On 14 December 1940 there had been an outbreak of rioting resulting in several bad injuries and one death. The cause was an ugly, brooding, hothouse atmosphere created by close surveillance, internment, frustration and a feeling among the internees that some stand had to be made.

The internees considered the food in the Curragh to be 'lousy bad', as Michael Traynor put it. It probably was, but it was the same food as army privates received, and when on 14 December the army's butter ration was reduced by a quarter this reduction was also extended to the internees' diet. It was the last straw. Peadar O'Flaherty, the prisoners' leader, lined them all up and gave a stirring address.

'Are we men or mice?' he asked, and gave the order to set fire to a prison hut.

Unfortunately, the fire spread to a number of other huts and six of them were destroyed with a great quantity of beds and bedding. And then, during investigations, it was discovered that the internees had been tunnelling for the whole summer and had almost reached the barbed wire.

Fierce fighting began when the military and military police went to put out the fires. Two internees and two members of the army were badly injured and taken to hospital. The internees were rounded up in the open, where they spent the day until being herded into two huts, one of them with a concrete floor. Being December this came to be known as the icebox. Throughout the night there was desultory shooting around the huts as trigger-happy military police fired at shadows. Inside the huts the internees were apprehensive that someone was going to be shot. For two days after the incident the men were kept in these two huts, only a cookhouse detail being allowed out to collect food and bring it back. Several of the internees had diarrhoea and dysentery, but the only sanitary facilities in the hut were buckets which provided an added dimension of unpleasantness.

The prisoners then refused to be counted and an armed guard had to be sent to the huts to check them. Only when it was certain that no escapes had occurred were the prisoners allowed to go to the dining hall. They lined up outside their huts facing a party of armed military police, nerves on both sides at breaking point. The military had been attacked during the fire with wooden trestle boards, iron trestle bars, broom handles and pieces of piping and fittings, and had replied with gun butts and rifle shots. In this instance the prisoners had no intention of rushing the armed party, but as their numbers swelled coming out of the huts, about fifty internees came to within ten yards of the armed party. Shooting broke out, one internee, Bernard Casey, of Co. Longford, being fatally wounded and another, Walter Mitchell, escaping with a bullet that lodged between the heel and the sole of his shoe.

Following this, a period of nearly two weeks of extreme tension ensued in the camp. The prisoners were penned into the icebox at night, hearing stray shots outside and fearing that something worse might occur. One night, a strong force of military police surrounded the camp and took selected leaders, among them Michael Traynor, to what was known as 'the glasshouse', a wing of the camp with a double row of cells under a high glass roof. Here, Traynor says, a fortnight of sheer horror followed. Jittery military policemen ran along iron stairs at night to quell suspected outbreaks. Beatings and kickings were more frequent than halfpence.

Readers who have seen Brendan Behan's play *Borstal Boy* will get an insight into the kind of fears that political prisoners engender in their captors. Traynor remembers his period here as a time of 'diabolical treatment'. Outside the camp, Sean MacBride tried to have the case of Bernard Casey brought into the open and debated publicly to focus attention on the appalling conditions in the camp, but this attempt failed. When those who were held to be the ringleaders of the disturbances were identified, they were brought before a military court and sentenced – to their great delight. Traynor, although he got five years, regarded being away from the military police 'as if I was in heaven'. They used the condemned cell in Mountjoy as a recreational centre and, with plenty of food parcels from outside, it was a relatively pleasant interlude for a man who had begun the year with a fifty-day hunger strike.

After Kelly's arrival things improved *vis-à-vis* the authorities. But for a time, among the internees, they got wrose. Basically the trouble stemmed from the unnatural atmosphere of the place and the divisions between the Dublin and Belfast wings of the IRA. But trouble also flared up over issues such as prisoners collecting their own coal, rather than having it delivered to the huts by the authorities; the reading of Stephen Hayes's 'confession'; and varying political views, Fascism versus Communism, or the issue of whether, in the event of an invasion, the internees should offer to sign out and fight in the hitherto hated Free State army, in a common defence of their homeland.

When Kelly arrived, the camp OC was Liam Leddy from Cork and he continued as such for some months until Kelly, Eoin MacNamee and Tom Cullimore decided that the only way to establish morale was by electing a new camp council. This trio made the Hayes 'confession' widely known throughout the camp although some prisoners were already aware of it. Joe Deighan, for instance, told me he had seen the 'confession' before Kelly showed up, but the publicity given to it by the trio led to their ostracism by the Leddy wing and they were 'sent to Coventry'. However, about 150 prisoners eventually came over to their side and by the end of the war, all the internees were on the Kelly side. For a time, relationships between the two wings were extremely bad. Any man caught talking to a member of the opposite camp was disdained by his own side and considered not to be a true Republican at all. But the position gradually eased over the years as the Kelly wing began to win concessions from the authority such as an ending of the physical punishment by the PAs,* an increase in the fuel allowance and facilities for hobbies and camp concerts. The Gaelic Athletic Association secretary, Padraig O'Caoimh, himself an old IRA man, sent in a set of footballs and medals that were keenly played for, and the prisoners got such control of their own affairs that one Christmas they acquired all the equipment and ingredients to manufacture a successful run of illicit alcohol.

'Gaelteachts', peopled entirely by Irish-speaking internees, were set up and Mairtin O'Cadain ran highly successful language classes. Other prisoners who had more education than these fellows also gave tutorials in their own special subjects and many a young country lad, who had left school at twelve, emerged from the Curragh with a far better education than he could possibly have acquired any other way.

---

* Military poicemen, Poli Airim in Irish, PAs for short. Prisoners in the Curragh complained to me that in the early days of the Curragh it was not unusual for prisoners found guilty of some breach of camp regulations to be forced to run a gauntlet of PAs armed with batons which they used to strike at the victims' limbs, their heads being protected by the mattress and blankets which they were forced to carry on their way to the 'glasshouse' for a sojourn on bread and water.

The even tenor of the prisoners' ways was threatened principally by the activities of Niall Verschoyle Gould, a devoted Communist who had been on the fringes of the Republican Congress movement and active in organizing strikes in Dublin. Gould formed the centre of a coterie of other Republican Communists, in particular Michael O'Riordan, Johnny Power and Dermot Walshe. These three had fought in the Spanish Civil War, and they elected Gould as their tutor in Russian.

Gould did not confine his activities to teaching Russian. As the central premise of Irish Catholicism was traditionally, before the Vatican Council II, an unthinking acceptance of authority, his clever dialectical approach undermined several fervent young Catholic internees. They were unaware of the Church's association with Britain in the enactment of the Act of Union and the subsequent quashing throughout the nineteenth century of every manifestation of Irish nationalism. He also undermined their faith in their nationalist gods, pointing out how John Mitchel had fought in the American Civil War on the side of the South and slavery, and he was well on the way to distracting the camp's attention from British oppression and/or de Valera, to that of the class struggle, when Kelly decided to take some action.

A message was smuggled out to the Bishop of Kildare and Leitrim, in whose diocese the camp was located, telling him that the morals of the camp were being perverted by a notorious Communist who was undermining the teachings of the Church and making the Curragh a hotbed of sedition and Marxism. Within three days Gould was removed from the camp and deposited in Mountjoy Jail. (To be a Communist in Ireland requires unusual self-control and discipline. While the tolerance of the people would rarely condone violence to a self-confessed Communist, such a declaration, even now, would inhibit his career in most fields, certainly in teaching.)[*]

In all some two thousand internees passed through the camp. The sort of men they were and the problems they faced are illustrated in this concluding passage from Kelly's camp memoirs describing the advice given to him by an old friend who had left the camp.

---

[*] Gould apparently taught his beliefs to his son. In 1957, years after the Curragh and the war, family estates in Longford came before the courts for a decision as to what should become of them. Evidence was given that a lawyer acting for the court had gone to Moscow and found Gould Jr working as a labourer digging a trench across a Moscow side street. The boy had refused to take any interest in his inheritance or to give any directions as to what should be done with it. The money was duly lodged in the court.

He urged me to get away out to the country where I would really appreciate freedom as he had done. The barbed wire had no terror for him then, he actually came to have a sort of regard for it when he found he could fondle it without being molested.

'Don't mind,' he added, 'if you find yourself talking to the animals in the fields. These were the first things I made friends with when I came home, for if the animal doesn't like you it walks away, and you know at once where you stand. One feels nearer to Heaven too, to stand on a hillside of a sunny evening in the harvest, and as far as the eye can carry to watch the corn and crops and grasses with their glorious hues and their waving in the breeze and the sun dancing on them. As to the people, 'tis little I can say about them, for even yet I can't fit in no matter where I go, and I hate crowds. Back of it all, I am at times conscious of a deep yearning for my old friends of Tintown.'

The last sad act of the IRA drama of the 1940s was a strip strike in Portlaoise Prison. In the Curragh, Arbour Hill or Mountjoy jails, the Republican prisoners were allowed to wear their own clothes. But on transfer to Portlaoise they had to wear convict uniform. When Sean McCaughey arrived there, in September 1941, like the men who had gone before him he refused to wear these clothes.

From then until the middle of 1943, he and the others were kept in solitary confinement. They were not even allowed out to the lavatory and the confinement was made doubly rigorous by having an empty cell on either side of them. In 1943, their conditions were relaxed somewhat. They were allowed out of their cells into a larger cell together for an hour in the morning and the afternoon and they were also permitted a paper per week and a letter per month. By refusing to wear the convict clothes, the prisoners had set themselves in defiance of the prison authorities, so very little else was done to make their stay there enjoyable. McCaughey was allowed no visitors during the four and three-quarter years he was in Portlaoise Jail.

Like the others, he spent all this time naked except for his prison blanket. Finally, on 19 April 1946, he went on hunger strike for release though it is alleged by his comrades that it was well understood by the prison authorities and by the government that he would have come off the strike if he had been removed to the Curragh. Whatever the truth of this, the early days of his hunger strike produced no result and five days later he went on thirst strike too. Seventeen days later Sean McCaughey died with his body in a condition better imagined than described. Patrick McLogan, who saw the body after death, said that McCaughey's tongue had shrunken 'to the size of a threepenny bit'.

The inquest was held in the prison and the deputy coroner refused to allow Seán MacBride, counsel for the next of kin, to cross-examine the governor. The following passage occurred during MacBride's cross-examination of the prison doctor:

> *Mr MacBride*: Are you aware that during the four and a half years he was here he was never out in the fresh air or sunlight?
>
> *Dr Duane*: As far as I am aware he was not.
>
> *Mr MacBride*: Would I be right in saying that up to twelve or eighteen months ago he was kept in solitary confinement and not allowed to speak or associate with any other persons?
>
> *Dr Duane*: That is right.
>
> *Mr MacBride*: Would you treat a dog in that fashion?
>
> *Mr McLoughlin*: That is not a proper question.
>
> *Mr MacBride*: If you had a dog would you treat it in that fashion?
>
> *Dr Duane* (after a pause): No.
>
> *Mr MacBride*: Did you have to attend the prisoner for a nervous breakdown?
>
> *Dr Duane*: He suffered from a nervous condition for a time.
>
> *Mr MacBride*: By reason of solitary confinement?
>
> *Dr Duane*: I don't know.

Replying to his own counsel, Major Barmys, the prison governor, said of McCaughey:

> He refused to wear prison clothes, and a man could not go out in the air without clothes, from the health point of view. Decency forbade it, and apart from that, his health would not stand it. You cannot have a naked man walking about a prison.

The jury's verdict was:

> That the conditions existing in the prison were not all that could be desired according to the evidence furnished; but there was no reflection on the Governor, Medical Officer or Staff intended.

So ended the Stephen Hayes affair. The only man who could really say what prompted his suspicions of the former chief of staff is dead. If the affair had not brought McCaughey southward he might have survived the war, though, given his temperament, he might have been killed in a police battle, been executed or died during one of the jail strikes.

The plight of the other prisoners in the jail, such as Thomas

MacCurtain, Michael Traynor, Liam Rice and Harry White, led to support for the new party which grew up around Sean MacBride in those years and which put Fianna Fail out of office in 1948. Just as Fianna Fail had come to power in 1932 to the echoes of 'Release the Prisoners', the same call sounded against them in 1948. One of the first acts of the new minister for justice, General Sean MacEoin, who as a member of the IRA had been sentenced to death by the British, was to 'release the prisoners'.

9

The IRA and the Nazis

No facet of IRA activities aroused so much distrust and alarm, at home and abroad, as did the organization's links, real or imagined, with the Nazis. These must, however, be assessed against the background of Irish neutrality.

On 5 September 1939, Winston Churchill wrote to the First Sea Lord and other top figures in the Admiralty demanding a 'vigilant watch' on the IRA in Ireland. He reasoned that 'if they throw bombs in London why should they not supply fuel to U-boats?' The IRA of course did not have any U-boat fuel, nor did anyone else in Southern Ireland. But the mere existence of the IRA made such a threat worth guarding against.

Churchill, moreover, was infuriated that in 1938 de Valera had negotiated both a satisfactory settlement of the economic war and an end to British rights, under the Anglo-Irish treaty of 1921, to what were known as the 'treaty ports'. Without control of these Irish neutrality would not have been possible. The ports were Berehaven and Cobh, both near the major southern port of Cork, and, to the north, Lough Swilly in Co. Donegal. From Lough Swilly the approaches to the Mersey and the Clyde could have been more easily guarded by British warships than from Derry, and from Cobh and Berehaven destroyers could have foraged westwards after the U-boats and linked up with incoming convoys far out to sea. Without them, such operations had to start from British bases such as Lamlash, Pembroke Dock or Falmouth, thereby reducing the British range of action by approximately four hundred miles.

Discussing a London *Times* comment on the 1938 agreement which said that 'The agreement releases the government of the United Kingdom from the . . . onerous and delicate task of defending the fortified harbours of Cork, Berehaven and Lough Swilly in the event of war', Churchill snarled in his memoirs: 'Further releases might have been attained by handing over Gibraltar to Spain and Malta to Italy. Neither touched the existence of our population more directly.' And during a victory broadcast on 13 May 1945, Churchill vented his irritation with de Valera in public, saying:

> Owing to the action of the Dublin government ... the approaches which the Southern Irish ports and airfields could so easily have guarded were closed by the hostile aircraft and U-boats.
>
> This was indeed a deadly moment in our life, and if it had not been for the loyalty and friendship of Northern Ireland, we should have been forced to come to close quarters with Mr de Valera, or perish forever from the earth. However, with a restraint and poise to which, I say, history will find new parallels, His Majesty's Government never laid a violent hand upon them, though at times it would have been quite easy and quite natural ...

Throughout the war British opinion continued to be puzzled by the Irish position, much as if Wales had opted for neutrality after several hundred years of association with Britain. The British had reluctantly approved de Valera's constitution in 1937 and the abolishment of the voice of governor-general, but nevertheless did not concede Ireland's right to have an ambassador accredited to her. The governor-general was not replaced for three years, and then only in ambiguous fashion: Sir John Maffey, who was actually retired at the time, was appointed British representative in Eire in November 1939. Britain still saw Ireland as belonging to the British Commonwealth, but Sir John could not be appointed as a high commissioner because the Irish did not recognize the Commonwealth, as Whitehall did not recognize the new Irish state. He was therefore designated a representative though with diplomatic status. In London, the Irish representative, John Dulanty, continued as he had since 1930 as high commissioner for Ireland.

Irish neutrality as regards Britain had been prepared for by de Valera as far back as 29 May 1935, when, in a debate in the Dail, he said: 'Our territory will never be permitted to be used as a base for attack upon Britain.' He reiterated this again on 25 April 1938, when signing the London agreements whereby he regained the treaty ports. He was equally far-sighted where Germany was concerned. Through Joseph Walsh, secretary to the Department of External Affairs, he had informed the German ambassador, Dr Edward Hempel, on 26 August 1937, that Ireland wished to stay neutral in any war, and would do so

unless attacked first, perhaps by bombing. (Even at that early stage
the Irish government learned to be more aware of the potential of
the Luftwaffe than did England.) Walsh also played the
Irish-American card adroitly at a lunch with Hempel, pointing out
that the Irish-Americans would set their faces against any Anglo-
Irish tie-up, and would do what they could to make Britain pause
before attempting to invade Ireland.

Hempel explained this position to Berlin and on 29 August the
German Foreign Ministry telegraphed him:

> In conformity with the previous friendly relations between the two
> countries the German government will refrain from all hostile activity
> towards Irish territory and will respect Ireland's integrity provided
> that for her part Ireland will observe strict neutrality towards Ger-
> many. In the event of war against England the German government
> will do its utmost to reduce to a minimum the resulting unavoidable
> disadvantage for Ireland and Irish trade. Germany is entirely clear as
> to the difficulties facing Ireland in consequence of her geographical
> position.

The Germans were not being altruistic about this. If the British *had*
tried to take over Ireland, Germany would not have been in a
position to prevent her. Also, as Paul Leverkuehn in *German Military Intelligence* shows, a central and crippling problem bedevilled
Nazi-IRA affairs. Apart from bad luck, spies being captured immediately on arrival and the IRA being 'riven with enmity', German
military intelligence found itself continually at loggerheads with
diplomats who effectively stymied all its schemes because of the
doctrine that 'military plans should play second fiddle to political
decisions'.

The American position was simple. As Professor Bob Stewart,
then of the Fletcher School of Diplomacy at Tufts University,
Boston, and wartime member of the State Department section dealing with Irish affairs, put it to me, 'I sure wanted Ireland in that
war.' To this end the ambassador to Ireland, David Gray, a relation
of Roosevelt and a wealthy man but not a career diplomat, exercised
a great deal of enthusiasm and energy, but little diplomacy, and as a
result was virtually *persona non grata* with the Irish government towards the end of the war. This was a pity because he was a man
who genuinely loved Ireland, but as he said, 'I had a job to do.'

The mind boggles at the way he sometimes went about his job. In one of his telegrams to the secretary of state (7 January 1941) we find him saying that he had told de Valera that 'he had capitalized on hatred of Great Britain for political reasons and so must take some responsibility for the existing popular state of mind'. Later he describes another interview with de Valera, saying:

> He began to talk about his rights. I told him that ... the only right that he and myself enjoyed was to believe in our religion, and be burned for it if need be. Every other right depended upon force to maintain it and that he was steering a very dangerous course if he thought otherwise. He called my views the greatest exponent of force he had ever met and made it clear that it was a case of facing reality. Curious, but almost friendly, I grow fond of Mr de Valera as we argue!

De Valera's determination to maintain neutrality seems to have checked this friendship and Gray, after an interview with de Valera in April, when, he says, 'de Valera flushed angrily and shouted that it was impertinent to question the statements of a head of state', reported:

> I think the effect of a stiff attitude will be sobering. It is the only way to impress him that there are realities closing in upon him. He always outmanoeuvred Chamberlain. I no longer hope to get anything from him by generosity and conciliation. He must be made to realize that it is possible that a situation is approaching in which if it be essential to survival his ports will be seized with the approval of the liberal sentiment of the world, that he will have only the choice of fighting on the side of Great Britain or Germany.

Gray later learned that de Valera told an opposition leader that Gray had misrepresented Ireland to the secretary of state and that if the situation were not so tense, and Gray not a friend of the president, de Valera would have asked for his recall.

Apart from all this, formal American policy frequently put the Irish national temperature up, particularly over the delays in supplying American ships to Ireland. Only two were made available. Then there was the unwillingness of the Americans to let Ireland have munitions and war supplies so long as she stayed neutral, the issue of conscription in Northern Ireland and the landing of American troops in the North. There was also the Americans' belief that the Japanese embassy in Dublin was filled with Japanese spies. In fact it contained four

Japanese nationalists who behaved with diplomatic decorum. The German embassy was also supposed to be a centre for transmission of information to Berlin, though the only broadcasts from the embassy occurred at the beginning of the war and consisted of weather reports for the Luftwaffe. These had ceased by 1942, as Hempel's wartime dispatches make quite clear. Even so the British and the Americans refused to believe they had ceased.

The conscription issue and the American landing were the most important episodes, raising the possibility of loss of life if the British tried to enforce conscription on Catholics in the North or the Americans attempted to cross the border. The conscription problem made the last fortnight of May 1941 a time of acute crisis. Southern Ireland and the Northern minority were inflamed at the proposal apparently motivated by the bombings in Belfast and the fact that very few volunteers were coming forward in the North. Even the pro-British Gray was aghast and on 24 May he cabled the secretary of state:

Opposition leaders yesterday informed me that conscription without a conscientious objector's escape clause for minority Catholic nationalists will constitute a major irretrievable and probably fatal political blunder at this time and play directly into de Valera's hands with grave possibilities for American interests. They predict draft riots, the escape of draft dodgers to Southern Ireland who will be acclaimed as hero martyrs by three-quarters of the population and the fomenting of trouble by Republicans and Fifth Columnists. The clearest headed leader predicts that de Valera will seize the opportunity to escape from economic and political realities by proclaiming himself the leader of the oppressed minority and with the blessings of the Cardinal will rouse anti-British feeling and call a Holy War. I think it a very likely prediction. All classes of opinion here unite in condemning the move as calamitous. It appears to be a repetition of the same fatal blunder made during the last war. The weak and failing Ulster Government is probably seeking to sustain itself by provoking a crisis. Unless Great Britain is prepared from a military point of view to seize the whole country it appears to be madness. So little can be gained and so much lost.

Eighty thousand Irish volunteers in the British army will be disaffected, there will be no material number of Nationalist conscripts, a government, a popular majority and an army inclined to be friendly to Great Britain rather than to the Axis will become definitely hostile, possibly giving active aid to Germany and most important of all the pro-British opposition will be helpless and the opportunity for dividing the country on the question of the ports will be lost for the duration.

The effect on Irish-American opinion at this juncture is not for me to estimate. This is a grave situation.

In London American Ambassador Winant saw Churchill and Eden in lengthy sessions. A stern message from de Valera warned the British against imposing conscription on Irishmen. The London meetings ended with Churchill's agreeing that Winant send the following dispatch to Hull:

The Ulster Government has weakened considerably over the weekend and in consequence the Cabinet is inclined to the view it would be more trouble than it's worth to go through with conscription. No immediate decision will be taken and in the meantime the less made of the affair the better.

That ended the proposal. My information from Unionist circles is that Northern Prime Minister Andrews had drawn back leaving Churchill with no option but to call off the attempt. Andrews apparently took the RUC's estimate of the situation more seriously than did the hardliners in the cabinet, notably Sir Basil Brooke, later Lord Brookeborough.

Relationships with the Americans were strained again when American combat troops armed with heavy artillery landed in the North on 26 January. De Valera protested against the violation of the sovereignty which the twenty-six counties claimed over the six, and most of the civilian population feared that the landings were a prelude to an invasion of the South.

Time put an end to these apprehensions and the unofficial co-operation which the Irish extended to the allies helped considerably to improve relationships. British flyers who crashed in Ireland were speedily put on the mail boat back to England or, if their planes were still serviceable, these were refuelled and returned. Many an RAF man got back to England this way with a cockpit load of butter, eggs and steak. His Luftwaffe counterpart ended up in the Curragh internment camp for the duration of the war. The Germans protested about this but de Valera had accepted the American argument that any allied plane forced to land in Ireland was clearly on a non-operational mission, whereas any German plane being so far from home was obviously operational. To return the flyer to Germany would be to infringe neutrality.

Sometimes it was necessary to intern British soldiers for the sake of appearances, but they managed to escape as a matter of routine. In contrast, the Germans were held behind bars until the end of the war. And when America's General Jacob L. Devers crash-landed in Ireland late in 1943 with a briefcase full of allied invasion plans concerning Operation Overlord (the D-Day code name) he was not subjected even to the pretence of internment. He was driven to the border in an official car and handed over to the Americans within a few hours of landing, his plans and his identity intact.

Also around the time of D-Day it became known in Dublin that the Irish officials were 'worried by the overcrowding in the Curragh, because of all the interned British airmen. There were so many of them that they were beginning to affect the health of the Germans.' A new camp was opened for these internees at Gormanstown in Co. Meath to the north of Dublin, and the internees were driven off by lorry. The lorries were stopped on the way and the internees, all badly needed flyers, were put into a fleet of waiting cars and driven to the border! The Irish government also allowed the Royal Observer Corps to set up plane spotting posts around the Irish coast. A British radio transmitter operating from a van went unremarked by the Irish authorities who took part in regular staff talks with the British army heads on the same basis of mutual trust and co-operation that the Irish Secret Service continually co-operated as a matter of routine with that of Britain.

But despite all these gestures of goodwill, Irish neutrality remained balanced against a precarious background of changing international conditions and every IRA action threatened it. The Irish government's position would have been swept away overnight had the Nazi-IRA links led to any serious trouble for the British. That they did not may be attributable to a number of factors: the efficiency of the Irish security forces, the ignorance of the Nazis about Irish affairs, German interdepartmental warfare and above all the disorganized nature of the IRA itself.

Sean Russell's departure to America had been disastrous for his bombing campaign in England and for the IRA at home. In Detroit on 6 June 1939, it became disastrous for him also in a manner which brought him into the arms of the Nazis, and to an extraordinary death. He was arrested by the Detroit police, apparently as a precautionary measure, because King George and Queen Elizabeth were at the time just across the border in Canada. The subject was raised in the House

of Representatives by Congressmen Sweeney of Ohio and MacGran-
ery of Pennsylvania, who called it 'a very stupid blunder on the part of
our Government which demonstrated British influence in the US'.
Russell was released on bail after McGarrity had put up a $5,000 bond
and some seventy members of congress had threatened to boycott the
royal visit.

A temporary bonanza of publicity boomeranged on Russell when he
was served with an expulsion order to quit America by 10 September.
He went on the run, but although he managed to stay hidden under the
Clann na Gael cloak, reduced wartime shipping prevented him from
getting a boat to Ireland. One chance remained. On 24 January 1940,
the German Foreign Office in Berlin received a telegram from the
German consul-general in Genoa asking 'whether the German Government would be prepared to provide transport to Ireland for Sean
Russell, Chief of Staff of the IRA, who unknown to the American
Government is still in New York. If this is possible, he will make his
way here by a new direct line from New York under an alias.'

Russell's arrival in Berlin from Genoa is recorded in the War Diary
of 3 May. Ambassador Hempel's objections to becoming involved with
Russell were overridden by the opinion of Wermann, the under-
secretary of state, who in a memorandum dated 10 February 1940,
pointed out that basically Fianna Fail and the IRA wanted the same
thing, the reunification of the country, and that their only difference
lay in their choice of methods. Wermann thought that 'by reason of
their militant attitude towards England, the IRA is Germany's natural
ally'.

An attempt to place Russell in contact with a German agent,
Captain Herman Goertz, who was setting out for Ireland at that time,
misfired because Goertz had taken off from Fritzlar airfield in the early
hours of 5 May, just a short time before Russell arrived at the airfield
to brief him. Russell was then enrolled in a course at Legal Laboratory
in, as the Abwehr Diary notes, 'the use of sabotage materials'. It was
while attending his bomb-making class that he was reunited with an
old friend – Frank Ryan, the Republican Congress leader who had
been captured by Franco's forces during the Spanish Civil War.

Ryan, an acting brigadier in the Lincoln Washington Brigade, had
been captured in the late summer of 1938 by a group of Italian troops.
This fact saved his life as the Italians hoped that they would be able to
exchange him for one of their own officers. Had the Spaniards
captured him he would have been treated like every other captured

member of the brigade and shot. The Italians failed to make an exchange but by the time they had turned Ryan over to Franco's troops some months had elapsed. In the meantime a group of American journalists, who had been allowed to speak to prisoners, discovered Ryan's presence and wrote about him. In Ireland people of all political persuasion signed petitions for his release. Somewhat pathetically IRA slogans – 'Release Frank Ryan or else' – appeared. Ireland had adopted a policy of non-intervention in the Spanish conflict and had an ambassador in Madrid but de Valera telegrammed Franco asking him to spare Ryan. No one in Ireland knew whether the telegram had any effect until after nine months Leslie Barry, Tom Barry's wife, and a sister of Michael Price, one of the principal figures in the Irish Red Cross, discovered his whereabouts through the agency of the Red Cross.

During this time Ryan lived in a cell with eighteen other condemned prisoners. Every morning nine of the eighteen were taken out and shot and their places filled by another nine. Ryan never knew which morning was to be his turn. All he could do was scratch his name on a comb which he hoped to be able to throw through the cell window of prisoners who had not been condemned and in this way leave behind some record of his fate. He had been wounded in the fighting and his slight deafness had become marked. In the terrifying isolation caused by deafness, imprisonment and language barriers, the arrival of Leslie Barry's first food parcel must have seemed like a message from heaven.

At the end of the Spanish war de Valera arranged through Leopold Kerney, the Irish ambassador in Madrid, for a Spanish lawyer for Ryan, and de Valera saw to it that the expenses of defending his former enemy were defrayed by the Irish state. Ryan's sentence was commuted to life imprisonment, and he was granted the further concession of a monthly visit from his lawyer, Señor Champourcin, and the right to receive food parcels. Meanwhile in Germany Dr Jupp Hoven and Helmut Clissmann,* who during their student days in Ireland had been friends of Ryan (a photograph of Ryan with Clissmann and Hoven appeared on the front page of *An Phoblacht* during Ryan's editorship), supported his case. Hoven officially notified the Abwehr that in his judgement the release of Ryan under German auspices would create a good impression in Ireland and would also place Ryan

---

* Clissmann became a businessman in Ireland and married an Irish girl.

at Germany's disposal. His idea was eventually taken up. The Nazis approached the Spanish police authorities and Ryan's lawyer contacted the Irish ambassador, who in turn got in touch with his government. All parties agreed to Ryan's release, and he was handed over to German custody at Irun-Hendaye on 15 July 1940. He was emaciated and haggard and almost completely deaf. The Nazis drove him to Paris and took him to eat at the Tour d'Argent where Kurt Haller, section leader in Abwehr (II) Office I West in Berlin, remembers that he was 'completely flabbergasted by the whole thing and thought he was dreaming'.

When Russell and Ryan were introduced, according to Haller they 'embraced one another like brothers who had not seen each other for many years'. Russell immediately agreed to take Ryan with him back to Ireland on 'Operation Dove', a loosely defined mission which left Russell free to take any action he saw fit in Ireland. It was finally sanctioned at a meeting on 5 August of Foreign Minister Ribbentrop, Admiral Canaris, Lieutenant Colonel Lahousen, the Abwehr head and Dr Veesenmayer, in charge of Irish affairs at the Foreign Office, who introduced Russell to Ribbentrop.

Ribbentrop was offensive to Russell, saying flatly that he doubted whether Russell was a genuine agent or indeed, if he were Russell at all. Apparently he disliked the Irish as a race. Despite this arrogance the Nazis thought enough of the Russell-Ryan mission to place a U-boat at their disposal, and it sailed from Wilhelmshaven on 8 August, captained by Commander Von Stockhausen.

Neither Russell nor the U-boat ever reached Ireland. On 14 August Sean Russell died in Frank Ryan's arms, when they were some one hundred miles west of Galway. He had been taken ill with agonizing pains in the stomach shortly after leaving and these got progressively worse. There was no doctor aboard, only a medical student as an orderly. Ryan persuaded this man to give Russell a purgative thinking that he was suffering from constipation. But it appears from the medical reports submitted to German doctors by Ryan, the orderly, the captain and the second in command of the U-boat, that Russell died from perforated ulcers.

He was buried at sea with full military honours, wrapped in a German flag. Not knowing what his mission was intended to be nor what conditions were like in Ireland, Ryan returned with the submarine to Germany. He never saw Ireland again. His last days were pathetic. On 15 January he suffered some sort of a stroke, and his condition deteriorated progressively. It was wartime, the hospitals were full of wounded, there was very little food, and the aerial bombardment grew heavier and heavier. As he was so deaf that he could not be left alone at night because he couldn't hear the sirens, he had to sit at cafés with a cup of coffee so that people could warn him when the sirens sounded. His friends and contacts in the German establishment were gradually transferred from Berlin. An Irish friend, Francis Stuart, the writer, who was lecturing at Berlin University, comforted him as best he could, occasionally taking him out for a drive to one of the Havel lakes to spend a day on the beach, and Stuart also attempted to get the Irish chargé d'affaires to arrange a passage for Ryan back to Ireland. But Ryan's health had deteriorated so badly that he was unable to travel. In January 1944 he was taken to a sanatorium at Dresden Loschwitz. He died on 10 June, after a period of agony during which his breathing was so painful that he had to be placed sitting in an armchair with the back of another before him so that he could rest his head on his arms before speaking. He was buried in the Dresden Loschwitz cemetery. A wooden cross giving his name as Francis Richard appears above the grave with his date of birth and of death inscribed on it.

Apart from the Russell-Ryan affairs the Nazis made a number of attempts to win over the IRA.

Oscar C. Phaus, journalist and founder of the German Bund, returned from America to Germany on 2 December 1938, and was approached by the Abwehr and asked to establish links with the IRA in Ireland. The Abwehr knew little about the IRA beyond the fact that if it carried out bombing attacks in England it must be a potential German ally. Phaus landed in Ireland on 3 February and tried to contact the IRA by approaching General Eoin O'Duffy, the former Blueshirt leader. If O'Duffy, on meeting a Nazi agent, did not actually put him in touch with the IRA he at least made no attempt to have him arrested. Within a matter of days Phaus had established contact and was driven by Maurice Twomey to meet members of the Army Council.

Various stories circulate about this meeting, one of them being that Phaus thought that he was going to have to shoot his way out, so unfriendly did the atmosphere become and so disbelieving was the attitude of those whom he met. A telegram from Germany, in reply to one which had been sent immediately upon his arrival at the meeting, confirmed his identity. The story seems a bit unlikely but, at all events, from then onwards Seamus O'Donovan became the principal Nazi link with the IRA and later in the month visited Phaus in Hamburg with a memorandum for the Abwehr setting out the IRA's policies and the strength of its equipment. Nothing was decided about sending equipment to the IRA but discussions took place about Nazi policy in the event of war between Germany and England.

O'Donovan again visited Germany in April and in August 1939, the third journey very nearly being the IRA's final contact with the Nazis. A row with the German customs infuriated O'Donovan. The Abwehr spent so much time trying to mollify him that it was only after he had left that the Abwehr realized it had arranged courier routes for messages and money, come to agreements on wireless transmissions and on possible arms and other supplies, but had forgotten to give O'Donovan the code word for the wireless exchange which would be needed to arrange these things. A few days after the outbreak of war a code phrase – 'House of Parliament' – was devised and sent to London via a Breton, Paul Moise, working for the Breton underground movement Breiz Atao.

It was not until 29 October that the first message to Germany was received from O'Donovan's transmitter. It asked about arms, but the Abwehr could not help as the message had not indicated any likely supply routes. (This transmitter was the one which the police seized on 29 December in the raid on Ashgrove House which captured D'Arcy and MacNeela.) Very little of value passed over the transmitters either from Berlin or Dublin. The IRA never did succeed in setting up a supply route, nor did it respond to the German requests to cease operations against de Valera and concentrate instead on military installations in Britain and the North. Indeed one of the messages which the Irish sent the Germans told of a direct rejection of advice – the report of the IRA raid on the Magazine Fort.

One can be reasonably certain about the valueless nature of the IRA's messages to Germany. Major Florence O'Donaghue and Colonel Dan Bryan, the leading figures in the Irish Secret Service during the war, both told me IRA transmissions were worthless. I also spoke to one of the chief broadcasters and script-writers connected with this transmitter – Seamus Byrne, a solicitor and playwright whom I had known since boyhood. (He was one of the four men arrested when the police raided the house.) I spoke too to the chief broadcaster from the transmitter which the IRA operated from Northern Ireland, Tarlach O'hUid, now a journalist. From the statements of all it appears virtually certain that the transmitter's main use was for the dissemination of internal propaganda to give an impression of a strength on the part of the IRA, which it did not really possess. In fact the discussion which the Southern radio occasioned worried German Ambassador Hempel so much that he telegraphed a strong warning to his foreign office about rumours circulating in Dublin concerning the IRA-German link-ups. Hempel felt that if the Germans were to be seen helping the IRA this would prejudice them in the eyes of both Irish and English – the Irish because there was a widespread sympathy towards Germany on religious grounds and the British because it might give them an excuse to breach Irish neutrality. Hempel's advice was not taken but the Germans would have saved life and money if they had listened to him.

The most important German spy in Ireland was Captain Herman Goertz who parachuted from a Heinkel on 5 May 1940, landing in County Meath near Summerhill and then managing to remain free for nineteen months. Some Irish army officers, who were not exactly pro-Nazi but were willing to make the war an opportunity for doing something about the partition issue, met Goertz. They decided against collaboration with him because of their contempt for IRA security and their distrust of all military powers. There were also some nationalists, and others who had some influence with the government through language circles such as the Gaelic League, who were disposed to assist Goertz in his mission of creating difficulties for the British in the North. But here again his involvement with the IRA stymied him.

He expressed a very low opinion of the movement in a series of articles, published posthumously in the *Irish Times* in August 1947. (Goertz had poisoned himself the previous May rather than face deportation back to Germany.) He wrote:

> The IRA had become an underground movement in its own national sphere, heavily suppressed by men who knew all their methods. Inside the IRA nobody knew what game was really played, not even their leader. Their internal means of communication were as primitive as boys playing police and brigands. They got no further than the open message in the sock of a girl. And what messages! There was no code –

they did not want to learn the most simple code, they preferred to sacrifice their men and women. They had not a single wireless operator; they made no attempt to learn messages discipline; their military training was nil. I once said to one of them whom I admired for his personal qualities: 'you know how to die for Ireland, but of how to fight for it you have not the slightest idea.' In spite of the fine qualities of individual IRA men, as a body I considered them worthless.

From the start the IRA had meant trouble for Goertz who, upon landing, had marched seventy miles to Laragh, Co. Wicklow, and the home of Mrs Iseult Stuart, wife of a man who had befriended him in Berlin and a sister of Sean MacBride. Mrs Stuart gave him hospitality and brought him clothing, but a few days later, contact with the IRA having been effected, he went, on IRA advice, to the home in Templeogue of Stephen Carroll Held, a businessman whose father was a naturalized German. On 23 May Held's house was raided by police who missed Goertz, but seized his transmitter and some $20,000 in notes. This seizure alarmed the government more than any development since the Magazine Fort raid. Five days later the all-party National Defence Council was formed and on 3 June 400 IRA suspects were rounded up and interned in the Curragh.

The money which Goertz had suggests that the Germans thought highly of him. In his articles he describes sending money to a transmitting station in the North and makes other references to helping the IRA financially. But it is very difficult to discover just what became of these sums. IRA leaders such as MacNamee, Kelly and McAteer impressed me as being among the most honest men I have ever met, and they all assured me that it was necessary to stage dangerous bank robberies in order to pay IRA debts. Nor did the equipment of the rank and file ever indicate any degree of affluence. Goertz's money seems to have vanished into that murky limbo of espionage where nothing flourishes but crookedness, mediocrity and betrayal.

Reading his articles, and knowing that the man who wrote them committed suicide, one could not help feeling sorry for Goertz. He describes how all his efforts to get back to Germany failed, either because of police vigilance or treachery. A plan to get him away by boat from Fenit, Co. Kerry, in February 1941 was scotched when the Irish authorities picked up his IRA collaborators, and a British patrol boat waited just outside the three mile limit. He actually got away from Brittas Bay in Co. Wicklow but his engine broke down and he had to remain. He tried again in September while German planes circled overhead but, he wrote, 'again my boat failed. It was extremely hard on me to stand on a broad field near the sea and watch those friendly aircraft overhead.'

Assessing the IRA and Goertz's role, Veesemayer, of the Irish Section in the Abwehr, in a lengthy report which he made on 24 November 1941, on a number of telegrams which Hempel had got from Dublin concerning the Hayes affair, said of Goertz: 'His communications are mostly one sided and therefore of a relatively valueless nature . . . both the Irish and the English police are informed as to his whereabouts . . . the value of his activity in Ireland has sunk to nil.'

The only spy other than Goertz to remain at liberty for any length of time was Ernest Weber-Drohl, a former strong man in a circus. He was sixty-one when he appeared in the Dublin District Court on 24 April 1940, charged with entering Ireland illegally. He convinced the court that he was, as he described himself, 'Atlas the Strong', that he had come to Ireland to look up two missing children by a sweetheart whom he had loved and lived with in Ireland in 1907 and that he landed in Ireland in a small boat from a tramp steamer which had taken him from Antwerp. The boat, he claimed, had overturned and he had to swim for his life, losing in the process his passport, marriage certificate, pipes and letters. Weber-Drohl went on to say that a sailor who had come with him from the tramp steamer in the little boat had assisted him in righting it, and that the sailor had then made his way safely back to the steamer.

The strong-man story was a nicely blended mixture of fact and fiction: the sailor had made his way back in the little boat but not to a steamer. He had come from a German U-boat that approached the Irish coast. In a rough sea, the little boat had overturned and a wireless transmitter, which Weber-Drohl was supposed to hand over to the IRA to replace the one seized in Rathmines, fell overboard. He had left Wilhelmshaven aboard U-boat U37, on 28 January 1940, so prior to his appearance in court he seems to have spent at least a month at liberty in Ireland. During this period he saw Jim O'Donovan and handed over money and code words to be used when another transmitter was found. This is about all Weber-Drohl achieved because three days after his acquittal the Secret Service picked him up.

The other German spies were caught almost on landing. One, Karl Anderson, was arrested in Kingsbridge Station in Dublin on 13 June 1940, the day after landing in Kerry, and three others were picked up in July. These three agents were called Tributh, Gaertner and Obed, and they had landed in Baltimore Bay on 18 July, with an incredible story of courageous seafaring behind them, having sailed from Brest in a yacht, the *Soizic*, rigged like a Breton fishing boat. The yacht had been commandeered for the voyage by a famous German yachtsman, Christian Nissen. They had passed close to British warships on a number of occasions on their thirty-six foot craft before landing and almost instant capture. Obed was an Indian, and three foreigners on a Cork road in wartime asking how to get to Dublin quite naturally attracted attention and they were arrested. None, of course, had made any contact with the IRA.

After 1941 the only German agent to make contact with Republican circles (and that only tangentially) was Gunther Schuetz, who made a spectacular escape from Mountjoy Jail in Dublin on 28 February 1942, after manufacturing a rope and grappling hook from some copper wire to scale the walls. He had earlier used some of the money given to him on departure from Amsterdam to buy women's clothes, allegedly for his fiancée, and dressed as a becoming young woman he made his way to the home of Kathleen Brugha (Cathal Brugha's widow), which was a centre of underground activity. Both Mrs Brugha and her daughter Noinin were active Republicans (Noinin afterwards married Sean O'Broin, one of the leaders of the raid on the Magazine Fort) and the police were actually coming to arrest her when they found Schuetz, who was using the name of Marschner. In the interval since his escape he had been put in contact with the IRA and it had been arranged that a boat would be provided to take him from Dingle to Germany. However, on 30 March, the day he was to go, the skipper of the boat, Charlie McGuinness, three men who were to act as crew, and the dining car attendant on the Belfast-Dublin train who was an IRA courier were all arrested.

Churchill's fears about the possibility of an IRA-Nazi tie-up proved groundless throughout the war. Eamon de Valera had wanted his country to be neutral and neutral it stayed, in one of the greatest diplomatic feats of the Second World War.

10

Republic and Republicans: I

The extraordinary doggedness of the Republican tradition persisting, despite many disasters, through the generations cannot be overlooked. Even with the disappearance of the border there would be some Republicans somewhere who would still claim to be the lawful inheritors of Ireland's revolutionary traditions, entitled to shed blood for what they believed a historically justified cause.

This sentiment was articulated on behalf of the Irish language by Diarmaid O Donnchadha* when he said:

> It is charged that we pay more heed to the words of dead heroes than we do to living leaders. We accept that charge as a compliment . . . Comparison between the statements of aim of living leaders and the writings and speeches of dead heroes is the only way to be certain that the living pursue the aims of the dead. We want to make sure, to echo the words of Pearse, that they are preaching the same gospel rather than perhaps a saner and a wiser gospel.

This 'gospel of continuity' was in part responsible for the outburst of activity that took place after the Second World War. The campaign of border raids during 1956–62 was in some ways the most costly of all post-1921 IRA activity. It occurred after the portcullis of years had been dropped on the events of the 1940s so that the bulk of those taking part knew of the leaders of other days only by hearsay – if at all.

And this is one of the extraordinary features of the IRA: the manner in which the tradition of continuity exists side by side with a blank ignorance of earlier events and personalities. It goes far to explain the IRA ethos, touching as it does on questions of Irish education

* Page 3. *The Case for the Defence; answers, based on facts and logic, to charges against the Irish Revival.*

generally, the IRA's own educative process of indoctrination, and the religio-political nature of the division of the country, all of which combine so that the young IRA man knows only as much about his country and Republicanism as the IRA lets him know. Before turning to the 1956–62 phase of activity it is necessary to examine these forces.

It must first be understood that 'a Republican' or 'the Republic' in IRA terms do not mean the same thing as they would, say, to a student of Plato, Rousseau or Jefferson.* A Republican is not merely a man who sees Ireland as one nation, a geographical and cultural unit, and who objects to that nation being partitioned and to the spectacle of the flag and troops of another country giving daily evidence of that partition. There are such men, of course, but let us see how the question, 'What exactly is a Republican?', is answered in a pamphlet issued to commemorate the death of Austin Stack on 27 April 1929.

Stack was condemned to death for his part in the 1916 Rising, but his sentence was commuted to penal servitude. He underwent many subsequent terms of imprisonment, and some incredible hunger strikes and other adventures, such as the smashing up of Belfast Jail in November 1918, when he was commandant of the prisoners there. He held various ministries in the underground Republican government, and during the Civil War itself was deputy chief of staff to Frank Aiken. He is venerated by his contemporaries as the very model of a perfect Republican.

> The name Republican in Ireland, as used amongst Republicans, bears no political meaning. It stands for the devout lover of his country, trying with might and main for his country's freedom.
>
> Such a man cannot be a slave. And if not a slave in heart or in act, he cannot be guilty of the slave vices. No coercion can breed them in the freeman.
>
> Fittingly, the question, What is a Republican? fails to be answered in our memorial number for Austin Stack, a man who bore and dared and suffered, remaining through it all and at the worst, the captain of his own soul . . . What then was Austin Stack, Republican?
>
> A great love of his country. A man without a crooked twist in him. One who thought straight, acted straight, walked the straight road unflinchingly and expected of others that they should walk it with him,

---

* We may also discount the definition of an IRA prisoner in Derry Jail who rose in disgust in the dining hall one Christmas Day, on being served with a herring, to proclaim as he held the offending object between finger and thumb, 'Any man who would eat these is no Republican.'

as simply as he did himself. No man could say or write of him: 'He had to do it.' That plea of the slave was not his. His duty, as conscience and love dictated, he did. The force of England, of the English Slave State, might try coercion, as they tried it many times. It made no difference. He went his way, suffered their will, and stood his ground doggedly, smiling now and again. His determination out-stood theirs, because it had a deeper foundation and a higher aim. Compromise, submission, the slave marks, did not and could not exist for him as touching himself, or the Cause for which he worked and fought, lived and died.

Fifty years after 1916 another Republican, Joe Christle, who himself took up arms in the 1950s, wrote an essay defining a Republic as he saw it. Christle split from the main body of the IRA during his period of activity, but the sentiments contained in his essay would be acceptable to most members of the IRA both past and present.

THE LIVING REPUBLIC!

The great purity of the Republic, the sublimity even of its object – the guarantee of equal rights and equal opportunities – is precisely that which makes our force and our weakness. Our force, because it gives us the ascendancy of truth over imposture and the rights of public interest over private interest. Our weakness, because it rallies against us all the vicious; all those who in their hearts meditate the robbery of the people, all those who having robbed them seek impunity, all those who have rejected equality as a personal calamity and above all, those who embrace politics as a family trade and the nation as a prey.

It must not be forgotten that the desecrating voice of the establishment raged equally loud in denouncing Pearse in 1916 as it did in denouncing South in 1956. In Ireland the voice of the establishment has been and still is the voice of criminal and here crime massacres innocence to reign. If now no man is led out blindfold to be executed in an Irish prison yard, it is because no man rebels against the criminal in power.

In this situation the first maxim of policy for the Republic should be to conduct the people by reason and the enemies of the people by strength . . .

Let us commune with them who declared the right of the people of Ireland to the ownership of Ireland with equal rights and equal opportunities for all citizens. The men who faced the firing squads of the establishment gave testimony to the truth of what had been declared and gave the lie to every Judas who would betray them.

The people can be relied upon to rally to take Republican ideals when Republicans themselves rally to the ideal ... equal rights and equal opportunities. It was for this the Republic was proclaimed and for this alone is there any meaning to Republic.

But the establishment will be heard to shout 'Oh No! Republic means Democracy and this formula is guarded by the Ballot-Box.' That is a deceit and this deceit founded the Free State and was used by clever men to cloak the surrender of 1922 as a stepping stone to the Republic. These clever men were heard to say that 'the people fought for the right to vote.' In other words the people fought for the right to choose their masters. But this is blatantly deceitful, for the Founders of the Republic wrote – the people shall be master; the people who wept in Gethsemane and who died naked on the Cross.

The Republic is not a formula to be dispensed at Ballot boxes once in every five years. It is the way of life. It is not that some are chosen to be masters for this would be 'Beggars change horseback but the lash goes on'; it is, that all have admitted the reality of equality ...

[The Republic] could not tolerate education based on privilege because in the Republic there can be no privilege ... the Republic would encourage the fullest expression by writers, poets and artists [and] could not have troops of an alien enemy occupying part of the national territory ...

We should with strength seek to destroy the establishment but not, after destroying it, seek wantonly to kill its agents for to do so would be to violate the honour of the Republic.

What made men join a movement dedicated to the establishment of such an ideal Republic? Family and environmental influences played a large part, as the careers of two of the IRA's outstanding figures show.

Sean O'Broin, one of the leaders of the Magazine Fort raid, comes from Kerry where the Civil War took a grisly turn. At Ballyseedy Republican prisoners were chained together and set to dismantle a mined barricade so that they were blown to pieces. Cathal Brugha's son Ruari, a successful businessman and Fianna Fail senator, gave me this statement:

'I joined the IRA at sixteen while I was still at school. It was the result of the environment in which I grew up. My father had been killed fighting in 1922 for the ideals of Easter Week, founded on a love of Ireland and its people, and an angry determination to save the nation from being completely smothered by English influences. In the struggle that followed 1916 against England, people had to endure many things. Hard decisions had to be made. Young men had been sent to their deaths in bitter fighting all over the country. Spies and informers had been executed but the leaders in this conflict were not fighting for military victory alone. The real struggle was for the mind and soul of a once proud nation, and now, at the end of it all, they were asked to swear allegiance to a foreign king and to acknowledge the right of the former enemy to keep troops in Ireland. These symbols of domination contrasted so violently with the inspiring vision of a free and independent Ireland that they were utterly unacceptable. This, I believe, is why my father made his sacrifice.

'Naturally, the atmosphere of my home was not only Republican and anti-treaty but also anti-Free State and generally derogatory of politics and politicians. I think my decision to join the IRA was inevitable because, with my upbringing and background, it would have been shirking a duty not to do so. In any case, for the very young, there was an element of excitement in it. Raids, arrests, secret parades, arms classes and the occasional public parade, which were a challenge to authority, helped to make it attractive. You felt you were part of something and had a sense of identity with the high ideals of the past.

'IRA policy, as I understood it, was confused. It was taken for granted that one joined the IRA to get an all-Ireland Republic of which Ireland had been cheated by England with the aid of some Irish politicians. I learned that the Free State was a British dominion created by an English act of Parliament; that there was a governor-general appointed by the king of England; that we were British subjects; that Ireland was partitioned by Britain and kept that way by British troops against the will of the majority of the people. I was led to believe that the ideals of anyone who went into politics (i.e. Leinster House) would be undermined or weakened; that he would become pro-British and that it was an act of treason to the Republic to acknowledge the state or the government. This was the type of doctrine one heard or read about in *An Phoblacht*.

'The things that stand out in my mind now as being significant did not seem so then. There was an instruction to the rank and file of the volunteers [IRA] to refuse to recognize the courts if charged with political offences. The theory of the *de jure* authority of the second Dail was used to justify the existence of an armed force. This theory rested on the fact that the second Dail had not been properly dissolved and that those who had refused to enter the Free State Dail retained the *de jure* authority of the second Dail. That argument was supported by reference to a statement [by de Valera] made in Leinster House that "the real authority lies outside this House". I think that the idea of the continuing authority of the second Dail had considerable influence on some of us at that time. This theory was being upheld despite successive governments being elected under a free franchise. We became the victims of an illusion that could never become a reality. It prevented constructive thought about the country and how best to serve it. But for a young person to turn his back on this teaching would have been seen as an abandonment of principle.

'To some, in that atmosphere, to do so would have been as impossible as changing one's religion. As a result, normal judgement could not be exercised and such political steps as the removal of the governor-general and the oath of allegiance, the introduction of the Irish Nationality and Citizenship Act, the recovery of the occupied ports, the new constitution with a president elected by the people – all of which were milestones in our development towards political independence and which would have been welcomed in 1922, were regarded by extreme Republicans as political stunts.

'I had resolved from the beginning to avoid gunfighting involving Irishmen because I rejected the idea of civil war. Many of the things which happened during the 1930s caused me to have misgivings. There were indiscriminate actions and shootings which were not consistent with the aims of the movement. Those in charge seemed unable to cope. All this led me to think critically and therefore independently and prevented me from becoming too deeply involved.

'As I see it now, the dilemma facing the leaders arose from their complete acceptance of the theory that force was the only way to achieve their aims. They felt committed to this policy partly through loyalty to those who had already lost their lives and also because of a deep distrust and dislike of political methods. Any deviation from the accepted principle appeared to them to be an abandonment of the struggle for Irish freedom and unity. This prevented them from considering other means.

'It is easy to criticise that campaign [Russell's against England]. However unrealistic and ill-advised that policy may have been it is true that some brave young Irishmen, acting in good faith, took part in it for the sake of their country. They carried out extremely difficult tasks in the most dangerous conditions. They suffered ill-treatment and long terms in British jails. Some of them never fully recovered from their experiences. Their sacrifices must appear on the credit side somewhere.

'In the autumn of 1940, I was interned. In the Curragh I was struck by a curious situation. Irish soldiers were guarding alike IRA and British and German internees in separate internment camps. I realized that Irish neutrality was a token of our sovereignty. I found it difficult to resent the government which had interned me because, in their view, I was not prepared to acknowledge their right to maintain order and defend the freedom of this part of Ireland. An unusual aspect of this situation was that many of us, certainly I myself, could have secured release simply by giving an undertaking. But this was what one could not do. It is one thing for a free man to declare his attitude of his own free will. It is quite a different thing for a detained political prisoner to do so in order to get out. And so many hundreds of men and some women (in Mountjoy Jail) remained in prison away from their families rather than "sign out" and lose their independence of mind and self-respect. As a result, many of them suffered torment – torn between responsibility for their dependants and loyalty to a cause.

'There is an interesting aspect of the later prison situation that is not generally known. During the invasion scare, sentenced IRA prisoners in Arbour Hill detention barracks decided that, if there was a British invasion of the twenty-six counties, they would volunteer for service in the Irish army. This may not seem peculiar today, but for them it would have meant putting on the uniform of the former Free State army with its memories of deaths, executions and civil war.

'Circumstances had brought them into a cul-de-sac; they had been taught no way of serving their country except by arms and sacrifice. These were some of the best elements in the nation. The stream of idealism that runs in every generation was at that time partly diverted, as it were, into the desert. They could have helped to supply some of the patriotism together with the dynamism essential in national politics. They sought nothing for themselves; they only wished to serve their country.

'It was obvious to me that the twenty-six counties were politically free and that the sort of activity in which the IRA had been engaged had not helped to end partition. The six counties is a largely planned area with all the ills that such areas possess wherever they exist in the world. There will be extremes of political differences and loyalties there for a long time. There is gerrymandering because of vested interests and because of inculcated mistrust and fear among the descendants of planter stock. We need to understand that the division in Ireland arises out of its tragic history and may not be quickly resolved.'

Another famous name in IRA history was that of Micksey Conway who, when I interviewed him in 1969, was Brother Maolmuire in the Cistercian community at Collon, Co. Meath. The formidable figure of the 1930s was no more. He was a low-sized, greying man with sincerity and decency radiating from blue, kindly eyes, from his weather-beaten, disciplined face and his warm, strong handshake. He was only a boy of twelve during the Civil War but he remembered incidents such as soldiers coming to Tipperary town and firing over the heads of looters who had taken butter from shop windows and were trampling it into the street.*

He told me he was first attracted to the IRA by the dedication and religious fervour he saw in its leaders. It matched his own religious feelings and made him see the IRA as something noble and pure. This dedication was to lead him into some pretty desperate situations. The Egan shooting, for instance, led to his death sentence, but when he was finally reprieved, he told me, he was disappointed. He had become resigned to the thought of death for imprisonment meant constant supervision by warders who sat beside him even while he slept, lest he attempt to strangle himself. This seemed a far worse fate than death in a cause he felt to be intrinsically good.†

Conway joined the Cistercians in 1951. When I met him seventeen years later he had been to Dublin only twice in the meantime. His normal daily routine was to get up at 4.15 and work all day, returning to bed at 8.30 p.m. – which he found trying in summer. He was very hopeful of the reforms and the renewal of the Church set in train by Vatican II. Driving back to Dublin after interviewing him, my abiding impression was that it would be difficult to meet a more sincere man.

---

* Tipperary, a rebel county, the home of Charles Kickham the Fenian writer, had its share of bitter Civil War memories, executions and divided families. One court-martial of two men who had betrayed IRA volunteers to Free State soldiers thereby causing their deaths, was guarded by a brother of one of the two accused, and subsequently executed, men.

† This is a common attitude towards loss of life in religious IRA men. Oscar Traynor, who commanded the Dublin brigade in the Anglo-Irish war, and had to initiate and sanction some pretty stern actions, told how one morning in Wicklow Street he met a man on his way to Mass in Clarendon Street Church and it emerged that the man was also going to receive communion. 'But,' asked Traynor, 'weren't you the man who carried out — last night? I've just bought a paper and it says he was killed outright?' 'Yes,' replied the gunman, 'of course I am, what's that got to do with it? That execution was sanctioned by the legal government of Ireland. I was only doing my duty.' With that he went off to receive communion.

The sort of influences playing on the idealistic mind of young IRA volunteers may be gauged from some typical Republican publications from the Civil War to the present day.

In an issue of a broadsheet, *The Fenian*, dated 13 September '7th year of the Republic', probably edited by Erskine Childers whose influence on Republican polemics has lasted until our day, one can trace the same threads of bitterness, high-mindedness, dedication and contempt for the institutions of the state other than those stemming from the mystical 'second Dail'. *The Fenian* always referred to the Free State as 'the Slave State' and defined its attitude thus:

> In answer to some correspondents we wish to say that is it not our intention to devote space daily to the reports of the proceedings of the so-called 'Parliament' now sitting in the very appropriate premises of the Royal Dublin Society. The only parliament entitled to legislate and govern in this country is Dail Eireann, The Parliament of the Irish Republic. The Kildare Street debating club is not the Dail. It therefore is entitled to no respect or obedience from the Irish people. The only use of interest its proceedings have for us is to afford a certain amount of amusement, or of insight into the minds of the men who have endeavoured to sell their birthright for a mess of English pottage.

Another Republican apologist, Frank Gallagher, in a pamphlet 'By What Authority?' published in London during the Civil War, defined the Republican position in a manner which would stand today for many Republicans:

> Before the Treaty was signed, Civil War in Ireland was impossible. What made it possible?
>
> For five terrible years the nation had remained united on three great principles:
>
> 1. The existence of the Republic founded in Easter Week, and confirmed by national plebiscite in 1918;
> 2. The sanctity of our national independence declared by the Sovereign National Assembly in January 1919; and
> 3. The territorial integrity of Ireland, which has outlasted history itself.

The Treaty violated these three fundamental principles, destroying the Republic, surrendering our national independence, partitioning our ancient nation.

The significance of the Government of Ireland Act meant nothing.

The question of the oath was responsible for voluminous literature in its own right. One of the more notable pamphlets, 'The Oath of Allegiance and All that It Implies', by 'Skellig' (J. J. O'Kelly, a member of Sinn Fein's first Dail, and a noted propagandist on the Republican side) devoted most of its animadversions on the oath to 'The Lustful Henry the Eighth's' machinations, and traced those supporting (in 1925) the Free State back to the days of Henry. Throughout the pamphlet references to the debauchery of the royal line made it clear that anybody subscribing to the contemporary oath of allegiance was, if not quite incestuous, homosexual and degenerate, at least very lacking in patriotism.

Lest there be any religious scruples in the minds of IRA men there was also a pamphlet entitled 'False Pastors' by Columban na Banban, who was very likely Father O'Flanagan, former vice-president of Sinn Fein, which said that the Irish bishops had the right and duty to lay down a code of behaviour for the faithful – except when they were in error. That the Irish bishops were very much in error we learn here:

> It is charged that through a long course of years they have been false to this nation; that they have time and again encouraged the enemy of our people; that they have blessed those amongst ourselves who stood for the compromise of our national principles and honour, and cursed the men who were ready to fight and die to win our liberty and independence. It is charged against them that when at last in 1921 victory seemed at hand, they sided with the men who betrayed the nation; and that then, encroaching on the purely temporal, prostituting their spiritual power and profaning the most sacred things, they conspired with a domestic enemy, the most terrible our people have ever known; and that they condoned by their criminal silence the perpetration of savage and inhuman deeds. It is charged against them that they are the principal cause of the blackest crimes which stain our history, not that they were the actual perpetrators, but because, by reason of their position and influence, the part they played makes them more responsible and guilty than the actual criminals.

The constitution of the IRA, published by the Republican Information Bureau in June 1932, contains a passage explaining how it is that on one hand the IRA might hold secret drill sessions, be bound by oaths and passwords, and on the other, drill openly, and publish newspapers and pamphlets:

It is well to emphasize here that the Irish Republican Army is not, and never has been, what is termed a 'Secret Society'. Its existence, constitution and policy are openly declared. Secrecy as to its activities is only maintained to safeguard it from attack. The policy of the Irish Republican Army is published and proclaimed in writing and speech as openly as circumstances permit.

The justification of having an army at all reads:

Until the Republic of Ireland is freed from foreign aggression and can function freely, the necessity for the Irish Republican Army will continue. Only to a Government of the Republic can the Army give allegiance. Should the time arrive when its services will be no longer necessary to defend the nation's sovereignty, it will disband.

The flexibility of this last principle is demonstrated by the fact that in June 1969, when armed attacks on the North had clearly failed, the IRA had turned itself to defending 'the nation's sovereignty' by burning down the homes of Germans who had bought land in Ireland.

Republican theology has always been subject to this kind of interpretation. One of Peadar O'Donnell's pamphlets, 'For Or Against The Ranchers?' printed by the *Mayo News* in Westport shortly after the outbreak of the economic war, tells small farmers that:

This rancher-based cattle trade versus tillage fight now is primarily a fight on the national issue. The ranchers are not fighting against exclusion from the British market; . . . It is in their role as Imperialists that the ranchers and big farmers are warring now, and it is in their role as Nationalists that the mass of the Irish people must overwhelm them. Any leadership that does not take its stand on the full Separatist platform must, therefore, fall short of the needs of the situation.

Young men reading *An Phoblacht* would find sentiments akin to those of O'Donnell. Its editorial for 26 March 1932 contained the following:

The enemy of Irish Independence, British Imperialism, is still entrenched and active. Its immediate aim will be to stir up conflict, seeking to drive a wedge into any movement that aims at its undoing. British Imperialism stands for the maintenance of the present Social and Economic system; it is for all National organizations accordingly to fight any influences that tend to foster internal strife, mobilizing en masse against the common enemy. The Treaty was imposed by force; its alternative ruthless war: it is unnatural and immoral. Partition, its changeling, is a degrading abomination, foisted upon us by the foreigner. To undo both is our obvious duty.

The *Irish Workers' Voice*, official organ of the Irish Communist Party endorsed this line in its publications. The Communist Party's inaugural meeting was held on 4 and 5 June 1933, in Dublin, where Sean Murray, the great figure in the Irish Communist Party in the 1930s, said that 'the manifesto was to be issued to the working men of Ireland, to all fellow Fighters for national freedom. The delegates here today from the four corners of Ireland are living proof that a society of United Irishmen can be formed in this twentieth century.'

The *Wolfe Tone Weekly*, which began under the editorship of Brian O'Higgins in September 1937, though not as popular as *An Phoblacht*, was a journal of some influence until its end in September 1939. Brian O'hUiginn (the Irish version of his name by which he was generally known) was a member of the first Dail. As a polemicist he lacked the grace and social content of Peadar O'Donnell, tending more towards Gaelic revivalism than socialism. The *Wolfe Tone Weekly* was, however, well edited and laid out, better than either *An Phoblacht* or the *Republican Congress.** O'hUiginn's first editorial set the tone for the two years of his paper's existence:

> What we believe in our hearts . . . of the heritage we have revived from the unconquered and breathless dead. When we think of the many men who, in the full vigour and glory of their manhood, lay down their lives without a murmur of complaint or regret, we must ask ourselves this question – for what did they die? And if we are honest we must answer in their own words, spoken with their dying breath – they died for the full and complete and untrammelled freedom of an Ireland, of every sod of Ireland. They did not die for a prosperous so-called 'Free State', nor did they die for a cosmopolitan Republic. They died endeavouring, in the words of Wolfe Tone, 'to break the connection with England, the never-failing source of all our political evil.' They died endeavouring to make the Sovereign Republic of all Ireland, in the inspired words of Padraig Pearse, 'Not free merely, but Gaelic as well; not Gaelic merely, but free as well.'

* O'hUiginn also produced tastefully designed Celtic art work. My father, who politically could hardly have differed more from him, would never allow any Christmas cards to be bought by our family other than those produced by O'hUiginn.

Since 1916 the most important influence on all sections of Republican thought has been Padraig Pearse. Pearse's writings* derive their strength from the manner in which they express the ideal of Irish separatism – 'Ireland Free is Ireland Gaelic, Ireland Gaelic is Ireland Free' – and from the themes of self-sacrifice and communion with the dead, which are common both in the Irish missionary tradition and in the typical Republican attitude towards serving Ireland.

'Patriotism,' he wrote, 'is in large part a memory of heroic dead men and a striving to accomplish same task left unfinished by them.' (This later appeared on a memorial programme issued by the IRA at Easter 1968.)

The way in which Pearse mixed revolution and religion was particularly powerful. His statement on 'freedom and the sword' embodies teachings learned by every Irish Catholic schoolchild of his time:

'One of the sins against Faith is presumption which is defined as: "A foolish expectation of salvation without making use of the necessary means to obtain it." Surely it is a sin against national faith to expect national freedom without accepting the necessary means to win and keep it. And I know of no other way than the way of the sword: History records no other, reason and experience suggest no other.'

This quotation appears on the late-page of a document on IRA policy published in June 1932 by the Republican Publicity Bureau. It is interesting to contrast it with an entry in the diary of Fergal O'Hanlon, nineteen, who was killed in the Brookeborough raid on New Year's Eve, 1957. Across two pages recording Easter Sunday and Monday 1956, Fergal wrote, 'I know of no way by which freedom can be obtained and when obtained maintained, except by armed men.'

The *Wolfe Tone Weekly* includes articles signed 'A Catholic Priest' on the 'Morality of Revolt', declaring that if one were revolting in the interests of the principles contained in the leading articles, one was not breaking the laws of God or man. The late Sean Dunne, a Labour

---

* Many of them, particularly a series entitled 'Tracts for the Times', showed a markedly socialist content, a preoccupation with death, a conviction that all must end in sadness. This theme cropped up in short stories like 'Eoineen na nEan (Eoineen of the Birds), 'Bridget of the Sorrows', in 'Isogain', in his poem 'The Mother' with the statement, 'I do not grudge thee Lord my two strong sons' (both Pearse and his brother Willie died before firing squads) and in his celebrated statement on the outbreak of the First World War. This trend towards morbidity may have been heightened by the death of his sweetheart, Elaine Nicholls, who was drowned off Great Blasket Island, off the coast of Kerry, while giving another girl a swimming lesson in 1909.

deputy who spent the war years interned in the Curragh for his youthful Republicanism, described this mentality to me as being that of a '— with a .45 wrapped in Rosary beads'. Earlier the *Weekly*, in a panel set in heavy black type that appeared in the issue of 16 April 1938, under the heading '1916' said, 'the men who took part in the Easter Week Rising were Irish in heart and soul, and their prayers were said on Irish Horn Rosary Beads. Do those who commemorate them follow their example?'

A poem in the *Wolfe Tone Weekly*, on 11 September 1937, from Jimmy Steel, at the time serving seven years, shows again how religion and Republicanism mingled.

A Prison Prayer

O, Sacred Heart of Jesus we pray to Thee today,
To aid our suffering Motherland
Upon her bloodstained way.
For loyalty to serve her,
For strength to set her free,
O, Sacred Heart of Jesus!
We send our prayer to Thee.

O, Sacred Heart of Jesus!
Look down on us today,
Make us strong and fearless soldiers,
Ever ready for the fray.
'Gainst thine and Ireland's enemies,
Wherever they may be,
O, Sacred Heart of Jesus!
We put our trust in Thee.

Another poem in the *Wolfe Tone Weekly*, in January 1938 was reprinted in many other Republican journals in Ireland and America. Entitled 'Who is Ireland's Enemy?', it included these stanzas:

Who is Ireland's enemy?
Not Germany, nor Spain,
Not Russia, France nor Austria;
They forged for her no chain,
Nor quenched her hearths,

Nor razed her homes,
Nor laid her altars low,
Nor sent her sons to tramp the hill
Amid the winter snow!

Who spiked the heads of Irish Priests
On Dublin Castle gate?
Who butchered helpless Irish babes,
The lust for blood to sate?
Who outraged Irish maidenhood,
And tortured aged sires,
And spread from Clare to Donegal,
The glare of midnight fires?
Who scourged our land in '98
Spread torture far and wide,
Till Ireland shrieked in woe and pain,
And hell seemed fair beside?
Who plied the pitch-cap and the sword,
The gibbet and the rack?
O God! that we should ever fail
To pay those devils back.

Who slew the three in Manchester,
One drear November dawn,
While round them howled in fury
The devil's hungry spawn?
Who shattered many a Fenian mind
In dungeons o're the foam,
And broke the loyal Fenian hearts
That pined for them at home?
Who shot down Clarke and Connolly
And Pearse at dawn of day,
And Plunkett and MacDiarmada
And all who died as they?
Who robbed us of McSwiney brave?
Who murdered Mellows too,
Sent Barry to a felon's grave
And slaughtered Cathal Brugha?

Not Germany nor Austria,
Not Russia, France nor Spain

That robbed and reaved this land of ours,
That forged her rusty chain;
But England of the wily words –
A crafty, treacherous foe –
'Twas England scourged our motherland,
'Twas England laid her low!

Rise up, o dead of Ireland!
And rouse her living men;
The chance will come to us at last
To win our own again;
To sweep the English enemy
From hill and glen and bay,
And in your name, o holy dead!
Our sacred debt to pay!

While most of this writing was propagandist rather than literary, the *Wolfe Tone Weekly* also provided a fifteen-year-old Dubliner, Brendan Behan, with a vehicle for his poetic view of the deaths of Rory O'Connor, Liam Mellows, Richard Barrett and Joe McKelvey during the Civil War. The poem appeared on 24 December 1938, under the heading 'Four Great Names'.

The tragic events of the war also provided a deluge of pamphlets and broadsheets. One of the most interesting was showered on Dublin on St Patrick's Day, 1942, after George Plant's execution. The leaflet set out the facts from the IRA point of view. But it is not the content so much as the manner of delivery that is memorable. With the aid of friends and relatives, including two Christian brothers, all of whom were subsequently arrested, Seamus G. O'Kelly, a victim of cerebral palsy but the father of four healthy children and a life-long IRA and Republican publicist, arranged for 5,000 copies to be run off and then, while de Valera was attending High Mass in the nearby Pro Cathedral, had them all scattered down on Dublin from the top of Nelson's Pillar.

Brian O'Higgins's *Wolfe Tone Annual* also came out during the war years. This was a compendium of articles on separatist history, something on the lines of the *Wolfe Tone Weekly* though less detailed. In October 1943 it was banned from appearing as a 1944 issue on the grounds that it contravened the Emergency Powers Order of 1939. It was subsequently published unaltered in 1945 and the banning reverberated through the Dail and the columns of letters to the editors for some years afterwards.

When a regular Republican newspaper, the *United Irishman*, began in July 1947, the mixture was as before, with articles about IRA leaders who had been executed, accounts of commemoration ceremonies, references to 1916 and a preoccupation with those who died for Ireland rather than with the living conditions of those who wished to live for her in the post-war years. As the younger spirits who masterminded the 1956–62 border campaign came to power, the paper developed a more militant tone and Eamonn Timmoney, OC of the IRA group in Derry in that campaign, said, 'This little paper played an important part in developing sympathies with, and support for, the Republican movement.'

It gave articles of interest to Republicans, told the new generation about the indignities suffered by Irish patriots at the hands of the British and Irish authorities in the past and blended Fenianism, commentary on the contemporary political situation in the North and attacks on the Fianna Fail and Coalition regimes in the South. As the campaign developed the paper devoted itself to accounts of great victories won and battles fought. (Many were more apparent to the editorial staff of the *United Irishman* than to the public at large.) The 1960s' *United Irishman* was well written and laid out though the Fenian content had been steadily diminishing and, while occasional photographs of commemorations (in particular of Bodenstown) occurred, it tended to consist of articles reminiscent of the old Saor Eire and Republican Congress days. Articles on Dublin's housing conditions, on emigration and attacks on Ireland's plan to join the Common Market formed the bulk of its contents. These, like the slogans defacing the walls around Dublin – 'EEC No!' – hardly carried the same impact as the old 'Up the IRA' which, leaping at you from dead walls, at least let you know where you stood.

But even in this more sophisticated era of Republicanism, the old dichotomy between armed force and cerebral political movement is still apparent in the movement's publications. Glossily produced, *The Separatist* sometimes appears on newstands showing a map of Ireland on page one with a Union-jacked hand lifting the six counties out of it, while in the foreground looms a figure of an IRA man with a tommy-gun. In its introduction, the publication states that:

> The IRA cannot be dismissed as mere gunmen screaming for blood. There is overwhelming support in the Republican movement today for a more realistic approach to Ireland's ills. This school of thought is disgusted with the way Ireland (32 counties) has been ruled for the past forty years and advocates sweeping social reforms especially in education.

They point out that Britain has changed its policy towards the 26 Counties and now rules by economic rather than by political means. They will fight this cheque-book invasion, changing tactics as it suits them. This does not mean that the IRA will lay down the gun, for they still believe that the final changing of power will come only with the threat of, if not the actual use of, physical force.

As a result of all this pressure towards a sombre, brooding type of patriotism, in which death was used with something of the same spirit of the Japanese suicide flyers in the Second World War, it is not surprising that the IRA should itself inflict death on some of its own members for real or imagined breaches of its code.

A man accused of a capital offence under IRA law is normally given the opportunity to defend himself in a court-martial (though this did not happen in at least one case). IRA court regulations stipulate that the accused be tried before three officers, that he be given the opportunity to nominate a defending counsel and that the prosecution be carried out in the same way as a lawyer for the state presents a case before a judge and jury in ordinary law cases. An accused man may summon witnesses and he is normally served with a copy of the convening order showing the personnel of the court, a copy of the charge sheet and a copy of any exhibits which may be produced, so that he and his 'counsel' may prepare a defence. The regulations provide for a number of oaths, modelled on those taken in legal courts. These are administered to all court members, the legal officer, witnesses and the shorthand clerk.

Much IRA time and energy went, and still goes, into the holding of such courts-martial, courts of enquiry into misdemeanours real or imagined and attendance at commemoration ceremonies. (These are tragically increased by the malfunctioning of some bomb, weapon or ambush.) The more legalistic attach importance to courts-martial, but these can prove to be fairly arbitrary affairs so far as justice is concerned. During the 'Belt and Boot Brigade' era in Belfast one court-martial occurred at which Tarlach O'hUid was the note-taker when sentence of death was pronounced for a not very heinous misdemeanour. For some reason the principal officer of the court hesitated about sentencing the accused. A discussion began and the officer asked O'hUid, 'Well, should we execute him, or what will we do with him?' O'hUid replied, 'How about reducing him in the ranks?' This compromise was accepted but a compromise was not always forthcoming and a number of 'disappearances' that took place during bombing raids on Belfast were not from falling masonry, but from IRA action. In one of these cases, the widow of the executed man was so well aware of the IRA's role that she asked a bishop to communicate with the IRA for a certificate stating that her husband had been executed. The insurance company would thus have proof of death and would pay the insurance she badly needed.

The IRA decided that such a comment would be too incriminating and refused her request so she never got her money.

No court-martial preceded the Admiral Somerville shooting but there was one for John Egan. I asked a member of the Army Council at the time (all such verdicts have to be sanctioned by the Army Council, in theory at least) how this action could be justified. He replied, 'These things are very necessary in an organization like the IRA. They are very good for morale and they serve to release tension.'

Of all the IRA courts-martial that of Dan Turley on 5 April 1933, in Dublin is probably the most contentious. Turley, who had been a gallant figure during the Anglo-Irish struggle and was for a time OC of the Belfast brigade, was at the time of his court-martial, intelligence officer to the brigade. The position of intelligence officer is a delicate one. To get information he has to make contacts with opposing forces, rendering him susceptible to their pressures and suspect to some of his colleagues. Turley fell under suspicion after a number of raids and arrests in Belfast pointed to an informer in the IRA camp. Because of his position and record he was not informed of the feeling against him and he accompanied two other senior IRA officers (one of whom supplied me with these details) from Belfast to Dublin where he learned that he was not being summoned to a convention but to a court-martial at which Michael Price was the prosecuting officer. He was found guilty of spying and sentenced to death, the sentence being commuted to banishment provided he never returned to the country again – on pain of being shot at sight.

Turley agreed to this and was taken to Glasgow by Sean Russell. However, Glasgow, for an insurance agent with his roots in Belfast and a young family to support, was not an attractive spot in the 1930s and after about six months he returned. Between then and 7 December 1937, when IRA men shot him dead on the way to Mass, Turley must have lived a haunted life. He remained in a secret room in his house most of the time. only venturing out at night. Several friends visited him and warned him that the IRA was going to kill him but he protested his innocence and refused to leave his native city. After his death his sons continued in the IRA, though refusing to believe their father guilty. With extraordinary loyalty to both their father's name and to the organization that had killed him they continued membership while attempting to build up a dossier proving his innocence.

In addition to Turley I was given the names of three men in the North who, it was claimed, were executed, and four more reputed to have 'disappeared' during bombing raids on Belfast.

North or south of the border, IRA training has always fallen into two categories – military and intelligence work. Recruits were trained in the use of rifles and small arms and in army drill. The guns used in these sessions were always carefully rushed away afterwards and only one or two weapons were ever available, even for a reasonably large company. This position did not greatly alter throughout the IRA's history between 1923 and 1963. Dumps have always been kept a closely guarded secret, but one that the police nevertheless penetrate. A Thompson gun at a drill session was a very rare event and the Derry unit of the IRA put down a motion at the 1953 convention that asked that limpet mines and silencers for sten guns be provided. But they were not available. The chief explosive was the highly volatile 'paxo', made from potassium chlorate and paraffin wax.

I went, while researching this book (1969), on a drill session with a group of young IRA men, and watched their military manoeuvres, mock attacks and advances over rough country under simulated war conditions, guns at the ready. This group seemed well armed, as a certain amount of surplus American war equipment inevitably finds its way into the hands of those willing to pay for it. The 'soldiers' wore green battledress with peaked caps and looked a little like Roman soldiers. Armament was fairly good, with modern looking sub-machine guns, automatic rifles, walkie-talkies, bomb-making equipment and useful looking revolvers. Physical fitness was excellent. As this was a military operation, nobody was anxious to fraternize with me, though all were courteous enough.

The countryside in many parts of Ireland, even quite close to Dublin, is mountainous and well covered so there is little difficulty about concealment. I was told that local farmers were friendly and interruption by police seemed unlikely. As a precaution, I was called for at five in the morning before it was light and I did not reach home again until after dark, so that I could not divulge the route, if questioned.

Everyone in that group of twenty-five to thirty people was a small farmer, a clerk or a labourer. The disquieting thing was that, apart from the obvious dangers to themselves and others, they had no coherent political or ideological creed, nor even a sense of humour. Particularly with the spread of the ecumenical movement and the lessening of the horrors attending the word 'Communist', the IRA, I would say, of all revolutionary movements in Europe, would have been the most vulnerable to a Communist takeover.

The groundwork for the IRA's intelligence network was established in a memorandum of 1 February 1924. The document said that the intelligence information needed was:

(a) GOVERNMENT OFFICES: A list of Officials, Clerks, etc., employed in Government Offices annotated as to whether they are friendly (R), hostile (FS), doubtful (D), or neutral (N).

(b) NEWSPAPERS: A list of the Staffs on all Dublin daily and weekly newspapers (Marked as above.)

(c) RAILWAYS: A list of the permanent employees at all Dublin Termini. (Marked as in (a).)

(d) OFFICES OF PUBLIC WORKS: A list of the Staffs and permanent Officials of Dublin Corporation, Dublin County Council, Rathmines Council, Employment Officers, Labour Exchange, etc. (Marked as in (a).)

(e) TRADE UNIONS: A list of Officials, Clerks, etc. of all Trade Unions. (Marked as in (a).)

(f) CONTRACTS: Names and addresses of all employers, gaffers, foremen, etc., who have the giving of jobs with particulars as to their political sympathies, and as to how best they could be approached to employ released prisoners.

Modifications were introduced to this scheme over the years. One could today safely add a dossier of television personnel sympathetic or otherwise. In the 1950s photographs of Special Branch members, their home addresses, telephone numbers and registration numbers of their cars were also collected. But the principle remains that each volunteer is considered to be an intelligence officer who reports to his company commander anything he considers may be of assistance to the movement. The amount of reportage depends on the ability of the individual.[*]

Another continuing source of Republican influence is the annual Bodenstown march, usually held on the Sunday after Wolfe Tone's birth date, 20 June. This occupies a position in the Republican calendar analogous to that of Easter in the Christian religion. Bodenstown is

___

[*] After the Second World War the paperback revolution inspired many young revolutionaries in the IRA. Eamonn Timmoney, OC of Derry, and Charlie Murphy, adjutant general of the movement in the early 1950s, both remarked on the influence of books by foreign underground leaders.

three miles from Sallins in Co. Kildare, about thirty-five miles south-west of Dublin. Visiting Tone's grave on Bodenstown Sunday in the 1960s I learned a great deal about the IRA, and about Ireland itself.

Until the worsening situation in the North caused the Army-Fianna Fail commemorations to be held on separate Sundays, it used to be the custom that the IRA also marched to Bodenstown on the same day, though after Fianna Fail and the Army had departed. The first procession of the day was by the Irish army. A wreath was laid on the tomb, reveille was sounded and honour paid to the founder of Irish Republicanism. A little later came the Fianna Fail procession, when the prime minister or some other leading figure laid a wreath to the man from whom the Fianna Fail party derives its inspiration. All was quiet, decorous and generally sunlit.

After lunch came the IRA, the illegal organization whose existence was not officially recognized, whose name could be mentioned publicly only while keeping a wary eye on the Offences Against the State act, and the grave of Wolfe Tone was again festooned with wreaths from various Republican organizations. Military commands were given, the flags of IRA detachments were displayed and there was a fiery denunciation of everything symbolized by the previous two processions.

The annual Bodenstown oration is more than a mere denunciation. It sets the tone for the coming year's Republicanism, explains the policies of the movement, justifies them against criticism and urges those present on to greater efforts. One can judge the direction of IRA policies by a study of the groups and personalities who attend Bodenstown in any given year. In 1931, for instance, though Cumann na Gael cancelled the special trains that normally run for the occasion, and police prevented some of the more openly militaristic from parading, the event was held with members of Fianna Fail marching together in a body. De Valera laid a wreath on Tone's grave after Peadar O'Donnell had called down the customary fire and brimstone on all those who stood in the path of IRA policy. But the following year Fianna Fail were in power and the links between the two movements were becoming more tenuous. In his oration, Sean Russell said of the Dublin parliament, now led by de Valera, what Wolfe Tone had two centuries ago said of Henry Grattan's planters' parliament:

> Of all parliaments beyond all comparison the most shameful and aban-doned of all sense of virtue, principle or even common decency, was the Dublin government.

However, politics are politics and, this said, Mrs Tom Clarke, widow of the 1916 hero and representing the Fianna Fail, laid a wreath on Tone's grave on behalf of the Fianna Fail national executive. On this particular occasion the official army parade was held a week later, for the times were not propitious for the army and politics to mix safely.

In 1935 Tone's graveyard again rang to the sound of blows between the two sections of the movement, further weakening and embittering both sides. The next year, following the murder of Admiral Somerville, the demonstration was banned altogether. It resumed in 1937 but was banned again in 1939. After the war it was the meeting place for those who initiated hostilities on the border in 1955, and was the venue for important public announcements, such as the speech by Christoir O'Neill in 1951 declaring that force would no longer be used against agents of the Southern Irish government but only against those maintaining the status quo in 'Occupied Ireland'.

But a casual observer is not normally aware of this significance. The Bodenstown marchers form up in assembly fields beside the shabby old limestone village of Sallins and then march out to the graveyard itself. All around the area there are encampments of various groups. Stalls do a roaring trade selling teas and ices and people go through the crowds selling booklets with the biographies of various patriots or distributing Republican literature. But the processional route is dotted at intervals by Special Branch cars with walkie-talkies and reputedly more lethal weapons. Special Branch photographers in plain clothes with miniature cameras normally mingle with the crowd taking pictures of those present.

Most of the marchers I have seen at Bodenstown were young men, generally from country districts, but there were also fathers and mothers wheeling prams, and elderly people. Behind the Republicans marched sympathetic groups. A contingent of Communists marched openly on at least one occasion. Here and there an American was to be seen, taking part in a pilgrimage. I once met one very fat old lady, barely able to walk, who had been coming for nearly fifty years. Although there were political overtones to her gesture she was making it in much the same spirit as any other woman of her generation would pay a visit to a noted shrine.

Even on my first visit men with wives and families chatted quite freely with me and, although the fact of my writing a book about the IRA had aroused controversy within the movement (and throughout the day I was shadowed by two young men detailed to watch me by a senior member of the movement who objected to my writing), no one offered me anything other than friendly conversation and the hope that, whatever my views, I would put their case fairly. That was in 1967.

The oration that year was delivered by Cathal Goulding, a good speech which marked a radical turn in Republican policy. He said frankly that the movement's concentration on the removal of partition was a mistake and that social and economic goals must be pursued. Disquietingly and paradoxically, however, he added that to achieve these the option of the use of force must be retained. It was the old bugbear of Republicans manifesting itself again. How to get recruits and retain the support of the militants if force is eschewed? And if it is used how can the support of responsible public opinion be retained?

By a coincidence I listened to his speech in the company of Jack Mulvenna and Roddy Connolly, James Connolly's son. They were old Republican Congress stalwarts who had been involved in fights with the IRA in 1934 and 1935 in that very graveyard for advocating the principles Goulding was putting forward then.

'It's fine but he's thirty years too late,' commented Mulvenna.

As we walked from the graveyard I was chatting with Charlie Murphy, one of the principal organizers of the 1956–62 border campaign. He paused to salute a neighbour, a friendly police superintendent in uniform.

'Force! My God, can you imagine anyone deliberately setting out to kill him?' commented Murphy.

Earlier I had noticed Murphy's wife Carmel standing rigidly to attention as the national anthem was played. She made an attractive picture against the sky, but she had tears in her eyes. As we drove home I asked her why.

'I was just thinking,' she said. 'Poor Wolfe Tone, the man who wanted to unite us all and there today we had three separate commemoration ceremonies and God know how much bitterness as well.'

Violence and tragedy also fringe the edges of the major Orange parade – that on 12 July to commemorate the Battle of the Boyne. It finishes at Finaghy, about three miles from the centre of Belfast, and thereby takes the Orangemen through Catholic areas, with a consequent rise in tension. The Orange banners are gorgeously sumptuous. Brocaded and tasselled they show in bright colours 'King Billy' on a white horse leading his followers across the Boyne, Queen Victoria bestowing a Bible on a blackamoor or dour-faced men with names and styles such as 'James McFettridge, Founder of the Royal Orange Lodge, Temperance Loyal Lodge, No. 708, Shankill Rd.' Union Jacks flutter everywhere and, indeed, the Northern Irish march under symbols of divided allegiance. In the South the Republicans, divided from the Dublin government, nevertheless carry their country's flag.

The Northern speeches are frequently concerned with religion and, since Vatican II, increasingly denunciatory of the ecumenical movement. The Orange processions with their bands, banners and bowlers have a marked Kiplingesque air about them. When passions and Paisleyism subside in the North it is to be hoped that the Orange commemoration will be maintained as a colourful remnant from the past – attended by Irishmen from all parts of Ireland, including those who walk at Bodenstown.

In sport, too, the ugly effects of partition can be felt. Rugby chooses its international team from both sides of the border, but soccer is split between the two states. The Gaelic Athletic Association (GAA), the largest sporting association in Ireland, confines itself to hurling, Gaelic football and handball, and its social occasions are devoted to the Irish language and céile dances. Until comparatively recently, anyone running foreign dances, or attempting to play 'foreign games' such as the former garrison games of rugby, soccer, cricket and hockey, is liable to be reported by the association's vigilante committee and expelled. There are very few Protestants in the GAA and in the North membership of the GAA carries political and religious overtones. Membership is denied to the British Army and the RUC. The authorities retaliate by sometimes harassing players on their way to training, or even, as in Crossmaglen, by damaging playing pitches and installations.

In athletics and cycling too, partition and the shadow of the IRA are noticeable. The Irish Athletic Association, founded in 1885, was the first athletic body to bring working-class people within its scope, thus becoming a national organization. In 1922, the GAA, by then more concerned with hurling and football, handed over control of athletic affairs to a new body, the National Athletics and Cycling Association. Most of the NACA trophies were presented by the IAA which joined the new NACA offering fine, Republican-sounding awards with names like the Lord Ardilaun Trophy and the Wakefield Cup.

A new athletic association was founded in 1937 to provide an international outlet after the suspension of the NACA in 1935 by the

International Federation – because the NACA maintained an 'anti-treaty' attitude and would not accept the border. The AAU 'accepted' the treaty to gain an outlet for international competitors from the South. Those from the six counties were represented by the Unionist-minded North of Ireland Amateur Athletic Association. In April 1967 the NACA and the AAU combined to form Bord Luithchleas na hEireann (BLE) (something similar, as far as NACA was concerned, to Fianna Fail entering the Dail in 1932), which was hailed as a tremendous advance in healing old scars. However, elements in the NACA refused to accept this settlement and led by ex-IRA men such as Jim Killeen, Jack Brady and Joe Christle, they could be said to be the contemporary 'Sinn Fein of Irish sport'.

BIE is recognized by the International Federation as controlling cycling and athletics in the Republic of Ireland, but the dissident wing of the NACA which, under Christle in the 1950s was perennially engaged in clashes with the RUC over carrying tricolours across the border during cycle races, is unworried by the lack of international outlet and this split will not readily heal.

The thirteen Irish language groups which would, on the face of it, appear to be IRA breeding grounds, tend more to enhance existing tendencies than to sow the seeds of Republicanism. The oldest language group, the Gaelic League, was the avenue through which Tarlach O'hUid, then a young man living in London and rejoicing in the name of Hood, first became interested in an Irish Ireland, and ultimately joined the IRA. But he was an exception. Almost all IRA men whom I questioned tended to regard the Gaelic movement as being 'parlour nationalist'. Interest in the language is a facet of their Republicanism rather than its motivating force.

Before 1916 the founder of the Gaelic League, Douglas Hyde, had quit the league because he resented the IRB's infiltration of it for political purposes. Nevertheless, so many IRA men join language classes, sometimes set up by the IRA as front organizations, that after the 1956–62 campaign a former chief of the Special Branch told me that the branch had to regard the language movement as an IRA stamping ground and to warn superiors of certain schools that individual Irish teachers were inciting classes towards militant Republicanism. Several times the police found that captured IRA lads were from a school class that had been influenced by an Irish language enthusiast.

11

Republic and Republicans: II

To understand the post-war IRA, it is vital to understand also the intellectual and religious atmosphere in Ireland at the time and to look at the educational system under which young IRA men had been raised.

Neutrality had screened Ireland from world affairs, leaving her with the literally insular political problems of partition and the IRA. Film and literary censorship had compounded the isolation, cutting off the flow of ideas and helping to stagnate the intellectual climate still further. Television had not come to Ireland except along the south-east coast where BBC programmes could be picked up faintly. And there were the country's religious beliefs affecting the Republican movement through the educational system.

The attitude of Catholics towards Protestants in the South was one of uncertainty rather than of bigotry. An Irish schoolchild speaking of a man who did not go to Mass would not have said: 'He is an agnostic.' He would have said: 'He's a Protestant', because, to the average child, it was only Protestants who did not go to Mass. Only 5 per cent of the South's population is Protestant, so there is no overt Protestant-Catholic clash. Such visible strains as exist are generally confined to rival pressure organizations with a religious character. For instance, it was a matter of pride to the Roman Catholic Knights of Columbus in Dublin that the order had successfully broken the monopoly of the Protestant Masons on the executive board of the Royal Dublin Society.

Nevertheless the religious divisions ran deep and cannot be overlooked. One of de Valera's undoubted achievements was his allaying of the fears of the Protestant minority at his election in 1932. The Protestant *Irish Times* had urged its readers to vote for the Protestant-aiding Cosgrave regime because, 'If Fianna Fail takes office, the wealth and security of every citizen, including the ex-Unionist, will be impaired and perhaps gravely imperilled.' But in office de Valera nominated Douglas Hyde, the Protestant founder of the Gaelic League, as president under his new constitution in 1937. (When Hyde died, the then prime minister, John Costello, and his cabinet did not attend his funeral service because before Vatican II Irish Catholics were forbidden to attend Protestant church services.)

While the fears of Protestants were aroused by the prospect of de Valera in power or by any manifestation of clerical influence, the arms-length attitude which such fears engendered among Protestants was compounded by the fact that, as school children, Catholics learned nothing of phenomena in Church history such as bad popes, the Spanish Inquisition, what the word 'anathema' once signified or that the pope of the day had ordered a *Te Deum* sung in thanksgiving when he heard the outcome of the Battle of the Boyne. But they did learn in their catechisms that, 'There is only one True Church and no one can be saved out of it.' The statement was generally mitigated by a reference to Christ's statement that 'In my Father's house are many mansions' but Protestants were obviously defined as being in a very humble place in the queue for salvation.

Almost no member of my own generation, who left school in the mid-1950s, had the slightest notion of why Protestants should have wanted to remain under British rule in the North, or how religion and politics had become so interwoven that, even in the South, the flags of British regiments can be seen displayed in many Church of Ireland churches and that many Catholic Irishmen will not attend Landsdowne Rugby football ground because there are prominently displayed there the names of former Landsdowne and Wanderers' Rugby Club members who died in the First World War. In some circles, the main entrance to St Stephen's Green Park at the head of Grafton Street, which is similarly inscribed, is known as 'Traitors' gate'.

The educational system, which furthered such prejudices, showed the marks of British influences and of the struggle between the claims of the Church and Irish nationalism which has been going on since the Act of Union in 1800.

The report of a council on education set up on 5 May 1950, to advise the government on the function of the primary school (for pupils under the age of thirteen) and its curriculum says:

'The school exists to assist and supplement the work of parents. Their first duty is to train the children in the fear and love of God. That duty becomes a first purpose of a Primary School . . . the child must *also* [my italics] take his place in human society as a citizen of the

State . . . His training for this is essentially religious and moral.'

Primary schools were under the control of a clerical manager, the local parish priest or vicar, who was responsible for the appointment of teachers and the maintenance of the schools.

So much for the influence of the Church. The Nationalists too have their share. An important guide for parents, *Education in the Irish Republic*, prepared by Professor John O'Meara in 1965, describes the curriculum of a typical primary school of the period as being chiefly concerned with religious doctrine, reading and writing in Irish, and English and arithmetic. In addition there were history, geography, music and (for girls' schools) needlework. One can assess the time spent on these subjects if one remembers the primacy accorded to religious instruction in the council's report and considers the findings of Father John McNamara in his study, *Bilingualism and Primary Education in Ireland*, in which he claims that 42 per cent* of the time spent teaching in national schools was devoted to Irish. Father McNamara was a lecturer in educational psychology in St Patrick's College, Dublin. In his book Father McNamara says that in an English test between two groups of twelve-year-olds, one Irish and the other English, the English children answered three times as many questions correctly as did the Irish. He says that the Irish children had all spent 42 per cent of their time at primary school learning Irish and only 22 per cent of their time learning English.

Arthur Griffith once complained that as a result of British influences, 'Irish education is a means of washing away the original sin of Irish birth'. But in the struggle between the claims of Irish nationalism and those of the Church, neither the Irish primary nor secondary schools' curriculum in the 1940s and 1950s would have given cause to retract his statement. And this was long after the British had left. The Irish language was not restored and if one examines the teaching of three subjects – history, English and Irish – one sees how the effect was to send young people out into the world generally unenlightened about the division of their country, with a strong anti-British bias but a paradoxically strong English bent towards literature, poetry and mode of expression. The courses for the three subjects during those years were laid down in the 'Rules and Programme for Secondary Schools', published annually by the Stationery Office.

---

* In the Dail on 22 July 1969, the minister for education put the figure at 38 per cent in primary school classes and 20 per cent in the senior classes.

History began with 'Early Christian Ireland, the Mission of St Patrick and the spread of Christianity' (which to Irish children, of course, meant the spread of Roman Catholicism) and ended with 'The Resurgence of 1916'. In between, the pupil learned of the invasions by Norsemen and Normans; the Elizabethan wars; the Plantation of Ulster; Cromwell; the Williamite wars; the penal laws; the famine, and the movements led by O'Connell, the Young Irelanders, the Fenians, Parnell and Arthur Griffith; and finally the 1916 Rising. European and world history were scarcely taught at all; only a smattering of European affairs was imparted, ending about the period of the French Revolution. Almost no Irish schoolchild, to my knowledge, learned anything about the pre-First World War era and from the Treaty of Versailles to Malta was a time unknown. Moreover the rules stipulated that, 'The Irish History Course will deal only with the period from 1014 to 1921.' This in practice meant that the teaching of history ended at 1916 and children never acquired a classroom knowledge of the Protestant drift away from Catholic power to the North and the emergence of a situation in which partition became possible, or the circumstances of the Anglo-Irish war and the Civil War. These were learned about later, either from the subjective viewpoint of relatives, or from polemic writings in Republican journals.

The English literature course gave the student very little assistance in broadening his mind, and shuts off his access to the writings of his fellow countrymen. A typical leaving certificate English course (that for 1951–52) offered one Shakespearian play, Hamlet and one poem each by Shakespeare, Milton, Wordsworth, Shelley, Coleridge, Tennyson, and one by Yeats ('The Lake Isle of Innishfree'). Essays by Lamb, Leigh Hunt, Grey, Thackeray, Belloc, Addison, Ruskin, Newman and R. L. Stevenson were also included. Earlier in the intermediate course pupils would have done slightly better, with one essay by an Irish author, Thomas Davis. Their poetry course would have included one poem each by Aubrey de Vere, Emily Lawless, D'Arcy Magee and James Clarence Mangan.

In the Irish course students read works about the 1916 period such as 'Mo Dhá Rosin' (My Two Rosaleens), a tale of young lovers parted by death in the 1916 Rising and 'Mo Sceal Fein', by An tAthair Peadar O'Laoghaire, the story of an Irish parish priest at the turn of the century. This story, describing the priest's battles with the British authorities, gave me, at any rate, the false impression that the clergy were on the side of the language revival. They were, in fact, anti-Irish because a knowledge of English enabled the Irish Church to spread throughout the British Empire.

Irish stories in the secondary school courses recreated the struggle between Church and nationalist ideologies by imparting both a propagandist and religious favour. Themes such as the great famine were balanced by those about outwitting the power of the devil, as in the book *Seadna*, or supernatural manifestations such as that of the Christ Child in Padraig Pearse's *Isogain*.

Both Church and state were faced with a difficulty in teaching history. The system of education had given the Church a powerful source of strength through its ability to channel so much of the energy and talent of Irish boys and girls into its ranks, and to control the quantity of Irish intellectual life. In Europe, at this time, Ireland, with a population North and South of four million, ranked next to the Netherlands in the actual number of Catholic missionaries sent abroad, and above Germany and France. During 1968, a year of special emphasis by the Church on missionary endeavour, Church apologists pointed with pride to the fact that the proportion of Ireland's resources expended on missionary activities was equal in percentage terms to American military expenditure in the Vietnam war.

This position was achieved by skilful Church diplomacy in playing ball with the British. But the British were, by definition, Ireland's enemies. How could this diplomacy be explained to children? For the state, after the Civil War, the problem was to give children a knowledge of highly contentious issues involving not only living persons in the two major political parties, and hundreds of thousands outside, but also the memories of recent deaths, imprisonments, hunger strikes, burnings and the many brutalities associated with the Civil War, partition and the settling of old scores. The simple answer decided on by both parties was to teach no history after 1916, and to outline very sketchily events of the nineteenth century.

In the North, a somewhat similar situation existed. The Catholic children received much the same historical instruction as do those of the South and some Irish was also taught. But the Protestant children learned almost nothing of Irish history and were instead instructed in the history of Britain. In both cases, North and South, Protestant and Catholic classrooms tended to impart the facts of the past with a gloss which took note of contemporary politics, though in both quality and volume the educational position has improved considerably since the 1950s. When I left school in Dublin in 1954 some six thousand secondary school pupils sat for their Leaving Certificate Examination. In 1969 this figure had increased to about seventy thousand.

A Telefís Eireann series of illustrated lectures on 'The Course of Irish History' during the 1916 celebrations, edited by Father F. X. Martin of University College, Dublin, and Professor Moody of Trinity College, Dublin, appeared in paperback and had an enormous sale. During this period I was shown in confidence a memorandum drawn up by a group of parents, educationalists and historians at the request of the government for use as a guide in creating more realistic history courses. It later became policy and helped to improve matters.* In the North a reappraisal of the history situation also got under way and the BBC did valuable work in televising a series of programmes similar to those by Telefís Eireann and reprinting them in book form. In general, in the wake of enthusiasm for the study of Irish history (generated by the commemoration of the 1916 Rising in 1966) and the goodwill that sprang from meetings between Republican Prime Minister Sean Lemass and the North's Captain Terence O'Neill in January and February, 1965, contemporary interest tended to focus on the civil rights movement rather than on how the border might be blown away – until the years after the 1969 upheavals.

It was the colourful Minister for Education, Donough O'Malley, who died in 1968, who led the move to improve the Southern Irish educational system – and it has improved out of all recognition. In the 1950s the kind of educational system I have outlined was the only one available to the vast majority of Irish schoolchildren. The governmental report, 'Investment in Education', prepared under the chairmanship of Professor Patrick Lynch, in 1966 revealed that over 50 per cent of Irish children left school at twelve.

Post-war politics had, of course, a great effect on the policies and organization of the IRA. The general election of February 1948 reaffirmed the high priority which partition and Republicanism were given in Irish affairs. Ireland had escaped the war but could not escape the post-war unemployment, high taxation, strikes and unrest. Fianna Fail had been in power for sixteen years and the country wanted a

* Also appearing in 1966 was my own effort to provide the first attempt at an objective survey of the years 1916–66, *Ireland Since the Rising*. It proved popular and was made recommended reading for university students of history.

change. But while these issues were prominently discussed during the campaign, the political reaction which they generated was canalized by the Republican movement, or more accurately by a part of it, Clann na Poblachta, which came into prominence concerned not so much with the new problems as with the old problem of partition.

The formation of Clann na Poblachta was the most important break in the ranks of 'physical force' Republicanism since the creation of Fianna Fail in 1926. For Eamon de Valera there was now Sean MacBride, and in place of the land annuities' question the tuberculosis issue presented itself. Some old Republicans, most notably Patrick MacLogan and Maurice Twomey, said 'No' to joining. However, a number of old Republicans, including Con Lehane, Michael Fitzpatrick, Nod Hartnett, Jim Killeen, Donal O'Donoghue, Dr Richard Battenbury and Finian Brenacht came together under MacBride's leadership. At public meetings throughout the country and at private ones in the Teachers' club in Dublin, the new party mushroomed into vigorous life, even enlisting people who had been on opposite sides in the Civil War.

The scheme that most caught the public imagination was a proposal to concentrate on the eradication of tuberculosis, which was then both a social and medical evil. For some reason syphilis carried less of a social stigma than did tuberculosis in 1948. The tuberculosis issue was the brainchild of Dr Noel Browne, not a Republican but a brilliant young socialist educated at Trinity. The Clann backed him in his programme for new sanatoria and immunization which proved a success (deaths from tuberculosis had fallen to 431 by 1961 from 3,101 in 1948) but deserted him in 1951 when the Church hierarchy objected to a health act which would have provided sex instruction from state medical staffs and would have thus taken what the hierarchy regarded as *moral* instruction out of the hands of the Church. The hierarchy also objected to free care for anyone, regardless of income. The government fell in the ensuing uproar.

The Clann also introduced the novel idea of seating Northerners in parliament, but as far as ending partition was concerned, this was a flop. In Dublin the seating of the two Northerners in the senate was taken as a sign of crossborder unity but in Belfast the move was regarded with deep suspicion. One of the men was Denis Ireland, who in the Unionist view had shown a renegade's colours by the foundation of the Irish Union movement. The other, Liam Kelly, was known to advocate the use of physical force and did in fact lead armed attacks against the North.

In the South, however, for the moment all was excitement and optimism. Clann na Poblachta, which got 173,166 votes, won ten seats in the elections of 4 February 1948, and Sean MacBride and Dr Noel Browne become ministers of external affairs and of health respectively on 18 February when the new Dail met.

The new prime minister was John A. Costello of Fine Gael. He led a heterogeneous coalition which ousted Fianna Fail, 75 votes to 68. The left-wing Clann na Poblachta formed a government with Labour, which was split into two factions: National Labour; and the right-wing Fine Gael. Costello said that 'the principal objective' on which these parties were agreed was the ending of partition.

In September, during a visit to Canada, Costello anounced that the government intended to repeal the External Relations Act. The statement aroused considerable surprise in Ireland. MacBride and William Norton of Labour were on record as favouring such a course, but Fine Gael during the election campaign had reaffirmed its traditional support of the Commonwealth and had subsequently said nothing to indicate a change of heart. But despite much controversy and debate the Dail unanimously agreed to pass the Republic of Ireland Act which received the president's signature on 21 December. The date when the bill would go into force was held over until the following year.

Then on 20 January 1949, the Northern premier, Sir Basil Brooke, announced that a general election would be held on 10 February. On 25 January, Costello invited the leaders of all political parties to confer on how their 'assistance can be given to the Anti-Partition candidates contesting seats at the General Election in the six NE Counties'. Two days later at an all-party meeting in the Mansion House, Dublin, it was decided that a public subscription should be opened to set up an anti-partition fund. This Mansion House committee and its offspring the Anti-Partition League provided a torrent of propaganda about partition and published a tide of pamphlets describing discrimination and gerrymandering.

The Mansion House committee collected more than fifty thousand pounds. Part was devoted to supporting anti-partition candidates in the North in the general election and the rest to purposes such as sending anti-partition speakers like Tom Barry and Denis Ireland on tours of America and Britain to inveigh against the border. (De Valera, too, went on a world tour to highlight the partition issue.) The all-party conference also chose the date of the Northern Ireland general election, 10 February, to announce 18 April – Easter Monday – as the date on which the Republic of Ireland Act would come into force.

All this of course played straight into the Unionists' hands. For years they had manipulated sectarian fears so that the average working-class Northern Protestant was conditioned to believe that if the border went, loyal Protestants would be trampled underfoot by hordes of IRA gunmen egged on by Catholic clergy. For one instance there is an alleged version of the Sinn Fein oath which circulates through the Orange Lodges. It was published in the April 1967 issue of the *Protestant Telegraph*, the organ of the Rev. Ian Paisley. The oath is supposed to read in part:

> These Protestant robbers and brutes, these unbelievers of our faith, will be driven like the swine they are into the sea by fire, the knife or by poison cup until we of the Catholic Faith and avowed supporters of all Sinn Fein action and principles, clear these heretics from our land . . .
>
> At any cost we must work and seek, using any method of deception to gain our ends towards the destruction of all Protestants and the advancement of the priesthood and the Catholic Faith until the Pope is complete ruler of the whole world . . .
>
> We must strike at every opportunity, using all methods of causing ill-feeling within the Protestant ranks and in their business. The employment of any means will be held by our earthly Fathers, the priests, and thrice blessed by His Holiness the Pope.
>
> So shall we of the Roman Catholic Church and Faith destroy with smiles of thanksgiving to our Holy Father the Pope all who shall not join us and accept our beliefs.

The Northern electorate rallied to the polls for the Unionists in such numbers as to blot out the Northern Ireland Labour party, even to the exclusion of the outstanding figure of Jack Beatty who had represented Mount Pottinger for twenty-four years, and to return the Unionists with the same majority as they held in 1921: 40 seats to 12.

In the South, however, the coalition government pressed ahead towards the Republic, which was born to the accompaniment of a twenty-one gun salute on Easter Monday. Fianna Fail boycotted the christening because de Valera said that the party stood for a thirty-two, not a twenty-six county Republic. The ceremony at the GPO building was emotional and impressive, recalling memories of 1916. I was a child of twelve at the time and as I stood with my mother on the reviewing platform (my father, the general secretary of Fine Gael, had died shortly before), the flags, the *feu de joie*, the marching soldiers, all raised within me emotions which, had I been older, could well have drawn me towards the IRA and its stand against the border.

Constitutionally as well as electorally the Unionists gained from the anti-partition campaign. In response to their alarm at the declaration of the Republic, British Prime Minister Clement Attlee introduced the Ireland Act in the House of Commons on 3 May. This contained the following provision:

'It is hereby declared that Northern Ireland remains part of Her Majesty's Dominions of the United Kingdom and it is hereby affirmed that in no event will Northern Ireland or any part thereof cease to be part of Her Majesty's Dominions and the United Kingdom without the consent of the Parliament of Northern Ireland.'

The new Republic was outraged at this reaction to its birth. In the Dail on 9 May all parties agreed to Costello's resolution proclaiming 'indignant protest against the introduction by the British Parliament of legislation purporting to endorse and continue the existing Partition of Ireland', and calling on the British government to 'end the present occupation of our six North Eastern Counties'. Costello in his speech added, 'We can hit the British in their pride, pocket and prestige and every effort we can make we will make if they present us with that horrible alternative.'

The country responded with mass meetings, county council resolutions, thunder from the letters to the editor and editorials in all the leading newspapers. Slogans on walls all over the country announced that the 'Border Must Go.' But the Ireland Act became law the following June and for the IRA, trying to pick itself up off the ground after the war years, nothing could have been more welcome than all this concentration on partition.

These were the constitutional events that aided the rebirth of violence and death, a cycle that had for so long characterized Irish Protestant and Catholic failure to stop hating each other.

In the unconstitutional IRA, the principal figure in the reorganization which took place when the detainees were released from the Curragh was the priest-like Anthony Magan, a bachelor and County Meath farmer who had given all his money, time and thought to the

IRA, a deeply religious man of the old-guard school of Irish Catholic-ism. In the Curragh he and Michael Conway had been the main leaders of the pro-Irish and pro-Gaelic culture group in the camp. Conway actually went into the Church and several people I inter-viewed told me that they felt that Magan belonged there too: when he was again interned in the Curragh during the 1956–62 campaign he organized a flourishing branch of the Legion of Mary. He was taken into the IRA by Jim Killeen but after Killeen helped to form Clann na Polbachta Magan ignored him. For a man who contributed most of his waking hours and all of his family inheritance to the Republican movement such deviation was treachery. He was continually in pain from rheumatism during the 1950s but he never allowed this to interfere with his lengthy drives, all-night meetings or day and night organizational activity. A stern, unbending figure whose intransigence drove many people out of the army, he nevertheless had a compassion for his men, especially noticeable after raids when his first question was never, 'How did it go?' but, 'Is everyone all right?'

When Magan, Conway, and to a lesser extent Sean McCool, began to reorganize the IRA the situation was vague and confused, almost like that after the end of the Civil War. Organization was practically non-existent and both the ex-internees and their sympathizers who had escaped the net were deeply divided. But Magan and Conway persevered. The first general meeting of Republicans came at Bodenstown in June 1945. There, in the inner assembly field, Magan, Conway and McCool suggested a reorganization. After Bodenstown the idea spread, very slowly, until an apparent reversal actually enhanced its chances and the post-war strength of the IRA increased.

This was the Ardee Street raid on 9 March 1946, in which a number of prominent Republicans were arrested, including Peadar O'Flaherty, Patrick Fleming, Cathal Goulding and John Joe McGirl. Magan and Conway were also picked up the following morning. What changed this apparent set-back into a springboard for further activity was that a document found at Fleming's home was read out in court and reprinted by the *Irish Press*. Republicans throughout the country were thus informed that an IRA reorganization was taking place. The document contained the following:

'That this meeting composed of representatives of the Cork and Dublin, Leitrim and Mayo units and of the surviving members of the 1938 Army Council resolves that the surviving members of the 1938–9 executive be summoned to a meeting for the purpose of bringing the executive up to full strength and electing an executive drawn from active volunteers.'

It was not realized at the time that publication would have an inspirational effect and Magan and Conway were convinced that disaster had befallen. They had arrived for the meeting in the Ardee Bar and found Special Branch men watching the premises as prominent Republicans walked past them, unknowingly, towards certain jail sentences. Their agitation was so great that they never thought of telephoning to warn those inside. Walking around the block, hoping to warn off late arrivals, they exchanged coats, but this ruse was noticed by the watching police who, however, allowed them to go free until the next morning. They were then both picked up at their digs, having spent a sleepless night trying to warn IRA men who might have known of the meeting to prepare for visits from the police. They were given four months each and the eight other young men picked up in the raid received nine to twelve months each.

The IRA also gained useful publicity that year from the death of McCaughey which occurred in the same month that the Stormont released a prominent IRA man, David Fleming, because of ill-health, and from the trial of Harry White. IRA drilling began again and, particularly in the North, 'the Army' began to infiltrate Irish language classes, debating classes, GAA clubs and kindred bodies. The Sinn Fein party was reactivated and a newspaper, the *United Irishman*, was started in July 1947. The stage was set for a new outbreak of violence.

12

Prelude to the Border Campaign

Reflecting on the disasters of the war years Magan originated a new policy, stating publicly that it was to be used solely against the Northern administration. This policy was proclaimed at Bodenstown in 1949 by Christoir O'Neill when he said:

'The aim of the Army is simply to drive the invader from the soil of Ireland and to restore the sovereign independent Republic proclaimed in 1916. To that end, the policy is to prosecute a successful military campaign against the British forces of occupation in the Six Counties.'

This aim was unpopular with many of the rank and file, who wanted 'the Army' to turn what they conceived to be its limitless legions against the Special Branch, members of the government, and, above all, against Stephen Hayes. The subject of his elimination was discussed continuously until during a particularly stormy meeting Magan suddenly produced a revolver, handed it to one fire-eater and said, 'Here, you execute him yourself.' The subject was never mentioned again. However, splinter group activities, or some undisciplined IRA man's firing of shots at a neighbour's house or letting off of gelignite bombs became magnified into nation-wide rumours of coups or assassination plots and the IRA had, from time to time, to repeat its avowal concerning the use of force solely against the North lest the Southern government be prompted to take action.

The Army Council statement of Easter 1950 said that 'in order that no excuse may be provided for using coercion and to define quite clearly that the Irish Republican Army had only one enemy, England, no sanction will be given for any type of aggressive military action in the Twenty-Six County area'. The statement for the following Easter said 'all types of aggression in the Twenty-Six County area are ruled out'. But it was not until after the Omagh raid of October 1954 that the Army Council formally told the various units that this was now official policy and incorporated it into the 'General

Army Orders'. From that month, Standing Order Number Eight read as follows:

1. Volunteers are strictly forbidden to take any militant action against 26-Co. Forces *under any circumstances whatsoever*. The importance of this Order in present circumstances especially in the Border areas cannot be over-emphasized.
2. Minimum arms drill shall be used in training in the Twenty-Six County areas. In the event of a raid every effort shall be made to get the arms away safely. If this fails, the arms shall be rendered useless and abandoned.
3. Maximum security precautions must be taken when meeting. Scouts must always be posted to warn of emergency. Volunteers arrested during training or in possession of arms will point out that the arms were for use against the British Forces of Occupation only. This statement should be repeated at all subsequent Court proceedings.
4. *At all times* Volunteers must make it clear that the policy of the Army is to drive the British Forces of Occupation out of Ireland.

Despite an occasional lapse, such as that which caused the death of Garda Clerkin (see later), the policy still holds as of today.

IRA influence over Sinn Fein grew between 1946 and 1949. Speaking at Bodenstown in 1949 Cristoir O'Neill, at the time vice-president of Sinn Fein, said:

'The Republican movement is divided into two main bodies – the Military and the Civil Arms, the Irish Republican Army and Sinn Fein. Each has an important task to do. In the final analysis the work of either is as important as that of the other.'

The drawbacks of a 'physical force' policy with the IRA's resources were very much apparent to the survivors of the violent era of the 1940s who now emerged as the principal Republican leaders – the 'three Macs', as they were popularly known, Anthony Magan, Thomas MacCurtain and Padraig MacLogan. For a period of almost ten years after the end of the Second World War they discouraged an armed campaign against the North, and the decade gives evidence of political rather than military activity.

MacLogan, OC of South Armagh during the Anglo-Irish war, was the chief political thinker of Sinn Fein. He operated a public house in Portlaoise and his name became familiar during the agitation to release the prisoners in Portlaoise jail at the end of the Second

World War. Like Magan, he was a man of deep religious conviction. Time-keeping in his pub was meticulous. No drunkenness or profanity was allowed. He met his wife on a pilgrimage to Lourdes and I think it symbolizes his combination of religious and conspiratorial outlook that he should have kept his secret IRA papers hidden in an altar that he made himself. He also headed the co-ordinating committee between Sinn Fein and the IRA, and one can see how the degree of control which the IRA exercised over the party had extended from the results of the Sinn Fein Ard Fheis of 7 October 1951.

Mrs Margaret Buckley, president of Sinn Fein throughout the war, was demoted to merely a member of the Ard Comhairle (the controlling body) which now included Anthony Magan. MacLogan became president and the vice-presidents were Michael Traynor and Tom Doyle, who had initiated the Magazine Fort raid. Charlie Murphy, who was shortly to become adjutant-general of the IRA, became joint secretary with Sean Kearney, who later left to become a priest. Patrick Doyle, who had been sentenced to life imprisonment in Belfast during the war, was also elected to the Ard Comhairle. (There were some differences in policy among them. Traynor, for instance, was not happy that the IRA's *de jure* position in the eyes of the movement should give the IRA control over democratically elected Sinn Fein representatives and he felt very strongly that the IRA should not control Sinn Fein).

Traynor and the 'three Macs' shared, however, the view that Ireland's fortunes would improve if the link with England were broken. They all wanted an end to partition.

They also favoured the social teachings of the papal encyclical *Rerum Novarum* – generally in Ireland in the early 1950s opinion favoured vocationalism – and they opposed the welfare state, which (though they failed to grasp the fact) was steadily driving a wedge between North and South as the standard of living in the North rose because of the British ties they were trying to persuade Northern Catholics to break. The entire Ard Comhairle felt that the welfare state destroyed the concept of the individual, who to them was not a tool to be brought out on election day but a being who should have a continuing influence on his own economic set-up.

Their major political activity then was to draft a Sinn Fein programme to embody these beliefs within a movement that had traditionally rallied mass support not for social and economic policies but for the use of force, and which also held to two basic concepts of Republicanism: Wolfe Tone's 'Breaking the link with England', and Terence MacSwiney's, 'When Ireland was wholly free Ireland was wholly Gaelic. When Ireland was wholly Gaelic, Ireland was wholly free.'

MacLogan, helped by Traynor and another prominent ex-internee, Frank MacGlynn, drew up a new constitution for Sinn Fein along with two other important plans: the 'National Unity and Independence Programme of Sinn Fein', and the 'Social and Economic Programme of Sinn Fein'. All were vetted by sympathetic clergy to ensure that they contained nothing contrary to Catholic teaching. The principles of the new constitution have a familiar look:

'That the allegiance of Irishmen and Irishwomen is due to the sovereign Irish Republic proclaimed in 1916.

'That the sovereignty and unity of the Republic are inalienable and non-judicable . . .'

Its objectives were:

The complete overthrow of English rule in Ireland.

To bring the Proclamation of the Republic, Easter 1916, into effective operation and to maintain and consolidate the Government of the Republic, representative of the people of all Ireland, based on that Proclamation.

To establish in the Republic a reign of social justice, based on Christian principles, by a just distribution and effective control of the Nation's wealth and resources, and to institute a system of government suited to the particular needs of the people.

To promote the restoration of the Irish Language and Irish Culture and the widest knowledge of Ireland's history; to make Irish citizens conscious and proud of their traditional and cultural heritage; and to educate the citizens of the Republic in their rights and responsibilities.

Other traditional IRA policies which were retained included the non-recognition of the courts and Dail Eireann. No barrier, however, was placed on membership of local government bodies which levied a large proportion of the taxes without which parliament could not have functioned.

As the Republican movement gathered strength after the war the 'three Macs' planned, not border raids and the blowing up of bridges, but a policy of passive resistance. Michel Traynor told me that a scheme for withholding rates was worked out: the IRA would protect the nationalist sympathizers who supported the idea. But the controversial question of the use of force caused a rupture within the movement as early as 1949 with the founding of the *United Irishman*. (Its first editor was Seamus G. O'Reilly, who worked from an office at 38, King St, Dublin, and produced the first issue in July 1948).

The paper was Republican in tone, but not controlled by the IRA, owing its origins to sixty pounds collected by members, principally Seamus Doyle and Tom Byrne, of a Republican club named after McCaughey. It was supported strongly by prominent Republicans no longer active in the IRA. But during 1948 the IRA became interested in it and MacLogan demanded representation on the editorial board. A row developed over the suggestion that the paper advocate the IRA's blowing up of customs huts along the border, to capitalize on anti-British feelings generated by recent political speeches. The row ended with Doyle, Byrne and Kelly severed from their connections with the paper.

Subsequent issues openly urged readers to 'Join the IRA'. The paper was against the 'Free State' (the change to a Republic altered neither the IRA's attitude nor terminology), anti-Free Mason, anti-Communist, anti-British, and opposed to Irish newspapers carrying advertisements for jobs in England. The difference between the opposing parties was succinctly put in a letter of resignation from the paper which Michael Traynor wrote on 4 January 1949:

'The difference between us is tactical, we are fully agreed on basic principles. Yet, I have stated time after time, on the committee and before the committee was formed, that I would not be a party to organizing the youth of Ireland to use force for the mere sake of using force.'

The difference between the activists and those who favoured passive resistance was more than 'tactical'. It was also the difference between one generation and another, between the men who had seen what 'action' could lead to and those who sought excitement without thinking of its consequences. As the movement gathered strength the activists gradually gained in influence and their urgings finally resulted in the campaign which began on 12 December 1956. But prior to this the exponents of force had incited the IRA to carry out six raids, of which four were unsuccessful, and to plan a number of other operations, none of which came off. In this period the movement also suffered three splits: those caused by Brendan O'Boyle, Liam Kelly and Joseph Christle.

Within the IRA proper the leading young activists were Charlie Murphy, Robert Russell, Eamonn Boyce, Tom Mitchell, Rory Brady and Joe Christle.

Charlie Murphy, a young Dubliner, was at the time a tall, striking-looking figure with prematurely grey hair. A clerk in the Guinness brewery, he had joined the IRA in 1950, at nineteen, after anti-partition slogans such as 'Let's Finish the Job' had put a match to the powder trail laid by a nationalist family and his boyhood reading about the War of Independence. He answered an advertisement seeking help for Republican prisoners and met Tom Doyle of Sinn Fein. From the start he showed an unusual aptitude for intelligence work, one of his exploits being to obtain a camera in the shape of a fountain pen with which he photographed the entire Special Branch and compiled a card index system giving their names, addresses and numbers of their automobiles.

Robert Russell joined the movement because of family influences; he was a nephew of Sean Russell. (He later married May Smith who became chair of Sinn Fein.)

Eamonn Boyce, who led the Omagh raid and was sentenced to ten years, later married and became a bus inspector. In 1953 he had not been aware of the IRA's existence until one day he passed a large hoarding advertising an English Sunday newspaper series about the IRA and showing a trench-coated figure carrying two guns. By chance, his companion at the time was Matty O'Neill, a former Curragh internee. He remarked on the garishness of the poster thinking that this portrayal had something to do with the War of Independence. He was surprised when Matty replied, 'Sure, them that's running it now don't mind.' Amazed that the IRA was still in existence, Boyce made further enquiries which led to his becoming a member when he was twenty-two.

Tom Mitchell, who was also sentenced to ten years for the Omagh raid, became leader of the prisoners at the Crumlin Road jail in Belfast. Elected to Westminster as MP for mid-Ulster he was un-seated as a convicted felon in 1955 and now works as an official with Dublin Corporation – appropriately enough inspecting dangerous buildings! A formative influence on him was a lay teacher at St Joseph's Christian Brothers school at Marino, North Co., Dublin. The teacher, later interned, was nationalistic in his interpretation of history and equated Republicanism with religion. Mitchell began to read about the wartime shootings and executions, attended Sinn Fein meetings in Abbey Street, enrolled in Sinn Fein and gravitated to the IRA.

Rory Brady is from Roscommon. His parents were dedicated Republicans and he himself took part in some of the most memorable events of the 1950s, including the Arborfield raid and an escape from the Curragh internment camp. He became chief of staff for a brief period in the later stages of the border campaign. (He was a vocational school teacher until 1969.)

These young men went on holidays together, chiefly to the Irish-speaking district in the west, the Gaelteacht, and, apart from their Republicanism, shared a common interest in the Irish language and culture. At the time none of them thought more deeply about the border issue than that the British should be driven out of the North and did not appreciate the part religion played in partition. The social or economic conditions which would follow if they succeeded in their objective did not trouble them greatly. They had only an undefined feeling that the new state ought to be somehow Gaelic.

In the 1940s and early 1950s the number of men coming and going seemed quite large but in fact the movement was neither strong nor widely spread. In Cork there was, of course, Thomas MacCurtain, and older Republicans such as Michael MacCarthy and Gerry MacCarthy (no relation), J. F. Reegan, who had fought with Frank Ryan in Spain, and a number of younger men of Murphy's and Mitchell's generation. In Limerick there was Willie Gleeson. In Portlaoise, MacLogan's base, there were some reliable men, in particular Terry O'Toole. In Lurgan there was Joe O'Hagan. In Leitrim, a county with a long tradition of rebellion, John Joe McGirl. In Drogheda Larry Grogan, who had signed the proclamation declaring the start of the bombing campaign against England. In Dundalk there was Liam Fagan. In Derry, Eamonn Timmoney and Seamus Ramsaigh were unusually good men.

In Belfast the movement was numerically strong – Charlie Murphy told me that he remembered inspecting parades, as adjutant-general, at which there must have been hundreds present. But the fire and passion which once animated the Republicans were missing. So was most of their motivation. There had been no sectarian rioting since 1935 and the comradeship of the years had taken some of the sting out of the Protestant-Catholic relationship. Nevertheless, the IRA group in Belfast was, willy-nilly, formed on a sectarian basis. No Protestants now attached themselves to the cause and the movement was almost entirely an armed Catholic one, although not representative of all Catholics. The welfare state having been introduced to the North many former Nationalists were secretly disposed to support the British link. Moreover security was weak. Incidents took place which made the Dublin IRA think that the RUC had sources of information in Belfast which would prejudice any attempted rising there. Bearing these in mind and also the possibility of inciting reprisals against the Catholics, whom they would not be strong enough to protect, the IRA Leaders decided to take no action in Belfast when the border campaign began.

The pendulum had swung from the time of the Hayes affair when Northerners went south to direct the IRA – now it was to be Southerners who largely controlled the movement and directed its energies northward.

The major raids initiated before the outreak of the border campaign were:

5 June 1951, Ebrington Barracks, Derry.
25 July 1953, Felstead School Officers' Training Corps, Essex.
12 June 1954, Gough Barracks, Armagh.
7 October 1954, Omagh Military Barracks.
24 April 1955, Eglington Naval Air Base, Derry.
13 August 1955, Arborfield Depot, Berkshire.

Neither the Ebrington raid nor that on Felstead attracted much attention but they did alert the RUC to the need for strengthening the Northern defence.

Before the Ebrington raid the Derry unit, like every other section of the IRA, had been subject to a high turnover of membership. The unit had been approximately one hundred and fifty strong in the years 1938–39 but wartime imprisonments cut down this strength and the unit was almost non-existent during 1943–45. However, following the release of internees in August 1945, some reorganization began, and by 1947 the unit was functioning again, at least to the extent of drilling. But this fact was so well concealed that no one was aware of the unit's existence until the IRA issued a statement from Dublin saying that an arms haul had been made.

Even then a number of people in the North believed that the raid was a figment of some B-Special's imagination. Hugh McAteer's brother Eddie, the Nationalist leader, issued a statement to this effect but the raid was genuine. The IRA seized twenty Lee Enfield rifles, twenty Sten machine-carbines, two Bren light machine-guns, six BESA 7.92 mm belt-fed machine-guns and a quantity of .303 and .9 mm ammunition.

After this raid the IRA drills attracted more members and a spate of incidents occurred. RUC intelligence improved and the RUC began to build up defences against any large-scale campaign. RUC commando units were formed, manned by personnel who had seen active service during the Second World War; wireless communications were improved, and security and fortifications at all military installations were considerably tightened.

The raid on the armoury of the Felstead School Officers' Training Corps was more ambitious and was initially successful. The raiders got away with ninety-nine rifles, eight Bren guns, ten Sten guns, a Piat anti-tank gun, a 2-inch mortar and a Browning machine-gun. But the next morning, at Bishop's Stortford, the police, noticing a suspicious van with its rear windows obscured by strips of paper and smeared with whitening material, stopped it and found the weapons inside. Three men were arrested: Cathal Goulding, Sean Stephenson and Manus Canning. The next October they were sentenced to eight years after a jury in Hertfordshire had taken one minute to find a verdict of guilty.

After sentence Goulding, who accepted responsibility as leader of the raid, said, 'We believe that the only way to drive the British Army from our country is by force of arms, for that purpose we think it no crime to capture arms from our enemies. We make no apology for our action.' However, this declaration by Goulding, a Dublin housepainter whose father had been active in the War of Independence, aroused little echo in Ireland as the raid had been a small one and had occurred in England. It was the Gough raid, in Armagh, which caught the Irish attention. It brought, furthermore, many young men into the movement as well as arousing considerable support in America.

Six months or so before the raid Leo McCormick, training officer for Dublin, noted on a visit to Armagh that the sentry outside the barracks had no magazine in his Sten gun. He felt that some use could be made of this discovery, but his plans were interrupted when he was picked up by the RUC for having incriminating documents on him and sent to jail. Charlie Murphy and Eamonn Boyce then decided that the thing to do was to plant someone in the barracks.

They called on another young Dubliner (nameless as he is still in the IRA) and told him they wanted him to join the British army. He agreed immediately and was posted to Armagh. To keep contact with him,

Murphy, Boyce and various girls used to travel to Armagh on Saturday nights to attend the soldiers' dances. They would leave the hall, ostensibly to court the girls but really to contact their plant and reconnoitre the barracks. In this way they learned enough to plan a raid for 12 June 1954.

The operation was launched from a farm outside Dundalk about a mile south of the border. There they struck a snag when the expected lorry didn't turn up. They therefore sent word to a local haulier telling him that there was a load of cattle to be shifted, and when he arrived they hustled him into a tent and took his lorry. They also had a car, the occupants of which were to take over the guardroom. There were nineteen raiders, armed with Thompsons, short-arms, grenades and burglary implements. Everything worked perfectly. It was nearly three o'clock on a busy Saturday afternoon when the car drove through the barracks' gate. The gang held up the guardroom, hurried the sentry away from the gate and in his place put a man who, because of his training in Ireland's equivalent of the Territorial Army, was able to march up and down in front of the gate in convincing fashion. (The lorry coming behind the car overshot the gate and had to reverse and a British army lorry, also making for the gate, courteously pulled up to allow the IRA in first and drove by without noticing anything amiss.)

Murphy raced up the stairs to the armoury ahead of the others. He had trouble getting his revolver out of his pocket and was further embarrassed when the two soldiers in the armoury refused to put up their hands. However, another IRA man arrived carrying a Thompson gun which overawed the pair. Positioning a Bren gun at the armoury window to command the barracks' square they started loading. As each IRA man came into the armoury he held out his arms and Murphy stacked him up with as many guns as he could carry. They got away with three hundred and forty rifles, fifty Sten guns, twelve Bren guns (most of which were non-operational), and a number of .22 mm arms.

During the course of the raid a woman, noticing that something was wrong, had stopped an officer in the street and urged him to go into the barracks and do something. Once inside the gate the officer was taken under control and, protesting that he was an officer and a gentleman, refused to be tied until a gun was put to his head. An NCO then noticed what was happening, got into a lorry and drove for the gate, intending to block the exit. But one of the raiders stood in the gate and brandishing a revolver said, 'Back', and forced the NCO to back the lorry across the barracks' square. Then he too was placed under guard in the guardroom.

The lorry containing the arms was driven away first, Boyce and the group in the car following after locking every gate and door for which they could find keys. (The keys were subsequently auctioned in America to raise funds for the IRA.) Luck attended the men in the lorry all the way back across the border. At the Monaghan side of the border an obliging RUC man gave them the right of way and they drove the remaining seven miles without incident. Boyce met them and handed over the small arms that he and the others had carted. Everyone got into the lorry and they drove on to a dump in Co. Meath where they met Magan. His first question was, 'Is everyone all right?'

The men were dismissed, some to find their way back to Dublin by bus, others, including Joe Christle and Eamonn Boyce, to return to Dublin in the lorry. Boyce sat in the body of the lorry but Christle got into the driver's cabin and, instead of following the pre-arranged route, he ordered the driver to go by the main road. On the outskirts of Dublin, a squad car, alerted to the fact that the raid had taken place, attempted to block their path. Christle ordered the driver to ram the squad car, which pulled out of the way. Later, when the lorry was being returned to its owner, two men in it were captured and interrogated. They were subsequently released as the Southern government was embarrassed by the whole affair and wished to make as little of it as possible. It was given out that nothing incriminating was found in the truck, although in fact two revolvers were seized.

The raid was a tremendous source of morale for the IRA but fears were aroused by an article in the *Irish Times* speculating that the arms were intended for use in the South. To prevent this idea gaining currency the speaker at Bodenstown the following Sunday, Gearoid O'Broin, repeated once again that IRA policy was directed solely against British forces in the North and said categorically that the guns would not be used against the Southern government or police force.

The raids which the IRA attempted between this time and 1956 were failures, yet the Omagh raid in October 1954, and its aftermath, brought both recruits and money to the IRA.

The raid (which resulted in eight young men going to prison) was made in an attempt to seize ammunition and arms. The IRA had not managed to obtain much information about the layout of the barracks until the same British army agent who had helped in the Armagh raid managed to spend a night in the barracks. With his briefing in hand the raid was fixed for the night of 16 October. A week before this date Magan arrived at a house in Dublin with some twenty machine-guns and gave them to Murphy and Eamonn Boyce, who was to lead the raid. Murphy, it had been decided, was too valuable a man in Dublin to risk.

Boyce had thirty-five men in his party, three armed with knives to silence the sentry who patrolled the back wall of the barracks (a duty very few were eager to undertake). Gearoid O'Broin was in charge of transport, which was to consist of two cars and a lorry, and he took equipment with which to start the British army lorries which the raiders hoped to commandeer.

Omagh Baracks, Co. Tyrone, backs on to marshes, its main gate opening on to a narrow street leading to the town. Three sentries patrolled the barracks: two watched the wall facing the town and those at right angles to it, and the third guarded the approximate one hundred yards of the back wall. The raid had been planned for the changing of these sentries, but O'Broin had trouble getting a lorry. Eventually he stole one but this had caused a three-hour delay. Boyce and fifteen men then scaled the wall at about 3.30 in the morning, the remaining twenty men staying outside the wall.

The men with the knives headed for an archway in which the sentry was expected to take shelter. When he did not the raiders attacked him, using not their knives but the butts of their revolvers with which they clubbed him. The sentry, however, was an exceptionally strong man and held off the attackers. His shouts both frightened other members of the raiding gang and alerted the British soldiers in the guardroom near the main entrance. In the event of something going wrong the IRA men had planned to use this gate to escape but the soldiers in the guardroom began shooting and made this impossible. The raiders retreated to the back wall and climbed it with no trouble. They escaped into the marshes, leaving their twenty comrades impotently standing outside the main entrance.

The invading party split up and disaster befell Boyce. He was unworried about immediate pursuit and returned towards the IRA lorry, watching for stragglers on his way. When he was fifty yards from the lorry it drove off. He ran for it but could not catch it and, still unworried, tried in vain to unlock an RUC car parked near by. He then began to walk towards the border twenty miles away but, exhausted, hungry and wet he was picked up as he attempted to take off his boiler suit in a ditch.

It is worth briefly examining here how IRA prisoners were treated at this time, not least because stories of their hardships influenced IRA policy and increased its recruitment. These stories also led to an IRA reprisal which cost innocent lives.

Prisoners were certainly roughed up to some degree. Boyce for instance was cuffed about and forced to strip naked and then dress again in his wet clothes six times. But the worst feature of the prisoners' treatment seems to have been the method of their transportation during the time of the taking of depositions. Under English law these had to be taken in the courthouse nearest the scene of the alleged crime. As a result, the IRA prisoners were taken from their cells at 5 a.m. each day, handcuffed to each other and to detectives and taken in a van across the province to Omagh.

Prisoners with weak stomachs got sick shortly after starting, and there was no sanitation available. The trips were never less than seventy miles, sometimes more. The vans often crossed into Donegal to avoid IRA ambushes against the convoy which accompanied the vans. Once in Omagh the police escort was changed but the prisoners, often after a court appearance of only a minute or two, faced another five-hour journey back to jail.

Once, however, the prisoners had been sentenced they were not harshly treated beyond, of course, having to endure normal prison routine. Here the great enemy was 'the bonk', a term coined by Philip Clarke, who, with Tom Mitchell, was elected to Westminster but was later unseated as a convicted felon. 'The bonk' described the terrible depression which would descend on even the best adjusted. One of its effects was that the prisoner became unpredictable, likely to strike out at anyone – a serious matter in such an environment. Prisoners seldom dared become too friendly with each other lest they weaken the will and self-reliance upon which they depended to get through their sentences.

The Arborfield raid led to the imprisonment of Donal Murphy, Charlie's brother. He had joined the IRA in Dublin by taking much the same route as had Charlie. Interested in history, he remembers being influenced in particular by the *Wolfe Tone Annual*, 'Scelig's' pamphlets and Tom Barry's book, *Guerrilla Days in Ireland*. Then came the familiar sequence of events: attending Sinn Fein meetings, quite casually at first, merely stopping for a few minutes after the pictures; meeting prominent Republican figures; driving speakers to Sinn Fein meetings at Charlie's request, and finally, in 1953, joining the Dublin unit of the IRA, aged twenty-one.

The following year a man who was to play an important role in IRA affairs contacted Donal's brother Charlie through the *United Irishman* offices, and set in train events which led to the IRA's most ambitious coup of the post-war period – and to Donal's being sentenced to life imprisonment. The man was Frank Skuse, who in autumn 1954 was a serving member of the British forces, stationed in Monmouth. Skuse had a magnificent presence being over six feet tall, red-haired and well proportioned. His father was a lieutenant commander in the British navy, and a brother is in the same organization today. Born in rebel Cork, he had sufficient Irish blood to make him eager to place such information as he possessed concerning the British military at the disposal of the IRA.

The Monmouth Barracks would have been easy for the IRA to attack because the surrounding walls were so low, but Skuse was transferred to Arborfield in Berkshire. There he familiarized himself with its layout and obtained maps for the IRA, which eventually decided to attack the Royal Electrical Mechanical Engineering Depot at Arborfield.

Donal Murphy only discovered what was planned by accident but he promptly volunteered for service. After a period of training, which laid special emphasis on things such as walking on tip-toes and small-arms drill, he and a group of eleven others, led by Rory Brady, were briefed in Dublin and shown a film of Arborfield, obtained by Charlie Murphy with Skuse's aid. On 11 August 1955, the party set off for England in the mail boat from Dun Laoghaire, pretending not to recognize each other. There were several other young Irishmen on board, either emigrating to England or returning after the holidays and one of them, in the bunk beneath Murphy, showed no surprise when Murphy's .45 slid out from underneath his pillow and bounced to the floor. Donal accepted the return of his revolver with the same courtesy with which he refused an offer of guidance from a policeman who came up to him at Euston station to ask if he could be of assistance. This time Donal was carrying two revolvers, a .38 and a .45!

The entire group spent the night in the same London hotel and set off at midnight, 12 August, for the raid. They had two hired vans and a car and had spent the day surveying the depot. About a quarter of a mile out Rory Brady lined them up at the roadside, in their dungarees and berets, and warned them not to fire first but if fired on to drop on one knee and aim low. Approaching the barracks they saw a red flare and feared something had gone wrong, but as this was followed by a green one they decided it was merely a routine drill and pressed on. They captured the sentry at the gate, took him into the depot, and left Skuse in his place.

Inside the guardroom the commander of the guard was cooking beans and sausages. He dropped the plate when they appeared and Donal grabbed a sausage – the last one he got for a long time. They tied up the eighteen-man guard without difficulty, but there were five men in the guardhouse serving punishment sentences and they had to use bootlaces and ties to secure them. Then they discovered that the keys to the armoury were not where Skuse had said they would be. He was summoned from the gate, after they had blindfolded the guardroom sergeant to prevent his recognizing Skuse, but he couldn't find them either (the armourer had taken them home) and they had to jemmy open the doors. In all they took five *tons* of guns and ammunition.

There were 82,000 rounds of ammunition in the van in which Donal was captured. He should have gone in the car, but Joseph Doyle was unsure of the route back to London and they went together. They were passing Ascot when a patrol car flagged them down on a routine check. They did not use their weapons because they feared that if the police failed to report to their radio control a general alert would ensue and trap their companions who were still in the armoury.

While Doyle and Murphy were being interrogated in Wokingham police station they heard the other van go by. But the raid had been futile. James Andrew Mary Murphy, in charge of the dump at Pentonville, had hired the vans in his own name and the police traced him easily. He was captured in his digs, lying in bed. The police had little difficulty in recovering the ammunition, although the rest of the raiders got away safely. All of them except Rory Brady were back in Ireland within four hours of the raids. Brady decided to hide out in the Channel Islands for a fortnight before returning to Dublin.

*   *   *

Donal Murphy's imprisonment led to some far-reaching contacts between the IRA and the wider world of revolution. Murphy had settled down to serve his sentence, determined that prison should not break him, when he became friendly with the Russian spy, Gordon Lonsdale, and a number of Greek Cypriots, including the guerrilla Nikos Samson. Lonsdale and he became particular friends and the Cypriots taught him Greek in return for lessons in Irish. Later these lessons developed into contacts between the IRA in Dublin and the Cypriots with a view to having EOKA recruits sent to Ireland to be trained in guerrilla warfare. The IRA also planned to rescue some of the Cypriots but the plans were rendered unnecessary by the signing of the London Agreements.

Murphy regarded Lonsdale as one of the most intelligent men he ever met. He had, Murphy said, an encyclopedic knowledge of world affairs and was able to talk informatively on all aspects of Irish foreign policy at the UN, Irish domestic policies, the Church and the economy to a degree not then usually equalled by many Irish elected representatives. The warders and the prisoners apparently looked up to him, but apart from Murphy he seems to have made no effort to be friendly with any of them. With Murphy, however, Lonsdale made a point of being friendly, perhaps reasoning that with him he could fulfil the need for companionship which even the most disciplined prisoner must feel without running the risk of being undermined by a British intelligence agent. He would politely decline offers of company from other prisoners on exercise walks, until Donal joined him, and he never attempted to indoctrinate the younger man into Communism. He confided in Donal to a remarkable degree. For instance, the IRA offered to help rescue him but he rejected the offer immediately, not because he thought that the plan could not succeed (at least that is what the IRA says!) but because he was confident that there was no question of his serving his twenty-five-year sentence. 'If anyone thinks there is,' he said, 'they're crazy. My people are just waiting to grab a suitable British spy and they'll exchange him for me.' He was so explicit and forthcoming on the subject that the moment Greville Wynne was arrested neither the Murphys nor anyone in touch with the plan to rescue Lonsdale had the slightest doubt that here was the requisite spy.

Donal was eventually released through the intercession of Carmel Murphy, Charlie's wife, with Cardinal Heenan, a distant relative. The cardinal interested Lord Longford in the case and the earl secured a pardon for him.

*   *   *

In 1956 Magan decided that Cathal Goulding, in prison for the Felstead raid, should be rescued. Plans were laid and during October Sean Cronin's wife Terry chartered an Aer Lingus DC-3 in the name of a fictitious drama group, the 'Scelligs Players' (the title was derived from the name of Cronin's birthplace, Ballinascellig). The plane was filled with Cumann na mBan women and IRA men, the women very curvaceous with sub-machine-gun parts, rope ladders and revolvers stashed in their underwear. Gouding was imprisoned in Wakefield and the plane was scheduled to touch down there. However, it was diverted because of bad weather to Huddersfield RAF base, and the party had to charter a bus to Wakefield. The group split up and made separate ways to the prison, intending to fling a rope ladder over the wall to Goulding, who was expecting the attempt. However, when the res- cuers got to the prison they found that there was a police patrol car circling the walls at regular intervals, and that alarm bells were sound- ing from within the prison. The raid was called off and the party regrouped at the bus and drove back over the mountains to the air base, unrecognized, and took off safely for Dublin.

The incident was in a way typical of the IRA attitude: concern for a captured comrade, great daring and ingenuity, and a wasteful expen- diture of money, energy and potentiality of personnel. The episode took £2,000 of the IRA's funds and had the police bring down the curtain on the 'Players' – practically all of the IRA leadership, with the exception of Magan, of whom Scotland Yard was known to have a description anyway, and MacCurtain, who lived in Cork, would have been arrested in England *two months* before the border campaign proper was scheduled to begin.

Another earlier scheme that never came to public knowledge took a tremendous amount of planning and cost life. This was the abortive second Armagh raid, intended as a reprisal for the severity of the sentences imposed on the men captured after the Omagh raid and their treatment. The raiders also wanted ammunition and to boost morale, after the Omagh failure.

Unlike the first Armagh raid this attempt was to have caused des- truction and, if necessary, taken life. There were between fifty and seventy picked men involved in the attempt, some of them experienced from the earlier raids. It was made clear to all that this was not merely a raid for arms, but an armed attack on a barracks which was to be burned down if possible. The raid was set for 6 March 1955, but when two trucks containing the raiding party, under Charlie Murphy, approached Keady village en route to Armagh they found it swarming with police.

Murphy decided to try another approach and sent a patrol ahead into Crossmaglen village. The main party retraced its route back over the border so as to reach Crossmaglen from a different direction. They arrived safely outside Crossmaglen, picked up their foot patrol and found that this village too was buzzing with police and B-Specials, and that barricades had been set across the roads. Murphy decided that to attack these forces would tarnish the IRA's reputation for attacking only British installations and personnel, a reputation which had been gained as a result of the Omagh raid, and he called the attack off. The party got back to Dublin unscathed, where it was learned through Joe O'Hagan of Lurgan, who had a contact on the force, that the RUC had expected a raid that weekend. (For reasons of their own Magan and Murphy decided that the leak in security had come from Belfast and this was a contributory factor in the decision not to begin hostilities in Belfast when the main campaign started the following year.)

The morning after the abortive Armagh raid it was discovered that a boy of eighteen, Arthur Leonard, had been killed when his van was fired on by a B-special patrol at Ready. Two other young people, a sixteen-year-old girl who was with Leonard and a man whose car was fired on by another jumpy B-Special patrol while driving in Co. Fermanagh, were wounded.

Ironically these happenings played into the hands of the IRA. It was widely assumed that the shootings had taken place as a result of Northern trigger happiness engendered by unnecessary mobilizations. Throughout the South, county councils denounced the Stormont regime and demanded that the B-Specials be disbanded. The force was likened to the Mau Mau, protest meetings were addressed by Sinn Fein polemicists and were widely attended by students and young people. In Belfast a visiting Labour deputy from Dublin, Sean Dunne, was expelled from the Distinguished Visitors Gallery for uttering shouts of 'murder' during a Stormont debate on the affair. Even the *Irish Times* became temporarily aggrieved at Stormont, observing huffily on 8 March that it was about time the Northern government developed a sense of proportion in its methods of law enforcement because 'paramilitary forces are an anachronism in a democratic society'.

Another destructive proposal which occupied a good deal of energy in the early part of 1955 was 'Operation Thermite', intended to inundate Eglington Naval Air Base, Derry, by blasting an embankment retaining the waters of the river Foyle. This scheme was eventually dropped, as was another plan to hijack an arms lorry from Omagh barracks. Throughout the period, and indeed as long as the IRA has existed, plans such as these were, and are, continually being made and discarded.

Hoaxes also characterized the period: one at Rhyl, North Wales, involving four junior army officers doing National Service caused a major alert throughout England. Affecting Irish accents the officers tied up a sentry at a royal artillery training camp, and threw him into a truck, making off into the night when another sentry gave the alarm.

This occurred only two days after the Arborfield raid, at a time when English public opinion was outraged by the disclosure that sentries on duty at Arborfield were armed only with pick-axe handles. As a result the minister for war had to return to London from holiday to make a report to the cabinet which also received a special report on IRA activities in Britain from the home secretary, Major Gwilym Lloyd George (later Lord Tenby). No sooner was this meeting over than the two ministers and the chief of the imperial general staff, Field Marshal Sir John Harding, were summoned to a further emergency conference with Prime Minister Sir Anthony Eden. The establishment was bracing itself for a repetition of the 1939 campaign when the four hoaxers confessed to their practical joke five days after the Eden conference, and the War Office issued a communique apologizing to the police for the trouble caused.

On 13 September more hoaxing came to light when it was announced that a sentry who had caused a widespread alarm by falsely reporting that three men had attacked him at St George's Barracks, Gosport, Hants, was to receive psychiatric treatment. On 26 October fifteen RAF stations in the north of England were placed on alert by a false rumour of impending IRA attack. Similar reports of bombs in planes and cinemas required checking and caused a not inconsiderable amount of inconvenience both in England and Ireland.

The public never learned, however, of the most extraordinary 'non-action' of the whole post-war period – the true story behind the attempts on the lives of the inspector general of the RUC, Sir Richard Pim, and his deputy, County Inspector A. H. Kennedy.

On 26 September 1957, as Kennedy and a friend. R. D. Ferris, were driving along University Road, Belfast, a bomb fastened underneath the car exploded. It was so slight a blast that the inspector garaged the car and continued his journey, believing merely that some mechanical failure had occurred. Investigation revealed what had happened and police realized that the attempt was similar to one the previous May. Then Sir Richard Pim and his wife were almost blown up by a bomb of the same type attached to their motor launch on Strangford Lough. Further investigation showed that the bombs had not been planted by the IRA, but by a disgruntled member of the Northern Security Forces who was, moreover, a relation of one of the leading figures in the Larne gun-running and in the creation of the Northern state. He had been disciplined after his drinking had led to repeated acts of bad conduct which, had they been committed by anyone else, would have resulted in instant dismissal. No influence could have saved him from charges of attempted murder after the bomb incidents, but, being tipped off by a friend, he entered a mental home as a voluntary patient.

In between the raids and abortive raids IRA training and reorganization went on. A month after the Armagh raid a big camp was established in Ballinascorney above Bohernabreena in the Dublin Mountains. Here over seventy men at a time from different parts of the country were trained for a week, each then returning home and training volunteers in their areas.

Security at this camp was ludicrous. On the normal weekend training sessions volunteers were expected to observe strict precautions to prevent their being followed: not speaking to each other in buses, approaching the camp site in ones and twos and so on. But no sooner would the Rockbrook bus have pulled away from its starting point in Dublin than someone would start singing the old IRA marching song, 'We're off to Dublin in the Green', and before long everyone in the bus would be joining in the chorus. The buses used to pass in front of my aunt's home in Kenilworth Square, in Rathgar, and I often encountered the young singers and thought they were campers. The police knew differently.

As Tom Mitchell put it to me, 'The Special Branch were at one end of a telescope and the IRA were at the other.' He remembers cycling up the Navan Road, a large suburban estate on the northern outskirts of Dublin, with a Bren gun strapped to the crossbar, dismounting under the noses of Special Branch men, who greeted him cheerfully, and then entering a field beside the main road to conduct an arms class in broad daylight.

Relations between the Special Branch and IRA (or at least parts of each group) had become so relaxed since the war that no one considered it unusual for a Special Branch man to greet an IRA man with a friendly 'Hello.' Both Special Branch and IRA members were younger now and had no personal knowledge of the Civil War. In fact some young recruits responded so effusively to the Special Branch that a rule was instructed forbidding volunteers to talk to Special Branch men. Even so, at Ballinascorney no one objected to Special Branch men watching as Charlie Murphy and Tom Mitchell shot a colour film of the training for use in America as propaganda. Bell tents were erected and the training sessions concluded with a shoot-off, using Bren guns, Lee Enfield rifles, a few Thompsons and revolvers.

The pattern of instruction at these training camps* was unrealistic for the conditions obtaining in the North. The theory of warfare used was taken from Tom Barry's book about events thirty years past. This overlooked the fact that in Barry's day reinforcements often took up to two days to arrive at a beleaguered barracks. These young men were going into action when it needed only ten minutes to bring troops, dogs and spotter planes to the scene of an attack. On top of this, of course, was the lack of modern heavy guns and armament.

Recruits were also taught ju jitsu and knife fighting. Some fainted at the thought of knifing (particularly at one especially realistic session in a hired room in Power's Hotel, Dublin, where a medical poster was attacked with carving knives and had a terminal effect on the careers of some would-be freedom fighters) but after the success of the Armagh raid there was great euphoria at classes and in camps. It was assumed that the British would run away when the IRA loomed up out of the night, the faces of the raiders smeared with blacking.

---

* At a camp at Kildare before the Omagh raid the IRA's armaments were almost lost. A short-sighted look-out dashed up to the officer in charge to inform him that there were 'tanks, red lights, white lights everythin' comin'.' As previously arranged, the officer immediately got all the weapons placed in a heap, set explosives around them and prepared to blow up the lot, when someone else reported that the 'tanks' etc. were nothing but the traffic on the main road some distance away!

13

Splits in the Ranks

While raids and training continued so did another familiar IRA activity – splits in the organization. In the decade after the war the policies of Brendan O'Boyle, Joseph Christle and Liam Kelly, all of whom diverged from the mainstream of 'physical force' Republicanism, occupied almost as much of the IRA's time as did preparations for the border campaign itself.

It is of interest here to turn briefly to America and the Irish-American societies in the post-war period.

The war and close surveillance by the FBI put an end to the Clann na Gael's activities in 1939–46, but in March 1946 it was reorganized following a convention of the various branches. Despite the war there was almost thirty thousand dollars in the kitty but a split occurred among the clubs and their members over whether this money should be used to build a monument in Dublin to Sean Russell or saved against the day when a new generation of IRA would arise in Ireland and require funds for another uprising. The pro-monument section, led by James Conaty and Joseph Stynes, won the day in 1949 and notified the anti-monument leaders by letter of their expulsion from the movement.

The anti-monument section led by Tadg Brosnan, Paddy Smith, Paddy Thornbury and James Brislanne, was still relatively powerful but it split in 1952, when Brendan O'Boyle went to New York looking for support for a campaign of his own. The pro-monument group healed its row with the Paddy Mahoney section, which had split over the speakeasy issue in 1930, through the good offices of the Dublin IRA which sent over a man called Monaghan to act as peace maker among all the sundered wings of the Clann. He failed, however, to heal the breach between the pro- and anti-monument sections and in fact the pro-monument section subsequently suffered a split itself in 1956.

Apart from the Clann, which was and is strongest in New York,

Chicago and Philadelphia, the many Irish-American groups which exist throughout the States were also likely supporters when bombs began to go off along the border. Some of these societies were little more than a joke. In 1969, I was given a circular seeking support for a group whose letter-heading proclaims that it has branches in New York, Boston, Philadelphia, Cleveland and San Francisco. Accompanying this was a handbill showing a starving, sad-eyed child behind barbed wire. The caption to the drawing reads:

'This child's father is in a concentration camp in occupied Ireland.'

Despite the claims of this circular, there were no concentration camps in Northern Ireland at this time. By 1979 of course, Long Kesh (see chapter 20) had been opened. The H Block issue had arisen and, in the grim, self-fulfilling prophecy nature of Anglo-Irish relations, what could be pointed to as uninformed Irish-American propaganda at the start of the decade was very near the truth at the close. Then came the hunger strikes. I will leave it to readers to draw their own moral, particularly when they have read Part II of this book describing in more detail what happened over the decade.

One day in the late 1960s I was visited in my office by Roddy Connolly, a lifelong Republican socialist. He was accompanied by a young Irish-American priest anxious to make contacts in the North on behalf of a civil rights movement founded in New England to help the Northern Catholics. Because he was in Connolly's company I contented myself with the quickest questioning of his background, and provided him with several introductions. Two days later Eoin MacNamee called in, fresh from Boston, where he told me that he had been told in Clann na Gael circles about a Protestant clergyman, who was seeking support for civil rights – a man of the same name as the young priest. I did not check into the Boston civil rights movement, but if I were in the IRA and a similar confusion arose over a Clann emissary I can understand the tensions and uncertainty which might arise.

Along with the splits and the confusions, the generosity of the average Irish American also exists and is a very real and all-pervasive fact of Irish-American life. Charlie Murphy told me he met with several acts of personal generosity from Americans. Men donated their personal savings to the movement when the border campaign began, or collected money for the movement like the member of the Red Branch Knights' Society of San Francisco who came to Ireland personally to hand over a cheque for $3,000 raised by the Branch. At its peak

American aid averaged about $3,000 a month, continuing the tradition of Irish Americans in every decade, whether they were supporting Tom Clarke and his newspaper *Irish Freedom*, or Maurice Twomey and *An Phoblacht*, or Brendan O'Boyle and his ill-fated campaign of 1952–55.

In the hot-house atmosphere of fears and splits after 1945 O'Boyle decided to form his own group. He had joined the IRA while a student at Queen's University, Belfast, in 1940, been captured the following year and was one of the escapees from Derry Jail in the big break-out of 20 March 1943.

His American funds campaign owed its inception to the merest fluke. A Mrs Tom Leonard, formerly of Co. Tyrone where her family and that of her husband were active in the IRB and IRA, was holidaying in Dublin with her daughter in 1947 when O'Boyle was pointed out to them in O'Connell Street as 'One of *them*. He's a good lad.' That was the only contact the Leonards had with O'Boyle until two years later when Mrs Leonard, attending a meeting in New York of the United Irish Counties Association, recognized him when he stood up to speak from the floor. He was on a business trip and, seeing the meeting advertised, went to it in the mistaken belief that the association might offer some prospect of revolutionary action. (It is, in fact, a highly constitutional body.) Mrs Leonard spoke to him after the meeting and invited him to her home the following Sunday. Among the guests was Harry Short, a kindly fanatic. Crippled from birth in his native Armagh, he had served with the Fianna in the War of Independence and emigrated to America afterwards. Like Joe McGarrity he devoted his life to the movement.

Short invited O'Boyle to meet some friends, including a member of the pro-monument group of the Clann. Realizing that O'Boyle did not have the support of the IRA – otherwise they would have been informed of his visit and he would not have been making himself known in circles like those of the United Irish Counties Association – Short and some other members of the group then took him to the home of Tadg Brosnan from Kerry, a former IRA leader and, since emigrating to New York, a worker for Clann na Gael.

After a time of probing and questioning O'Boyle ventured as a general observation the fact that 'there's a good group at home, if they got support. Do you people think they could get support?' The others thought this quite possible despite problems. The Clann was split; O'Boyle was not 'official'; the Clann men were all in their late fifties or early sixties; and American law does not look kindly on the use of its territory and resources for the fomenting of revolution in other countries (unless of course such activities are confined to the hands of government agencies), so there were likely to be difficulties with the FBI. (Indeed it is because of these difficulties that I must omit dates and names of surviving group members who still live in the US lest they find themselves behind bars in the evening of their lives.)

O'Boyle returned to Ireland and tried to get control of the younger element of the IRA and become chief of staff. The group in America was to raise funds, purchase and arrange for the shipping of arms and ammunition to Ireland.

O'Boyle wrote to Short in August saying that he would require about ten thousand dollars, five hundred Thompson sub-machine guns and substantial numbers of rifles, ammunition and hand grenades. He would need these to achieve any sort of success against the Stormont government, plus the men to use them and a back-up of friendly houses, doctors, intelligence service and transport, would be required. However, in the conditions obtaining in Ireland at the time both the request and its execution were doomed to end in failure and misery. The IRA mistrusted O'Boyle and thought he was getting money for personal use. Murphy and Magan had him shadowed constantly and the Special Branch also watched him because they suspected him of smuggling across the border.

In America also opinion was divided as to the wisdom of helping O'Boyle. One of the most influential figures on the Irish-American scene, the chief representative of the Irish Hospitals Sweepstake's organization, himself an executive of the Clann and a man who could smuggle elephants in and out of America if he chose, warned Short on the 'Sweep' grapevine to have nothing to do with the campaign. But Short decided to persevere. He told me that he reasoned, 'O'Boyle is a Northerner. We'll have the fight in Ulster and not in the South. We'll get away from bloody civil war in the South.'

With this in view Short contacted a group of Northern Irish emigrants who, with the addition of one Kerry man, formed the Northern Action Committee. Its members were Felix O'Byrne, Paddy Thornbury, Tom Leonard, Frank Curran, Frank Donnelly, Tommy Guy, like the others a former IRA man but who had taken the Free State side in the Civil War, and Tadg Brosnan, the only non-Ulsterman.

They met in August 1949 in a hotel in Times Square (no minutes were taken for obvious reaons), and Short read O'Boyle's letter to them. The committee was then set up.

Committee organization was simple. For secrecy the members decided that in correspondence they would always sign their mothers' names. The only hard and fast organizational rule was that if Short thought the subject warranted it any member of the group must be prepared to meet him without delay at any time. The committee asked for contributions of $100 from friends and associates and had impressive receipt forms printed from a design invented by Joe McGarrity's daughter. In all the group sent about fifteen thousand dollars to Ireland betwen 1949 and 1960. (About two-thirds of this was sent to Brendan O'Boyle and when he was killed the group transferred its support to Liam Kelly.) They tapped all the county associations for money but the greatest support was from Kerry, Cork, Tipperary, Down, Armagh and Tyrone.

The *modus operandi* for raising funds was to show arms to representatives of different groups and explain the purpose of both weapons and collection, but the committee's motives were sometimes questioned. A problem also arose because part of the Clann was supporting the 'official' IRA and opposed O'Boyle's schemes. Some prominent Irish-Americans, such as the 'Sweep' executive, also continually used their influence to scotch support for either organization on the grounds that both were equally suicidal and futile. Then, too, the minimal secrecy which the committee imposed was sometimes sufficient to cause trouble. One holidaying Tyrone man met Liam Kelly in Ireland and, remembering his subscription in New York, thought that the money was being sent to Kelly. Kelly understandably made it known that he had no money and this caused controversy. Another prominent Irish-American, John MacIvor, wrote to Charles MacGleenan (one of the staunchest and best informed Republicans in the country) in Armagh to ask him what he knew about an IRA man called Mac-Allister who was planning an uprising in the North. Not knowing that O'Boyle was using the name MacAllister, MacGleenan replied that he had never heard of him. This kind of incident was always sorted out, but there was enough gossip, among other problems, to make O'Boyle's plans for a campaign very difficult to put into action.

The committee did do away with one convention which had been a continuing source of friction between the IRA and Clann na Gael. Historically the Clann and the IRA were on an equal footing so far as leadership of the joint movement was concerned, but the committee agreed to place itself entirely under the command of O'Boyle, and to ask nothing of him except leadership. Short secretly hoped that O'Boyle would prove himself the strong man of an all-Ireland Republic.

Great ingenuity and daring were shown in securing arms and transporting them to Ireland, not only under the noses of the American and Irish authorities, but also of the hostile wing of the Clann in America and of the equally hostile IRA in Ireland who were ready at any time to commandeer arms intended for O'Boyle. One shipment of ten revolvers and five tear-gas pencil-guns consigned to him at a Dublin hotel was, in fact, hijacked by the IRA.

The story of the arms procurement activities of the committee reads at times like a film scenario. On the Pulaski Skyway outside New York one evening a car driven by one of O'Boyle's sympathizers developed a flat tyre, which was fixed with the aid of a helpful policeman who duly received a five-dollar bill for his services, unaware that in the boot of the car were two 100 lb. tins of napalm which had just been stolen from the Brooklyn Naval Yard.

One of the most useful suppliers of arms was a gangster whom a member of the group met accidentally. It was he who supplied the tear-gas guns and he was making excellent progress with the supply of revolvers when he decided to expand his activities and began turning up machine-guns. This ceased following a gangland murder involving the use of a machine-gun taken from Brooklyn Pier. The police circulated the serial numbers of stolen weapons and the committee discovered it had been given weapons in the missing serial range.

O'Boyle too proved himself an expert in customs' evasion. He had an almost incredible network of contacts. He once, thanks to a contact, cleared Idlewild Airport with his papers in order but carrying in his luggage several dozen revolvers and many thousand rounds of ammunition. He had the customs at Cobh, where the transatlantic liners from America traditionally call, particularly well organized. A shipment from New York of nine cases of ammunition was once sent to him at Cobh without him being told of the number of cases in the consignment. He only collected eight. One case was left aboard the liner and made a round-the-world cruise before the liner again docked at Cobh and a horrified O'Boyle was telephoned in Dublin by a customs official who told him that there was a case addressed to him awaiting clearance at the docks. His customary helper was off duty when he arrived but he managed to get his case through the customs without opening it to declare the contents.

But all his daring and ingenuity were not proof against the weight of gossip and intrigue that gradually crushed down O'Boyle's spirit. The dour reality of the Northern political scene caused his organization to dwindle away. By July 1952 he was dependent on a neighbour and his wife, who were not members of his group, to go with him on a mission to blow up Stormont telephone exchange. When the neighbour's baby fell sick O'Boyle's wife Carmel offered to take her place. They got to their destination safely and Carmel and the neighbour stepped out of the car leaving Brendan making adjustments to a mine. Suddenly there was an explosion.

The neighbour led Carmel away from the car, urging her, 'Don't look back.' She was taken to hospital and treated for shock. The neighbour made his escape and despite her terrible condition Carmel resisted all police questioning and refused to reveal the dead man's identity. The Unionists would not allow her to attend her husband's funeral but no charges were brought against her. Ultimately Cardinal d'Alton intervened privately to have her released.

The Liam Kelly split forced its way into the public consciousness on 26 November 1955, when a mine tore the side out of the Roslea RUC Barracks, Co. Fermanagh.

Kelly, who had led the raid, was the founder of two Republican organizations, Saor Uladh (Free Ulster), the military wing, and Fianna Uladh, its political arm, which ceased to count for very much after the year of its foundation, 1953. Kelly was a figure of some standing in East Tyrone and in Nationalist circles generally, having been imprisoned for nine months in 1953 for sedition shortly after his election to Stormont for mid-Tyrone. On his release his homecoming to the town of Pomeroy was marked by severe clashes between police and Kelly's sympathizers – afterwards referred to in the North as the Pomeroy riots.

The IRA denounced the Roslea raid on the day after it occurred and issued a statement appealing to young men 'not to join sentimental or microscopic organizations such as those who attacked the RUC Barracks at Roslea'. (The IRA also attacked it with equal lack of success on 11 October 1957.) However, Kelly refused to admit to the raid and issued a statement through Fianna Uladh on 28 November which said:

'Fianna Uladh neither admits nor denies responsibility for the raid.

'It is our policy now and always not to felon-set, to inform on political prisoners or to give any information whatsoever to the usurpers of our country that would aid the process of elimination, which in our opinion helps the English army of occupation and its satellites.'

At the time it was not generally realized that there were two militant Republican groups at work. Nor did the public or the IRA know that Connie Green, who had formerly served with the British army and was a member of the Saor Uladh attacking party, had been shot in the raid. His death, or rather the irregularities surrounding the inquest into his death, caused such a storm that Saor Uladh was finally forced to issue a statement, in the Fianna Uladh journal *Gair Uladh* on 16 December, accepting responsibility for the raid. The statement also showed the differences between the IRA and Kelly's groups. It said:

'Saor Uladh accepts the Constitution of the Republic enacted on 1 July 1937, and recognizes that Oireachtas Eireann is the sole legitimate authority in Ireland.

'Saor Uladh is organized solely in the Six Counties. Application of the laws enacted under the Constitution is by the Constitution itself restricted to the Twenty-Six County area. It is apparent therefore that these laws are not applicable in the case of Saor Uladh.'

These points are clearly at variance with what was then IRA policy, and there was also the attitude of Magan and the older members of the IRA executive to be considered. Their orthodox Republicanism precluded any official liaison between the IRA and Kelly, although younger members did make unofficial contact with the Kelly organization. Charlie Murphy told me that Kelly once gave him a large quantity of ammunition for use by the IRA but MacLogan later ordered it to be returned and another young IRA man, Terry O'Toole, told me that when he was on the run he found the Kelly organization both more helpful and more efficient than that of the IRA network in the North.

This, of course, was because Kelly was a Northerner and despite the fact that many Northerners were acting in the IRA the IRA's concept of the North was of a place 'up there'. It had to be attacked from the South, according to a plan masterminded from Dublin, which, when the attacks were over, was to be the safe resting place and recruitment area. Militarily, however, Kelly saw the Northern situation as one to be solved by Northerners. His campaign failed for the usual reasons: lack of popular support and scarcity of weapons of a sufficiently high calibre to breach the defences of RUC barracks (although he tried to purchase arms in America). Like the IRA he also attempted to drive out the British by attacking the Irish constabulary.

While the Fianna Uladh admission of responsibility was important in clarifying the internal situation for Republicans, it was almost completely overshadowed in the public's mind by the events of the raid itself. These show the hesitancy and confusion of governmental policy towards the Republican movement at this time.

The raid began at 5.40 am when a mine went off at the end of the barracks. The debris blocked the doorway from the guardroom which the attackers entered through the breach. As the rubble was being removed Sergeant William Robert Morrow, who was living in the barracks at the time with his wife and two little boys, leaped from bed, grabbed a Sten gun, and beat off the attack, which lasted about fifteen minutes. (He was awarded the George Medal for this.) In the shooting, a Constable Knowles was hit seven times, but recovered later and after the raid it was believed that he was the only casualty.

But rumours, which the *Sunday Independent* published on 28 November, persisted that one of the attackers had been shot in the raid and buried secretly in Monaghan after an inquest had been held and a coroner had made the usual order for burial. After enquiries by journalists the Government Information Bureau in Dublin made the following announcement:

'In answer to enquiries it was ascertained through the Government Information Bureau that on Saturday afternoon the Coroner for North Eastern Monaghan was informed that the body of an unknown man who appeared to have died from gunshot wounds was lying in a farmhouse in his district. An inquest was held in the evening when it was found by the jury that the unknown man had died from shock and haemorrhage and that there was no evidence to show how the injuries had been received.'

The GIB refused to make any further comment, but a leading Irish journalist, John Healy, succeeded in getting the coroner, Dr Thomas Leonard (aged 77), to talk to him. The old man revealed that prior to the GIB announcement 'no information was to have been given by anyone who participated in the inquest'.

'That,' he said, 'was the position until today. Then Dublin let us down with this announcement . . . it was no longer a secret . . . that is why I am able to talk to you now.'

Leonard said that the man had died on the morning following the attack. He had been attended by a local doctor who had sent for a priest to give the man the last rites. That afternoon the doctor and two other men called on Leonard, told him that a man had died (without telling him when or where) and asked him to hold an inquest. Leonard explained that he could not do this without informing the authorities and the men left, apparently to do just this. Leonard then got in touch with the Gardai and was visited by a superintendent who at first said he knew nothing about the affair. He later returned and told Leonard that he would be called for at 8 p.m. to carry out an inquest.

That evening Leonard was taken to a farmhouse where he found the body of a 'fine looking man' already in a coffin, and six men ready to act as jurors. Leonard swore them in. The superintendent presided and the inquest was held in his presence and that of a solicitor, a detective, the owner of the farmhouse and the doctor who had examined the man while he was dying. Uniformed guards and members of the detective force were stationed outside the house. Evidence was taken from the owner of the farmhouse and from the doctor, who said that the dead man had had a bullet wound in his left side. A verdict that death was due to shock and haemorrhage was returned.

Leonard went home and made out the death certificate which he described as a 'most unusual one. There is no name. I could not say if the man was married or single, what occupation he had. In the age column I wrote "about 30". That was all.' (The body was buried the following morning at Carrickroe cemetery, about twelve miles north of Monaghan, with the full rites of the church.)

The background to all this was that Liam Kelly sought to have Connie Green buried without an inquest but the doctor insisted that this would not be possible. Kelly telephoned a Clann na Poblachta member who was highly placed in the coalition government, to obtain the permission. However, when the Clann na Poblachta contact sought the co-operation of Michael Keyes, the Minister for Justice, he was informed that an inquest would have to be held but it could be held in secrecy.

The entire episode aroused the strongest feelings both North and South and in England. John J. Horgan of Cork, at the time one of the senior coroners of Ireland, wrote to one of the papers saying that a secret inquest, at which the coroner made no attempt to identify the deceased or ascertain the cause of death, and following which he denied all knowledge of the event, constituted 'a breach of both law and practice'. The *Irish Times* printed an interview with 'a prominent barrister' who was quoted as saying:

'Let us take an extreme case. Suppose I and some friends of mine decided to commit a murder. Apparently all we have to do is to take out the victim, shoot him, and bring him to the nearest coroner for an inquest and then to a graveyard for burial. We don't even need to say who he was.'

These two quotations reveal the principal worries and the criticisms of the public in the South at the time, though there were subsidiary considerations arising out of there being only six jurymen empanelled. But in the North, where tension had been steadily rising from the time of the Ebrington Barracks raid of 1951, the Roslea affair aroused much sharper reactions and criticism.

During a debate at Stormont a day after Healy's story, Lord Brookeborough said:

'It is unbelievable that any civilized country which has outlawed the IRA is yet afraid to take action which any civilized country would take to prevent blackguards and scoundrels coming here to commit murder and create antagonism among the people.'

He added that if and when it became necessary to increase the size of the B-Specials, men would join and do their duty 'as their fathers had done in the past . . . We want to assure these blackguards that we won't be shoved around. Nothing is going to put us out of the United Kingdom.'

In the same debate Minister for Home Affairs George B. Hanna announced the banning of Saor Uladh and referring to the inquest said:

'The wisdom of our fathers in refusing to join with the South is evident when one considers the procedure at that inquest, which could not take place in any properly conducted community . . . I charge the Government in the South as being morally responsible for the raid.'

He gave instances of cases wherein the Stormont authorities had given information to the Southern authorities concerning illegal drilling on the Southern side of their border, 'but they took no steps to stop it'. Hanna also pointed out that the Nationalist members who had walked out of the debate claimed to represent the Roman Catholic Church. 'Had the Church no views on what had happened?' he asked. (The Church did in fact have something to say, but it was said too late to have any bearing on the immediate controversy.)

A significant point which emerged from the Stormont debate was the fact that Lord Brookeborough had been in touch with the British prime minister with a view to getting Great Britain to seek an extradition treaty with the Republic. In London, *The Times* seized on this point in a leader headed 'Murder and the IRA':

'Whatever the technicalities in bringing the offenders to book, it should be a point of honour with all three governments . . . to co-operate in overcoming them. If further agreements between the three governments are required they should at once be negotiated . . . these men are, like pirates, the common enemies of all civilized states and it behoves all governments to combine against them.'

In Belfast the *News Letter* capitalized the feelings of Orangemen at the time, saying:

'Events since the Roslea raid make the Dublin Government look extremely foolish . . . If the Government is not pursuing a policy of hushing up the affair, and thereby shielding the men who were engaged in it, then its authority is being defied in its own territory, it is a week-kneed and incompetent Administration, and no credit even to the Irish Republic.

'It is the duty of all to give whatever assistance they can and to prove that Ulstermen in 1955 are just as capable of defending themselves, and as ready to do so, as the men who manned the Border and patrolled the gunmen's roads in 1921 and 1922.'

The following day, 30 November, the Northern Ireland Minister of Finance Brian Maginess pressed home the attack on the Dublin government saying:

'Those in the North who look southwards saw a people who were afraid to speak out, and afraid to condemn murderous attacks on police and military establishments. They saw a government that was weak and vacillating. As they saw these things they could thank God that we are part of the United Kingdom.'

On the same day Southern Prime Minister Costello made a major speech in the Dail in the course of which he made three central points:

'We must assert and vindicate the people's right to determine national policy and the right of the Oireachtas and the Government to maintain and to uphold the authority that reposes in them . . .

'We are bound to ensure that unlawful activities of a military character shall cease, and we are resolved to use, if necessary, all the powers and forces at our disposal to bring such activities effectively to an end . . .

'In order to prevent any future controversy or discussion on this point . . . there can be no question of our handing over, either to the British or to the Six-County authorities, persons whom they may accuse of armed political activities in Britain or in the Six Counties.'

Both Fianna Fail and Clann na Poblachta supported Costello in his stand and on 4 December he attempted to deal with the alleged government complicity in the secrecy surrounding the Monaghan inquest. Speaking at Abbeyfeale, Co. Limerick he said:

'No order or direction to hold the inquest in secrecy or to maintain secrecy was given or suggested by the Government or any member of the Government or by any member of any Government Department, or by the Commissioner or any officer or member of the Guards.' He went on to add that as soon as he had heard of the affair he had given a personal direction that 'there should be publication forthwith'.

(I would be inclined to assess Costello's statement as entirely honest in the light of the information available to him. He was after all the leader of only one party in a coalition supported by Clann na Poblachta which had made Liam Kelly a senator.)

A courageous motion by Dr Owen Sheehy Skeffington in the Senate on 15 December which welcomed the general tenor of Costello's speech, but regretted that he had not actually taken steps to halt 'this crazy militarism, however high its ideals or self-sacrificing its members', failed to attract a seconder.

Nor did church leaders get much further in their efforts to check 'crazy militarism'. At midnight Mass on Christmas Eve Cardinal d'Alton appealed to young men not to use violence in support of their aim in uniting the country, and on 19 January the standing committee of the Irish hierarchy issued a statement condemning the use of force and pointing out the dangers of civil war. The statement was also read out at Masses but it had no effect on the IRA's recruiting or planning. As Charlie Murphy put it to me, 'When the bishops called down fire and brimstone not a man stirred but when Joe Christle fecked off half the shagging IRA followed him!'

Before describing the 'fecking off' of Joe Christle it is important to pick up the threads of the 'official' IRA's activities.

Following the Arborfield raid and the severe sentences on his brother and friends, Charlie Murphy began to feel personally responsible for both these and the Omagh imprisonments. A sense of guilt coupled with the exhaustion engendered by years of sleepless nights and punishing travel, almost drove him out of the IRA. This point came one day in November when he found Michael O'Donovan, a life-long Republican, sitting in an office of the *United Irishman*. He had just been dropped from the staff by Magan. O'Donovan, or 'Pasha' as he was generally known, was such a keen Irish-speaker that he even spoke to his dog in Irish and Murphy like everyone else in the movement had a soft spot for the old man. He tried to get Magan to reinstate him and when he failed he resigned from the headquarters staff of the IRA although he remained an ordinary member of the Dublin unit. A few days later, the Roslea raid took place. Realizing that it was not an IRA job but fearing that it might mean a round-up of IRA men Murphy set off for the hills around Dublin in a car and warned the groups drilling there to lie low. Magan then asked him to return, which he did and so began an association that led to large-scale hostilities against the North.

Sean Cronin was thirty-three when he came back from America. He had become known in Clann na Gael circles in New York, and was accepted into the IRA by Magan. He had been an officer in the regular army before emigrating to America where he worked as a journalist and on his return he joined the *Evening Press* as a sub-editor. (Ironically he had known of the editor, Douglas Gageby, in the army where Gageby had earned a reputation for his wartime work in intelligence, as has been mentioned earlier.) From the start Cronin made headway in both the IRA and on the *Evening Press*. On the newspaper he was meticulous about time and used to appear five minutes early in the office every morning. Cronin's American accent earned him the name 'Sheriff' among his colleagues. The staff all liked him and was sorry when he resigned, ostensibly because he had a commission from a newspaper chain in America. A few days later he was picked up on the border and we realized what the commission was and how apt had been his nickname.

I had nearly stumbled on the truth some months earlier when I happened to notice him coming out of the *United Irishman* offices. We knew that he used to write for the paper, but pretending not to know this I said to him the next day in the office, 'I hear, Sean, that you're getting very prominent in Sinn Fein circles.' He nearly rose out of the chair with surprise, grabbed my arm and barked at me, 'What? Where did you hear that? What do you mean?'

He was so intense that I thought he was afraid that I might say something which would harm his prospects on the *Evening Press* and I relented and told him that I had seen him the previous day and was only joking. I was not aware that his relief stemmed from the fact that the IRA had just agreed to a full-scale attack on the North along the lines of a plan drawn up by himself.

From the moment that he arrived back in Dublin in October 1955 Cronin had been keen on action, but as he had to go through a recruits' course like everyone else it was not until January 1956 that he began to be listened to in the inner councils of the IRA. Then Charlie Murphy invited him to join him as a co-training officer, because of his military background. (At the time, apart from an active service unit of perhaps fifty men who had taken part in raids, the vast majority of the rank and file of the IRA had no experience what-soever of soldiering.) Cronin gave Murphy a plan, 'Operation Harvest', for an attack on the North aimed at destroying communications, military installations and public property on such a scale as to paralyse the six county area. Murphy turned the plan over to Magan. It had, of course, very little practical relevance but Magan liked it, and in April 1956 appointed Murphy and Cronin as joint operating staff. Murphy and Cronin then began repeated visits to the North to meet local IRA units and to reconnoitre targets.

In July 1956 Murphy and his colleagues arranged for the biggest single operation the IRA carried out, apart from the campaign itself – a battle school in the Wicklow Mountains. The course was devised by a former British officer, a veteran of the Burmese war who had also fought on the Republican side in the Civil War. The site could only be reached by a rope wall over a stream, but he could cross it like a cat, whereas the IRA lads puffed and floundered and very often had to be pushed over.

The day began at 5 a.m. and training involved the use of live ammunition and simulated attacks over the ground along which charges of gelignite had been laid to be detonated by Murphy and Cronin. (A film of this exercise was shot and sent to America.) The school lasted for a fortnight and involved making a considerable amount of noise, but there was no interference from either the Special Branch or the regular army, which during lulls in the firing could be heard at their own practice ranges in the Glen of Imaal just over the mountains. The only complaint received was from traders in a nearby town who objected that the IRA had not bought its supplies locally and to allay such criticism it was decided to invite the locals to a supper which was so lavish[*] that one shepherd remarked as he laid

---

[*] This generosity was a cause of the IRA's running out of meat during the exercise, but despite the presence of large numbers of sheep in the vicinity, no effort was made to eat them, not through honesty but because, despite the fact that the course was held to increase expertise in human slaughter, no one liked the idea of killing a sheep!

into a second helping, 'Be Jasus lads if this be war let there never be peace!'

However, no date was set for the start of a campaign, nor for security reasons were the rank and file informed of what was afoot. In view of the security position this was necessary but it helped to bring about the Christle split, when most of the active service unit, unaware of what was being planned by the 'Official Army of the Republic', followed Joe Christle in breaking from the IRA because he stood for action against the North and the IRA apparently did not.

Joe Christle had a quality that I can only describe as 'whoosh' – energy, anarchy, male supremacy and learning all canalized into a brand of patriotism that found its outlet in everything from fomenting strikes and laying up explosives to bicycle racing. Apart from organizing the marathon round-Ireland Ras Tailteann he cycled twenty miles before work every day himself. His home in Rathgar, Dublin was continually in turmoil. Phones rang. People rushed in and out. Beethoven boomed from the record player. Large young men in track suits carried bicycles through the hall. (Like most things surrounding Christle there was more purpose to the activity than met the eye.) His three friendly young sons were trained to wash dishes and do housework. They were intelligent lads who instead of toy guns were given books at Christmas. One evening chatting with them while waiting for Joe, I was particularly impressed by their knowledge of Greek mythology.

In 1945, when Christle was still a schoolboy at St James's Christian Brothers School, he founded his first revolutionary circle. He was sixteen. He made efforts to contact the IRA but failed and joined the FCA (An Forsa Cosanta Atiuil), the Irish equivalent of the British territorial army. As membership involves taking an oath of allegiance to the state I asked Christle how he squared this with his conscience.

'Oh,' he said, 'we took the oath like Dev did. To break the oath.'

In the FCA summer camps he would distribute leaflets asking his fellow FCA members what were they defending, twenty-six or thirty-two counties? He found a good deal of support for his views and the authorities removed him and a number of like-minded enthusiasts in the summer of 1949. By then he had also joined the Gaelic League and was a member of its Ard Craobh (literally 'high branch') of which de Valera was chairman. That year also he founded the Gate Cycling Club, joined what was left of the NCA and was taken into the IRA by

'Pasha' O'Donovan. Everyone in the Gate Club was a member of the IRA and on the Armagh raid six of the twenty raiders were club members.

He joined the John Mitchel Club of Sinn Fein in 1952 and became one of its principal speakers along with Myles Shevlin and Seamus Sorahan. He saw that 'action' brought a mushroom growth in recruiting and he felt that the movement was too preoccupied with form and not enough with substance. Because of this view and as that suspicious person, a university student, he gradually found himself isolated from the older leaders of the movement, in particular Anthony Magan, Michel Traynor and Patrick MacLogan. They felt he wanted to take over the movement for himself – and certainly Joe was a leader rather than a follower.

Never a man to allow revolution to interfere with his lawful activities he sat for part of his bachelor of law examination on the morning of the Armagh raid. He had just completed a question asking, 'What are the safeguards in the Irish Constitution against armed insurrection and rebellion?' when he was called for and driven off to take part in a little 'armed insurrection and rebellion' against the Northern Ireland constitution.

He emerged from both tests with second-class honours, hearing from the university some weeks later and being censured by the IRA for taking it on himself to give orders for the disposal of an arms lorry after the raid, an action which resulted in the lorry's being captured. In August he organized the first of his annual eight-day cycling events, the round-Ireland Ras Tailteann. In October he took part in the Omagh raid. In November he organized the National Students Council, embracing every student society in University College, Dublin. He was wounded during the Omagh raid and was on sick leave from his job in the state-run Electricity Supply Board, when he and Martin Campbell, who had been an important IRA fundraiser around Chicago in 1921–23, set off in December around the country in a car with the slogan 'Let Christmas Day be Prisoners Day', and was so successful that on Christmas Day he and Campbell carried literally buckets of money into the Castle Hotel in Denmark Street for the Prisoners' Dependants Fund.

Christle continued on his ebullient way during 1955 in a manner gravely upsetting to the older men. As part of their contribution towards helping the election of Mitchell and Clarke three of the Christle group decided that if they could get the support of the veteran

Nationalist priest, Canon Maguire of Newtownbutler, Co. Fermanagh, they would have gone a long way towards persuading the Nationalists not to stand against either Mitchell or Clarke and so avoid splitting the vote. The three were Seamus Sorahan, a law student and at the time the best public speaker in Sinn Fein, and the brothers Willie and Joe Fogarty. They drafted a letter seeking the canon's cooperation and had it signed by hundreds of students as coming from '. . . University College, Dublin, where Philip Clarke studied and so often spoke of you as the leader of Nationalist thought in Occupied Ireland . . .'

As far as anyone knew at the time Clarke had never mentioned the formidable old canon in his life, but Sorahan and Willie Fogarty had Fáinnes (gold circles which proclaimed the wearers fluent Irish speakers and Pioneer Pins which proclaimed them teetotallers, which they were not) fixed to their lapels and set off with a letter to the canon. The emissaries and letter so appealed to the old man that he promised to help them.

The IRA leadership, particularly Magan, MacLogan and Mac-Curtain, eventually decided that Christle would have to go. In June 1956, Charlie Murphy was ordered to hand him his dismissal notice, ostensibly for addressing a Sinn Fein meeting without permission. This had the easily foreseeable result that those who thought like Christle also left the IRA. The bulk of the most active and best trained volunteers, including most of the active service unit and twelve out of fifteen of the officer corps, followed him. Like Christle they were unaware that a campaign was being planned by the IRA leadership. But their secession and subsequent activities were so embarrassing to the 'official' leaders that they spent as much time between then and December 1956 trying to dissuade others from following Christle as on planning the campaign itself.

On his dismissal Christle approached Liam Kelly and those sections of Clann na Gael which would always support 'action'. Kelly, however, was not too happy and at first suspected Christle of being an IRA plant, but the two groups, about seventy men in all, finally came to agreement in August 1956 at a meeting in Dublin at which the Northerners arrived carrying arms. The first joint Christle-Kelly operation took place on Armistice Day 1956 when they burned down customs huts along a 150-mile stretch – almost the entire length of the border. The group carried out about twelve attacks, blowing up customs huts, telephone exchanges, bridges, B-Special drill halls, and demolishing the lough gates at Newry.

Kelly and Christle accompanied their groups on all the raids and on a number of ambushes which failed when the RUC, the B-Specials or British military did not arrive. Another plot which Christle hatched but which failed through lack of cooperation from his own supporters, including Kelly whom it horrified, was a plan to seize the town of Newry, with the help of the Catholic population, thus forcing the British to engage them and, he reasoned, forcing the Irish army to become involved also. This, Christle hoped, would lead to a situation in which the United Nations would intervene and send a peace-keeping force to replace the British in the North!

There was some evidence of sympathy for Christle's scheme in high places. Michael Fitzpatrick, chief whip of Clann na Poblachta, told me that he favoured sending the Irish army to the border on manoeuvres just to see what the Orangemen would do – engage the Southerners, he hoped. I have also been told about Dail deputies parking outside Leinster House with car boots laden with arms and ammunition which they were transporting for the IRA. On at least one occasion a minis-terial car was used to transport ammunition for Thompson guns from Kerry to Dublin and Christle did have many contacts in the army. (So much so that on one occasion a serving officer, still in the army, took part in a border raid and was very nearly captured, but had the good fortune to find a farmhouse whose occupants put him in contact with a priest who spirited him safely back across the border. Whether or not Christle had intended him to be captured and so provoke a crisis within the army is still a subject of debate.)

Kelly differed from Christle on other matters also. Christle wanted to 'ostracize' British servicemen by using the EOKA tactics of bomb-ing cafés, pubs and dance halls patronized by British soldiers. Kelly disagreed because Catholics might be killed and this he felt would be murder – an attitude towards taking life typical of the thinking concer-ning the use of force and the IRA. It is best illustrated by a story from the 1930s. A man wanted to have a farmer shot because of a dispute over land. The chosen IRA man asked him if he had any sons. He had three, all in their early twenties. Could they not handle the problem for him. The man was horrified.

'My sons shoot him is it? Sure that'd be *murder*.'

Kelly and Christle disagreed again on what the outcome of a suc-cessful revolution should be. Kelly did not care who ruled Ireland so long as she were free. Christle saw himself as a socialist revolutionary wanting to create a revolutionary situation by violent methods. To the

Northerners, the police were only guarding the peace. Christle argued, 'Let's break the peace so!'

Both men had to acknowledge one fact although in different ways: Kelly by suddenly departing to the States without telling Christle and Christle by laying down his gun, though not his belief in the use of force. The fact was that a campaign such as theirs could not change the position of the Northern Irish government.

In the event the Kelly-Christle partnership cost no lives nor did they lose a man on the border. When in January 1959, a group of Christle's men were caught by the Gardai and interned he ordered them to sign out. He was arrested himself but was later released.

Readers will see for themselves how in the decade 1969–79 scruples of Kelly's sort were laid aside as irrelevant as a newer and more ruthless breed of IRA man decided that there was no such thing as justifiable or murderous force – there was only effective or ineffective force, and effective force was decided on whatever the cost.

Padraig Pearse, commander of the Easter Rising, addressing a meeting in Ireland in 1915. His writings and ideas formed the philosophical basis of modern Republicanism. He was executed by the British in 1916.

An early group of Volunteers in uniform.

Volunteers Jack Doyle and Tom McGrath inside the Dublin G.P.O. during the Easter Rising of 1916.

Republican prisoners being marched to the Dublin docks for transport to British prison camps after the 1916 Easter Rising.

The G.P.O. photographed from the top of Nelson's Column just after the Easter Rising.

The view of Nelson's Column (destroyed by an I.R.A. bomb in March 1966) down Henry Street, showing the devastation in central Dublin after the Easter Rising.

Michael Collins, Commander-in-Chief of the Irish Republican forces, brought the British to the bargaining table and headed the team which negotiated the Treaty of Irish Independence.

Sir Hammer Greenwood inspecting a unit of the much feared group of British Army Auxilaries. (*Hulton Picture Library*)

On the brink of the Civil War, anti-Treaty I.R.A. gunmen patrol Grafton Street, Dublin, July 1922. (*Hulton Picture Library*)

An I.R.A. patrol on the border between Donegal and Tyrone, May 1922. (*Belfast Telegraph*)

An early group of B-Specials. First organized by Lord Brookeborough in 1920, this Protestant Unionist volunteer militia rapidly spread to all parts of the Six Counties.

A group of I.R.A. men tunnelled out of a Derry jail in March 1943, and fled across the border in a truck. They were picked up by Southern soldiers and interned. This photograph of their arrest was taken by a woman who stood unnoticed behind a hedge.

An R.U.C. man with a Sten gun outside his barracks in 1957. The poster offers a reward for information about the death of R.U.C. Sgt. Arthur Ovens.

Irish-American "Minute Men" picket the British consulate in New York in April 1958. They were protesting against the trial and ill treatment of two men from County Tyrone for taking part in a booby-trap murder of R.U.C. Sgt. Arthur Ovens.

A British soldier describes his narrow escape from the I.R.A to his compatriots, 1954. The photograph was taken through a hole in the wall surrounding the barracks, unbeknownst to those inside. (*Colman Doyle*)

A British Army patrol from the Royal Warwickshire Regiment on the streets of Belfast in the mid-1950s.

Rev. Ian Paisley's Ulster Constitution Defence Committee blocking Armagh city centre to civil rights marchers, November 1968. Their cudgels had nails driven through them. (*Colman Doyle*)

Rev. Ian Paisley during his first campaign for election to Stormont. (*Colman Doyle*)

B-Specials in Derry, August 1969. The handkerchiefs are for protection against gas. (*Colman Doyle*)

A young Nationalist citizen of Derry faces the R.U.C. during the Battle of the Bogside, August 1969. (*Colman Doyle*)

A canister of tear gas lands on the Bogside barricades, August 1969. (*Colman Doyle*)

At the height of the Battle of the Bogside, an R.U.C. armoured car burns in William Street. (*Colman Doyle*)

Massed Loyalists jeer in the background as British troops charge Nationalists, firing rubber bullets. Belfast, May 1971. (*Colman Doyle*)

The chaos of 30 January 1972 – Bloody Sunday – as British troops fired on the peaceful demonstration, killing thirteen unarmed civilians and injuring many more. (*Colman Doyle*)

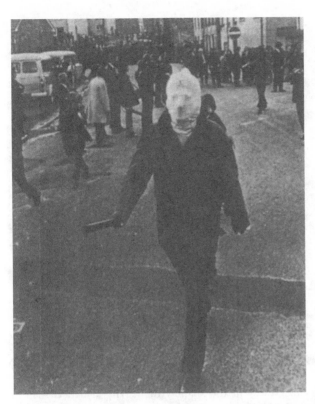

U.D.A. march in
Armagh, June 1972.

The coffin of Lord
Mountbatten being
borne by Irish troops
on to an aeroplane
for return to
Britain, 1979.

Civil rights marchers in Newry in the shadow of heavily armed British forces in 1972. (*Colman Doyle*)

British Army soldiers on patrol in Northern Ireland. (*Colman Doyle*)

14

The Border Campaign: 1956–62

While the border was the prime source of political discontent in Ireland during 1956, it was also the principal source of revenue for anyone in the area wanting to get rich quickly. Politics and smuggling, to a certain extent, are still the main preoccupations in a belt of land reaching about forty miles into the hinterland on both sides of the border, which stretches from Derry in the North to Carlingford Lough at its southernmost extremity. Not only does the border divide North from South, it also divides the North. Donegal, which is in the Republic, is more northerly than any spot in the Six Counties and the bewildering loops and curves of the red line marking the division on the map are even more bewildering to an observer standing on a hill a couple of miles north of any of the border counties.

Politically, to the east of the Bann river 80 per cent of the population is Unionist. This is where the good land lies. Driving through the North once with a knowledgeable commentator pointing out the Protestant and Catholic areas to me, I could soon tell for myself which was which – the Orangemen had all the fertile low-lying land, the Catholics generally lived in the hilly marginal areas west of the Bann in east and mid-Tyrone, south Down, west Armagh, south Armagh, south Fermanagh and in the Derry area. At the time of the border campaign these areas were described politically as 'Nationalist'. Apart from a brief interlude of enthusiasm for a Civil Rights policy of reform within the system, circa 1967–69, they could again be so described, and to a heightened degree today.

Geographically the 'North' can be either left or right of you, turning in behind you, running along before you, or all unknown to you falling further and further behind as you drive along an 'unapproved road', one on which a customs patrol can stop you when you fondly imagine you are still in the Republic. Of course, if you come to a sign post you can tell immediately: if you are in the North the names are printed only in English, in the Republic they are given in both Irish and English. Also, rural electrification is further advanced in the Republic and you can tell by the large number of poles and overhead wires where you are. In 1956 it was usually possible to tell North from South by the way the fields were kept. Those in the South looked the way the country-side looks in childhood or on Christmas cards: overgrown, bounded by enormous hedges and ditches and as likely to be occupied by rabbits, hares, flocks of crows, flights of pigeons, or occasional foxes and badgers as by cattle or sheep. The fields in the North were neat trim agricultural units.

As the South's agriculture improved, it became increasingly hard to tell the two sides apart by looking at the landscape – and even more difficult to find someone who knew from living there. Emigration to England, to America and to the towns on either side of the border, drained away the people at a rate that could be measured better visually than statistically. Standing on a hill in 1969 at an old IRA jumping-off point such as Knockatallon, six miles north of Monaghan town, you could see the remains of perhaps thirty homesteads from which people had gone in the last five or six years.

The man on whose land I stood had memories of a boyhood and adolescence filled with dances and card games, cups of tea in neigh-bours' houses, rabbit hunting, haymaking, bringing in the harvest with the labour shared between one farmer and another, and the excitement distributed evenly among the hordes of children. His children had no one to play with. It was two miles to the nearest shop and three to the local school. They had no car and by the time his wife had looked after the large family she was lucky if she could manage more than two or three visits a year to Monaghan. This man was in the IRA and 'immediate and violent revolution' was his solution to the problems of life in north Co. Monaghan. It may not be a good solution but you could at least have understood his feelings if you looked over his empty countryside on a wet winter's day. He was a skilful man who could have made good money in Dublin, but his father was a widower in his seventies, and would not leave his farm, his only reassurance in his old age, and my friend could not leave his father alone in the green desert where the pressures of economics had left only the rushes and furze to chase men off the land.

Life was traditionally hard in these counties, which is why the natives made poteen to keep out the cold and the reality. Then came the border and they started to smuggle after the land annuities dispute and the economic warfare made a field across the road a part of England so far as tariffs were concerned. It was a smuggler's paradise.

The pattern of smuggling changed with the times. During the war any food was welcome in the North. Car batteries, tyres, razor blades and nylons fetched good prices in the Republic. Butter was a perennial favourite, because the cheap food policy of British governments had left a gap ranging from sixpence to two shillings in the pound between the price of butter in the Republic and the North. Whatever the fluctuation, there was always an inducement for someone with a lorry to run four or five tons of butter down south. Dramatic confrontations between customs men and smugglers, midnight car chases and rammings were so frequent that they rarely made any sort of headlines unless the Dublin evening papers were stuck for news.

The border runs through farms, and even through houses, as in the village of Pettigoe, divided between Donegal and Fermanagh and the entire area is a mass of small, winding roads without signposts. There is a tradition of secrecy in the area as well as the normal suspicion of the law that exists in the Irish countryside. Children mistrust strangers and are trained to regard even the most innocent questions as being aimed at their family's liberty.

While I was driving around the border, inspecting the jumping-off points for raids and the places that were attacked a school teacher told a story which illustrated the local attitude to the police perfectly. A patrolling squad car had picked up a child wandering along the side of a by-road, at a time in the morning which suggested that the child was either lost or a truant from school. The child, a boy of about seven, appeared not to know his own name or where he lived. Neither did anyone at the farms at which the squad car called. Eventually the police sought the teacher's help and he immediately recognized the child as one of his pupils, the son of an established local family. Everyone the police had called on earlier must have known this also, but they, and the child, mistrusted the police's motive in trying to identify the boy. 'Tell them nothing', is the motto of the border counties.

Such were the traditions of the countryside in which the IRA launched, on 12 December 1956, a campaign against the North.

The actual beginning of the campaign was as untidy and as straggling as the countryside itself. One cannot point to a quickly implemented decision to start the campaign, but shortly after 'Operation Harvest' was proposed the IRA leadership decided that some such scheme should be put into effect. The 'three Macs' were not, however, enthusiastic. MacCurtain argued that they had no armaments to justify such a campaign, but the urge for 'action', founded on a lack of appreciation of the real partition problem and fired by the optimism of youth, overcame his and other objections (Magan was irresolute for a time and MacLogan and Traynor were not happy either). Murphy, Russell, Cronin, Brady and the younger element in the leadership carried the day, and from April 1956 on the IRA made plans for the campaign.

In these early days of the campaign and its planning Charlie Murphy was comparatively little known. He was, however, a key man in organizing the campaign, was later involved in a *cause célèbre* and was the central figure in a dispute which split the IRA internally.

On 13 January 1957, a month after the campaign had officially started, Murphy, Magan, MacCurtain and Sean Cronin (not the Cronin of the IRA leadership but a namesake) were arrested at Murphy's home after they had attended Mass. The arrests were made by Detective Inspector Philip MacMahon, later head of the Special Branch and the man who was to prove the nemesis of Murphy and the movement. Along with the men the police seized incriminating lists of money sent from America to the IRA.

MacMahon turned the captured evidence over to the state solicitor's office and ten days later it was produced in court before Judge Michael Lennon.[*] Lennon created something of a sensation by openly siding with the accused men. When the prosecutor produced a copy of the declaration which brought the Offences Against the State Act into force, Lennon remarked ironically, 'This proclamation does not end with the words "God save the King".' The prosecutor asked if he were expected to reply and the judge said, 'Yes. I remember proclamations

---

[*] In 1931 Lennon had attacked James Joyce, in the American *Catholic World*. He revealed that mixture of shame and chauvinism which so many Irish intellectuals show to the 'one who got away', because they feel that such a person is condemning them by force of example to the role of timeservers in a land where, as Joyce put it, 'Christ and Caesar are hand in glove'. The attack so infuriated Joyce that six years later he wrote to his friend Constantine Curran refusing to visit Dublin because to him the map of Ireland was marked 'Hic Sunt Lennones'.

of the kind made in relation to myself and they always ended with the words, "God save the King".'

Further exchanges followed and at a later hearing Lennon ordered that the property belonging to the two IRA men before him – Magan and MacCurtain – be returned to them. The 'property' consisted of ammunition and, order or no order, MacMahon refused to hand it back.

Lennon's actions cost him his judgeship. After an inquiry he was retired on a not very impressive pension. But this stern treatment of an eccentric but humane judge should be assessed against the background of a time during which many judges were reluctant to include IRA cases on their lists and sentences on IRA defendants tended to be of the order of three to six months. At the same time the IRA was attempting not to recognize the courts.

Murphy had meanwhile served three months and he was to remain at liberty for almost a year. He married on 6 February 1958, the day of the abortive raid on the Blandford military barracks in Dorset, England. (This was another example of daring and planning going to waste. Before the raid Murphy and Frank Skuse paid several visits to the camp and familiarized themselves with the layout. The raiding party of nine men was led by Sean Cronin and included Skuse but the attack was completely bungled. The only result was that a British soldier was shot in the stomach; no arms or ammunition were seized and the raiders were forced to abandon a new car obtained for the occasion.) Shortly afterwards the IRA learned that the Special Branch was about to arrest a captain in the regular army who had been helping the IRA. Someone had to warn him and Murphy volunteered. MacMahon immediately learned of this (the Special Branch by this stage had the IRA riddled with informers) and MacMahon was waiting.

Murphy went back to prison and MacMahon then singled him out as the victim of a ploy designed to split the IRA down the middle – which it did very successfully. Murphy was depressed at his capture, the various disastrous raids and the failure of the campaign in general and was disposed to listen to tales of the hardships which families of imprisoned IRA men were suffering. For several days MacMahon tried in vain to talk with Murphy, but eventually MacMahon got him to accept a week's parole during which he was to contact the Army Council and report that if the campaign were called off all the prisoners would be released.

Sean Cronin, the leading man of the hour, was furious at Murphy's action. Cronin believed that if the IRA decided to end the campaign the prisoners would automatically be released, an assumption which was open to question in the light of what had happened during the war. Having encountered great hostility, Murphy returned to jail after two days and refused from then on to have any dealings with MacMahon. But the damage had been done. The IRA was subsequently riven by controversy as to the rights and wrongs of Murphy's action.

The first decision the campaign planners made was to send organizers to a number of centres: north Antrim, south Derry, south-east Derry, south Fermanagh, south Down, south Armagh, Derry city. These were all Nationalist areas and all were easily reached from the border. Belfast did not require a special organizer as Paddy Doyle lived there. Then this was interrupted by the Joe Christle split in June, and the energies of the IRA were devoted to dissuading volunteers from following Christle. (When twelve out of the fifteen officers in the Dublin area did follow him, eighteen-year-olds in some cases succeeded them.) For a time Christle's followers kept their weapons, but tensions subsided when these were handed back. As a result the organizers were not sent in until August, but they managed to remain undetected, despite their Southern accents, until the outbreak of hostilities. There were approximately twenty of these organizers and their job was to train volunteers locally, act as intelligence agents, pick out targets and report back to Dublin in person at regular intervals.

The Army Council had voted to begin the campaign in November 1956, but the irresolution of some members of the council, and a number of other snags pushed the date into December. During the planning period Paddy Doyle was captured with a Belfast newsletter to local units and the council decided to cut Belfast out of the campaign altogether. It had been feared all along that the IRA might be too weak to defend Belfast Catholics and this setback decided the issue. Then there was a row between the emissary sent from Dublin to Derry concerning the smuggling of arms into the North. Derry had been chosen as the entry point but as a result of the row it was decided to send the arms in by south Fermanagh. This caused a twenty-four-hour delay on the very eve of the campaign, almost getting Charlie Murphy captured on 10 December. He had to drive through the border areas postponing everything and between the psychological let-down and the exhaustion caused by travel and lack of sleep he failed to notice that he was driving without his lights on. He was stopped by an RUC man in Pomeroy, Co. Tyrone, but was let off with a caution. (On Armistice Day he had an even narrower escape when Joe Christle and Liam Kelly burned down custom huts. Murphy, Noel Kavanagh and Sean Daly were in the North casing likely targets. Their method of operation was to drop a petrol cap off their car as they passed an RUC barracks and then get out to look for it, inspecting the area as they did so. They were doing this outside an RUC barracks when charges went off under the customs huts, but they escaped.)

Approximately one hundred and fifty men took part in the opening night of the campaign which between then and its end in 1962, was to cost, according to figures supplied to me by a Stormont spokesman, £1 million in outright damage (paid for by the British exchequer) and approximately £10 million in increased police and military patrols. Six young RUC men and eleven Republicans were killed. In the South increased patrols and the opening of the Curragh internment camp cost in the region of £400,000 a year for the campaign's duration. The campaign was certainly a factor in the fall of the government in Dublin in 1957, and had other effects. An official concerned with attracting new industry to Ireland told me that some British and Continental investment was scared off by the disturbances.

But though matters appeared serious to foreigners, and poisoned the relations of Dublin with both Belfast and London, the Irish, both North and South, viewed it with less excitement. In the North the Nationalists refer to the campaign today as 'the incidents', because that is in fact what it was: a series of incidents along the border, impinging very little on Belfast and annoying rather than terrifying the Northern administration. It did, of course, arouse terror in the hearts of Unionist sympathizers living along the border – even on the Southern side. In the early stages of the campaign some Southern Protestants living in border areas made a practice of crossing over to earn pocket money as B-Specials, but after it became known that the IRA was aware of this practice the Gardai warned moonlighting B-men that it would be impossible to guarantee their safety in the South. In the South public interest flared up for the first few days of the campaign or at dramatic moments like the Brookeborough raid with its subsequent emotive funerals; the opening of the internment camps; the trial which led to Judge Lennon's dismissal; Sean Cronin's trial at which 'Operation Harvest' was read out in court, and the trial of two young Co. Tyrone men for the murder of an RUC sergeant blown to pieces in a booby-trapped cottage. But once it became obvious that the campaign could have no effect on the permanency of the Northern regime public interest diminished.

Interest reached its highest point in the Republic's elections in 1957, when Sinn Fein candidates polled 66,000 votes, but by the 1961 election this total had fallen by half and no Sinn Fein candidates were elected. At no time did this interest even betoken any hostility to England or indeed towards the North. Most people in the Republic were rather puzzled by the whole thing and were inclined to write the whole thing off as 'the IRA at it again', without any clear appreciation of why it should have been at it again. British tourists were as welcome as ever in the South. In fact, except for a time of great emotion such as the 1916 Rising, or the time of the 'Troubles', and isolated episodes which we shall come to later, such as the killing of Lord Mountbatten or the burning of the British Embassy, it is difficult to find a time in this century when anyone in Ireland would attack an Englishman – despite the efforts of some schoolteachers and politicians who, failing any coherent philosophy of their own, often do make efforts to equate being pro-Irish with being anti-British.

One incident which I can authenticate shows the degree of incomprehension that exists in Irish-English affairs. It occurred at the time of the 1955 Ras Tailteann, the day after the Northern authorities had prohibited the carrying of the tricolour in Northern areas by Ras cyclists. The prohibition, and its breach by some cyclists, had led to violence and a number of cyclists were beaten up by Orangemen. An NCA supporter, employed at Killarney Mental Hospital and normally one of the gentlest of men, was so incensed when he read of this that he swore to take retributory action if he could. He was on his rounds as a van driver on a deserted country road when he saw a British car coming towards him. He stopped his van, halted the car, seized the Union Jack fluttering from the bonnet and tore it into pieces and jumped on them while the middle-aged couple in the car, both visitors from the north of England, looked on in astonishment. The destruction accomplished he drove off leaving Mum saying to Dad (as they later reported), 'Eeh lad. The man in Aer Lingus never said owt about anything like that!' But as the van drove over the hill they noticed in large letters on the rear doors 'Killarney Mental Hospital' and the whole incident thereupon (wrongly) lost all political significance.

*   *   *

The campaign began with a satisfactory bang. Ten different areas were attacked on the night of 12 December 1956, in a ring from Antrim round to Derry. The targets included the BBC relay transmitter at Rosemount, Derry, which was demolished, and Gough Barracks, Armagh, which survived. A Territorial Army headquarters, being built at Enniskillen, was blown down. The Magherafelt Quarter Sessions Courthouse, Co. Derry, was burned down. Near Magherafelt, Toome Bridge was destroyed. At Newtownbutler, Lady Brooke Bridge was damaged and Carry Bridge at Inishmore Island also suffered. In Newry, a B-Special hut was partly burned.

Most of the explosions took place early in the morning and in Charlie Murphy's words, 'The place looked like the western front. Bombs going off, flames, Very lights, Sten guns – the lot.' He, together with Magan, Robert Russell and others, directed operations from Monaghan, a campaign centre. A guard on his rounds wanted to know what was going on and finally Russell told him that he was a chicken farmer up early to catch the market – a remark rendered nearly inaudible by a loud explosion a few miles to the north. The guard went off complaining that he would have to make a report about this.

The raids were greeted with predictable denunciations in Dublin, London and Belfast, but not in Moscow. On 29 December *Pravda* denied British claims that the raids were only 'isolated actions without popular support' saying: 'The Irish patriots cannot agree with Britain transforming the Six Counties into one of its main military bases in the Atlantic pact.'

In Dublin the government a day later said it would take every action needed to prevent loss of life. In London the government ordered the British ambassador in Dublin, Sir Alexander Clutterbuck, to express Britain's 'very great concern' at the incidents and the hope that Dublin would live up to its promise.

In Belfast of course reaction was more decisive. Lord Brooke-borough referred to the IRA as 'hooligans who raid this country' in a speech on 13 December to a meeting of the Shankill Unionist Association which was also addressed by the chairman of the British Conservative party, Oliver Poole. Poole pledged support for the Unionists and promised that as soon as Sir Anthony Eden, then on a visit to Jamaica, returned to London he would inform him of the raids. At this time Eden was under heavy attack from the 'Suez rebels' and the twelve Unionists at Westminster could not be lightly lost by the Conservative government. The price of their support was seen in a strong statement which Eden made in the House of Commons on 19 December.

Before this the North had already looked to its own defences. The Special Powers Act's regulations were reintroduced on 15 December (providing for arrest and internment without warrant or trial) and further orders provided for the imposition of curfew, the immobilization of cars and a strengthened police force. On 22 December the RUC guided British support in the drastic step of blowing up unapproved roads in border areas, destroying bridges and spiking roads at intervals. Deep craters greatly restricted transport along the border and the only usable roads were guarded by police and customs posts. Three thousand RUC men and 12,000 B-specials were called into action, and the North became an armed camp.

South of the border the number of guards in border areas was doubled and despite the fact that Belfast continually thundered that Dublin was not doing enough to curb the raids it was in fact the Southern Gardai who brought off the first large-scale capture of IRA men and who throughout the campaign posed a greater threat to the IRA than did the RUC. It was also the Gardai who eventually seized the 'three Macs', Murphy, Cronin, Laurence Grogan and the rest of the principal leaders. If the Southern authorities had not been so vigilant the campaign would have certainly been more destructive.

On 16 December the Gardai and units of the Irish army surrounded a farmhouse at Knockatallon and seized Murphy, Cronin and eleven other IRA members but this time released them the same day. Their release caused great annoyance in Stormont where the Minister for Home Affairs, W. B. Topping, observed that he hoped that this was not the sort of 'necessary and appropriate' action which the Southern government had referred to in its statement of 14 December.

Unionist MP Nat Minford, replying to Topping, said that he did not think that the British government was treating the situation seriously enough to 'bring to justice those damned scoundrels nor to bring pressure to bear on the Dublin authorities to stamp out IRA drilling and prevent the raids'.

'We Protestants,' he declaimed, 'are running this country, and are going to run it. We want to live in a country where peace will prevail. If we find that these attacks are going to continue, then we Protestants ourselves will have to determine what the future will be. I'm not content to sit back and see these things continue.'

It was Lord Brookeborough who calmed the atmosphere, saying that Eden had assured him that the North would get the same support in defending itself as any other part of the United Kingdom. He counselled against any efforts to meet force with force, 'no matter how tempted', because such action 'would put the country in a state of chaos, bloodshed and hatred . . . the defence of the country must rest with the government and no one should take any action on their own.' Eden said the next day that 'The safety of Northern Ireland and of its inhabitants is therefore a direct responsibility on Her Majesty's Government, which they will of course discharge.'

Costello replied to Eden, reiterating his statement of 30 November 1955, saying that the six-county area was a part of the Irish national territory and that any claim that the six counties were 'an integral part of the United Kingdom' could never be accepted by any Irish government. He called on Britain, as being primarily responsible for partition, to take the initiative in doing away with it and wound up by saying again that the government would do everything it could to bring 'unlawful military activities to an end'.

But Costello's government had less influence on the campaign than the campaign had on the government. The campaign helped in bringing down the coalition government, returning Fianna Fail to power and thus ultimately leading to the downfall of the IRA. Untroubled by divided councils, as was a coalition having to deal with IRA sympathizers in Clann na Poblachta, Fianna Fail was able to take vigorous and successful action against the movement.

The end of the coalition came on 28 January 1957, when, on behalf of Clann na Poblachta, Sean MacBride moved a vote of no confidence in the government on economic grounds and because of its 'failure to formulate and to pursue any positive policy calculated to bring about the reunification of Ireland'. Deprived of the Clann's support, Costello had no option but to dissolve the Dail which he did on 12 February 1957. A general election was held on 5 March and in the post-Suez economic crisis the coalition took a bad beating, Fianna Fail winning fourteen more seats than it had held in 1954. Clann na Poblachta lost some thirty thousand of the fifty thousand votes it had got in 1954, but Sinn Fein won almost sixty-six thousand. (Their four seats meant nothing because the candidates refused to sit in the Dail and thus lost, if nothing else, the chance of a national platform to state their case.)

One of the most interesting developments of this period was an attempt on the part of the Church to find a solution to the border problem. On 3 March, Cardinal d'Alton put forward a plan proposing that each of the six counties be allowed to choose between Dublin and Belfast. If the North agreed to federation with the South, Ireland was then to associate with the Commonwealth as an independent republic on the same basis as India, and offer bases to NATO. (At the time the cardinal's idea was a non-starter, but so far as Dublin and Westminster were concerned, relations were so harmonious, behind the scenes, on the partition issue that something could well have been worked out. The 'not-an-inch' extremists of the North of course remained a big stumbling block, but even these were considerably weakened by having Harold, rather than Sir Henry, Wilson, in London's Corridors of Power. Had Edward Heath found himself dependent on the ten Unionist back-benchers it might have been a different proposition, however.)

In the campaign itself the organization was of course poor as is obvious from the experiences of a typical IRA organizer. Gerry Higginbothom was nineteen when he attended a Sinn Fein meeting in Middle Abbey Street, Dublin, after the Omagh raid in 1954, and he joined first Sinn Fein and then the IRA. His feelings about partition were simply a vague notion that Ireland would be better off with thirty-two counties than twenty-six, and he was personally anti-British. He was shaken by the Church's letter of January 1955, but after a chat with a Jesuit he decided that this need not affect his political activities. An amiable, able lad, the gap left by the Christle defections brought him to the fore rapidly, and in September 1956 he resigned his job as a clerk and went to Fermanagh under the name of Gerry Cronin. He was joined there by Dave O'Connell from Cork and they began training in Fermanagh and Tyrone.

Young Higginbothom always felt that the predominantly Catholic counties of Derry, Fermanagh and Tyrone, of which he had personal knowledge, were never suitably organized for lengthy guerrilla warfare or even for hit-and-run operations. Training with Thompson and Sten guns and rifles was carried out across the border in Monaghan and was confined to groups of approximately twenty young men at a time. Everyone thought that the movement would snowball when the campaign began, but they were shattered when the Southern police began picking up columns as they recrossed the border and it very soon became clear that no one was going to replace the captured men.

Only luck had kept Higginbothom from being caught before the campaign began. His car had broken down at Derrygonnelly, Co. Fermanagh, and an RUC sergeant asked him his name and what he was doing in the area. Gerry explained that he was interested in exploring caves but he could not answer the policeman's request for the correct name for such activity (he called it archaeology instead of speleology). The sergeant walked off saying resignedly, 'I suppose you'll be coming back some night to put something against the gable end.'

When the campaign began Higginbothom's chosen gable end was Lisanelly Barracks, not far from Omagh. The attack called for the use of gelignite to breach the rear wall, but after obtaining the gelignite from Mountfield quarry, seven miles away, his lorry stuck in a ditch. While the lorry was being extricated sirens went off as other points were attacked and when Higginbothom and his group finally got back to the mustering point the rest of the raiding party had disappeared. Only their possession of two Thompson guns enabled him and his companions to secure a night's lodgings in a mountain farmhouse. (Another young IRA man of the period, Terry O'Toole, told me that in his experience food and lodging had become so hard to find by 1958 as the campaign wore on that he frequently had to brandish a revolver to get in for a night.) There followed eighteen days in a shack with food being supplied at intervals by local sympathizers.

On New Year's Eve 1957 he and his column were ready to attack Carrickmore Barracks about ten miles away from their hideout when they learned of the Brookeborough affair (described below) and Carrickmore had to be abandoned because the area was alive with police and soldiers. They were advised to retreat to Strabane where Saor Uladh members put them up. They crossed the border with the aid of friendly girls who paired off with them as if they were going across to the Republic for a 'court'. In Dublin Higginbothom made contact with the leadership and was asked to return to the North, to Donegal, and to attempt to recross the border and organize a column around Strabane.

By this time, however, the more reliable men in Strabane had been picked up and he could get nothing done. In desperation he took twelve men to Clady one night and let off a mine at an old bridge in the hope that the military would be attracted to the scene and that an ambush could be carried out. However, the RUC made it a policy to ignore things that went bang in the night and this ploy failed. He returned to Strabane later dressed as a Franciscan friar and was saluted with due reverence. But he spent the first afternoon in dread because there was a woman dying nearby and for a time it seemed likely that he would be called on to administer the last rites. In the end he gave himself away in a shop by asking for a brand of Southern cigarettes that was not sold in the North. There are no Franciscans in the North anyhow and this slip enabled the RUC to apprehend him. The campaign knew him no more.

A farmhouse at Knockatallon was intended as the operational HQ for the border area, the place from which raids could be launched and to which men could return. It was only about a mile and a half to the border from the house but on 13 December, a cold, sleety night, to avoid the roads which were alive with police an IRA patrol led by Charlie Murphy followed a route thirty miles over mountain and bog to attack the RUC barracks in the town of Lisnaskea. In the town there were some anxious moments when it was learned than an IRA suspect had been captured and was in a cell at the rear of the barracks. It was feared (wrongly) that he might have given away the raid and while Murphy and the others were going over the final plans in an outhouse not far from the barracks, the woman whose husband owned the farm burst in and exclaimed, 'That fucking bollocks has spilt the beans.' Murphy was thunderstruck, not because of the suspected leakage but because he had never heard a woman swear before. However, they decided to go ahead.

Lisnaskea Barracks is a three-storeyed building in the main street of Lisnaskea with houses on either side, one of them the local curate's, who was then a Father Fergusson. Across the road lived the parish priest, Canon Donnelly. The IRA party got word to him that they were shortly going to free 'occupied Ireland' and would he care to vacate his part of it in case something nasty came through his window during the war of liberation?

(Solicitude for the welfare of parish priests is not normally a characteristic of the IRA, but all had received confession a short time earlier from a Republican-minded young chaplain who had turned his Volkswagen into a roadside confessional.) The old canon sent back word that at his time of life death might as well come to him in his own house and he stayed put.

As the raid began Murphy was just removing a mine from the back of a truck when the driver put his foot on the accelerator instead of the brake, the truck moved forward and the mine dropped at Charlie's feet. The mine, which was made of gelignite, failed to explode. Half of the group then dashed across the road with it, and placed it in position. It went off perfectly at 1.20 a.m. and blew in the side of the barracks, and with it the staircase, which meant that the attackers could not get at the fourteen RUC men. The aim of the raid had been to destroy the barracks and take whatever arms were available, but without heavy weaponry this was impossible. Neither of the two Bren guns used by the attackers functioned properly. The police replied with Sten guns and revolvers and between them the two parties managed to break almost every window in the town. After twenty minutes the IRA broke off the attack and made off in the truck, sheets of tracer bullets pouring down the street after it. 'It made a very pretty sight' one of the residents of the town told me.

Derrylin Barracks was also attacked that night without any damage. Two bridges outside Lisnaskea were blown up to delay pursuit. Everyone concerned got back safely to Knockatallon, arriving in broad daylight, much to Sean Cronin's horror. Here they heard Costello's statement about 'appropriate action' and decided that weapons not immediately needed should be dumped.

The main column then returned across the border hoping to ambush a patrol. Cronin, Murphy and eleven others stayed on, Murphy intending to go next day to south Fermanagh with a sack of ammunition for Noel Kavanagh. He then fell asleep and was shaken awake a few hours later to find that police and soldiers had surrounded the farm and that the kitchen was full of police. Everyone was very polite. 'Excuse me, sir,' said the soldier who had awakened him. 'Not at all,' he replied and when police and soldiers vanished upon discovering a mine upstairs, Murphy rendered it harmless for them.

There were a number of incriminating documents in the house and when the party was taken to Monaghan police station none of them expected to see home again for some time. But the police officer in charge of the operation telephoned Dublin from the room in which they were detained and to their incredulity they realized from the conversation that they might not be charged.

'No sir, they'd no ammunition,' they heard him say and they were told that they could go – whereupon they immediately refused to move unless they were given transport! The police contended that they had no transport, but Cronin and Murphy persisted and finally two taxis were hired and paid for by the police and the whole party driven to Dublin, Murphy and Cronin in a squad car. The pair walked up

Emmet Road, where Murphy lived, in their American army battle dress, but finding that Mrs Murphy had gone to England to visit Donal they called round to a neighbour for breakfast.

A little later Magan came and told them that the campaign had been called off because of their arrest and that Laurence Grogan was in Drogheda contacting those concerned to tell them this. After much argument an Army Council meeting was called and it decided to reactivate the campaign, the men on the border being recalled, however, not only for Christmas but also to regroup and reorganize.

In a sense the Brookeborough ambush explains everything about the IRA and its hold on Irish tradition. It shows all the courage, the self-sacrifice, the blundering and the emotional appeal that have characterized and kept alive the IRA spirit for centuries. The two young men who lost their lives in the Brookeborough affair, Fergal O'Hanlon and Sean South, were given two of the biggest funerals in living memory – but during their lives there was never sufficient public support for their aims for them to receive proper military instruction or even to be correctly briefed on the target that claimed their lives: the RUC barracks in the centre of the little Fermanagh town of Brookeborough.

O'Hanlon was nineteen at the time of his death and South twenty-seven. South was cut from the same cloth as Pearse or Liam Lynch. A clerk in his native Limerick city, he was a prominent member of An Realt, the Irish-speaking branch of the Legion of Mary. The Legion, the physical manifestation of the Mariolatry which characterizes so much of Irish Catholicism, is dedicated to social worker and missionary activity in the developing countries for the Roman Catholic Church. South showed himself in his few writings to be a staunch though not uncritical Catholic and possessed of a social conscience. His attraction to the military calling is shown by the fact that the only photograph of him in circulation shows him in his uniform as an officer in the FCA, the regular Irish army reserve.

O'Hanlon was also an outstanding young man in his native Monaghan town. A keen footballer interested in Gaelic culture, he leaves several references in his diaries to the need for training and self-discipline in order to do his duty for Ireland. His IRA comrades remember him as a particularly winning and promising boy.

I once called on O'Hanlon's parents and visited the farm where he died. Mrs O'Hanlon looked and acted like the mother of a martyred saint. She had the same passionate dedication to the cause which claimed him as had her son and she spoke about his death as something holy as well as patriotic. It hurt her to hear anyone suggest that the cause should be abandoned or that the Republican movement should forswear force as a means of reuniting Ireland. To her, this was a betrayal of all that Fergal and those who went before him died for.

After a meal his father drove me to the place called Baxter's Cross. Hard by the Cross there stands an old-fashioned, two-storeyed farmhouse and beside it a cowbyre. It was in this byre that the bodies of O'Hanlon and South were found. A few miles away to the north is Brookeborough. (Ironically things had become so peaceful that the barracks which was the scene of the raid had become a private house occupied by a family.) Both the farmhouse and the byre at Baxter's Cross are deserted. There are no windows or doors in the byre and one has to look closely to pick out the bullet holes in the wall and the two tiny crosses which Mrs O'Hanlon set into the cement at the spots where her son and his comrade died.

It was frustration after so many failures that led to the Brookeborough raid, plus the fact that the raiders, who had been out on long, fruitless patrol duty, had been supplied with detailed plans of the barracks by a local. On the night of the raid, January 1957, the raiding party got its first full meal since Christmas at a friendly house and set off in a truck for the attack.

Brookeborough is an Irish town of the sort best described by the quip, 'It has only one Main street and the further you go, the mainer it gets.' The barracks was located in the middle of the town in a house which looked no different from those adjoining. The plan was for the truck to pull up outside the barracks, five men acting as a cover group staying in the truck to open fire and divert attention while an assault group armed with two mines, two Thompson guns and four rifles, augmented by a half-dozen or so home-made grenades, breached the barracks walls and gained entrance. While this was going on, two other men would keep watch on the roads leading into the town.

There was nothing to distinguish the barracks and in the badly lit street the driver, Vincent Conlon, who had given up a job in America to come home when he read of the raids, almost missed it. However, one member of the party, a local man, shouted out, 'Oh Jasus, there's the barracks,' and the truck stopped immediately outside the building.

The cover group opened fire with a Bren gun and four rifles while the assault group attempted to let off a landmine. It failed to explode and the party had to dash back and get a second mine from the truck. This also misfired, even when someone tried to trigger it by shooting at it. Then South's Bren gun ran out of ammunition – they had only three magazines for it, a microscopic amount for such a quick-firing gun. As soon as its noise died away the raiders realized that the occupants of the barracks were returning their fire. South was hit first; like the others in the truck he was a sitting target from the upper windows of the barracks. One of the attackers threw a grenade at the barracks, but it bounced off a window-sill and fell under the truck. Just as this happened a burst of Bren-gun fire wounded Phil O'Donoghue, Sean Garland and Fergal O'Hanlon. Then the grenade went off and O'Donoghue was blown off the truck; as he hit the road he was struck by three bullets, one of which ran right around his stomach under his belt without scratching him. All it left was a red weal.

Despite the rain of bullets, the party somehow scrambled back into the truck while the RUC concentrated its fire on the driver. The windscreen was cracked and frosted by the bullets. Conlon could not see where he was going, but one of the men who had been guarding the approach to the town came back directly under the windows of the barracks and broke in the windscreen with his rifle butt. Conlon was unhurt but the truck's tipper gears had been shot to pieces and every time the truck went over a bridge or bump its back went up in the air and everyone in it slipped to the rear. Conlon managed to keep going for a few miles despite this damage and the ruined tyres and then at Baxter's Cross the party halted, realizing that the RUC must be close behind and that Roslea which lay ahead would be alerted.

There was no one in the farmhouse and the only shelter for O'Hanlon and South, who were both unconscious, was the open cow-byre. Four other members of the party were wounded and one, Sean Garland, wanted them to leave him behind so that he could make a fight of it and gain time for the rest to escape. He was dissuaded and the survivors retreated up the hill a few hundred yards in the direction of the border. About ten minutes later the RUC drove up, stopped by the abandoned truck and, taking no chances, opened fire on it for what seemed like five minutes. A few minutes later the IRA party heard one long burst of fire coming from the direction of the cowbyre and they believed afterwards that this was the *coup de grâce* being administered to O'Hanlon and South. However, Pat Regan (upon whose personal account I have based this description of the raid) went back to the spot some years later and found that the line of bullet holes was approximately waist to chest high on the wall facing the cow-byre entrance and he concluded that none of these bullets struck either O'Hanlon or South, unless perhaps by ricochet. He attributed the firing on the cowbyre to the normal military tactics, employed when approaching a strongpoint supposedly held by the enemy, of falling on one knee and firing a burst. However, this explanation did not percolate through IRA circles for some years and the deaths of O'Hanlon and South were a source of immense bitterness.

The survivors reached the Monaghan border safely where, after resting in a friendly house, they gave themselves up to obtain medical attention for the wounded. They were treated in the Mater Hospital, Dublin, and although the police were supposedly keeping a keen eye on them, and their names were printed in the papers, they all managed to leave their sick beds at varying intervals and get out of the hospital, which has a long Nationalist tradition, without being detained.

The greatest single disaster of the entire campagin was Edentubber explosion in Co. Louth which claimed five lives in November 1957. In some parts of the Irish countryside where tragedy has walked across some green corner it is possible to recreate the event from a relic of some sort – a tumbled-down church, a ruin, a cross perhaps, but at Eden-tubber today all that remains is a five-barred gate leading into an empty field. Not a stone stands to mark the spot where four young IRA men and the owner of the forester's cottage were blown to pieces when a home-made landmine went off just before the four set off to cross the Louth border a few yards away. Behind the hill there is a lane which leads to a Mass rock inscribed with a cross, a memento of the religious division of the penal days that began the whole affair. Behind rise the Carlingford mountains, ahead lies Newry, home of one of the dead boys, Oliver Craven, nineteen. In the distance there is Armagh, the birthplace of a second victim, Paul Smith, also nineteen, and away to the south far beyond the reach of eye is Co. Wexford, which gave a title to one of President Kennedy's favourite songs, 'The Boys of Wexford':

We are the Boys of Wexford,
We fought with heart and hand
To burst in twain our Captive Chains
And free our native land.

George Keegan, twenty-nine, and Patrick Parle, twenty-seven, had been singing that song since boyhood, and on the night of 12 November 1957, they had left their native Wexford to play a part, as they saw it, in freeing their native land. The fifty-five-year-old bachelor who went to his death with them had lived alone since his mother died. His life and death were symbolic of the Irish: love of his mother denied him a wife; love of his fatherland took his life. Little wonder that the news of this affair shocked Murphy and Cronin. Murphy in particular became prey to a melancholy, suffering for years afterwards, losing weight and frequently waking up sweating in the grip of nightmares.

It is here worth looking briefly at the career of a prominent IRA man of the border campaign period – Terry O'Toole. He saw much active service over a long period, was one of the 'activists' while interned in the Curragh and was very aware of the intrigues and splits that affected the movement.

O'Toole joined the IRA in June 1954, influenced by the Armagh raid and by the fact that his uncle, Tom Maguire of Mayo, was and is a life-long Republican. He joined the Heath unit (named from the heath near Portlaoise, another traditionally Republican area where Mac-Logan had his pub). Nothing happened beyond routine drilling and meetings until August 1957, despite repeated appeals by Terry and the unit to be sent north. MacLogan was the leading figure in the area and was not in favour of such action.

Then in August word came from Dublin that five men were required immediately for active service. Terry could not supply the request and went to Galmoy in neighbouring Kilkenny to get two volunteers. With these he went to Dublin and was directed to Donegal. The first operation was to be an ambush of British soldiers from Omagh Barracks along the Omagh-Derry road. However, the ambush party, about fifteen strong, was forestalled and a police raid seized 150 lbs of gelignite which had been made into mines.

O'Toole and the others withdrew to Mountfield in south Tyrone and began to train about fourteen local youths, there and in Carrick-more.* The local people were friendly but the IRA was very poorly

---

* Carrickmore became a flash-point in Anglo-Irish relations during October–November 1979, when at a time following Mountbatten's death, the British were pressing the Irish on security, the IRA again took over the village for several hours, for the BBC's *Panorama* programme, under the noses of the nearby, and unsuspecting, British army.

organized and Frank Morris of Convoy, Co. Donegal, who was strictly speaking in Saor Uladh, was their mentor in the area. It was to him that they looked for guidance rather than to Dublin. O'Toole and his group worked with local farmers cutting turf and sharing farmhouse chores. There was no difficulty about freedom of movement by day but night raids by police on suspected houses became so heavy that accommodation was hard to find.

It was decided to build a dug-out in a farmhouse which was used as a piggery by a friendly farmer. Working at night, they removed the floor of one room and dug down eight feet, scattering the yellow clay in a nearby potato field lest it attract attention. The hole was then covered with railway sleepers provided by sympathizers, and the sleepers were covered with concrete. Entry was provided by a shaft which was cut from under a small porch outside the house. Covered by a camouflaged trap-door the shaft and dug-out were completely hidden. After giving the concrete a week to settle straw was sprinkled over it and the pigs were allowed back in. In all it took ten days to build during which the IRA group lived on packets of chicken noodle soup and potatoes from nearby fields. It seemed a small price to pay in return for the safety of the dug-out, but in fact the hiding place nearly killed them all. When they woke up after the first night in the shelter all of them were suffering from excruciating headaches. There was such an acute lack of oxygen that matches would not strike. Worse, they could not force open the trap-door, because the pigs were lying on it. Eventually the tallest man in the group managed to get his shoulder to the door and forced it and a surprised pig into the air. He almost collapsed from the effort. Had his strength not sustained him for the moment all those in the dug-out would have died.

Supplies were now needed for their raids as they had only approximately two hundred rounds of Thompson and three hundred rounds of revolver ammunition. Intelligence was another problem for although the locals were friendly their information was usually so outdated as to be useless. Information about troop movements was finally obtained only after several nights were spent in the open watching B-Specials setting up road blocks a few yards away from them. Then, having discovered when and where to carry out ambushes the supplies problem reasserted itself; four separate lots of equipment sent from Dublin were all seized.

In a hopeless position they decided to move to Monaghan where they thought organization and opportunities would be better. It took them two days on foot, sleeping out at night, and when they got there they learned that two of their number were named in an RUC leaflet as being wanted in connection with the death of a sergeant the previous August. They could all have faced a capital charge had they been caught, and the fact that they were not informed of the leaflet earlier is indicative of the lack of communication between border units and GHQ in Dublin. Then in December O'Toole, Sean Cronin and J. B. O'Hagan, the leading figure in the North, decided that O'Toole's column should be broken up and that he would try to organize the adjoining areas of Lifford, Co. Donegal, and Strabane, Co. Tyrone.

Between Christmas and Easter his group succeeded in blowing up four transformers on a line between Lifford and Derry, a customs hut and an RAF hut. The plan in each case was to attract the military to the scene and ambush them. The Northerners refused to be drawn and neither shooting nor loss of life took place.

Another operation that failed to materialize was planned for Easter under the direction of a Dubliner, Jimmy McGilligan. Over sixty men were to have taken over the village of Clady and made a stand there, similar to that envisaged by Tom Barry in the 1930s. The approaches to Clady were to have been ambushed for some considerable distance so that Easter Monday 1958 would rival Easter Monday 1916. The scheme fell through when the extra men required from Dublin were not forthcoming. Instead Sean Cronin ordered a 'demonstration' in the village.

Seven men accordingly entered the village on Easter Monday night. The Army Council's Easter message was read out, a number of IRA leaflets were distributed and the proceedings concluded with the hoisting of the tricolour and the firing of a volley over the post office. The group waited outside the town hoping to stage an ambush but nothing happened until the following day when a tank arrived at the village to supervise the removal of the tricolour. The next day O'Toole and his group had planned to blow up a B-Special hut but their hideout was discovered and they were taken in handcuffs to the Curragh.

While the bombs continued to go off during 1958, particularly during July, the most significant IRA activity was hidden from the public and in fact took place within the Curragh internment camp.

After a number of skirmishes on the border and raids on quarries in the Republic for gelignite de Valera had reintroduced the Offences Against the State Act on 4 July. Sixty men were picked up in one sweep on 8 July and by the following March a total of 131 were interned in the reopened Curragh. (The camp, however, did not remain open long. The campaign fell into such disarray that the last of the internees were released on 11 March 1959.)

Compared to the rigours of the war years the Curragh now was almost a rest camp. The food was plentiful if unvaried and could be supplemented from outside or by meals cooked in the huts on electric rings. Tea could be obtained from an immersion boiler. There were four huts at the peak of the internment containing about forty detainees in each. Each hut had its own OC and there was a camp council of prisoners with Thomas MacCurtain as OC. The huts were opened at 7 a.m. and breakfast was served in the dining hall at 8. Anyone who was sick got breakfast in his hut, served by a member of the Legion of Mary, until he recovered or was transferred to hospital. Everyone did a spell of orderly duty, cleaning out the lavatory (renamed 'Boland's' in honour of the Minister for Justice), or washing dishes and generally tidying up. Showers were compulsory once a week, and could be had more often. A nearby field was made available for games and the prisoners were also encouraged to read or to make wallets and crosses which were sold outside the camp to raise funds.

The worst feature of internment was the lack of privacy. No one could ever get away from his fellows, or from the sound of chipping and snipping as yet another wallet or cross began its journey to the outside. To a sensitive person the conditions were hell, but several of the internees told me that if you overlooked the defences the place was 'more like a factory than a camp'.

The camp was protected by five sets of fences. Two lay between the camp and a trench six feet deep and eight feet wide, which was booby-trapped with flares and tripwires, and three more fences had to be surmounted when and if this was negotiated. At the four corners of the camp elevated sentry posts were manned by an armed guard. In addition the perimeter was patrolled by guards armed with revolvers and ammonia grenades.

The prisoners were divided among themselves as to escaping. The camp council frowned on escape attempts believing it best to avoid doing anything that might get someone killed. The activists thought this a cowardly attitude and felt that the proper course for Republicans was to make life difficult for their jailers in the time-honoured manner.

Two of the activist group, O'Toole and Conlon, the driver at the Brookeborough raid, brought the debate to a head by trying to escape without the sanction of the camp council.

On first being interned O'Toole was almost glad of the rest and food apart from the 'patriotic eggs', which were so called because, he claims, when cooked they assumed the national colours of green, white and orange and were apt to turn into concrete if left on a plate. But the novelty wore off soon and he gladly fell in with Conlon's suggestion that they escape. At the time the two men were receiving treatment for slight illnesses in the camp hospital and Conlon thought they could get out through a window in the shower cubicle which was protected only by two iron bars. This window also opened on to clear ground away from the camp defences.

On Whit Sunday they attacked the bars, taking a shower each on each guard's watch and by the following night, although somewhat chilled from their series of unwanted showers, they had sawn through the bars with saws from the handicraft classes. A third occupant of the ward, a young volunteer named Kelly, was to accompany them and he unwittingly caused the escape to fail. Conlon, as arranged, went into the shower first leaving O'Toole playing draughts. A few moments later O'Toole also went to the shower, on the pretext of washing some shirts and underwear. This was the signal for Kelly to follow, first putting some turf on the fire and thus necessitating his washing his hands.

Conlon, a large man, stuck in the window for a moment and had to be pushed through. O'Toole followed more easily. They waited for five minutes for Kelly, unaware that the guard had begun chatting with him just as he made for the shower, and then decided to head for Kilcullen, a village on the main Dublin road. Incredibly, they had made no plans for hiding places, although Terry was reared less than twenty miles from the Curragh. After about ten minutes the pursuit began but they got away safely to a place called Yellow Bog, about six miles from the camp. They then decided to knock on the first house they came to, and by good fortune it turned out to be the home of a member of Sinn Fein.

They stayed there for the night, but did not dare to sleep. Next day planes circled the area and soldiers appeared nearby. Kelly, who had finally escaped, had been in the vicinity, attempting unsuccessfully to gain admission to three neighbouring houses, so that their presence in the area was known. They left through the back of the house, deciding not to cross the Liffey which flowed nearby. Later in the day a lorry dropped some troops near their hiding place and they made a run for it. It was now Tuesday and as they had had no sleep since the previous Sunday they slept in a ditch, covering themselves with sacks.

O'Toole awoke to find a young soldier prodding him with a bayonet and that was the end of the escape bid – a fact which was not made any the more pleasant by the officer in charge telling them that had they crossed the Liffey they would have got away as the far side was not being searched.

This short-lived burst for freedom renewed the issue of escape especially when militant members, in particular Charlie Murphy, J. B. O'Hagan and Willie Gleeson, were picked up and interned. These grouped under Murphy's leadership, along with O'Toole and Frank Driver, a phenomenal character who never allows his humorous brand of anti-clericalism (based mainly on the position of the bishops on the Act of Union issue in 1800) to interfere with his Christian charity.

Driver was particularly active in planning escapes. One suggestion of his was that the wife of an internee who had ten children should take them all to the house of the Most Rev. Dr John Charles McQuaid, Archbishop of Dublin, and deposit them on his doorstep for safekeeping until her husband was released. Another was that the wives, female relatives and sympathizers of the internees should make a mass march on the barbed wire from the outside, cutting their way in with wire cutters. 'Jesus,' said Frank. 'Think of the publicity if one of them got shot.' The camp council thought of it and turned the proposal down with horror.

When Murphy arrived in camp there were two escape projects in train. One involved cutting a tunnel under the wire, but it came to nothing as a sergeant spotted some of the clay from the tunnel that had been carelessly dumped on a path. The second one worked though not the way the activists had intended.

A blanket was taken from the hut where most of the activists lived (it was called 'Little Rock' after the Arkansas trouble spot) and covered with grass in a corner of the playing field. Two detainees slipped under it while another group stood around to mask them from the sentries. When it was dark the two simply slid under the wire while back in the huts two dummy beds were made up so that the customary inspection found nothing wrong. The trouble was that when the camp council, which had been pressed into sponsoring the escape, sent word to Sean Cronin about the scheme, he nominated Dave O'Connell and Rory

Brady as his candidates for escape whereas those in the camp wanted Murphy and O'Hagan to go out. Cronin's men went.

Cronin himself was interned not long before the camp elections to choose a new OC. It had been expected that MacCurtain might stand down and that Murphy would stand in his place, but in the event MacCurtain went forward and Murphy preferred not to stand against him. J. B. O'Hagan stood in Murphy's place and was narrowly defeated. Cronin remained neutral until the night of the election when he advised that policy be left as it was, in the hands of the official leadership, the 'three Macs'.

To the militants the election result meant that if they wanted action they would have to bring it about themselves, and that Murphy was the only leader they could look to to support such a policy. The activist group now gained two supporters, Frank Armstrong, and a young Limerick man, Jimmy Devereux, an expert fitter who could make wire-cutting equipment. The hacksaws used in making souvenirs had all been withdrawn and their only wire-cutting tool was a pair of pliers which a detainee had hidden. But using angle-irons and a six-foot-long poker from the laundry Devereux made three wire-cutters, tempering the steel in the hut fire while members of the group lounged around screening the operation not only from the camp authorities but also from the supporters of the 'no escape' policy, who would certainly have attempted to stymie the attempt if they could. The poker was used to make extended arms for the cutters.

The escape was planned for December 1958. Twenty-six men were to take part and after getting away they intended to go to Meath to regroup and recommence operations on the border. Everyone went to confession before the escape bid, which in the event failed to come off on the chosen date for it was discovered that soldiers were stationed all around the big trench. The minister for justice was visiting the camp and a general stand-to had been ordered.

The next day, Willie Gleeson, Tom Ferris, Terry O'Toole and Devereux cut their way through the first fence before the guards realized what was happening. Then a guard ran up firing two revolver shots which struck no one. O'Toole noticed as he ran that the sentry in the elevated post nearest to him had his rifle in the air and this seemed to confirm the theory that the escapees would not be fired on. He ran on, passing within eight feet of the guard who was firing the revolver, not knowing that behind him Brian Boylan had already been shot. Charlie Murphy, who had stayed at the gap assisting the others through, went to Boylan's assistance. The rest of the group cleared the second and third fences and reached the dyke without further casualties. Then ammonia grenades were thrown at them. Hampered as they were by trip wires that set off flares, they floundered among the coils of barbed wire, everyone injured or cut or temporarily blinded. O'Toole was shot in the right thigh, but kept going. By the time the last fence was reached the cutters had been abandoned and the group, by now reduced to ten, attacked the fence with bare hands and clawed it down while the ground was cut up by flying bullets.*

It was approximately a mile to the nearest cover, a field with a thick ditch, where they carried out what first aid they could. One of them, Pat McGirl, was completely blind from the ammonia gas and was later captured as was Liam Fagan who had been shot in the knee and had to crawl on his stomach. First aid had to be abandoned as the soldiers drew near again and the group split up. Some of them then went to Moone, near the camp, and called inadvertently at a house where a man was being waked. The widow was not a Republican herself, but her husband had been one and she paused in her grief to arrange that the escapees be taken to friendly houses.

Equipped with maps O'Toole and his companions (Gleeson, Devereux, Gerry Houghey, and Dan Donaghy) circled Kildare and headed for Portarlington town, following a route that took them thirty-five miles instead of the normal eighteen. They reached a friendly house on the outskirts of Portarlington the next morning, wounded and exhausted, and a doctor was sent for (he turned out to be a state medical officer). He tended their wounds and the others moved on but O'Toole's leg prevented him from travelling. He stayed there for two days until the woman of the house dressed him as a woman and drove him to the west of Ireland where a sympathetic surgeon got him into a hospital, and the bullet was removed from his leg, nearly four days after he was shot.

Back in the camp and in the ranks of the IRA throughout the country the escape deepened the split in the movement. To the official

* The Republicans were particularly bitter about this shooting, but in fairness it should be underlined that the sentries in the elevated posts could probably have killed many of the escapees had they wished. The number of leg wounds seems to indicate that they deliberately aimed low. The soldier with the revolver who first inflicted casualties was disarmed by an officer as he prepared to fire at some of the escapees from point-blank range.

leadership, that is to say the remnant that remained of an organization, the escapees had put themselves outside the movement and almost every Army Council meeting between then and June was devoted to discussing what should be done about them. And on top of this issue there was heated argument over the control of Sinn Fein. Should the party be autonomous or should it be controlled by the IRA?

There was one distraction during this arguing. Joseph Christle dumped an unwanted hero into the IRA ranks, James Andrew Mary Murphy whom he had rescued from Wakefield Prison, 12 February 1959. Then the London *Daily Express*, whose Irish correspondent, Seamus Brady, was known to be particularly well informed about all levels of Irish politics, constitutional and otherwise, printed a report asking, 'Is Murphy Skuse?' Controversy blew up within and without the IRA as to whether he was Skuse and, if he was, whether he should be extradited to England. Ultimately he was not but for a time this issue drew attention away from what was left of the campaign and from the controversy within the movement, most of it directed against Charlie Murphy for his acceptance of parole at the time of the MacMahon incident and his leadership of the escape.

There were two legal proceedings during the campaign of which mention must be made here. The more important was the case of Gerrard Lawless – the first to be judged by the Court of Human Rights in Strasbourg.

Lawless, who had an IRA record, was arrested by Detective Inspector MacMahon on 11 July 1957, just as he was about to leave Ireland for England. Lawless said that MacMahon offered him a job and money if he would give information about the IRA but that he had refused, claiming that he was not in the IRA (he had sided with Christle in the split). He was then interned in the Curragh where he was, in fact, ostracized by the IRA detainees.

From the Curragh Lawless contacted a Dublin lawyer, Ciaran Mac An Ali, asking him to take his case. Some of the finest lawyers* in Ireland joined Mac An Ali in doing so and on 8 November 1957, an application on behalf of Lawless was filed before the European Commission on Human Rights asking immediate release from the Curragh, payment of compensation and damages, and payment of all costs

---

* Senior counsels Sean MacBride and Tommy Connolly, junior counsel Seamus Sorahan and one of the country's leading solicitors, P. C. Moore. They continued the tradition of defending the IRA men without payment.

before both the Irish courts and the Court of Human Rights. On the advice of his lawyers Lawless then reluctantly availed himself of the machinery for release from the camp by signing an 'undertaking' and he was freed on 10 December.

After a lengthy argument, first through the European Commission and then through the Court of Human Rights to which the Commission's judges had referred the case, judgement was given against Lawless on 1 July 1961, but despite this some important principles were set out. Lawless's lawyers established that the 'undertaking' which Curragh internees signed to release themselves had no legal status as it was not provided for by the Offences Against the State Act to which it referred. More significantly the court set the precedent that it did not have to accept a member country's own opinion as to whether a state of emergency existed within that country sufficient to warrant such measures as internment, but that it could exercise its own judgement as to the extent of the internal crisis, and consequently could rule on the measures adopted to deal with that crisis.

This decision had a direct effect upon Irish politics. When the border campaign flared up again temporarily in 1961–62 the government did not resort to internment camps but instead had recourse to military courts. These imposed sentences of several years – which were quickly commuted to months when the IRA called off the campaign. It is, indeed, doubtful that any Irish government will use internment camps again except in the gravest emergency.

The most dramatic court case of the entire period was the 'Mallon and Talbot affair' which, although it received far more publicity than the Lawless case, had far less long-term significance.

The affair began on 17 August 1957, when RUC Sergeant Arthur Ovens kicked open the door of an unused cottage near Coalisland, Co. Tyrone, and was blown to bits by a mine. The RUC, understandably enraged by the death of a colleague who was also the father of three children, nearly took Coalisland apart looking for those responsible. After lengthy interrogations the RUC came up with Kevin Mallon and Patrick Talbot, both twenty-one, as the chief suspects.

In Dublin (where to this day it is not known exactly who set the booby-trap) Charlie Murphy and Sean Cronin decided that regardless of the policy of not recognizing the courts Mallon and Talbot would have to be defended or they would be hanged. Again Sean MacBride came to the rescue after Murphy and Cronin had failed to get another Dublin lawyer interested in the case. MacBride advised them that no

Unionist lawyer would take the case, that a Nationalist would be too timorous and that the best thing to do was to get an Englishman. He then arranged for Elwyn Jones, later a Labour attorney general, to defend the two young men. A vigorous publicity campaign (in which the *New Statesman* was prominent) highlighted the tortures to which Mallon and Talbot were allegedly subjected and a special committee was formed in Dublin to raise funds for the defence. As a result of this, and of Jones's effort, Mallon and Talbot were sentenced to prison rather than to execution and they were freed when the campaign ended.

The campaign had manifestly failed, although with Irish doggedness the movement was on one hand looking for a scapegoat to blame for the failure and on the other trying to prolong the attacks on the border. It eventually did find a formula whereby the Curragh escapees could be received back into the fold. They signed readmission forms, which were a sort of admission that they had been thrown out but now accepted the authority of the official section of the movement. In fact O'Toole and the others planned to eject the 'pacifist' section of the movement at the convention elections in June 1959, but for the moment they co-operated with the existing leadership.

By June the rift in the IRA had become public knowledge. Reports of a split appeared in the papers and denials by the IRA publicity bureau certainly failed to convince the Special Branch at least whose members frequently accosted IRA men in the streets and asked them, 'Which IRA do you belong to, Charlie Murphy's or the official IRA?' without even bothering to arrest any of them. Worse, the authorities publicly showed their contempt for the movement by gradually releasing the men in the Curragh. By March 1959 the movement was no longer a real threat, despite the British ambassador's formal protest against the releases and de Valera's angry exchange with British Prime Minister Harold Macmillan. Yet even after de Valera retired on 17 June 1959 (he became President) IRA activity continued to poison British-Irish relationships. De Valera's successor, Sean Lemass, worked unavailingly for a revision of the Anglo-Irish Free Trade Agreement of 1948, which by the terms of the Agreement should have been revised by 1959. It was not until 1965 under the Labour government that the Irish secured a new and satisfactory trade agreement.

Within the IRA, the campaign against Charlie Murphy reached a poisonous intensity, and Myles Shevlin tried to heal the rift at a meeting in Monasterevan, Co. Kildare, on Spy Wednesday, April 1959. Everyone reacted amicably and parted friendly but nothing came of the meeting. In fact for a time relations got worse when, after the June convention the Murphy wing, having failed to secure his elevation and the overthrow of the 'pacifists', resolved to carry out border raids on its own and commandeered weapons from the 'official' IRA. These were given back after Cronin informed O'Toole that his section had a series of operations planned along the border. When Murphy heard this he realized that the situation was drifting not towards war against the North, but towards war within the IRA and he ordered that the captured weapons be handed back.

Charge and counter-charge flew with the dum-dum destructiveness of character that the Irish can so well employ. When Murphy tried to clear his name by calling for an inquiry the report praised Murphy with faint damns in such a way as neither to make the past forgettable nor the future attractive. Murphy resigned and entered a black period of self-doubt, financial stringency and readjustment. Throughout this time the kindness of Sean MacBride was one of the things that kept him sane. Murphy's wife Carmel worked as a waitress and he was taken back by the Guinness brewery. He and Carmel became the most law abiding and popular members of their suburban community, devoting their energies to nothing more revolutionary than residents' associations and bring-and-buy sales. Myles Shevlin and Thomas MacCurtain also parted with the movement shortly after the Monasterevan meeting and Sean Cronin was made the subject of an inquiry after allegations of Communism were directed against him. The inquiry found no substance in the allegations but Cronin too resigned from the army. He is now a successful journalist in America.

During all this time blood was still being shed. On 2 July 1958, a police patrol fired on an IRA patrol near Clontivern, Co. Fermanagh, and killed the column leader, Aloysius Hand, a twenty-year-old unemployed labourer. He had a loaded Thompson gun, and according to the evidence given at the inquest had fired two bursts before the RUC shot. A verdict of justifiable homicide was returned.

Later on 15, 16 and 17 July the campaign flared up all along the border in the major show of activity since its inception in December 1956. Explosions took place from Down to Derry, resulting in two deaths, a number of injuries and some destruction to customs huts and to bridges.

The first death was deliberate. Constable H. B. Ross, Forkhill, was cycling through Moircastle on the south Armagh border when an electrically triggered mine was detonated from behind a hedge. Although he was badly injured he managed to walk to a nearby house to wait for an ambulance. He died in hospital the next day leaving a wife and child. The second death was caused by the IRA's faulty bomb-making. Patrick MacManus, twenty-seven, the principal IRA leader at liberty in the North, was removing a gelignite mine, made in a biscuit box, from a cache on the roadside at Drumask, Co. Cavan, when it went off, blowing him to pieces. The physical damage wrought in this short-lived offensive ranged from the destruction of the biggest customs post between North and South, the Killeen post on the main Dundalk–Belfast road, which was wrecked, to craters blown in unapproved roads.

One particularly distasteful killing occurred on 24 August 1958: the shooting of James Crossan by the RUC in ambiguous circumstances at the customs post at Mullan, Co. Fermanagh.

The IRA claimed that Crossan was murdered and this is how his death is described in its roll of honour. The RUC said in a statement that 'the suspicions of a police patrol on duty near the British Customs post at Mullan, Co. Fermanagh, were aroused by persons approaching the post from the direction of Eire. Police called on these persons to halt, whereupon they bolted towards the Border . . . They again called on them to halt. One man stopped but the others continued running. Police opened fire and later . . . the dead body of a young man was found. The other man, who like the dead man is a native of Eire, has been detained.'

However, a statement from 'An Enniskillen correspondent', in the *Irish Press* said, 'Crossan and McHugh parted from three Fermanagh friends, two of them Unionists, on the Fermanagh side of the Border at Mullan at about 3.30 a.m. The three Fermanagh friends drove off in a van towards Kinawley and the two Cavan men were walking back again to another van which had brought the five to the Cavan [Southern] side of the Border when Mr Crossan was shot dead by Six County police who had taken up positions near the Customs hut.'

At the inquest a verdict of justifiable homicide was returned and this was met by an indignant press release from the IRA saying that '. . . James Crossan was unarmed. The suggestion that he and Ben

McHugh were on a reconnaissance mission at Mullan British Customs post is ridiculous.'

While 1960 was uneventful, 1961 began and ended with deaths, and of all the deaths of the campaign these are the least defensible. Public support for the 'physical force' policy had been falling away and this, combined with new political preoccupations and new political figures and philosophies that greatly improved the standard of living in the South, pushed the whole border question well into the background. (In the general election of 1961, Sinn Fein lost all four seats and its poll fell by over 50 per cent.)

Nevertheless the militants struck again. On 27 January 1961, a young RUC man, Corporal Norman Anderson, was taken up a lane shortly after he had said goodnight to his sweetheart, and thirty-four bullets were shot into his back. The IRA believed that he had been spying on its movements. In the wake of condemnation, South and North, the IRA pulled in its horns for the summer, but on 12 November, a police patrol was ambushed at Jonesborough, Co. Armagh, and another policeman, Constable William Hunter, was shot dead. There were protests from Belfast, from the British government and from Dublin and the Southern government decided to act.

On 22 November, it was announced that the government was setting up the Special Criminal Court again. The court was composed of army officers and there was no doubt that the government, and in particular the new minister for justice, Charles Haughey, a young man who had come to the fore after the 1961 election, were determined to take the most drastic measures to scotch not only the campaign but also the IRA at the next possible opportunity. The IRA decided not to give them that opportunity.

On 26 February 1962, the Irish Republican Publicity Bureau announced that:

'The Leadership of the Resistance Movement has ordered the termination of "The Campaign of Resistance to British Occupation" . . . all arms and other materials have been dumped and all full-time active service volunteers have been withdrawn.'

The statement added that one factor responsible for the decision had been the attitude of the public, 'whose minds have been deliberately distracted from the supreme issue facing the Irish people – the unity and freedom of Ireland'. Another juncture had been reached in Irish history in which it appeared that the IRA were finished once and for all.

15

New Initiatives: 1962–70

After the campaign ended the dissension within the ranks of the Republicans continued. The dispute centred upon who should control the Republican movement henceforth and again the situation resembled that at the end of the Civil War. The 'physical force' men had been beaten; disillusion and depression had set in; scapegoats had to be found, and there was no clear leadership.

Eamonn Boyce is an example of what IRA men were like at the time and of what they encountered. Boyce emerged from prison to find that his mother had suffered through the loss of his income and through helping his colleagues. She had slept for months with several hundredweights of gelignite under her bed, worried by his absence and the presence of the explosives and, as Boyce said, 'wondering where she got the headaches'. Eventually he found a job as a bus conductor, but first he had to master his nerves so that he could cross a road unaided, make a simple purchase in a shop, sign on at a Labour Exchange, or do any of the normal things which prison keeps a man from doing. Many of Boyce's comrades decided they could take no more and dropped out of the movement completely. Patrick MacLogan was found dead in his back garden with a revolver beside him, causing allegations and counter-allegations in the IRA as to how he died.

Gradually, after 1964 the movement began to build itself up again, and a Republican debating society, the Wolfe Tone Society, became popular in circles outside the IRA. The most significant single individual was perhaps Roy Johnston, a young Marxist computer scientist who became so trusted by the IRA leaders that he was appointed to the Army Council as a kind of education officer cum political commissar. Under his influence IRA policy moved steadily left. The absence of a strong ideological grounding (apart from the crusading to end partition by force) made this a relatively easy process, at least at leadership level; among the grass-roots members and those of a right-wing cast of mind the new developments were worrying.

In 1965 the political arm of the movement, Sinn Fein, announced that it would continue to sit on local government bodies but would also continue to boycott Stormont, the Dail and Westminster. However, the party decided, somewhat paradoxically, that in the event of Sinn Fein winning an overall majority, which would enable it to take over the Dail, the party would do so: constitutionalism, too, was growing during this period. In the North Sean McCaughey, who had been a vice-president of Sinn Fein, resigned and concentrated on building up an Irish union movement along much the same lines as Denis Ireland's efforts of the 1940s. Helped by the emotionalism of the 1916 anniversary celebrations in 1966 Sinn Fein increased its strength, openly in the South and in the North under the guise of Republican clubs. At the 1966 Ard Fheis Sinn Fein was pledged by its president, Tomas McGoilla, to an effort to win a majority in the Dail within five years. At Bodenstown in 1967 Cathal Goulding made his speech in favour of socialist policies and decried the movement's concentration on the 'physical force' policy found in the writings of Dan Breen.

But the activist tradition inevitably re-emerged and throughout 1966 several incidents and bombings took place, the most celebrated being the destruction of Nelson's Pillar. One young Republican, Richard Behal, in jail in Limerick on charges arising out of a visit to Ireland by Princess Margaret, made a dramatic escape at midnight on New Year's Eve 1966, and for the greater part of the year, on the run from both the left-wing IRA and the Special Branch, was openly associated with some of these incidents. Another group of Republicans which favoured the use of force began to coalesce into what became known as the Saor Eire Action Group and this took a hand at bank raids. Between 1967 and mid-April 1970 either it or the IRA carried out seventeen bank raids. In the last, disavowed by the official IRA, a garda was killed.

Throughout this period the *United Irishman* struck up a medley of Fenian and Marxist airs despite the fact that there were rumblings from Clann na Gael in America that the leftward swing was not to its liking. In England the movement made some ground by dropping the title Sinn Fein and trying to amalgamate all the various emigré Irish parties and associations under the banner of a new grouping: Clann na hEireann, 'the family of Gaels'. In Dublin the Republicans' greatest success in terms of publicity was the sponsorship of the Dublin

Housing Action Committee, a body which existed independently of the IRA to do something for Dublin's homeless. The IRA put muscle into its demonstrations and sit-ins, and in the country also, wherever disputes arose over small farmers seeking to have large estates broken up, the IRA became active in land leagues. Foreigners who owned land in Ireland or who held Irish ground-rents were singled out for verbal and sometimes physical attack. In May 1968 the IRA burned out £60,000 worth of buses used to take workers to a factory owned by an American company, the EI Company of Shannon, during a dispute over union recognition. In the west, in Rossaveal on the Connemara coast, a £6,000 fishing boat owned by an American-financed company was wrecked in August by an IRA bomb, and in June 1969, a number of buildings on farms owned by Germans were set alight.

But the IRA's most significant initiative was its behind-the-scenes involvement in the Northern Civil Rights movement. The broad-based Civil Rights movement, which captured the world's headlines, began appropriately enough in the fiftieth anniversary year of 1916 with a private meeting of interested parties in Derry at the home of a prominent Derry Republican, Kevin Agnew, a solicitor, in August 1966, and a public meeting the following November in Belfast. Cathal Goulding attended the Derry meeting and while he said frankly that he did not think it would work, he pledged the IRA to give it a trial. When the North of Ireland Civil Rights Association was officially founded in Belfast at a meeting in the International Hotel on 29 January 1967, the broad-based Committee of 13 which was founded to run the movement included, apart from a number of communists, trade unionists and reform-minded individuals such as Dr Con McCluskey, Agnew and two Wolfe Tone Society Representatives as treasurer and PRO, Fred Heatley and Jack Bennett. The association worked brilliantly: Unionist spokesmen continually thundered that CRA (Civil Rights Association) was only another way of saying IRA, but never a shot was fired, never an IRA man showed himself as such and the IRA deserves some of the credit for the great success of the Civil Rights movement, although politically it got swallowed by it much as it did in Fianna Fail's success in 1932.

As the Civil Rights movement spread figures such as John Hume, Ivan Cooper, Gerry Fitt and Bernadette Devlin came to national and then international prominence and the radical movement, People's Democracy, received much publicity. Behind the scenes, however, many older Republicans of the generation of 1940 disagreed violently with the passive resistance policy. The idea of going up to a policeman at a barricade and allowing him to baton one into the ground without any attempt at retaliation was common ground with the Southern opponents of the socialist policy generally but all criticism was stifled by the enormous publicity the Civil Rights movement received after 5 October 1968. Then a peaceful march in Derry was batoned by the RUC and there began the decline into anarchy, the erosion of respect for the RUC as an impartial force and the build-up of Protestant feeling which on 2 August 1969 made of the Apprentice Boys' march in Derry a torch that very nearly lit a powder keg in all Ireland.

As Protestant passions mounted, inside Stormont hardline Unionists such as William Craig began to rail against Prime Minister Terence O'Neill and his policy of liberal Unionism and a gradualistic approach to friendship with Dublin. Unconstitutional leaders and movements began to make themselves felt on the Protestant side. The Ulster Volunteer Force was heard of again and in May 1969 a group of IRA leaders in Belfast became worried enough at the build-up of Protestant strength and emotion that it went to Dublin to ask the Army Council for large supplies of arms without delay.

The request was not granted. In the first place the IRA had become almost demilitarized – most of its weapons had been sold to Welsh nationalists – and was virtually without funds. (The *United Irishman* was only saved by an emergency appeal for money.) To have given the few arms at its disposal to Belfast would have left the IRA in the South unarmed. Then too, in the event of weapons being discovered in the North, the work for the Civil Rights movement would have been discredited and a stick given to Stormont to beat the IRA out into the open from behind its facade of Republican clubs. Moreover, Belfast had not distinguished itself during the border campaign and the conversion to militancy did not wholly convince the Dublin leaders. The Northerners went away unhappy and from then on there were suggestions that a separate Northern Command be formed.

On 12 August the Apprentice Boys were allowed to hold their traditional march in Derry despite warnings that this could lead to a bloodbath. In the event, the procession passed off peaceably enough but eventually, maddened by the provocations of some Catholic hooligans who had been pelting them with stones, the RUC instead of being withdrawn from the Bogside area baton-charged its assailants and hurled stones back at them. Batons and bricks failed to dislodge the Bogsiders from behind their barricades and, for several days, there was enacted another siege of Derry. This time history was reversed and the Catholic defenders withstood the Protestant onslaught.

In Dublin the prime minister was Jack Lynch, a quiet, pipe-smoking Corkman who had never shown himself a militant in any sense. He had continued the hands-across-the-border policy initiated by his pre-decessor, Sean Lemass, visiting Stormont and being entertained by O'Neill, and having O'Neill on a return visit to Dublin. But Lynch now escalated the partition issue to a plane it had not reached since the days of the treaty debates. Speaking mildly, with sincerity in his voice and a haggard look about the eyes, he went on television to announce that he had moved units of the Irish army up to the border and was opening field hospitals so that people injured in the Bogside battles could be treated without fear of being reported to the RUC. Refugee centres were set up in military installations in the South.

London was immediately forced to take notice of a situation which raised the spectre of Irish troops being engaged against British forces. In Belfast the news was received with fear and horror by Protestant extremists and rioting broke out in which millions of pounds' worth of property and some lives were lost. Whether the rioting would have come anyway as a result of the summer's build-up of tension and the fighting in Derry or whether the Irish government's action precipitated it will always be arguable but, once and for all, it forced the British government to take the most decisive action it had taken on the North of Ireland since the creation of the state itself. British troops poured into the North and British politicians poured in after them; a spate of commissions and tribunals ensued, and the British government guaranteed, publicly, that all the reforms sought by the Civil Rights movement would be conceded and, privately, that if the government of Major Chichester Clarke, who had succeeded O'Neill, fell, there would be no further Northern government. Westminster would take over.

It seemed for a moment that in one year the Civil Rights movement had done more to end injustice than fifty years of anti-partition policies had begun to do. Where was the IRA during all this? Apparently not there at all as an organized body. As far as can be reasonably ascer-tained, approximately six Republicans took to the streets of Belfast during the rioting which broke out after 12 August to defend the Catholic areas. One of these, at least, was a middle-aged man who had not been active since the 1940s. He somewhere got a tommy-gun and for his exploits that night has forever earned himself an honoured place in the hearts of Belfast Catholics. There seems little doubt that had the handful of IRA men not been present, Orange mobs led by B-Specials would have burned the Falls Road to the ground and, with it, every Catholic family which did not flee. But this circumstance, much as it may have rebounded to the credit of the individuals concerned, rebounded very badly indeed on the IRA's public image.

The principal public activity of the IRA during this period was to issue a ridiculous statement claiming that units of the IRA were active in the North and ready to take any and every action, short of throwing the British Crown into the Thames, in the defence of Catholics and liberation of the North. It did nothing except bolster the charges by hard-line Unionists that the CRA and the IRA were identical. Relations between Belfast and Dublin reached their nadir. Republicans congregated in farmhouses along the border waiting for arms from Dublin that never came and once again the Northern IRA decided to act on its own and the plan for a Northern Command began to take shape. Distraught Republicans began scurrying around the country to lay hands on weapons to give to the desperate Catholics – with sometimes bizarre results. A Dublin Capuchin monk, for instance, gave five rounds of revolver bullets and a Dominican dressed five IRA men as priests to enable them to get into Belfast undetected.

Concomitant with the IRA troop movements, the Irish government mounted an ill-advised publicity campaign to draw world attention to the partition issue, a campaign which recalled the anti-partition efforts of 1948. The government also appealed to the United Nations, through Irish Foreign Minister Dr Patrick Hillery, where he made a seemingly strong effort (at the time the Irish army had only enough ammunition for 72 hours' firing) to get a UN presence into the North. For a time the Americans were sympathetic but the British mounted what an Arab delegate told me during a subsequent visit to the UN was the 'strongest diplomatic offensive of their history since Suez' and swayed the Americans with the argument: 'This is a Civil Rights issue, domestic to the UK. You have Civil Rights issues too, domestically (Martin Luther King was still alive and marching). If international observers are admitted to the UK's domestic affairs a precedent will have been set and you will have UN observers, possibly Russians and Chinese, in Selma ... do you want that?'

Shudderingly, the US said it did not want that and, debating from a position of having to because of the sudden eruption rather than because of long-felt, planned-for conviction, the Irish were not altogether displeased to let the issue slip having been seen to raise it honourably and loudly – Ireland was after all applying for an EEC membership for which Britain's support would one day be essential, even though a prime reason for joining was to gain more independence of Britain economically and hence politically.

In fact, subsequently, though Ireland did take Britain to the Court of Human Rights it is arguable that her preoccupation with the problems and prosperity of EEC membership, its fat subsidy for farmers, its butter mountains, MCAs and wine lakes, fish quotas and the rest of it, did distract Ireland's relatively small Foreign Affairs Department and her decision makers in the cabinet from concentrating on the North. As the main thrust of government policy swung towards Europe and international investment, away from the old catch cries about 'reintegration of the national territories', arguments about *de jure* and *de facto* recognition and so on, one sometimes got the impression that the baby of interest in the North was thrown out along with the bathwater of shibboleth.

But this is to anticipate. Along with the UN initiatives some of Lynch's colleagues reportedly began taking more private and unconventional initiatives. Some monies and arms found their way into IRA hands. Northern Catholics could also receive training in the Donegal area and at some of the military centres set up in the South for refugees. Reports that six Irish army officers were sent across the border to co-ordinate Citizens' Defence Committees, again with Republican co-operation, circulated in Dublin.

These matters were shrouded in the deepest secrecy, and will be dealt with in context later (see pages 372 *et seq.*). Publicly however it was clear that the Fianna Fail government appeared to speak at times with two voices on the North. Two ministers in particular, Neil T. Blaney and Kevin Boland, took harder attitudes than did Lynch. Boland laid the continuing blame on Britain and Blaney repeatedly said that the use of force was not ruled out on the part of the Irish government as a means of ending partition. Rumours that some of Lynch's colleagues had not wished him to stop short of the border but to push on to Derry gained currency; but on 28 December Lynch gave a very frank radio interview in which he said that he had had a 'firm chat' with Blaney. 'He understands,' Lynch said, 'that the members of the government must adhere to government policy. In fact, he does.'

Whether this broadcast had anything to do with governmental policy towards the IRA is a matter of conjecture, but it is a fact that six Derry youths who had been training openly under arms near Buncrana, Co

Donegal, were suddenly arrested in early January 1970, charged under the Firearms Act and lodged in prison in Dublin before being released under the Probation Act. Despite this leniency the arrests were clearly designed to indicate that the blind-eye policy regarding drilling was at an end and Lynch won a thunderous ovation at the Fianna Fail Ard Fheis on 18 January when he again ruled out force, challenged anybody (his audience included Blaney and Boland) to oppose him, refused to allow organizing for Fianna Fail in the North and said frankly that the South would have to recognize the fact that the majority of the North's inhabitants wanted to remain linked with Britain.

Exactly one week before Lynch's speech the Republican movement had split down the middle in a crisis that was as public and almost as damaging as that which led to the formation of Fianna Fail itself. The stated issue was the recognition of the 'partition parliaments' of Dublin, Stormont and Westminster. The IRA had held a secret convention in mid-December which had voted 39 to 12 in favour of recognition and the Sinn Fein Ard Fheis meeting (in the incongruous surroundings of the American-financed Intercontinental Hotel) was supported to do likewise and give Sinn Fein a mandate to oppose foreign investment and set about the 'reconquest of Ireland, shop by shop and factory by factory'. There seemed little doubt that the Ard Fheis would give the required two-thirds majority.

A commission set up by the 1968 Ard Fheis to examine the movement and make recommendations as to its future had circulated a report, 'Ireland Today', in March 1969 saying that there was no need for the leadership of Sinn Fein and the IRA to be amalgamated as 'the present degree of mutual understanding of overall policy and strategy renders any such amalgamation unnecessary'. The usual overlapping of membership had occurred and many of those who had voted to recognize the parliaments at the IRA convention were highly placed on the Sinn Fein executive.

News of the IRA vote was leaked to the press and the *Sunday Press* carried the story two weeks after the convention, on 28 December. The report helped to crystallize opposition to the new policies. The March document had recommended that 'all embargoes on political participation in parliament be removed from the Constitution and Rules of both bodies [Sinn Fein and IRA]', but this was accompanied by a directive 'that the undermining of confidence in existing parliaments and eventual abstention from them in order to establish an alternative form of government must be a major objective of the movement'. Now, however, it was out in the public press that Sinn Fein was going to recognize the 'partition parliaments' without any provisos. A new 'provisional' Army Council was set up and various IRA units and Sinn Fein bodies around the country gave the 'provisional' council their allegiance. These groups included important figures such as Tom Maguire, John Joe Sheehy and eighty-nine-year-old Joe Clarke, who fought in 1916. By the time the crucial vote was taken at the Ard Fheis on 11 January, the traditionalists had so rallied their forces that the proposal to abandon the abstentionist policy was only carried by 153 votes to 104, less than the required two-thirds majority. There may have been other, deeper motives behind the proposals to enter parliament. The 'Ireland Today' document posed the possibility of a link-up with the Southern Irish Communist Party and, interestingly enough, in mid-March the Southern and Northern Communist Parties completed a merger at a meeting attended by several Russian journalists. The idea of a 'National Liberation Front' had come very close to giving Moscow a voice in an Irish national movement for the first time in history.

Far from agreeing on the 'creation of the National Liberation Front' called for by the March policy document, Sinn Fein was as split as ever it was. The 'Provisional Army Council' had brought out its own newspaper, *An Phoblacht*, and it was hard to prophesy what the future held.

The IRA tradition is mainly one of physical action and separatism. It is not an intellectual one, which is why I have carefully refrained from discussing events or personalities which some historians might feel were influential in the Republican story: the constitution of 1937 or the declaration of a Republic in Ireland in 1948, for examples on the political side, or the writings of Sean O'Faolain or of Brendan Behan on the literary one. These are not important to Republicans of the 'physical force' school. For them what counted was deaths, commemorations, a holding firm with the past, laced with an indomitable sense of lunatic humour, epitomized for me, at this stage, by a letter (published in the *Irish Press*, 6 November 1969) to his mother from Conor Lynch, son of a prominent IRA man of the 1930s, who had just received a seven-year sentence in England.

'Cheer up, Mother,' he wrote. 'It could have been worse, I could have got seven years and a month.'

In the next chapter, we will see how this stage gave way to a new era and a new IRA.

PART II

1969–1979

16

The Roots of the Conflict

How did the blackened, almost unarmed and certainly very largely discredited IRA resurrect itself to become a national force moving the North of Ireland issue to the fore throughout all the dismaying events of the 1970s? At the time of the IRA's initial regrouping following the setting up of the Provisional Caretaker Executive, I met an IRA friend who had been picking up the threads of family and business life but now appeared to be going downhill again through becoming involved in IRA activities. As he told me both of his hardships in the past and of what he was doing at that time, I remember saying to him: 'Eamon, you are mad! You have done your bit for your cause and now you risk wrecking your own happiness and everyone else's to join a splinter of a splinter group.' For that was how most people in Southern Ireland would certainly have described the IRA in the early part of 1970; but as it happened I was both completely right and totally wrong. My friend did undergo terrible traumas but the IRA blossomed into one of the major guerrilla organizations to emerge since World War II.

Events moved at two levels – the constitutional and the paramilitary. They also moved in a number of different arenas, in a way that makes understanding very difficult. Let us, nevertheless, make a start by taking the constitutional level as it affected the major actors in the drama in London, Belfast, and Dublin.

The catalyst in Northern Ireland was the Civil Rights movement – though the British Education Acts also contributed to ensuring that in the ranks of this movement there would be several young men and women equally, if not better, educated than their Unionist opponents, and well able to hold their own on television and in political techniques. But these factors were compounded by the particularly obdurate type of resistance with which the Unionist hierarchy and those who wished to join it – or control it – like the Rev. Ian Paisley, met the Civil Rights demands.

It is hardly an over-simplification to say that the Catholics were forced off the streets into the arms of the IRA who were subsequently maintained in their recruiting by the activities both of the Protestant paramilitary mirror organizations which grew up to combat the IRA and of the British army.

Yet while all the old wounds of Irish history were re-opened by the contemporary political situation and the bloody conflict began, it became clear that no side had enough strength to deliver the knock-out punch necessary to achieve its aims.

The strongest partner in the dilemma was the British government. Yet though it had an army, large resources and a native 'Ulster security force' at its disposal, it could never hope entirely to exterminate the IRA, for the following reasons:

1. *The high birth rate* in the Catholic ghettoes of Belfast, Derry and elsewhere.

2. *The supply of money and guns* from America and later, to some degree, training, weapons and money from the Arab States.

3. *The support generated for the IRA by events*: the growth of the Civil Rights movement, the Falls Road curfew of July 1970, the unilateral introduction of internment in August 1971, when no Protestants were interned, stimulated the Catholic population to extend a far greater degree of support to the IRA than had existed at any time since the end of the Anglo-Irish War of 1916–21 and arguably even during it. This support, which probably peaked in 1972 when Stormont fell, suffered many rises and falls but never wholly disappeared. It is arguable whether tradition, fear, the need for protection against sectarian assassinations, or the popularity generated by IRA activity itself through daring raids, spectacular exploits, dramatic hunger strikes and so on was the stronger reinforcement of this support.

4. *British policy*: this was certainly hard to overestimate in terms of its benefit to the IRA. For although the troops entered Derry and Belfast as 'saviours', it might have been predicted that the troops would inevitably be drawn into conflict with the civilian population – given the nature of armies, and the fact that as soon as it had mustered itself into any semblance of organization the IRA did its utmost to make pariahs of the soldiers and to turn the population against them. The army, to be an effective impartial peacekeeping force, should have been briefed to counteract this. But the army seems to have been unnecessarily psyched up against the situation – for instance, the Sinn Fein 'oath' in Chapter 17 of this book was reproduced from the first

edition as the genuine article in the manual issued to every soldier who came to Northern Ireland. The manual was withdrawn from circulation and the 'oath' deleted after I published the manual's contents in the *Irish Press*.

Not only the troops and police warders, but British personnel generally seemed either to have a natural antipathy for the Irish or to have been indoctrinated against them. I remember a young Protestant ex-warder at Long Kesh telling me why he left the prison service. 'I don't like the "Ra" [IRA],' he said. 'You see that "knuckle",' he said, showing me his hand – 'I broke that on a Ra man's head one day. But I'd always use my hands and I'd never hit a man unless I had to. But you should hear the way the fellows over from England talk. "The Paddys", they call us Protestants and Catholics. They treat the prisoners like scum. They'd use boots, batons, anything. They sickened me, and I got out.'

There were and are many individual exceptions; soldiers and police who tried to understand the people and involve themselves in helping the community. But where these were not regarded with outright suspicion and hatred as potential spies, they came up against the inevitable 'them' and 'us' syndrome which a young soldier from Dublin encountered one night when he stopped a Belfast architect of my acquaintance at a roadblock and tried to show his friendliness towards him while going through the motions of searching his car. He was coldly rebuffed. 'But,' he tried, 'I'm one of you. I'm a Catholic – from Dublin.'

'Your bullets are just as hard,' said the architect.

Thus the way in which the police and military assessed the situation was a key element – one which affected not only the decision to opt for internment or to impose the Falls Road curfew but other vital happenings in the province.

For instance, the internment swoop was seen solely as an anti-Republican and Catholic measure to be carried out in the same spirit and against the same type of foe as it had been in the 1950s. Accordingly no Protestants were seized although there was a litany of criminal activity on that side of the fence visible for all to see – if they wanted to see. (The first killings of any sort, the Malvern Street murder, the first explosion and the first constable killed in the North, Constable Arbuckle, were all carried out by Protestants.) Moreover the Catholics who were locked up for the most part had little or nothing to do with the IRA, a fact which, magnified by the ill-treatment the internees received, did however considerably boost the IRA's support.

The Bloody Sunday massacre of 30 January 1972, when British paratroopers fired on one unarmed Civil Rights procession through Derry was another example of the British lack of understanding of the overall situation. Thirteen people were shot dead and, in the country-wide wave of indignation which followed, the British Embassy in Dublin was burned down. The subsequent inquiry by Lord Widgery (published on 19 April 1972) into the shootings exonerated the para-troopers whose basic case was that they thought they were in danger of their lives, shots having been fired at them. However, no one else in Derry that day, including some journalist eyewitnesses of the calibre of Simon Winchester, then of the *Guardian*, heard any shots until the army began firing. Nor was it ever explained why the army viewed that particular march with such anticipation. It was banned in advance, and was therefore technically illegal, but this in itself would not explain the heavy concentration of top military figures present in Derry that day, nor the type of orders the soldiers were evidently acting on. On the evidence it would appear that either the army simply wanted to teach the natives a lesson or that they were given a heightened and mislead-ing impression of what was likely to happen.

Less publicized outside the country but still of invaluable benefit to IRA propaganda was the tactic of road cratering in border areas which the army initiated on 11 October 1971. As a measure aimed at diminishing guerrilla activity it was like damming a stream with pal-ings. Moreover British statistics put the total number of border in-cidents (out of the total number of violent acts since the trouble began) at 3 per cent by September of 1979. What the cratering was meant to achieve in 1971 is beyond belief.

Another circumstance affecting the troops' morale and behaviour was the fact that they were left to find a military solution, in a society divided by hate, to a problem which was essentially political. Their responses to IRA provocations were military ones, invariably involving and alienating anti-IRA members of the Catholic community so that they soon became pro-. It's just not possible to fire CS canisters down narrow teeming streets and affect only IRA lungs.

But instead of being reined in while the politicians got down to sorting out the mess, the troops were left to blunder forward. The result was a morass of brutality, and propaganda fodder – kicked-down doors, ripped-up floorboards, beaten-up young men and, worse, occasional bursts of ill-directed rifle fire that claimed civilian life and helped on the one hand eventually to land Britain before the European Court of Human Rights and on the other to build up the IRA's strength. In the crucial formative period of 1970–1, the man directly responsible for Northern Ireland was Reginald Maudling. He did absolutely nothing to halt the drift into anarchy and is chiefly remembered for a remark he made on leaving Belfast in an aeroplane after inspecting his new field of responsibility: 'Christ,' he said, calling for a large Scotch, 'what a bloody awful country.'

Under Labour the army was considerably restricted in its operations, the Minister of Defence at Westminster, Roy Hattersley, keeping a day-to-day check on army operations such as their use of the water cannons in crowd control. And the Unionist squirearchy and its bigotry was becoming increasingly distasteful to the Labour Cabinet in which James Callaghan was one of the most powerful advocates of a 'seize them neck and crop' attitude to the Unionists – by suspending Stormont, for instance.

However, the Tories were, apart from Maudling's lack of drive, encumbered by the traditional relationship with the Unionists so that the army was allowed to fall from an impartial role of peacekeeping between Protestant and Catholic to one of implementing Unionist-inspired policy.

The Falls Road curfew, known to this day by the inhabitants as The Rape of the Falls is a classic example of this. Power changed hands at a general election on 18 June, the Tories formed a Government and the effects were felt in Belfast as early as 3 July. An area of the Falls Road was cordoned off, placed under curfew, saturated by troops and a most vigorous and rough handed search for arms was undertaken. From 3–5 July the area was saturated with CS gas. There was wide scale violence in which, the figures are disputed, either three or five people were killed. Sixty civilians and fifteen soldiers were treated for injuries. Homes were wrecked, furniture smashed and thrown into the streets, and needless, petty offence offered to the Catholics. For example, there were some incidents, which lost nothing in the subsequent recounting, of crucifixes being smashed and holy pictures thrown into lavatories. For the Army had compounded the search blunder by using young Scottish Protestant soldiers in the operation. When the search concluded the Army added insult to injury by taking two Unionist ministers on a tour of the area to survey the pacified natives from an army vehicle. One of the Ministers was Lord Brookeborough's son

John. However, when the Irish Foreign Minister, Dr Patrick Hillery, drove up from Dublin to inspect the Falls area, as a result of Nationalists' protests to the Irish Government, there was outrage in the British press at this outsider's presumption! Paddy Devlin, a Labour MP at Stormont, summed up the Catholic mood when he issued a statement following the shooting of a Catholic youth by the Army.[*]

> The Army are deliberately provoking trouble in certain selected areas where Catholics live to justify saturation of these areas by troops . . . With the restraining hand of Mr James Callaghan gone from the Home Office . . .

The outrage provoked by the Falls incident provided a huge increase in Provisional recruitment. But even this was dwarfed by the supply of manpower and support generated by internment. This time amidst the several hundreds of internees 'lifted' there was one Protestant, the SDLP Stormont MP Ivan Cooper. The entire Nationalist community was inflamed. The SDLP and the Civil Rights movement combined to spearhead a civil disobedience campaign which included a rent and rates strike. If some IRA strategist had been able to implement his dream scenario for building a support base he could not have done better.

5. *Reform policy*: though reform was introduced, often with a genuine desire on the part of a wide section of British public opinion (if not of some decision-taking mandarins in Whitehall) to do something positive about the problem, these changes were like fixing sticking plaster to a broken limb.

This point deserves examination in some detail, especially as in Ireland, in a situation of tremendous political passion, events of profound significance have often been masked by more exciting, but ultimately far less important happenings. For example in 1920 the Government of Ireland Act was passed. Few Nationalists of the time, preoccupied as they were with the course of the Anglo-Irish war, saw this Act for what it was – permanent statutory recognition by the British of the strength of Unionist and Conservative politicians. For the rest of Ireland the notion that a once-universal Protestant domina-

[*] The full statement is quoted in Coogan, p. 209 *Disillusioned Decades*, Gill & Macmillan, Dublin, 1987.

tion of Ireland should be ceded from the Crown to Catholic and Nationalist control was now becoming an inevitable part of political philosophy.

Not surprisingly, during the next fifty years Unionist hegemony, deriving from the 1920 Act, offered very little in the way of democracy to the Catholics, and Britain did equally little to ensure that it should.

Now in August 1969, as the Catholics protested against their situation in a new Civil Rights fashion to the tune and inspiration of 'We Shall Overcome' rather than 'The Soldier's Song', Britain too seemed to be moving in a new way to redress old grievances. Harold Wilson, the British Prime Minister, met the North of Ireland Prime Minister, James Chichester-Clarke, a cousin of Terence O'Neill, who had fallen in the uproar of Unionist and in particular Paisleyite disapproval of his reformist policies. Following the meeting (on 20 August), Wilson drafted and issued the Downing Street Declaration.

This stated that Catholics were to become equal under the law; local government was to be democratized; and housing was to be reallocated. But, and it was a very big 'but' to the Unionist mind, anything in the way of a fair share for a Catholic meant less of a share for a Unionist – and a possible weakening of his privileged position derived, as he saw it, from and through his cherished link with England.

The Joint Communiqué pledged itself to reform in three major areas thereby, of course, implicitly forcing a Stormont administration to admit publicly that such reform was needed. The three areas were:

(i) the fair allocation of housing by public authorities;
(ii) the avoidance of any discrimination in any form of public employment; and
(iii) the promotion of good community relations by methods including the prohibition of incitement to religious hatred.

Some of the disabilities Catholics laboured under were physical, i.e. jobs and housing, and some had a legal and psychological effect – though these could have an acutely physical outcome also, as for instance, in the operation of the Flags and Emblems Act of 1954.

The Flags and Emblems (Display) Act (Northern Ireland) 1954 'gives special protection to the occupier of land or premises who wishes to display a Union Jack. It is an offence to prevent or threaten forcibly to interfere with such display. In respect of other emblems any police

officer may, if he apprehends a breach of the peace, require the person
displaying the emblem to remove it, and in the event of failure to comply
may enter the premises to remove and detain it. Failure to remove such
emblems on police request constitutes an offence.'

The 'other emblems' referred to usually meant the tricolour which if
displayed by a Catholic, say around St Patrick's Day or at election time,
could be deemed an incitement to riot and subversion whereas the
Union Jack had to be treated with respect even while its symbolism was
visibly being misused so as to make of it a symbol of supremacy and
injustice.

For instance one of the principal stepping stones in Paisley's rise to
power was the 'Cromac Square' saga which began during the Westminster election of 1964 with Paisley holding a Union Jack leading a
demonstration to the Catholic district of Cromac Square in West
Belfast in protest against a tricolour being displayed in the window of a
Republican candidate's election HQ. After days of riots and bus
burnings the tricolour was eventually removed by the police, though it
was acknowledged at the time that had Paisley not seized on the
opportunity for self-publicity, very few people in Belfast would have
known of the flag's existence and fewer taken offence at it. But once
singled out, the law decreed that it was the display of the tricolour and
not Paisley's opportunism which caused the disturbances.

Similarly the local government laws allowed the Unionists to pack the
local bodies which allocated County Council housing so that there was
blatant injustice and discrimination against Catholics in housing.
Limited companies and occupiers of premises with a rateable valuation
of £10 could appoint nominees – as could companies for each £10 of
their valuations – under a system of plural voting, which even allowed
such votes to be cast in another constituency (where Catholics might
have a majority) so that the poorer Catholic community was in effect
electorally disenfranchised.

The electoral laws were finally reformed (by the Electoral Act of
1968–9) and as a result of this and the lowering of the voting age to
eighteen the local government electorate rose from 694,483 in 1967 to
1,031,694 in 1972, almost a 50 per cent increase. However, as we shall
see, 1972 was one of the worst years in the history of the North and the
benefit passed unheeded. Over fifty years of injustice had created a
disease for which the cure had come too late.

One has to see the situation on the ground to understand how the

Unionists used it to their own advantage. For instance, in Fermanagh and Derry, Civil Rights protesters could point to the fact that the numbers of Catholics exceeded those of Protestants yet the Protestants returned more representatives!

In Fermanagh, where the Catholic electorate for Stormont elections outnumbered Protestants by 29,400 votes to 23,500, the Unionists created three seats (Enniskillen, Lisnaskea, South Fermanagh) so that the first two areas lost much of the Catholic representation and a majority Catholic area returned two Unionists while the Catholics could only elect one Nationalist, in South Fermanagh. In local government elections the result was worse: the minority Unionists element managed to return twenty Unionists to only six Nationalists.

Derry city, which had 36,049 Catholics and 17,695 Protestants, was carved up so that it returned a Unionist.

The plural voting system which, of course, favoured the commercially dominant interests, coupled with the gerrymandering produced results which could be seen in their darkest colours in Derry where the Unionists managed so to arrange matters that their 9,235 electors returned twelve representatives whereas the 14,325 Nationalists could only return eight members.

Dungannon, which I mentioned at the outset as being a particularly black spot for violence during the troubles, was 53 per cent Catholic in 1969, yet returned fourteen Unionists as against only seven Nationalists (the electoral figures may not justify but they help one to understand the bombing statistics).

An article in the *Belfast Telegraph* on 30 January 1969 summed up the position thus: 'Roughly a quarter of the total adult population is denied a local council vote . . . '

This manipulation was not carried out for reasons of abstract political power – to maintain laws of significance to the Protestant conscience, for instance. It was intended to achieve a specific result in jobs and housing too.

For instance, again taking Dungannon, we find that a housing survey carried out by a team led by Austin Currie (January 1968) discovered that between 1945 and 1968 the allocation of new houses to Protestants and Catholics on a percentage basis was Protestants 71 per cent, Catholics 28.9 per cent. It was no accident that the entire Civil Rights movement should have taken its rise in the Dungannon area, being led first by Dr Con McCluskey and his wife Patricia who compiled statistics on discrimination, and then receiving a tremendous impetus from a sit-in joined by Austin Currie at Caledon – over the allocation of a house to the eighteen-year-old secretary of a prominent local Special who was jumped over a housing waiting list that included Catholic families with up to a dozen children (see page 747).

In Derry at the time of the Civil Rights genesis, there were practically no Protestants unhoused whereas the younger, faster growing, majority Catholic population had 2,000 unhoused families.

In fact it was gerrymandering that caused the Unionists' downfall ultimately in Derry because the high-rise flats, which the Unionists had built to pen the Catholics into the Bogside area so that they could not spread out and dilute the Protestant vote, were the stronghold from which Catholic petrol bombers successfully withstood the charges of B-Specials and RUC jointly trying to enter the area during the August 1969 rioting that first brought the troops to Northern Ireland.

One could go on for pages itemizing further instances of discrimination. Sufficient to say that apart from its existence in private commercial firms or large-scale government-subsidized firms like the Harland and Wolff Shipping Company, which at the time had probably less than 100 Catholics employed out of 10,000 workers, the practice was also part of the public employment system. In Derry, for instance, as the Civil Rights movement began, the heads of all fifteen departments in Derry City Council were Unionists. Catholics held only 33 per cent of the County Council jobs – the lower paid ones, as 79 per cent of all salaries were paid to Unionists and the general Catholic representation in Public Service Boards (transport authority, etc.) was only 11.1 per cent. Out of such percentages are gunmen made.

Though the Downing Street Declaration threw a fair light on specific Catholic grievances, it was drafted in such a way as to shed very little light on Nationalist aspirations – a fact which in the welter of debate about the reforms proposed in the Declaration was not very extensively discussed. So far as the link with England was concerned the Declaration was a direct extension of the 1920 Government of Ireland Act and its lineal descendant the Ireland Act of 1949 which stated that no change would take place in the statutory position of Northern Ireland without the consent of the majority of that state – the Unionists.

The significant portion of the Declaration read as follows:

> The United Kingdom Government reaffirm that nothing which has happened in recent years in Northern Ireland derogates from the clear

pledges made by successive United Kingdom governments that Northern Ireland should not cease to be a part of the United Kingdom
without the consent of the people of Northern Ireland or from the
provision in Section I of the Ireland Act 1949 that in no event was
Northern Ireland or any part thereof to cease to be part of the United
Kingdom without the consent of the Parliament of Northern Ireland.
The Border is not an issue.

In the same spirit of giving with one hand, but taking with the other,
the Declaration both emphasized Britain's responsibility for law and
order and stressed at the same time that its military presence was not
limitless. To the Protestant or Republican extremist the Declaration
might be taken as encouragement to try to push Northern Ireland in
the direction either desired.

But in constitutional terms the Declaration meant that Unionism
continued to receive the British government's underscoring of its
legitimacy.

However, while the British angered the national-minded amongst
the Catholics by continuing to affirm the link with England and the
sanctity of the Union, they also incurred the disapprobation of the
Protestants by dismembering what they considered to be fundamentals
of their state. The B-Specials were stood down. The Royal Ulster
Constabulary were disarmed. Plural voting was abolished. And, finally,
Stormont was suppressed. However, having initiated these developments, the British then backed down when the Loyalists staged their
largest and most definitive stand against British policy in the Ulster
Workers Council Strike of July 1974.

After Stormont was suspended in March 1972, William Whitelaw
was appointed to administer Direct Rule from Whitehall as Secretary
of State for Northern Ireland – giving rise to the Dublin joke that the
tricolour would henceforth be green, orange and Whitelaw. He
demonstrably tried to break new political ground from the word go, as
we shall see, holding talks with the Provisionals that July, and on 25
September opening talks at Darlington on the future of Northern
Ireland which eventually, through a series of conferences and Green
and White Papers, led on to the Sunningdale Agreement.

The Sunningdale Agreement was named after the conference between the British and Irish governments and representatives of some
sections of Unionism (but not Paisley or the extremists like the Ulster
Defence Association and of course the IRA) – the Alliance Party and

the Catholic Social Democratic and Labour Party (SDLP) – which all met at Sunningdale from 6 to 9 December 1973.

The Agreement reiterated the Downing Street Declaration stipulation that no change would be made in the status of Northern Ireland without the consent of the majority. It envisaged the setting up of an Executive to run Northern Ireland which would share power between the Catholic and Protestant elements. There was to be an all-Ireland court procedure which would combat terrorism and at the same time recognize the existence of the two separate states by trying suspects within the jurisdiction in which they had been apprehended.

But recognizing at least the fact that Ireland was one island the Agreement also provided for the setting up of a Council of Ireland which would provide a link between Belfast and Dublin, provide an 'Irish Dimension' to meet with the aspiration of the SDLP towards eventual peaceful unity, and would carry out tasks of mutual benefit to North and South in the realms of EEC membership, agriculture, trials, terrorism and so on.

Lest this should be seen as a diminution of the North's constitutional status in Unionist eyes, it was proposed to register the Declaration at the UN.

However, domestic British problems rate higher than those of the 'UK Overseas' and the very day after the Agreement was signed, Whitelaw was transferred back to England to deal with the miners. Lesser men succeeded him; power swung back to Labour which showed itself unable to control either the army or mob rule, and the North was allowed to degenerate into the bloody political slum it has since become.

The UN proviso did not assuage Loyalist anger at this ultimate 'betrayal' coupled with all that had gone before, and a province-wide strike was embarked on which, as we shall see later, wrecked both the Agreement and Faulkner's political position. The fact that the British security forces subsequently arrested and imprisoned Loyalists, although still to nothing approaching the degree to which they had tried to suppress Catholic organizations, had the effect of increasing the move towards an 'Ulster consciousness' among the Loyalists.

Protestants began to feel that the British were one day going to do them down and depart, 'stopping only to write a large cheque' as a Protestant apologist put it to me once. Loyalists for the first time in a position of conflict with the British began to experience something of an identity crisis. Just where were his roots? What in 1970–80 terms is the percentage in shooting Catholics? Who gains?

At this time there were small but definite signs that some of the Protestant paramilitary leaders had become imbued not only with these feelings but also with the belief that they should have had some of the powers, and trappings, which the Unionist ascendancy traditionally garnered to themselves. These trappings were the rewards of a society whose values were secured by the efforts of the Orange paramilitary overlap with the regular police, and sometimes the army in keeping the 'White Niggers', the Catholics, in their place. Now the paramilitary leaders were thinking seriously of what the position would be *when* the British withdraw, not *if.* They did not welcome such a possibility but they envisaged it as being likely to occur at some stage in the undetermined future. And they wanted some of the political spoils which would be going begging when this happened.

17

The Constitutional Participants in the Drama

1. THE BRITISH

The question which one often hears and which logically arises at this juncture is, why don't the British pull out? Why haven't they gone already? Why go on putting up with their soldiers being shot and with bombs going off in the UK mainland when the problem of the Northern Ireland Protestant and Catholic is outside their power to control?

Regrettably the answer is not what British apologists would have us believe, that they are holding the ring out of a sense of duty, because they can see no way of withdrawing from their 'Northern Ireland commitment' without leaving behind a situation where Protestants slaughter Catholics. The fact is that the Tories are by tradition and definition the Conservative and Unionist Party and the traditional Unionist alliances (which generally represent about ten Westminster Unionist pro-Tory seats) and sympathies were clearly and disastrously shown when within a matter of days after the election of June 1970, which returned them to power, the Tories allowed the British army to be used to ransack the Falls Road during a period of two days' curfew which recalled nothing so much as General Massu's descent on the Casbah during the Algerian War. The anger that this episode aroused gave the Provisional IRA a strength in Belfast which it possesses to at least some degree to this day. There certainly were some scores, probably even a few hundreds, of weapons in the Falls Road – acquired at this stage as much for defence as offence by the Republicans of both Official and Provisional wings. But this should be compared to the revelation in Hansard that at this period the Protestants held 107,000 *licensed* weapons including two machine guns, for which an obliging Justice of the Peace had issued a licence to a gentleman who said that he needed them 'to kill otters'. The Shankill, however, was not curfewed.

The Queen is still the Queen of Britain, the United Kingdom and Northern Ireland, and on BBC TV the weather maps still show the weather for England and the top right-hand corner of Ireland. The strong Nationalist movements in Scotland and to a lesser degree Wales were a powerful disincentive to a British government to 'let Northern Ireland go'. Though these waned in strength during the late 1970s they also made clear the possibility that if one part of the UK broke off, others could too. The Scots Nationalists' slogan, after all, was 'It's *our* oil!' Jim Callaghan's coming to power generated a good deal of optimism in Ireland.

Yet neither Labour administrations of the period had the power or the will to do anything substantive. The British Labour Party leadership is a balancing act between contending forces within the party, at the best of times.

Under James Callaghan the party suffered from the additional need to maintain itself in power with the aid of minority groups in parliament.

As readers are by now aware, successive British administrations had concluded that the Unionists were not to be trusted with power. They had progressively dismantled or attempted to reform all the instruments through which that power was administered, local government, the B-Specials, the RUC, the housing executive, and finally Stormont, the seat of government itself. There could be no more damning indictment of a regime than this concluding stripping away of all its executive powers. Nevertheless when dependent on the Lib-Lab pact and on the smaller parties, Jim Callaghan in a desperate attempt to prolong his stay in office for another six months actually did a deal with the Westminster Unionists whereby, in return for their support, he would give the Unionists more power by introducing proportional representation into the North – which was estimated as possibly meaning an extra five seats for the Unionists.

Appalled at this opportunism, Gerry Fitt, a life-long supporter of Labour, which meant in Belfast risking his life, abstained in the crucial vote of no-confidence moved by Margaret Thatcher which brought on the 1979 election that returned the Tories to power. Callaghan lost by one vote – the Unionists of course voted with their traditional allies, the Conservatives; had Fitt voted, there would have been a tie – the Speaker would have voted for the status quo and Callaghan would have survived.

Yet, although the Irish issue in a sense brought on the General

Election, the 'bi-partisan policy', as the all-party agreement not to rock the boat over Ireland was euphemistically termed, meant that the Irish question was not raised during the election campaign despite the murder of Airey Neave.

The fact that Mrs Thatcher had a comfortable majority (and nothing to the right of her over Northern Ireland) might on the surface have given grounds for optimism concerning her administration, though her stated approach had been a militarized, 'Northern Ireland is British' one. But the only real indications of what her policy was had been the customary diffusing emphasis in British and Irish ministry pronouncement following the first official visit to Dublin of the new Northern Ireland Secretary, Humphrey Atkins, in July 1979, and more importantly, following the murder of Mountbatten; although it should perhaps also be noted that the first Head of State received by Mrs Thatcher after her election was Jack Lynch. The Irish spoke of the need for a political initiative, the British the need for increased security.

2. THE NORTHERN IRISH

Looking at the period 1969–79, one got a false impression of movement. Northern Irish political life appeared to be changing radically. The once monolithic Unionist Party burst apart under the strain of the times. Terence O'Neill and his cousin Chichester-Clarke who succeeded him, a captain and a major respectively, were of the old ascendancy Church of Ireland type, landowners with British army records. Brian Faulkner, who took over from Chichester-Clarke on 20 March 1971, represented the triumph of the Presbyterian business tradition of the North over the landowners. He was not to enjoy his premiership for long. A decision he strongly advocated – the introduction of internment on 9 August 1971 – helped to create such turmoil throughout the province that Stormont was suspended on 24 March the following year. Effectively speaking, with the exception of the Power-Sharing Executive set up as a result of the Sunningdale Agreement of 9 December 1973, which collapsed in May 1974, the North has been governed by direct rule from London since Stormont fell on 24 March 1972.

Bereft of a British initiative, constitutional North of Ireland politics did not develop, they simply polarized. Brian Faulkner was killed in a riding accident and succeeded by an innocuous Fermanagh farmer,

Harry West, who, after his poor showing in the June 1979 election, was succeeded by James Molyneaux. but already by June 1978, the Unionist Party was in a situation analogous to that of the IRA. There was an 'Official' Unionist Party and a number of rival groupings, the more vigorous of these being the Rev. Ian Paisley's Democratic Unionist Party. How democratic the organization is, is open to question, but it is beyond question that Ian Kyle Paisley, the fundamentalist Free Presbyterian with a doctorate from Bob Jones's Bible Belt University, lungs like the Bull of Basham and a theology from the Apocalypse, has established himself as the leading political figure in Northern Ireland. Certainly in the early days of the Northern conflagration it was he above all others, including even William Craig, who was at the time Minister for Home Affairs, who incited opposition to the Civil Rights marchers. He would have appeared to have been a prime target for the Provisionals but they let him live for two reasons: 1. his onslaughts on the Unionist Party leadership had the effect of bursting the party asunder; 2. 'he only says publicly what the rest of them say privately; he shows them all up,' explained a Provisional spokesman.

Paisley, whose church grew richer by the week, continually attracted new recruits from the Church of Ireland. He still sits in both the Westminster and European Parliaments, being returned by unassailable majorities.

In fact it was to be a noteworthy feature of the period that the murder of politicians was about the one form of killing generally, if not totally, eschewed by all groups. The Official IRA did kill two Senators, one Northern (Senator Barnhill), one Southern (Senator Billy Fox), but neither was premeditated. John Taylor, the Unionist MP, was their most considered target and he survived his wounds. The Provisional IRA shot one MP, the Rev. Robert Bradford, the Official Unionist MP for South Belfast. He was shot, on 4 November 1981, because the Provisionals accused him of being a key figure in the 'Sectarian Murder Machine'. The INLA made an attempt on Ian Paisley's life in 1985 which could have had horrific repercussions had the attempt not failed, mercifully. Subsequently the INLA carried out bomb and gun attacks against Councillors who were members of Paisley's party, the DUP. In one, during 1987, Councillor David Calvert was badly wounded. And, for their condemnation of the IRA violence, Austin Currie of the SDLP and Gerry Fitt, its leader, both had their homes raked with gunfire by Provisional supporters, a mob of whom on one occasion broke into Fitt's home in West Belfast, but were held off by him with a revolver until the police came. Fitt showed me the revolver once after a meeting in Queen's University. 'It won't save me from an assassin,' he said, 'but they won't be able to kidnap me – they won't get me into that car.'

Apart from the fact of having to contend with hostility from the differing wings of Republican extremism, who detested the SDLP almost as much as the Unionists, the SDLP also had cause to fear Orange extremists. A third member of the party was his election agent, Senator Paddy Wilson, who did not carry a gun. Not long afterwards in Belfast on 26 June 1973, Senator Wilson and Miss Irene Andrews, a Protestant, were found beside his car, ritually murdered. Senator Wilson's body had been stabbed literally dozens of times; the Ulster Freedom Fighters, a Protestant paramilitary group, claimed responsibility for the murders. And Protestant paramilitaries were also responsible for the other major killing on the Catholic side, that of Maire Drumm, vice-president of Sinn Fein, on 28 October 1976, while she was staying in the Mater Hospital, Belfast, for cataract treatment.

The foregoing is a grisly list of horrors but mercifully short in relation to the high visibility and vulnerability of politicians in Northern Ireland.

The middle of the road and middle-class Unionist Party, the Alliance grouping led by Oliver Napier, a solicitor, at one stage seemed to offer the possibility of a new departure for Unionism. A leading member of the party, driving to London with me after a meeting at Cambridge, confided that he could see himself 'coming out in favour of a United Ireland one of these days'. That interesting political phenomenon – a Unionist supporting a United Ireland – disappeared in the years which have elapsed since, and it seems unlikely that it will be seen in the years which lie ahead. It would be reassuring to feel that the new situation created by the 1994 ceasefire would change Northern Irish political figures from being, in effect, nothing but media spokesmen for the differing Northern viewpoints into people who could actually 'deliver'.

The most unfortunate examples of this paralysis are the members of the Catholic Social Democratic and Labour Party. The party contained some of the brightest political talent to appear on the Irish scene for years, including the outstanding figures of Gerry Fitt, John Hume, Seamus Mallon and Austin Currie. Growing out of the Civil Rights movement, the SDLP built on the foundations of the old 'Green' Nationalist Party but appeared to offer a chance of progress to the old

Northern problems, being reformist rather than preoccupied with the border. This could have had profound reprisals on Southern opinion and in America. Until mid-1971 it appeared to many people in Ireland that the fluent, articulate SDLP men who ran rings around their Boer-like Unionist adversaries on TV were inevitably destined to move world and domestic opinion (particularly in Ireland) to a degree that was certain to bring change and reform in all the traditional areas of Northern bitterness.

However, the conflicting currents of the Provisional campaign, Loyalist reaction to the Provisionals and army response to the general situation, produced a tidal wave of disorder that washed the SDLP out of effective political life in July of 1971 when, following the shooting of two innocent Derry men, Seamus Cusack and Desmond Beattie, by the army on 8 July, the party's deputy leader, John Hume, came under such pressure from his electorate that he persuaded his colleagues to withdraw from Stormont a week later, to the annoyance of Fitt who constantly withstood similar pressure in Belfast. The TV screen can mislead those who appear on it as to their effectiveness just as much as those who view it. From being forced into adopting the Abstentionist tactics of the Nationalist Party, the SDLP was ultimately driven, as the decade ended, to adopting the central policy of Eddie MacAteer's party, what was known as The Full National Demand of Irish Nationalists down through the years – a British withdrawal from Ireland, however long-term this aspiration might appear.

The SDLP did make some important contributions to developments during the decade – particularly in influencing Dublin's policy towards the North and, largely through John Hume, in persuading American politicians of Irish descent into taking an interest in the Irish issue. Edward Kennedy in particular took a keen and continuing interest in the North, getting a regular weekly briefing on the day-to-day situation; and Tip O'Neill, then Speaker of the House of Representatives in Washington, actively embroiled himself in controversy through his criticism of British policy. He appeared to have been quite genuinely shocked at Callaghan's opportunistic deal with the Unionists. Other distinguished figures such as Governor Carey of New York, Patrick Moynihan and Hugh Byrne, along with life-long campaigners for Irish interests such as Paul O'Dwyer, the Civil Rights lawyer, or Judge James Comeford, former Chairman of the New York St Patrick's Day Parade, that annual assertion of Irish strength in the US, were increasingly making their voices heard on specific issues such as the behaviour of the security forces. President Carter, too, had interested himself in the Northern issue. American politicians' statements had almost inevitably condemned violence and then gone on to ask Britain to do something about her responsibilities in the area.

The American dimension has not been regarded as an unalloyed plus by the Dublin governments. First, the Irish in America have long supported force as a tactic for achieving reunification – a tactic to which Dublin is straightforwardly opposed. Opposed in fact to a degree which may have proved counter-productive because a succession of Irish Prime Ministers and Ministers going out to America since the troubles began, warning Americans against subscribing to the Provisionals, have certainly created something of a backlash against the idea of foreigners coming to the US to tell Uncle Sam how he should spend the dollars in his pocket; and the Provisionals have in fact thus been given some subscriptions which they would not otherwise have received.

Secondly, some American politicians who interested themselves in the Irish issue were too close to the physical force aspect in Dublin's view – most notably Congressman Mario Biaggi whose ad hoc committee on Northern Ireland claimed the support of over 130 senators and congressmen. This sizeable lobby of pro-Irish sentiment was outweighed in value in Dublin's view by virtue of Biaggi's close links with the Northern Aid Committee (the Provisionals' major support group in the state led by the old-time Tipperary Republican Michael Flannery), and later with the Irish Caucus (an umbrella committee of Irish-American organizations, led by Fred Burns O'Brien, an Irish-American civil servant, and by Father Sean MacManus, the Redemptorist priest who helped to get Sean MacStiofain off his hunger strike [see Chapter 21] and whose brother Jackie was killed in the 1956 campaign). Although in true Irish style all these organizations related to each other in a manner which proved they were Republican – they almost immediately split – nevertheless, as a result of these cross currents in Irish-American sentiment, as much of the Irish Embassy in Washington's time was spent on anti-Provisional activities as was devoted to positive lobbying on the Northern issue. It was the old dilemma of trying to be pro-Irish or sometimes anti an aspect of British policy without *inter alia* helping the IRA.

Britain's response to the American influence was low-key, subtle and so far quite effective. The style of the State Department tends to be English in the sense that the style of diplomacy generally tended once to be French. Tea, tweeds and a posting to the Court of St James tend to be highly favoured. This natural sympathy to the British position – combined with the fact that most media coverage of the North of Ireland tends to come through agencies, correspondents and TV crews based in London – makes for an understanding approach to Britain's difficulties in 'Ulster'.

In this period the calibre of America's ambassadors to Dublin had risen sharply; men like John Moore, Walter Curley and William Shannon, a former policy maker at the *New York Times* and author of a standard work on the Irish in America, had performed that rare feat of furthering both their own country's interests and those of the country to which they had been accredited. But the view from Dublin was not as readily accepted in Foggy Bottom as that from St James and the dispatches of William Shannon had sometimes to contend with those of Kingman Brewster, his counterpart in London. However, as a US Presidential election neared, one in which the importance of men like Edward Kennedy and Tip O'Neill did not need to be stressed, the odds appeared to favour a view more sympathetic to Dublin. 1979 saw more interest in, and speechifying about, Ireland than America had seen in any other time in that troubled decade.

3. THE SOUTHERN IRISH

Finally to the last principal set of actors on the constitutional stage – the Dublin administrators and in particular Jack Lynch and Fianna Fail. For although by one of the ironies of history it was the Coalition – which by tradition might be expected to be less than enthusiastic concerning the fulfilment of Republican goals just as it was John A. Costello's Coalition of 1948 which declared a Republic so it was the Coalition of 1973 between Fine Gael and Labour (the latter containing such an avowedly anti-Republican figure as Dr Conor Cruise O'Brien) – that came nearest in the period under review to furthering Republican ambitions with the Sunningdale Agreement.

Nevertheless Fianna Fail were in power for nearly twice as long as the 1973–7 Coalition since the troubles began and were the major Irish constitutional force to be reckoned with during the era. As it is also the constitutional embodiment of Republicanism, the party whose leader drafted the constitution, Article 3 of which lays claim to Northern Ireland, it was the party on which the moral responsibility for finding a solution to the problem lay heaviest. But although a Fianna

Fail study group was working to produce a full policy on the implications of unity, there was as yet in existence no detailed blueprint as to what exactly the party intended to do to create a peaceful, post-British-withdrawal Ireland in which Protestant fears would be assuaged and liberties protected. In a general atmosphere of 'Oh Lord make me good but not yet', one was aware that the party was generally in favour of unity, this to be achieved at an unspecified future date, at some sort of conference at which the Protestants' reservations about the South's constitution and laws would be resolved.

The main line pushed abroad – in Washington, for instance – was that Dublin would like to see Britain withdraw her 1949 guarantee to the Unionists so as to make them more amenable to negotiation. Of course, as we have seen, the Downing Street Declaration reinforced rather than dismantled this barrier. The keystone of the Lynch policy was that, while distancing itself from the IRA demand that Britain should make a declaration of intent to withdraw from Northern Ireland, she should nevertheless exercise herself towards working for unity, rather than checkmating it. There is no doubt that a sizeable segment of the rank-and-file of Fianna Fail favoured a more activist policy than that of Lynch.

In July 1979, before the parliament recessed for the summer, there were angry parliamentary party Caucus meetings protesting at aspects of the party's performance including its policy on the North; and finally Lynch had to devote a full day to a parliamentary meeting at which the various grievances were aired. While these were as much related to the handling of the economy as to the North and to a damaging strike in the postal service, the North was the issue which was viewed almost in theological terms. And for a very good reason: apart from their undoubted ancestral feelings on the issue, the party was aware that the substantial portion of their huge majority, gained because of the Northern situation two years earlier, was in imminent danger of being lost to them. For the West of Ireland had returned Neil Blaney, one of the men sacked over the Arms Trial affair, as its member for Europe – against Fianna Fail's nominee. Blaney has always maintained that he hadn't left Fianna Fail; Fianna Fail had left him! Blaney was not to be heard referring to the Provisionals as terrorists – he called them Freedom Fighters. From all this, Charles Haughey, that other major figure of the Arms Crisis, emerged to become Lynch's main rival for the leadership.

On top of these symptoms of Northern-occasioned disquiet, Lynch had to endure another particularly unwelcome challenge just four days after he had returned from seeing Margaret Thatcher in London to discuss the North in the wake of the Mountbatten murder.

He unsuccessfully sought to prevent Síle De Valera, the youngest deputy in the Dail, and a granddaughter of Eamon De Valera, from delivering a speech at the Commemoration of Liam Lynch on 9 September in Fermoy, Co Cork. He had seen an advance copy of her script, which she had circulated early to gain publicity. It was couched in old-fashioned, *An Phoblacht*-style rhetoric, and seemed both by its timing and content to be an effort to undermine Lynch. He had to issue a statement publicly rebuking her and to call a special parliamentary party meeting to discuss the issue on the eve of the Pope's visit so that the details would be lost in the coverage of the Pope's visit. Lynch weathered that storm, occasioned not so much by the speech or the age of the girl concerned as by her surname, but it served to highlight the weakness of his regime in other areas, economic as well as political, so that ultimately the death of Lord Mountbatten brought other unlooked-for results for the IRA.

One other circumstance which aided the IRA tremendously should be noted here. Despite all the apparently genuine efforts that had been made at reform, all the expenditure of life, money and effort, a report published by the Fair Employment Agency in January 1978 showed that though adult Catholics number only one-third of the population of Northern Ireland, they contributed twice as many unemployed than the numerically superior Protestants. In fact, due to the higher birth rate, Catholic children were generally reckoned to be in a majority of 52 to 48 per cent to Protestant children at school-going age. But the employment situation was like the ring the Chinese fishermen place around trained cormorants' necks to prevent them swallowing the fish they catch – Catholic children could catch an education but this could not necessarily enable them to earn their daily bread – hence they had to emigrate.

Discrimination and political inertia ensured both a continuity and a steady recruitment to the IRA. The obvious analogies between the situation of Irish Catholics and of the Palestinians (whose

poverty and lack of opportunity provided a continuing stream of recruits to the PLO) meant inevitable contact between the IRA, the PLO
and other such organizations.

So much for the story of the progress of the constitutional actors in the
drama of Ireland over the ten years from August 1969 to 1979. To
turn now to the activities of the unconstitutional actors who in a sense
both brought up the curtain and refused to let it drop – the Provisional
IRA.

18

The Provisional IRA –
the Rebirth of a Movement

As the IRA themselves put it, their strategy in the years which saw the rebirth of the 'movement' between 1969 and 1971 fell under three headings:

1. Defence
2. Retaliation
3. Offence (in 1971 and continuing apart from various truces to 1994)

A Provisional apologist given the history and theology of the movement could make a case under all three headings, defence being the most obvious. Around 1969/1970, Belfast was the cockpit of activity in Northern Ireland. Later, as we shall see, other areas such as Crossmaglen in Co. Armagh were to become scenes of bloody and momentous deeds, and some towns, apart from the obvious centres of Belfast and Derry, were particularly badly hit during the troubles. Three of these were Dungannon, Strabane and Coleraine which were devastated several times by bombings.*

However, Belfast remained the key area for a number of reasons. The Protestants struck there most continuously, and there was both a plentiful source of recruitment and a nucleus of older leaders so that the Provisionals regrouped there as a result. There was, for instance, William McKee, later to become OC of the Belfast Brigade of the Provisional IRA, who was badly wounded as he conducted a successful defence of St Matthew's Church off the Newtownards Road, in the face of determined Protestant efforts to burn it down in July 1969. The Protestant mobs who also attempted with some success to burn out

---

* One of the worst of these occurred on 12 June 1973, when a bomb killed six people in Coleraine and injured thirty-three more, some, in hospital parlance, 'very seriously', i.e. crippled for life.

areas in the Falls Road in August 1969, were in the minds both of the Catholics and, in some cases, of themselves, always ready to return to finish off the work so begun. So the need for defence was a powerful motive force in the strengthening of the Provisional IRA in the early 1970s.

The Provisionals, or Provos* as they became generally known, began to group in the Falls area generally. For instance, the Andersonstown branch of Sinn Fein, the Rodger McCorley Cumann, split from the Official IRA of Cathal Goulding when the section led by Albert Price – father of the Price sisters, Dolores and Marion, who went on hunger strike in Brixton prison after being sentenced for their part in the London bombings (see Chapter 21) – differed from the socialist policy of the rest of the Cumann and reverted to the traditional Republican aim of getting the British out of occupied Ireland. This sort of re-alignment of forces went on everywhere there was a Sinn Fein branch. But most notably in districts like the Clonard area, in which the Bombay Street burning had occurred, and in which other deeds of Republican significance had also taken place. For instance, it was in the 'little India' area of the Clonard district in Cawnpore Street that Tommy Williams and his companions were arrested after the fatal shooting of an RUC man, for which Williams was subsequently executed. Amongst his companions who escaped the noose was Joe Cahill, who now became something of a household name through his appearance at press conferences as he and other figures from the past – 'forties men' – who had seen active service in that area began to come together and re-organize.

Within the ranks of the IRA as a whole Sean MacStiofain (in English, John Stephenson) was emerging as the principal leader. He became Chief of Staff of the Provisionals after the Intercontinental walk-out. Born in England of an Irish mother, service in the Royal Air Force as John Stephenson had accentuated rather than dulled his ancestral nationalism, and a capacity for mastering the internecine politicking of the IRA carried him upwards through the ranks of the movement, which he had joined along with various Irish Language movements during the 1950s. He served a jail term with Cathal Goulding, who now faced him across the ideological divide, for his

* The Provisionals came to be known as Provos or Provies or Pinheads. This last is not a term of abuse but to differentiate them from the 'Stickies', the Officials, who used gum to affix their Easter Lilies to their lapels as opposed to the Provisionals' pins.

part in the Arborfield raid. Apart from the fact that his was the hand on the throttle that moved the IRA from 'neutral' to 'go' in the organizational build-up period of 1969–71, his principal contribution to Republican strategy was the introduction of the snipers' technique of only firing one shot before disappearing, which claimed several soldiers' lives.

Daithi O'Connell, who is credited with being the architect of the car bomb, and later became one of the movement's principal political thinkers, had taken part in the famous Brookeborough ambush and escaped from the Curragh internment camp in the 'Three Macs' era, as we saw with another young IRA man who was also to become a household name during the post-1969 hostilities – Ruairi O'Bradaigh, President of the Provisional wing of Sinn Fein.

Little India, full of Victorian red-bricked, dry-closet houses born to huddle and hate under the shadow of long-silent mills, now began to echo to the murmur of old aspirations and old leadership. The Kashmir Road, Cupar Street, Bombay Street, Cawnpore Street, and many other names from England's colonial past, began to come alive in contemporary Ireland in a manner that was to provide John Bull with one of his last and worst heartaches of the Empire.

As the Shankill Road loops around the Clonard district, there was, in its early days, little need for the IRA leaders to stress the need for 'no-go areas'. Later, barricades manned by vigilantes met both the Catholics' requirements for security and the Republicans' instinct to deny Britain's security forces a right of access.

The IRA had an odd sort of life of its own, as much based on the fears and aspirations of the Catholic population as on separatist theology. It is literally true, for instance, that in August 1969 the only weapons known to be available to the IRA were ten guns. Subsequent to the Bombay Street burnings, Jack McCabe, with another Republican sympathizer, Myles Shevlin, a solicitor, smuggled in some guns to the North which had been cached since the 1950s campaign – one of them a Schmeisser machine-gun. McCabe, a veteran of the forties who subsequently blew himself up when a spark from a shovel with which he was mixing explosives on the floor of a garage in his home on the Swords Road, Dublin, sent the explosives off, injuring him terribly and fatally, was probably the main IRA bomb supplier of the period. His eyes and testicles were blown away but on his deathbed he used his last strength to give Shevlin details of what had gone wrong so that someone else would not make the same mistake. 'An iron man,'

Shevlin told me, 'an iron man.' After his death, on 30 December 1971, the Northern hydra was to ensure that many others with expertise gained in armies both at home and abroad would be found to follow in his footsteps.

Immediately after the burning and appearance of troops on the streets, anyone in the Falls Road area who could lay their hands on a weapon did so, for defence. It was out of this maelstrom of emotion that what I described earlier as 'unconventional initiatives' (on page 336) emerged from influential Dublin political circles. There is in some circles an erroneous belief, fostered by both British Intelligence, and, for their own ends, by some Irish politicians and polemicists, that the Provisional IRA was born as a result of these initiatives. This is untrue, the Dublin plotting was both dangerous, and grossly unprofessional, but ultimately largely inefficient, and in sum only added up to a tiny push along the road to strength for the Provisional movement. Its birth, and subsequent life, stems from deep roots in Irish history, or more accurately, Anglo-Irish history. Nevertheless a conspiracy theory of the Provos' origins is frequently regurgitated. The theory is based less on fact than on an antipathy to Fianna Fail and Irish Nationalism in general, and to some Fianna Fail politicians in particular. One of the principal proponents of this theory is Dr Conor Cruise O'Brien. In a foreword to Martin Dillon's otherwise excellent book, *The Dirty War*[*], which contains a first-class account of the Fianna Fail–Provo contact, he writes:

> The deal that launched the Provos was essentially this: certain members of the Lynch Government approached those leading members of the IRA who were known to be disgusted with the Marxist leadership, on both nationalist and Catholic grounds, and also on operational grounds. These leaders – who were to become the leaders of the Provisional IRA – were offered money, arms and general support if they would abjure operations against the Republic, and concentrate on operations inside Northern Ireland. The Provisional-leaders-to-be agreed. The new policy, in exchange for which the emerging Provos received support from the then Dublin government, is enshrined in the IRA's General Order No. 8, which is still in force and is set out in the IRA's Green Book, published for the first time in the Appendix to *The Dirty War*, General Order No. 8 runs as follows . . . [Dr O'Brien then quotes the Order and concludes]: 'Thus the Provos were born, and the dirty war began.'

[*] Martin Dillon *The Dirty War*, Arrow, London, 1990, pp. xiv–xv

There are serious factual errors in this analysis. Firstly, as readers will no doubt have noted (pp. 256–7) for themselves, the Order was developed not in the 1969–70 period, but many years earlier – in the years 1950–54 when it was formally incorporated into the IRA's General Orders. Secondly, far from having to 'abjure' operations against the Republic, the IRA split because amidst the fires of 1969 it was still observing the cease fire which it had declared in 1962. On a lesser plane I would also point out that the contents of *The Green Book* had appeared in earlier editions of this book long before Dr O'Brien penned his foreword!

The Fianna Fail–IRA links took place against a deteriorating security situation in Northern Ireland. Catholics were arriving south of the border in their thousands. Refugee camps were set up at various centres under the auspices of the Irish army. A Government sub-committee was formed to deal with the problem. A contingency plan, which was never implemented, was drawn up for an Irish army invasion of the North to protect Catholics. This was dropped when unofficial soundings revealed that the British would not be prepared to turn a blind eye to the incursion. It was also pointed out by military experts that by the time the Army secured even the town of Newry, close to the Border, wholesale slaughter would have occurred amongst Catholics in further away Belfast.

In this pervervid atmosphere all sorts of contacts were being established during the period. Inflamed Nationalist leaders, many of them Republican sympathizers, were coming to Dublin to seek aid and protection. To some this meant UN intervention, to others simply: 'give us the guns.' Government sources in turn were making contacts of their own throughout the North. What was going to happen? Were the Catholics really in imminent danger of slaughter? Would the Irish army have to become involved? Could the IRA protect Catholic areas? Would the IRA fight under its present leadership? These were the questions of the hour. While answers were being sought a hawks and doves debate raged throughout Fianna Fail. To the doves, involvement with Northern Ireland was madness which could only end in destruction for both parts of the island. To the hawks, it was the bounden duty of Fianna Fail, the Republican Party, as it liked to style itself, to both protect its Nationalist brethren and, if possible, get back the 'Fourth Green Field'.

Cathal Goulding, the then Chief of Staff of the IRA, is on record[*] as

---

[*] He taped an interview for the BBC's *Timewatch* programme with Martin Dillon which was not screened. The transcripts of the interview are in the author's possession.

saying that he was contacted and asked to go to London to discuss the
provision of funds for the IRA. Here, he says, in an Irish Centre he
met Jock Haughey, whose brother Charles was Minister for Finance
and a member of the Cabinet sub-committee. The Haugheys' father,
Sean, had been a member of the IRA in the Anglo-Irish war, which
resulted in the emergence of the Northern Statelet. He had also been a
prominent figure in Michael Collins's subsequent attempt to surrep-
titiously help the Catholics of the day, who in 1922 were in similar
situations of peril to those of 1969. Unknown to his Cabinet colleagues
Collins, the head of Government, had weapons smuggled into the Six
Counties to arm the IRA. Sean Haughey had been one of the most
effective smugglers.

Goulding told Jock Haughey that it would take £50,000 to buy the
arms required. Haughey gave him some £3000. There were a number
of other such meetings, but no more money changed hands. One
gathering was held in the Intercontinental Hotel, Dublin, attended by
a number of well-known Irish businessmen and a Fianna Fail Minister, to put a proposal to a prominent Co. Derry IRA man: that he
should help to organize a more militant wing of the IRA in the North.
He had consulted with Goulding first and Goulding advised him to go
to the meeting and agree to take the promised money and car. The car
would have been in the IRA man's name and Goulding reasoned that,
as it could not be taken off him, 'at least we'll have got something out
of them.' But neither money nor car was ever produced.

However, arising out of these contacts, arrangements were made
that allowed a consignment of arms to pass through Dublin Airport
and into the hands of the IRA in October of 1969. That shipment
effectively ended the period when anything tangible came the way of
the Goulding faction of the IRA. The Government had a number of
agents on the ground in Northern Ireland, of whom Captain Jimmy
Kelly, of Irish Military Intelligence, was the most active. He too made
contact with Republican circles in the course of his duties. All his
actions were undertaken in the belief that he was carrying out official
Government policy. Kelly had access to bank accounts opened by the
Northern Ireland Cabinet sub-committee.

This money, some £100,000 in all, was, according to a Government
announcement of 21 August 1969, supposedly to be administered
through the Red Cross, for the alleviation of distress, not for causing it.
And indeed a great deal of the funds disbursed with official approval at
that time were used for charitable purposes. Around £24,000 was

given to Cardinal Conway for use at his discretion. Other monies were spent on the work of the Belfast Central Citizens Defence Committees. These Committees were staffed with representatives of Goulding's wing of the IRA, the emerging Provisional element, 'bishops' men', representatives of the Church, and of Labour and other political parties. They were as their name suggested, Defence Committees, born out of the climate of fear which prevailed in Belfast's Catholic areas at the time. Much of the money went on assisting victims of rioting, but they also provided a vehicle for IRA recruitment, of a Provisional nature. The Committees began to split when the 'bishops men' element moved against Jim Sullivan, their Chairman, and installed a Catholic businessman, Tom Conaty, in his place. The Committees finally split when the clerical party objected to money being given to the families of IRA men on the run.

With the assistance of Albert Luyks, a Belgian friend of Blaney's, Captain Kelly made contact with a Hamburg arms dealer. On 19 February 1970 in Dortmund Kelly handed over £10,000 to the dealer for a consignment of arms which were to be shipped to Dublin from Antwerp. Customs clearance in Dublin had been agreed on the basis that the arms would be treated as described on the manifest: steel plates. However, British intelligence, who had monitored Kelly's contacts, arranged for an employee of the arms dealer's to ensure that proper documentation was not forthcoming. The consignment was held up. All that came to Dublin were some bulletproof vests. The resourceful Kelly then arranged for a private plane to fly the arms to Dublin Airport from Vienna on 19 April. A document supplied from the Department of Finance was furnished by Kelly to the Airport authorities requesting that the cargo be passed through customs. However, the hawks and doves factor within Fianna Fail and the Irish Civil Service now began to combine with the activities of both British Intelligence and the Irish Special Branch to frustrate the importation.

Acting principally on the instructions of the Secretary of the Department of Justice, Peter Berry, the Gardai placed a cordon around Dublin Airport on 18 April. John Kelly, a prominent Belfast Provisional, was tipped off and flew to Vienna to warn Captain Kelly (no relation) to abort the mission. The guns never arrived in Dublin, but apparently word from British Intelligence sources did. Liam Cosgrave, the leader of Fine Gael, received a letter, ostensibly from the Gardai, telling him something of what was going on. He went to see the Taoiseach, Jack Lynch, who somehow until then had managed to remain unaware of what had been going on. The greatest political upheaval to affect the Republic since the foundation of the State ensued. Sackings and resignations became the order of the day. Haughey and Blaney were dismissed. They, Jock Haughey, Captain Kelly and Albert Luyks were all subsequently acquitted by Dublin courts when arraigned on arms smuggling charges.

The famous 'Arms Crisis' exploded as the result of a chain of events which included the allocation by the Southern government of public monies for the relief of distress in the wake of the burnings (there was a very wide-ranging set of appeals from the North to help the Catholic population). This was not done under IRA auspices, although the IRA of course did begin sending emissaries far and near to search for armaments. There was also a general feeling in the South that somehow all the momentous happenings in the North were in some way going to help the South 'to get back the six'.

It became known that an Irish army officer, Captain James Kelly, had been moving in different circles north of the border, and in the subsequent court proceedings it was revealed that he and Jock Haughey had indeed gone to Germany on an arms mission. Kelly believed sincerely that he was acting with official government knowledge during this time. But in fact the mission which he was given, and undertook in good faith, appears to have been originally conceived as a result of ad hoc personal initiatives on the part of senior politicians. The result was that Kelly departed from the army and abandoned his military career in the wake of the dismissals and resignations of other political figures. The most ironic resignation was that of Kevin Boland, a son of the wartime Fianna Fail Minister of Justice who had had the task of carrying out De Valera's stern policy towards the IRA of the war years. The contemporary Minister for Justice, Michael O'Morain, also resigned.

John Kelly, the Belfast man whose sincerity when on trial in October 1970 impressed even opponents of Republicanism, said bitterly in the course of an oration that ranks in the best tradition of Irish speeches from the dock: 'We did not ask for blankets or feeding bottles. We asked for guns – and no one from Taoiseach Lynch down denied our request or told us this was contrary to government policy.'

I remember one enthusiastic Dublin public relations practitioner whose services had been engaged at this juncture breezing into the office of the *Irish Press* to give me a preview of what one minister, whose name he liberally quoted, had planned to 'get the word out to the rest of the world when the banging started'. The PRO envisaged that in order to bring the matter to UN attention, the Irish army was going to be used to cross the border to seize 'even a football field'; and the Irish government had, he assured us, a communication network set up through Paris in case the British seized the lines through London.

The only tangible evidence of the communications which emerged from all this was a newspaper, the *Voice of the North*, produced by another former *Irish Press* (and *Daily Express*!) journalist, Seamus Brady, a confidant of Neil Blaney, and a brief appearance on the Irish scene of Markpress, the publicity organization which had acquired some experience of wartime propaganda during the Biafran conflict.

Such, in outline, were the events of what became known as the 'Arms Case'. A Dail Committee set up to investigate the incidents after the Courts cleared the Haugheys, Blaney and Co., failed to either elucidate the facts or get back the money for the arms that did not arrive from Vienna. Albert Luyks has since died and taken his secrets with him. But it is quite obvious from both the scale of the monies and arms involved that the events of approximately eight months in 1969–70 could not, and did not, have a lasting effect on the Provisionals' growth.

Meanwhile, as these events were in progress, back in Belfast IRA leaders from the past negotiated under the guise of community leadership with the British military authorities, particularly General Farrar-Hockley, on issues such as whether or not the barricades should come down and on law and order problems. These talks were held to have broken down when Farrar-Hockley named on television four of the principals with whom he had negotiated. They were Liam Hannaway, Billy McKee, Leo Smith and Frank Card – or Proinsias MacAirt as he prefers to be known.

The principal military activity in the IRA at this time (1969–71) was stone-throwing and sometimes petrol-bombing, which could just as easily have been attributed to high spirits on the part of local youths who had inherited, along with the attitude of the urban, unemployed proletariat anywhere towards uniforms, the particularly Irish ancestral antipathy for 'their law' and 'their order', as manifested by 'their' troops and 'their' RUC.

To the outside eye, nothing very significant in terms of IRA development seemed to be happening, apart from acts of hooliganism and destruction, and the fact that the Protestant apologists and Ian Paisley were working themselves into paroxysms of rage at the spectacle of members of Her Majesty's security forces being denied access to part of the United Kingdom by Republicans in parts of Belfast and Derry. These finally came to an end when on 31 July 1971 'Operation Motorman', a major, motorized, British army thrust into Derry's IRA controlled areas, brought an end to the no-go areas – but not to the IRA who simply were not there when the troops arrived and re-emerged to fight another day.

Within the movement, as new faces and new ideas emerged, an old debate also re-surfaced the idea of 'going political'. The debate was not on the customary lines of force versus constitutional action (the Provisionals were clearly in favour of force), but of having a political programme to put forward to show that the Provisionals were not merely mindless gunmen. O'Bradaigh and Daithi O'Connell were strongly in favour of a political programme, but MacStiofain and his supporters, chiefly the Northerners, were mistrustful of anything that might dilute the military effort. However, the politicals ultimately won out to the extent that a socialist-sounding policy for a new order in Ireland, the 'Eire Nua' (New Ireland Policy), was adopted.

A part of the new policy revealed to the public on 21 August 1971 in Monaghan Town (the venue was chosen because it was in the South but near the border) contained one fundamental new idea, namely that there should be four regional parliaments for Ireland, catering for regions drawn up on the old provinces of Leinster, Munster, Connacht and Ulster. Ulster was to be restored to its original nine counties with its own parliament, Dail Uladh, the idea being that the Protestants would gain three more counties, albeit with a much reduced overall majority, which would on the one hand reduce their fears of being swamped by Catholics and at the same time give the Catholics a larger share in the running of the new Dail Uladh. The idea was keenly discussed at least in Republican circles, though I for one could never see that the Unionists, having sown the dragon's teeth they did with six counties, could be expected to do any better with nine.

The Provisionals also drew up a five-point programme which was issued on the eve of the Lynch-Heath meetings at Chequers on 6 September 1971, and which subsequently formed the basis of discussions on a cease-fire with Whitelaw. The five points, though dismissed by everyone concerned, are a useful thumbnail description of the Provisionals' aims and still stand, though the provision regarding Stormont clearly no longer applies. They asked that the British government should:

1. End its campaign of violence against the Irish people.
2. Abolish Stormont.
3. Hold free elections to establish a regional parliament for the Province of Ulster as a first step towards a new government for the thirty-two counties.
4. Release all Irish political prisoners, tried or untried, in England and Ireland.
5. Compensate all those who had suffered as a result of British violence.

Still the only overt signs of IRA activity on the streets of Belfast were riots, stone-throwing youths and 'up the IRA' graffiti. But behind the walls of the redbricked terraced houses a stranger, had he penetrated, might have observed here and there groups of men sitting around walkie-talkies imported from America and heard exchanges like these:

'Foot patrol coming up Kashmir Road . . .'

'Roger, will open up a second front in Dunville Street.'

The 'second front' might have consisted of five or six youths armed with stones or an occasional petrol bomb. But their activities would have diverted the patrol from the Kashmir Road and from possibly finding an arms cache or radio transmitter, and in any event another group of soldiers was pinned down. Also at this time (roughly late summer of 1970/early spring 1971) one began to read of the soldiers being taken to hospital after 'accidentally discharging their own weapons'. I remember a hospital orderly in Musgrave Military Hospital in Lisburn telling me that his ward at that stage was already filled with gunshot victims – 'shotgun pellets, twenty-twos, everything' – but the army were not issued with those types of guns and yet 'they were making out that it was accidental discharges that did it', said the orderly. Yet despite the obviously deadly nature of the steadily fermenting yeast, the first British soldier to die in the troubles, Gunner Curtis, was not shot until February 1971.

The ultimate object of the campaign that began to get off the ground was not to gain an outright victory over the British army, which was clearly impossible, but to render the existing state inoperable so that the army would have to withdraw. The army is still there but the IRA certainly succeeded in making the state a heavy liability to Britain. The British government estimated at the end of August 1979 the operational cost since the army first moved in, on 15 August 1969, at around £404.3 million; the daily cost of terrorism was said to be running at about £500,000 or £5.50 a second.[*] The overall bill for holding on to the North was £1 billion annually – the same as Britain contributed to the EEC.

After a period in 1971/2 following the introduction of internment, which was characterized by riots, bus burnings and prolonged gun battles with troops, costly in terms of ammunition, the pattern changed; rioting gradually died away and the campaign developed along a three-fold path.

1. The shooting of personnel – security forces, police, members of the Ulster Defence Regiment and so on,
2. The use of bombs, placed both in premises – some large, but some ludicrously small, 'soft' targets such as insignificant shops and pubs – and in parked cars. One of the biggest single 'economic targets' was destroyed on 17 July 1971, when the Provos blew up the £2m *Daily Mirror* plant at Dunmurry outside Belfast (one of the most advanced in Europe), partially because it was regarded as the 'Soldiers'' paper. Despite, or perhaps in part because of this, the *Daily Mirror* in London published an editorial in August 1978, calling for a British troop withdrawal.
3. The use of propaganda, at which the Provisionals soon proved themselves to be enormously adept. Another related field at which the Provisionals were to show considerable prowess was intelligence.

All through the decade they proved themselves able to get hold of top secret information which had both a military and a propaganda value. For instance, in 1969 they learned of internment in advance so that instead of being a crushing blow, it proved a launching pad – so few of their key personnel being picked up that the blow fell mainly on the innocent, with consequent enormously damaging repercussions for the authorities. They learned that British intelligence was operating behind the cover of at least one seemingly ordinary business and brutally crippled this endeavour by eliminating the team, including a woman, that operated in Belfast behind the cover of the Four Square Laundry. In early 1979 they brought off a coup which really displayed

[*] *Sunday Independent*, 26 August 1979.

arcane knowledge, taking from the English mails a top-secret British military assessment (published in *An Phoblacht* in May) of their own strength in which the British concluded, among a number of other judgements, that the IRA could not be defeated – an incredible morale booster to receive from an enemy.

Recruitment was very largely from the young of working-class Catholic strongholds in Belfast, Derry, Armagh, Down and Tyrone, though later, as the campaign began stretching on and on, Southerners started to be drawn into the ranks also. The widespread nature of IRA support in ghetto areas, though it contained inherent weakness in terms both of its potential for infiltration and for ghastly errors of timing and inefficiency which led some British security forces to sneer at the 'Paddy factor', did offer great advantages to a guerrilla movement.

The 'Paddy factor' arose because much of the movement was young, working class, limited in vision and experience, very often cut off from central direction by the duress of the circumstance, and had to rely therefore on 'targets of opportunity' or personal initiative. These last two circumstances in particular were sometimes responsible for awful tragedies of bungled warnings as to bomb explosions, or for unforeseen tragedies such as the kidnapping of Dr Niedemayer.

A bomb could be made in one place, transported to a second and picked up by a third party who might not have known either of the others, for delivery to the target – be it a restaurant, hotel, public building, shop or pub. In all cases the basic motivation was the same, the waging of economic warfare. This particular aim was pursued to its extreme limits with the policy, later on in the decade, of actually shooting industrialists and businessmen. This began in January 1976, causing widespread criticism even amongst IRA supporters, particularly after the very able managing director of Dupont in Derry, a man who had done a great deal to attract investment to the province, Mr Jeffrey Agate, was shot. The IRA did try to justify the businessmen's killing, issuing a statement on 22 March 1977:

In all cases, those executed by the IRA played a prominent role in the effort to stabilize the British-orientated Six County economy.

This economy has never served the interests of the people. It is geared completely to their exploitation and is to the benefit of those in control. The war is not merely a conflict between Republican and

British forces. It is a conflict between the interests which these forces represent. Those involved in the management of the economy serve British interests – they represent and maintain economic interests which make war necessary.

But despite the foregoing, the campaign was recognized for what it was, an ugly and unpopular affair, and was quietly dropped without public declaration. But as we shall see in our examination of the events of 'Bloody Monday' on 27 August 1979, in which Earl Mountbatten was blown up at Mullaghmore, Co. Sligo, the idea of striking at the prestigious continued intermittently to be reactivated by the movement to a point where it became major policy.

The IRA benefited from the traditional passive support given to the movement. The bed for the night, the blind eye, the co-operation in money or services. For instance, the IRA were not invulnerable, bullets did wound them, but one very rarely heard* of a doctor or a hospital reporting the fact that a wounded man was receiving treatment – 'traffic accidents' were widespread! But political support, in the form of the vote, continued to be withheld – or rather the type of person who might have drawn the vote continued to stand aloof from the movement.

All through the decade both the cause of constitutionalism (as represented by the SDLP) and of physical force suffered because the two wings of Catholic assertion were divided. This in a sense makes the IRA's struggle all the more remarkable. It was far more lengthy and costly in life and destruction than the Anglo-Irish war of the 1916–21 era but, unlike that era, it was carried out without a significant political movement and, hence, without the sanction of being able to point to a voting support for its activities.

The changing times forced new techniques on the Provisionals as the campaign wore on and British surveillance and technology improved. For instance, during March 1973, because searches and heavily increased surveillance were making bombing more difficult, the IRA introduced the tactic of proxy car-bombing, i.e. forcing the driver of a hijacked lorry to drive his own vehicle to the target under the threat of his own or his family's death and leaving the driver to raise the alarm. On 28 March of that year, one of the most spectacular of such bombs caused three-quarters of a million pounds'-worth of

---

* In fact in the South, never.

damage in the centre of Belfast.* At different times, as we shall see, judges, businessmen and prison warders were added to the death lists. On 8 April 1976, the first prison warder claimed as a 'legitimate target' was shot dead. (The hitting of one such legitimate target on 17 April 1979 well exemplified the increasing inhumanity of the campaign; he was at a wedding holding the hand of a three-year-old child at the time.)

Up to the summer of 1978, when a re-organization of the movement into a cell system, not unlike the old IRB model, was carried out, the IRA was modelled on the old army-style lines and engaged in activities under familiar banners: the IRA itself; Sinn Fein, its political wing; Cumann na mBan, the women's wing; Na Fianna Eireann, the youth organization; and one new departure, the IRA auxiliary, which did not show itself in overt operation but existed as low-profile support groups of considerable value to the movement as a whole. As the campaign wore on, the movement issued a wide variety of pamphlets and newspapers, the principal being the *Republican News* in Belfast and *An Phoblacht* in Dublin, which were subsequently merged into *An Phoblacht*.

Apart from the premeditated direct attacks carried out by the IRA on security forces, warders, informers, loyalists and the organization's own disciplinary activities, which could and did include shaving off women's hair, tarring and feathering, kneecapping and even death, there was the loss of life as a by-product of the IRA's activities. For instance – not including the enraged response against innocent Catholics by Protestant killer squads such as the UVF, the Tara Organization or the Shankill Butchers Gang, all of which tortured and killed Catholics as a direct consequence of the IRA campaign – there were the members of the public, and of the IRA itself, accidentally killed as a result of premature explosion or a faulty warning system.

When thinking of the IRA operatives one should not visualize hardened neo-psychopaths of ice-cold nerve. There are a few, but they are a minority. This may sometimes, particularly in the wake of a miscalculation which cost civilian casualties, seem very hard to accept, but the IRA made a firm and fixed distinction between attacks on UDR and RUC personnel and sectarian assassination. It was official

---

* The principal destructive agent used in the North was gelignite, although more modern substances including napalm bombs which destroyed La Mon, for instance, were used. The gelignite was obtained under the traditional guise of 'Staff exports' from quarries all over Ireland and England and from America where in New York it took five years and a suspiciously large amount of explosives to blast out the New York City water tunnel.

IRA policy (broken only very rarely and in exceptional circumstances – see Chapter 24) that a Protestant was not a target for his religion. It was the status of the target as an upholder of the Northern status quo which determined the choice of target.

The only time civilian casualties were deliberately caused was during the British campaign.

The majority of volunteers are young working-class men and women of varying degrees of education, intelligence, nerve and experience. Some grew tougher under the duress of circumstances, jail, interrogation, placing bombs and so on. Some did it as a matter of reluctant necessity. Some, a few, may even enjoy killing – the near sexual satisfaction of a gun. Many, many caught up in all sides of the conflict drank far more than was good for them or the people on whom their decisions had impact. Drink must be more of a factor in this campaign than in any other.

The bulk of Northern volunteers also come from a background in which the system is regarded as so evil that any evil may legitimately be used to destroy it. This and the sense of historical continuity of keeping faith with the patriots who have died in this and earlier struggles made up the 'justification factor'.

I remember one IRA-supporting housewife on the Falls Road saying dismissively of a Protestant housewife (like herself a good mother to a young family) who had lost a brother and a husband to IRA action, 'Ah sure, what is she but an auld orangie?' The more havoc the IRA wreaked, the more the Loyalists lashed out at Catholics – any Catholics – and the more action and reaction intertwined, the more callous everyone got.

The IRA women who lured three British sergeants to a party on the Antrim Road in Belfast one evening so that they could be lined up and machine-gunned to death, or the IRA squad who caught two off-duty RUC sergeants, who were buying wine to take home to their evening meal with their families, and forced them to lie on the floor for 'execution', had one thing in common: they weren't killing flesh-and-blood people, they were destroying cyphers. 'We've nothing against them personally. It's the uniform we are after. It's just business,' said one IRA apologist to me in a comment that might have come straight out of *The Godfather*.

Yet that spokesman and the bulk of his movement would have been highly insulted at being compared to the Mafia. The 'justification factor' is compounded of a combination of 'the cause' and dialectic.

Basically the IRA man felt that he was fighting for freedom, for an end to injustice, while his opponents sought supremacy, so the end justified the means.

It was, after all, though at another place and in another time, another Republican upheaval which caused Madame Roland to exclaim as they took her to the guillotine, 'Oh Liberty, what crimes are committed in thy name.' The other component of the 'justification factor', the dialectic one, means that all action can be rationalized in de-personalized language.

An opponent is not murdered. He is 'hit', 'done', 'knocked off' or 'executed'. A bungled bombing which cost civilian life is defended by pointing out that 'civilians die in war. It's a regrettable inevitability.' So much for the 'them'. If one of 'us' gets killed it is a matter for empathizing with the families, and a ritualistic black berets, military-style funeral perhaps, but certainly an occasion for human emotion.

The ranks of the 'them', the security forces and in particular the Loyalists, see the Catholics in a similarly de-personalized, demonized guise, of course.

Out of this medley of emotion one gets a cold statistic of nearly 2,000 dead in the troubles to mid-1979 (see table overleaf).

But then if one analyses how and why some of them died, names and events swim through the haze of incident – The Abercorn, McGurk's, Donegall Street, Bloody Friday, La Mon – in a confusing yet ultimately all too explicable montage.

McGurk's bar was blown up by Loyalists in reprisal for IRA activity because it was owned and frequented by Catholics. Fifteen people died including Mrs McGurk and most of her family. This was one of the first of innumerable other premises destroyed for sectarian reasons. The Abercorn could have been the work of Loyalists also, or it could have been caused by a Provisional bomb in transit to another target. Anyway, one nondescript March day in 1972, a bomb exploded amongst a restaurant full of women and children, killing two people and leaving some of the hundred injured without arms, legs, eyes, and with psychological trauma probably never to be eradicated.

That year also, bungled communications were responsible for two awful incidents, the Donegall Street explosion (20 March) which killed six people, and the Bloody Friday explosions (21 July) which killed nine.

In the case of the Donegall Street blast, a car bomb went off in a street crowded with children who had been cleared from a street

A partial breakdown of the statistics involved in the death toll, 1971–79

	1971	1972	1973	1974	1975	1976	1977	1978	Jan.–March 1979
Shooting incidents	1,756	10,628	5,018	3,206	1,803	1,908	1,081	755	189
Explosions	1,022	1,382	978	685	399	766	366	455	90
Bombs neutralized	493	471	542	428	236	426	169	178	35
Weight of explosives (in lbs)[1]									
In explosions	10,972	47,462	47,472	46,435	13,753	17,596	2,839	5,443	2,015.5
Neutralized	3,001	19,978	32,450	27,094	11,159	16,252	2,188	5,860.5	559.5
Armed robberies	437	1,931	1,215	1,231	1,201	813	591	439	132
Amount stolen (in £s)	303,787	790,687	612,015	572,951	572,105	545,497	446,980	231,250	64,354
Malicious fires[2]			587	636	248	453	432	269	58
Deaths: civilians[2] (sectarian, interfactional & intra-factional assassinations shown in brackets)	115	322 (122)	171 (87)	166 (95)	216 (144)	245 (121)	69 (42)	50 (14)	7 (1)
Deaths: army/UDR	48	129	66	35	20	29	29	21	3
Deaths: RUC/RUC'R'	11	17	13	15	11	23	14	10	–
Injuries: civilians	1,838	3,813	1,812	1,680	2,044	2,162	1,027	548	113
Injuries: Army/UDR	390	578	548	483	167	264	188	117	22
Injuries: RUC/RUC'R'	315	485	291	235	263	303	183	274	51
Houses searched[3]	17,262	36,617	74,556	71,914	30,092	34,939	20,724	15,462	1,285
Finds: firearms	717	1,264	1,595	1,260	825	837	590	400	95
Finds: ammunition (in rounds)	157,944	183,410	187,399	147,202	73,604	70,306	52,091	43,511	8,419
Finds: explosives (in lbs)	2,748	41,488	38,418	26,120	11,565	21,714	3,809	2,108	744.25

Apart from the figures for deaths and explosives, a breakdown of violence over the period gives an idea of the scale of the upheaval, of the enormous outpouring in energy and resources involved. Either the shooting incidents for 1972 (over 10,000) or the house searches for 1973 (over 70,000) tell a story of disruption and danger that was all the more acute by virtue of so much of it being compressed into a small area that made up many of the Catholic districts of West Belfast and the working-class ghetto areas of the Catholic towns throughout the North. Then if one thinks of all the security and legal personnel involved in the apprehension, prosecution and ultimate detention of those involved in the figures below, the scale of the war really emerges. And those figures are of course not financial. One has also to think of the figures for compensation, for injury, death or destruction.

Persons charged with serious security-type offences[2]

	31 July–31 Dec. 1972	1973	1974	1975	1976	1977	1978	Jan–March 1979
Murder	13	71	75	138	120	131	60	11
Attempted murder	16	85	75	88	121	135	79	13
Firearms offences	242	631	544	460	353	301	225	49
Explosives offences	86	236	161	100	215	146	79	9
Theft act	111	186	232	314	188	203	151	42
Other	63	205	275	97	279	392	249	63
Total	531	1,414	1,362	1,197	1,276	1,308	843	187

[1] Estimated weight only
[2] Consolidated figures not available for earlier years.
[3] Includes occupied and unoccupied houses searched.

nearby by troops who had received a bomb warning. The Provisionals claimed that the security forces deliberately misunderstood their warning so as to maximize the casualties. But it is more likely, in the tension and confusion of Belfast, that the Provisionals over-estimated the capacity of their opponents to deal with a profusion of bomb scares, phoned in moreover by excited, possibly very youthful, callers.

The Bloody Friday bombs, for instance, involved twenty-two separate explosions in a one-mile radius of the Belfast city centre over a period of forty-five minutes. Between them the explosions injured about three hundred people, crippling some of them for life. It's one thing to phone a warning, it's another to estimate how soon it will take effect. In the La Mon disaster nearly eight years later, warnings were phoned but not sufficient time elapsed between the time they were received and the bomb going off to avoid carnage: the bungled napalm bombing of the La Mon Restaurant in the Protestant district of Comber in February 1978 in which twelve people died was one of the worst episodes of the entire period.

But to hark back to the 'justification factor', an IRA spokesman whom I met after the La Mon bombing, though he showed himself mindful of the loss of life and of the possible Orange retaliation, was at least equally disgusted at the fact that the news had blanketed the reports of the IRA's achievement in shooting down an army helicopter. *An Phoblacht*, for instance, led the issue following La Mon with the helicopter story and recorded La Mon on a back page under a list of the week's happenings.

To look back through the pub bombings, tortures and assassinations for one year, that of 1972, we see that the total killed in that one twelve-month period was 468 persons. Most of these were civilians – 323. Some 103 were army, the rest RUC and UDR. The happenings deserve to be reckoned alongside the Munich Olympics massacre, or the kidnappings of Signor Aldo Moro or Herr Schleyer, but they become lost in the welter of Northern Ireland horror – hence but one of the reasons why the Provisionals decided to try for a British campaign and later for 'prestige targets'.

19

The British Campaign

As in Sean Russell's day, there was always a body of opinion within the movement which favoured 'having the war on England's sod'. Theoreticians like Daithi O'Connell reasoned, regrettably correctly, that the Irish could kill each other off until Tibbs Eve, and even throw a bunch of working-class British soldiers into the deadly stew for good measure, without anyone in England becoming unduly worried – but should a few of the bombs which went up so frequently in Belfast go off in Britain, then the public consciousness would be galvanized – hopefully into action on a British withdrawal.

The difference between Sean Russell's day and the contemporary campaign was that the contemporary one was better organized. Those opposed to the IRA could point to the ease with which the police captured some of the bombers – after, for example, Scotland Yard explosions, arrests were made within hours of the blasts as groups of young men and women were apprehended trying to buy air and rail tickets back to Ireland – but it was more protracted and destructive than the earlier campaign and had, as the bombings in December 1978 and January 1979 showed, more potential for being re-started should the IRA so decide.

Although many of the bombers and gunmen were new to the British scene and inexperienced in getaway techniques, others were trained according to the lessons of the IRA's past and of post-World War II guerrilla experience generally. Men took names and used them to acquire passports – inspired by those appearing on tombstones over graves whose occupants, had they lived, would have been the same age as their impersonators. 'Sleepers' (people who had lived for years in England without mixing with other Irish) came to life and went into action. The means used embraced everything from petrol bombs, fire bombs, explosive bombs to direct assassination.

The list of incidents which began on 8 March 1972, with explosions at the Old Bailey and Whitehall (the Aldershot bombing of February that year was an Official IRA reprisal for Bloody Sunday) was to include episodes as diverse and bloody as the Birmingham bombings which killed 21 people and injured 168, and shootings and bombings in the West End of London which for a period in 1974-5 severely affected the commercial and social life in the area.

The campaign often looked meaningless and cruel – a bomb in the Tower of London, frequented almost exclusively by tourists, in July 1974, for instance, injured forty-one innocent children and killed a woman; but apart from the general theory of spreading the war to England there was also often a specific reason for individual actions.

The coach bombing on the M62 motorway in which nine soldiers, a woman and her two children were killed in February 1974, the pub bombings at Guildford and Woolwich in October of that year, which between them claimed seven lives, all occurred during election periods and were designed to underline the fact that Britain had not yet found an answer to the Irish question. Ross McWhirter, the compiler of the *Guinness Book of Records*, was shot because he was sponsoring a reward scheme for the apprehension of those responsible for the campaign.

The most striking example of how the IRA could tie their British campaign to specific demands of the moment probably occurred during a set of truce talks in 1975 between the Provisionals and British civil servants (James Allan and Michael Oatley under the direction of Sir Frank Cooper, Permanent Secretary to the Secretary of State for Northern Ireland, then Merlyn Rees). The British told the IRA negotiators, James Drumm and Pronsias MacAirt, that they could not control the British bombers whom they alleged were simply IRA mavericks. The IRA men replied to the civil servants (after consultation with their principals) that there would be a spate of bombings until midnight on 27 January and that then an undeclared truce would occur. Sure enough, the 27th was punctuated by a series of explosions. The truce was formally agreed to at a meeting on 10 February, but it, like the others, was to peter out.*

The IRA intended to resume operations in England very shortly

* Although it was subsequently denied from the British side, one of the most interesting side-effects of the talks seems to have been the channelling of British public monies to the Provisionals via Provisional-minded builders under the auspices of the Northern housing executive. No sane author would attempt to describe the labyrinthine world of the Belfast housing executive with complete authority. But it does appear that a substantial amount of what seemed like legitimate building activity was in fact only a Provo fundraising front which the authorities tried to crack down on.

after Balcombe Street (described below), and would have done so had not the Gardai in Dublin succeeded in breaking a captured IRA man, an epileptic, and seized a load of explosives en route to England. The man who talked was subsequently executed by the IRA in a Dublin pub. A little later in the year, two IRA men were arrested in England. Both went to jail, in England and in Belfast, although on somewhat lesser charges than they might have incurred had they been captured after some of their planned operations.

Operations did resume, as mentioned earlier, in the late winter of 1978 and, though peaks and valleys in the campaign occurred, the will to wage such a campaign remained constant.

While it would be impossible within the present compass to deal fully with the entire bombing campaign, the career of the 'Balcombe Street four', as the IRA unit became known after they were sentenced at the Old Bailey on 10 February 1977, to a total of over thirty years apiece by Mr Justice Cantley, is worth examining in some detail.

Readers will readily see the similarities in the attitude and background of the young men concerned to those involved in the pre-World War II campaign, but the difference in the degree of sophistication, training and ruthlessness will also be readily apparent.

The four were Martin O'Connell, a native of Co. Clare, who came to London in August 1974; two months later Eddie Butler and Harry Duggan arrived, and Hugh O'Doherty did not arrive until March 1975. They were convicted of six murders; one manslaughter; a series of bomb attacks; possessing firearms with intent to endanger life (at Scott's Restaurant, Mayfair); using guns to resist arrest; kidnapping John Matthews and his wife Sheila, who were held hostage during the six-day Balcombe Street siege; plotting to cause explosions; and plotting to discharge firearms with intent to endanger life. In all they caused fourteen explosions in London and one in Surrey.

Another member of the unit, Brendan Dowd, is also serving life imprisonment for other IRA offences. The five were operating together until the murder of a policeman, Constable Tibble, after which Dowd left London for Manchester.

In just over a year of guerrilla activity the four averaged more than one attack a week. Their slide into capture began on the night of 6

December 1975, when, from a stolen car with all four aboard – the first and last time they had all gone on a mission together – they raked Scott's with gunfire; the second time they had hit the building, but they were pursued by police and then sought refuge in Balcombe Street where they commandeered a flat and eventually surrendered after a six-day siege, leaving the owners of the flat (Mr and Mrs Matthews) unharmed.

Until January 1975 the unit was under orders to attack military targets, including pubs frequented by soldiers. The principal aim was *not* to kill, but in the bitterness after the end of the six-month ceasefire in 1975, the orders from Dublin switched to killing.

The four were then living in two flats in different parts of North London: O'Connell and Duggan in Milton Grove, Stoke Newington; the others in Crouch Hill. Both areas were filled with coloured immigrants, but contained very few Irish; they avoided pubs and districts frequented by the Irish. They got their money and supplies via couriers who visited them monthly from Ireland – their identities (they were mostly women) still remain secret. They kept social life to a minimum – a film, perhaps, or a football match, but rarely drinking or going out with girls.

On a mission the normal *modus operandi* was for only two to take part, usually one employed in planting the bomb and one keeping an armed watch. The night Ross McWhirter was shot, for instance, Duggan did the actual shooting (with an Astral Magnum) and Doherty drove the getaway car belonging to Mrs McWhirter.

Duggan planted the bomb under Edward Heath's car in November 1975, but O'Connell made it. As well as making most of the bombs, O'Connell organized the intelligence and drew the maps of target areas. Duggan came next in seniority. Doherty mostly did reconnaissance, and Butler generally acted as back-up man.

Normally the unit chose its own targets, though occasionally Dublin might recommend something or someone in particular, and they concentrated their attacks on the wealthier areas and strata of society.

Harry Duggan was born in Kilburn. His parents were told in 1973 that he was dead, 'killed in action in the North'. He was supposed to have been buried in Feakle, Co. Clare, at that time. Eddie Butler, from Castleconnell, went missing soon after Duggan's 'death', in December 1973. Hitherto he had had a background of minor IRA activity, selling Republican papers on a Sunday and so on. Hugh

Doherty met the others in London. He had spent most of his life in Scotland, his parents having emigrated, like many Donegal folk before them, to the transported orange and green rancours of Glasgow. During the period of the campaign all four were in their middle twenties.

Ironically Duggan might not have been involved at all had the Canadian authorities not turned down his application for a visa to Canada where he had an opportunity of working as a carpenter during the early 1970s. He then rejoined the IRA and took part in a number of operations including the £8 million robbery of paintings from Sir Alfred Beit's collection in Co. Wicklow (see Chapter 20).

Duggan's 'death' and resurrection formed part of a Provisional plan to utilize key men in specialized operations under a cloak of anonymity gained by announcing their deaths after explosions in which victims could not be identified. (Incidentally a variant of this idea was used by the British army to cloak their casualties, some of whose Northern losses have been attributed to accidents suffered by BAOR personnel while in Germany so as to delude the Provisionals and possibly the British public. The Protestant paramilitaries also buried their dead secretly for a time to avoid giving the IRA the satisfaction of learning their casualties.)

It was only during the siege at Balcombe Street that Irish finger-prints experts discovered that Scotland Yard had fingerprints which matched those found at an abandoned house near Charleston, Co. Mayo, after Duggan and another IRA man had shot their way out of a Garda force which had surrounded the house after the art robbery.

Scotland Yard had no inkling of the four's whereabouts until the Scott's episode when by chance they ran into one of the police patrols saturating the West End as a result of the bombings. The Yard had hitherto been concentrating its surveillance on known Irish haunts and on known Sinn Fein sympathizers, all of whom the group of course sedulously avoided. Until they were captured they terrorized the West End to such a degree that I once crossed Oxford Street at rush hour without having to watch for traffic!

The explosions and killings caused by the Balcombe Street group, which, of course, had their effect heightened by other occurrences such as the Birmingham, Woolwich and Guildford death tolls, left an ancillary trail of maimings and shock. This explains, though it does not forgive, a phenomena closely related to the bombing campaign, the treatment meted out to the captured IRA men while in custody.

The *Irish Press* and the *Guardian* newspapers were instrumental in revealing the ill-treatment of the six Northern Irishmen arrested for the Birmingham killings. To say that the 'confessions' on which their successful prosecutions were based were not yielded voluntarily is to understate very considerably what happened. It is a tradition of the bombing campaigns against England undertaken by Irish extremists, stretching back through the days of the Coventry explosions to the Fenian times, that Irish captured as a result of the activities invariably receive rough justice when apprehended. Brendan Behan, who gave a glimpse of this facet of the age-old struggle between the Irish and English, carried an indentation on his forehead to the grave; a memento from the Liverpool police who arrested him for his part in Sean Russell's campaign.

Warders at Hull prison were brought before the courts on charges arising out of the treatment of Irish prisoners, and in Parkhurst prison on the Isle of Wight, Irish prisoners voluntarily sought solitary confinement to escape their fellow prisoners who, led at one stage by both the infamous Kray brothers, offered them violence and threats of death without interference from the warders. (The moving of one Kray brother to a criminal lunatic institution didn't improve the situation.)

Hatred between political prisoners and their captors is not a phenomenon confined to the IRA in England. As noted elsewhere, there were riots and incidents involving a high degree of brutality in Mountjoy and Portlaoise jails in Ireland also, to say nothing, of course, of what transpired in jails in Northern Ireland, such as Long Kesh or Crumlin Road, or, above all, in interrogation at centres like Hollywood and Palace Barracks.

Such bitterness is probably inevitable in a situation where not only are people losing life, liberty, limbs and happiness, but the freedoms of democratic society are being utilized by their assailants to carry on their campaign. What is really surprising is not the bitterness but the degree of apathy in Britain about the whole Northern Ireland position, despite all the catalogue of horrors listed above.

Nor are things much different in the South of Ireland. For instance, the worst single set of happenings of the entire course of events was the simultaneous bombings in Dublin and Monaghan in which over thirty people were killed outright and scores more were maimed. Yet within a matter of days after Dublin had seen gutters run with blood, bodies fused together with the force of the explosion, arms and legs blown across pavements and through shop windows, it was as though there was a social determination to forget the horrors, and the subject dropped completely out of conversation except for the families of those directly involved. In fact in the case of Dublin there was a determination to forget or more particularly to forgive, lest the episode spark off an unimaginable escalation of revenge. But the absence of response from London had the effect of goading the IRA to see just what action was required to provoke the response which they sought. And so more young Irishmen went to their destiny.

Although nothing can restore life (or limb), in some ways the most pathetic victims of the bombing campaigns are those innocently caught up afterwards. Those wrongfully sentenced for the Birmingham–Guildford bombings would not have come any closer to bomb situations than the television screen had they not been North of Ireland Catholics.

The names of those falsely imprisoned for life for the Birmingham-Woolwich-Guildford bombs were Gerry Hunter, Richard McIlkenny, William Power, Hugh Callaghan, Patrick Hill. All are from Belfast. The sixth, John Walker, is from Derry. All have consistently asserted their innocence. Leave to appeal was refused in 1977. The Woolwich-Guildford four also sentenced to life imprisonment were Paul Hill, Patrick Armstrong, Gerald Conlon and Carole Richardson. The three men are all from Belfast; the woman is from London. Hill, who was twenty-one at the time of sentence, was also given a life sentence for the murder of a soldier. His girl-friend Eugenie Clarke gave birth to his child seven weeks before the sentence was passed. A disturbing circumstance that surrounded the whole affair was that after their arrest the Balcombe Street four, who refused to take any other part in the proceedings against them, claimed that it was they who were responsible for the Woolwich and Guildford attacks and not any of the foregoing. And so, innocent people served terms of imprisonment ranging between ten and eighteen years.

Guiseppe Conlon, Gerald Conlon's father who died in prison in England in February 1980, was entirely innocent of any crime. He was a very sick man entirely unconnected with the IRA when he learned of his son's arrest. He set off from Belfast for London to do what he could for his son; but he was arrested, accusing of having had explosives in his possession and, on the basis of a 'scientific' test, jailed, and he died in prison.

20

Response to Violence

One of the unpleasant truths concerning the attitudes of the various constitutional parties to the Northern turmoil was (and is) the degree of hypocrisy that permeated everyone's dealings with the situation. Once the Civil Rights movement stalled in the face of Protestant extremism, it became evident that what kept the situation moving was the activities of the hard men on the extremes of Republicanism and Protestantism – particularly the Republicans and specifically the Provisional IRA.

Yet the common cry on all sides was 'no talking to gunmen'. The only acceptable political activity concerning the gunmen was to denounce them, legislate against them, imprison them, torture them and generally to devote most of one's political waking hours to them, but never, never to negotiate with them. Not surprisingly, after a decade of this the problem had neither gone away nor been solved, but neither had there been any formal acknowledgement that they, or more importantly their cause, existed.

While maintaining this public posture, however, the British did in fact 'talk' to the IRA on a number of separate occasions. The first came during a visit by Harold Wilson to Dublin (on 13 March 1972) when he took a break from his official duties to talk with top Provisionals including Sean MacStiofain and Daithi O'Connell. Nothing came of these discussions. The most substantial contact occurred in July 1972, when there was a dramatic meeting in London between William Whitelaw and a top-level IRA delegation comprising Sean MacStiofain, Daithi O'Connell, Seamus Twomey (then OC of the Belfast battalion), Martin McGuinness (then OC of the Derry battalion), and Ivor Bell and Gerry Adams, the senior officers in the Belfast command structure. A Dublin lawyer, Myles Shevlin, acted as secretary to the IRA delegation.

The IRA men were first flown to Belfast in a British army helicopter for trans-shipment to Oxfordshire in an RAF turbo-prop Andover; and the worst moment of the entire talks (for them) occurred then because the helicopter circled for a time, and they feared, though they couldn't show it, that at any moment they could be shot down by an IRA rocket. Although the talks were in a sense historic – in Anglo-Irish terms the first in which Irish guerrillas had fought their way to a conference with the British Government since Michael Collins had debated with Lloyd George – they were also abortive. The British army refused to honour the Agreement made at the talks to counter Protestant militarism. At that stage, despite the history of the movement, the IRA seemed to be merely one component, and a rather uncertain and gangsterish one at that, of the Irish problem. One can only conjecture as to whether or not there would have been a Protestant backlash had the British kept to the Agreement. A backlash certainly seemed more possible then than it does now. But if one looks at the loss of life subsequently one sighs over what the Agreement could have led to had the meeting justified its hopes.

It was held at 96, Cheyne Walk, Chelsea, the home of Paul Channon, a Guinness heir and a member of William Whitelaw's team of junior ministers. Quite apart from the complexities of the situation outside the room, the cultural gap within it was such that meaningful understanding would have been difficult to arrive at anyhow. The Scottish landowner Whitelaw, the millionaire Channon, the suave career civil servants, David Steel and Phillip Woodfield, and the IRA delegation came from yawningly different backgrounds. Seamus Twomey had been a bookmakers' 'runner' in Belfast, invaluable training for street warfare but not for Cheyne Walk; Martin McGuinness had been a butcher's assistant, Gerry Adams a barman, Ivor Bell a mechanic. Only O'Connell, who had been a teacher, and Myles Shevlin, had a degree of academic training.

O'Connell impressed the British most, but the others, conscious of the historic dangers encountered by Irish insurgents in dealing with British statesmen, displayed a kind of rough sincerity that came across unimpressively. As so often happens in Republican affairs, a man's natural intelligence and, very often, qualities of character and judgement, are belied by the theology of the movement, its symbolism and anti-Britishness. A British informant on the talks wonderingly described one of the Irish participants to me afterwards as being 'like a dog'.

For their part the British gave an impression of condescension and heartlessness that repelled the IRA – 'Whitelaw is a ruthless bastard.

"We can accept the casualties," he said, "we probably lose as many soldiers in accidents in Germany." ' That sort of philosophy, which was not confined to Whitelaw, was a major factor in the IRA's decision to have a bombing campaign in England – where the casualties would not be 'acceptable'.

The meeting had been foreshadowed by an IRA ceasefire which had followed the granting of political status to IRA and Loyalist prisoners on hunger strike in Crumlin Road jail and a diminution of British army activities in Catholic ghetto areas. There was a general mood in favour of conciliation on the part of the Catholic community which Whitelaw, who by now realized what an enormous blunder internment had been and understood better the historical position of the Catholic minority, was anxious to build on. But he was thinking in small-scale terms – not of acceding to Irish wishes for a United Ireland.

He had opened by saying that the Provisionals had observed their ceasefire undertakings honourably, and went on:

I hope that the trust set between us is reinforced by this meeting. I record that the histories of our two countries give the Irish grounds for suspicion. I hope that in me you will see a British Minister you can trust.

Look on me as a man who will not make a promise that he will not keep.

He told the IRA team to make any point they wished; he had come there to listen to them. MacStiofain called for a general amnesty for all political prisoners, in Irish and British prisons, all internees and detainees and all persons on the wanted list; a suspension of offensive operations by the British army and an immediate end to internment.

Whitelaw said he noted the Republican attitude in relation to internment and said, 'without agreeing entirely' with Mr MacStiofain, that he understood the feelings of the Republican movement on the matter. 'I hope you understand our difficulties at this time of year with the 12th of July coming upon us. Any moves on my part might bring about a worse situation,' he said. 'Give me the time and the opportunities and I will surprise you gentlemen with the rapidity with which I will act.'

Whitelaw said that recognition of this principle (the principle of the right of the people of Ireland as a unit to decide the future of Ireland – the central IRA demand) would have to be 'very carefully discussed' with his cabinet colleagues. Both the Tory and Labour parties had given repeated assurances to the majority in the North on this point and this very point had been given 'statutory fact' in the Government of Ireland Act.

At this stage the Irish delegation intervened, saying that if Mr Whitelaw was going to quote the Government of Ireland Act, then any negotiations would become sterile. They told Whitelaw that this was 'the very root of the trouble' and discussion on this line would serve no useful purpose.

'Neither of us is a plenipotentiary. I am an Englishman in an Irish situation. The minority in the North have been deprived of their rights. I set myself the task of conquering this. You can give me some help in the matter,' said Whitelaw.

MacStiofain said that the best contribution England could make would be to rescind the principle involved in the Government of Ireland Act. 'We have had talks with many shades of Unionism and are satisfied that there is a growing realization that such a declaration [rescinding of the Government of Ireland Act] by the British government would bring home to many Unionists the realities of the situation.'

The Irish side made a number of proposals of which the following were crucial:

1. Britain should make a public declaration that it is for the whole people of Ireland, acting and voting as a unit, to decide the future of Ireland.
2. The British government should give an immediate declaration of its intent to withdraw from Irish soil, such withdrawal to be completed on or before the first of January 1975.

From the foregoing it is obvious how wide apart were the objectives which the Irish and the British were seeking.

One side wanted full-scale independence; the other a peaceful return to the status quo albeit to a reformed and more just one.

Daithi O'Connell said there had been too much talk about a 'Protestant backlash' and this and previous British governments had been intimidated by such talk. 'These are our people,' he said, 'and we do not desire nor would we welcome a clash with them. But the fact must be faced that they cannot be allowed to intimidate and hold out on the whole people of Ireland.'

During the meeting the IRA delegation told Whitelaw and his officials that it was desirable to use the term 'Unionist' rather than 'Protestant'. They stressed that a confrontation with the UDA was not being sought, but that the possibility of it could not be ignored.

Despite the divergence in the two points of view, a four-point agreement was hammered out:

1. A bilateral suspension of offensive operations would continue until 14 July.
2. In the event of a resumption of hostilities, twenty-four hours' notice would be given.
3. On 14 July, a further meeting would take place at which the British government's submissions and documents in reply to points one and two would be made known.
4. In the event of the documents being unacceptable to the Irish, they would be at liberty to resume offensive operations without notice.

Two days later it all came to nothing – ostensibly over a nondescript housing estate called Lenadoon on the western fringe of Andersonstown. Some time earlier, Protestant extremist leaders had visited the Protestant residents of this area and 'advised' them to leave their homes because, it was stated, they were in danger from their Catholic neighbours. Catholics in the area said the real reason was because the UDA wanted a clear field of fire at the Catholics when *Der Tag* dawned. Whatever the reason, the houses lay empty and it was decided that Catholic families who had been intimidated out of their homes from elsewhere in Belfast should be rehoused there. However, when the Catholics sought to take up their allotment the UDA said they would burn them out.

The army decided not to accept this challenge and barricaded the area. Outraged Catholic crowds gathered as, after a period of negotiation, Seamus Twomey sought to get an army barricade removed to allow through a Catholic owner with a lorry piled high with the furniture belonging to one of the homeless families. At this stage Protestants were carrying arms openly behind the troops who were using CS gas, a water cannon and rubber bullets to keep back the Catholic crowds. At Twomey's insistence the troops disarmed a revolver-carrying UDA man, but then they used a Saracen armoured car to ram the furniture lorry. As Whitelaw had not proved responsive to the barrage of frenzied Provisional phone calls which preceded this incident, Twomey took the ramming as the signal that the ceasefire was over – and very speedily shots rang out and battle recommenced.

Whether the IRA were wise to attempt to force the housing issue during the July period or whether the truce would have ever come to anything is arguable – what is certain is the ensuing death toll.

While it was largely conducted on Irish soil and had none of the drama involved in flying Irish terrorists under safe-conduct in British aircraft to meet with British statesmen in London, what became known as the 'Feakle' peace initiative both led to the most important truce of the decade and was certainly the most effective peace movement of the decade.

Prior to the foundation of the Peace Movement two years later, there had been other peace groupings in the North aimed at improving community relations and the cessation of violence. PACE – Protestants and Catholic Encounter; Peace Point, an offshoot of the New Ulster Movement; and the would-be ecumenical 'Women Together'. All of these seemed in working-class eyes (whether Protestant or Catholic) a little too middle class and where the IRA were concerned they were all viewed as actual or potential British front organizations working to sap their war effort.

The Rev. William Arlow and a group of Protestant fellow clergymen did not do what the other peace movements did – largely confine themselves to attacking the IRA – but instead tried to understand them. The Rev. Arlow and the group, all active in the Irish Council of Churches, had had their interest in trying to promote ecumenical contact in Ireland whetted by their experience in meeting Catholics in Holland and when it was suggested – according to a popular Belfast story, by a Republican on the plane home – that they should try this ecumenism a little nearer to home, Arlow agreed and began making contacts with Sinn Fein.

It had been a very bad year both in Ireland, which had seen, apart from the collapse of Sunningdale and the hopes placed in a power-sharing executive, a ferocious outburst of murder of all sorts, including the Dublin bombings, and in England which had suffered a spate of bombing both in London and in centres such as Aldershot, Birmingham, Bath and Bristol. Accordingly, Arlow's seeds fell on fertile soil. First the Provisionals showed meaningful intent by turning up at the little Clare town of Feakle on 20 December 1974, in an inconspicuous hotel, with a heavyweight delegation. Three of these, Seamus Twomey, Kevin Mallon and J. B. O'Hagan, later went to prison. The others were Ruairi O'Bradaigh, Seamus Loughran, Billy McKee and Daithi O'Connell. The only woman present, the best known in the leadership of the Republican movement, Maire Drumm, was subsequently murdered in her hospital bed.

Apart from Arlow, the Protestants present at the meeting were: Dr Arthur Butler, Church of Ireland, Archbishop of Armagh; Rev. A. J. Weir, Clerk of the Assembly of the Presbyterian Church in Ireland; the Rev. Eric Gallagher, former President of the Methodist Church in Ireland; the Rev. Ralph Baxter, Secretary of the Irish Council of Churches; the Rev. Harry Morton, General Secretary British Council of Churches; the Rev. Arthur McArthur, Moderator of the General Assembly of the United Reformed Church of England and Wales; Stanley Worrall, former Headmaster of the Methodist College, Belfast.

Arlow had also contacted Sir Frank Cooper, Permanent Secretary to the Northern Office, Stormont, so everyone present knew they were not talking in a vacuum. However, before anything definite could be decided, they were informed that the Special Branch were on their way – the Provisionals had eyes and ears in all sorts of unexpected places – and the immediate aftermath of the meeting appeared to be nothing more than an inquiry initiated by an angry Irish Prime Minster (Liam Cosgrave) to find out where the leak was in the Special Branch. It was never discovered but meanwhile, though interrupted, underground Feakle continued to bear fruit! The Provisionals decided to declare a ceasefire from 22 December to the following 2 January – a hopeful way to begin the New Year. Merlyn Rees said three days before the ceasefire ended that in the event of a 'genuine and sustained cessation of violence', the British government 'would not be found wanting in its response'. The next day, New Year's Day, 1975, the Provisionals announced a fortnight's extension of the ceasefire. It seemed like a breakthrough but on 16 January 1975 came the depressing announcement that for a variety of reasons, including a British failure to reply to a demand that the army withdraw to barracks and an escalation of British military activity, the ceasefire would end.

This was not the first time over the period that the various British parties appeared to go in different directions. Not only did the army frequently appear to chafe at the restraints imposed by politicians and civil servants, but there was also a considerable and continuing rivalry between the army and the RUC.* During the talks one of the civil

---

* On 11 January 1977, the RUC were appointed the principal security force in the province, but this primacy was damaged by the IRA blows struck against Lord Mountbatten and the British army on 27 August 1979. Subsequently Sir Maurice Oldfield, the intelligence supremo, was appointed from London to try to co-ordinate security.

servants surprised the Provisional side by remarking when in a discussion of army attitudes which the IRA called for, following which the Provisionals had lashed out, killing a number of soldiers, 'Oh well, we will play at soldiering won't we . . .' However, Arlow, the Provisionals and the Foreign Office persisted, and on 19 January Arlow introduced Proinsias MacAirt and James Drumm, husband of Maire and holder of the hardwon distinction of being the most imprisoned Republican in Northern Ireland, to the Foreign Office officials, James Allan and Michael Oatley.

After a frigid opening session, the meeting led to more talks which resulted in a number of important, tangible developments. On 12 February for instance, Rees publicly announced the opening of a number of 'incident centres', which were ostensibly to monitor a hoped-for ceasefire but were also to provide, in Provisional eyes and in the eyes of their foes, a base for local political and community involvement. The Provisionals gave point to the discussion by displaying an ability to turn the off-stage bombing on and off like a tap until finally, on 9 February, there was an IRA announcement of a ceasefire to take effect from the following day. This was matched by a British commitment to maintaining the army at a 'low profile' from 10 February. The 'incident centres', each with a 'hot-line' to Stormont Castle, followed.

This was a hopeful and important breakthrough but it ultimately petered out the following October in the closure of the incident centres, a spate of bombings and a number of other episodes, such as IRA feuding, unrelated to but affecting the ceasefire. The principal factor ending the ceasefire was that each side wanted different things from it. The IRA wanted a formal British declaration of intent to withdraw from Ireland. This, it seems, they were certainly led to believe they were getting, but the smooth Foreign Office diplomats, skilled in the art of the misleading nuance, had not actually committed their masters (who were of course bound to the Downing Street Declaration) to this Holy Grail of Republicans.

What the British sought, and got, was a respite from Provisional harassment of the security forces, and a somewhat improved climate in which an effort could be made to bring the various factions together in a convention and perhaps to rescue something from the midst of Sunningdale, just as in the wake of 1916 the British had tried to quell awakened Nationalist sentiment by staging a convention to be attended by all political factions. However, elections were held on 1 May 1975. The anti-Sunningdale Loyalists won forty-seven seats to thirty-one.

The summer bled on, and it became clear that there was no hope of a new power-sharing formula emerging from the 'politicals'. In their innermost hearts the British could not really have expected a 'convention' held in the wake of Sunningdale's collapse to do what Sunningdale could not, but it provided at least a political figleaf to cover the real lack of will and hopelessness, where Ireland was concerned, in the Labour government.

Meanwhile, throughout 1975, although the IRA and the army left each other more or less alone, some of the cruellest and most dramatic events of the decade occurred. Maddened by the suspicions engendered by the talks and the establishment of the 'incident centres', the Loyalist paramilitaries lashed out at innocent Catholics both by means of pub bombings and individual killings, in a wave of murder that reached a crescendo with a slaughter at Bessbrook the following January (see Chapter 24). All three major paramilitary groups had their splits and feuds. The Provisionals with the Officials. The Officials with the Irish Republican Socialist Party. And the UDA within itself – Charles Harding Smith, shot on 6 February, being the most notable victim of this feud.

While this was going on, Southern Ireland had its share of incident with episodes like the effort by the Provisionals to break into Portlaoise with an armoured bulldozer, the Larry White shooting in Cork, the Herrema siege at Monasterevin and a UDA bombing of Dublin airport. England had its share of bombing throughout the autumn until the Balcombe Street siege rang down the curtain on that particular chapter of events. The incident centres were closed down in October after a month in which one of their OCs, Seamus MacOsguir of New Lodge, was shot in the Officials-Provisional split.

As with the Boal/MacBride talks (described later in Chapter 24) the situation, still *sub regnum* Downing Street Declaration, had not matured to the point where unilateral talks involving just one section of the combatants could end the violence. Also ended that year was detention which in effect meant nothing as the prisoners were still held; only the methods of seizing and prosecuting changed, and an end was signalled for political status for prisoners from 1 March of the following year.

The last was a decision that was to provide much adverse publicity for the British and to provide a rallying point for Provisionals during the low point of their campaign from the end of 1977 to the summer of 1979.

*				*				*

Finally to the most publicized response to violence, the Peace Movement which began on 10 August 1976, when British troops in hot pursuit of a car driven by Danny Lennon, a member of the Provisional IRA, fired on him, fatally wounding him and causing the car to go out of control on Finaghy Road North, mounting the pavement and killing the three young Maguire children, Joanna (aged eight), John (two-and-a-half) and baby Andrew (six weeks), before the eyes of their traumatized mother, Mrs Anne Maguire, and their aunt, Mrs Pat O'Connor, whose children mercifully escaped unhurt.

Watching another aunt, Mairead Corrigan, weeping on TV that evening, Mrs Betty Williams, no relation, decided that the afternoon's slaughter of the innocents was just too much and she contacted Mairead Corrigan and the pair began circulating a peace petition.

Spontaneously the Peace Movement mushroomed into the biggest mass movement of the decade. It was aided by Ciaran McKeown, then an *Irish Press* journalist, who wrote them a prayer for the movement. Some of its rallies were spectacular, particularly an early march down the Shankill Road which was genuinely inspirational. In full view of the cameras Protestant women embraced marching Catholic nuns. Very large sums of money were collected, particularly in Norway, and Corrigan and Williams were awarded the 1977 Nobel Peace Prize.

However, the movement allowed itself to give the appearance of being more anti-IRA than anti *all* forms of violence, understandably, perhaps, in view of its genesis, and was used by the Northern Ireland Office as a smokescreen for political inertia and ultimately left no lasting imprint on the campaign.

21

Prison: Riots, Escapes, Unlucky Freedoms, Personalities and a Place Called Crossmaglen

The decision in 1975 to end political status for prisoners after 1 March 1976 led to the H Block blanket protest where the IRA prisoners sought to win back political status by not wearing prison clothes. There was a consequent withdrawal of privileges and the situation escalated until the prisoners ended up in cells befouled with their own excrement, wearing nothing but blankets, sometimes for periods of over three years.

The Provisionals managed to smuggle out a film showing the conditions inside the block and this had a considerable impact when it was shown on television. The impact was heightened and spread by the *Washington Post* columnist Jack Anderson who gave American readers a bombshell insight into the H Block affair in his widely syndicated column. The situation escalated to one of far greater anguish and danger than any other prison drama of the period, with warders shot dead outside the jails situated in the Long Kesh compound area – and beatings, bad diet and conditions of indescribable filth inside the jail provoking many humanitarian people including Cardinal O'Fiaich to call for an end to the horror.

As in other areas, prison occupied a real place in the IRA's mind and in publicity. How to avoid it, how to beat the system either by riot or hunger strike and, above all, how to get out.

'The Crumlin Kangaroos' was the name of a popular ballad written about a group of nine men who escaped from the Crumlin Road Jail, Belfast, on 16 November 1971. Two were recaptured but the other seven reached the Republic safety having had the benefit of the traditional right of sanctuary in a Cistercian Monastery in Tyrone. This was the first major escape of the period and it also provided marvellous propaganda opportunities for the Provisionals to provide living refutation of the Compton Report's attempt to whitewash reports of army brutality.

Less than two weeks after the 'Kangaroos' episode, on 2 December 1971, two of the Provisionals' toughest volunteers, Martin Meehan and Dutch Doherty, were amongst a trio (the other was Hugh McCann) who again escaped from over the Crumlin Road wall. The prison at the time was bursting at the seams with over 900 inmates, and supervision was not what it normally was, allowing the three, with the aid of a friendly warder, to get away using knotted blankets and sheets.

They, too, gave evidence of being tortured. The army tried to refute this, using a doctored picture of Doherty allegedly pleading for mercy which was published in the *Daily Mirror*, in an attempt to show that the pair had 'squealed'. However, the army boot in his ribs was airbrushed out.

Meehan's escape, in particular, jolted the army who were anxious to interview him. It jolted the South, too, where there was always the danger that war could spread from the North. On 27 January 1972, Meehan and his henchmen both compounded this risk and added to the South's difficulties in trying to refute Unionist claims that it was not a haven for terrorists, by engaging the British army in a four-hour cross-border gun battle. Later that day, Meehan nonchalantly told reporters, 'We pasted them. You could have heard them squealing for miles.' No one suffered in the incident, the only casualty being London-Dublin understanding.[*]

On 17 January 1972 another seven-man escape team made head-lines by following the example of a seal. They were being detained on the *Maidstone* prison ship in Belfast Lough when a member of the group spotted a seal slipping through a gap in the barbed wire draped around the ship, and it was decided that if the seal could come in, they could go out. This they did, camouflaged in black boot-polish and smeared in butter to keep out the cold. Though badly cut by the wire, they managed to get safely through the icy water to shore although some of them could scarcely swim. They hijacked a bus and drove to the Catholic markets area of Belfast where they disappeared only to reappear at another propaganda-bonanza press conference.

The foregoing were all, as it were, the 'acceptable face' of the IRA legend. Such episodes fitted into the movement's daring, romantic side

[*] Again that year (9 July) Provisional sympathizers demonstrated at the Curragh, hurling abuse, physical as well as verbal filth, at the soldiers who did not respond even while stones were hurled. Ultimately CS gas was fired and the crowd was dispersed harmlessly.

and involved no loss of life; but they came early on in the decade before the dull, horrific campaign was well under way. Later a grimmer note was to enter the prison saga. The hunger strikers and the bitterness of Portlaoise jail are described elsewhere.

Mountjoy jail in Dublin had its riots and damage but the principal flare-up of the period occurred in the North. On 13 October 1974 Long Kesh went up in smoke with the Republican prisoners attacking warders (over the food) and being subdued by soldiers. To complete the subjugation process helicopters dropped CS gas into the wire-enclosed compounds.

As the burned-out Long Kesh huts were still smouldering, women IRA prisoners in Armagh prison seized the governor and three prison officers and imprisoned them! There was a sympathetic riot in Crumlin Road for which troops and police were called out; and at Magilligan prison camp in Derry the IRA also burned their huts. Subsequently there were conflicting claims as to how many were injured in the riots, the Provisionals claiming one hundred and the North of Ireland Office a third of this number.

The Armagh governor was surrendered uninjured after two days but the Provisional prisoners were left for some days afterwards to weigh the effects of the publicity they had gained against their bruises and their discomfort in trying to sleep amidst ashes and muck.

Probably the most dramatic escape of all occurred in Dublin, giving rise to yet another ballad, 'The Provie Bird'. The Provie Bird was the name given to the helicopter which, with a suborned pilot at the controls, dropped into the exercise yard of Mountjoy jail on the afternoon of 31 October 1973, and took off again with three of the most important IRA men in the country while the other prisoners stood around and cheered and the warders made a futile attempt to get through the cheering throngs.

This escape really created a sensation not only because of the dramatic means but because the three prisoners were Seamus Twomey, Chief of Staff; J. B. O'Hagan, a pillar of the movement from Lurgan; and Kevin Mallon who, toughened and hardened from the days of his beatings as one of the two prime suspects in the Sergeant Ovens case, had become one of the most formidable and daring IRA figures of the century. He is yet another example of how IRA men get hammered out in the anvil of circumstances: sometimes the beatings and jailings break them but when they don't, a Joe Cahill or a Kevin Mallon emerges.

*   *   *

Many of these escapees would have been better off had they stayed in jail, because here and there, without headlines, as the campaign wore on, several who had reported back to duty were either killed or re-arrested and charged with more serious crimes committed after their escapes.

One of the more ironic cases was that of John Francis Green whose escape from Long Kesh on 9 September 1973 dressed as a priest caused a great deal of knowing head-shaking; his brother, Fr Gerrard Green, who had been visiting him prior to the escape, was found after it, tied up in a compound. Green went back on active service and was found shot dead in a farmhouse south of the border twenty-two months later. The Provisionals blamed the SAS and cited his death as one of the reasons for ending their ceasefire on 16 January 1975.

Because of the nature of the campaign and sometimes of the theatre in which it was waged, splits, or at least cases of 'separate identity', within the Provisional movement also occurred, in and out of prison. Apart from the ideological reasons recorded elsewhere, two of the most celebrated centred around personalities on the one hand and a place (see Chapter 20) on the other. We will look at the personality difference first, that of one of those who was to find freedom unfortunate.

Some of the loudest headlines generated by the IRA were detonated from within the Provisionals by an active service unit (ASU) which the IRA heartily detested by the time it was run to ground. It was led by Eddie Gallagher, the son of a small farmer in Co. Donegal, who while working in London met the woman who was to bear his child and eventually to marry him in Limerick Jail, Rose Dugdale, the English heiress. She was active in a sit-in at the London School of Economics (which, incidentally, attracted a number of young Irish revolutionaries whose Republicanism thus became impacted on to socialism) that had caught his attention.

The ASU began 1974 by seizing a helicopter and forcing the pilot to fly them to Strabane where they dropped two milk churns filled with explosives on an RUC barracks. Neither exploded. On 23 February Manchester Magistrates Court issued a warrant for Dr Dugdale on the charge of conspiracy to smuggle arms and explosives to Northern Ireland and it became known also that the British army were anxious to discuss milk-churn delivery, as practised in Strabane, with the lady in question.

But the Garda Siochana in Southern Ireland became even more eager to make contact with her when in an uncharacteristic display of appreciation for the finer things of life, an IRA squad raided Russborough House, near Blessington, Co. Wicklow, and departed with the cream of Sir Albert Beit's collection of art valued at eight million pounds sterling.

Rose Dugdale was arrested, and the paintings recovered, on 4 May in a house rented by her in Glandore, Co. Cork. On 25 June she was sentenced to nine years for the theft of the paintings.

Eddie Gallagher was also picked up later that year and consigned to Portlaoise jail on 15 August. Four days later he was free again, one of the group that blasted its way out of the jail with smuggled explosives. Gallagher, who was also suspected of the Lord and Lady Donoughmore kidnapping, was one of those who would have been better off staying in jail. For he really hit the headlines the following autumn before police ran him and Marion Coyle to ground on 21 October 1975, in a house in Monasterevin, Co. Kildare, some forty miles south-west of Dublin, with Dr Tiede Herrema, the managing director of Ferenka Limited, a subsidiary of the giant Dutch multi-national Akzo, whom they had kidnapped in Limerick earlier in the month.

After a seventeen-day siege, all were released unharmed. But there were some consequences apart from the fact that Marion Coyle joined Rose Dugdale in Limerick instead of securing her release, which was one of the objects of the kidnapping (along with freeing Kevin Mallon, who had been recaptured, and James Hyland); and Eddie Gallagher returned to Portlaoise, this time with a thirty-year sentence.

One side-effect was that many Republican sympathizers visited by the police during the search for Herrema were so disgusted by the kidnapping that they volunteered valuable information about other Provisional activities.

Another was that because of this and the generally unfavourable and unwelcome publicity surrounding Gallagher and company's activities, the Provisionals placed him at or near the top of their black-list.

A third was that Ferenka closed down with the loss of 1,500 jobs. This was largely due to labour relations and the fact that the tyre manufacturing process carried on at the factory had been rendered near obsolete by newer technology, but the kidnapping will always linger on in some people's minds as the main causative factor.

However, though Dr Herrema was subjected to a ghastly ordeal through no fault of his own, he was at least able to live to tell the tale. Not so another kidnap victim of the IRA prison saga, Thomas Niede-mayer, the German Consul in Belfast and head of the North of Ireland branch of Grundig. Like Herrema a highly popular figure in the community, he was kidnapped without authorization by an IRA party on 27 December 1973, acting on impulse in a confused gesture of retaliation for the ordeal of the Price sisters and the other hunger strikers in jail in England. He suffered a heart attack as a result and died. His body was subsequently disposed of and his wife and family were left to mourn his loss in an agony of uncertainty.

The final and most improbable footnote of the Gallagher saga is that a sizeable strike of uranium has been made on land in Co. Donegal owned by – Eddie Gallagher.

The place which gave rise to a state of 'separateness' within the Provisionals, amounting almost to a sort of 'independent Republic' within the physical force spectrum as a whole, is of course the Provisional-oriented area of Crossmaglen. Ironically, Crossmaglen – or more specifically the district of South Armagh in which it is situated – gave both the British army and the Provisionals two of their most authentic heroes of the period. Captain Nairac, whom the Provisionals captured, beat severely and shot while he was on under-cover work in South Armagh, certainly would be accounted a hero on the British side. On the Provisional side was Michael McVerry, whose short life was shaped through being born not only to a parish but to a history.

The market town of Crossmaglen in South Armagh boasts the largest square in Ireland but this is not why Crossmaglen is a name that strikes a disturbing chord in the mind of any British soldier who has served in Northern Ireland since 1971. Set in a little 'U' of land enclosed in Northern Ireland by the border, Crossmaglen is the prime example of the Unionists' chickens coming home to roost.

By tradition and religion it is a Gaelic-minded Catholic enclave with a minuscule Protestant population. Lying in the shadow of the Sliabh Gullion mountains in a cobweb of narrow twisting roads, bordered by high overgrown hedges, its inaccessibility from the rest of the North meant that in centuries gone by rebels flourished there long after the rest of the country was conquered. Naturally the people of Crossmaglen turn towards the South for all the things that make up a cultural pattern – shopping, holidays, careers.

Only the most mindless gerrymandering could have included Crossmaglen, or nearby Cullyhanna for that matter, into a state of proclaiming itself Protestant and British. But included it was, and today the lists of British soldiers 'killed in action' bear witness to that folly. Unionists claim, as they have done throughout the fifty years of the state's existence, that it was the proximity of the border which made South Armagh such an IRA hot-bed. The IRA were able, they say, to take advantage of the terrain and retreat to Dundalk.

The IRA of the Crossmaglen district didn't retreat anywhere. After they had set off their tripwire bombs – or radio-controlled bombs – fired their lethal snipers' bullets or even, on one celebrated occasion, downed a helicopter (the day of the La Mon débâcle in Belfast), they simply went home, protected by the unseeing eyes of their families, friends and neighbours.

There was also a flourishing GAA club at Crossmaglen which the soldiers have frequently disrupted. Deplorable though this conduct was, I felt I had an insight into it, one day, when on a visit to the town I saw part of a group of young soldiers watching a rugby international on a television set in a shop window. The other part faced outward, guns at the ready. The British garrison there had to be serviced by helicopter because the roads were too easily and too frequently ambushed.

The archetypal Crossmaglen IRA figure, one of the folk heroes of the decade, was Michael McVerry who was killed on 15 November 1973, during an attack on Keady RUC barracks in Co. Armagh. Aged twenty-three, McVerry was the officer commanding the First South Armagh Battalion. He was a native of the townland of Skerriff near Cullyhanna.

McVerry exploited the countryside he knew so well to the full, sometimes opening fire on troop-carrying vehicles from a car and being chased by them blazing away like something out of a film until he lost his pursuers. Apart from using bombs and timing devices, he used bluff and sheer cheek as well – as for instance when having caused an explosion in a shop in Crossmaglen he made no effort to get away but, picking up a child, stood with the child on his shoulders talking to the soldiers while the debris was shifted.

A young man of McVerry's dedication could not understand or accept that the IRA leadership could descend to internecine politicking and position-seeking. Even for an outsider it is sometimes very unpleasant to go to a public occasion, a funeral say, or to Bodenstown and to watch the preening and publicity-seeking of some of the movement's top figures. It's hard to accept that men who have risked, and taken, life for 'the cause' could behave like any ordinary small-time self-seeking politician, seeking public notoriety. At times like that one may be forgiven for speculating that in some cases intense dedication to the cause may be a cover for some deep-rooted lack in character rather than a sincere, thought-out resolve.

Towards the end of his brief career McVerry also seems to have become somewhat disillusioned by the type of recruit coming into the movement. There was a good deal of drinking, general laxity and a falling away from the high standards he set himself. He felt that the war was not being pushed with sufficient vigour and was attempting to heighten the tempo of activities with a barracks raid carried out in the unfamiliar district of Keady, Co. Armagh, where he was killed.

Today his memory is recalled by an imposing memorial – a set of inscribed gold-leafed tablets reached up a flight of steps in Cully-hanna. The effect of this memorial is to provide both a source of inspiration to like-minded young men of the district and, as such, a source of affront to the security forces and the Loyalists who each sometimes daub the memorial with insults and obscenities, a regrettable but apposite example of what a 'them' name on a monument means to an 'us' in Northern Ireland.

22

Hunger Striking: the IRA Reach
Beyond the Bars

Of all the facets of the decade-long campaign, the most typically Irish was hunger-striking, that powerfully weak form of protest in which, as we have seen in other eras, the case of the participant seems to the public to get morally stronger as the victim gets physically weaker.

There were six major incidents of hunger striking in the course of the post-1969 campaign. Five of these ended in failure – although one, a mass strike at Portlaoise, was to have far-reaching effects as we shall see. Two of the strikes ended in death and only one resulted in the prisoners' demands being met.

The first involved Joe Cahill and the O'Bradaigh brothers, Ruairi and Sean. Just a week after the Republic voted by a majority of approximately five to one in favour of the government's proposal to join the Common Market, Lynch felt strong enough to move against the IRA after the Mountjoy jail riots of 18 May 1972. He brought in an Emergency Bill to enable civilian prisoners to be transferred to military custody and followed this up a few days later on 31 May with the setting up of Special Courts under the 1939 Offences Against the State Act.

The Special Courts consisted, of three judges who sat without a jury. The IRA decided to respond to this tactic by hunger striking and for eight, thirteen and nineteen days respectively Sean O'Bradaigh who was director of Sinn Fein publicity, Ruairi O'Bradaigh who was its president, and Joe Cahill who was on the IRA army council went on hunger strike after being picked up as part of a new drive. All were released for lack of evidence and though the strike aroused some publicity – O'Bradaigh's sister also joined in – it caused nothing like the controversy which was to develop over subsequent strikes.

The successful strike was the strike which included the Price sisters, Dolores and Marian, who were arrested with five others after car bombings in London in March 1973, and who went on strike in order to be sent back to Ireland to serve their sentences. Two of the men arrested with them, Hugh Feeney and Gerard Kelly, also went on hunger strike with the same demand and were also force fed for a period which lasted over 200 days, and were also ultimately successful. But somehow the men's struggle never captured the public's imagination in the same way that the girls did. Apart from the fact of being women, Dolores wrote poetry and Marian had a descriptive touch about her writings which made her letters on forced feeding particularly arresting. For instance a letter which another Price sister, Claire, was prevented from reading on Radio Eireann contained the following:

> Well this morning we had our force-feeds. Dolores was a bit sick and I was the sickest I have ever been. As soon as the tube went down I started to retch and then when the liquid was poured in, it all came up again, so half way through the doctor pulled up the tube and started all over again.
>
> I don't think that helps much because I still puked the remainder up. Very unpleasant, but this is the first day of the New Year and if I have to go through the same for the next 364 days I will.

However she concluded:

> We read in the paper about Dolores being at 'Death's door'; she did not think that she looked that bad on the visit, but I don't suppose we are very good judges. Anyway, don't be worrying about us because I assure you we are both still alive and kicking and living in Brixton.

During their captivity the girls were transferred from Brixton prison to Durham and Dolores wrote a poem which read in part as follows:

> The light has gone out of my existence
> No reason left but the great one
> The one that overrides all others.
> That takes my whole being
> Reserves and demands it.
> Still there is a longing for the little ones.
> The wave of your hand
> That stirs my heart and makes me smile
> To think that for me it is there
> The sound of your voice,
> That I know from among many

That too is one of the little.
Perhaps it is the little that is great,
The great just is.
And I could say such things to you
Could tell you of my dreams,
How once there was a little girl
Who danced in summer streams,
And sat upon a mountain,
And thought that she was God,
Knowing in her innocence,
All things that she must solve
Then I could show the woman
Still so much the child
Who knows to hold your hand in hers,
If only for a while
And would you gladly give yourself
To one who soon may die . . .

A very sizeable publicity campaign built up in support of the girls' demands and respected public figures as disparate as Bishop Daly of Derry, the SDLP Assembly man, Paddy Devlin, Lord Longford, Fenner Brockway, the Labour MP, joined in the campaign to have their requests granted. The girls finally ended the strike on 7 June 1974 but they were not transferred to Armagh jail until 18 March 1975, because the bombing campaign in England in the interim made their transfer politically inadvisable. Ironically it was the deteriorating position of the Provisional ceasefire which helped Roy Jenkins, the then Home Secretary, to make up his mind in March 1975, that the transfer of the Price sisters might have a beneficial effect on the situation. Ultimately it had no bearing on it, but for a time the conciliatory attitude gave hope of better things to come. Kelly and Feeney were transferred the following month as was a member of the UVF, William Campbell, who had been in jail in Glasgow on explosive charges.

At one stage the Price sisters' affair looked like being compounded by deaths other than their own, when the popular Tipperary peer, Lord Donoughmore and his wife were kidnapped by IRA elements in support of the Price sisters' case. This was one of those sidebar dramas, as was the kidnapping of Dr Herrema, that were thrown up by a mixture of impulsiveness, daring, and a lack of foresight by groups within the IRA which in themselves did the IRA considerable damage and could have done even more had they not ended without bloodshed.

The Donoughmores are a particularly popular family in Ireland. Their son, Mark Hely-Hutchinson, a leading amateur jockey in his time, is the managing director of the Guinness Brewing Company and the family were known to be sympathetic to Sinn Fein during the Anglo-Irish war of the 1920s. The Donoughmores' ordeal came to an end when the news of the Price sisters' transfer broke and though they came to have a high regard for their captors there was an ominous note of what might have been, in the words used by one of them when he broke the news of the Price girls' victory to Lord Donoughmore: 'You're lucky,' he said.

The hunger strike of Sean MacStiofain actually occurred before that of the Price girls and could have had more damaging long-term effects because he was at the time chief of staff of the IRA. But again, by some benign turn of fate, confrontation and bloodshed were avoided. His arrest came as the result of an interview on Telefis Eireann, the Irish television station. As a consequence the government later cracked down on Telefis Eireann and fired the nine-member Authority which the government appoints as watchdogs of what is transmitted.

Despite the presence of this board of governors and with the war in the North hotting up, the government had earlier in the year introduced an additional safeguard in the shape of a loosely worded addendum to the Broadcasting Act, Section 31 (now referred to in Ireland in much the same way as the phrase Catch 22 is used in America). Aimed at debarring IRA spokesmen or propaganda from the station, Section 31 is very difficult to interpret but government lawyers have advised the government what it can be taken to mean in a particular circumstance.

The particular circumstance that brought down the government's wrath on RTE was an interview with Sean MacStiofain by Kevin O'Kelly, at the time news features editor of RTE.

The government killed two birds with the one stone by arresting MacStiofain in the early hours of Sunday morning, 19 November 1972, as he drove away from O'Kelly's home where he had given the interview, and then by sacking the RTE Authority for allowing the interview to be transmitted later that day.

MacStiofain heightened the atmosphere of drama by going on a

hunger and thirst strike and he was sentenced to six months' imprisonment on 25 November for IRA membership. That evening bombs
went off in Dublin causing injuries to some forty people. Kevin
O'Kelly was sentenced to three months' imprisonment for contempt of
court, for refusing to answer a question about the interview, and the
RTE Radio and TV service closed down for a forty-eight-hour strike.
Large meetings were held in Dublin, addressed by Provisional spokesmen, demanding that MacStiofain be released; and armed men
dressed as priests burst into the Mater Hospital to which MacStiofain
had been transferred in an unsuccessful attempt to rescue him. Shots
were fired in the hospital itself but mercifully no one was injured.
MacStiofain's would-be rescuers were all captured and sentenced to
seven years' imprisonment. MacStiofain himself was transferred by
army helicopter to the Military Hospital at the Curragh to prevent any
further rescue attempts. He continued his hunger strike but accepted
water and glucose.

The backdrop to his incarceration turned particularly rancorous
because of the visits to MacStiofain in hospital by both the present
Catholic Archbishop of Dublin, Most Rev. Dr Dermot Ryan, and his
predecessor, Dr John Charles McQuaid.

Critics of the IRA and of clerical influence in the Republic had a
field day with both visits, which were particularly Irish crises of conscience for both prelates. Once they were asked to visit a man who
through hunger and thirst strike could be termed in *articulo mortis* (and
whose death moreover, if he did die, could be the cause of widespread
bloodshed with the Northern conflict once and for all engulfing the
South), both had a moral and a spiritual obligation to visit him.

But politically, of course, the visits exposed both men to attacks from
critics in the Republic and in the North. In the Dail, Dr Noel Browne,
TD, an old political opponent of Dr McQuaid, was particularly
scathing on the visit to a gunman by his old 'Mother and Child'
scheme adversary.

The Dail was convulsed at the time with far more weighty matters,
because at a juncture in the passage of the second stage of the
Offences Against the State Amendment Bill when it looked as though
the proposal might founder, two bombs suddenly went off in Dublin
on Friday night, 1 December 1972, in Sackville Place and at Liberty
Hall (blowing in the windows of my office). To this day many people in
Dublin swear that the bombs were planted by British intelligence. Two
people were killed and scores were injured. The Bill passed by seventy-

six to twenty-three at four a.m. the following Saturday morning. Ironically, one man blown into the division lobbies on the amendment side had hitherto been one of the Bill's sternest critics, Patrick Cooney, of Fine Gael who, when power changed hands in the election on 28 February 1973, became Minister for Justice and was to become one of the most controversial law and order figures to hold that office in the history of the state.

MacStiofain stayed on strike for fifty-seven days and finally came off it the following January when the IRA army council asked him to. A statement issued by the council said that 'after fifty-seven days of hunger strike no useful purpose will be served by Mr MacStiofain continuing his protest against unjust imprisonment.'

MacStiofain never again regained the position of power he had held in the Provisionals. It was alleged that he had sought the statement from the Provisional leader which enabled him to come off the strike to save his face. The Dublin wags of the time had it that his telephone number was Curragh 888 but from his biography it is clear that he suffered considerably during the strike and certainly for a time it appeared that if he were to die the result would be civil war in the South of Ireland.

The two saddest occurrences of the hunger-striking episodes were the deaths of Michael Guaghan and Frank Stagg, the former in Parkhurst on the Isle of Wight on 3 June 1974, and the latter on 12 February 1976, at Wakefield prison. Stagg had initially gone on hunger strike with Gaughan on his death-fast and though he decided not to make the supreme sacrifice on the first strike, he followed the route of Terence McSwiney, Terence McCaughey, D'Arcy and MacNeela on the second occasion.

The basic demands of both men were for political status, the right to wear their own clothes and not to be forced to do prison work. Gaughan, the eldest of six children, was twenty-one when he was sentenced for his part in a bank robbery in Hornsey in North London which netted only £530 for the Republican movement. He was in fact a member of the Official IRA through its English wing, Clann na hEireann. Stagg, who was two years older than Gaughan, also came from Mayo and unlike Gaughan was married. He was sentenced to ten years in October 1973, on charges of conspiracy after being arrested with Father Patrick Fell and five others – the Coventry seven, as they were known.

Gaughan's death was made all the more poignant by virtue of the fact that it came a week after the successful Loyalist strike to which the government capitulated. But there was to be no capitulation to the demands of a lone IRA hunger striker in a British jail. He went on hunger strike on 31 March, was artificially fed from 22 April, but refused medical treatment and died of pneumonia eventually. The two men could only be seen by their relations through a glass screen during visits supervised by police and prison warders. In these circumstances Gaughan received a single visit from his mother three weeks before he died and in describing the visit afterwards, Gaughan's brother John said: 'They both cried.'

His death raised a controversy in English medical circles as to whether doctors should render medical assistance in a case like his even though some forms of treatment, if given without a patient's consent, could have led to charges at law of technical assault. In fact the use of hunger striking as a political weapon posed the same dilemma for doctors as voluntary euthanasia – 'does the patient have the right to end his own life?'

However, a discussion of the issues by the British Medical Association's ethical committee later in the month in which Gaughan died, failed either to yield an answer to the problem or to avert Stagg's death two years later.

A far greater controversy obscured this issue when Gaughan was buried with the full IRA honours in Ballina in his native Mayo after a funeral, which took place following a procession from the east to the west of Ireland, virtually closed down the town of Ballina with IRA supporters. This created vast publicity for the Provisionals and an even greater headache for the government, which did not want to allow itself to be drawn into confrontation with the Provisionals during the funeral and so generate worldwide publicity. The Provisionals got their publicity anyhow.

The government was annoyed on a number of fronts: the domestic flouting of its authority; the criticisms which the television and newspaper accounts of the proceedings gave rise to in England; the consequent pressure this brought on from London; and, no small consideration this, the very evident proof of its strength which the Provisional IRA had openly given in moving in very large numbers from Dublin airport in the east (where Gaughan's body was landed) right across the country to Ballina in the west.

Consequently when Stagg died on 12 February 1976, having been on hunger strike for sixty-two days, the government took a decision expressly to deny Stagg what according to his lawyer, Michael Connolly, was his principal last request, namely that he be given a military funeral along a route from Dublin to Ballina which he specified. The Provisionals were equally determined that a major propaganda funeral should be held and the stage was set for a confrontation.

The situation was made all the more distressing by virtue of the fact that a split developed between members of the Stagg family over the affair. His widow Bridie, who with Stagg's seventy-year-old mother was present at his bedside when he died in the hospital wing of Wakefield prison – having shrunk to approximately four stone in weight and gone blind in the process – blamed the Provisionals as much as the British Home Office for his death. His brother Emmet also held the Provisionals responsible and objected to a military-style funeral, but other members of the family, in particular another brother, Joseph Stagg, supported the idea. Apart from the family bitterness which this split engendered there was so much pressure and intimidation from Provisional sources on Emmet Stagg and the widow that for months afterwards Emmet Stagg had to have police protection.

Against this unseemly backdrop an almost tangible state of national tension built up as the media of the world waited at Dublin airport for the plane bringing Stagg's body back from Yorkshire and for the expected clash between the authorities and the Provisionals.

However, while the plane was en route to Ireland the government diverted it to Shannon and despite some scuffling with Provisional sympathizers, successfully whisked the coffin away to Ballina where it was buried on 20 February in Leigue Cemetery near Gaughan, but not in the same Republican plot as Stagg had wished.

The next day, Joe Cahill who, with a party of other prominent Republicans including the President of Sinn Fein, Ruairi O'Bradaigh, had had a fruitless wait at Dublin airport for the fought-over, wasted corpse, delivered a funeral oration over the grave promising that one day Stagg would lie in the Republican plot.

Stagg was buried in a grave dug by police which was concreted in to a depth of eighteen inches and watched over round the clock by police; but the guard was withdrawn some six months later and shortly after midnight on 6 November 1976, a group of Provisionals accompanied by a priest dug through the night to tunnel under the concrete, recover the coffin, bless and re-inter it in the Republican plot a hundred yards away.

Today there are three tombstones bearing Frank Stagg's name in Leigue Cemetery: one over the concreted grave erected by his wife and some other members of the family; another over an empty plot bought by his brother George; and the third includes his name amongst those buried in the Republican plot.

But the most potent inscription of all is the invisible one, in the pantheon of Republican martyrs which, if the Northern Irish situation is not resolved, will one day surely inspire some other young Irishman to follow Stagg's example – with possibly more deadly consequences.

The largest outbreak of hunger striking of the period, a mass strike by Republican prisoners at Portlaoise led by Daithi O'Connell, Leo Martin and Dan Hoban, lasted for forty-seven days and ended deceptively on 22 April 1977, in apparent failure. However, it proved subsequently to have very far-reaching effects, and contributed to the downfall of the Irish government.

The strike itself was called off to the sound of a national sigh of relief after a Catholic bishop, Bishop James Kavanagh of the Dublin diocese, interceded. He had been collected by the nationalist-minded Senator Michael Mullen, General Secretary of the largest Irish union, the Irish Transport and General Workers Union, at the behest of IRA sympathizers to see if intercession might get the prisoners, the authorities and the country off the hook. The prospects of mass death appalled everyone.

The prisoners failed to get any concessions as a result of their strike in the short term but the circumstances and personalities involved are worth examining in some detail, as they do illustrate how the Northern issue and the IRA can suddenly erupt from being a peripheral issue to become once again *the* Irish political concern.

The economic situation had contributed to the downfall of Fianna Fail in the General Election of 28 February 1973, and the return to power of a coalition between Fine Gael and Labour led by Liam Cosgrave, son of William T. Cosgrave, the first Prime Minister of the Irish Free State after independence.

But Fianna Fail had been in power for sixteen years and the accretions of office had done their work. There was a general wish for improvement throughout the country when the Coalition took office and an expectation that new faces, particularly in the Labour Party which included intellectuals like Dr Conor Cruise O'Brien and Justin

Keating, would provide a leavening of brilliance rare to the normal atmosphere of Irish parliamentary debate.

In fact Irish political debate is not noticeably below the level of, for example, the standards of West European parliamentary debate, but Fianna Fail has the tradition of machine politics in which the leader is habitually the central figure and spokesman for the government, and ministers are expected to be competent rather than compelling in their public persona which very readily leads to the charge that Fianna Fail are the duds and the Opposition, the intellectuals.

The presence of figures such as I have mentioned and of Dr Garret FitzGerald, then leader of the Fine Gael party, certainly added substance to the charge in the abstract, but, tested in the reality of politics, the result was a great disappointment for people who felt that Fianna Fail had gone stale and needed a rest to regroup and rethink, and that a change would be good for the country.

Part of the problem stemmed from the interaction of the personalities of two very different men, Liam Cosgrave and Dr Cruise O'Brien. Both in different ways anathematized the IRA: Cosgrave because his father had led the Treaty side into victory in the civil war by taking stern action against the Republicans whom he saw as attempting to wreck the country, and the son shared the father's feelings towards the IRA; O'Brien, because he objected to the nationalist movement on principle, feeling that the 1916 revolution had delivered the country into the hands of bogmen, priests and Fenians.

He had a belief that to have credibility and integrity in Irish politics one had to confront both these forces and though he never became noticeably embroiled in controversy over the Church he was not alone in assailing the IRA with great vigour at the time of his election. He subsequently espoused a course of confrontation of all the Irish nationalistic beliefs – or myths, as he and his at one time large body of supporters, would have seen them.

He publicly stated on more than one occasion that he did not think it helpful to work for Irish unity and he continually said that if the British left Northern Ireland the result would be a holocaust.

He was appointed Minister of Posts and Telegraphs and as such the operations of Radio Telefis Eireann fell within his purview. He believed that the Provisional IRA, if not in actual occupation of the building, at least greatly influenced programme-making and found himself the centre of a controversy on censorship which gradually had the effect of alienating a considerable body of Irish public opinion from the new government.

Meanwhile Cosgrave through his Minister for Justice, Patrick Cooney, who as mentioned earlier had been a liberal during the course of the passage of the Offences Against the State Act Amendment Bill, pursued a particularly tough law and order line. A few major developments may be mentioned here to exemplify the attitude of those years.

One was the introduction of an Emergency Powers Bill which gave the police the right to hold suspects in detention for seven days without charges; in other words subjecting them to duress and stress during that period in order to extract damning evidence. The other was more difficult to identify: the formation of what became known as the 'Heavy Gang', a flying squad of policemen who conducted interrogations with suspected IRA men in different parts of the country and whose activities again gave rise to the very considerable disquiet and widespread allegations of police brutality.

Since it has been fashionable in England, particularly in the popular press, to say that if the Irish government stepped up its security measures then the IRA would be defeated, it will, I think, be instructive to look at what happened when an Irish government did take an unusually harsh line on the IRA. (After years of conflict it should not be necessary to point this out – since the components of the problem should be known to everyone in a senior position in Fleet Street and the British media generally.)

As Mary Holland pointed out writing in the *New Statesman* (7 September 1979):

> The nadir of recent British experience in Northern Ireland was reached precisely when the army, spurred on by a Unionist government at Stormont, had control of the fight against the terrorists in the province. Those were the years that produced internment, no-go areas, Bloody Sunday, the complete alienation of the Catholic community and a situation of such volatility in the South that the Irish government was unable to prevent the burning down of the British embassy.
>
> It was the closest Ireland has come this time around to the much prophesied civil war, and what averted it was the suspension of Stormont in 1972 and the arrival of William Whitelaw, who immediately saw that his first priority must be to tie the army's hands back where they belonged.

Fate decreed that I and the *Irish Press* played a role in inflicting the first defeat on the Coalition and then bringing about the resignation of an Irish President, Cearbhall O'Dalaigh. These events, particularly as can be imagined the resignation of the President, led to vast public controversies and ultimately, as the subsequent election results were to show, built up into one of the few occasions in Irish history when under native government the public refused to go along with a government in measures aimed at the IRA.

The affair began when in August 1976, after five men had blasted their way out of the basement of the Special Criminal Court at Green Street in Dublin, the government decided it was time to really put the boot into the IRA. Using the Offences Against the State Act, a State of Emergency was declared and some draconian legislation was drawn up under an Emergency Powers Bill. It was proposed to increase the length of time wherein IRA men could be held in detention for questioning from two to seven days and no one was under any misapprehension that the extra five days were intended to provide the suspects with a more thorough knowledge of prison cooking. In addition the penalty for IRA membership was increased from two to seven years. Additional powers of search and arrest were conferred on the army, and in another bill, the Criminal Law Bill, there was a provision aimed specifically at the media, and, as it turned out, even more specifically at myself and the *Irish Press*, section 3 of which read as follows:

> Any person who expressly or by implication directly or through another person or persons or by advertisement, propaganda, or any other means, incites or invites another person (or persons) generally to join an unlawful organization or to take part in, support or assist in its activities shall be guilty of an offence and shall be liable on conviction on indictment for a term not exceeding ten years.

The distinguished *Washington Post* journalist, Bernard Nossiter, then the paper's correspondent in London, came to Dublin to interview Dr Conor Cruise O'Brien about the package which at the time, though it was not liked, was expected to go through the Dail, with the veiled assistance of Fianna Fail – accepted as just another distasteful procedure necessitated by the situation in Northern Ireland. Nossiter's interview changed that.

He discovered that O'Brien had intentions beyond the stated scope of the bill. He wished also to 'cleanse the culture' of such malignities as revolutionary ballads and if necessary he agreed that the bill could be used against teachers of history who glorified Irish revolutionary heroes (readers will remember that earlier in the book I referred to the link between the teaching of history and IRA recruitment).

These targets intrigued Nossiter but what shook him was O'Brien's pulling open of a desk drawer to produce a collection of cuttings of 'Letters to the Editor' from the *Irish Press* as further examples of the sort of thing the bill would put a stop to. He did not propose, he said, to use the bill against the authors of such letters, but against the editor of the paper. He left Nossiter in no doubt that an editor 'offending' in such a fashion would find himself in trouble.

Immediately on leaving O'Brien, Nossiter contacted me and warned me to look out for myself. I declared editorial war on O'Brien, reprinting the *Washington Post* interview which appeared on 3 September 1976, and printing a series of strong editorial attacks on the bill.

Politically the climate altered sharply. It was one thing to swallow distasteful security measures against the IRA, it was another to use the IRA to cloak the launching of a vendetta against the press. (Though no one should really have been surprised at this for as far back as 3 August 1973, Eamon MacThomas, editor of *An Phoblacht*, had already been given fifteen months for IRA membership when his activities which were strictly confined to the paper.) Accordingly, after a period of uproar in the media and in the Dail, the government backed down – the first time it had suffered a defeat of any sort since taking office.

The Minister for Justice, Patrick Cooney, announced that the bill was not intended for the prosecution of editors, and the wording was watered down to give effect to their promise; and there the matter should have ended.

However, while the foregoing had been taking place, President O'Dalaigh, whose office had certain powers in relation to the legislation, had been becoming increasingly disturbed about the drift of events. O'Dalaigh had made Irish legal history in 1946 when at the age of thirty-five he became the youngest-ever Attorney General. He then went on to become Chief Justice and a Judge of the Court of the European Communities. But above all, for the purposes of this narrative, he was also a former Irish editor of the *Irish Press* (from 1931 to 1942). His late brother Aengus was, in addition to being one 'of the few Saints in contemporary Irish history, the *Irish Press* librarian.

Over the years I had known O'Dalaigh to take a keen interest in matters affecting the welfare of the press generally, sending me documentation on EEC legislation concerning press freedom, newspaper taxation, or newspaper cuttings on related topics which he thought I should read.

Although he had been an all-party-agreed presidential nominee in 1974 on the death of his predecessor Erskine Childers – he had been, prior to his Chief Justiceship, firmly in the Fianna Fail camp and now, two years after his accession to the presidency, he was, in addition to his disquiet over the danger of a curtailment of press and other freedoms, feeling the draught of Coalition antipathy to this background. His very office derived, of course, from a constitution which scrapped the one drawn up by Liam Cosgrave's father; and he found that he was being offered petty slights to his own and the presidential dignity. For instance, he told me that an invitation to the Head of State to attend the canonization of Blessed Oliver Plunkett ceremonies in Rome was taken up instantly by Cosgrave without reference to him.

Perturbed at the authoritarian drift of events and by the legislation, he decided (as he was entitled to under the constitution) after a four-hour consultation with the Council of State not automatically to sign the bill into law as expected but to refer the Emergency Powers Bill to the Supreme Court to be tested for repugnancy to the constitution. This bill was found not to be repugnant and was duly signed by him and passed into law. (Both bills, including the Criminal Law Bill containing the now famous, but sanitized Section 3, had been drawn to the attention of the Council of State.) There the matter apparently ended.

However, on 18 October 1976, at an army ceremony at St Columb's Barracks, Mullingar, the then Minister for Defence, the convivial Patrick Donnegan, a County Louth politician, spoke of the President's referring of the legislation to the Supreme Court and referred to him as a 'thundering disgrace', saying in the same breath that 'the army must stand behind the state'. O'Dalaigh took this as a clear implication that the minister who was probably only voicing the cabinet's opinion felt that the President did not stand behind the state. He felt that in addition to anything personal which might be derived from Donnegan's statement there was an open affront to the dignity of the office of President in whom the constitution vests the supreme control of the defence forces, all commissioned officers, on the government's nomination, holding their commissions from the President.

Accordingly, following the utterance of Donnegan's statement in the presence of an army audience, O'Dalaigh felt that he had no way of preserving the dignity of the presidency save to resign which he did on 22 October.

The combination of Section 3, the O'Dalaigh affair and the Portlaoise hunger strike affair so moved public opinion that the security issue exploded in the faces of the government the following February, and the old Clann na Poblachta vote resurfaced to help give Jack Lynch his overwhelming total of eighty-four seats.

Neither he nor the IRA welcomed the support. The IRA leadership in particular, knowing that Fianna Fail would be more subtle adversaries than the Coalition in power, but equally opposed to subversion, vainly tried to prevent a stampede of their sympathizers to vote and campaign for Fianna Fail. In fact, though Fianna Fail's popularity had waned, chiefly on economic grounds, by the time of the European Elections two years later in June 1979, but also because of lack of progress on the Northern issue, this Republican component was still strong enough to work the other way, against Fianna Fail, some of whose supporters turned against their own party to assist Neil T. Blaney, who had been sacked by Jack Lynch over the Arms Crisis in 1970, but who always averred that he had not left Fianna Fail (Fianna Fail had left him), to a resounding victory over a Fianna Fail candidate.

The other legacy from the Coalition's over-zealous pursuit of 'security' has been the fact that because of the increase in the penalty for IRA membership to seven years, many senior IRA men now recognize the courts, plead their cases and get off to fight another day, much to the chagrin of the security forces on both sides of the border.

It was an era of considerable significance for anyone who had believed that there was no difference intrinsically between Fianna Fail and Fine Gael. Arguably there isn't on matters of social and economic policy to any very marked degree; but when it came to dealing with the IRA the essential division certainly showed up.

Fianna Fail have taken stern action against the IRA on occasion. But they manage to convey whilst doing this that it is a question merely of a government being only concerned with the putting down of unlawful acts and meeting the challenge posed by the IRA and of a second authority raising its head in the state.

Fine Gael, however, gave the impression of pursuing the second course in a mood of theological righteousness. 'We did it during the civil war and we'll do it again,' was an attitude one encountered in government circles at the time. There was a prevailing zeal – a desire to hunt, to root out the devil and his works and props rather than an objective governmental attitude towards dealing with a problem which has bedevilled Irish administrations since the foundation of the state.

In fairness to the Cosgrave administration, one would not have required any theological aversion to the IRA to have found government in 1973 a particularly difficult task in Ireland. Specifically where prison conditions were concerned, the IRA had already distinguished themselves under Fianna Fail by burning down a new prison during a riot in Mountjoy jail, Dublin, and so leading to the transfer of some of them to the Curragh under military custody. Accordingly the question of internment continually flickered around the edges of Irish political debate, though public opinion was generally against it in the wake of the fiasco of the Northern experience in August 1971. However, it always remained an option in the wings and the Curragh transfer had overtones of internment policy. The transfer was not in effect a backdoor effort to bring in internment but a recognition of the fact that prison conditions in Ireland were woefully inadequate to cope with the rise of urban crime, let alone the IRA. The principal prisons with which the IRA were connected were Portlaoise and, to a degree, the women's prison in Limerick. The prison service was so inadequate that the women warders had to be augmented by policewomen – Ban Gardai – in Limerick, and after the transfer there for the Alfred Beit robberies and the Herrema kidnapping respectively, of Rose Dugdale and Marion Coyle, the pair drew attention to these shortcomings by throwing boiling water in the face of a Ban Garda which led to some more prison staff being employed. In Portlaoise there was pretty rough fighting between prisoners and warders which left both sides battered in the extreme.

But the worst single episode of this phase of the Portlaoise saga occurred outside the jail in the early hours of 16 October 1976, when a booby-trap bomb in a deserted cottage near the town claimed the life of one policeman, Garda Clerkin, and blinded a second for life. Not only was this a deliberate, planned murder – the Gardai were lured to the cottage by a phone call – but it was a calculated breach of the Standing Order No. 8 policy which the Provisionals had hitherto (and subsequently) observed and which could have had very far-reaching consequences indeed, including the implementation of the death penalty,* against whoever was found guilty of the crime.

It was against this backdrop that the Provisionals launched their mass hunger strike seeking political status.

Portlaoise was still the vile place in which Sean McCaughey died in the 1940s. Governments had been reluctant to expend money on 'coddling' prisoners and the influx of politically motivated Provisionals into the Irish prisons was totally unforeseen.

But the contemporary Provisional prisoner was quite different to anybody who had gone before: he was highly motivated, highly organized, and his only contact with the prison authorities came through his spokesman. On the other hand the government had an absolutely rigid attitude, as outlined earlier, and when I visited the prison myself in November 1977, after the turbulence had subsided, some of the prison staff and justice officers confided to me that 'we were pushed all the time' to ensure that the Provisionals were confronted at every hand's turn, when the familiar Republican defiance of prison regulations began. Between them, the two sides made of Portlaoise a pressure cooker within which temperatures steadily rose and common humanity boiled away. (Outside also, since the Gardai were ordered to baton protesters away from the gates when a demonstration began.)

My visit came as a result of the national disquiet which became widespread as reports of prison conditions spread and the incoming Fianna Fail administration invited the editors of the three national daily papers to tour the prisons to see that all was well under their benign tenure.

Of course by the time the journalists were invited, all was comparatively well, given the archaic nature of the buildings and the fact that the existing prison regulations were written in the last century. But evidence of tension still remained, besides the fact that there were armed soldiers on the roof and gun emplacements on the walls. There were sixteen members of the uniformed Gardai patrolling one door of the jail alone, in addition to the normal staff. Since sixteen visible

---

* The death penalty was very nearly carried out against the Murrays – a husband and wife team who were responsible for the death of the off-duty Garda Reynolds who pursued the pair after an attempt at bank robbery (on 11 September 1975) at the Dublin suburb of Clontarf. The Murrays, who belonged to a revolutionary socialist group unconnected with the Provisionals, had their sentence commuted at the last moment by the Supreme Court. By then the death cell at Mountjoy had been readied and the cabinet, I am told, were determined, had the appeal failed, to carry out the execution, even though there was a woman involved, Mrs Murray, who actually fired the fatal shot.

Gardai in this forty-hour-week era means that when holidays are included a total of forty-two men are involved in all, one can see what the concentration of police power in the prison must have meant to the crime statistics outside.

Under the Coalition, its obsession with 'security' and the checkmating of 'subversives' as the political prisoners are known in department of justice circles, this payment in manpower was willingly made against a backdrop which included episodes like a bombing which nearly cost the life of a prison governor's wife – part of an iron railing was blown into her kitchen. Another abortive effort if it had gone off would have claimed the life of Governor O'Reilly or the lives of his family, but before it had a chance to detonate, a bomb under his car was defused. Provisional prisoners made a daring escape by blowing their way out of the jail in August 1974, using explosives smuggled in a box of Lucky Number sweets. Another attempt to smuggle explosives into the prison was foiled when a lady visitor to the jail was discovered in the act of passing over a string to a prisoner she was visiting in the jail, the cord being attached to a contraceptive, crammed with explosives, inserted in her person. On yet another occasion the following year a prisoner was shot dead by soldiers on duty at the jail during an unsuccessful raid on the jail in which an armoured bulldozer was used in an attempt to batter down a side door.

The prisoners' protest resulted in all forms of concessions being withdrawn – handicrafts, study and reading facilities, television viewing. The strictest surveillance was made of visitors whose conversations were conducted through a thick wire mesh in the presence of prison warders.

Surveillance was so tight that one woman who had travelled from Donegal almost 200 miles away, getting up at 4 a.m. in order to catch the bus to see her son, had her visit terminated within seconds because she addressed him in the Irish that the family normally used in their Gaelteacht district. There were reports of prisoners' relations being left standing in the rain outside the jail; of people being denied visits after making long journeys to see relatives; parcels of all kinds were forbidden after the Lucky Numbers episode and another involving the smuggling in of explosives to prisoners in a hollowed-out shoe heel (this resulted in a dramatic escape by prisoners appearing on remand in Green Street Court before appearing in the Special Criminal Court).

But the most degrading and most detested form of retaliation was the incessant strip searching whereby prisoners, sometimes several times a day, were stripped and searched in a procedure which involved manual parting of the buttocks and inspection of the testicles (prisoners had been known to hide explosives by taping them behind their testicles). The strike lasted for forty-seven days without any apparent gain for the strikers but it did have the more far-reaching effects already outlined. The situation in Portlaoise was, under Fianna Fail, at least contained as a result of those days' experiences.

23

Arms

One of the side effects of the violence was that groups of young men, uprooted by the troubles, roamed around the country pulling off robberies, either on behalf of some paramilitary organization or for themselves – it was, and is, often very difficult to tell which – the skills and the guns required for such activities becoming all too easily available in the disorder of the times. But on top of this one could never be sure whether a bank robbery or a payroll snatch, both of which happened, North and South of the border, so often that no one raised an eyebrow any more (the police reckon in the Republic some £2 million was taken between January 1978 and August 1979), even if they did not appear to be politically motivated, could in fact be the work of a front organization working for the IRA, like the Saor Eire activists; or a joint venture between two Republican organizations – for example, the Provisionals and the Irish National Liberation Army or even an outside criminal hired by one or other organization for the job. For instance, a train robbery at Sallins, Co. Kildare, appropriately enough not far from Wolfe Tone's birthplace, netted the Provisionals some £¼ million.

But a group of young men from the Irish Republican Socialist Party were found guilty of the crime after confessions were extracted from them by methods which had aroused widespread controversy and unrest. I was approached by a Provisional source to explain to the government that they had done the robbery but obviously couldn't claim it publicly. My informant said that they found this circumstance particularly embarrassing because Deisun Breannacht, the father of one of those sentenced over the Sallins robbery, Osgur Breannacht, was at the time editor of the Provisional newspaper, *An Phoblacht*. But in the welter of confusion surrounding the robberies, which of course the government found outrageous, officialdom did not show itself to be impressed by the Provisionals' submission which, in view of the calibre of the source who approached me, I feel could be true; Brean-nacht and the others were later released.

Another Kildare fundraising venture which the IRA found highly embarrassing concerned a haul of cannabis worth approximately £1 million which the Gardai seized on 25 August 1979, near Naas, also in Kildare, and by coincidence near to Sallins.

One of the three men seized by the Gardai in this swoop was James 'the Fox' McCann, known to the popular press as the 'Green Pimpernel' of Republicans because he succeeded in escaping from Crumlin Road jail by cutting his way through his cell bars. But Fox's escape seems to have been doubly unlucky for him. Apart from being captured by the police in very serious circumstances, he was badly kicked and beaten by Provisional prisoners when transferred to Portlaoise jail, and into the bargain the Provisionals issued a statement denying any connection with him or the drugs.

Drugs, or rather drug traffickers, have at times been the subject of very severe IRA punishments. Even women have not been exempt, and the fact of being implicated through the capture of a man once prominently associated with the IRA in drug-running was both infuriating and, particularly where their conservative supporters both in Ireland and America were concerned, was potentially highly damaging to the Provisionals.

The captured British army document referred to earlier put the Provisionals' annual income at around £1½ million. I would be inclined to assess it higher. Apart from the foregoing, there is the American connection, the various drinking clubs controlled by the Provisionals such as the Prisoners' Defence Fund Club in Andersonstown or in what is known as the Pound Loney area off the Falls Road, the very large Pound Loney Club.

The Provisionals also control pubs, hold collections, levy 'protection' and in fact so control West Belfast that no builder could operate there without Provisional consent. In fact it is highly doubtful if any builder can survive there anyhow, because ripping off the system has become such a way of life in Belfast that between materials 'falling off lorries', never getting put on lorries in the first place, and being removed from sites when and if they ever get there, building in Belfast – including East Belfast where the UDA holds similar sway to the IRA – has become one of the world's most bankruptcy-prone professions, as a talk with any Northern accountant will speedily verify. What all this has done to the character of people is of course a matter of conjecture, worth a study in itself.

Yet despite the manner in which it is acquired (there was much talk about racketeering and 'Godfathers of Crime' in the media during and since Merlyn Rees's tenure in office when a determined effort to 'criminalize' the IRA was set in train as part of the British propaganda effort), the money generally speaking – there is of course some incidence of outright pilfering – is administered for 'legitimate purposes'. These include the welfare of prisoners' relatives and supporting men on the run and their families, and above all the purchase of arms and explosives.

In the earlier stages of the campaign the IRA mainly relied on couriers to transport relatively crudely made, highly volatile bombs to the point of detonation. But the army's techniques of cordoning off shopping areas and searching everyone who entered, forced a change of method on the Provisionals. Firstly the car bomb was favoured – hijacking a car, putting a bomb in it and parking it outside the chosen target. As noted already, this technique, though devastating, had the drawback that synchronising the warning often posed problems. Then came radio bombs and other more sophisticated methods. The IRA began to use radio-controlled devices, trip wires and 'sleeper bombs' that could be planted weeks in advance of the arrival of a VIP and then detonated.

The 'sleeper bomb's' most illustrious target was Her Majesty, Queen Elizabeth II of England. One of these devices went off some hours after she had visited Coleraine University during her visit to the North in August 1977. The then Secretary of State, Roy Mason, claimed at the time that the bomb was thrown over the university perimeter before it exploded. Mason had been most zealous in lobbying for the visit even though it occurred during the worst possible week as far as Catholic sensibilities were concerned – one which combined both the anniversaries of internment and the Apprentice Boys' Parade in Derry. It was this parade which had first put a torch to the situation in 1969. The week after the visit, on 19 August, the army's chief bomb disposal officer, Lt-Col. Derrick Patrick, stated that the Provisionals did have a sleeping bomb.

For the rest of Mason's reign, Ulster Television's nightly broadcasts faded out with a clip of film showing Her Majesty arriving from a helicopter with the ineffable Mr Mason smirking in the background (good taste finally prevailed and the clip was removed).

Despite some spectacular captures both while arms were en route to Ireland and when they were found in dumps, the IRA managed to build up a sizeable armoury over the years. Russian RPG-7 rockets have been used and Russian Kalashnikov and Chinese Simarol rifles have been found in arms raids, but the principal Provisional weapon became the Armalite, whether it be the M16 or the AR180 version. These are very high velocity weapons which weigh only seven pounds and have a collapsible butt which enables them to be used both lethally and inconspicuously.'[*] Apart from these, the Provisionals laid hands on a small quantity of a variety of weapons from all over the world: a few German Landmann .22 hunting weapons, some Magnum French hunting rifles, also .22 calibre, some Garand semi-automatic rifles, Springfields, Lee Enfields, a few Thompson sub-machine guns, the lawyer's German Schmeisser sub-machine gun made its appearance as did a wide variety of revolvers, hunting guns, petrol bombs, nail bombs, hand grenades – in fact practically every device of the smaller sort which man developed to kill man in recent years showed up in Belfast.

And not all of the smaller sort either. It was confirmed that the Provisionals had acquired M60 machine guns which fire NATO issue 7.62 bullets, and I had from time to time been given indications that the Provisionals possessed even more deadly heavyweight equipment which for various reasons – the risk of civilian losses being one – had not been used yet. This consideration would not apply in the type of situation which might arise should wholesale warfare break out between Protestant and Catholic, and in conversation with UDA leaders one day, I found that they too believed that the Provisionals had more heavy armaments in stock and had a healthy regard for them.

British intelligence was particularly effective in halting any major flow of arms from the Middle East, although at different times organizations such as Al Fatah and the PLO have declared themselves sympathetic to the Provisionals (although Yasser Arafat distanced himself from the Provisionals at the time of the Mountbatten murder).

The skill of British intelligence in priming the relevant authorities was shown in the seizure of a number of major consignments of armaments destined for the IRA at Holland, Canada and off the Irish coast (one could include the shipments which precipitated the famous Arms Trial but it was a small consignment involving only some hundreds of pistols intended primarily for the defence of Catholics in the North against Loyalist mobs – not as part of an aggressive war on the British army). The major seizures occurred:

---

[*] The guns are manufactured under licence by the Stirling Armament Company Ltd of Great Britain which means in fact that the British manufactured the guns the Provisionals used to kill British soldiers.

1. 17 October 1971, when Dutch police swooped at Schipol Airport, Amsterdam.
2. On Wednesday, 28 March 1973, when the Irish government seized a shipment of arms aboard a 298-ton motor vessel registered in Cyprus as the *Claudia* which was intercepted off the coast of Waterford: 250 rifles, 240 small arms, anti-tank mines and explosives.
3. On 4 July 1975, in Canada when the Mounties swooped on a number of centres: Toronto, St Catherines, Tavistock and at Windsor, Ontario. The Mounties captured a variety of weapons including machine guns, Sten guns, semi-automatic weapons, hand grenades and ammunition, but the raids did not have the impact of the other two seizures which, of course, occurred much nearer home.
4. On 21 December 1977 when a triphammer blow fell on further arms importation on a large scale from countries other than the USA as the Dublin police pulled off a 'two-for-the-price-of- one' coup (as they had done with the arrest of Sean MacStiofain) by picking up both Seamus Twomey, who had been at large since the Mountjoy helicopter escape, and another important IRA figure, Seamus McCullum.

The Schipol haul of Czech-made armaments including Bazookas, rocket-launchers, hand grenades, machine guns and rifles was so large that it filled 166 crates and it created a sensation partly because the IRA had sent a pretty young woman along with Daithi O'Connell to Amsterdam to finalize the deal. She was Maria Maguire whom the Provisionals took into the movement because she seemed the type of university-educated, politically minded type which the movement was then trying to attract. However, the following year Miss Maguire left the movement and wrote a series of articles for the *Observer* which were highly critical of the Provisionals and of Sean MacStiofain in particular. She followed this up with a book, *To Take Arms*, which gave a penetrating but to the Provisionals a highly unwelcome[*]

---

[*] Apart from Miss Maguire, the second most celebrated departure from the ranks of the Provisionals during the decade was Peter McMullen who wrote his 'Life in the Provisionals' story for the *Boston Globe* in September 1979. He was a former British paratrooper who deserted, after bombing his own barracks. Before deserting the Provisionals he bombed other targets including Claro Barracks in Ripon, Yorkshire, and is wanted by both Britain and the Provisionals. At the time of writing he is fighting extradition from America on the grounds that his offences were political.

portrait of the movement and of MacStiofain who was then temporarily in obscurity.

The Amsterdam affair was a non-starter from the word go because as O'Connell and Maguire arrived in the city, the *Daily Telegraph*, generally regarded in Ireland as the mouthpiece of Whitehall and of British intelligence, came out with a report that O'Connell was on the Continent, involved in an arms deal. The nearest the pair actually got to the arms was watching them on Dutch television being inspected by a Scotland Yard detective, although in the end the publicity gained may have made up for the arms lost.

The *Claudia* affair too caused great discussion in Ireland. This arms shipment, which occurred following a visit by Daithi O'Connell to Tripoli, was apparently monitored by British intelligence until it was practically in the arms of the Irish security services – the *Claudia* crew reported seeing a British submarine shortly before they were picked up. As a result the irrepressible Minister for Defence, Patrick Donnegan, commented: 'We gave her [the *Claudia*] a good kick up the transom.' In fact the ship was allowed to go free eventually.

McCullum had been using a false name, Robin Kingsley, owner of the Progress Electro Company, Middle Abbey Street, Dublin, to cloak his real name and purpose – the importation of a large shipment of arms from Cyprus. McCullum, who also had a prison record in England for possession of explosives, had been interned during the 'Three Macs' era and used the name of a dead Dubliner, John O'Neill, to secure a valid passport for travelling purposes.

He managed to get two huge transformers, weighing over three tons each, shipped aboard the *Tower Stream* filled with a wide variety of arms supplied by Al Fatah. However, the scratch-my-back-and-I'll-scratch-yours world of intelligence services soon buzzed with the information that the Israelis had news of an Arab shipment headed for Dublin. The British saw to it that the Belgians prevented the shipment getting any farther than Antwerp, and McCullum getting any farther than Martello Terrace, Sandycove, Co. Dublin, in the shadow of James Joyce's tower, where his Ulyssian Odyssey began. McCullum's ended in the arms of the Irish Special Branch. Twomey was picked up a little later in the afternoon having been shadowed from a visit to McCullum.

The seized shipment included two Bren guns, twenty-nine Kalashnikov rifles, twenty-nine sub-machine guns, over a hundred hand grenades, thousands of rounds of ammunition of different kinds, large amounts of TNT, rocket-launchers and rockets to go with them, and substantial amounts of plastic explosives.

An obvious source of armaments on the face of it was the Soviet Union. But the conditions described at the time of the Russell-Boland-Cooney visit hadn't changed all that much. Ireland still hadn't shot any bishops; although in his book *The Secret Work of Society Secret Agents*, John Barron, the former American intelligence operative, says:

> The KGB has worked secretly through Czech, Cuban and Arab terro-rist intermediaries to arm and train both wings of the IRA. The Cuban operational plan for 1972 drafted under KGB supervision stipulated that the Cubans would train Irish Republican army personnel in the tactics of terrorism and guerrilla war.

Barron's views, considering his sources, have to be treated with some respect, but while the Russians were obviously keen on infiltration in Ireland, the conservatism of the Moscow regime and the manner in which they went about implementing their policies had to be taken into consideration. One Provisional leader, with disgust in his voice, said to me at the time: 'The Russians don't recognize revolutionary move-ments, they only recognize revolutionary governments.'

At Russian Embassy parties in Dublin one noticed the respect accorded to figures on the revolutionary left, not the revolutionary illegal who were not invited. Tomas MacGiolla, President of Sinn Fein, the Workers' Party (the old official wing), for instance, was usually to be seen encircled by Russian 'diplomats'. The 'Workers' Party' tag was adopted to differentiate further the Official IRA's political wing from Provisional Sinn Fein and to give the party more distinction of identity and purpose in the minds of potential young recruits, who might not be attracted to banners inscribed merely Sinn Fein (Gardner Street) Officials or Sinn Fein (Kevin Street) Pro-visionals.

One also learned that the Russians, who were supposed to account for their movements when going outside Dublin, did not always do so, and Russian Embassy personnel were observed crossing the border at unguarded points.

The main thrust of Russian influence would appear to have been educational and propagandist. It was directed at the Official IRA, the Irish Republican Socialist Party and its military offshoot the Irish National Liberation Army (INLA) which is described below. There was certainly some form of Russian-PLO involvement in providing training for both Provisionals and the INLA at Middle Eastern centres.

This was confirmed by both the Irish police and the Israeli Embassy in London which issued a booklet (on 15 February 1978) on IRA-PLO links.

The Provisionals also had links with other separatist guerrilla movements. For instance, with the Basque ETA. These were acknowledged as far back as March 1974 when a spokesman for ETA was quoted in *Der Spiegel* as saying that ETA had 'good, very good relations with the IRA'. Perhaps the 'goodness' of these relations may be assessed in the light of the continuing reports one heard that IRA training and experience contributed to such ETA activities as the blowing up of Señor Blanqui, or the spate of bombings at Spanish holiday resorts in the summer of 1978.

But the principal source of weapons and money for the Provisionals was the United States. Anyone who has an Irish-American entrée in the States will very speedily learn this for themselves. I encountered IRA collections on the east and west coasts, and, of all places, in Peoria, Illinois. The American connection also limited the IRA's freedom of movement in making Communist bloc contact because the ultra-conservative Irish-American trade unionists, on whom the IRA relied to get the hardware through the docks, would have turned in horror upon any sort of Red involvement.

Congressman Aspin said (on 2 September 1975) that the IRA had stolen weapons from US bases. Quoting from a US army report, he said that the IRA were amongst the extremist groups who between 1971 and 1974 had stolen enough arms and ammunition from US depots to arm ten battalions or 8,000 men. Apart from the fact that there had been an evident penetration of the American network which resulted in the capture of a consignment of Armalites and two M60 machine guns at Dublin docks from an American ship on 1 November 1979, this ideological balancing act continued until the demise of the Communist bloc.

A Provisional leader told me on leaving prison that they found it nearly impossible in jails and camps to interest the young volunteers in traditionalist Republican indoctrination. A diet of socialism and Marxism was required. And the Provisional assessment of the temper of its Belfast Brigade was that it was unlikely, following the attitude of the Church over the decade, that the Provisionals would have gone to the aid of a church as Billy McKee did over St Matthews in 1969. Ireland today has the youngest electorate – over 50 per cent under the age of twenty-five – of any country in Western Europe. It also has one of the highest rates of youth unemployment, a potentially highly important consideration for any future IRA – and for whoever controls it.

The educated unemployed who have had the benefit of the revolution in Irish education, which has occurred since universal free secondary education (and a consequent increase in university numbers) was introduced in the 1960s, are not likely to be as passive as the traditional dole queues in the acceptance of their lot.

24

The Use of Torture

The question of the use of torture has been, as can be imagined, highly emotive. Although constantly alleged by the IRA, it was not until the *Sunday Times* published the fact that the army were using such techniques that 'respectable' opinion in Ireland accepted its existence and the Irish Department of Foreign Affairs began opening a file on torture with a view to governmental action.

The law case of Ireland against the United Kingdom and Northern Ireland began before 1971 ended (the Irish application was introduced before the Commission of Human Rights on 16 December) and did not end until 1978 began, when, on 18 January, the European Court of Human Rights delivered its verdict.

The court found that the following five techniques were used:
1. hooding the detainees except during interrogation;
2. making them stand continuously against a wall in a spreadeagled and painful posture for prolonged periods of some hours;
3. submitting them to continuous and monotonous noise;
4. depriving them of sleep; and
5. restricting them to a diet of one round of bread and one pint of water at six-hourly intervals.

It found therefore: 'By sixteen votes to one that the use of the five techniques in August and October 1971 constituted a practice of inhuman and degrading treatment, which practice was in breach of Article 3.' (Article 3 of the Convention on Human Rights states that 'No one shall be subjected to torture or to inhuman or degrading treatment or punishment.')

However, the court found 'that the said use of the five techniques did not constitute a practice of torture within the meaning of the Article'. The court did not visit the barracks mentioned – Palace, Girdwood, Hollywood – nor did they go to Northern Ireland at all. Judges did visit Greece during the Greek torture hearings to interview witnesses but not during the Irish ones because the British had claimed that the lives of witnesses would be imperilled, though this consideration was not advanced during the Widgery and other tribunals.

The one vote against the other sixteen judges in the finding of the breach of Article 3 was Judge Sir Gerald Fitzmaurice. He had this to say: 'According to my idea of the correct handling of languages and concepts, to call the treatment involved by the use of the five techniques "inhuman" is excessive and distorting, unless the term is being employed loosely and merely figuratively.' The Judge went on to give examples of figurative use within most people's experience:

'One hears it said, "I call that inhuman", the reference being to the fact that there is no dining-car on the train. "It's degrading for the poor man," one hears with reference to an employee who is being given all the unpleasant jobs. "It's absolute torture to me," and what the speaker means is having to sit through a boring lecture or sermon. There is a lesson to be learnt here on the potential dangers of hyperbole.'

Sir Gerald's semantics are one of the classic examples of how a lawyer can use words so as totally to dehydrate a case of all humanity or reality, and recalled to me an occasion some years earlier when I discussed without 'hyperbole' with Kevin Hannaway, one of the hooded men and like his father Liam a life-long Republican, the experience which had led to the Belfast courts awarding him damages for his experiences. 'After they arrested me, I was thrown into a lorry where I got a kicking. Then I was taken to another barracks where I got another kicking and they took me up in a helicopter and told me they were going to throw me out. I thought we were hundreds of feet up but we were only a few feet up. They set Alsatians on me, my thigh was all torn, and they made me run in my bare feet over broken glass.' Following these happenings, Hannaway underwent the 'five techniques'. When it was all over, he told me, lowering his voice because his wife was in the room, 'My privates were the size of a football from the kicking.'

How did you manage to get through it all, I asked him? 'I kept thinking of *The Last Words*, and I thought of what those men went through and I said to myself, sure what am I getting – nothing! So I stuck it out.'

(*The Last Words* is a book about the last words and writings of the executed 1916 leaders. It is doubtful if any political science course includes it on its reading list but such works have more relevance to the making of a revolutionary than the learned tomes that are written about them afterwards.)

The case caused a good deal of rancour between successive governments in both Britain and Ireland while it proceeded – the British continually sought to have it dropped – but not amongst lawyers who made large sums of money from it. Some of the victims were also compensated.

However, despite Strasbourg, torture as described (however the word is interpreted) continued to be used by the security forces.

On 20 December 1972, the British government published and accepted the report of Lord Diplock's commission into the administration of law in Northern Ireland. Stemming from Diplock, an Emergency Provisions Bill was introduced at Westminster the following April tightening up the conditions on which bail was granted, shifting the burden of proof of innocence to the accused in the 'terrorist' type cases and enabling such cases to be heard without a jury because of fear of intimidation. The IRA, Cumann na mBan, Fianna Eireann, Saor Eire, Sinn Fein and the UVF were produced under the bill. Under Roy Mason pressure mounted on police to obtain convictions and the statistics show that from 75 per cent to 80 per cent of convictions in these 'Diplock' courts were obtained on the basis of 'confessions'.

Concern over reports of torture led to the Amnesty report which was sent to Mason on 2 May 1978. The revelations in the document destroyed Sir Kenneth Newman's allegation that prisoners 'were injuring themselves as part of an IRA propaganda campaign against the police', and in June 1978, a committee of inquiry was set up under Judge Harry Bennett, QC, to investigate police interrogation procedures in Northern Ireland. On 16 March the Bennett report confirmed that there had been mistreatment. A number of police doctors had already protested about the statement and one of them, Dr Robert Irwin, had gone on television just before the Bennett report was published to describe what was going on at Castlereagh where he was police surgeon. The North of Ireland Office's response was to orchestrate a campaign against him, using the fact that his wife had been raped, to try to belittle his witness. In the welter of disclosures surrounding the Irwin affair it also became known that the police authority had three separate meetings with Sir Kenneth Newman to discuss the doctors' complaints during which they told him that having appointed him they could fire him. He quoted the Northern Ireland Police Act to prove that they could only hire him – not fire him!

There did not seem to be any great grounds for optimism either that the matter was simply one of replacing Sir Kenneth. His deputy, who succeeded him, Deputy Chief Constable Jack Hermon, was as involved as Newman in what happened.

The problem lay at the very heart of the British connection. On the one hand, the North of Ireland was officially regarded as being as much a part of England as Bradford or Leeds. On the other hand, to continue her presence in 'the UK overseas', Britain was forced to adopt methods which would drive those responsible out of public life for ever, were they to be employed in the 'UK mainland'. Even if one were to adopt the *Realpolitik* morality that the Provisionals' record leaves them open to any sort of treatment, the problem was that a great deal of the time the treatment was meted out to people who were not Provisionals. I had a graphic illustration of the nature of the problem one evening in Belfast while doing research for this book.

I was driven to a pleasant middle-class suburb, as remote from the slums where the IRA flourish as one could imagine, to meet the IRA leadership. The people who owned the house were apparently returning from a continental holiday and all was bustle and suntan and reminiscence; a world removed from the preoccupation of the people drinking tea and eating cake in their living-room. One of the group was a businessman who, it transpired, used his various bank accounts to cover the movement of IRA funds.

Apart from discussing IRA policy, our conversation switched for a time to the RUC. There was bitter condemnation of the force for their unfair treatment of a group of students whom those present apparently knew in a non-IRA capacity. Seemingly the students were picked up one evening, taken to a barracks, questioned all night and then charged with loitering, drunkenness and other misdemeanours of a like nature. The charges necessitated appearing in court on the eve of their exams. All the students were represented by lawyers when the cases came to court and they were found not guilty and acquitted. The point the IRA men made was there was never any question of the lads behaving as charged because of the proximity of their examinations. They had simply been harassed because they were Catholics, and in the hope of interrupting their studies. I could not of course evaluate the allegation but I found it fascinating to hear these men, law-abiding in one compartment of their minds, sworn to bloody revolution in another, complaining about the police force not because on one level they were at war with them – the RUC are 'legitimate targets' to the IRA – but because they regarded them as 'bent coppers'.

For their part, the RUC are formed by the traditional view of the Catholics as either potentially or actually disloyal, killed and maimed by the IRA and baffled by the IRA's code of secrecy – a code most terribly enforced on those who would break it – and by the knowledge that houses like the one I was driven to actually do exist. The RUC attempted to overcome their difficulties by using tactics which Europeans associate with pre-war Germany, rather than EC England and the reforms proposed by the Bennett report had a near impossible task in attempting to change that situation.

The level of feeling towards the RUC Special Branch investigators on the part of the IRA may be gauged from the fact that some in the IRA say that if they ultimately win, as some day they confidently expect to, the one category of their opponents for whom there will be no amnesty are the 'police torturers'. 'They'll have to get out or be shot' I was told bluntly by an IRA spokesman. However, I feel that if the 1994 ceasefires lead to reorganization and reform of the RUC, even this deep-rooted antagonism could be overcome. The Provisionals' leadership are likely to conclude that peace is worth a policeman or two.

25

Sectarian Murder

Sectarian assassination is such a feature of the struggle that it deserves a special examination, as do the Protestant paramilitary forces and their endeavours. The sectarian assassin can be either a bigoted racialist or a genuine patriot. He can strike to punish, as he sees it, treacherous and rebellious members of a sub-species which is threatening life, love, liberty and the pursuit of happiness. This is how many Protestant assassins, particularly in the UVF, see their actions. Or he can coldbloodedly retaliate for an earlier killing as the IRA did at Bessbrook in South Armagh on 5 January 1976, when ten Protestant workmen were machine-gunned to death after they had been ordered out of their mini-bus and forced to line up for death, one of the few occasions when the IRA went in for outright sectarian murder.

Why? I asked an IRA spokesman. Looking me straight in the eye he replied: 'Why not? It stopped the sectarian killings in the area, didn't it?' Unfortunately he was right. Five Catholics had been killed in two attacks in that area on the previous day. The attacks stopped immediately.

However, a very hopeful rapprochement between the UDA and the IRA was aborted by the killings. The UDA had actually prepared documents on what they saw as the way forward for exchange with the IRA when the news of the massacre broke; but when the UDA leadership turned up to discuss the exchange the morning after the shootings, the projected discussion instead took the form of one man picking up a copy of the *Daily Mirror*, with a massacre headline on page one, from the table and saying, 'How could you exchange papers with the people who would do *that?*' It was one of the many episodes throughout the course of the ten-year tragedy in which overall development was stunted by individual action at ground level – though, as we shall see, there were many attempts at IRA-UDA contact then and before. Still, the massacre must rank, apart from its intrinsic horror, as being one of the most unfortunate turning points of the decade no matter what claims can be made for its effect on sectarian assassination.

Assassination reached the peak during 1972 when of the total of 322 civilian deaths, 122 were classified by the RUC as assassination; of these 82 were Catholic and 40 Protestant.

Things have improved since then. It is possible that I may have contributed to the improvement, since at a certain juncture early in 1978 I was able to use the contacts I had built up over the years to help arrange an unofficial agreement whereby in return for the IRA abandoning the use of car bombs the UDA forswore sectarian assassinations. Although an occasional car bomb went off, more as a result of a local IRA unit's initiative than because of official policy, the pact more or less held up until the time of Mountbatten's murder.

In fact there were signs of strain showing before Mountbatten. The reorganization, and the revelations about RUC interrogation methods had visibly strengthened the Provisionals and cut the number of security 'successes' when at a Provisional rally in Belfast's Casement Park, GAA Ground, during August, Provisional volunteers displayed modern automatic weapons – enraging Loyalists.

The UDA deemed it advisable to respond with a statement promising 'a shift of emphasis towards a more positive paramilitary role'. That this did not go far enough was demonstrated later in the month – on the very morning of Mountbatten and Warrenpoint – on 27 August, when it was announced that some members of the UDA, the UVF and the Red Hand Commandos were going to assassinate known members of the IRA and of the INLA. In fact prior to this announcement a number of assassinations and assassination attempts had been made on known IRA men and on innocents mistaken for IRA men.

In one of these, the previous April, the assassins called at the home of Billy Carson, who was a member of the Provisionals, and waited for him to return, chatting to his children and watching television, till he walked into the house and they shot him dead. Then after Mountbatten, the UFF (generally regarded as a UDA hit group which can be disowned if necessary) called a press conference to announce that they would retaliate for the deaths of 27 August; a number of shootings resulted. However, all this killing was remarkably small-scale in the light of what happened and, though they sometimes made ghastly mistakes, UDA or Protestant paramilitary attacks were carried out at least on the initial presumption that the victim was an IRA man – not merely a Catholic.

This was a considerable advance on the type of selection made earlier in the decade when Protestant 'hit men' would sit on a bus until it passed a Catholic church, watch who blessed themselves, shoot them and then get off.

Of course, long before it was possible for any outside initiative to be undertaken the Protestant paramilitary organization had matured and altered almost beyond recognition. There were two reasons for this; one external, the other internal. The UDA's fastest growth was principally in the year 1972 – a year of particular Unionist ferment; it was the year which saw the growth of William Craig's Ulster Vanguard movement with its Grand Old Duke of York militarism (his speeches marched his hearers up the hill of apparently strong action but then contrived to march them down again without actually committing anyone to violence). The Loyalist Association of Workers (LAW) led by Billy Hull, a prominent shop-steward at the Harland and Wolff shipyards, also preached traditionally Protestant politics. It was of course also the year in which Stormont fell.

The Vanguard movement (the Ulster was speedily dropped) soon found itself uncertain how to advance. But the UDA and the UVF had no such inhibitions. There was only one way that its members wanted to or could reply to what the IRA were doing, which was to meet force with force. Interestingly enough, a principal force in the UDA's rise in late 1971 and in the early months of 1972 was the influence of militant Protestant women. These said to their husbands and boyfriends (in some cases even to their sons) in effect, 'What are you doing about it all? You are not men at all. You are letting the IRA get away with it.'

The traditional response of the Protestant establishment when the natives became restive had always been to crack down hard. The appearance of the UDA in military formation and paramilitary battle-dress was in some senses the gut reaction of Ulster Protestantism to the feeling that somehow, somewhere, its traditional leaders had sold them out.

The UDA's birthing stages were almost an exact mirror image of those of the IRA. Men scurried around looking for weapons; a few Smith and Wessons, some Webleys and some automatic pistols from Czechoslovakia. Some weapons were bought by sympathizers in Scotland, others from armament factories in Britain which did not seem unduly curious as to why all the gentlemen with North of Ireland accents should want so many of the trade-in police guns and the old rifles. These did not cost much – about £15 to £35 – because they were in bad condition, but the traditional engineering skills of the Ulster Protestant soon had them in good working order again.

While this was going on community relations in Belfast were worsening. As always in times of communal tension, mixed districts were the first to feel threatened; Ballymurphy and New Barnsley rapidly lost their Protestant admixture and the Catholics in districts like Finaghy, Woodvale and the Newtownards Road became even thinner on the ground.

I remember feeling at the time as I went about the various districts, shepherded by either a Protestant or a Catholic interlocutor, that fear wasn't just a feeling, it was as easy to see and as ugly as facial cancer.

Here one met a shaken Catholic family after an intimidatory visit by UDA men in masks who warned that a home must be abandoned or the visitors 'could not be responsible for the actions of people in the neighbourhood'. There one met a Protestant lady whose furniture had just been thrown out on the street by her Catholic neighbours.

And so the fears and the confusion, the inculcated bigotry, the hates were fed into the mindless computer of Belfast history and the answer came out in bullets.

Scores of young Catholics were found with hoods over their heads and bullets through their brains. Others were found in a condition better imagined than described, with mutilations, throat cuttings and every form of atrocity.

Modelling itself on the IRA, the UDA held its first military-style funeral (for a UDA man, J. L. Brown, found shot to death a few days earlier) on 28 June 1972 – the same day that the Provisional IRA issued its policy document, Eire Nua ('a New Ireland'), in Dublin. A murder trial in October the following year, in which Albert 'Ginger' Baker got life for the murders of four Catholics and for some eleven robberies totalling £15,000, revealed the activities of the 'romper room' – a torture chamber in the Shankill Road. Hoisting torture victims ceiling-high by means of a pulley and then letting them crash to the floor was only one of the techniques used there.

Men were done to death in every conceivable and inconceivable way. There was a feeling among the Protestants that the IRA were no better than animals and should be treated as such. They adapted and improved on such IRA tactics as kneecapping by using a Black and Decker drill.

But eventually this wave passed, though not before the UDA had detonated a number of bombs in Dublin and Monaghan on 17 May 1974. The Dublin bombs killed twenty-five people, and those in Monaghan killed six.

It was as if in Mafia terms the organization had 'made its bones', killing to prove its manhood to show that it could do in Dublin what the IRA did in Belfast. Within the movement there was a dawning realization that this sort of brutality alienated not only the Catholic population but also a very large section of the Protestant community on which the UDA would have to rely if it ever intended to be taken seriously as a political movement or even for funds to continue as a paramilitary movement. (Interestingly enough, these are not as readily forthcoming as formerly, and there is a marked difference in attitude between now and the time of the successful Loyalist strike of May 1974.)

On 25 May 1974 Harold Wilson went on British television to castigate the Loyalist strikers and call them spongers on the British public. But the effects of the Dublin bombings and the Loyalist strike proved stronger than his rhetoric. Three days later on 28 May, Merlyn Rees issued a statement saying that 'there is now no statutory basis for the Northern Ireland Executive'. In other words, Faulkner had lost support in the Assembly.

There was more than a whiff of the Curragh Mutiny about the army's attitude during the Loyalist strike. British soldiers were photographed talking amiably to UDA members at barricades and the GOC, Lieutenant-General Sir Frank King, refused to take his 17,500-strong force into action against the strikers on the grounds that he hadn't enough men. The army saw its role as fighting the IRA only. The RUC did absolutely nothing to restrain the strikers either, and several of them told journalists that their orders in fact precluded them from doing anything.* This was at a time when *per contra* the Secretary of State for Northern Ireland, Merlyn Rees, and his civil servants were vainly attempting to prod the force into action.

The elasticity with which Protestant groupings could stretch to cover the constitutional and unconstitutional wings of the Loyalist spectrum was well exemplified by the formation of the Ulster Army Council on 10 December 1973. This was founded to oppose the

---

* The best account of this crisis is Robert Fisk's *Point of No Return*, an excellent guide to the Northern problem generally.

Council of Ireland idea contained in the Sunningdale pact. The Ulster Army Council was influenced, as is so much Protestant paramilitary thinking, by the IRA, whose supreme governing body is of course the 'Army Council'.

Its membership included the UDA, the UVF, the Ulster Special Constabulary Association (the former B-Specials) and the Red Hand Commandos who had played such a distinctive role in the August 1969 burnings in Belfast. It is worth noting that Glenn Barr,[*] who was an Assembly man representing Vanguard at Stormont, was also a UDA Commander. The Down Orange Welfare organization which with the Vanguard took part in the Ulster Workers' Council, the body which organized the strike, had at its head a former British Army Colonel, Peter Brush. Catholics did not enjoy witnessing such a grouping taking place but the only difference for them was that on this occasion the paramilitaries were offering their services and encouragement to the politicians, rather than the other way around.

It is worth digressing here to note that this trend continued following the Mountbatten murder. John Taylor, a particularly venomous Unionist apologist, made a 'hold-me-back, let-me-at-them' speech saying that if there was going to be retaliation by Loyalist paramilitaries then he hoped that it would be directed against the South. The Official Unionist Party Secretary, Norman Hutton, concurred in this statement saying that the remarks by Taylor, a member of the European Parliament, were official Unionist policy. However, Sam Duddy, speaking for the UDA, said that the organization would not be retaliating on behalf of Mr Taylor or anyone else in the Unionist Party, and disassociated itself from Taylor's remarks.

In the case of the Loyalist strike, the politicians who were being helped by the paramilitaries were the Loyalists opposing Faulkner over Sunningdale (Ian Paisley, William Craig, and Harry West). The more perceptive of its leaders came to accept that the role of the organization was not simply to exist to do the dirty work for Unionist politicians who could and would disown them when the going got rough. A newer, more reactive breed of leadership began to emerge particularly after the Loyalist strike when it became evident that men like Glenn Barr, Andy Tyrie, Harry Chicken, Sam Lyttle and others were thinking on political lines, although they continued to make extremist Protestant

---

[*] Barr said after the strike that the army could have broken it, had it wished, by moving early in its development.

noises. Privately, however, men like these would admit in conversation with people like myself that some form of Irish Ireland appeared inevitable; that the British would go one day and that their dilemma was to try to win public support for some form of acceptance for these ideas while at the same time keeping their more extremist followers in check by making the usual threatening noises.

As one leader said to me with grim humour, 'There's no redundancy in my job!' After the second Loyalist strike, called in 1977, flopped because the electricity workers would not join in this time, the UDA became increasingly bitter against the British who began increasingly to mete out to them the same type of treatment which the IRA and the Catholic community had long experienced.

This process was accelerated on the British side by a growing realization that the policy of 'the enemy of my enemy is my friend' had severe limitations, in particular when it gave rise to wholesale protection rackets and to internecine bloodshed. Several leading members of the UDA including Tommy Heron, Ernie Elliott and Sammy Smith were murdered by their own people, and some like Charles Harding-Smith and Vogel had to flee the country for their lives.

These pressures combined to produce a situation where the UDA was short of funds (since it had nothing even remotely approaching the IRA's overseas sources of money) and driven to a realization that protection rackets, knifings and sectarian assassination were counter-productive in terms of political advancement, actually launched a political campaign in March 1979, to gain support for the UDA goal of an Independent Ulster. Independent of both Dublin and London, that is. This idea, though still mistrusted by old-time Belfast Republicans like Billy McKee and Proinsias MacAirt who felt that it in some way was a policy that would result in a continuing British presence, was nevertheless the subject of continuing secret contact which had begun some years earlier between the UDA and IRA.

The principal figures involved in the earlier talks were two lawyers outside the ranks of the paramilitaries. On the IRA side one of the most distinguished living Irishmen, Sean MacBride, a top UN administrator, Nobel Peace Prize winner, Clann na Poblachta founder, and former Chief-of-Staff of the IRA; and, for the UDA,* Desmond Boal,

---

* Strictly speaking, Boal was speaking on behalf of the Ulster Loyalist Central Coordination Committee. But without the UDA there would have been very little need for 'coordination'!

a politician and a confidant of Paisley. He is a noted traveller and a Protestant apologist who had been flickering around the edges of religious controversy in Ireland since the mid-1950s.[*]

From the end of 1976 to around April the following year these talks proceeded more or less fruitfully. The framework of an agreement between the two factions appeared feasible – at least to the negotiators! It was intended that the European Convention on Human Rights would be used to safeguard both Protestant and Catholic, North and South of the border. The North was, under this safeguard, to have a kind of independence with, however, some links to the South which would both reassure the Northern Catholics that in some way the South's numbers could if needed be used to weigh in their favour, and loose enough to prevent the Protestants fearing that they would be engulfed in an All-Ireland Catholic state. There was to be a ceasefire during which, most surprising of all, the document was to be presented to London – accompanied by a ULCCC-Provisional IRA demand for a British withdrawal from Ireland.

However, the situation simply had not matured sufficiently to bear the weight of all this. During April on the Provisional side attention was distracted by a renewed outburst of warfare between the 'stickies' and the 'pin-heads', and on the Loyalist side Paisley diverted action by calling for a second Loyalist strike. He wanted more action against the Provisionals at a time when because of their internal reorganization overt activity was at a low ebb and Roy Mason mistakenly thought that the security forces were winning. Mason had since mid-January sanctioned an agreement whereby the prime responsibility for security shifted to the RUC. Paisley also wanted, or said he wanted, a restoration of Stormont. More likely he simply wanted to show that he was still a power in the land.

In any event the strike began on Monday, 2 May 1977, and petered out a few days later. Mason did not bow to the intimidation this time; London and Belfast had learned the lessons of 1974 when it was realized too late that a firm attitude at the start could have prevented the situation escalating. The Protestant paramilitaries were

---

[*] He then figured as a negotiator in a national controversy which erupted over mixed marriage in which a Protestant lady left her husband, a Catholic, in Fethard-on-Sea in Co. Wexford and returned with her children to the North and to Protestantism rather than submit any longer to the dictates of the Ne Temere decree. There was for a time a boycott by Catholics of Protestants in the area as a result.

discredited by the failure of the strike and on both sides the paramilitaries' powers appeared to be on the wane.

Against this background it proved possible to salvage something from the carnage and chaos – civilian casualties went down from 145 (in 1976) to 69 (in 1977), principally due to a decline in sectarian assassination which thus provided a basis for the 'no car bombing' pact which survived even the La Mon carnage described below. In fact with the exception of the occasional inevitable breach on either side the pact could have been said to have lasted until after the Mountbatten murder. Following this the Ulster Freedom Fighters called a press conference while Andy Tyrie, either for reasons of strategy or relaxation, was on holiday, to announce a resumption of retaliatory killing, but even this subsequently proved to be considerably less than was feared.

Against the scale of deaths in the decade the agreement over car bombing and the MacBride-Boal talks do not bulk large. But without them these things might have been incalculably worse. To the question, 'What did you do in the war, Daddy?' it is at least possible to reply: 'We tried.'

One of the main architects of the UDA's shift in emphasis from the bullet and the knife to political activity was Andy Tyrie, a skilled mechanical worker who was forced out of the leadership in 1988 by younger and more bloodthirsty elements. At moments of crisis, such as in the aftermath of the La Mon bombing when he was besieged by heated calls for a resumption of the assassination campaign, he had been known to throw a list of top IRA men's names on to a table and with them a gun, saying, 'Those are the men you want, pick up the gun and I will give you as many more as you want to do the job – but there's no use shooting Catholics just for revenge.'

Neither the list nor the gun was picked up. On another occasion Tyrie, who had successfully negotiated for a UDA man, Freddy Parkinson, who was at the time serving a sentence for attempted arson in Mountjoy jail, Dublin, to be released for his mother's funeral in Belfast, completed his side of the bargain by personally picking up the reluctant Parkinson on the Shankill Road and driving him to Dublin to complete his sentence.

On the UVF front (the UVF is largely subsumed into the UDA, particularly in Belfast, but it does have an identity of its own), a similar metamorphosis took place. This was attributable to the twin pressures of attrition, jail and internment and the dawning realization that their idealism or hatred had been misdirected. Jail is a great leveller. Many an ardent Orange supremacist who went into Long Kesh for his UVF activities became so unsettled in his traditional beliefs by observing Republican fellow prisoners and by his own treatment at the hands of the warders and soldiers that he changed to the extent of actually learning Irish. To be sure some kept up the brave pretence that they were only doing so for the same reasons that the Americans used Indian dialects during World War II, because it was a language that the Germans could not understand. Similarly, the Protestants wanted to find out what the Catholics were saying.

Many of the younger UVF men in particular had been imbued with patriotism, myth and prejudice to the extent that the only way they could see of 'defending the Protestant heritage, the liberty of religion and the British connection', was to take a gun and shoot some seventeen-year-old Catholic of their own class.

However, as the time in jail passed, remorse began to set in –and conscience has proved a powerful causative factor in bringing about a change of heart in many a youthful killer. Remorse apparently ended one of the biggest murder hunts of the decade, that for the killers of UDA leader Hugh McVeigh, and a lesser UDA figure, volunteer David Douglas, who were done to death by the UVF on 7 April 1975. The idea behind the murders seemingly was to try to provoke the UDA into taking action (and so to shatter the ceasefire between the IRA and the army) against the Provisionals who were widely assumed to have done the killings. Eventually, almost two years later, however, in a four-hour reserved judgement, Mr Justice McDermott handed out a total of 700 years in sentences to twenty-six UVF men whom he held to be guilty not only of the murders but of a series of other crimes as well.

It was the evidence of one man, 'Witness A', as he was referred to all during the trial, which formed the basis of the breakthrough which led to the finding of the murdered men's bodies and the ultimate sentencing of the killers. Witness A had taken to going at regular intervals and praying beside their grave and these pangs of conscience were causing people in the district to wonder at his actions and leading his colleagues apparently to think of silencing him and this led him to go to the police. Witness A was spirited out of the country following the trial after threats were made to him from the dock.

However, after a spell in jail, young men like these begin to ponder on the nature of their heritage and on the fact that it was the British uniform which they were trained to revere which was now keeping them behind lock and key. It was the British handing out beatings, whenever tension arose in the camp, over prisoners' demands or infringement of rules. It's a hard thing for a young man barely out of adolescence to find that he has gone into prison believing himself to be a patriot and to find himself christened a murderer instead. It's even harder when unlike his young IRA counterpart, who has a far greater historical continuity to look to, he finds that his cause and his culture crumble under examination into a crisis of identity (rather like the disappearance of the Blueshirt movement of the 1930s while many of its members were in jail). Hence there has come on the Protestant side a general consciousness of being Irish – an Ulsterization process, as some commentators put it. They know at least that they belong to Ulster; that much is safe and sure, as Dublin looms closer and London apparently prepares to betray them.

In the Protestant dilemma there is a hope for the future. A voyage of self-discovery has begun and it is a giant step forward. Until the murder of Mountbatten one could have said with reasonable confidence – nothing is of course certain in the Northern Ireland morass – that a backlash from the Protestant side would not necessarily occur if the British left. And though events since the murder weakened that confidence, they did not wreck it.

One of the more distressing aspects of the IRA campaign was the tactic of shooting off-duty Ulster Defence Regiment personnel, sometimes in circumstances of particular horror, such as when they are taking their children to school, or in their homes watching television. In some of the talks between the UDA and the IRA which have flickered on and off through the years, these shootings have been used as a bargaining counter for a cessation by the UDA of its sectarian assassination campaign.

Partly this was because many UDA men are in the UDR but the reason for the UDR killings goes deeper than anger at this or the need to have a bargaining position in the grisly subterranean horse-trading. I have written earlier about the role of the B-Specials and their formation by Lord Brookeborough. Readers will therefore be aware of the key position the corps occupied in the maintenance of Protestant hegemony and then consequent detestation by the Catholic population whose leaders frequently called for the force's disbandment.

Catholic detestation came to a head with the events of August 1969, in which B-Specials took part in the acts of burning and violence not as a legitimate aid to the forces patrolling the border but as a Protestant militia seeking to extirpate the Catholics in the centre of cities exactly as their forefathers had done.

Some of the episodes in which the B-Specials were involved were shown on British television (during the Falls Road burnings of August 1969) and enlightened English public opinion was enraged. Harold Wilson, the then British Prime Minister, expressed himself strongly on the corps in the House of Commons during a debate on Northern Ireland, and a committee of inquiry into the activities of the police and the B-Specials was set up under Sir John Hunt, the Everest conqueror. His report was published in October 1969, and accepted by the government that day – an alacrity that was as pleasing to the Catholics as it was dismaying to the Protestants.

Sir John recommended that the B-Specials be disbanded and replaced by another body, the Ulster Defence Regiment. Protestant sentiment was so outraged by the disbandment of the 'Specials' that some replacement had to be found. But it was hoped that the new corps, which was finally set up during April 1970, being ultimately responsible to the GOC Northern Ireland, would therefore be more susceptible to orthodox discipline since security was henceforth to be a matter not for militias but for Whitehall.

Sir John Hunt had proposed that the UDR be 2,000 strong but by 1979 it had just under 8,000 members and a women's auxiliary unit, the Greenfinches, which had 600, with about 1,000 members on duty every evening and 2,000 at weekends. A strong advertising campaign on television and in newspapers sought to keep those numbers up despite the IRA's attrition. Initially the force was not a 'legitimate target' for the IRA but it was not long in operation before there were Catholic complaints that the new UDR was just the old B-Specials in a new guise. Initially the force had a 16 per cent Catholic enrolment. This had fallen to 8 per cent by the end of a year (Hansard, 25 November) and must be virtually non-existent now.

I noticed when driving in the North with Catholic friends that they appeared to be more fearful of being stopped by the UDR at road blocks than by the army. As I have never encountered anything but courtesy myself whenever I have been stopped in the North by either the UDR or the army I cannot add anything by way of firsthand experience to this observation. In the abrasion of Northern Irish life both the Catholic population and the IRA very obviously could, and after reports of UDR involvement in the various killings of Catholics and, of course, in the arrests and weakening of the IRA – the IRA declared open season on the UDR in 1971 when five members of the force were shot in the course of the year. By the end of 1979, some eighty members of the force, including two women, had been assassinated. At first sight that figure would seem to indicate that the UDR had been most foully set upon – and in some cases its members were – but there is another figure which should be considered in this context.

In March of 1979 the RUC admitted that UDR members had been involved in thirty known cases of murder, the two most spectacular or horrific examples of which were the massacre of the Miami Showband, a Southern group whose members were ambushed, three being murdered and two wounded on 1 August 1975, near the border,* and by the activities of the Shankill murder gang known as the 'Butchers'.

The 'Butchers' day of reckoning came on 20 February 1979, in Belfast when Mr Justice O'Donnell sentenced a group of eight 'Butchers' to a total of forty-two life sentences for nineteen deaths. One of the most prominent members of the group, Robert 'Basher' Bates, was an ex-UDR man. To anyone familiar with the North it was inconceivable that a group not actively connected with either of the major sources of paramilitary activity could have got away with the spate of torture, throat cuttings and shootings which the 'Butchers' practised over a period of several years. Yet this apparently was the case, even though the 'Butchers' met regularly and openly in such Belfast haunts as the Lawnbrook drinking club and in other Protestant pubs.

Many Catholics believed that the authorities connived at or at least turned a blind eye to such activities, because, acting on the theory that 'the enemy of my enemy is my friend', it was felt that such pressures would 'soften up the Papes' and make them more willing to yield up the guerrillas in their midst, the IRA.

The official version of the 'Butchers' downfall is that they had left one victim, Gerard McLaverty, a Catholic, for dead, but through a change in their *modus operandi*, he recovered and with the aid of excellent police work on the part of two police officers, Detective Chief Inspector James Nesbitt and Detective Sergeant Chambers, was able to identify his assailants standing outside a pub.

Instead of using a meat cleaver or an axe on McLaverty, after the customary bout of torture, they tied a bootlace around his throat to silence him and then slashed his wrists with knives and threw him in an

---

* In a botched effort to blow up the Miami van two UVF men died on the same occasion.

alleyway where his blood congealed in the cold so that the bleeding stopped and saved his life.

Sentencing the killers, Mr Justice O'Donnell made it clear that in the case of two of them, William Moore and the ex-UDR man, Bates, life was to mean life and that no reason was to be accepted for terminating this sentence save terminal illness.

The most substantial journalistic effort to prove the links between the security forces and the paramilitaries came in October 1973, when *Political Murder in Northern Ireland* was published by Martin Dillon and Dennis Lehane. But Loyalist paramilitaries' spokesmen, post the Sunningdale strike, made public claims about their UDR links (I was flatly told during one visit to the UDA HQ that 'you can take it we more or less control the UDR') and there was a notorious case in the Bawnmore district of Belfast in September of 1979 in which a Catholic who had spent three years in jail on an arms charge was murdered within minutes of a UDR patrol passing by.

Wherever the truth lies, the development of the UDR, the subsequent onslaught on it and its involvement with episodes like the 'Miami' affair and the 'Butchers'' activities help to illustrate yet again why to Catholics in the ghetto the term 'law and order' has to be defined as to whose law and whose order. To the people of Andersonstown, Ballymurphy, the Clonard and so on, the RUC and the UDR and any similar grouping are either instruments of oppression in themselves or sources of information for their associates in the ranks of sectarian assassins.

As readers will be aware by now, a characteristic of 'The Movement' is its tendency to split whether over ideology or personality. This trait also asserted itelf strongly in the 1969-79 decade.

While the Provisionals are of course the principal physical force unit within the Republican movement, it is just conceivable that they will not always remain so. For just as when the Provisionals split from the Officials they seemed to be but a splinter group, and then established themselves as the strongest guerrilla movement in Europe, so too might an Irish National Liberation Army type-movement prove in the long run to be even stronger than the Provisionals. Apart from the speculation, and the fact that the organization was responsible for assassinating Airey Neave, the birth and survival of the INLA is significant inasmuch as it shows yet again the strength of the revolutionary current which constitutes extreme Republicanism in Ireland and the impossibility of that current ever being completely short-circuited so long as the border issue remains – British uniform in Ireland is an irritant in the political oyster around which no pearl will ever form.

. Like the Provisionals, the INLA was born out of a feud within the Official IRA. This came to a head in a bloody feud which began with the shooting of Hugh Ferguson (IRSP) on 20 February 1975, and lasted until May as the Officials tried unsuccessfully to put down the mutiny. Apart from Ferguson, the shootings and counter shootings included Sean Garland, badly wounded in Dublin a few days later on 1 March. Within the Official movement he was regarded as one of the heroes of the IRA having been wounded in the Brooksborough ambush. The following month Billy McMillen, the Officials' leader in Belfast, also a respected figure inside and outside the movement, was murdered on 28 April and an unsuccessful attempt was made to machine gun Seamus Costello as he was overtaken by a motor-cycle while driving from a meeting in Waterford on 7 May.

The INLA support centred for a time on Divis Flats in the Falls Road and there was for a time a joke about the nickname given to the flats based on the initials of the INLA's political wing – the Irish Republican Socialist Party. The flats were called 'Planet of the IRPS', but no one is laughing now after episodes like the assassination of Airey Neave, and bank robberies of the scale of the one carried out in June 1979, at Barnagh Gap, Co. Limerick, which netted £500,000. The Irish Republican Socialist Party has its own newspaper and disclaims any connection, save a shared aim, with the INLA. This aim is a united socialist (thirty-two county) Irish Republic achieved through physical force. The IRSP was set up by and under the leadership of Bernadette McAliskey (née Devlin) and Seamus Costello in 1974 but she split from the party a year later because of its 'militarism' and Seamus Costello was assassinated in 1977. Miriam Daly, who for a time ran the IRSP, was later also murdered, by a Loyalist undercover squad who, it is alleged, was working for British intelligence.

The INLA is largely financed through raiding banks in Ireland and by Middle Eastern subventions. It has carried out a number of attacks against the army, UDR and RUC which were for a long time ascribed to the Provisionals because it was not until after the Neave killing that the very tightly knit, secretive, Republican unit publicly claimed an operation. It is now known that the INLA also attacked UDA and UVF

members because, it says, of their known sectarian activities. The
INLA is known to be close to the Provisionals, possibly to the extent of
engaging in what in business circles are known as 'joint ventures',
while remaining bitterly opposed to the Officials and other left-wing
groupings, Trotskyites, socialists, and so on. They had, before the
Provisionals themselves tightened up, a tighter recruitment policy than
the Provisionals, screening applicants for membership rigorously and
keeping numbers small and anonymous – though the organization
claims at the same time to be organized in all the important Irish towns
and certainly has strong support in the Falls Road district of Belfast
and in Derry.

The sophistication of its weaponry – which include Kalashnikov
(AK47) rifles, Russian hand grenades – taken together with the
bomb-making skills, so potently demonstrated in the mercury-
triggered device which killed Airey Neave as he drove his car from the
House of Commons car park, made the INLA a formidable foe indeed. The organization decided to kill Neave because he had been
calling for a strengthening of the SAS and the UDR and for the introduction of hanging and the reintroduction of internment. As he was
expected to succeed Roy Mason those views could well have become
policy for Northern Ireland where his intelligence background would
have been of further assistance to him and a drawback to the revolutionary groups opposing him.

As for the Officials themselves during the period, the story is no
more cheerful than for any of the other parties concerned. After the
split the Officials continued in being, attracting numbers of young
people by their blend of Marxism and revolutionary Republicanism
which, after 29 May 1972, did not even carry the risk of the Provisionals' brand – death – because on that day, the Officials declared a
ceasefire. This ceasefire has held more or less intact to the time of
writing, barring some feuding with the Provisionals, and more especially with the Irish National Liberation Army which split from them.
Had the Provisionals not been preoccupied with their anti-British
activities, the original Provisionals' split might have had a different and
a bloodier end – one of the Provisionals shot and permanently injured
by the Officials, for instance, was Thomas Cahill, Joe Cahill's brother.
As it was, a short vicious spate of fighting between the two wings in
October 1975 claimed eleven deaths and fifty wounded before two
priests, Father Alex Reid and Father Desmond Wilson, managed to
negotiate a settlement.

The stated aim of the Officials – to unite Protestant and Catholic workers in an All-Ireland Socialist Republic – does not have a snowball's chance in hell of succeeding and it would be easy to dismiss them as pretentious and unreal rhetoricians. There is a joke told in Belfast concerning an army haul from the Provisionals, the UVF and the Officials. The Provisionals yielded some bombs, Armalites and machine guns, the UVF some rifles and revolvers, and the Officials 'five thousand copies of *The Thoughts of Chairman Mao*, five thousand copies of *Das Kapital* and a library of books on world revolution'.

In addition to this, their record of military operations is a litany of brutal bungling.

A bombing at an army billet in Aldershot, in retaliation for Bloody Sunday, killed a Catholic chaplain and some cleaning women – 'workers of the world unite'! And their other activities included the assassination of Senator Barnhill;* an attempted assassination of John Taylor (which failed, according to Belfast gallows humour, because they shot him in the head!); the dragging of a UDR man, who was also a bus driver, off a school bus and shooting him dead in front of the screaming children; and finally the murder of a popular young Derry lad, Ranger William Best, who was home on holidays from the British army and who had been known to join his friends in the Provisionals in throwing stones at the British army. This last murder precipitated a wave of condemnation for the Officials and the ceasefire.

However, despite this record of literally murderous folly, the 'Stickies'' appeal – or perhaps more correctly that of left-wing Republicanism – is not to be underestimated. For instance, when after the ceasefire the Officials' Belfast leader, Joe McCann, was shot by British troops, Gusty Spence, the UVF leader, wrote to his widow in sympathy and appreciation of McCann's views; and in the 1974 Westminster General Election the Republican Clubs, as the Officials' political wing is known in the North (in the South, it is Sinn Fein, the Workers' Party), received 21,633 votes, a thousand more than Brian Faulkner's wing of the Unionist Party. It may not be the Official IRA wing which ultimately benefits from this residual support, but the

---

* The Stickies only intended to destroy his home in Co. Tyrone as part of their 'class warfare', but the Senator put up a struggle and was killed more or less accidentally. His home was then destroyed.

hard men in the INLA, some of whom were mixed up in the Best affair and in other murders of a similar nature both since and before the split.

But certainly in a country with high unemployment and the youthful electorate already referred to, this smouldering socialist torch was one that the authorities were very keenly aware could put sparks to the political fabric of the country, if circumstances were right.

To wind up the litany of fractiousness, it might be noted that Saor Eire* too had a split which yielded an offshoot, 'Saoirse Eire'. Larry White, one of its members, was shot dead in Cork on 10 June 1975. I was to acquire a particular interest in this last death because as a result of publishing allegations concerning police brutality towards the men accused of his murder, made by their solicitor, I found myself in the High Court, successfully defending, I am happy to say, a contempt of court charge.

One of the tactics used by the Coalition was to try and muzzle the papers on the subject of the IRA by using the contempt of court laws. The four major newspaper groups in the Republic and even the weekly opinion journal *Hibernia* were all prosecuted by the state between 1974 and 1977. In this unprecedented outburst of state legal assault, the *Irish Press* was the only paper successfully to defend itself.

Apart from the difficulty of trying to determine who shot who and why in Northern Ireland (generally over guns or money, which one side or the other probably felt belonged to it), there is also the fact that sometimes 'contract' killers were used by both sides – Republican and Protestant. On top of this, the activities of the SAS and the 'dirty tricks' brigade have never been satisfactorily explained.

One of the issues which continually caused trouble between London and Dublin was the vexed question of extradition. For the Dublin governments, bound by history and the Irish constitution, the position remained exactly that enunciated by John A. Costello on 30 November 1955, when he said (Chapter 13) '... there can be no question of handing over either to the British or to the Six County authorities, persons whom they may accuse of armed political activities in Britain or in the Six Counties.'

---

* Saor Eire officially went out of business on 27 June when a statement was issued on behalf of the organization saying that it was suspending operations 'in the interests of the working class'.

After Sunningdale a 'law enforcement commission' was set up which reported on the advisability of an all-Ireland court which would try offenders within the jurisdiction within which they were apprehended, for instance Dublin could try an IRA bomber wanted by the British without having to hand him over for trial; but the British never availed of this facility and continued to seek extradition.

This pressure was accompanied by a publicity campaign which, apart from the irritation it caused in Dublin, sometimes backfired – at least once with tragic results, in the case of Margaret McKearney. In September 1975, Miss McKearney was twenty-one, a native of Moy, Co. Tyrone, a member of a fiercely Republican family in which two of her brothers had been jailed and one, Sean, killed with a comrade[*] in a premature bomb explosion. She was also, according to Scotland Yard, 'possibly the most dangerous woman terrorist in Britain'.

She was wanted in connection with a number of the British bombings, London, Liverpool, Southampton, Glasgow and Manchester, police believing that she was one of the team of women who brought over supplies, money and instructions to the IRA units in Britain. However, Scotland Yard issued the Press Association with a picture of her, allegedly taken at a dance in Dublin. This was later said, however, to have been found during a raid in Manchester and it also became known that at the time that Scotland Yard was allegedly seeking help in apprehending 'the most wanted girl in Britain' she was known to be back in Ireland. Moreover the Irish Special Branch were able to substantiate the fact that Miss McKearney was also in Ireland on dates when the Yard claimed she was active in Britain.

The discrepancy in the dates gave rise to a belief that the British authorities were using the McKearney affair to bring pressure to bear on the Irish government over extradition and there was a resultant flurry of diplomatic activity between the two governments.

However, while the matter was still being discussed privately and diplomatically, publicly and bloodily a group of Loyalist assassins took a hand in the affair by shooting an innocent couple (on 23 October) in their garden – Peter McKearney and his wife Jane, who were mistaken for Margaret's parents. They were in fact unrelated.

British intelligence was of course far from quiescent over the period. An obvious centre of activity was and is the embassy. Sir John Peck, the popular British diplomat who had the doubtful privilege of having

---

[*] Eugene Martin of Charlemont.

his embassy burned down[*] after Bloody Sunday, had an intelligence background in the Middle East – though neither he nor the Irish saw any reason why this should prevent him settling down subsequently to an enjoyable retirement in Dublin. A successor of his, Christopher Ewart-Biggs, was of course apparently struck down because of intelligence considerations. One IRA version of the reasons for his deathwish I was given was that it was the military attaché, not the ambassador, who was the real target.

This would at least be a more convincing explanation than the fact that Brian Cubbon, Permanent Ulster Secretary of the Northern Ireland Office, who was in the car at the time of the explosions, was the reason for the attack. For while it would not be difficult to monitor the ambassador's movements with a view to ambushing him, it would be very difficult indeed without up-to-date information from the embassy itself or the security forces guarding it to say just when Cubbon would be in the car. Cubbon, incidentally, survived the blast and has lived unattacked since, as has Merlyn Rees, another supposed passenger in the car.

Obviously over the decade I, like other journalists, had heard stories of an espionage connection with some leading Fleet Street journalists who had come to Ireland because of the troubles (and sometimes similar stories concerning people residing in the Republic). But it is better not to dwell on these and to give only concrete proved examples. I will content myself with two; one involving Britons, the other an Irishman. The Britons, of course, were the celebrated Littlejohn brothers, Kenneth and Keith, whose British army background was apparently put to other uses by the British authorities. On 19 February 1973, this pair lost their appeal in the London High Court against being sent back to Ireland to face charges arising out of the armed robbery of £67,000 from the Allied Irish Bank in Grafton Street, Dublin, the previous October. For the offence Kenneth received twenty years and Keith fifteen from the Special Criminal Court. Stiff sentences for mere bank robbery nowadays. The London case was heard in camera because the Attorney General said that 'matters of national interest' might be involved.

What these matters might be became somewhat clearer in the

---

[*] Perhaps the Foreign Office made a point of sending to Dublin men versed in incendiarism; Peck's predecessor, Sir Andrew Gilchrist, was also present at the burning of the Dublin Embassy in Jakarta.

Dublin proceedings during which it was revealed that the money was thought to have gone to the Official IRA whom the Littlejohns had infiltrated, quoting as their authority for this action the British Ministry of Defence. They named a number of leading figures in public life as being party to their actions, saying that in particular, Geoffrey Johnson Smith, Minister of State in the Ministry of Defence, knew about them.

It never became clear at what point the Littlejohns came to be regarded not as agents but as bank-robbers by the British, thus allowing them to be returned to Dublin. Nor did the full extent of their activities – some of them known to be carried out in border areas – ever become public. But the Irish government sent its ambassador to the Court of St James, Donal O'Sullivan, to lodge a protest over the affair on 9 August. And it also took the unusual step of issuing a statement through the government information office expressing 'dissatisfaction' with the British government's assurances concerning espionage in the Republic, saying that spying was 'unacceptable' and 'counterproductive'. (The British government took some of the sting out of the exchange by pointing out that it had officially informed Lynch of the Littlejohns' activities. He acknowledged this but pleaded a 'lapse of memory').

The file on the case involving the Irish citizen, which presumably formed part of the 'unacceptable' background to the O'Sullivan protest, was closed at the Special Criminal Court on 27 February of that year, 1973, when Patrick Crinnion of Dublin was found guilty of a number of charges under the Official Secrets Act and sentenced to three months' imprisonment which he did not have to serve as he had been in custody since the previous December. John Wyman, the Englishman to whom he had been supplying the information, received a similar sentence and discharge from the court. One can only hazard a guess as to what Wyman's real job was – but before he was found out, Crinnion had been a member of the Irish Special Branch, a fact which caused very great annoyance in government circles. To this day, no one can say with certainty whether or not there are Crinnions engaged on the Provisionals' interest in the Special Branch but no decision-takers in the Department of Justice will, or can, rule out the possibility entirely.

26

Return to Secrecy and Discipline

After eight years of the foregoing, and much, much else, some of which will probably never be known even after cabinet, police and army records are laid bare, the IRA found itself under heavy pressure. British technology, war weariness, attrition North and South of the border and a number of other factors were taking their toll. Losses mounted and Roy Mason was talking about squeezing the IRA like 'toothpaste'.

Talks about the IRA as being 'finished', 'degenerating into Chicago-type gangsters' and so on became common.

However, where the IRA is concerned such talk can be highly misleading.

It was not that much of what the IRA was seen to be doing – kneecapping, bank-robbery, increasing civilian casualties, shootings of off-duty UDR men and so on – did not come well within the 'Chicago' description. What was important was what they were not seen to be doing – planning and reorganization.

But over and above the reorganization there are paramount considerations about the current IRA campaign which differentiates it from all earlier Fenian or IRA activity and that is the way in which it departs from the normal pattern of cyclical violence. In this case it is not a matter of generations coming to maturity and striking a blow to maintain the Fenian tradition of a Rising in every generation. This time the pattern is continuous – the IRA's fresh 'generation' is next year's school leaver, or his younger brother or sister. Consequently when the IRA started to reorganize it had something to reorganize (unlike the fifties' campaign when the tactic of attacking barracks, as in Tom Barry's day, was found to fail in the face of modern communications). This time the issue was not targets or how to attack them. As has been demonstrated, the IRA could choose and hit these all too effectively. The problem was largely structural. The 'Army' was modelled on an outmoded pattern which was proving susceptible to penetration. Belfast, for instance, had a 'Brigade' structure in which Andersonstown, Ballymurphy and most of the Upper Falls Road area were organized into the 'First Battalion'. The Lower Falls and Clonard were the Second Battalion, and northern and eastern Belfast (also with large Protestant populations), the Third Battalion.

One only had to stroll into an IRA haunt like the Prisoners Defence Fund Club in Andersonstown and listen to the audience join in a rousing rebel chorus to the music of the Wolfehounds or some other group, popular in Republican areas, to tell where the spectators came from – they used to raise their arms in the air, swaying in time to the music, holding up one, two or three fingers on each hand to show which battalion they belonged to, supported, or lived under the aegis of. In either case a useful starting point for any police agent present.

It was decided to change the battalion system to a cell structure and to move younger, unknown figures into positions of responsibility leaving well-known, established, older men in a high-profile position as front men (The social conditions ensured that the supply of young men was never in doubt.)

A blueprint was drawn up incorporating these and other sweeping changes that envisaged transforming the shape of the IRA into a more deadly, more secretive organization. By a double irony, the blueprint became public – being seized at the time of Twomey's recapture on 2 December 1977. However the reorganization did become more secretive and more effective.

The document was entitled simply 'Staff Report' and included the following:

> The three-day and seven-day detention* orders are breaking volunteers and it is the Republican Army's fault for not indoctrinating volunteers with the psychological strength to resist interrogation.
>
> Coupled with this factor which is contributing to our defeat we are burdened with an inefficient infrastructure of commands, brigades, battalions and companies. This old system with which the Brits and Branch are familiar has to be changed. We recommend reorganization and remotivation, the building of a new Irish Republican Army.
>
> We emphasize a return to secrecy and strict discipline. Army men must be in total control of all sections of the movement.

* The North's Special Powers Act, like the South's Offences Against the State Act, can be altered as the moment dictates to bring in any security remedies called for.

1) A new rank of Education Officer must be created.

GHQ must have a department of education with officers available for lectures and discussions at weapons training camps. Anti-interrogation lectures must be given in conjunction with indoctrination lectures. The ideal outcome should be that no Volunteer should be charged unless caught red-handed.

It should be pointed out to new recruits the failure of our past structures – the number of men who have been arrested and who signed their freedom away. The commonsense methods of personal security should be thrashed out. Any new recruit mixing with known volunteers should be suspended pending discipline.

We must gear ourselves towards Long Term Armed Struggle based on putting unknown men and new recruits into a new structure. This new structure shall be a cell system.

2) Ideally a cell should consist of four people. Rural areas, we decided, should be treated as separate cases to that of city and town Brigade/Command areas.

For this reason our proposals will affect mainly city and town areas, where the majority of our operations are carried out, and where the biggest proportion of our support lies anyway.

CELLS; as we have already said, as from now, all new recruits are to be passed into a cell structure.

Existing Battalion and Company Staffs must be dissolved over a period of months with present Brigades then deciding who passes into the (reorganized) cell structure and who goes into the Brigade controlled and departmentalized Civil Administration (explained later).

The cells of four volunteers will be controlled militarily by the Brigade's/Command's Operations Officers, and will be advised by Brigade's/Command's Intelligence Officer.

Cells will be financed through their cell leader, who will be funded through the OC co-ordinator. That is, for wages, for running costs, financing of operations (expenses, etc., will be dealt with through the OC).

Cells must be specialized into IO cells, sniping cells, executions, bombings, robberies, etc.

The cell will have no control of weapons or explosives, but should be capable of dumping weapons overnight (in the case of a postponed operation).

The weapons and explosives should be under the complete control of the Brigade's/Command's OC and EC respectively.

Cells should operate as often as possible outside of their own areas; both to confuse Brit Intelligence (which would thus increase our security) and to expand our operational areas.

Disguises should be made use of in all operations. The breaking up of present structure into administration sections and operational cells will make for maximum military effectiveness, greater security, a more efficient back-up structure to increase support and cater for our people's problems.

Thus our Operations Officer can go straight into an area and deal exclusively with Military Operations and problems.

All present volunteers under old structure must be re-educated and given up-dated lectures in combating new interrogation techniques.

Women and girls have greater roles to play as military activists and as leaders in sections of civil administration in propaganda and publicity.

Cumann na mBan, we propose, should be dissolved with the best being incorporated in IRA cells structure and the rest going into Civil and Military administration.

Na Fianna Eireann should return to being an underground organization with little or no public image. They should be educated and organized decisively to pass into IRA cell structure when of age.

IRA AUXILIARIES: To be trained for defence, but with an increasing emphasis on a policing role under Brigade civil administration.

Aux. Batt. Structures (in Belfast) should be maintained. The present IRA should use them less and less, with Brig. QM's having discretion to pick out potential workers. These Aux. structures should be transferred under co-ordination department.

CLUBS; clubs are bases of support, places of cultural activity and fund-raising venues. Clubs should now be expanded into Community services (e.g. for the youth, mothers, pensioners, etc.)

SINN FEIN: Sinn Fein should come under Army organizers at all levels. Sinn Fein should employ full-time organizers in big Republican areas.

Sinn Fein should be radicalized (under Army direction) and should agitate around social and economic issues which attack the welfare of the people. SF should be directed to infiltrate other organizations to win support for, and sympathy to, the Movement. SF should be re-educated and have a big role to play in publicity and propaganda departments.

How effective was the 'building of a new Irish Republican Army'? The answer to that question is best explained in a British army document seized in the mails by the Provisionals and reproduced triumphantly (after being vetted for some months by IRA intelligence) in *An Phoblacht* on 10 May 1979, a few months before the Mountbatten killing underlined the accuracy of the army's appraisal.

It said that the Provisionals were acquiring weapons at a faster rate than the army could recover them and it predicted that the Provisionals may acquire more sophisticated Soviet-designed anti-aircraft missiles, the SA7, similar to those used by Nkomo's guerrillas to shoot down two Rhodesian Viscounts near Lake Kariba in 1978.

The document said:

> The Provisional IRA (PIRA) has the dedication and the sinews of war to raise violence intermittently to at least the level of early 1978, certainly for the foreseeable future.
>
> Even if 'peace' is restored, the motivation for political inspired violence will remain. Arms will be readily available and there will be many who are able and willing to use them. Any peace will be superficial and brittle. A new campaign may well erupt in the years ahead.

Commenting on the calibre of Provisional IRA volunteers the report said:

> LEADERSHIP – PIRA is essentially a working-class organization based in the ghetto areas of the cities and in the poorer rural areas. Thus if members of the middle class and graduates become more deeply involved, they have to forfeit their lifestyle ... Nevertheless, there is a stratum of intelligent, astute and experienced terrorists who provide the backbone of the organization ...
>
> TECHNICAL EXPERTISE – PIRA has an adequate supply of members who are skilled in the production of explosive devices.
>
> RANK AND FILE – Our evidence of the calibre of rank and file terrorists does not support the view that they are mindless hooligans drawn from the unemployed and unemployable.
>
> TREND IN CALIBRE – The mature terrorists, including, for instance, the leading bomb makers, are sufficiently cunning to avoid arrest. They are continually learning from mistakes and developing their expertise.

The report contained the first official admission of the risk faced by Queen Elizabeth during her visit to the North during her Silver Jubilee in August 1977. At Coleraine University, which was visited by the Queen, an IRA bomb exploded several hours after she left.

The report concluded:

> The Provisionals' campaign of violence is likely to continue while the British remain in Northern Ireland. We see little prospect of political development of a kind which would seriously undermine the Pro-

visionals' position. (Nor can anyone else see such a 'political development' on the horizon.)

The murder of Lord Mountbatten on 27 August 1979 in a Sligo bay was the most shocking single political assassination in Irish history, ranking in importance, if not exceeding it, with the Burke and Cavendish slayings in Phoenix Park in Parnell's time, marking a high-water mark in ferocity for the Provisionals' campaign and a correspondingly low one in Anglo-Irish relations. The IRA's hammer blow smashed into the world's consciousness with a force that was underlined when as the wavelets were still lapping up wreckage from the Earl's bombed launch at Mullaghmore in the West of Ireland, eighteen members of the Second Battalion Parachute Regiment including a Lieutenant Colonel were blown up on the northeast coast at Narrow Water Castle near Warrenpoint in County Down.

This last was in fact the better planned of the two, and in numbers alone the more horrific; the families of working-class soldiers also feel grief, after all, and there were more of these affected than in the Mountbatten party. There were two explosions, the first designed not only to kill the soldiers in a vehicle in a passing army convoy but to lure more troops to the scene. The Provisionals reckoned (correctly) that these would be helicopter-borne and that they would take refuge in a nearby castle gate. They did and a Provisional unit which had remained at the scene then detonated a second bomb, inflicting the greater part of the day's casualties.

But neither blow was unprecedented. Soldiers had been bombed before and more significantly. Although no one realized it fully after Mullaghmore, the IRA had declared it was going after 'prestige targets' as early as November 1974. Daithi O'Connell, when speaking on an ITN programme during an interview with Mary Holland, the English journalist who most consistently and most informatively reported[*] on the Irish scene, said unequivocally that not only would there be more bombing in England, but that the IRA would strike at targets of an 'economic, judicial, military and political nature'. On 21 November the sound of the Birmingham explosions gave a grisly resonance to his words.

[*] A small coterie of English journalists have reported on Ireland with accuracy and insight all through the Troubles. John Whale, and the Insight team of the *Sunday Times*, Keith Kyle, the Dimblebys and the *Tonight* programme-makers on BBC being prominent among them.

Even before Birmingham the interview created a furore, more because of O'Connell's demeanour, and the mere fact that he was allowed on the air at all, than for what he threatened. But even before the interview the Official IRA had tried to shift their war out of the ranks of the working class and the unemployed and move death up the social scale. Within the Provisionals there had been condemnation of the Officials when they, prior to their ceasefire, began making attacks on targets other than installations or military figures. 'Look at that,' said a Provisional leader to me one day, showing me a clipping from the *Irish News* in which the Officials claimed responsibility for an attack on a director of the no-Catholics-need-apply firm of Mackies, the engineers. 'Just look at that. Sheer class warfare, that's what it is.'

However, prior to Mullaghmore, the Provisionals themselves were already deeply involved in 'class warfare' on 'prestige targets', as they chose to call them. Apart from the businessmen campaign already described and dropped, judges had been shot* – Rory Conaghan, Martin MacBirney and Liam Staunton; there was the murder of the British Ambassador to Dublin, Ewart-Biggs, followed in the year of Mullaghmore by that of Sir Richard Sykes, British Ambassador to the Netherlands, on 22 March 1979, whom the British had placed in charge of the investigation. And of course there had been a spate of upper-class targets in England during the various bombing splurges of the decade. The Adjutant-General of the British army, General Sir Cecil Blacker, had had a narrow escape as far back as 4 January 1974, when a thirty-pound bomb was found outside his home in London. As that year ended, a bomb was thrown into Edward Heath's Belgravia home causing material damage only. Apart from Ross McWhirter, the Balcombe Street group were wanted for an unintended death in the upper-social register, that of Professor Gordon Hamilton-Fairley whose accidental and very regrettable loss to medicine occurred as he passed a booby-trapped car owned by Hugh Fraser, Conservative MP. Above all, the Provisionals made a

---

* Prior to these killings, a study of court cases for the previous two years, published on 18 October 1973, in Belfast by two university lecturers, Tom Hayden and Paddy Hilliard, found that there was marked discrimination against Catholics in the judicial system. However, two of the murdered judges mentioned above, Conaghan and Staunton, were Catholics, and Conaghan, a well-loved figure on all sides of the community, had actually once sent Paisley to prison! MacBirney was well known through his appearance on a BBC Radio Quiz programme.

much more deadly and much more serious attempt than was generally realized at the time on the person of Her Majesty, Queen Elizabeth II herself when she visited Northern Ireland.

Nevertheless, despite the foregoing, the death of Lord Mountbatten and three members of his party, the Dowager Baroness of Brabourne, his fourteen-year-old grandson, and another fourteen-year-old, Paul Maxwell, a local lad, who was aboard acting as a pilot but was no relation of the Mountbattens, produced a reaction of shock, anger and incredulity which elevated the Mountbatten episode to a new place in all the outrage that had gone before. Ireland, and in particular Jack Lynch, was placed in the dock of British public opinion, and security emerged as the key issue for the British.

Lynch found himself the target for attack particularly in the *Irish Times*, because he did not immediately cut short his holiday in Portugal on hearing of the Mountbatten murder (a decision which contrasted with Mrs Thatcher's descent on Northern Ireland to comfort the troops after Warrenpoint). The two sets of killings did not produce comparable results, of course. In the case of Mountbatten the public reaction in Ireland, no less than in England, was caused by the felling of a Titan in world affairs and a well-loved gentleman in private life. But in the British army, Warrenpoint set up a crisis of morale in a corps that was already unenthusiastic about service in Northern Ireland, whose recruitment was falling off and whose general commanding officer, General Creasey, and presumably other officers were already highly resentful at not being able to take the gloves off *à la* Oman (where Creasey had served) and where water supplies could be blown up or poisoned, villages destroyed and a welter of parallel activities engaged in without any fear of meddling press publicity.

If Mrs Thatcher had not gone to Northern Ireland there might have been no army to go to a little later. (A 'troops out' march held at the time attracted, instead of the usual few hundred marchers, a following of over 10,000.)

Papers like the *Star* and the *Express* had banner headlines calling the IRA 'bastards', and editorials, particularly in the Beaverbrook group, referring to Ireland in terms in which the description a 'stinking country' passed almost unnoticed. Against this background it was decided to set up a top-level meeting between the Irish and British governments to discuss the situation on the afternoon of the service in Westminster Abbey for Lord Mountbatten.

After a morning feeling the effects of the full weight of British ceremonial at its best and taking part in a sad and moving ceremony (witnessed amongst others by six kings and three queens) necessitated by the activities of Irish assassins, the Irish Prime Minister met the fourth British Prime Minster he had dealt with since the troubles began years earlier.

To say the least of it, it was not the best psychological backdrop for such a meeting, in which the Irish pressed for a political solution and the British stressed only the need for improved security. Moreover in an effort to prove the genuineness of his desire for reconciliation and to promote a political settlement, Lynch had said in a radio broadcast (Radio Eireann, 2 September 1979) prior to the talks that he would seek simply a power-sharing form of devolved government in the North without insisting on an Irish dimension, e.g. a Council of Ireland. Lynch left himself open to the charge of being intimidated and falling far short of the Full National Demand. However, insofar as the IRA were concerned this would have been an irrelevancy anyhow, as five years after Sunningdale something considerably less than that package could only be expected to be ignored by them. Where the general Irish public was concerned, anything that was not too obviously a climb-down in the face of British pressure would have been acceptable after years of the Northern horror – at least temporarily after Mullaghmore. But four days after the Thatcher meeting, the first of a promised series of talks, the explosive nature of the Republican issue for Fianna Fail was dramatically illustrated yet again by the speech delivered by Sile de Valera at the annual commemoration of Liam Lynch. By holding the party meeting which the speech necessitated on the eve of the Pope's visit to Ireland (28 September) Lynch effectively dodged press scrutiny of the meeting which in the end supported him. However, coupled with the bad showing of the party in the Euro elections of June 1979, Lynch was irretrievably on a slide; and the Northern issue, combined with rising inflation, resulted in his losing the two by-elections in his own native county of Cork in November 1979. The particular *causus belli* was an agreement which is still not fully understood by the public at large, or anybody else in the Republic for that matter, whereby apparently an 'air corridor' was created along the border so that Irish and British helicopters could fly into each other's territories for a distance of some kilometres.

Lynch apparently agreed to something of this nature at a meeting with Mrs Thatcher and her cabinet after the Mountbatten funeral. Militarily speaking the arrangement was totally ineffective as a means of suppressing the IRA but evidently it was a project dear to the heart of the British military authorities who favoured 'hot pursuit of the IRA' across the border.

The notion of British troops or aircraft infringing Irish sovereignty awoke every sleeping fibre of Nationalism there was in the Fianna Fail party – as well as widespread fears that Irish helicopters might be shot down by the IRA in mistake for British ones; and after some pretty severe internal in-fighting within Fianna Fail, Lynch resigned on 11 December 1979, and was succeeded by Charles Haughey after some even more intense in-fighting with Deputy Prime Minister George Colley. Haughey elevated the Northern issue, at least in terms of verbal republicanism, in Fianna Fail's priorities at the annual party conference on 15 February 1980. He said Northern Ireland was *the* political challenge facing the government and said flatly that the Northern state had failed.

The SDLP also acquired a change of leader when Gerry Fitt found himself in a minority of one within the party because of his enthusiastic endorsement of Britain's proposals for a constitutional conference which the incoming Thatcher administration offered as a means of solving the imbroglio – specifically excluding the Irish dimension contained in the Sunningdale pact. John Hume succeeded him.

Where the IRA itself was concerned, *An Phoblacht* in the issue after Mullaghmore/Warrenpoint (1 September) served to reveal how far the IRA had come in targets, language and sentiment from the time Billy McKee got himself shot to pieces in a gun-fight that killed four Protestants defending St Matthew's Church. Above a photograph of Mountbatten with 'Executed' emblazoned across it, a sneering half-page article signed by 'the Brigadier' described how the Queen took the news without a blink, merely informing the butler that 'there would be one fewer for dinner' but 'groaned in anguish' when 'the Brigadier' accidentally smashed the Meissen tea set. 'Personally,' said the Brigadier, 'I never had much time for the old fool, but *noblesse oblige* and *de mortuis nihil nisi* slobber . . .' *An Phoblacht* also marked the occasion by printing a cartoon, headed, in a play on the pop song title, 'I hate Mondays'.

The official *An Phoblacht* statement was headed 'Execution of Soldier Mountbatten' and it went on:

In claiming responsibility for the execution of Lord Mountbatten (former Chief of the United Kingdom Defence Staff, cousin of the Queen

of England and symbol of all that is imperial Britain) the Irish Republican Army stated that the bombing was a 'discriminate operation to
bring to the attention of the English people the continuing occupation
of our country'.

The statement went on:

> The British army acknowledge that after ten years of war it cannot
> defeat us but yet the British government continue with the oppression of
> our people and the torture of our comrades in the H-Blocks. Well, for
> this we will tear out their sentimental imperialist heart. The death of
> Mountbatten and the tributes paid to him will be seen in sharp contrast
> to the apathy of the British government and the English people to the
> deaths of over three hundred British soldiers, and the deaths of Irish
> men, women and children at the hands of their forces.

On the same day in the *Irish Times*, talking with Niall Kiely, a Provisional spokesman gave one of the most chilling – and important –
interviews of the entire decade. To underline its importance *An
Phoblacht* reprinted it in its next issue.

In one sentence it laid down IRA policy for the future:

> We will do exactly the same thing again – against prestige targets.

That was the language of the brutal and the brutalized. It was the
authentic note of Belfast 1979 – ten years on from the Falls Road
burnings and the Downing Street Declaration and still nowhere near a
solution.

PART III

1979–1986

27

The Ignition of the Crisis

'Pat' was an important figure in the IRA's command structure. Middle thirties, five foot nine, black haired, moustached, an unremarkable, windcheatered figure, he might just as easily be blond and wearing pin-stripes when, and if, I see him again. We met in Belfast and 'Pat' devoted an afternoon to the interview. He was friendly, knowledgeable, and completely frank in his replies to my questions; he answered precisely what was asked, volunteering nothing. A shortened version of the upshot is reproduced here in his own words; it gives some impression of the effect of the war on the thinking of the IRA of the mid-1980s and the changes that had taken place over the past decade.

In the early seventies the IRA was hugely popular. We had big companies. Everyone was volunteering. Lads would be well known in this area. They'd be known to the Brits too. So they began to be picked up. There was internment, Sunningdale, all that, and a bit of war weariness set in. Young people began dropping off. So the numbers in units got smaller. Remember there was the truce with the Brits. After the Miami the numbers went up. But in the Truce the Brits got wind of us. Touts, then Mason and the stuff about 'squeezing the IRA like toothpaste' – numbers started going down again.

We had the Brigade structure, at least formally and they were on to us. The Peace People. Everything was coming down on us. Seventy-six was a very significant year. We began going over to the Cells generally, with ASUs [Active Service Units] operating independently. We had to contend with the war weariness. We had the problem of people looking for protection. We were trying to organize local policing. Paisley's strike was terrifying our people. There was talk of Civil War. Numbers were definitely down. I think an average volunteer only lasted about three months then. Anti-interrogation became the big thing. We started going over to the *Green Book* philosophy. Mason was one of the best things to happen to us.

Also La Mon made us realize the need to politicize the struggle.

Implementation of the Cell structure really took over and by 1979 I'd say we were on the way to defeating Castlereagh and the Conveyor-Belt System. Everyone knew what happened if you got caught. We started operating only on the 'need to know'.

The prisoners understood what the Brits were about. Volunteers were politicized: the *Green Book* philosophy took over. There was analysis of history. Lectures on how to deal with isolation. The rhetoric definitely changed from 1916 and Pearse, Connolly and so on. We began looking at other struggles. Vietnam especially. The hunger strike cemented the position about education. Don't mind that talk about Libya. The Libyans were trained in conventional warfare. They couldn't teach us anything. There's no international conspiracy. The IRA makes its own news. We have waiting lists waiting to join up.

There's always a debate of course about soldiers against politicians. But the war's about people, not kills. Destroying the economic infrastructure* wouldn't help the people. A thing like the Agate thing was different. Mason was in the States trying to encourage American investment. In theory American businessmen support the MacBride principles†, in practice no.

GHQ men went through the Brigade areas talking to the ASUs explaining electoral strategy, explaining how military decisions could affect people's attitudes. A lot of the Army were apathetic to Sinn Fein. They weren't interested in politics. We had to argue Standing Order No. 8 through with them. They see the Gardai as Brits in different uniforms. But Standing Order No. 8 is a realistic policy even though the Gardai and the RUC are collaborating. They talk to each other across the border on radio. The Free State's security policy, in essence, is a pro-Brit policy. The danger is the Brits will manage to get some permanent foothold on the island through the Free State security co-operation. They've got a strategic NATO interest. They don't want the Republic neutral.

If Section 31‡ were removed it would help Sinn Fein but it wouldn't affect the IRA. The arms seized on the *Marita Ann* are standard issue to the IRA. We already had that type of armament. We'd have preferred of

---

* Pubs were favourite targets for IRA bombings in the early '70s, as well as factories and shops. However, local opposition and changes in compensation awards systems altered this.

† Named after Sean MacBride, the Nobel and Lenin Peace Prize winner, these are analogous to the Sullivan Principles, and relate to the participation of American companies in South Africa under apartheid. They attempt to lay down ground rules for fair employment, between not black and white but Protestant and Catholic.

‡ Section 31 of the Broadcasting Act prevented Sinn Fein spokesmen being interviewed on RTE.

course that the particular shipment got through but you can draw your own conclusions about the weapons position from the fact that the *Marita Ann* stuff was already standard issue, before the capture.

Getting arms, or explosives or planning anything is the same for us as for anyone, the BA or the RUC, except we don't have recourse to back-room 'boffins' with resources, science and so on to bear down on any problem. Our back rooms can be raided or under surveillance at any time, but still we do analyse any situation we come to, though it takes us longer than our enemies. The analysis and adaption goes on all the time. Sometimes people think the IRA is on the run. The truth is the IRA is *always* on the run, and always learning,[*] reading about other struggles, the history of colonialism; it videos films like *The End of Empire* or Julian Pettifer on Vietnam. Analysing things that happen to us like the super-grass thing. We realize the need for volunteers to have a stable, committed background. We try to pick people who'll last the distance, we recruit the over-twenties for preference – an eighteen-year-old might be inclined to marry and give up, maybe joining up out of a sense of identity and local status, but he mightn't have the commitment. We do have some Protestants in the IRA, mostly in rural areas, but they're mostly Catholic. We have some university types – mostly in Sinn Fein. Yes, of course a volunteer can leave when he wants to. He's expected not to talk, of course.

Our aim is to create such psychological damage to the Brits that they'll withdraw. Sick of the expense, the hassle, the coffins coming back to England. But we know we can't defeat them in a military sense, no more than they can beat us. So there's a kind of stalemate. But we always retain the ability to bring the situation to a crisis. Bomb a county target to switch the troops from the cities. Then hit city targets. Or do a Brighton, a Mountbatten. We analyse each result and act accordingly. If it doesn't work *then* we'll worry, but remember, we live here; Maggie Thatcher doesn't. Yes, we have plans for a Doomsday situation.

We're organized into cells, as you know, five to ten people, independent of the organization except for the OC who knows the Brigade Adjutant. He (and his own men of course) get his orders from him. The Cell has its own pool of weapons, and explosives, intelligence. It arranges houses and transport outside the organization. There are five to six Cells active in greater Belfast. Single men get £10 a week. Married men £20. You're so busy you don't need money. But there's the dole and people help out, food and so on. You learn to live with the

---

[*] The 'Republican University' Jail, North and South of the border, produces its quota of university graduates and third level qualifications. One can see the lights blazing in the cells of Portlaoise in the small hours of any morning as the prisoners avidly make use of study opportunity.

risk, the threat of prison – I've been in prison myself. Yes, I've taken life, or at least I must have done judging by the casualties after operations I've been in. But I was never conscious of hitting anyone at the time. You're so keyed up during the operation. You lead two lives. One for the family. You're always at risk. There's a Shoot to Kill policy in Armagh just now. But that's nothing new. Remember Ronnie Bunting, Miriam Daly, Bernadette, a lot of innocent people get . . . caught up. No, I'm not talking about the likes of the Stronges. If you encourage sectarianism, you pay for it. Look at the people in for the Birmingham and Guildford bombings. They're completely innocent.

There's a lot of talk about Marxism and left-right splits about, but that's nonsense. Everyone knows they have to hang together. You get political discussion in any organization. The main thought is to get the Brits out. Everyone can follow his own political theory then. Danger makes for pragmatism not grand theory. The IRA is not riddled with racketeers and Godfathers. There's strict control of weapons.[*]

If some 'loose horse' IRA men did decide to go in for bank robberies, with their training they'd be inclined to go for a million. No, most of the crime in Belfast is either INLA or 'sticky' off-shoots, hoods, or petty criminals.

We're stripped down for a long war.

The awful authenticity of the Provisional IRA was tested and proven in the crucible of the H Blocks of Long Kesh in 1980 and 1981. In those years the IRA's capacity for endurance – the obverse side of the coin of infliction – was brought under the microscope of the international media and was seen to triumph in death in a manner which captured the attention of the world. The 'armed struggle' was elevated from being almost exclusively a matter of guerrilla warfare to a political plane on which Sinn Fein succeeded in winning nearly half the votes of the Nationalist population of the Six Counties and gained a degree of purchase in the affections of sympathizers throughout the island which it still retains. For the contemporary Provisional IRA, where Northern Ireland is concerned, the outcome of the hunger strike led by Bobby Sands was the equivalent of the 1916 Rebellion aftermath to the Nationalists of that era.

Like bankruptcy the crisis came in two ways, gradually and

---

[*] How strict I can vouch for. One day a friend brought a pleasant young fellow into my office for me to autograph a copy of the book. Well dressed, good looking, he seemed like an accountant or a lawyer. I asked after him a year later and found that he had been an active service volunteer. He had sold some guns from a dump – and was executed.

suddenly. The public at large were unaware of what was building up in the H Blocks; to them the IRA meant deeds like La Mon and the Mountbatten killing. These were what got the headlines. But the situation inside the H Blocks increasingly became the IRA's own focal point.

These H Blocks are named from their construction: cells down each arm are linked in the middle by the administration offices, like an H. They were built on the site of the Second World War airstrip of Long Kesh, ten miles west of Belfast, as the result of a conscious political decision to criminalize the IRA. Since internment in August 1971, IRA prisoners (and subsequently Loyalist ones also, though separately) had been housed in wire compounds in a corner of the site. Here, they behaved like prisoners of war, responsible only to their officers, acting in a military manner, but – central to what happened subsequently – wearing their own clothes. They also received a plentiful supply of parcels, news and mail from outside. As we have seen, their virtual prisoner of war status, certainly a *de facto* version of it known as 'Special Category Status', came about as a result of an effort made by the British to neutralize the IRA after the fall of Stormont in 1972, when a top level conference took place in London between Cabinet Ministers and an IRA delegation. From the IRA side the price of this conference was the calling off of Billy McKee's hunger strike in Crumlin Road jail in return for conceding in substance to his demands for political status.

For roughly four years the IRA prisoners enjoyed Special Category Status, but increasingly Unionist and Tory anger became focused on the 'Sandhurst of terror', on which was conferred a near Libyan bogeyman status. Concurrent with this burgeoning distaste, the British themselves were evolving a new counter-insurgency strategy. Like the Americans in Vietnam they decided to 'Vietnamize' the conflict, that is, let the natives do the fighting, chiefly the RUC and the UDR. This policy became known as 'Ulsterization'. A second wing of the strategy, 'Normalization', meant what it said: an attempt to restore the Province to an appearance of normality so as to counteract the IRA's economic campaign and its efforts at sabotaging whatever dignity the Special Category Status conferred and making the IRA not an organization with a political ambition and its roots in history, but a mafia-like conspiracy differing only in its methods from what the North of Ireland Secretary of the time, the hapless Merlyn Rees, termed 'ODCs' – Ordinary Decent Criminals.

The crucial step towards the ignition of the H Blocks crisis was taken on 30 January 1975, with the publication of a report from Lord Gardiner, a former Lord Chancellor, who had been asked by the Government post-Sunningdale to consider 'in the context of Civil Liberties and Human Rights, measures to deal with terrorism in Northern Ireland'. Lord Gardiner reported as follows:

> The introduction of Special Category Status was a serious mistake . . . It should be made absolutely clear that Special Category prisoners can expect no amnesty and will have to serve their sentences . . . We recommend that the earliest practicable opportunity should be taken to end the Special Category.

This did not altogether escape the attention of the IRA negotiators, who told the British that any tampering with Special Category would mean a drastic IRA response, including the shooting of warders – a threat which was duly carried out. However, at the time of its publication, debate centred on another recommendation in the report.

In the best British tradition of calling a spade an agricultural implement – which caused Long Kesh to be rechristened 'The Maze' – the unpopular term of 'internment' disappeared but 'detention' remained. In effect this was internment by another name; once picked up or 'detained', prisoners were remanded in custody almost indefinitely – thus adding to, rather than lessening the problem, as by the time Lord Gardiner made his report, prison numbers had risen from a total of 727 in the early days of the Civil Rights Movement to 2,848. As almost 1,200 of these were Special Category prisoners Britain had an embarrassing number of political prisoners on her hands to account for internationally. Lord Gardiner decided to get rid of them and their type of accommodation at one fell swoop, recommending the building of the H Blocks:

> 71% of male prisoners, 1,881 out of a total of 2,648, are now in temporary prisons of the compound type rather than in conventional cellular accommodation.
>
> Prisons of the compound type, each compound holding up to 90 prisoners, are thoroughly unsatisfactory from every point of view; their major disadvantage is that there is virtually a total loss of disciplinary control by the prison authorities inside the compounds. The layout and construction of the compounds make close and continued supervision impossible.

From the British point of view the phrase 'thoroughly unsatisfactory' accurately sums up what happened following the adoption of Lord Gardiner's report. Prison totals continued to rise, to over 3,500, largely because of an essential component of the 'Conveyor-Belt System': the extra-judicial 'Diplock' courts. These were set up as a result of Lord Diplock's Commission, which reported to Parliament on:

> What arrangements for the administration of justice in Northern Ireland could be made in order to deal more effectively with terrorist organizations by bringing to book, otherwise than by internment by the Executive, individuals involved in terrorist activities, particularly those who plan and direct, but do not necessarily take part in, terrorist acts, and to make recommendations.

Lord Diplock's recommendations, which Parliament accepted immediately (20 December 1972), were far-reaching indeed. After analysing the problem he said:

> We are thus driven inescapably to the conclusion that until the current terrorism by the extremist organizations of both factions in Northern Ireland can be eradicated, there will continue to be some dangerous terrorists against whom it will not be possible to obtain convictions by any form of criminal trial which we regard as appropriate to a court of law; and these will include many of those who plan and organize terrorist acts by other members of the organization in which they take no first-hand part themselves.
>
> We are also driven inescapably to the conclusion that so long as these remain at liberty to operate in Northern Ireland, it will not be possible to find witnesses prepared to testify against them in the criminal courts, except those serving in the Army or the police ... The only hope of restoring the efficiency of criminal courts of law in Northern Ireland to deal with terrorist crimes is by using an extra-judicial process to deprive of their ability to operate in Northern Ireland those terrorists whose activities result in the-intimidation of witnesses. With an easily penetrable border to the South and West the only way of doing this is to put them in detention by an executive act and to keep them confined, until they can be released without danger to the public safety and to the administration of criminal justice.
>
> Deprivation of liberty as a result of an extra-judicial process we call 'detention', following the nomenclature of The Detention of Terrorists (Northern Ireland Order, 1972). It does not mean imprisonment at the arbitrary diktat of the Executive Government, which to many people is a

common connotation of the term 'internment'. We use it to describe depriving a man of his liberty as a result of an investigation of the facts which inculpate the detainee by an impartial person or tribunal by making use of a procedure which, however fair to him, is inappropriate to a court of law because it does not comply with Article 6 of the European Convention.

For so long as 'the troubles' lasted, Lord Diplock prescribed that certain types of offences, murder, possession of arms or explosives, grievous bodily harm – in short the type of offence commonly associated with terrorism – should now be termed 'scheduled offences' and dealt with as follows:

1. Trials of scheduled offences should be by a Judge of the High Court, or a County Court Judge, sitting alone with no jury, with the usual rights of appeal.
2. The armed services should be given power to arrest people suspected of having been involved in, or having information about, offences and detain them for up to four hours in order to establish their identity.
3. Bail in cases involving a scheduled offence should not be granted except by the High Court and then only if stringent requirements are met.
4. The onus of proof as to the possession of firearms and explosives should be altered so as to require a person found in certain circumstances to prove on the balance of probabilities that he did not know and had no reason to suspect that arms or explosives were where they were found.
5. A confession made by the accused should be admissible as evidence in cases involving the scheduled offences unless it was obtained by torture or inhuman or degrading treatment.
6. A signed written statement made to anyone charged with investigating a scheduled offence should be admissible if the person who made it cannot be produced in court for specific reasons, and the statement contains material which would have been admissible if that person had been present in court to give oral evidence.

The paragraph concerning confessions was destined to create lasting bitterness throughout Northern Ireland. In effect it contains the third element of the 'Conveyor-Belt System', for despite Lord Diplock's stipulation as to the use of torture, it became an accepted fact of life that the way to get confessions out of suspects was to brutalize them.

In November 1977 thirty solicitors who did most of the work in the 'Diplock' courts wrote to the Secretary of State for Northern Ireland, Roy Mason, stating:

> Ill treatment of suspects by police officers, with the object of obtaining confessions, is now common practice, and . . . most often, but not always takes place at Castlereagh RUC station and other police stations, throughout Northern Ireland.

As I have indicated earlier (see Chapter 24) this complaint was only the tip of the iceberg. Throughout the 1970s there was a whole series of official investigations arising out of the methods used to obtain confessions. These generally concurred in substance if not in form with the findings of Lord Parker of Waddington's Report (adopted 31 January 1982), which found that the methods then in use were illegal under UK law, though not 'immoral' given the circumstances of the time. Interestingly enough in view of his H Block report, a minority report from Lord Gardiner held that even where terrorists were concerned such methods were immoral.

Britain would probably not have been prepared to go even as far as commissioning Lord Parker's Report had not another brutality investigation a few months earlier aroused such derision when it appeared in November 1977 that the Government felt it had to be seen to give the issue serious attention.

Lord Compton had been charged with finding out the truth behind the widespread belief that the treatment of suspects during the internment swoops of August 1981 had been very brutal. He investigated the techniques used and reported that 'our investigations have not led us to conclude that any of the grouped or individual complainants suffered physical brutality as we understand the term'.

As the reader has in earlier chapters studied these techniques, I will leave the matter there, with the obvious comment that prisoners treated by the above listed 'Special' methods of interrogation, courts, and imprisonment felt with a burning conviction that they belonged to a 'Special Category' in both name and deed, as did their families when the time came to support them in public protest.

28

Five Demands and Hunger Strikes

Knowing that the IRA would resist the abolition of Special Category Status, the British attempted to negotiate away the prisoners' opposition, dealing through their leader of the period, David Morley. They offered special treatment and concessions, the most notable of which was a sort of Head Office of terrorism which the authorities intended to provide in downtown Belfast, in Rosemary Street. There, not only the IRA, but also the UVF, UDA and sectarian killers of all persuasions were apparently supposed to meet in paramilitary ecumenical bliss under the one roof so that the British could safely keep tabs on them all. However, as the prisoners in the Long Kesh compound saw before their eyes the H Blocks growing daily, other offers, such as increased recreational and educational facilities, fell on increasingly hostile and deaf ears.

Realizing this, the British took quite extraordinary steps during the negotiating period, allowing Morley to go not only out of jail to negotiate with Northern IRA leaders, but down to the Republic, which was outside the State's jurisdiction. Ostensibly this was to confer with IRA leaders there, though in reality, as Morley himself told me, for no other purpose than to see how far the IRA could stretch British credulity. Morley even sought for and obtained the right to carry a gun on these jaunts. The only stipulation was that, having signed for it, he had to give it back to the authorities on his return.

Something of a division in medium-term objectives developed at this time between the IRA members inside and those outside the jails.

Outside, they were preoccupied with such phenomena as the adverse effect of the Peace People campaign and the fallout from catastrophes like the La Mon bombing. Action took the form of intensive debate on how the structure of the IRA might be reorganized (the outcome of which chapter and verse will be detailed later) and, most importantly, how to resist the new British counter-insurgency techniques of the 'Conveyer-Belt System', which were not only adversely affecting the campaign, but also swelling the prison totals quite dramatically. The Army Council was also preoccupied with drawing up a philosophy for dealing with interrogation and for articulating Republicanism in the contemporary era. These various strands were drawn together to become one of the IRA's most secret and highly prized documents, the *Green Book*. Like Colonel Gaddafi's *Green Book*, it sets down all one needs to know about the philosophy of the Revolution, its history, and the means whereby the struggle is to be prosecuted, and after much internal debate, it came to be the IRA's bible.

As I have explained elsewhere, IRA prisoners lose their rank, revert to the position of volunteer, and endeavour to carry on the war from within, practically speaking responding to the command structure in the prison rather than to that outside. As they had traditionally done, prisoners now defied the British efforts at criminalization. The first man to lose Special Category status, Ciaran Nugent, refused to wear prison clothes, saying after his sentence in 1976, 'They'll have to nail them to my back.' He served out three and a half years with nothing but a blanket to wrap around himself in a cell from which all furniture had been removed as a punishment for his refusal to wear the official garb. He was denied outdoor exercise, visits, parcels and educational facilities.

Nugent's example was followed by hundreds of others as the 'Conveyor-Belt System' went into overdrive. The Republic at large was unaware of what was happening, although Castlereagh, the barracks in which many of the interrogations were conducted, became notorious, partly because of the effect of its name alone. The original Lord Castlereagh, prime architect of the Union of 1800 which the IRA off the 1970s were trying to break, is best known to most Irish people today from Don Byrne's couplet:

> *I met murder on the way*
> *and he had a face like Castlereagh.*

But inside the jails the pressure cooker boiled up dangerously. The situation became both more horrific and more farcical. Certain Loyalist warders had developed the practice of kicking over the prisoners' slop bowls in the mornings so that the contents spilled over the cell. This resulted in the prisoners refusing to 'slop out' and spreading excrement on the wall instead. (An earlier attempt to throw it out of the windows was foiled by warders who threw it back in again.) The 'battle of the bowels' resulted in the prison cells, the most modern in Europe, becoming filthy, maggot-infested caves, in which young men stood naked save for their hate and a prison blanket. This phrase 'on the blanket' was to acquire a new dimension in Irish prison history, though initially not one welcomed by the IRA outside.

The H Block prisoners were also engaged in debate. They were going back into history, to the memory of Terence McSwiney, the events of the 1940s, and the example of IRA prisoners from time immemorial who, when all else was taken from them, fought the battle with the only weapon left, their wills, crystallizing into a stark and skeletal resolution: to fast to the death. Preoccupied with its own external reorganization, and mindful of the potential disaster should a strike break out and be defeated – 'break the lads in jail and you break the movement' is a fundamental IRA tenet – the IRA failed until 1980 to realize the potential which the H Block issue held, and sought instead to avert a strike.

By an accident of fate, in January 1980 I came to be involved in these events, and I am convinced that the principal IRA thrust of the period was aimed at keeping the hunger strike at bay, not encouraging it. Prison chaplains, prisoners' families and others with whom I was friendly at this period, all feared that the situation would escalate out of control and that the prisoners would put into operation their declared intention of having a hunger strike, with or without IRA sanction and with potentially devastating effects on themselves, their families and the community as a whole. In an effect to head off the potentially explosive situation, I highlighted the problem of the dirty protest in the book *On the Blanket.* As a result of my research, I was quite clear at the time that a magnanimous gesture on the part of the British Government, coming down, as such things often do, to simple pieces of symbolism – such as in this case the right of prisoners to wear their own clothes – could have brought about a complete change in the position. It was not to be. Ironically, my book appeared on the very same day that the European court passed an adverse judgement on a case brought by a Belfast solicitor on behalf of a number of prisoners in Northern Ireland seeking to have themselves declared 'political'.

* Ward River Press, Dublin, June 1980.

Their 'five demands' were:

1. The right to wear their own clothes.
2. The right not to do prison work.
3. Free association with fellow prisoners.
4. Full 50% remission of their sentences.
5. Normal visits, parcels, education and recreational facilities.

The situation worsened and eventually the prisoners, under the leadership of Brendan Hughes, decided that unless the 'five demands' were met, they would go on hunger strike.

These demands were not conceded despite warnings as to the possible consequences of a hunger strike and high level negotiations with the British, involving figures such as Cardinal O'Fiaich and Charles Haughey. A hunger strike duly broke out on 27 October and lasted until 18 December when an eleventh hour settlement, reached after frenzied negotiations between Dublin, London, Belfast and various mediators, including myself, seemingly produced a formula which got everyone off the hook, while allowing prisoners the crucial right to wear their own clothes. It turned out to be a false dawn and both the strike and its aftermath produced a lasting bitterness which was ultimately to lead to another, fatal hunger strike. To understand how this came about it is necessary to examine the situation which developed both before and during the first strike (December 1980).

As the pressure on the prisoners built up (prior to the commencement of the October 1980 strike) they, in turn, began to look for ways to put pressure on the authorities to alleviate the situation. Off-duty warders were shot. Prisoners' relatives formed H Block defence committees, and the spectacle of women in blankets walking barefoot on Belfast (and eventually on Dublin) streets began to be seen. Influential people in the Nationalist community began to be perturbed about what was happening. In February 1980 Cardinal O'Fiaich held a series of meetings with Humphrey Atkins, the Northern Ireland Secretary of State, and he and Bishop Edward Daly of Derry urged Atkins to find a formula which would get both parties off the hook before a full-blown hunger strike broke out. They pinned their hopes on the definition of prison work being broadened and permission being granted to allow the prisoners to wear their own clothes.

The relationship between prisoners and warders is an abrasive affair at any time. But in the summer and autumn of 1980, after years of defiance on the part of the prisoners, retaliation by the mostly Loyalist warders, and the IRA campaign of shooting them when they were off-duty, relationships in the prison were at such an appalling level that informed people began to worry that something unique and dangerous was brewing in Northern Ireland. Messages to this effect went to the British Government from a variety of sources including the Government in Dublin, to no avail, but as the storm clouds built up to the point where a hunger strike appeared inevitable, a breakthrough apparently occurred on 23 October. The Northern Ireland Office announced that instead of prison uniform the men would be permitted to wear civilian clothes. This gave rise to great hopes, which were dashed and turned to even greater anger when it was discovered that what the Northern Ireland Office meant was 'prison issue civilian clothes'. The difference between these and the prisoners' 'own clothes', the first of the 'five demands', may not appear much at first sight but in the cauldron of Long Kesh symbolism was all. The prisoners were determined that having, as they saw it, come from an unjust society, through an unjust legal system, fighting for a just cause, they were not going to admit that they were wrong, or that their enemies were right, by allowing themselves to be 'criminalized' in any particular. A hunger strike duly broke out four days later on 27 October. It was led by Brendan Hughes and his six companions were Tom McFeeley (with Hughes Joint OC of the Provisional prisoners), Sean McKenna, Leo Greene, Tommy McKearney and Raymond McCartney. John Nixon, OC of the INLA prisoners, a much smaller group than the Provisionals, was accepted as a member of the hunger striking party.

As the hunger strike wore on the seven men in Long Kesh were joined by three women in Armagh jail, Mairead Farrell, OC of the Armagh Provisional prisoners, Mairead Nugent and Mary Doyle. Like the men in Long Kesh they had been on a dirty protest from 7 February of that year. This protest began when male warders attempted to seize the berets and black shirts from which the women had fashioned a type of uniform. During the raids for this clothing, several women were injured, and as a protest, having been locked in their cells and refused the use of toilet facilities, used the same method as the men to make their objections known.

I visited Long Kesh and Armagh during the strike and found the Armagh conditions the worst, a combination of the prison building itself being older and the fact that in addition to faeces, the women's menstrual blood was smeared on the walls of the cells, which I found particularly nauseating. The women had neither washed, brushed their teeth nor received a change of clothes or underwear for ninety days. Prior to the strike, prisoners had only been allowed one hour's outdoor exercise per day; those on dirty protest now lost this hour as punishment.

Understandably, responsible people in many walks of life throughout the country were deeply perturbed by the possible consequences of all this. As the publicity generated by the strike built up, it appeared that the British were prepared to go along the same face-saving lines as had the Republic in order to defuse the Portlaoise situation, and come to some agreement over the 'Five Demands' which would concede substance without name. There was continual communication between Charles Haughey's office and Downing Street throughout the period and, amongst others, Cardinal O'Fiaich maintained his efforts. All this seemed to bear fruit when on 10 December 1980 an official of the North of Ireland Office spoke to the hunger strikers. After this visit a very lengthy document, some thirty-four pages, and a statement which Humphrey Atkins was about to make in the House of Commons, were given to the prisoners.

The part which influenced the IRA read:

> I want to spell out for you and your families what will happen when the protest ends. First of all, any such prisoner will be put into a clean cell as, I hope, all prisoners end their protest. We shall have the task of cleaning out all the cells right away and this should take a week or 10 days.
>
> Within a few days clothing provided by the families will be given to any prisoners giving up their protest so that they can wear it during recreation, association and visits . . .

It was hoped that a formula based on the fact that the prisoners would get 'clothes provided by their families' would do the trick. The prison issue civilian clothing would be distributed, or so the prisoners believed, after their families' garments arrived, and the prisoners for their part would come off the dirty protest and consequently off the 'blanket' as well. This was the message with which Bobby Sands, who had succeeded Hughes as the prisoners' OC, accompanied by two prison chaplains (Fathers John Murphy and Tom Toner), went through the wings of the prison on 18 December. The hunger strike was ended.

There was one very important element in Sands's acceptance of the settlement terms: the condition of one of the hunger strikers, Sean McKenna. He was a particularly tragic product of the troubles. His father was one of those who, after the 1971 internment swoops, received the type of treatment which led to the Dublin Government bringing Britain before the European Commission of Human Rights. The treatment meted out to McKenna senior was some of the worst to have been suffered by anyone and when he died in 1975, at the age of forty-two, it was generally accepted by his friends, family and neighbours that it was the 'inhuman and degrading treatment' that had brought him to an early grave.

Young McKenna was an embittered IRA activist during 1976 and living in the Republic at Edentubber (near where the four IRA men were blown up in the 1956–62 campaign) when he was kidnapped, it is believed by the SAS, and taken across the border to Bessborough Barracks, Co. Armagh. There he underwent the customary brutalizing treatment before being placed on the 'Conveyor Belt' that eventually landed him in Long Kesh. By the forty-eighth day of the strike he had gone blind and his mental condition was giving rise to concern amongst his comrades. He had begun the strike with an indifference to the prospect of death, described to me by a priest who visited him as 'tantamount to a death-wish'; and then, as the strike progressed, he apparently moved in the other direction, recalling his father and expressing a wish not to die – though not seeking to come off the strike.

I was close to people in Dublin taking part in negotiations with the British at the time, and thus in a position to know that one of the arguments used against Dublin's wish that concessions be made was the fact that the British felt that the strike was going to end shortly in collapse anyhow because of McKenna's failing health. Apparently, also, Sands and his friends decided not to tease out the documents or to have more extensive discussions with the prisoners before calling off the strike because they feared that by the time this process was completed, McKenna would be dead. Accordingly, when over Christmas and in early January it became apparent that the Atkins proposal contained a chicken and egg element, Sands felt particularly embittered and betrayed.

As rumblings that all was not well reached me in Dublin from sources as different as Father Brendan Meagher, who had been in the jail bringing messages from Dublin, and from Father Faul, who was the most active of the prison chaplains and at that time the one most respected by the prisoners, I made some inquiries myself. During these I remember Padraic O'Hannrachain, Charles Haughey's political assistant, saying worriedly: 'Maybe it's just a case that all these fellows in Whitehall have gone home for the Christmas and they're watching television and everything will be all right when the holidays end . . .'

Things were far from all right after Christmas. What none of us had realized at the time was, as Mr Michael Alison, the minister in charge of prisons, was to put it later: 'There was a lady in the case.' Mrs Thatcher remembered Airey Neave. 'Crime was crime', as she was to repeat subsequently, and the combination of her inflexible nature and the Loyalist prison administration's reluctance to concede anything to Republicans completed the lighting of the powder fuse.

As early as 2 January, the IRA obviously realized that there was trouble ahead and released the following statement (from the Republican Press Centre in Belfast): The statement deserves to be read in full as its significance was not at the time appreciated, nor was it as widely publicized as hindsight suggests it might have been:

> Belfast Republican Press Centre Tel. 46841
> 2nd January, 1981

We have been asked to issue the following supplied statement to our office from the PRO of the protesting prisoners in H Blocks 3, 4, 5, and 6, Long Kesh:

On Thursday, 18th December 1980, the British Government presented the Republican hunger-strikers and our O/C with documents which contained in our estimate 'the requirements of our five demands'.

In response to this development, and against a background of apparent flexibility and co-operation within the prison, we the blanket men were hopeful that the ending of the blanket and no wash protest would follow quickly.

This depended obviously upon 'a responsible and sensible attitude from the British Government in implementing their proposals'. Given the above we declared that we would make a positive response.

Immediately before Christmas, with a noticeable absence of movement from the British, we issued a further statement drawing public attention to the manner in which the British Government, contrary to earlier indications and assurances, was handling the situation.

We feel we must again draw the public's attention to the continuing deadlock. The British are intent on deliberately creating as much confusion as possible and upon protracting the deadlock in order to sow suspicion and dissension among our supporters and families.

The blanket/no wash protest can be resolved quite simply. The British Government and their prison administration are fully aware of this, but it appears to us that they lack the will to resolve this issue and that they are committed to going back on their original assurances, including Humphrey Atkins' statement about what would happen as the protest was deescalated.

So, we call upon all those in authority, in Church and State, who urged the British to act in a sensible manner, to immediately and publicly bring pressure to bear upon the British to ensure the speedy resolution of the blanket/no wash protest and the defusing of the H Block/Armagh prison crises.

We ask our relatives and supporters to remain alert and vigilant. We assure them that we will not continue indefinitely to accept the present unsatisfactory situation. The British Government are past masters of deceit and double-dealing. We were aware of this when we accepted, with some qualifications, their document. We were dubious about the sincerity of their intentions, but were convinced that even they would not be stupid enough to waste yet another opportunity to settle this issue.

Should they remain intransigent we will be forced to fall back upon our own resources. In that event our only guarantors, the masses who supported us during the recent hunger-strike, will once again be called upon by us to take to the streets.

If the British Government cling to the forlorn hope that they can yet break the men and women of the H Blocks and Armagh, they have but to look at their failures during the last 4½ years of our protests.

We will not be found lacking in illustrating our ability and will to, if necessary, once again escalate our protest.

Signed PRO, H Blocks 3, 4, 5 and 6, Long Kesh

However, the statement had no effect on the situation in the prison and Bobby Sands obviously began to feel that a hunger strike was inevitable. It has been suggested that this strike was orchestrated from without by the IRA, but, as I think the following hitherto unpublished letter from Sands himself makes clear, this was not the case.

The letter was written on a sheet of toilet tissue paper, in tiny lettering and smuggled out. Readers will need a little explanation as to some of its contents. For instance, 'Brownie' was Gerry Adams.

'Comm' is a communication. 'Rat' was the prison governor, Mr Stanley Hillditch'. 'Sid' was Sidney Breathnach, Sands's adjutant: 'Angel' was Father Brendan Meagher. 'The Germans' was probably a reference to a German Jesuit who was visiting the prison at the time and attempting to mediate. 'Marcella' was the name of Sands's sister, with which he often signed letters and statements. 'A move' was generally accompanied by violence as it involved forcibly washing the prisoners, often with wire brushes and carbolic soap, in water that was either too hot or too cold. The purpose was to move the prisoners to clean cells to allow the dirty ones to be cleaned up. Finally the reference to the IRSP, 'accept one on HS', illustrates the respect given to the hunger-striking tactic. It was felt that the IRSP prisoners deserved the honour of joining the hunger strike and Patsy O'Hara was the prisoner selected as a result of initiative.

14.1.81 5 p.m. Brownie.
Comrade: Got your comm (date 9 p.m. 13.1.81) read to me at pipe today at dinner. Then I asked for Rat directly after dinner lock-up (2.30 p.m.) saw him almost immediately with No. 2 Rat, A Chief and P/O. Now I went at him very delicately on clothes. I said relatives were confused and that we had considered statement telling only those in moved wings to bring up our clothes on Friday. I said perhaps we could avoid that by informing them personally etc. I went on to subtly suggest that simultaneous gesture of clothing would be handy to everyone and that we'd immediately wash upon receiving them. I read into his statement given to us to-day using the 'request of clothes' and 'encouragement to come off protest'. Now I didn't get to how could relatives best do this, i.e. deliver clothes, what amount etc. when I came under attack from the old attitude again. Firstly, the Rat called the simultaneous delivery farcical, but I beat that back and he said okay, I will forget the principle involved in that, and then said, but we must be clear, what will happen on Monday morning, will prisoners be standing at their doors in prison issue clothing? I said we're talking about a step by step procedure bla, bla, and tried to get off the point. He kept hitting me up the face with it. I said I don't know, it depends on what happens. He said your own clothing is a privilege, you're asking for a privilege before you declare that you are a conforming prisoner who is so available for industry work etc., etc. He asked me then, 'if you were to get clothes together would you be a conforming prisoner?' I said if we got clothes, and we washed and put clothes on we'd be nonprotesting prisoners. He questioned this. I elaborated, i.e. we'd not be on blanket/ non-wash. He quoted document, prisoners to come off protest

altogether and emphasized 'altogether' and repeated work etc. He mentioned education once and said that it was only for sub-normal people, i.e., remedial education. Any way comrade, I was throwing him every sort of chance and had to make my stand on having achieved clothes that is only a step and there must be further steps and suggestions, etc. I kept getting Secretary of State's statement on the prison regime shoved down my throat etc. At the end up, I said well what of the simultaneous clothes delivery and so on. He said he'd have to consider all this and that I should read Atkins' rubbish. He said he'd get back to me. I didn't try to get visit with Sid, the climate wasn't favourable. I was militant enough, but only when I had no choice. Rat said that as it stands now that anyone who leaves clothes in for prisoners will be leaving it in for to be held in reception until prisoner ends his protest.

So, there you have it, comrade. Now I'll comm Sid on this as soon as I can. My impressions were, they could have been seeking a major compromise on our behalf or weakness, but am more convinced that they are just downright intransigent, and want us at the very least off non-wash protest. We can't hold back for very long. Other 8 wings will be moved soon. So, I'll wait and see if Rat changes tune, (I doubt it). I was expecting Angel never saw him. I doubt if he has anything helpful. Screws in this block believe we're winning. Screws in H 5 the opposite. It's all my running around here does that. Still think Germans are trying to defuse issue. Got comm from IRSP accepting one on H/S. So 'if' we go (which I think we'll have to do) we'll go with 3 Provos and one IRSP. We thought that this morning's document, i.e. Rat's statement, left some manoeuvrability, shows you how wrong you can be. Yahoo!! Well, that's about it. Think you may hold statement on clothes now cause if they don't come across they'll just hold them in reception and people will think we have them. Okay, comrade, I'll get back to you.

Marcella XXXXX.

The fatal sparks were struck by the events of the weekend of Friday, 23 January 1981.

The prisoners were given to understand that a selected group of twenty men would wash, shave and have their hair cut, after which they would collect their own clothes for that weekend. The clothes were delivered at eleven o'clock on Friday morning by the prisoners' relatives. Sands contacted the Governor and formally told him that the prisoners wished to end the protest and wanted washing facilities and their own clothes. The Governor, Mr Stanley Hillditch, said he would reply later. After consultation Hillditch returned at two-thirty that afternoon with word that the men could wash and shave, though he added that they would not get their own clothes until there was 'strict conformity'. The washing and shaving went ahead and at four o'clock all should have been well. (According to prison rules the week ends on Friday and there is no prison work to be done after four o'clock.) The custom was that prisoners who conformed to regulations normally were allowed to wear their own clothes throughout the weekend. However, despite repeated requests, the prisoners were refused the clothes which their relatives had brought in. On 23 January Sands circulated a statement within the prison, which contained a clear warning of his intentions:

For our part we must realize that another hunger strike, should it collapse, would present the Movement with disastrous consequences. Therefore a second hunger strike cannot and will not end in defeat because as I have said before, when the balance of conformity outweighs that of resistance, then criminalization is indeed winning . . . So, comrades, once again under the duress of the British barbarity and in the ugly face of further British intransigence, we are forced to embark upon a hunger strike in the coming weeks. The announcement of this should be made public, along with the date, on Friday, 30 January. The number of hunger strikers shall be small, myself and three others, amongst them of course a representative of the IRSP . . .

I accept now that men will sacrifice their lives on this hunger strike. But you must all cast aside everything for total unity within these blocks – unity and steadfastness. You should, when a comrade dies, remain steadfast. Because, comrades, at the end of the day, men will die and the responsibility of ending this protest for once and for all will not lie with dead comrades, but with you. Because only your unflinching resistance and steadfastness will force an end to this protest.

Therefore, stand together and give your fullest support to the OC of these blocks. And in one way or another, comrades, victory will be ours, because we have the will to win. And we will win.

Just over a month later on 1 March 1981, Bobby Sands began his passage into Republican immortality. He was to be joined by nine others: Francis Hughes, Raymond McCreish, Patsy O'Hara (INLA), Joe McDonnell, Martin Hurson, Kevin Lynch, Kieran Doherty, Tom McElrea and Mickie Devine. They were all carefully screened before beginning the protest; there could be no oscillation between determination and despair, as in the McKenna case. The strikers came from each of the North's Six Counties and, in addition, they were outstanding figures within the Republican movement.

Everything that was known or could be ascertained about hunger striking was studied. The IRA even contacted a Palestinian who had survived a hunger and thirst strike for a lengthy period, so that his experiences could be put to use. The H Block committees were revived, though with some misgivings, because as always the IRA outside the prison was fearful that a collapse of the strike would have harmful effects on the movement as a whole. However, the temper of those outside proved to be almost as determined as that within, and despite its reservations Sinn Fein, having as I know from my own sources attempted and failed to dissuade the strikers from going ahead, gave its full support.

This time the strike was a staged affair, with prisoners joining at intervals; in all it lasted 217 days until officially being called off on 3 October 1981. By the time it ended Anglo-Irish relationships had been badly soured and Sinn Fein itself had come from behind to threaten to obliterate the SDLP. Its new leaders, Gerry Adams, Martin McGuinness, Danny Morrison, Joe Austin, Richard McAuley, Jim Gibney, Tom Hartley and Owen Carron persuasively talked their way into the public consciousness via television, newspapers and radio in a myriad of interviews. The character of Sands himself made a powerful impression on the country as a whole. The circumstances of his life and his treatment in Castlereagh could have served as the stereotype of the thousands of Catholic lads whom Sands came to symbolize in Northern Ireland.

Born in 1954, he lived with his Catholic, but not Republican, family in the predominantly Protestant district of Rathcoole, from where the family were driven by Loyalist gangs after the troubles escalated in the 1960s. Bobby Sands thus lost not only his home but his apprenticeship as a coach builder. They moved to Twinbrook where apparently after the Burntullet March intimidation of the family, combined with attacks on the People's Democracy marches, induced him to join the IRA at the age of eighteen. Shortly afterwards a number of guns were found in a house and Sands was charged with possession. He received three years in the cages of Long Kesh, where at that time Special Category Status was in full swing, and devoted his time to a programme of reading and learning Irish. After being released in 1976 he again became active in the IRA, married and had a son. The marriage did not last under the duress of the times but the affiliation with the IRA did. Sands became prominent in his district in the address of local grievances, edited a newspaper, *Liberty*, and developed the talent, which he later showed in Long Kesh, for producing articles and letters in great quantities. A good singer, much in demand at parties, and subsequently in jail for prison concerts, he appears to have become fascinated with the story of the skylark who, when placed in a cage, refused to sing. Its owner then covered the cage with a black cloth, so that eventually the bird died. Sands would later write a book which had a powerful effect on the younger members of the IRA in particular, *The Skylark Singing Her Lonely Song*, a compendium of his thoughts on prison experiences.

He went to jail again in October 1976, for his part in the fire bombing of the Balmoral Furniture Company. One of those involved with him in that operation was Joe McDonnell who, like Sands, would die on hunger strike in Long Kesh. Sands received the customary treatment in Castlereagh, a six-day programme of kicks and blows, sleep deprivation and lack of food aimed at producing a confession. He refused to sign this, and resolved that the important thing was not to give up. His companions of the time say that he found consolation in the Prophet Sirach: 'Blessed is he whose heart does not condemn him, and who does not give up hope.' He coined an Irish phrase which was to resound around the country, 'tiocfaidh ár lá' ('our day will come'), and constantly preached that the treatment of IRA prisoners was part of the British effort to criminalize the Nationalists outside the jail. No matter how bad the beatings or the pangs of hunger, the important thing was to withstand them as Terence McSwiney had done, and some day '*tiocfaidh ár lá*'. To Sands, as to thousands of young men of his type, life in a Nationalist ghetto was merely a sojourn in a larger prison while awaiting one's time to be picked up and sent via the 'Conveyor Belt' to the smaller prison of Long Kesh. Both systems had to be destroyed.

What was known about Sands's personality and record, and the fact of his being on hunger strike, made him an attractive candidate, and when the Sinn Feiners out-manoeuvred the SDLP into not contesting the vacant Fermanagh–South Tyrone seat after the death of Frank Maguire in March 1981, Sands was the sole candidate for the Nationalist vote. On 9 April, he won the seat. It was a media event of the first magnitude – the campaign had been closely followed by the world's press and TV cameras, Civil Rights-minded young people had come from as far away as America to campaign for him – and the publicity, his personality and the hunger strike combined to overcome reluctance that a vote for Sands was a vote for the IRA.

However, although he won political status at the polls, and died a member of the British parliament, he did not manage to move Margaret Thatcher. He continued his fast despite visits to his cell from members of the European parliament, the European Commission of Human Rights, and the Pope's private secretary, and the publicity attendant on refusals to grant permission to visit him to such notables as Ramsey Clark, the former United States Attorney General, or the American anti-Vietnam campaigner, Father Daniel Berrigan, SJ. He died on Tuesday, 5 May, and it is estimated that close to a hundred thousand people attended his funeral in West Belfast. All over the world his death was marked by signs of respect – in New Delhi, for example, the Indian parliament observed a minute's silence – but apart from Northern Ireland, it was in America that the hunger strike had the most lasting effect. The heightening of the consciousness of being Irish resulted in people of all classes rediscovering their ancestry, with tangible results. For instance, in 1985–86, opposition by Democratic Senators in the debate on the Anglo-Irish aid package significantly watered down the extradition clause so prized by Margaret Thatcher, so that the Republican Senators failed to link extradition to the Aid Bill in any meaningful way. It is worth noting here that apart from the constitutional clout shown by the Irish-American, the underground physical force factor is being increased almost daily by illegal immigration. Young people are going into America from both sides of the border on tourist visas and then disappearing into the Irish network to work in bars and on building sites. Some ultimately get 'green cards', most live just one jump ahead of the FBI and the social welfare system, unable to return home for a family wedding or funeral lest they are not allowed back again. These young people, many of whom are understandably bitter towards the society which educated them and then failed to provide them with employment, support revolutionary groups far more uncritically than they would, say, the SDLP or Fianna Fail.

The month after Sands died, hunger-striking candidates were proposed as candidates in the General Election called by Charles Haughey in the Republic. One of these, Kieran Doherty, was actually elected in County Cavan, and in a number of other constituencies, Fianna Fail's loss of the H Block vote was enough to turn the balance of power in favour of the Coalition. Margaret Thatcher still held firm.

One after another Sands's nine skeletal companions followed him to their graves. Eventually the strike was called off in circumstances of considerable controversy and bitterness, with Republicans contending that Father Faul had induced the families of hunger strikers to pressurize their men into ending it.

One of the ironies of the whole affair was that in so far as actual prison conditions were concerned, by December the prisoners had (*de facto* if not *de jure*) won most of the concessions for which the hunger strike was held. They were wearing their own clothes; they had 50% of the full remission they had sought (despite the fact that Lord Gardiner whose recommendation it was that the H Blocks should be built in the first place, had stipulated that it was essential that there should not be an 'amnesty' and the prisoners should serve their full sentences); prison work was confined to around ten things which they could agree to do or not, but only under orders from their own OC. They were allowed a form of 'association', so that some forty prisoners in a wing were able to gather at one time, in the presence of only five warders, which meant that prisoners could not be intimidated. They had the facility of leaving their cells every night for some two hours after dinner time, and also an hour's exercise in the fresh air during the day. Their command structure was recognized implicitly, though not officially, by the prison staff, a prisoner making a request did so through his OC, not directly to the Governor. And some of the more degrading customs of the jail which had had a bearing on the strike – the hated mirror search, for instance, in which prisoners were spreadeagled naked over a mirror so that an anal inspection could take place – were also abolished. In a word, much the same situation as had been reached in Portlaoise in 1977, and has continued with only intermittent hiccups of confrontation ever since, was also arrived at in Long Kesh, but only after ten deaths and far-reaching political changes.

29

The Test of the Ballot Box

The younger street-wise, Northern activists whom I mentioned as coming to the fore in Sinn Fein, had been pressing for the adoption of the *Green Book* philosophy by the Republican Movement as a whole. After the hunger strike, the largely abstentionist-minded Sinn Fein became not a mere appendage of the IRA, but a serious constitutional threat to the SDLP in Northern Ireland and, for a short time apparently, also to the constitutional parties in the Republic. The votes won by the nine H Block candidates who stood in the Republic during the June 1981 election totalled some 10.2% of the vote, though candidates stood under the banner of 'H Block'. In February 1982 Sinn Fein stood as a party in its own right, but its vote fell by over 50% in the June election; the party won no seats and did not contest the November 1982 election.

However, in the North the momentum of the hunger strike continued. The Northerners were, in fact, more keen on political action than the Southerners, and it was for this reason that at the 1981 Ard Fheis, Danny Morrison asked the celebrated rhetorical question: whether the delegates would object if Sinn Fein took power 'with a ballot box paper in one hand and an armalite in the other.' Many constitutionalists outside the Movement recoiled in horror at such a prospect but in Northern Ireland the argument served to reassure those who thought along the traditional lines, that seeking political power meant going soft on physical force. The next year's Ard Fheis again showed the influence of the Northerners' 'no sops to Loyalists' policy, and the Eire Nua Federal policy was dropped. A single unitary state was the preferred goal and the Ard Fheis passed unanimously a resolution which sought: 'that all candidates in national and local elections and all campaign material be unambivalent in support of the armed struggle'. The armalite was clutched in the hand as firmly as any ballot paper. The young tigers were cock-a-hoop at that Ard Fheis.

A week earlier Sinn Fein had taken just over 10% of all votes cast at the Northern Ireland Assembly Elections and the party went on to win 13.4% of all the votes – approximately 40% of the Nationalist vote – in the Westminster election in June 1983.

These external changes were reflected in the internal balance of power the following November when the Sinn Fein Ard Fheis saw Ruairi O'Bradaigh and Daithi O'Connell stand down as President and Vice President. Their stated reason was that as they were the main architects of the Aire Nua Federal policy opposed to Dail elections and taking seats in the European parliament, there was no point in continuing in their posts. The real reason was that the hunger strike had made out of Sinn Fein a Northern movement led by Northerners; and Gerry Adams and his cohorts were now firmly in the saddle. Adams, who personally defeated Gerry Fitt in the West Belfast Westminster election in June of that year, was a particularly potent figure, the equal of anyone who had come to the fore in constitutional politics, North or South of the Border. Highly politicized, with a background of the 'Republican University' and street politics, and an unusually well-developed gift for political analysis, Adams believed that the time was ripe for a Sinn Fein electoral onslaught on the Republic, given the widespread alienation, particularly of the young, from established parties as a result of unemployment. His analysis might well have been proved correct. Up to the time of the hunger strike the penetration of the Northern conflict throughout the island as a whole had been remarkably slight, given the size of the country and the scale of what had happened over the previous sixteen years. It seemed inevitable that at some stage the Northern knell would begin to toll in Southern constitutional policies.

However, shortly before Christmas 1983 the unacceptable face of Sinn Fein showed itself in the fatal events at Ballinamore, Co. Leitrim. Gardai and Army seeking to free the captured English industrialist Don Tidey were fired upon by IRA men and a Garda and a soldier were killed. Subsequently there was controversy as to whether at least one of these deaths was caused by blind shooting from their own side – there was considerable confusion amongst the security forces at the time – but the fact of the deaths themselves, combined with the revulsion felt throughout the island at the kidnapping, had the effect of creating a serious setback for Sinn Fein. Indeed, from that date it is true to say that Sinn Fein went backwards, winning only 4.9% of the vote in the June 1984 European parliament election, thus bringing home to Sinn Fein the difficulty of operating a national movement from North of the border. Accordingly, the Adams faction persuaded the November 1986 Sinn Fein Ard Fheis to drop the Abstention Policy, causing traditionalists led by Ruairi O'Bradaigh and Daithi O'Connell to set up a new movement: Republican Sinn Fein. Whatever chance this movement might have had of achieving any sort of success faded with the sudden death, from natural causes, of Daithi O'Connell, on New Year's Eve, 1990.

Writing in the prestigious American foreign policy journal *Foreign Affairs* in April 1986, the former American Ambassador to Ireland, William B. Shannon, an authoritative commentator on Irish and Irish-American affairs said:

> Prime Minister Thatcher, by refusing any of the graceful compromises that were offered to her by the Irish Catholic Bishops and other intermediaries early in the strike, may be seen by history to have made a major strategic error. The hunger strike was the greatest political propaganda coup for the IRA in the last decade.

Watching the rise of Sinn Fein in the early post hunger strike period, the British Government certainly did not make any public statement of agreement with Shannon's sentiment, or those of like-minded people, but it certainly acted as though it agreed. In particular James Prior, a leading 'wet' in Mrs Thatcher's Cabinet, who was appointed Secretary of State for Northern Ireland in 1981 and lasted there until 1984, decided that something new was called for.

Starting in the spring of 1982, Prior attempted to breathe life into at least that part of the Sunningdale Agreement which provided for a Power Sharing Executive. He worked to resurrect a Northern Ireland Assembly but did not seek as a prerequisite from those taking part that they would share power. The assembly was to start from small beginnings, to have legislative not executive powers, and to elect committees which would hold inquiries or examine Civil Servants. If this experiment were to succeed, the Committee Chairmen could, it was thought, evolve into full-blown Cabinet Ministers with Government Departments at their disposal. This experiment in 'Rolling Devolution'* as it was known, was in fact the brainchild of a

---

* The idea was that the committee deal would 'roll on' to a stage where the province would achieve full devolution with the exception of London's control over security.

Unionist-minded Tory back-bencher Dr Brian Mawhinney, who in fact became a Minister in the Assembly. Unionists of all stripes eventually agreed to co-operate, while Sinn Fein said it would contest the-elections but boycott the Assembly. The influence of Sinn Fein at the time was such that the SDLP followed suit and also declared a boycott.

The SDLP's position requires some explanation as it illustrates how the hunger strike impacted on the larger political scene outside Sinn Fein's own particular following. As I indicated earlier, the intervention of H Block candidates cost Fianna Fail the 1981 General Election. It also cost Dublin, or London, depending how one looks at it, the friendship of the other administration. Early in his Premiership, on 21 May 1980, Haughey had gone to Downing Street and presented Mrs Thatcher with a Georgian silver teapot. After their meeting, which according to him had gone swimmingly, particularly their *tête-à-tête* session, glowing accounts of progress between the two leaders were put out by Haughey.

Those who, like myself, thought they were too glowing and overly optimistic had their doubts somewhat reassured when the most tangible evidence of Haughey's claims emerged in the shape of a top-level delegation visiting Dublin in December 1980, after which one of the most far-reaching communiqués in the history of Anglo-Irish relations was issued. Prime Minister Thatcher was accompanied by Lord Carrington, Sir Geoffrey Howe, and Humphrey Atkins; Haughey, by his Deputy Taoiseach, Brian Lenihan, the Minister of Foreign Affairs, and by Michael O'Kennedy, the Minister for Finance. The communiqué noted that the meeting had been the first agreed in the May summit and spelt out a wide range of national and international issues on which the two Governments agreed to cooperate, but the key was the sixth paragraph.

> They accordingly decided to devote their next meeting in London during the coming year to special consideration of the *totality of relationships* [my italics] within these islands. For this purpose they have commissioned joint studies, covering a range of issues including possible institutional structures, citizens rights, security matters, economic co-operation and measures to encourage mutual understanding.

That paragraph contained the seed of subsequent Anglo-Irish developments but, for the time being at least, it was blown out of the water by the issue referred to in paragraph seven – H Blocks, concerning which the two leaders merely reiterated the hope that 'the issues could be resolved'.

In the event they were not. After the December meeting Haughey said in a speech typical of his rhetoric of the period that what had happened had been an 'historic breakthrough which did not rule out *any* possibility including a new type of federal or confederal arrangement involving Ireland, Britain and Northern Ireland'. Mrs Thatcher said at her press conference, however, that there was 'absolutely no possibility of a confederation flowing from the agreements reached'. Despite this, in Anglo-Irish relationships, fairly predictable disagreement on what words meant, all sides agreed that a very significant step had been taken and pointed unofficially, in the off-the-record briefings to journalists, to the fact that it was hoped that by the time the next Summit was held the following June, substantive proposals would have been worked out for signature. By next June however, Anglo-Irish relationships were at their worst since the de Valera-Churchill animosities of the Second World War.

The H Block issue had cost Haughey his Premiership and so embittered him that when he regained it the following February (1982), he stood aside from the EEC support for Britain in the Falklands War, directing the Irish delegation at the UN to abstain also, which meant in effect that Ireland was opposing sanctions against Argentina. He also criticized the Prior Assembly, saying that Northern Ireland was a 'failed political entity' requiring direct Dublin and London talks leading to reunification to resolve the problem. With Sinn Fein (also favouring unity) riding high in the opinion polls and popularity stakes of the time, the SDLP leader, John Hume, tacitly concurred with this view, and turned his attention from the Assembly and Prior's efforts to a campaign aimed at getting a new consensus from the South and from constitutional politicians in Northern Ireland and Britain. A tall order, but one he went very far with.

Hume got on better with Jack Lynch and Garret FitzGerald than he did with Haughey. Therefore he was probably aided in his efforts by the fact that Haughey again fell from power in November 1982, and FitzGerald returned once more as Prime Minister. At all events, Hume succeeded in getting all-party agreement to his ideas so that on 14 April 1983, Fianna Fail, Fine Gael, Labour and the SDLP met to announce that they were setting up a Forum to examine the realities of a United Ireland. The Unionist parties boycotted the proceedings and Sinn Fein, whose success had occasioned the whole thing, was deliberately not invited. The deliberations, held in Dublin Castle, were to be for constitutionalists only: the armalite had to be laid aside while the test of the ballot box was being applied.

The initiative was probably somewhat oversold as it could not of itself produce anything – substantive progress, of course, depended on London – but there was something high-minded about the whole affair which caught the Irish public's imagination. The reports of economic policy, the legal systems North and South, the cost of violence, the cost of the division of Ireland since 1920, and all the other matters which the Forum went into in its eleven months of painstaking analysis earned respect. In particular, the fact that all the Nationalist parties took part in the discussion had a comparable effect on public opinion as would have occurred in England had the Conservatives, Labour, and Alliance parties participated in a single political task.

Accordingly, when the Forum reported its major findings on 2 May 1984, there was considerable expectation in Ireland that something was going to happen as a result. It defined three possible models for a New Ireland, the most favoured being a unitary state governed from Dublin. Alternatives were a federation or confederation of the two parts of Ireland, something along the lines of the Haughey-Thatcher communiqué of 1981, or joint authority in which Britain and Ireland would share the governance of the North. But the Forum also pledged itself to 'remain open to discuss other views which may contribute to political development', in the unrealized expectation that the Unionists might want to come forward even at that late stage.

The Unionists, of course, never did. There was some initial skirmishing after the Forum report was published, Haughey contending that the only resolution acceptable to Fianna Fail was the unitary option. On 2 July 1984, just two months after the report had been published, Prior, who had announced that he was leaving the North of Ireland Secretaryship and the Government to go into business, opened the North of Ireland debate in the House of Commons. Mrs Thatcher sat beside him as if to underline the importance of what he had to say. In a few paragraphs he indicated that none of the three major options defined by the Forum was likely to receive British Governmental support, though he angled for Dublin co-operation on security and there were indications that the joint sovereignty option might be a runner. This was the most dangerous course from Dublin's point of view because it involved the South in the responsibility of security without giving it the authority to control organizations such as the UDR and the RUC.

Senior Civil Servants continued the discussions in Dublin and London throughout the summer and autumn, and finally at yet another Anglo-Irish Summit on 18 and 19 November in London, FitzGerald and Thatcher met again. Mrs Thatcher, as always, was determined that Britain retain its sovereignty in Northern Ireland, and her major concern at the time was that the Ulsterization policy should continue. However, while the communiqué issued by the two leaders did not build anything substantial on the Forum workings, neither did it diminish the status of the exercise.

At their subsequent press conference, however, a chasm opened. While FitzGerald was clearly concerned to keep the talks alive at all costs, Mrs Thatcher displayed all the intransigence which she had shown over the hunger strike issue itself – with this difference: she did it before Irish television cameras. Speaking of the three models put forward by the New Ireland Forum she said: 'I have made it quite clear, and so did Mr Prior, when he was Secretary of State, that a unified Ireland was one thing that was *out*. A second solution was a confederation system: that was *out*. A third solution was joint authority: that is *out*.'

I can speak with some authority when I say that for once the vast majority of the Irish people agreed with the editorial I wrote in the *Irish Press* for the next day, in which I said that Mrs Thatcher managed to make 'out' sound like a four-letter word.

Not only was constitutional Irish public opinion outraged; Mrs Thatcher was criticized internationally, particularly in America. Gradually the realization sank in in Whitehall that she had made a mistake and that as a result Garret FitzGerald was damaged. They met again in Milan in June 1985, at a European Community Conference and FitzGerald took the opportunity to impress on her how damaging to the SDLP and beneficial to Sinn Fein her attitude had been.

She got the same message from Washington. It was pointed out to her, by a friendly administration into the bargain, that if she failed to find an accommodation with the moderate Hume or FitzGerald she was unlikely to find it with any Irish politician. Accordingly she went back to the drawing board. Negotiations recommenced between top-level British and Irish Civil Servants. On the British side the team was led by Sir Robert Armstrong, the head of the British Civil Service, a man of considerable ability and one whose observation of the Unionists' behaviour over the years at close quarters had not endeared him to their cause. On the Irish side the team was led by the able Sean Donlon, Secretary of the Department of Foreign Affairs, who was close to both FitzGerald and Hume – so much so that Haughey, when in office, once tried unsuccessfully to shift him from his post as Irish Ambassador to Washington.

What the two teams worked out between them, and eventually unveiled at Hillsborough Castle outside Belfast (symbolically the former seat of the Governors of Northern Ireland) on 15 November 1985, was another version of the Forum's joint sovereignty option based on the 'totality of relationships' clause in the December 1980 Dublin Communiqué. Haughey rejected the agreement immediately, saying it was a 'sell-out', thus bringing to a head a party split, and Mr Desmond O'Malley left, taking three other deputies with him to found a new party, the Progressive Democrats. Nationalist opinion North and South of the border, however, was more welcoming and Haughey eventually modified his position.

The Hillsborough Agreement provided for an Irish Minister being designated as the permanent Irish Ministerial Representative, with the British Secretary of State for Northern Ireland as co-Chairman of an inter-governmental conference which was to meet at Maryfield not far from the sacred precincts of Stormont itself. The conference was to discuss all matters of interest to both North and South, to meet at 'regular and frequent' intervals, and the Agreement stipulated that 'the United Kingdom Government accept that the Irish Government will put forward views and proposals on matters relating to Northern Ireland'.

So far as Unionists were concerned the plain meaning of the Agreement was that an Irish Minister and Dublin Civil Servants were North of the border as of right, Dublin accents could be heard in Stormont as of right, and after all the years of murder and mayhem on the part of the IRA, the Fenians and their Dublin allies had at long last triumphed. In fact the Agreement stipulated that there was to be no change in the constitutional position of Northern Ireland for so long as the majority wished to remain in the United Kingdom. Apart from thus consenting to legitimize partition in an Agreement which was more-over to be lodged at the United Nations, the Irish Government also had to swallow the bitter pill of being seen in the Nationalist community to take responsibility for the UDR, the 'Diplock' courts, strip-searching in Armagh and such like, without having the power to address these grievances – in effect this was the joint sovereignty option by another name. However, the Nationalist community perceived that whatever was making the Unionists mad must have something in it to make *them* joyful, and at this time it was difficult to say what the long-term outcome of the accord would be.

As a respected UDA confidant of mine said: 'Look, you surely don't think any of our people *read* the Agreement, do you? We don't have to. We *know* what's in it.' Obviously it represented, for the Protestant community, a high-water mark of Nationalist influence, at least on the symbolic front.

The Unionist response was to withdraw from Westminster immediately on learning the Agreement's contents and to organize a series of protests at every level throughout the Province. Broadly speaking these may be defined as falling in stages into three categories, all equally ineffectual:

1. Withdrawal from Westminster and from participation in County Councils, Corporations and so forth.
2. A campaign of civil disobedience.
3. A campaign of violence, including violence directed against Southern targets.

The earlier stages were not long lasting and the last stage was not reached, although it was abundantly telegraphed by statements from Loyalist spokesmen and by deeds such as the continual intimidation of RUC men who sought to uphold the Agreement and the burning out of policemen's families in Protestant areas.

Where Sinn Fein was concerned, the effect was not long lasting either. British determination overcame RUC recalcitrance – the three RUC men who appeared on British television on 21 April 1986, wearing masks and saying that they would not uphold the Hillsborough Accord, were not reflective of a general resolve within the force. As briefers on the Accord put it in Dublin and London, the aim was to give the 'alienated' Nationalist supporters something to look forward to (code for 'win support back from Sinn Fein').

I am aware from contacts in the Gardai and in the Army that UVF cars were seen, presumably on scouting missions, in the vicinity of police and military installations on the Republic side of the border. It is very difficult to work out which strand of Loyalism actually means what. I have given above the three main Loyalist responses to the Agreement. The people making these responses may be sub-divided as follows.

On 23 January 1986, the election necessitated by the withdrawal of the Unionists from Westminster gave them 418,000 votes, a seeming rebuff as both Paisleyites and the official Unionists had called for a poll of 500,000 votes. In the election they actually lost a seat to Seamus Mallon, Deputy Leader of the SDLP. Constitutional Nationalists now had two forceful and articulate spokesmen at Westminster, John Hume being the other. (One question posed here, of course, is what would happen to the remaining fourteen Unionist seats should a hung parliament loom. Would these return to whichever party promised to scuttle the hated Agreement?) On the actual ground level, however, the 418,000 votes were less significant in themselves than which strand of Unionism would win out. Currently the hard men of the UDA and of bodies such as the Ulster Clubs, which have sprang up just as did the Ulster Loyalist Council in the wake of the Sunningdale Agreement, are the actual motor force of militant 'Loyalism'. It is they, not the Democratic Unionist Party led by Ian Paisley and his increasingly thrustful Deputy Peter Robinson, nor the Official Unionist Party led by Jim Molyneaux, which count. However, it should be noted that Robinson distinguished, or disgraced himself, depending on how one looks at it, by being arrested by Gardai in the company of a group of marked, cudgel-carrying men who took over the border town of Clontibret on the Republic side of the border at 2 a.m. one night, thereby, of course, terrifying the inhabitants of that County Monaghan town. The invasion was ostensibly staged to highlight security lacunae, but at the time, in August 1986, Ian Paisley was abroad. Paisley returned to the subsequent court hearing so promptly that it was widely commented that he was concerned about Robinson's stunt – a highly dangerous one in the tense border area – not because of its physical dangers but because of its political one to his leadership. The initial court hearing sparked off riots in Dundalk. The affair ultimately ended in farce. Robinson, who had been reported as intending to refuse to pay his fine, ultimately escaped any consequences of his action. Someone paid the fine anonymously. Robinson added to his unsavoury reputation after the American raids on Baghdad in June 1993. He proposed that the RAF should emulate the American example and bomb what he termed the 'IRA strongholds' in Dublin and elsewhere in the Republic. It was a highly irresponsible piece of incitement at any time, but doubly so coming during the North's traditionally perfervid 'marching season'. But certainly Clontibret was the first occasion on which any Westminster MP led a paramilitary invasion into the Republic's territory. Meanwhile, in the underworld of Loyalism a debate raged as to whether the correct course to follow is UDI; a repartition; closer integration with Britain – or outright sectarian warfare. The outcome of Northern Ireland's present ceasefire will be dependent to a large extent on which of these schools of thought wins. Ominously, the years 1991–3 showed a decided tilt towards the sectarian option. But, more promisingly, the internal debate following the loyalist paramilitaries' emulation of the Provisionals' ceasefire in 1994 has shown a less sanguinary orientation, and a tilt towards 'the peace-niks', as one leading loyalist described the current paramilitary leadership to me.

But should either orange or green peace-niks lose out the IRA always maintain the capacity to create a crisis unexpectedly. It could not strike a decisive blow at the British to achieve its objective, nor could the British crush the organization, a familiar pattern, as readers of these pages will by now have grasped. Personally, I doubted that the IRA or Sinn Fein could be defeated. They must be part of any settlement which brings a final resolution to the Northern agony. As readers have seen already in the interview with the IRA leader 'Pat' and will see later in the extracts from the *Green Book*, the 'army' was stripped down for a long hard war. And the statistics show that six months after the Accord was signed, one of its main effects was thwarted already: the hope that Unionist opposition could be overcome through increased Garda-RUC cooperation, resulting in a defeat for the IRA. The IRA killed more than two dozen members of the security forces in that time and the tempo of attacks, both shootings and bombings, was stepped up after an initial three months' lull, during which the strategists digested the effects of the Agreement. The Army Council had obviously deduced correctly that these could be withstood.

Things would have been different had Mrs Thatcher allowed Bobby Sands the right to wear his own clothes while he was a prisoner in Long Kesh Jail.

30

Bombs in Britain and Counter-Insurgency

Let us turn our attention to some of the other principal developments caused or influenced by the Republicans in the period 1980–86.

Unquestionably the major event was the hunger strike and its chain reaction effect of bringing about the Anglo-Irish Accord of November 1985. But other incidents also had a bearing in bringing about that Accord, occurrences in England, the Brighton bombing in particular, the Harrods bombing and the attack on Chelsea Barracks. In Ireland the 'highlights' of those years, if that is the correct term, included a spate of kidnappings, sometimes with fatal results, the massive jail break from Long Kesh, attacks on security forces, such as the mortar bombing of Newry Barracks, the seizure of the *Marita Ann*'s cargo of arms off the Kerry Coast; and one must also take note of the depredations of the INLA, the bombing at the Droppin' Well in Ballycastle, Co. Down, the Darkley Massacre and the great controversy surrounding the extradition of the INLA leader Dominic McGlinchey. All of these will be examined in the following pages, but let us begin with the British bombing campaign.

Curiously, it was the bomb which claimed the lives of animals as well as people that created the greatest controversy of the period. On 20 July 1982, two bombs detonated in London killed a total of eleven soldiers, four of them members of the Household Cavalry and seven members of a band of the Royal Greenjackets.

The Cavalry were ambushed by a bomb set off by a radio signal in Hyde Park, which contained 25lbs of gelignite and about 30lbs of nails. This killed and maimed a number of horses, which seemed to create as great an outrage both in England and Ireland as the deaths of the soldiers. In Dublin the Royal Dublin Society replaced the horses which had been destroyed, and some £50,000 were raised, apart from the RDS gesture, for the families of the soldiers.

I happened to be in London the week after the explosions. People were still laying wreaths on the spot in Hyde Park where the horses were killed, but I saw no signs of activity in Regent's Park where the bandsmen were blown up. My strongest impression at the time was the remarkable lack of anti-Irish feeling that my Irish accent elicited, even though the TV pictures, nightly it seemed, carried pictures and reports of the surviving horses' condition, giving these greater prominence than the medical bulletins for the surviving soldiers.

Eight days before Christmas 1983, a car bomb exploded outside Harrods, one of the world's best-known stores, claiming the lives of six people and injuring ninety others, some of them very drastically – PC John Gordon, for instance, lost a leg in the blast. Apart from horrifying the public all over the world, this cruelly underlined the deep-rooted nature of the IRA problem. Hans Crescent, where the bomb was planted is just around the corner from Hans Place, where the Irish delegation stayed in 1921 during the Treaty negotiations which were supposed to have solved the Irish problem once and for all. Exactly why that target was chosen during that week has never satisfactorily been explained. Did the planners of the raid deliberately set out to take life in a shocking context and at a particularly shocking time? A quite high-ranking Republican figure did flatly say to me that it was 'deliberate'. However, while there was a continuing desire to export as much of the terror and destruction of the Northern conflict as is possible to the British mainland, it must be said that this theory, like much else about the IRA, remains to be proven.

Other IRA apologists told me that the bombing was just 'a job that went wrong', one of the inevitabilities of war. They pointed to the fact that Natalino Vella, a Dublin fish and chip merchant who was sentenced at the Old Bailey on 7 March 1985 to fifteen years on a variety of arms charges, was apparently an IRA 'quartermaster' who had been sent over to London especially to find out what had gone wrong with the Harrods bombing and to order the unit responsible back to Ireland. Mr Justice McCowan, who sentenced Vella, also condemned Paul Kavanagh and Thomas Quigley, both of Belfast, to thirty-five years in prison on the same occasion. They were found guilty of the Ebury Bridge nail-bomb blast near Chelsea Barracks on 10 October 1981, which killed a widow, Mrs Nora Field, and a teenager, John Patrick Breslin, instead of the intended victims, Irish Guardsmen returning to their barracks in a bus. Mr Ken Howorth, a bomb disposal expert, was killed on 26 October, when a bomb which Kavanagh and Quigley were accused of setting went off in an Oxford Street Wimpy

Bar. The Judge also found them guilty of the attempted bombing of Debenhams in Oxford Street, also in October, and of the explosion at the Attorney General's Wimbledon home on 13 November.

The police believed that it was an IRA unit run by Kavanagh which planted the Harrods bomb. Apparently they stumbled on the unit more or less by accident when estate workers at Pangbourne, Berkshire, discovered an arms cache in which Kavanagh's and Quigley's fingerprints were found, along with the car keys used in the Chelsea Barracks bombing. When Vella came over to London after the Harrods bombing he walked into a police trap. He had ordered Quigley and Kavanagh to show him where their arms and explosives were hidden; police tailed them to two dumps, one at Salcey Forest in Northants. and another at Annesley Forest in Nottinghamshire, where they found what the prosecuting Counsel described at the Old Bailey as 'a comprehensive collection of terrorist hardware'. In his statement, Vella, whom the prosecution alleged had supplied 'the terrorist hardware' for the 1983 campaign, said that he had not known that Harrods was to be a target. 'I would rather hit the economy of England than see people killed,' he said. 'Things went badly wrong. The unit stepped outside its instructions. There was a lot of trouble about Harrods. We didn't want all those people killed. We didn't know if they had given the general forty-five-minute warning. Anyhow it shouldn't have been the target.'

This pretty comprehensive disavowal would, I know, be in line with a good deal of IRA thinking on the outrage, but where such statements are concerned in an era of Castlereagh-type interrogations and super-grasses, one has to be somewhat wary of accepting statements at their face value. However, there is no doubt that there was no division whatever within the IRA over the target chosen for the attack on 12 October 1984: the Grand Hotel in Brighton, at which Mrs Thatcher and members of her cabinet were staying during the British Tory Conference. There were five people killed in the blast: Sir Anthony Berry, Tory MP; Mrs Roberta Wakeham, wife of the Conservative Chief Whip; Mrs Jeanne Shattock, wife of the Chairman of the Party's western area; Mr Eric Taylor; and Mrs Muriel MacLean.

Apart from the deaths and the television footage showing the victims being recovered, notably Mr Norman Tebbit whose wife was very badly injured in the blast, the idea that the entire British Cabinet had nearly been wiped out by the IRA traumatized people both in England and Ireland and caused considerable alarm as to the possible repercussions. Mrs Thatcher herself only escaped by a hair's breadth: she had used the bathroom which took the full brunt of the explosion only minutes before the bomb went off. The IRA could have planted the bomb at the previous year's Tory Conference but decided that their chances of a major coup were better if they waited until Mrs Thatcher herself would be reasonably certain to be in the line of the blast. One of the brutal simplicities of terrorism is that despite intelligence, counter-insurgency and sophisticated equipment of all sorts, it is virtually impossible to guard against the obvious. In this case the world and his wife knew with certainty that the one place during the year that anyone could be sure of finding Mrs Thatcher was at the hub of her own Party Conference. The idea of hitting the British Government is not new in Republican circles. During the Anglo-Irish War, for instance, Cathal Brugha devised a scheme which involved taking a suicide squad into the House of Commons and mowing down the front bench. Individual members of any British Administration who deal with Ireland can incur an outstanding amount of opprobrium – for instance, Mr Roy Mason is still very badly thought of by Republicans and others. The Brighton blast was the result of more than simply a desire to 'get the people responsible'. It was a direct and calculated response to Mrs Thatcher's handling of the hunger strike and was intended to avenge the deaths of the ten strikers. It was also an underlining of a cardinal feature of IRA strategy.

Speaking to me in 1986, an Army Council spokesman said: 'We can't be beaten; there is no question of us winning in the sense of driving the British Army into the sea. But we always maintain the capacity to bring the situation to a crisis at some stage.'

In the wake of such a deep-rooted problem it is inevitable that the innocent of all sides suffer along with the guilty. I referred earlier (see Chapter 19) to the treatment of Irish prisoners in England and to the fact that claims of innocence had been made by those convicted for serious crimes. In my interview with the Army Council spokesman I raised this issue and was categorically assured, as I had been on earlier occasions, that the prisoners in jail for the Birmingham and Guildford bombings were totally innocent. This claim was not new – this had been the contention of Civil Rights campaigners like Father Faul for several years and there had been sporadic media interest in the subject but the conversation revealed details, known to the authorities for years, which made me realize how immoral the cover-up had been and the scale of the injustice suffered by the victims.

While those serving long sentences, as in the Birmingham and Guildford cases, are the worst examples, it is also true that the inevitable prejudice excited by the IRA had resulted in some very small-minded and unjust actions being carried out against Irish prisoners. Strip-searching in Armagh jail for instance, has apparently been employed as a tool to break the prisoners' morale and is seen by the Northern Ireland Office in much the same light as the issue of prison uniforms was during the hunger strike.

The official reason for the introduction of strip-searching in Armagh jail in November 1982 was given in Hansard on 15 March 1983: 'On 22 October in the course of a detailed search of cells two keys were found in the possession of two remand prisoners.' Since then, however, prisoners have been searched, not merely on admission to the prison, or before, or after, a court appearance when there might be a possibility of something being smuggled to them, but on random occasions when they have not left the prison for weeks or had any visitors. According to statistics provided by the Irish Information Partnership in November 1985, the prisoners were searched thirty times per capita of the average number of inmates between 1982 and 1985. According to the prisoners themselves the number of searches was much higher and the women in particular regarded it as a direct tool of humiliation. They described being asked to remove sanitary towels or tampons and place them in a bag while the search was in progress; being searched while five and six months pregnant; and there were also ancillary complaints such as the searching of members of their families, including children, during prison visits. Independent witnesses such as the Tribunal on Strip-Searching, set up by the Irish Trade Union Movement in Dublin and comprising not only trade unionists but academics, politicians, clergy and journalists (including myself), established that the allegations were broadly true.

One can imagine the impact of this practice on two girls in Brixton Prison, Martina Anderson and Ella O'Dwyer, who were remanded on charges of conspiracy to cause explosions in Britain and found guilty on 11 June 1986. It was accepted in Ireland that these girls were strip-searched hundreds of times during their period on remand. The authorities may have stated otherwise but this belief was strongly reinforced by the continuing impact of the Maguire family saga. I referred earlier to the Guildford affair. The controversy surrounding this heated up in Ireland in April 1985, when the prestigious RTE current affairs programme *Today Tonight* screened a two-hour investigation of the trial which had linked the Maguire family to the bombing. Subsequently the programme led to the case being examined on Channel 4 and on Yorkshire Television.

In the programme, the *Today Tonight* team led by editor Joe Mulholland, proved through the interviewing of expert witnesses that the evidence which convicted the Maguire family was extremely shaky. The prosecution case centred exclusively on scientific tests which 'proved' that there were traces of explosives on the defendants. However, the tests were carried out by a seventeen-year-old apprentice and the results could never be challenged as the samples were destroyed in the process. Even Dr Yallop, the scientist who invented the test, said that it was not reliable evidence as cigarettes or household cleaning agents could have given similar readings. Nevertheless the Maguires were sentenced in a trial in which the prosecution admitted that no explosives were ever found. Despite this anomaly Annie Maguire served nine years of a fourteen-year sentence imposed in 1976 when she was forty years of age. Her husband Patrick, her sons Vincent and Patrick, her brother William Joseph Smith, her brother-in-law Patrick Giuseppe Conlon, who died serving his sentence, and a family friend Patrick O'Neill, were all found guilty at the Old Bailey of possessing nitroglycerine. The Maguires were devastated by the trial and lived for several months in great penury after Annie was released in February 1985. Their flat in Kilburn had no furniture and they encountered bureaucratic difficulties in getting council grants.

Understandably all this had considerable impact on Irish public opinion, and particularly Northern Irish public opinion. Out of such dragons teeth issues have IRA men traditionally sprung.

The efforts to curb the IRA have resulted in some tactics being employed which would not be countenanced elsewhere in Western Europe, and can only be justified in counter-insurgency terms, not legal ones. One of the best known and most odious of these is the use of so-called 'supergrasses'.

The supergrass phenomenon was first seen in action in the trial of four IRA men who in March 1980 were sent away on the word of an informer, Stephen McWilliams. Later that year, in September, another one, James Kennedy, put twelve more men behind bars.

Supergrasses who retracted their evidence have mentioned astronomical sums of money being offered to them if they implicate Republicans. One such, David Lean, told reporters that he was offered £300,000 to implicate Gerry Adams, Danny Morrison and Martin McGuinness. 'The sky was the limit' was how he termed his offers. But this is only the start. After the supergrass has done his work he has to be protected for the rest of his life. The RUC say that the police can only offer an informer a top payment of £5,000 and that the rest comes from British intelligence, from the so-called 'reptiles fund' which pays for the informer's new life abroad, including a new name, new home and a new face with plastic surgery.

Giving details of such figures in March 1985, the Northern Ireland Secretary, Mr Douglas Hurd, said that in the previous seven years the British Government had spent almost £1½ million in protecting and resettling informers who gave evidence in court. He said this figure represented total 'direct expenditure' for such items as paid information, hotels, living allowances, pocket money, assistance in finding accommodation and jobs abroad, but the total cost must be far higher. By March 1985 there had been twenty-seven supergrasses who were given total immunity for their own crimes in order to implicate others but Hurd's figures only referred to eight of the twenty-seven, who by that time had *disappeared* to start new lives abroad under new names, but very much under the same old dread. His figures did not include such 'indirect spending' as wages and overtime for the RUC men assigned to rehearse the supergrasses in their evidence pre-trial – often in luxury hotels out of the country – and the amount spent afterwards in guarding not only the informers themselves, but their relatives. It was known by March 1985 that the taxpayer had spent more than £5 million on court costs alone for these trials. One case, that of Christopher Black, whose evidence convicted thirty-five people on IRA-linked charges, cost £600,000.

The supergrasses' evidence, which the 'Diplock' courts naturally accept *without corroboration*, became less valuable as community and other pressures built up.

In a fourteen-month period during the years 1980–81 the IRA executed six men they found guilty of informing and in their own words 'took less drastic action against others' (anything from kneecapping to exile). Of the first twenty-seven supergrasses, from the years

1980–85, fifteen retracted their evidence, and Lord Gifford, himself a former judge, said in a report on the system published in 1984 that the supergrass system was 'not justice', that it led to 'telling of lies' and to the conviction of the innocent. He accepted the fact that the RUC regularly programmed supergrasses to 'concoct and rehearse statements'.

Lord Gifford's view was echoed by Mr Justice Higgins, who described one 'supergrass', William 'Budgie' Allan, as a 'liar' and threw out charges, based on his 'evidence', against forty-four Loyalists who were brought to trial in 1983. The waste of money and time involved in this trial can only be guessed at. Nevertheless, Allan, a former UVF activist who at the time of the trial was serving a fourteen-year sentence on a total of fifty-two charges, including attempted murder, was granted the Royal Prerogative of Mercy by the Secretary of State for Northern Ireland, Mr Tom King, on 11 May 1986, following a deal done between Allan and the Chief Constable, Sir John Hermon.

The supergrass system thus differs from the ordinary use of informers, who are, of course, also used in the Province, though merely as spies to collect information. The RUC adopted the system after they began to find it increasingly difficult to obtain confessions in the absence of full internment (a variant of which still exists: internment by remand) and institutionalized torture, which was ruled out in the wake of reports by Amnesty International, the European courts and the Bennett Report. It comes in for heavy criticism for reasons other than the use of uncorroborated evidence. Many of those used either to manufacture or to give evidence were themselves convicted killers who thus got immunity from their crimes. However, in the early stages of the system the RUC and the Unionists were able to weather the storm by pointing to the number of suspects rounded up; by March 1983 there were three hundred behind bars of whom eighty-two were actually convicted. Privately Unionists were cock-a-hoop at such results. One prominent Unionist politician said to me in London at a convivial occasion one evening: 'The Republican Army has always been vulnerable to informers. We have them now – that is if the Rescue Brigade, the do-gooders like yourself, don't manage to bugger up things!'

The Chief Constable, Sir John Hermon (Annual Report 1985) was more restrained. He said that the 'converted terrorist process', as he termed it, 'undoubtedly dealt a severe blow to the morale of both Republican and Loyalist terrorist organizations and to their ability to murder and destroy'. He claimed that in one area of Belfast alone, 'terrorist murders dropped by 73% and all terrorist crimes by 61% following information supplied by this process'.

But it was neither the activities of the 'Rescue Brigade', nor of Lord Gifford, who recommended that trial by jury should be restored, albeit with safeguards for the security and identities of jury members – that dealt the supergrass process a telling blow. This came when supergrasses themselves began to retract their evidence. The RUC attempted to counteract this failure of nerve by invoking an archaic legal measure, the Bill of Indictment, which had the effect of bypassing the customary preliminary hearing of evidence so that defendants were automatically returned for trial, thereby giving the police a fresh chance to apply psychological tactics on the waverer.

At present, the supergrass tactic, while much diminished in effectiveness, is still in operation. It was revealed by a Northern Ireland spokesman during August 1986, that since the previous month 'the four remaining supergrasses who were serving jail terms are now held at Maghaberry'. Behind this bland statement lies an astonishing tale of expense, deceit, and muddle. Maghaberry took ten years to build, and cost £40 million, but, at the time of the statement, the prison, situated some twenty miles from Belfast, housed nobody but the four supergrasses as the Government still felt it was insufficiently secure. However, the supergrasses probably didn't complain. They had been housed in a specially designed cell block containing private bathrooms, gym, library, and other comforts such as arm-chairs, videos and television. Although these four must have been the most at risk, both from Loyalists and the IRA enemies, of any prisoners in the world, they were probably better off than their twenty or so counterparts who lived in Britain because other countries of their choice had refused to take them.

Both inside and outside prison the wretched supergrasses were both a symptom and a cause of the disease they were intended to cure: the poisonous political scene in Northern Ireland.

31

Action in Ireland

If the hunger strikes displayed the 'acceptable' face of the IRA, on the other side of the coin were the detestable features of kidnapping. The need to provide the sinews of war and the attrition of the security forces campaign drove kidnapping further up the Movement's scale of priorities, especially at times when certain personalities, people less susceptible to the nuances of Irish public opinion than other, more experienced members of the Army Council might have been, held particular influence. Alongside this unwelcome development was the fact that criminal gangs sometimes got in on the act so that a spate of actual or threatened kidnappings accompanied the IRA campaign, particularly from 1979 onwards, when the exigencies of the time seemed to have overcome the revulsion caused by the Herrema affair four years earlier. In that year there was a series of raids in Dublin and Wicklow directed at the families of bank managers, and money was paid over before the Gardai became involved. This type of extortion had been common in the North for a long time, though it was officially denied by the banks. It attracted widespread publicity when in December 1979 the Gardai succeeded in rescuing Mrs Margaret Fennelly, the wife of a Cobh bank manager, before a ransom of £60,000 could be paid. Two years later they captured a gang with extremely dubious political connections which had sought to extort £100,000 from Mrs Anne Hudson of Enniscorthy, Co. Wexford, who had been kidnapped in Courtown. Mrs Hudson was eventually discovered in a flat in my own area of Glenageary, Co. Dublin. Later that year the Gardai were paid a back-handed tribute when the Provisionals kidnapped the Dublin businessman Ben Dunne and held him for five days North of the border, releasing him on 23 October in South Armagh. There was considerable controversy over whether or not a ransom was paid for Mr Dunne. I have heard the sum of £750,000 being discussed in Republican circles. Crossborder kidnappings continued with the snatching of two bank managers' daughters, one from Dundalk and the other from Ardee, who were released in Newry after £50,000 had been handed over in each case.

It is thought that kidnappings in June and August 1983 may have been connected with the INLA, not the Provisionals. Certainly, Mr Richard Hill and his daughter Dianna, who were seized in a holiday home in Co. Mayo, are thought to have been taken by the INLA. The Hills, like Mrs Heloise Jones seized earlier in the year in Co. Dublin, were released safely. In August, after a wild shootout, the Gardai arrested five Provos who were subsequently sentenced for the attempted kidnapping of Mr Galen Weston, the Canadian multi-millionaire. The Special Branch had been lying in wait at Mr Weston's home in Roundwood, Co. Wicklow, obviously acting on a tip-off, when the Provisionals drove up. Later that year, kidnapping mania led to the seizure of Mrs Alma Manina, who was released by the Gardai after being kidnapped in Greystones, Co. Wicklow on 21 October. A number of local men were arrested but it is not clear what happened to the £60,000 ransom.

The two most celebrated kidnappings to occur in 1983 were, of course, the stealing of the thoroughbred horse Shergar, the Derby winner from Ballymoney Stud at the Curragh on 8 February, and the Don Tidey drama in December. Shergar was apparently put down by his kidnappers when the syndicate led by the Aga Khan which owned the horse failed to pay the ransom. The horse's body was never recovered. This kidnapping is associated with one particular maverick IRA man whose daring exploits have often been in the news.

The Don Tidey kidnapping made appalling headlines. A policeman and a soldier were killed in the fusillade which broke out as the security forces closed in on the dugout where the Provisionals had hidden him, in Ballinamore, Co. Leitrim. Mr Tidey, who was employed by the international combine Associated British Foods, apparently cost the insurers some £2 million. Garret FitzGerald had intervened personally with Mrs Thatcher to ensure that no ransom would be paid and received assurances in this regard. However, I understand that the Gardai believe that the money was handed over by the insurance company in Switzerland. Subsequently the Gardai began an action against a prominent Irish-American businessman, having arranged the seizure of some millions of his money from Irish bank accounts.

One bizarre side-effect of the affair was the leaking by RUC sources to Loyalist paramilitaries of the fact that the ranson had been paid to the IRA.

The Loyalist paramilitaries promptly counter-attacked by demanding a like amount of money from the stores owned by Associated British Foods in Ireland. There were some reports of vegetables being poisoned, causing the Quinnsworth chain to install videos carrying warnings to shoppers and requests to report anything suspicious. This episode petered out without it being ascertained whether or not the Loyalists had received any money.

After the Ballinamore débâcle the IRA went cold on kidnapping and there was a merciful respite of the practice in Ireland until an English criminal gang seized Mrs Jennifer Guinness, the wife of a prominent Dublin merchant banker, in April 1986. She was released by the Gardai on 16 April unhurt and without a ransom being paid. The only good thing to be said about kidnappings in the period under review is that the Gardai showed a consistent and successful record against them.

The power of the Irish-American link was amply demonstrated on 29 September 1984, when some seven tons of arms were seized by the Irish authorities aboard the *Marita Ann* off the Kerry Coast. The five men arrested aboard the trawler were Gavin Mortimer, Martin Ferris, John McCarthy, John Patrick Crowley, and Michael Browne, the skipper and a member of one of Ireland's best-known fishing families.

The *Marita Ann* was captured by the Irish naval vessels the *Emer* and the *Aisling* after being fired at by tracer bullets. The trawler had transhipped the arms from a bigger American trawler, the *Valhalla*, which had crossed the Atlantic from Boston (and was seized there by US Customs on 16 October). The arrangements for the purchase and shipping of the arms were well known to some members of the Boston police force, whose help in providing bodyguards, and advice in guiding the purchases through the underworld of American arms dealers, greatly assisted the *Marita Ann* project – initially, that is. Although the capture was hailed as a triumph of FBI detection coupled with satellite surveillance, which was supposed to have monitored the *Valhalla*'s progress across the Atlantic, it was the age-old Irish role of the informer which played the most important part. At the time of the seizure, in an effort to protect the identity of their 'moles', a story was issued by 'Washington sources' and printed by the papers, stating that the capture 'was connected with a top-secret US Customs operation code-named Leprechaun which has been underway in New York for two years' (*Sunday Press*, 30 September 1984). However, the IRA, my sources tell me, were not thrown off the scent by this theory. The IRA shot one man in connection with the event and other deaths may have followed. The power of the IRA's 'doctrine of continuity' was ironically underlined by the occasion: some of those arrested were caught waiting at Banna Strand, a place made famous by its association with the capture of Sir Roger Casement, who was hanged for his part in the attempt to smuggle arms from Germany in the *Aud* prior to 1916. The ballad about Sir Roger and 'the lonely Banna Strand' is one of the most popular in Ireland and, though the authorities were naturally delighted by the arms seizure, the song – and its symoblism – received a renewed burst of popularity.

Garret FitzGerald also was delighted by the *Marita Ann* episode, for two reasons. Firstly, he hoped that this demonstration of Anglo-Irish security co-operation, in the most spectacular arms seizure since that of the *Claudia* off the coast of Waterford eleven years earlier, would help incline Margaret Thatcher favourably towards the Forum proposals; and secondly – as his statement of congratulation to the Security Forces indicated – because the arms had been prevented 'from coming into the country to murder people both North and South of the Border'.

It was the IRA statement[*] on the affair, however, which eventually proved to contain the correct long-term pointer to the outcome of the seizure. After criticizing the Dublin Government for continually postponing Ireland's freedom by acting as Britain's agent, the statement promised that the IRA's campaign 'would not be curtailed'. Decoded, this meant that though deprived of a highly important arms shipment, they could and would improvise. The degree of efficiency with which they could do this was demonstrated a few months after the *Marita Ann*'s seizure. An attack was launched on Newry RUC Barracks at 6.30 p.m. on 28 February 1985, using home-made mortars fired at a range of two hundred metres from steel tubes four and a half feet long and bolted to the floor of a hijacked lorry. The mortars wiped out a

[*] *Sunday Press*, 30 September 1984.

canteen made from two portacabins that had been filled with a teatime crowd. The attack was obviously launched with a great deal of local knowledge; nine members of the RUC were killed (including two women) and thirty-two others were injured. It was the highest single death toll suffered by the RUC since the troubles began. The dead* included a chief inspector and a sergeant.

But shattering as the blow was to the morale of the force, it was only the bloody tip of an iceberg continuously grinding away at it. Apart from outright attacks and threats of attacks, there was a constant campaign afoot to isolate the police by various methods, including shooting contractors who repair RUC barracks or provide them with supplies. I have even known of a band which played at an RUC Social Club to be warned to desist.†

The IRA broadened the 'legitimate' target list with their announcement on 7 August 1986 that they would attack civilians who work not only on military contracts, such as barracks and so on, but for government installations such as British Telecom.

Apart from provoking fear and resentment amongst Catholics, for whom such employment is the only possible work opportunity, this provoked a backlash from the UVF. Hooded spokesmen appeared on television reading out what amounted to a tit-for-tat death threat against Catholic workers in Protestant firms, and this particular threat was further underlined on 18 August, when a group, thought to be from within the UDA, having first stolen the clocking-in cards of the few Catholics allowed to work at Shorts Brothers, announced that it would take action against them.

This firm had just won an important American defence contract with the assistance of John Hume, in the teeth of opposition mounted by Irish-American spokesmen such as Father MacManus of the Irish-American Caucus, on the grounds that there was discrimination against Catholics in the factory, in flagrant contravention of the McBride principles, among others. However, the real point about Shorts is that the number of Catholics was so small, approximately 3% of a workforce of 7,000, even though the management had the full backing of all the firm's trade unions in its threat to dismiss anyone

---

* The names of those killed were: Chief Inspector Alexander Donaldson; Sergeant John Dowd; Constables David Topping, Ivy Kelly, Rosemary McGookin; Reserve Constables Geoffrey Campbell, Sean McHenry, Paul McFerran and Denis Price.
† Members of the group were Catholics. The threat was a boon to their careers, as they emigrated to Ibiza where they became highly successful.

found guilty of stealing the clocking-in cards, or engaging in sectarian intimidation.

The Shorts situation merely serves to underline the continuing facts of life of Northern Ireland employment, whereas the IRA threat added a new dimension of terror to both Protestants and Catholics in the Province, a further step in their aim of isolating British installations.

The strain on the RUC in dealing with attacks mounted by Loyalists after the signing of the Anglo-Irish Agreement can well be imagined. But although the Agreement is widely and deeply resented within the RUC as it is within the wider Loyalist community, the force has not shown any great difficulty in controlling Loyalist mobs if ordered to do so (and sometimes the 'if' is highly relevant, as was apparent during the Loyalists' Province-wide work stoppage of 3 March 1986, when intimidation was widespread and unchecked) despite the spate of attacks on individual policemen's homes. The RUC is a highly trained force, particularly in counter-insurgency, to a degree that gave rise to a belief within the IRA that fear of Loyalist backlash from paramilitaries should more properly be directed at the RUC, who had training, equipment and local knowledge. It remains to be seen how the RUC's reaction to the new situation created by the Republican-led ceasefires affects that calculation.

Despite the fact that, post Hillsborough, the RUC obviously did enough impartial policing to enrage the Loyalists, the Stalker affair confirmed Nationalist suspicions that the force was not to be trusted. One of the most controversial aspects of the RUC's activities was highlighted by this affair. Following complaints from Nationalist leaders, in particular Seamus Mallon, Deputy Leader of the SDLP, and repeated representations by clerical leaders, most notably Cardinal O'Fiaich, on 24 May 1984, Mr John Stalker, Deputy Chief Constable of Greater Manchester, was appointed to head an eight man team of detectives investigating reports of an RUC 'Shoot to Kill' policy in Armagh, which had claimed the lives of at least six people in the preceding months. His report was handed over to Sir John Hermon on 18 September 1985, and little was heard of it officially until it was sent to the Director of Public Prosecutions on 13 February 1986. On 4 March is became known that the DPP had asked for further information. Unofficially, however, there was widespread discussion about a series of leaks which held that Mr Stalker had recommended prosecuting a number of high-ranking officers and had severely critic-ized some of the RUC's operations in South Armagh. Then, on 6 June 1986, it was officially announced that Mr Stalker was being replaced as leader of the inquiry by the Chief Constable of West Yorkshire, Mr Colin Sampson. He was suspended from duty pending the outcome of an internal police investigation in England concerning an alleged serious breach of the disciplinary code. Apparently this stemmed from a trip he had made to Miami with a local businessman, Mr Kevin Taylor. The same day, he gave a press conference accompanied by his solicitor, at which he stated that he was completely innocent of any wrongdoing and did not know what the suspension related to. British newspapers, however, speculated freely that he had uncovered highly embarrassing information about the RUC and that efforts were being made to silence him. Mr Stalker himself refused to be drawn on reports that the RUC had shown a lack of co-operation.

In Northern Ireland experienced observers shook their heads and recalled the Irwin case. Doctor Irwin's report was eventually con-firmed, but not before the North of Ireland Office and the RUC had orchestrated a smear campaign against him, using the fact that his wife had been raped in an effort to discredit him.

The BBC's *Panorama* programme of 16 June 1986 did a great deal to substantiate fears that Mr Stalker had in fact been 'set up'. The official inquiry found so little to criticize in Stalker's conduct that he was restored to duty – making people wonder all the more why it had been found necessary to suspend such an apparently conscientious officer in the first place. The wonderment was shared by the SDP which held a full-scale debate on the affair at its Harrogate conference on 16 September 1986. Not surprisingly, Stalker subsequently found the atmosphere in the police force uncongenial and retired. He has since done well for himself through activities as diverse as writing a book, *Stalker*, TV appearances, and acting as a security consultant to a football team. Nevertheless, as he has said himself publicly many times on both sides of the Atlantic, he would have preferred to continue working as a police officer because: 'It's what I do best.'

Apart from the immediate publicity attracted by the hunger strikes, a series of escape attempts ensured that the prisoners remained the focus both of tension and media attention. In the 1980s prisons in both the Republic and the North flickered into the headlines briefly, as

escape attempts were discovered and foiled, not unusual for a movement which during the first five years after internment dug so many
tunnels under Long Kesh – more than two hundred of them – that it was
afterwards revealed (*Irish Press*, 26 September 1983) that had the
tunnelling continued, there was a real danger of the place collapsing.
The tunnel diggers were apparently defeated by underground sound
detectors and infra-red cameras mounted on helicopters, but in a
manner typical of the IRA's method of coping with its enemies'
technological advances – shown also in the armament field, for example
in the case of the Newry home-made mortar attack – they went back to
the drawing board and succeeded in 'springing' thirty-eight prisoners
on 22 September 1983. This break-out had a significant effect on the
IRA because of its scale and the calibre of the men who were thus
released back into the movement.

The escape took some four months to plan. The prisoners made a
virtue out of necessity, using the work which had been enjoined on them
by the hunger strike and visiting the workshops to gather intelligence on
the prison layout, becoming so diligent in cleaning duties that often they
were found polishing and scrubbing areas normally out of bounds. H
Block 7 was chosen as the wing for the escape because the adjoining
block was being renovated and its gates were deserted. Six handguns
fitted with silencers were smuggled into the prisoners. Armed with
these, and led by Brendan McFarlane, who had succeeded Bobby
Sands as the prisoners' leader, at 2.15 p.m. on a quiet Sunday afternoon
prisoners moved into the central accommodation block of H Block 7, on
the pretext of cleaning out the store and the Medical Officer's office.
Within half an hour they had the block under control and were scanning
files both to gain information and to destroy anything which might lead
to their identification and capture. They climbed into a lorry which had
brought supplies to the prison, one keeping a gun on the driver. They
cruised effortlessly through the first two security gates and stopped at
the van pool near a lodge at a prison exit, where they encountered about
a score of warders coming on duty, stopped and attempted to hold them
up. Fierce fighting broke out. Some of the prisoners had knives as well
as guns and the warders were armed with truncheons. One warder was
stabbed to death, five others received stab wounds and a man on each
side was shot. The prisoners had intended to drive out of jail but the exit
was blocked by warders' cars, so they made off on foot across the fields.

Some hijacked cars, others hid in barns or took over houses. Several
were captured or, like Seamus McElwaine (shot on 24 April 1985),

killed in subsequent encounters with the security forces. One of the saddest cases was that of Kieran Flemming, aged 24. He had spent more than a quarter of his life in jail after being imprisoned for an indefinite period in 1976 for his part in an ambush which resulted in the death of policewoman Linda Baggley. His colleagues told me that he was badly hurt in the swirling bludgeoning that broke out in the van pool, and had to be urged on by his comrades to face the second bout of fighting that broke out at the blocked prison gate, where he again suffered injury. He escaped and recovered from his wounds, but while on active service on a cold sleety day on 2 December, he and a colleague, Anthony MacBride, ran into an SAS patrol near Beleek, Co. Cavan, close to the border. MacBride and a soldier were killed and Flemming escaped, only to find his route barred by the River Bannagh on the Fermanagh side of the border. He suffered from a fear of the water, and often had nightmares about drowning, a colleague told me. With the SAS behind and the river ahead he made an attempt to cross, but drowned, probably out of shock and horror.

The escape was both a body-blow to the Northern authorities and a corresponding lift to the IRA's morale. Following an enquiry conducted on behalf of the Government by Sir James Hennessy, the prison Governor, Mr Ernest Whittingham, resigned. He was replaced by the formidable figure of Mr Stanley Hillditch, who had governed the prison during the grim days of the hunger strike. It was felt in many quarters that others should have followed Mr Whittingham at the political level but neither Mr Prior nor Mr Nicholas Scott, the North's prison minister, acceded to the resignation calls from enraged Unionists and prison officers.

Apart from morale, the IRA gained from the expertise of the men released. Brendan McFarlane in prison in Holland, fighting attempts to extradite him back to Ireland, speedily acquired folk hero status within the Republican movement. He has been credited – whether correctly or not is a matter for conjecture – with being the brains behind almost every noteworthy IRA activity to occur subsequent to his escape, and something of the calibre of the others may be judged from the following potted history of their careers to the date of their escape.

Kevin Barry Artt (24) of Madden Gardens, Belfast. Life for murdering assistant governor, Maze prison, Mr Albert Miles, 1978, convicted in Christopher Black 'Supergrass' trial.

Brendan McFarlane (31) of Ardoyne, Belfast. Life for murdering five people in a bomb attack on Shankill Road bar, in 1976. Succeeded Bobby Sands as prison leader during the hunger strike.

Hugh Joseph Corey (27) of Moneymore, Co. Derry. Life for murdering part-time UDR man in 1976.

Terence Damien Kirby (27) of Andersonstown, Belfast. Life for murdering 77-year-old garage owner, William Creighton, in 1976.

Seamus Joseph Clarke (27) of Holmdene Gardens, Belfast. Life for murdering five people in Shankill Road bar explosion.

Kieran Gerard Flemming (23) of Nelson Drive, Derry. Indefinite sentence for murdering, when he was a minor, policewoman Linda Baggley in an ambush in 1976.

Anthony McAllister (25) of New Barnsley, Belfast. Life for murdering a soldier in 1979.

Seamus Turlough McElwaine (22) of Knockna Cullion, Co. Monaghan. Life for murdering a UDR man and RUC Reserve Constable in 1980.

Anthony Edward Kelly (22) of Garvan Place, Derry. Indefinite sentence for murdering as a minor an RUC Reserve Constable in 1976.

Brendan James Mead (25) of Rockdale Street, Belfast. Life in 1980 for his part in the murder of a UDA man.

James Joseph Smyth (38) of Ladbrooke Drive, Belfast. Jailed for 20 years in 1978 for the attempted murder of a prison officer, possession of illegal documents.

Gerard Patrick McDonnell (32) of Rockmount Street, Belfast. Jailed for 16 years in 1978 for having bomb-making material and illegal documents.

Robert Peter Russell (25) of Springhill Crescent, Belfast. Jailed for 20 years for the attempted murder of an RUC superintendent in Belfast in 1978.

Dermot Joseph McNally (26) of Lurgan. Life in 1977 for causing explosions and other serious crimes.

Gerard Kelly (30) of Moyard Crescent, Belfast. Life in 1973 for his part in the Old Bailey bomb blast. He and the Price sisters, Dolores and Marian, were transferred from English prisons to Long Kesh in 1975.

Dermont Finnucan (22) of Buncrana Gardens, Belfast. Jailed for 18 years for possessing arms used in a murder bid on an Army patrol in 1981.

Paul Brennan (30) of Flenalina Park, Belfast. Jailed for 16 years in 1977, for having a bomb.

Paul Anthony Kane (28) of Nortwick Drive, Belfast. Jailed for 18 years on evidence given by Christopher Black of attempted murder and having firearms.

Patrick Oliver McKearney of Moy. Jailed for 14 years in 1981 for having a loaded gun.

Patrick John McIntyre (25) of Letterkenny. Jailed for 15 years for murdering a UDR man.

James Pius Clarke (27) of Letterkenny. Jailed for 18 years for attempted murder in June 1979.

Gerard John Friers (24) of Ardmonagh Gardens, Belfast. Jailed for 14 years in 1981 for having a lorry bomb near Dungannon.

Sean McGlinchy (27) of Balaghy. Life for murdering six people in car bomb explosions in Coleraine in 1973.

William Gerard Gorman (24) of Carlisle Road, Belfast. Indefinite sentence, as a minor in 1980, for murdering a policeman in 1974.

James Joseph Burns (34) of Lenadoon, Belfast. Jailed for a minimum of 30 years for murdering a man at Suffolk.

Henry Harrison Murray (35) of Lenadoon, Belfast. Life in December 1979, minimum 30 years, for murdering an RUC man.

Peter Christopher Hamilton (29) of Butler Street, Ardoyne. Life for murdering five people in a Shankill Road bar in 1975.

Robert Kerr (27) of Pim Street, Belfast. Life in 1979 for killing a woman civilian searcher, and a soldier at city centre security gates.

James Gary Roberts (24) of Riverdale Park Drive, Belfast. Indefinite sentence, as a minor, for murdering a 64-year-old grandfather in a Dunmurray pub.

Dennis Martin Cummings (31) of Stewardstown. Life for murder.

Edward Joseph O'Connor (24) of no address. Life for murder.

James Patrick McCann (27) of Andersonstown. Jailed for 25 years in 1977 for the attempted murder of soldiers and policeman.

James Gerard Donnelly (21) of Ardoyne. Jailed for 15 years for conspiracy to murder, and other offences on evidence of informer Black.

Marcus Laurence Murray (22) of Lisnaskea. Jailed for 20 years for conspiracy to murder, and possession of firearms.

Martin Gerard McManus (27) of Moyard Crescent, Belfast. Jailed for 15 years in 1979 for possessing guns and ammunition.

Robert Storey (27) of Riverdale, Belfast. Jailed for 18 years, for the attempted murder of soldiers.

Joseph Simpson (30) of Gweedore Park, Belfast. Jailed for 20 years in 1981 for the attempted murder of policeman and possessing incendiaries.

32

The INLA: 1980–93

The history of the INLA in the five years from 1980–85 was largely that of one man, the extraordinary Dominic McGlinchey, who acquired a latterday Ned Kelly reputation largely through his habit of stripping Gardai of their uniforms after hold-ups.

McGlinchey had a strong Republican background. He was the third eldest of a family of eleven, of whom one brother, Sean, is currently serving a life sentence for a bombing in Coleraine; another, Paul, got a fourteen-year sentence for attempted murder; and at the time of his capture on St Patrick's Day (17 March) in 1984, his brother Michael had been sentenced for IRA membership. McGlinchey, labelled by the media as 'Ireland's Most Wanted Man' or 'Mad Dog', was leader of the INLA and, on his own admission, a killer thirty times over with some two hundred 'active service' operations behind him before his arrest by Gardai in Co. Clare. His road to notoriety began, as did that of so many other young IRA activists of the time, with internment. He was picked up at the age of seventeen in Bellaghy, Co. Derry, during the fatal August of 1971, and for five days sustained the sort of treatment which, as I have indicated, led to Britain's being arraigned before the Bar of Europe. During the next ten months he was held in Ballykelly Camp, Magilligan, and finally Long Kesh, the 'Republican University'.

Prior to his incarceration McGlinchey had taken no interest in politics beyond attending any Civil Rights marches which occurred in his area, but when he was released in the summer of 1972, by order of the then Secretary of State for Northern Ireland, William Whitelaw, he embarked on the course of conduct which gained him notoriety.

The year after his release he was back inside again, this time for eighteen months, having been one of the first to be tried by the 'Diplock' courts, for possession of arms. The sentence served, he joined up with another young man, Francis Hughes, who had become active in the IRA after getting a bad beating from soldiers one evening at a road block. Hughes was destined to be the second man to die in the Long Kesh hunger strike, after Bobby Sands. With a third South Derry Provo, Ian Milne, (subsequently imprisoned in Long Kesh) they became a legend, so much so that the RUC took the unprecedented step of issuing 'wanted' posters for them, categorizing a long list of murders, shootings, bombings and hijackings, which they had perpetrated by 1976. However, it was not the RUC but the Gardai who captured McGlinchey in November 1977, on charges of hijacking a Garda car, resisting arrest and threatening a Garda with a gun, and he was not released until February 1982.

Given the temper of the Southern courts at the time, the question of extraditing him back to the North did not arise. Nor did the question of his going back to the IRA, as in jail he had clashed with the leadership. Prior to going to Portlaoise he had been Operations Officer for South Derry; now he assumed the same position for the INLA and in less than six months became its Chief-of-Staff. At the time the organization was riven by feuding, which in some cases had resulted in deaths (I have been told of at least four such killings), and was based mainly in Dublin and Belfast. McGlinchey stopped the feuding, ruthlessly it is said, and built up the organization throughout the country, so that cells started operating from South Armagh, South Down, Tyrone, Louth, Donegal and many other places. There were several robberies in the North and South during his time as Chief-of-Staff, two of which in Cork netted over £300,000, and by the end of 1982, his first year in office, the INLA had claimed responsibility for the deaths of twenty members of the British security forces.

McGlinchey did not plant the bomb in the Droppin' Well Inn at Ballykelly, which killed eleven soldiers and six civilians in December 1982, but he admitted to being 'involved' in the attack and argued that prior to the incident there had been six warnings about soldiers using the pub.

In 1983 a number of Catholics in the Portadown area were shot by members of the UDR, who afterwards boasted openly not only that they had committed the murders, but that they would continue to kill other members of the dead men's families. One family warned the police that unless action was taken something drastic would occur. Nothing happened, so the brother of the dead man contacted the INLA leader, McGlinchey, and requested a weapon with which to kill a known UVF man. He was given a Ruger semi-automatic rifle but, clearly deranged by the death of his brother, used it instead to attack the Darkley Gospel Hall, where he shot three church elders and wounded people later described by McGlinchey as 'entirely innocent hill-billy folk'. After the massacre, the man again warned the police that unless they took action, 'what happened at Darkley Hall will look like a picnic'. This time, arrests followed.

Other 'innocent folk' were killed as a result of McGlinchey's campaign. For instance, in June 1982, a sixteen-year-old boy's head was blown off when an INLA bomb went off on the back of a parked motor-bike, and in September of that year, a nail bomb claimed the life of a British soldier in the Divis Flats complex and also killed two children. But McGlinchey, who felt the need to explain himself to the media after the Darkley shooting, said that 'never at any time have I killed or been responsible for killing civilians'. He said of his victims, be they UDR, Army or RUC 'they are agents of an oppressive and violent state'. Where the Gardai were concerned, apart from repeatedly holding them up and taking their uniforms, he operated a Standing Order No. 8 policy.

'I genuinely wish,' he said, 'that there were other ways of dealing with repression, but I believe it is the only way. Therefore I do what has to be done and don't think about it thereafter. I take no pleasure whatever in it as some people would like to suggest.'

McGlinchey has admitted to planting several bombs personally, at Magherafelt, Toomebridge, Bellaghy, Portglenone, Castledawson, Ballymena, and many other places. He said of his *modus operandi* when shooting someone: 'I like to get close to minimize the risk for myself. It's usually just a matter of getting in first and by getting in close you put your man down first . . .'

In the midst of this lurid career he managed to get married (on 5 July 1975, at Toomebridge) to Mary O'Neill, with whom he had two sons, Declan and Dominic. His career ended, temporarily at least, when Gardai surrounded a cottage near Newmarket-on-Fergus, Co. Clare. McGlinchey was captured after a fierce shootout, but the controversy he generated continued.

There were of course extradition warrants against him, and immediately after his capture it was proposed that he be sent back to face charges in Northern Ireland. His lawyers objected to this, and in the High Court Mr Justice Barrington granted a temporary injunction against his extradition. However, although there were a variety of serious charges which could have been laid against him in the Republic, that same day the State made a decisive and successful effort to extradite him. A special sitting of the Supreme Court was held, with Justices Griffin and Henchy sitting in company with the Chief Justice Mr Tom O'Higgins, a former Fine Gael presidential candidate and a nephew of Kevin O'Higgins, whom three IRA men had shot in 1927, thus creating a political climate which forced Fianna Fail into the Dail. Now, in 1984, the political climate was one in which a Fine Gael Taoiseach, whose father (Desmond FitzGerald) had succeeded the murdered O'Higgins in the 1927 Cabinet, wanted to create circumstances favourable to impressing both the Unionists and the British as the Forum deliberations continued. Extradition had long been something stoutly argued for by the Unionists and rejected by the Republic.

After a two-hour hearing Chief Justice O'Higgins ordered that McGlinchey be extradited. He said:

> To prove that an offence was political, an appellant must demonstrate that he or she was engaged in what reasonable, civilized people would regard as political activity.
>
> This court is invited to assume that because of the existence of widespread violence organized by paramilitary groups in Northern Ireland, any charge associated with terrorist activity should be regarded as a charge in respect of a political offence or an offence connected with a political offence. I am not prepared to make any such assumption.

McGlinchey, the 'Mad Dog', the 'most wanted man in Ireland', was driven North to face what everyone assumed would be an immediate court appearance on a variety of charges. Back in Dublin the decision was criticized on the grounds that the haste with which he had been passed across the border indicated a supine attitude on the part of the Irish authorities, who should at least have had the national self-respect to try him for crimes committed against the Irish State before caving in on the important principle of extradition. This controversy worsened as the months dragged by and, despite the speed with which the 'most wanted' man had been extradited, it became evident that the Northern authorities had little or no evidence on which to justify McGlinchey's presence in their custody. It took over six months to bring him to trial, for the murder of a sixty-seven-year-old post-mistress in her home at Toomebridge, Co. Antrim, eight years earlier. The death of Mrs Hester McMullen was what the Pentagon would term a 'collateral casualty' of one of McGlinchey's many raids, and he received life imprisonment for it on Christmas Eve, 1984.

However, the following October Belfast Appeal Court quashed this conviction. Mr Justice Gibson said that the evidence against McGlinchey consisted solely of two fingerprints found on the getaway car and two affidavits which he made in Dublin to resist his extradition. He held that the fingerprints could have been made at any time before the murder and were therefore insufficient evidence on which to base a conviction, and he ruled that the affidavits were inadmissible. Two days after the trial, on 12 October, McGlinchey was handed back to the Gardai, just a few days short of two full years after they had first apprehended him. He was sentenced on 12 March in the Dublin Special Criminal Court to ten years in Portlaoise for firearms charges in connection with the Co. Clare shootout. By then the pendulum of public opinion had swung back towards him considerably. The pictures in the papers and on TV made him seem less terrible than his reputation; there was considerable sympathy for his attractive wife and children and, as the Presiding Judge Mr Justice McMahon said while sentencing him, it was to his credit that on a number of previous occasions he had not fired on Gardai while in a position to do so. It was widely felt that had he wished it, a marksman of McGlinchey's calibre could have accounted for some of the Gardai in the Co. Clare gunbattle; he had previously stated that he would never be taken alive. Many people sympathized with, if they did not condone his Counsel's version of events. Mr Paul Callan SC said that on the day of his arrest, McGlinchey had arranged to meet his children and had reacted instinctively when surrounded. (One Garda was hit in the shoulder by a bullet when McGlinchey aimed a burst of submachine-gun fire at a Garda car). He continued: 'He is an intelligent man of ability and great energy and, but for the fact that he was born in the Community of South Derry, it is highly unlikely that he would ever be before any court . . .' With the names and the places changed, one could probably say the same about thousands of young men in Northern Ireland, both Republican and Loyalist.

The Chief Justice who originally tried McGlinchey's case, Mr Justice Tom O'Higgins, a neighbour of mine, was immediately placed under twenty-four-hour armed guard; his house was floodlit with detectives stationed in huts at the front and rear. He had once been his country's most prestigious judge, the sort of man one met walking his dog, driving in the district, or occasionally sipping a pint of Guinness; he now became an incessantly guarded hate-object. Eventually he resigned and took up a post in Europe, saying frankly that the strain was too much for him and his family.

During his time in Portlaoise, McGlinchey had asked me to visit him. I found a low-sized, slight, balding man of whom prison and other happenings had taken their toll. Shortly before I visited him his wife Mary had been shot dead as she bathed their two children. I knew that there was considerable tension within the prison, because a man, popularly suspected of the murder, had recently been captured and sent to Portlaoise also. I asked McGlinchey how he felt about his coming to the jail. To my surprise McGlinchey answered: 'I don't think that he had anything to do with my wife's death.' McGlinchey seemed to harbour no animosity towards anyone, except, to a degree, the RUC, who had made such a song and dance about extraditing him and then, having subjected him to the stress of this process, tamely sent him back to the Republic. All he wanted to do, he said, was to serve his sentence and be re-united with his sons. At the time, though well-cared for by relatives, the children were being subjected to considerable harassment and bullying by Loyalist kids.

I was subsequently informed that McGlinchey was correct in exonerating the man of complicity in his wife's death. According to my informant, Mrs McGlinchey, who had run McGlinchey's operation for a time in his absence, had been shot in reprisal for a killing for which, rightly or wrongly, she had been held responsible. The dead man's brothers had returned from the US, shot Mary McGlinchey with borrowed weapons, and were back on the plane to America next day. McGlinchey was released in March 1993, and immediately set about making good his promise to spend time with his children.

Amongst other treats he took them on a holiday to the Aran Islands, the Irish-speaking islands off the coast of Galway. On a Saturday evening, shortly after his return (on 12 June 1993), he went to a party arranged for them at Darver, near Ardee, Co. Louth. A car drew up which McGlinchey mistakenly assumed to contain Garda Special Branch. He left the children, aged 9 and 12, in the car and went to talk to the occupants. A man got out carrying a machine gun. He moved to cock the weapon and McGlinchey grabbed it. A burst of fire caught him in the head and side, but he succeeded in jamming the gun. The attacker then produced a handgun, but miraculously, though wounded in the head, arms and side, McGlinchey succeeded in grabbing this also. As he struggled, his would-be killer emptied the pistol at him. McGlinchey was shot twice more, but managed to escape into some shrubbery. A second man in his assailant's car called to McGlinchey's attacker, who got into the car and drove off. At this, McGlinchey's twelve-year-old ran out into the road to take the number. The car stopped and the gunman got out and made towards the children, who ran into the house where the party was to have been held.

McGlinchey recovered from his attack and said that it had been carried out by British agents. 'They had English accents and the man who attacked me was a trained man. He was wearing a flak jacket under his coat. They meant to shoot me and the children in the car. Only I made the mistake of thinking they were Gardai, and got out and surprised them or they would have killed us all.' He denied that he was still a member of the INLA or its splinter organization the Irish People's Liberation Army (IPLO). He said that Republican or Nationalist movements would not have had any interest in attacking him. The only people who would gain from his going 'home to Bellaghy in a box were the British', McGlinchey said.

I simply cannot evaluate McGlinchey's claims. In the murky under-world of the splinters of splinters of the paramilitary organizations it would be a brave man who would say where the truth lies. However, as with so much of the McGlinchey saga, there are contradictory reports about this, reports which McGlinchey's subsequent tragic fate would tend to substantiate. A spokesman for the group of former members of the IPLO told the *Irish Press* (June 1993) that they were responsible for the attack. Either they, or some like-minded figures, finally caught up with McGlinchey in a phone box on a street in Drogheda at 11.10 p.m., on Thursday, 10 February 1994. While his horrified sixteen-year-old son Dominic, who had also witnessed the murder of his mother, looked on helplessly from their car, another car pulled up suddenly at the phone box. Two men jumped out, carrying pump action shot guns and a handgun. McGlinchey was pulled from the box, punched and kicked to the ground, and shot in both knees. Thus immobilized, he was then dispatched by two blasts to the head.

The seedy horror of his death was compounded by briefings given by Garda Special Branch members to journalists in the days after the murder. There were rumours of involvement in drugs smuggling. Stories, such as that carried by the *Sunday Independent* (13/2/94), alleging that he had linked up with a criminal gang. According to the paper McGlinchey had struck up an association with Dublin's most notorious criminal whereby the criminal disposed of the contents of trucks which McGlinchey hi-jacked along the Border. One of the pall bearers at his funeral, Bernadette McAliskey, was applauded by the crowd at the cemetery, when she described journalists as:

> curs and dogs. May everyone of them rot in hell. They have taken away Dominic McGlinchey's character and they will stand judgement for it. He was the finest Republican of them all. He never dishon- oured the cause he believed in. His war was with the armed soldiers and police of this state.

McGlinchey's funeral was a dignified affair, devoid of paramilitary trappings. Martin McGuinness, of Provisional Sinn Fein, attended. McGlinchey is still respected within the Provisionals for his services to the movement. Mourners from a thousand strong cortège took turns to carry the coffin, changing every forty yards or so. Many of them were women. He was buried in his native Bellaghy, Co. Derry. All the terror and the tumult of Ireland's tragedy inevitably comes to such quiet places. McGlinchey lies alongside his wife and an infant daughter who had died of meningitis. Not far away is the grave of his former comrade Francis Hughes. Another hunger striker, Thomas McIlwee, is also buried in the cemetery.

The serenity of the graveyard is not however mirrored in the history of what created the INLA and what it gave birth to – more graves, sometimes reached via ghastly tortures. Even the briefest glimpse of the INLA landscape gives a chilling picture of the vio- lence that the Northern Ireland conflict has spawned. I knew one of its victims slightly, Seamus Ruddy, a Newry schoolteacher. He was an intelligent, likeable figure with a good sense of humour. He came into my office to brief me of his own accord, because he had happened to hear that I was interested in finding out what were the policies and goals of the INLA. He was a prominent figure in both the INLA and the IRSP and was involved in gun smuggling on the Continent. In 1982 he severed all links with the INLA. Subsequen- tly he devoted his time to teaching in Paris and to his English girlfriend, Cecilia Moore.

But in 1985 the INLA needed weapons, and its then chief of staff, John O'Reilly, came to Paris with a hit team in an attempt to procure them. O'Reilly refused to accept that Ruddy was no longer involved and had no information for him. Ruddy was savagely beaten and then murdered. His body has never been found. O'Reilly himself was one of those who was killed in a murderous feud that broke out after the Irish People's Liberation Organization split from the INLA in June of 1986. The IPLO came to be led by Gerald Steenson, a legendary figure in Belfast's underworld. He was only sixteen when he murdered the Commander of the Official IRA, Billy McMillen, as his contribution to the feud, then in progress, between the Officials and the Provos. This, and his subsequent sanguinary career, earned him the soubriquet, 'Dr Death'.

One of O'Reilly's allies was one of the gang, who also had a long history of murder and prison sentences.

An effort to bring the two wings of the INLA together erupted in blood. 'Dr Death' took advantage of a 'peace-meeting' at a Drogheda hotel in January 1987 to murder both O'Reilly and a friend, 'Ta' Power, who had arranged the meeting. Several other killings followed over the next few months, including that of 'Dr Death', until a truce was agreed in March. It was in the course of the feud that Mrs McGlinchey was shot (on 31 January 1987). One man who took an active part in a number of the killings blamed Tony McCluskey for 'setting-up' O'Reilly. The man chopped off McCluskey's fingers with bolt-cutters. He was quoted as saying that he wanted to give him a 'hard death'. In his book, *War and an Irish Town**, Eammon McCann quotes a young man who took part in the murder of a man suspected of being an informer. The lad, that is all he was, told McCann: 'We cut off the fucking finger he dialled with and stuck it up his arse before we killed him. Good, eh?' Another victim of the feuding was also found to have had his fingers cut off. Their whereabouts were discovered when an autopsy revealed the contents of his stomach.

The murderer, who for a time was the most wanted man in Ireland, was finally captured by Gardai and is now in jail. But before being caught he had kidnapped a wealthy Dublin dentist, John O'Grady, and cut off his fingertips in chagrin at not being paid a ransom. The Provisional IRA moved against the IPLO on 31 October 1992, wiping

* *War and an Irish Town*, Eamonn McCann, p. 16, New Edition, Pluto, London and Boulder, Colorado, 1993.

out the organization in a series of punishment shootings in which one man was killed and between twenty and thirty wounded. But the INLA is still alive – and capable of killing again should the cease fires breakdown.

33

The Green Book: I

As we have seen, the IRA prepared a structural plan based on the cell system which became public when Seamus Twomey was captured in 1977. The report found on him isolated the IRA's central problem as follows.

> The three-day and seven-day detention orders are breaking volunteers and it is the Republican Army's fault for not indoctrinating volunteers with the psychological strength to resist interrogation.

What did not become public was the *Green Book*, an important blueprint drawn up to give recruits the ability both to withstand outside pressures and to constantly keep political goals in mind. While it dealt with all aspects of training and the movement's aims, it clearly regarded the most important thing for a volunteer as being not so much what he carried in his hands, or what shape his organization took – though such considerations are crucial – but what he carried around in his head and heart.

One of the first documents drawn to every recruit's attention, equal on a plane of importance with the 1916 Proclamation, is the Democratic Programme of the First Dail which met after the Sinn Fein landslide victory in the 'khaki election' of 1918 with a mandate for the whole of Ireland. In the first lecture of the *Green Book* the recruit is told:

> Commitment to the Republican Movement is the firm belief that its struggle both military and political is morally justified, that war is morally justified and that the Army is the direct representative of the 1918 Dail Eireann Parliament, and that as such they are the legal and lawful government of the Irish Republic, which has the moral right to pass laws for, and to claim jurisdiction over the territory, air space,

mineral resources, means of production, distribution and exchange and all of its people regardless of creed or loyalty.

In the same lecture he is warned:

> The most important thing is security, that means you:
> DON'T TALK IN PUBLIC PLACES:
> YOU DON'T TELL YOUR FAMILY, FRIENDS, GIRL-FRIENDS OR WORK-MATES THAT YOU ARE A MEMBER OF THE IRA. DON'T EXPRESS VIEWS ABOUT MILITARY MATTERS, IN OTHER WORDS YOU SAY NOTHING to any person. Don't be seen in public marches, demonstrations or protests. Don't be seen in the company of known Republicans, don't frequent known Republican houses. Your prime duty is to remain unknown to the enemy forces and the public at large.

Being an Irish Revolution, drink of course has to be taken careful note of.

> Another important thing volunteers must realize and understand is the danger involved in drinking alcohol and the very real danger of over-drinking. Quite a large body of information has been gathered in the past by enemy forces and their touts from volunteers who drank.
> Volunteers are warned that drink-induced loose talk is the MOST POTENTIAL DANGER facing any organization, and in a military organization it is SUICIDE.

The recruit learns from Day One that:

> The Irish Republican Army, as the legal representatives of the Irish people, are morally justified in carrying out a campaign of resistance against foreign occupation forces and domestic collaborators. All volunteers are and must feel morally justified in carrying out the dictates of the legal government, they as the Army are the legal and lawful Army of the Irish Republic which has been forced underground by overwhelming forces.

The recruit is told that 'the British Army is an occupying force', and the RUC, Gardai, UDR and Free State Army are 'illegal armies and illegal forces whose main tasks are treasonable and as such morally wrong, politically unacceptable and ethically inexcusable'. The volunteer is, as we have seen, told under 'Standing Order No. 8' that 'the Southern forces are not to be regarded as targets'. This, as we saw, was an acknowledgement of the fact that times had changed in the Republic and that any other attitude would be unacceptable to the public. The recruit is also made aware of the importance of another tenet forced on the IRA by harsh experience: motivation. Mindful of the splits and informers which grew out of both internment and more particularly the IRA's own blanket style of recruiting, he is warned:

> The Army as an organization claims and expects your total allegiance without reservation. It enters into every aspect of your life. It invades the privacy of your home life, it fragments your family and friends, in other words claims your total allegiance.
>
> All potential volunteers must realize that the threat of capture and of long jail sentences are a very real danger and a shadow which hangs over every volunteer. Many in the past joined the Army out of romantic notions, or sheer adventure, but when captured and jailed they had after-thoughts about their allegiance to the Army. They realized at too late a stage that they had no real interest in being volunteers. This causes splits and dissension inside prisons and divided families and neighbours outside. Another important aspect all potential volunteers should think about is their ability to obey orders from a superior officer. All volunteers must obey orders issued to them by a superior officer regardless of whether they like the particular officer or not.

This motivation is not merely expected to carry the volunteer through vicissitudes such as capture, interrogation and prison; it is expected to sustain him to the movement's ultimate political goal – a socialist Republic. It is dinned into him that military action is an extension of political action, therefore the military campaign of the IRA is in effect a political campaign. The recruit is told bluntly: 'people with no political concepts have no place in the Army.' Furthermore, those concepts must be of a particular type: 'All potential volunteers must be socialist in outlook.' The recruit is given a very clear-eyed vision of the facts.

> Before any potential volunteer decides to join the Irish Republican Army he should understand fully and clearly the issues involved. He should not join the Army because of emotionalism, sensationalism, or adventurism. He should examine fully his own motives, knowing the dangers involved and knowing that he will find no romance within the Movement. Again he should examine his political motives bearing in mind that the Army are intent on creating a Socialist Republic.

Nowhere are the facts spelt out more specifically than in the briefing given on how political goals are to be arrived at by military action.

> Volunteers are expected to wage a military war of liberation against a numerically superior force. This involves the use of arms and explosives. Firstly the use of arms. When volunteers are trained in the use of arms they must fully understand that guns are dangerous, and their main purpose is to take human life, in other words to kill people, and volunteers are trained to kill people. It is not an easy thing to take up a gun and go out to kill some person without strong convictions or justification. The Army, its motivating force, is based upon strong convictions which bonds the Army into one force and before any potential volunteer decides to join the Army he must have these strong convictions. Convictions which are strong enough to give him confidence to kill someone without hesitation and without regret. The same can be said about a bombing campaign. Again all people wishing to join the Army must fully realize that when life is being taken, that very well could mean their own. If you go out to shoot soldiers or police you must fully realize that they too can shoot you.
>
> Life in an underground army is extremely harsh and hard, cruel and disillusioning at times. So before any person decides to join the Army he should think seriously about the whole thing.

He should indeed.

'Analysis' is a word which a recruit soon becomes aware of; it figures prominently in all IRA teaching. For, having warned the would-be guerrilla of what he is up against and told him what he is striving for, it is then of course essential to explain how both the 'for' and 'against' arose.

> The nationhood of all Ireland has been an accepted fact for more than 1,500 years and has been recognized internationally as a fact. Professor Edmund Curtis, writing of Ireland in 800 AD, says that 'she was the first nation North of the Alps to produce a whole body of literature in her own speech', and he is told how the Danes were driven out or assimilated by a people 'whose civilization was a shining light throughout Europe', prior to the Norman invasion of 1169 with which there 'commenced more than 8 centuries of RELENTLESS AND UN-REMITTING WARFARE that has lasted down to this very day'.
>
> The objective of the 800 years of oppression 'is economic exploitation with the unjustly partitioned 6 counties remaining Britain's directly controlled old-style colony' and the South under the 'continuing social,

cultural and economic domination of London'. This last led to Irish savings being invested in England 'for a higher interest rate' and many hundreds of thousands of boys and girls from this country had to emigrate to England to seek the employment which those exported savings created.

Another aspect of economic imperialism at work is the export of raw, unprocessed materials: live cattle on the hoof, mineral wealth, fish caught by foreign trawlers, etc. Further, from 1958 on, the Free State abandoned all attempts to secure an independent economy, and brought in foreign multi-national companies to create jobs instead of buying their skills and then sending them home gradually.

'Africanization' is the word for this process elsewhere. Control of our affairs in all of Ireland lies more than ever since 1921 outside the hands of the Irish people.

The logical outcome of all this was full immersion in the EEC in the 1970s. The Republican Movement opposed this North and South in 1972 and 1975 and continues to do so. It is against such political economic power blocs East and West and military alliances such as NATO and the Warsaw Pact.

It stands with our Celtic brothers and other subject nations of Europe, and with the neutral and non-aligned peoples of the Third World; it seeks a third, socialist alternative which transcends both Western individualistic capitalism and Eastern state capitalism, which is in accordance with our best revolutionary traditions as a people.

It can be imagined how potent this teaching was (and is) to an unemployed young man in Andersonstown, Ballymurphy or the Bogside with British soldiers patrolling the streets. But as the hunger strikers lay dying, moved by their ordeal and by his own circumstances, such a young man would even more readily accept the fact that:

The position of the Irish Republican Army since its foundation in 1916 has been one of sustained resistance and implacable hostility to the forces of imperialism, always keeping in the forefront of the most advanced revolutionary thinking and the latest guerrilla warfare techniques in the world.

He would accept the legitimacy of linking 'the 1916 Rising, the Black-and-Tan War, the War against the Free State and the new Six-County State, the Bombing Campaign in England 1939–40, the Resistance Campaign 1956–62 and finally the present most heroic campaign of all dedicated to final victory . . .' He would also be moved and recognize grace notes struck in his own day by the description of those dates, albeit with hyperbole as:

> The milestones, the battle honours won, the blood-stained trail of sacrifice, imprisonment, hunger strikes, executions, yet with telling blows delivered to the enemy, often in the heart of British imperialism itself, commanding the open admiration of freedom-loving peoples around the world.

And finally, with hammer-blows of moralistic continuity, any remaining doubts he might have of himself setting out to follow those 'milestones' would be broken down with the following:

> NOTE. The moral position of the Irish Republican Army, its right to engage in warfare, is based on: (a) the right to resist foreign aggression; (b) the right to revolt against tyranny and oppression; and (c) the direct lineal succession with the Provisional Government of 1916, the first Dail of 1919 and the second Dail of 1921.

Regarding point (c), the first Dail declared itself the successor to the signatories of the 1916 Proclamation when it met in January 1919. Later, in March 1921, it declared that if enemy action reduced its ranks to a minimum, the remaining Deputies should hand over executive powers of government to the Army of the Republic, which would constitute itself as a Provisional Government. In 1922, when the majority of the Dail approved the Treaty of Surrender, and were thus guilty of treachery, the IRA withdrew its allegiance from the Dail. Later that year it recognized the minority of the 1921 Deputies as the 'final custodians to the Republic'.

> In 1938 the seven surviving faithful Republican Deputies delegated executive powers to the Army Council of the IRA as per the 1921 resolution. In 1969 the sole surviving Deputy, Joseph Clarke, reaffirmed publicly that the then Provisional Army Council and its successors were the inheritors of the first and second Dail as a Provisional Government.

From that point on the recruit would accept the IRA premise that it was fighting 'a long war of liberation' on the three grounds outlined above. It is then explained that the type of society the recruit sees around him is a product of economic and cultural imperialism manifested in the 'living conditions, life style and political power of the minority in comparison with those of the majority'.

> Economic imperialism is evident on every main road and city street of Ireland: in Banking, Insurance, Merchant Marine, the Motor Industry, Mining, Fisheries, Industry in General, ICI, Courtaulds, Pye, Phillips, Grundig, Shell-BP, Wimpey etc.; and cultural imperialism, epitomized in the Conor Cruise O'Briens of this Island, has been reinforced since the Treaty sell-out by successive Free State Governments via mass media, RTE, and the press and through education.

He is taught that a Republican must fight these and all other forms of imperialism and neo-colonialism so as to overthrow the unjust systems prevailing in both Free State and Six Counties.

> The injustice of being as an individual politically impotent, the injustice of unemployment, poverty, poor housing, inadequate social security, the injustice of the exploitation of our labour, our intelligence and our natural resources, the injustice of the bloody-minded destruction of our culture, our language, music, art, drama, customs, the inherent injustice of the state repression which is necessary to maintain the present system as a whole.

So long as partition lasts, a unified national concentration on correcting these injustices is not possible. 'We must therefore first of all break the British connection.' The IRA promises a democratic and socialist state:

> A Government system which will give every individual the opportunity to partake in the decisions which affect him or her: by decentralizing political power to the smallest social unit practicable where we would all have the opportunity to wield political power both individually and collectively in the interests of ourselves and the nation as a whole. Socially and economically we will enact a policy aimed at eradicating the Social Imperialism of today, by returning the ownership of the wealth of Ireland to the people of Ireland through a system of co-operativism, worker ownership, and control of Industry, Agriculture and the Fisheries.
>
> Culturally we would hope to restore Gaelic, not from the motivation of national chauvinism but from the viewpoint of achieving with the aid of a cultural revival the distinctive new Irish Socialist State: as a bulwark against imperialist encroachments from whatever quarter. Inter-

nationally our alignment would hopefully be with the progressive Governments or former colonies like ourselves with the dual purpose of mutual advantage and of curbing the endeavours of imperialistic military and economic power blocs throughout the world.

In order to achieve the long-term goal of the Democratic Socialist State every member of the movement is urged to concentrate on short-term objectives which might be accomplished en route to the long-term goal.

A new recruit's immediate obstacle is the removal of his (her) ignorance about how to handle weapons, military tactics, security, interrogations etc. An OC's might be how to put a unit on a military footing; an IO's how to create an effective intelligence network; a Cumann Chairman's how best to mount a campaign on a given issue, e.g. H Blocks etc., and for all members of the movement regardless of which branch we belong to, to enhance our commitment to and participation in the struggle through gaining as comprehensive an understanding as possible for our present society and the proposed Republican alternative through self and group education.

The approach of the *Green Book* is a cunningly thought out mixture of philosophy and guide to action. Each lesson or lecture is in part repetitious, in part a thinking forward to the next stage, a constant preoccupation with the problem of how to win friends and influence people while at the same time killing others and setting off explosions. The basic formula chosen to deal with this lethal paradox is 'get your defensive before your offensive'. This is explained to the recruit thus:

Before we go on the offensive politically or militarily we take the greatest defensive precautions possible to ensure success, e.g. we do not advocate a United Ireland without being able to justify our right to such a state as opposed to partition; we do not employ revolutionary violence as our means without being able to illustrate that we have no recourse to any other means. Or in more everyday simple terms: we do not claim that we are going to escalate the war if we cannot do just that; we do not mount an operation without first having ensured that we have taken the necessary defensive precautions of accurate intelligence, security, that weapons are in proper working order with proper ammunition and that the volunteers involved know how to handle interrogations in the event of their capture etc., and of course that the operation itself enhances rather than alienates our supporters.

The book does not hesitate to point out the IRA's own mistakes in order to highlight this point. It warns about how the enemy can exploit for publicity reasons bomb situations, there having been some horrific cases of bombs going off before buildings could be cleared:

> Even the given situations of adequate bomb warnings are exploited which is again our mistake in not having sufficiently considered our defensive before going on the offensive: the so-called Bloody Friday being the prime example. Either we did not stop to consider that the enemy would 'Dirty Joe' us on the warnings or we overestimated the Brits' ability to handle so many operations. But regardless of which is the case we made the mistake and the enemy exploited it.
>
> Other more everyday examples: [the enemy] exploits the mistake of a volunteer who stays in his own home by arresting him; he exploits the careless dumping of war materials by lifting them or, as is the more recent tactic, by assassinating volunteers who return to pick the materials up; he exploits IRA-sticky* confrontations by staying out of the way to allow the subsequent detrimental publicity and effect on support to run its course; he exploits IRA-Loyalist confrontations by moving in behind the IRA unit and attacking it, plus again the detrimental international publicity.

But the recruit is also taught how to exploit the enemy's mistakes.

> We exploit these mistakes by propagating the facts. So it was with their murderous mistakes of the Falls Road curfew, Bloody Sunday and internment, which were exploited to our advantage support-wise as was the murder of John Boyle in Dunloy.

The grim flexibility of the IRA, which can 'legitimize' a target at the drop of an ideological hat, is contained in the directive on tactics.

> Tactics are dictated by the existing conditions. Here again the logic is quite simple. Without support Volunteers, Dumps, Weapons, Finance, etc., we cannot mount an operation, much less a campaign. In September 1969 the existing conditions dictated that Brits were not to be shot, but after the Falls curfew all Brits were to the people acceptable targets. The existing conditions had been changed.
>
> Likewise at present, for example, although the leadership of the SDLP has proved itself to be collaborationist and thus an enemy of the people. At various stages since 1974 we could have employed the tactic

* Official IRA.

of making them subjects of ridicule by tarring and feathering them when for instance they were members of an Executive which tortured and interned Irishmen, which penalized rent and rate strikers, etc., or when they recently declared at Westminster in a debate on H Block that 'Life should mean Life and there should be no Political Status'. The defensive precaution in the latter example being of course that the people be made aware beforehand that they actually did make such an utterance.

The rule of thumb for all our actions can therefore be clearly seen to be that we must explain by whatever means we have at our disposal why we bomb, why we punish criminals, why we execute informers etc.

In that concluding phase, the 'etc.' can be the most important – and deadly – word. The 'existing conditions' can indicate a chilling range of 'etceteras'. For instance, the businessman Jeffrey Agate was shot because at the time the Secretary of State for Northern Ireland Roy Mason was touring the US trying to attract investment to the Province. Sir Norman Stronge and his son were shot and their home burned because sectarian assassinations were claiming the lives of Catholics. The death of Sir Norman, a former Speaker of the parliament of Stormont and one of the Province's leading Orangemen, made the sectarian assassins give up their campaign – at least temporarily. Edgar Graham, the Unionist Assemblyman, was shot because it was discovered that he had been aiding the prisons administration with advice which was felt to be outside a politician's normal term of reference. The Carrolls, a husband and wife who had been 'turned' by the RUC, were executed both as informers and to respond to the tactic of 'turning'. Whole categories of people can be declared 'legitimate targets' for a period. During the H Block crisis, for instance, over a score of warders were shot; throughout 1985 and 1986 contractors who either did building work on RUC barracks or even performed catering duties were targets.

So far as the IRA were concerned, these people were helping to 'service the war-machine' of their enemies. And the *Green Book* itself says:

We do not exclude taking an action which does not completely fill the criteria of this analysis on how to conduct the struggle. Many instances have arisen and will arise again when we have had to step outside these general terms of reference to our immediate detriment propaganda-wise and support-wise. However, even in such an eventuality, if we rationalize our action, get our defensive before our offensive, try to ensure that we have an alternative, relatively unaffected area of support from which to operate if the support in the area in which the detrimental but unavoidable action takes place, we are adhering as best as possible under the circumstances to the proper conduct of the war.

The young recruit is left under no illusion as to the power and extent of the enemies ranged against the IRA both from outside and within.

THE ENEMY: CATEGORIZE – CURE: The enemy, generally speaking, are all those opposed to our short-term or long-term objectives. But having said that, we must realize that all our enemies are not the same and therefore there is no common cure for their enmity. The conclusion then is that we must categorize and then suggest cures for each category.

Some examples: We have enemies through ignorance, through our own fault or default and of course the main enemy is the establishment.

The enemy through ignorance we attempt to cure through education though such an attempt is obviously futile if we do not firstly educate ourselves. Our means are marches, demonstrations, wall slogans, press statements, Republican press and publications and of course person to person communication. But as already has been stated, we must first educate ourselves, we must organize the protests and demonstrations efficiently, we must be prepared to paint the wall slogans and to sell and contribute to Republican press, Publications and Press statements.

The enemy through our own fault or default is the one we create ourselves through our personal conduct and through our collective conduct of the struggle: the wee woman whose gate or back door gets pulled off its hinges by a volunteer evading arrest and who doesn't get an apology as soon as possible afterwards or more preferably has the damage repaired by one of our supporters; the family friends and neighbours of a criminal or informer who has been punished without their being informed why. In brief our personal conduct as well as our conduct of our Republican activities must be aimed at if not enhancing support, at least at not creating enemies unnecessarily.

The establishment is all those who have a vested interest in maintaining the present status quo in politicians, media, judiciary, certain business elements and the Brit war machine comprising, the Brit Army, the UDR, RUC (r) [reserve], Screws, Civilian Searchers. The cure for these armed branches of the establishment is well known and documented. But with the possible exceptions of the Brit Ministers in the 'Northern Ireland Office' and certain members of the judiciary, the overtly unarmed branches of the establishment are not so clearly identifiable to the people as our enemies as say armed Brits or RUC.

It is our task therefore to clearly identify them to the people as such and again depending on the existing conditions and our ability to get our defensive before our offensive, effect a cure. Execution, as earlier stated, is not the only way of making this category of establishment enemy ineffective: we can variously expose them as liars, hypocrites, collaborators, make them subjects of ridicule etc., e.g. The 'Mason–Superthug' poster image, the 'Captain Nervewreck' cartoon strip, the Conor 'Booze' O'Brien pun etc.

If Dr O'Brien did in fact 'booze' to the extent the IRA pun attempts to suggest, he would not have created the body of writing which makes him the object of their propaganda. But as has been said before it is an Irish Revolution, and no opportunity for humour, however slight, can be lost sight of even when summing up something as important as the movement's strategy (as opposed to tactics).

GUERRILLA STRATEGY: Many figures of speech have been used to describe Guerrilla Warfare, one of the most apt being 'The War of the Flea' which conjured up the image of a flea harrying a creature of by comparison elephantine size into fleeing (forgive the pun). Thus it is with a Guerrilla Army such as the IRA which employs hit and run tactics against the Brits while at the same time striking at the soft economic underbelly of the enemy, not with the hope of physically driving them into the sea but nevertheless expecting to effect their withdrawal by an effective campaign of continuing harassment contained in a fivefold guerrilla strategy.

The strategy is:

1. A war of attrition against enemy personnel which is aimed at causing as many casualties and deaths as possible so as to create a demand from their people at home for their withdrawal.
2. A bombing campaign aimed at making the enemy's financial interest in our country unprofitable while at the same time curbing long term financial investment in our country.
3. To make the Six Counties as at present and for the past several years ungovernable except by colonial military rule.
4. To sustain the war and gain support for its ends by National and International propaganda and publicity campaigns.
5. By defending the war of liberation by punishing criminals, collaborators and informers.

The greatest threat posed to the IRA is that of penetration either by enemy agents and informers or by the supergrass system. To guard against this threat, volunteers learn tactics such as anti-interrogation techniques, which the *Green Book* concentrates on in particular – an indication of how importantly this is viewed by the IRA, and which we will examine shortly. But even more important than the counter-interrogation techniques is the creation of a good self-image on the part of the volunteer, by dinning into him the justice of his cause and his personal superiority to the 'Brit' enemy, who has 'not only the sympathy of, but a degree of control over the elements which largely formulate people's opinions – TV, Radio, the large circulation press'.

> While one of our chief considerations in deciding tactics is the concern for our friends, relatives, neighbours, our people in the midst of whom we operate, the enemy is simply dealing with an impersonal, inferior foreigner, a 'Paddy', 'Muck-Savage' or 'Bog-Wog', and with the great added advantage of all the resources and back up of a conventional army, paramilitary police, etc., e.g. MRF, SAS, plain clothes units, covert surveillance teams etc.
>
> At this juncture the most obvious differences between the Brit and the IRA volunteer, apart from the fact that the Brit is an uninvited armed foreigner who has no moral or historical justification for being here in the first place, are those of support, motivation and freedom of personal initiative.
>
> The Brit's support, his billets, dumps, weapons, wages etc., are all as stated earlier provided for by involuntary taxation. His people who pay the taxes have never indicated nor indeed have they been asked to indicate by any democratic means their assent to his being here at their expense.
>
> The IRA volunteer receives all his support voluntarily from his people.

It is pointed out to the volunteer that 'the Brit, apart from the adventurist elements, has no motivation for being here'.

> A member of the IRA is such by his own choice, his convictions being the only factor which compels him to volunteer, his objectives the political freedom and social and economic justice for his people. Apart from the few minutes in the career of the average Brit that he comes under attack, the Brit has no freedom or personal initiative. He is told when to sleep, where to sleep, when to get up, where to spend his free time etc.

The IRA volunteer, except when carrying out a specific army task, acts most of the time on his own initiative and must therefore shoulder that responsibility in such a way that he enhances our necessary stated task of ensuring that his conduct is not a contributory factor to the Brit attempt to isolate us from our people.

The threat of capture looms over all IRA activity, even more omnipresent than death. It is a situation from which the IRA can draw either defeat as in earlier confrontations with the Curragh for instance, or victory in death as in the H Block struggle. But capture and interrogation are circumstances for which all volunteers have to be prepared en route to the Movement's long-term objective of a Democratic Socialist Republic, before the actual prison, or rather interrogation programming commences. Immediately before the subject of interrogation is dealt with all that a volunteer has learned to date is summarized in chart form as shown on the following page.

The summary continues:

> By now it is clear that our task is not only to kill as many enemy personnel as possible but of equal importance to create support which will carry us not only through a war of liberation which could last another decade but which will support us past the 'Brits Out' stage to the ultimate aim of a Democratic Socialist Republic.
>
> Resistance must be channelled into active and passive support with an on-going process through our actions, our education programmes, our policies, of attempting to turn the passive supporter into a dump holder, a member of the movement, a paper-seller etc., with the purpose of building protective support barriers between the enemy and ourselves, thus curbing the enemy's attempted isolation policy. And of course the more barriers there are, the harder it is for the enemy to get at us while at the same time we increase the potential for active support in its various forms.
>
> The immediate protective barriers are of course, our own security, the other branches of the movement, our billets etc. But we must build up other barriers by championing the various causes in our support areas through involvement in the various enemy structures which have been brought down as a result of the war: Policing, Transport, Bin-Collection, Advice-Centres, etc.
>
> The alternative to our plotting such a course is obvious. IF, for example, we have an area with a unit of IRA volunteers and nothing else: no Sinn Fein Cumann, no Green Cross committee, no local involvement etc., after a period, regardless of how successful they have

been against the Brits, they end up in jail leaving no structures behind: no potential for resistance, recruits, education or general enhancing of support.

It will be seen from the foregoing that despite all the political and military training and advice, the recruit must be warned that jail is something he will almost inevitably experience. Interrogations are frequently simulated in training to increase the volunteers' awareness of what confronts them.

LONG TERM OBJECTIVE: Democratic Socialist Republic
SHORT TERM OBJECTIVE: Brits out

34

The Green Book: II

It is when studying what the volunteer is told will happen to him in the eventuality of capture that one fully realizes the commitment of the rank-and-file IRA man to the 'Cause'. The use of interrogation techniques has been documented in a variety of ways: reports by Amnesty, Lord Compton, Judge Bennett; the case brought by the Government of the Republic before the Court of Human Rights at Strasbourg over the treatment of men caught in the internment swoop of August 1971; and the accounts given by individuals seeking damages for experiences which befell them while in custody. From my own research into prisoners' experiences, particularly for my book *On The Blanket*, I have found that, if anything, the *Green Book* lectures *understate* the horror of what lies in store for a captured IRA man. Certainly whatever makes them face such risks, it is not the £10 a week (£20 for a married man) which was the standard pay in the mid 1980s.

In view of the important light it sheds on a volunteer's conditioning, I am reprinting this section of the *Green Book* at some length:

ANTI-INTERROGATION

1 ARREST

Most volunteers are arrested on or as the result of a military operation. This causes an initial shock resulting in tension and anxiety. All volunteers feel that they have failed, resulting in a deep sense of disappointment. The police are aware of this feeling of disappointment and act upon this weakness by insults such as 'you did not do very well: you are only an amateur: you are only second class or worse'. While being arrested the police use heavy handed 'shock' tactics in order to frighten the prisoner and break down his resistance. The prisoner is usually dragged along the road to the waiting police wagon, flung into it, followed by the arresting personnel, e.g., police or Army. On the journey to the detention centre the prisoner is kicked, punched and the insults start. On arrival he is dragged from the police wagon through a gauntlet of kicks, punches and insults and flung into a cell.

What A Volunteer Should Do When Arrested

1. The most important thing to bear in mind when arrested is that you are a volunteer of a revolutionary army, that you have been captured by an enemy force, that your cause is a just one, that you are right and that the enemy is wrong and that as a soldier you have taken the chance expected of a soldier and that there is nothing to be ashamed of in being captured.

2. You must bear in mind that the treatment meted out to you is designed to break you and so bleed you of all the information you may have with regard to the organization to which you belong.

3. They will attempt to intimidate you by sheer numbers and by brutality. Volunteers who may feel disappointed are entering the first dangerous threshold because the police will act upon this disappointment to the detriment of the volunteer and to the furtherment of their own ends. Volunteers must condition themselves to the obvious fact that they can be arrested and if and when arrested they should expect the worst and be prepared for it.

II · INTERROGATION

After the prisoner has been placed in a cell, he may be left for some time alone. During this lull, police officers, 'The Interrogators', will crowd around the outside of the cell door from time to time, shouting threats and insults, telling the prisoner what they will do to him when they go into the cell.

After some time the interrogators will enter the cell and ask the prisoner to make a confession. During this period he may be subjected to assaults and abusive language, depending on the circumstances surrounding the charge. At this stage he will be fingerprinted and other questions will be put to him, related to the specific charge or other charges. Usually his name and address will be taken, place of employment, occupation, educational standard and so forth. After this he will be again isolated in his cell while his 'interrogators' check his identity, usually with local police, his home and place of employment. In this period of time the police will try to establish his political beliefs, if any, his associates, his police record, if any, and in this way build up a file on him. Most probably 'his associates' and general pattern of movement will give a pretty good idea to the police, if the person is involved in or is sympathetic to a political organization. Armed with this body of information the police will re-enter the cell and accuse the prisoner of all sorts of activity. If the evidence does not indicate a degree of guilt on the specific charge, he will be accused of all kinds of vague activity.

The purpose of these vague accusations is to implant a feeling of guilt in the prisoner. If, however, the police have some evidence or strong beliefs, linking him with a specific charge, pressure will be applied immediately. This pressure will take the form of physical and psychological torture, most probably he will be punched and kicked around the cell while they scream at him to make a confession, indicating to him that they know all. One or more of the interrogating officers will act in a particular and brutal manner, if they fail to get a confession or an admission of guilt they will leave the cell, telling the prisoner they will be back and threatening him with the most barbaric forms of torture, implying that they extracted confessions from better men than he.

Another set of interrogators will enter the cell, possibly carrying a file with the prisoner's name written on it. They will act quite friendly and sympathetic towards him, telling him that they do not condone the activity of the previous interrogators, that they were mad, crazy and possibly they may kill him when they come in later, they will go to extremes to impress the prisoner of their own sympathy towards him, and ask him to make a confession to them indicating that they do not want the previous interrogators 'to get at him again'.

They will probably guarantee him that if he makes the confession they will not allow the former interrogators to re-enter the cell, this will be coupled with a warning that otherwise they cannot guarantee him safety. When the prisoner refuses to confess they will pretend to become very annoyed and disappointed at his lack of co-operation. They may strike him across the face or in the stomach while telling him that he ought to be thankful to them, that they saved him from the previous interrogators and indicating that his behaviour and attitude is a thankless way to repay their kindness.

The interrogators will then open up the file and pretend to read extracts from it, related to the prisoner's past life and activities, even the most intimate and private aspects of his life will be read to him, and possibly a general account of his movements and associates. Most of this information may have been supplied by his friends, employer, school, family, or girlfriend, it may also be 'Pub Talk', local gossip, information supplied by touts or information extracted from other prisoners. This detailed information is designed to frighten the prisoner and to shatter his confidence in his associates and his organization. If, however, they get no confession, they will leave the cell, but before doing so they will give the prisoner their names and tell him to ask for them at any time he wishes to, again indicating that the next set of interrogators are crazy, drunk, and will do him severe damage, then they leave the cell.

After a period of time another set of interrogators will enter the cell, again these interrogators will be particularly brutal and nasty towards him. They will attack him immediately in a most hostile and vicious manner, suggesting to him that if he did not confess to the former interrogators he will confess to them, they will let him know that they have a reputation of getting confessions from people like him, implying that everyone they met confessed before they were finished with them. The torture used will now take on a three-fold purpose:

1 Physical Torture.
2 Subtle Psychological Torture.
3 Humiliation.

1 Physical Torture

The physical torture will be in the form of beatings, kicking, punching and twisting of limbs, it may even be burning from cigarette ends.

2 Psychological Torture

This will be in the form of threats to his family, his friends and himself, e.g. threats of assassination and threats to castrate him.

3 Humiliation

This takes the form of stripping the prisoner of his clothes and remarks passed about his sexual organs. This period of interrogation may last for as long as two hours or more and at the end of that period they may produce a factual or faked confession from an associate. Failing to get their confession they leave the cell, telling him they will be back and when they do come back they will break every bone in his body.

This process can continue for seven days without a break, the minimum of sleep is allowed and if they deem it necessary, no sleep will be allowed. Lack of sleep causes the prisoner to become confused.

Because of the existing laws which authorize the police to detain a person for seven days, it means in effect that the process of interrogation can continue to disorientate their victim, due in the main to lack of sleep.

Interrogation can have many different phases, depending on the evidence or information which the police have gathered. It is obvious that a volunteer captured carrying out an operation is already seen to be guilty, especially if captured with a weapon bomb, etc., in this case the police have all the evidence needed to obtain a conviction and interrogation becomes unnecessary. Most likely the volunteer will be beaten up in the police stations for what he has done, not for what he knows. If interrogated under these circumstances it will be to get information on the organization to which he belongs and on his comrades. Another shady aspect directly related to interrogation is blackmail and bribe. When the police cannot obtain a confession they may attempt to blackmail the volunteer, this may be in the form of threats to spread scandalous stories about the volunteer, stories or threats may be designed to hit at the character of the volunteer such as a threat to tell his comrades or his organization that he told everything or that he had been working for them for years. The other phase of this shady interrogation is bribe. A volunteer may be promised money, a passport and a safe passage to any country he so desires if he co-operates.

THE INTERROGATION – ANALYSIS

The best defence in anti-interrogation techniques is to understand the techniques as practised by police forces. The purpose of interrogation is to get a confession. If the interrogators knew what they were searching for then there would be no need for interrogation, therefore interrogation is necessary only when the police are unaware of information, which would lead to a conviction. The best anti-interrogation is to SAY NOTHING . . . All police forces work from a story suspicion or a clue, therefore when a volunteer is arrested they strive to build that clue on that suspicion and the only way that can be done is to obtain information from their victim. They usually start by questioning their victim, writing down a recording of what he says, comparing this information with information already in their possession, looking for differences which contradict the information previously gained, going back to their victim, pointing out these differences, resulting in the victim changing his alibi in order to suit this difference. The police will again check this new story with other information and again look for a difference or mistake narrowing the prisoner's alibi down until finally it breaks. All of these changes in his statements will be recorded and used as evidence against him, evidence which will without doubt be accepted by the court and so lead to his conviction. This cannot be over stressed: when arrested SAY NOTHING . . . Ask to see your solicitor and doctor immediately and keep on doing so.

DO NOT INDULGE IN CONVERSATION WITH THE POLICE

After the prisoner had been placed in his cell, we have seen earlier in the lecture how the police had crowded outside the cell door shouting insults and banging on the door. The purpose of this exercise is to frighten the prisoner and so arouse anxiety in their victim. When anxiety has been aroused all natural, rational defence barriers break down or weaken. When this happens the prisoner becomes irrational and becomes more prone to interrogation, in other words an anxious or frightened man is easier to intimidate by interrogation than a cool, calculating person. During the time the prisoner is left alone in the cell, he should, in as far as is possible, ignore the police, the threats and the insults and he should marshall all facts surrounding his arrest. He should bear in mind that he can be detained for no more than seven days and he should understand clearly the issue involved, detention for seven days if he remains silent or possibly years in prison if he speaks. Most volunteers speak from a sense of fear thinking mistakenly that if they speak, torture or ill treatment will not be used. It is a recorded fact that interrogators are guided by a simple rule of thumb: 'If a prisoner won't speak he may be innocent and interrogation may be a waste of time, if he speaks a little there is always more and so interrogation is necessary', therefore the prisoner who speaks a little in order to avoid abuse is in effect inviting more abuse from his interrogators who will always assume there is something more. Therefore the best defence is to remain COOL, COLLECTED, CALM, and SAY NOTHING.

We have seen earlier in the lecture how the first batch of interrogators will enter the cell usually insulting, shouting and beating the prisoner. Volunteers should understand that this first batch of interrogators usually fingerprint, ask name, address etc. At this stage a little is known about the prisoner and therefore the task of the interrogator is to identify him positively. Again the prisoner must bear in mind that everything he says will be recorded and compared with existing information in the possession of the police. The purpose of abusing the prisoner at this stage is called the 'softening up period', usually one or more will act in a particularly nasty manner. This interrogation period may last no more than one hour and is only a preliminary investigation. The purpose of using heavy handed techniques and sheer hostility is an opening for the following batch of interrogators, whom we have seen act in a particularly sympathetic manner.

This set of interrogators, we have seen, acted in a friendly and sympathetic manner towards the prisoner, offering him cigarettes and friendship. Volunteers should be well aware and on guard against their feigned friendship. These interrogators pretend to be sympathetic towards the aims and objects of the movement, going to lengths to impress the volunteer, pretending that they too believe in a united Ireland. They will, no doubt, tell the volunteer that their father or grandfather was in the same organization and that they were forced by economic circumstances to join the police force and that they are now merely passing the time until they are pensioned off. They will try to convince the volunteer that it is in his interest to make a confession, that they advise him to make a confession to them in order to escape from the previous interrogators who, they claim, are anti-Republican and are not interested in getting a confession but are only interested in beating the prisoner up. The volunteer should understand that these seemingly kind police officers may be acting the tough cop with his comrades who had been or are arrested. Finally, we have seen how these interrogators, pretending to become upset, have stretched forward and beat the volunteer about the face and body, declaring that their advice and friendship was being returned or repaid with a stubborn attitude and a refusal to make EVEN PART OF A CONFESSION. This technique is as old as police forces, they attempt to win over the friendship and trust of the prisoner, hoping that if their prisoner falls into that trap he will become upset, not so much at the punching about the face which he received from them but at his own refusal to co-operate: this perhaps is the most dangerous type of interrogation and one which leaves the prisoner in a psychologically vulnerable position.

Another technique is called TOP SECRET FILE TECHNIQUE, this involves the interrogators bringing into the cell a file with the prisoner's name printed on it. The police will open this file in the presence of the prisoner as we have seen earlier in the lecture. They proceed to read from this file parts of the prisoner's past life, even to the most intimate details, and a general account of his movements and friends, especially those associated with or known to have contacts or sympathies with a political organization, e.g., Sinn Fein. They also have information gathered from various sources such as employer, neighbours, PUB TALK OR LOCAL GOSSIP. Very often the PUB TALK and gossip is factual, this arises from the volunteer or volunteers in general speaking in pubs under the influence of alcohol, telling close friends and girl friends and boasting in a bravado manner about their exploits and the exploits of others. This type of bravado is POSITIVELY DANGEROUS, not only to the volunteer and his associates but to the Movement in general. Another dangerous aspect of interrogation is 'an associate's confession', this involves an interrogator approaching the volunteer with a signed or unsigned, factual or unfactual confession of an associate. Volunteers must understand (in the first place) this confession may be a hoax and in the second, even if it is a factual confession of his associate, this confession is not an indication of guilt and will not be accepted in court unless his associate who made the confession is prepared to turn State or Crown witness and is prepared to swear its truth in the witness box. Very often a volunteer may break under severe physical and psychological torture and make a confession, but rarely is prepared to turn Crown or State witness and swear against his comrades. If this technique is employed by the police DON'T FALL FOR IT, it is a trick to weaken the volunteer and so get him to make and sign a statement.

Another dangerous technique employed, is bringing the prisoner who made a statement into the same room as the volunteer who refuses to co-operate, usually they are left on their own and the prisoner who made a statement may try to entice his comrade to do likewise. If this happens to you always bear in mind that you are not alone because the room is always bugged and any talk is recorded. Another important point to bear in mind is when the prisoner who confessed and perhaps implicated you approaches, don't launch into a verbal attack on him because this verbal attack on him would be an implication of your guilt, always speak friendly to him and suggest he must be mistaken, that he is ill and advise him to seek medical attention.

Another important point to be remembered and one which is extremely important, DON'T GET INVOLVED IN A POLITICAL CONVERSATION, this technique is a universal tactic and one which recurs repeatedly. When volunteers refuse to make a confession and when all other tactics of interrogation have failed, the police usually, if not always, attempt to get the volunteer to speak on political matters. This is a technique which many volunteers fail to recognize, its purpose is to fling the volunteer off balance, to sound out his political thinking, to break his silence and so make it easier for him to speak freely. This tactic has been used against volunteers and very often to their own detriment. When a volunteer has been arrested and the usual terror tactics used against him, this display of friendship has a weakening effect upon him and can be explained in psychological terms.

As we have seen earlier in this lecture, these seemingly friendly interrogators will give their names to the prisoner before they leave the cell, telling him that the next set of interrogators are crazy, anti-Republicans who are out to do him harm, they will tell him to call upon them at any time he so wishes and they will do their best to save him from brutal treatment. All volunteers must understand and understand in the clearest possible way that no interrogator is his friend, that they are the enemy, the instruments of coercion, the tools of suppression and a more dangerous enemy than the interrogators who will beat him up. These people act a part in a well-rehearsed play, and are using subtle psychological techniques in order to undermine the morale of the volunteer. All volunteers are well versed in brutal treatment as practised by the police and Army. They understand what physical torture means, but now you will have to understand the meaning and application of psychological torture, perhaps the term is an uncommon one, but its effects are far reaching.

We have seen earlier in this lecture how the 'heavy squad' now enters the scene and proceeds to attack the volunteer in a most vicious and brutal manner.

This shock treatment is well rehearsed and is meant to push the volunteer into a physical and mental corner, in other words they hope that their shock treatment will knock the volunteer off balance, and off guard in the hope that he will confess. They will shout statements to the effect that they have a reputation for extracting confessions, that they have never yet failed and that he will not fool them. Now we must analyse this approach, the first thing we note of importance is, the shouting in conjunction with the physical torture, the shouting as we shall see is a more important interrogation technique than the physical torture. Again, why shout? Why boast? Why tell the volunteer that they are experts at extracting information? This shouting and boasting is merely an assurance to the police that they can get a confession, it is the first obvious sign of their own weakness, a compensation for their own shortcomings and all volunteers should and ought to look upon this display as a modern war dance. Just as primitive peoples held war dances, and built totem poles in order to compensate themselves for their own known weakness, so too frustrated interrogators will shout and boast in front of the prisoner to compensate themselves for their own weakness. The best anti-interrogation technique when a volunteer finds himself in this situation, is to look upon the police interrogators as he would look upon primitive people, wearing the head of a dead animal, hoping that by doing this they gain the strength or cunning of the animal whose head they wear. All volunteers should look upon shouting, boasting policemen as they would look upon primitive people doing a war dance.

While the sole object of this frightening lecture is to defeat the British and all British influences, reading the following passage one could be forgiven for thinking that the IRA, for all their Irishness, had acquired the peculiarly British characteristic of understatement.

PSYCHOLOGICAL TORTURE

We have seen that this type of torture is widespread and usually in the form of threats to the volunteer in question, to his friends and family, threats to assassinate him, to blacken his character, to castrate him; loss of sleep, poor quality food and continuous noise. This in conjunction with physical torture and the fear of physical torture builds up anxiety and borders on hysteria. All of this is designed to smash down the volunteer's natural defence mechanism, usually a person held for a period of time, perhaps seven days, living in an environment of fear and indecision, constantly being threatened, cut off from all natural contacts, deprived of his usual social surroundings, lack of sleep etc. This can and does form disorientation and disillusionment: during this period the volunteer will get no sleep or very little sleep, living this type of vague existence for a number of days can leave its mark and deserves an independent lecture.

The sexual overtones of some interrogation techniques are graphically described in a section devoted to humiliation.

HUMILIATION

We have seen that this type of interrogation technique invariably is stripping the prisoner of all his clothes and remarks passed about his sexual organs. Volunteers should be aware of the proven fact that clothes are an important aspect of the individual's character or make up. By removing his clothes the interrogators hope to remove the volunteer's character and make up, psychologically this is symbolic and by doing this the police like to humiliate the volunteer and so lift away the barriers, just as they find barriers preventing them from getting a confession. A person's clothes become symbolic of this barrier and by removing them they hope to remove the natural defence mechanism of the volunteer.

The second part of humiliation is to pass derogatory remarks about the volunteer's sexual organs. This is quite common in all police stations, North, South and in England. Volunteers should attempt to understand the mentality which underlies this act and so be better prepared to meet this angle if and when it happens to them. Just as they removed the volunteer's clothes which symbolized a defence mechanism or natural barrier so too by passing derogatory remarks about the volunteer's sexual organs they attempt to humiliate the volunteer and by so doing to weaken his will to resist. The mere act of doing this has deeper undertones than one would guess. Volunteers should understand that from a psychological point of view this act is called a penis complex. This complex is inherent in the homosexual and although the interrogators themselves may be married men with a family it indicates suppressed homosexual tendencies. When the volunteer realizes and under-

Uniformed U.D.A. paramilitaries with British Army protection. Belfast, 1972. (*Colman Doyle*)

Provisional I.R.A. leaders (left to right) Martin McGuinness, Daithi O Connell, Sean MacStiofain, and Seamus Twomey, on 23 June 1972. (*Pacemaker*)

Michael Gaughan's funeral as it passed through Dublin, 8 June 1974. Gaughan, of Ballina, County Mayo, died on hungerstrike in Parkhurst prison, Isle of Wight, England. (*Colman Doyle*)

Michael Gaughan, who died on hungerstrike in a English prison in June 1974.

Bobby Sands became an icon of the Republican movement in 1981 when he died on hungerstrike while in Long Kesh Prison.

Prisoners inside Long Kesh Prison during internment in the 1970s. This snapshot was taken by one of the prisoners and smuggled out.

Members of the R.U.C. search Republican suspects before making an arrest in 1970s Belfast. (*Colman Doyle*)

The presence of the British Army is an aspect of everyday life in Belfast (as shown here in the 1970s) throughout the Troubles, and right up to the present day. (*Colman Doyle*)

Arms from the United States bound for the I.R.A. captured aboard the trawler *Marita Ann* off the Kerry Coast on 29 September 1984. (*Irish Times*)

Inside the Grand Hotel, Brighton, England, after the I.R.A. bomb exploded on 12 October 1984. British Prime Minister Margaret Thatcher narrowly escaped death in the explosion which killed five people and injured many more. (*Press Association*)

Sefton, the Household Cavalry horse and his rider, Trooper Michael Pederson, both badly injured in the Hyde Park bombing of 20 July 1982. (*Press Association*)

Remains of the Austin 1100 used in the car bomb attack outside Harrods on 17 December 1983. (*Press Association*)

Mortar launches used in I.R.A. attack on Newry R.U.C. Barracks on 28 February 1985. Nine members of the R.U.C. were killed and thirty-two injured. (*Pacemaker*)

Plain clothed policemen and Army at the scene of the shooting of Sinn Fein President Gerry Adams in 1984. (*Pacemaker*)

Signing of the Anglo-Irish Agreement on 15 November 1985, at Hills-
borough, County Down, by Irish Prime Minister Garrett FitzGerald and
British Prime Minister Margaret Thatcher. The three men standing in the
centre are, from left to right, Irish Deputy Prime Minister Dick Spring,
Northern Ireland Secretary Tom King, and British Foreign Secretary, Sir
Geoffrey Howe. (*Pacemaker*)

Rev. Ian Paisley salutes the crowd gathered at City Hall, Belfast, during
the massive Loyalist demonstration against the Anglo-Irish Agreement on
23 November 1985. (*Pacemaker*)

Sinn Fein President Gerry Adams carries the coffin of James Lynagh, an I.R.A. unit commander killed by the S.A.S. in a shoot-to-kill ambush at Loughall, County Armagh, on 8 May 1987. (*Colman Doyle*)

The scene at Enniskillen on 8 November 1987, where an I.R.A. bomb exploded during the annual Remembrance Day commemoration. Eleven civilians were killed and sixty-three were injured in what is one of the worst I.R.A. atrocities of the Troubles. (*Pacemaker*)

Two scenes of the violence that broke out in the streets of Belfast in March 1988, in the wake of the killing of three I.R.A. members in Gibraltar by the S.A.S. in a shoot-to-kill operation. (*Pacemaker*)

Gerald Conlon, one of the Guildford Four, outside the Old Bailey court in London after his release on 19 October 1989. He served fifteen years for a crime that he was totally innocent of. (*Press Association*)

Hugh Callaghan, one of the Birmingham Six, in Dublin after his release in March 1991. (*Colman Doyle*)

A Scotland Yard security picture showing the devastation to the City of London by the massive I.R.A. bomb on 24 April 1993.

Smoke billows from the burning van in Whitehall, London after the mortar bomb attack on Prime Minister John Major and his Cabinet in 10 Downing Street on 2 February 1991. (*Press Association*)

Loyalist demonstrators in the Shankhill Road mark the announcement of the IRA ceasefire. (*Martin McCullough/Press Association*)

One of the hundreds of Republicans who turned out to listen to the speech given by Sinn Fein president, Gerry Adams, at Connolly House, Belfast, following the IRA ceasefire announcement, 31 August 1994. (*Martin McCullough/Press Association*)

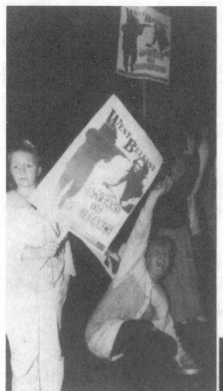

Nationalists in celebratory mood gathered outside Springfield Road police station minutes after the IRA ceasefire came into effect. (*Martin McCullough/Press Association*)

Loyalists from east Belfast walk to the City Hall in the early hours to celebrate the Loyalist paramilitary groups' ceasefire, October 1994. (*Martin McCullough/Press Association*)

Falls Road after a
bomb explosion.
(*Press Association/
Topham*)

Adams, Reynolds
and Hume in Dublin,
1994. (*Pacemaker*)

Aftermath of the
Canary Wharf bomb,
11 February 1996.
(*Popperfoto*)

Prime Minister Tony Blair and Taoiseach Bertie Aherne sign the Good Friday Agreement, 10 April 1998. (*Popperfoto*)

The Omagh bomb of 15 August 1998, killed 29 people. (*PA News*)

Father Sean Larkin celebrates mass on the front line of the Garvaghy Road, Portadown, where the massive security operation in place for an orange order march prevented his congregation from attending their church, 6 July 1997. (*Topham Picturepoint*)

Peter Mandelson replaced Mo Mowlam as Secretary of State for Northern Ireland, 11 October 1999. (*PA News*) stands this proven fact he should not have great difficulty in triumphing over his interrogators. He should look upon them as homosexuals with the immunity of the establishment, as people who become sadistic from the homosexual tendencies which underlie them.

BRIBERY and BLACKMAIL are also discussed with a grim warning for those who succumb to such techniques.

The police sometimes attempt to use blackmail and bribe in the last vain attempt to obtain a confession. All volunteers should ignore this type of carrot-dangling. Blackmail rarely works effectively and can backfire against the police in libellous action and so bad publicity. Bribery never works, despite the fact that a volunteer may be offered money and protection in exchange for information. He should bear in mind that when he is of no further use to the police they drop him and the protection means nothing, for example, Kenneth Lennon.[*]

To avoid ending up like the unfortunate Lennon, volunteers are finally given some advice on how to make MIND triumph over MATTER.

While being tortured in a brutal, physical manner it is important that the volunteer should consolidate his position, he should realize that it's seven days if he keeps silent, perhaps seventeen years if he speaks. It's no easy thing to dismiss physical torture as a small meaningless thing. It is by no means small and by no means meaningless to the receiver. From time immemorial, from histories recorded as far back as the Babylonian Empire up through the days of Imperial Rome, from the Spanish Inquisition to Nazi Concentration Camps, Free State and British police stations, come stories of how people coped and defeated the attempts of police to beat information from prisoners.

One notable technique was the prisoners' ability to form images in their minds or on the surrounding walls. People who were brutalized found that by directing their powers of concentration away from their interrogators and diverting it to images formed in their own mind they could in effect overcome the physical pain. Some people pictured images in their own mind or in the mind's eye, this picture may have been a flickering candlelight, a leaf or a flower, but by concentrating upon it, by building it and by stabilizing it, it seemed to attract their concentration so strongly in fact, that physical abuse became meaningless. This mental exercise is called by some psychologists mind over matter and is said to be a highly successful and invincible anti-interrogation technique.

[*] Lennon was found shot dead in a ditch after the IRA tracked him down – in England.

Little is known of the laws surrounding this technique but all authorities associated with its research maintain that people under severe physical and mental pressure seem to adapt themselves to this state. People without previous experience or knowledge of the subject, but who under interrogation stumble across this technique maintained that it worked but they did not know why.

Again, some people found that by staring at a certain spot on a cell wall they experienced a similar sensation. It may be that the ancient Indian practice of Yoga has close or similar sensations, but one thing is certain that when a person's concentration is directed away from his interrogators he seems to triumph and perhaps torture is a method employed by the police to hold the prisoner's attention on them. This advice should be at least considered by volunteers.

In conclusion, if and when arrested:

SAY NOTHING, SIGN NOTHING, SEE NOTHING, HEAR NOTHING.

But to illustrate just what one has to train the mind to deal with, the most shocking warning on psychological torture is kept until the end.

A technique at present being practised by the Brits and Police is one of shock aimed psychologically. This involves exposing blown up photographs, usually of dead bomb victims, dead soldiers and policemen and more often than not the corpses of the suspect's comrades. The technique behind this tactic is to arouse emotions of hysteria in the suspect and by so doing to disorientate him temporarily. All volunteers must understand and be fully aware of the anxiety, the shock and the hysteria it can arouse in the unprotected suspect.

By understanding this technique and by looking at it logically and the tactic behind it, volunteers should be ready to meet the situation of that nature, with confidence in the knowledge that its purpose is to shock the volunteer into confession. Another tactic of this nature is throwing the limb or limbs of a corpse into the cell of the suspect. To the best of our knowledge this tactic has been used only once, but successfully, again in the Miami Showband case.[*]

The best protection while being interrogated is LOYALTY to the Movement. This implies LOYALTY to all YOUR COMRADES and PROTECTION of all members of the Movement. Again commitment to the aims and objectives of the Movement, a deep and unmoving POLITICAL COMMITMENT to the ideas of the Socialist Republic, CONSTANT AWARENESS

[*] Members of the Miami Showband, a popular group from the Republic, were ambushed and murdered during the wave of sectarian assassinations (see Chapter 25) in Armagh. An attempt was made to destroy their bus and bodies with bombs.

that you are a REVOLUTIONARY with a sound POLITICAL base, NOBLE and JUSTIFIABLE CAUSE, and a deep and firm belief that those holding you and interrogating you are MORALLY WRONG, that you are SUPERIOR in all respects, because your cause is RIGHT and JUSTIFIED.

PART IV

1986–1993

35

The Enemy of My Enemy is My Friend

Legitimate Targets and Shoot-to-Kill

The years that have elapsed since 1986 were filled with incident. An attempt to chronicle all that happened within the present compass would result in just that, a chronicle, a litany of horror, salami of the mind. Instead, I propose to concentrate on a selected number of the major developments of the period; episodes which made world news, or which I know from some involvement of my own to be especially significant.

In their battle against the IRA the British relied more and more on the talents of the Special Air Services (SAS). Based in Hereford, the SAS are the British Army's elite hit-unit. They are particularly effective when deployed on behalf of friendly sultans in Brunei or Oman – away from the media. SAS commandos are highly paid and trained to an unusual pitch of fitness. SAS men commonly perform operations such as waiting for days in a hole in the ground for a suspect to show up. In this time they will remain immobile, sleeping in wet clothes, and defecating into plastic bags. The suspect, if he arrives, ceases to be regarded as a suspect and becomes a target. SAS men are trained to shoot to kill.

The SAS played a leading role in one of the worst blows suffered by the IRA since 1986 in the village of Loughall, County Armagh, on 8 May 1987. Nine men were killed, one of them an innocent passerby, Anthony Hughes, a Protestant, whose car was fired on by the SAS. The eight IRA men who were killed included at least four senior IRA figures, James Lynagh, James Lynch, Patrick Kelly and Patrick McKearney. Lynch, from Tully, County Monaghan, had done several jail terms, but though released, was on the RUC's 'most wanted' list. Kelly was the principal leader of the IRA in County Tyrone. Lynagh, the commander of a particularly active unit which, amongst many other operations, is thought to have carried out the 1981 attack on the home of Sir Normal Stronge and his son James, two of the North's leading Unionists, in which both men were killed. McKearney was one of the men who led the Great Escape from Long Kesh in 1983.

The conventional wisdom is that the security forces had an informer close to Kelly and Lynagh – a woman called Colette O'Neill was later kidnapped by the IRA for this reason, but was rescued by the RUC –and that both men were kept under close surveillance as they planned an attack on Loughall RUC station. The resulting intelligence enabled the SAS to be in waiting as the raiding party drove up to the barracks, shortly after seven p.m. In the resulting shoot-out all the IRA men were killed. Like the curate's egg the story is good in parts. The IRA attack was expected and a shoot-to-kill policy was applied with ruthless efficiency. Indeed it is said that an IRA killing was allowed to go ahead less than two weeks earlier, on 25 April, so that the stake-out would be successful.

In this fatal incident a member of the UDR, William Graham, was shot dead in front of his wife at Pomeroy, County Tyrone. The link with Loughall was established in two ways. Weapons captured at Loughall were proved to have been used to shoot Graham. Moreover, a footprint left by one of his killers matched that of one of the Loughall dead. It is said that the RUC informer had warned of Graham's intended murder but I do not have any first hand knowledge on this point. What I can say with certainty is that, apart from encapsulating in a single incident all the brutality of the Northern conflict, Loughall was highly significant in a number of other ways.

There was the importance of the IRA unit which was taken out; the demonstration of the existence of the oft denied 'shoot-to-kill' policy on the part of the British; and the manner in which both psychological warfare and straightforward happenstance play a part in the war. History has ingrained into the IRA a deep-rooted fear and detestation of informers. The RUC seek to increase the fears and uncertainties by allowing it to be believed that their informants are more effective than they are in fact. As a result, acting on the principle that just because you are paranoid does not mean they are not out to get you, the IRA are sometimes driven to act in a manner damaging to their own side. Misplaced suspicions are thought to have cost the lives of some IRA victims wrongly executed as 'touts'.

It happened that at the time of the Loughall incident I was acting as an intermediary in discussions between a Republican contact and a high-ranking Dublin Government figure. The contact had been originated by

Roman Catholic clergy who were trying to further dialogue between the various parties to the conflict. The process eventually led, amongst other conversations, to the talks between the Sinn Fein President, Gerry Adams and the leader of the SDLP, John Hume. Loughall occurred shortly after I had introduced my Northern contact to the Dublin cabinet member, who asked if I could find out what had really happened. I did so and my contact came to Dublin to deliver his report in person, in my presence. Significantly his account contradicted the official SAS version. As I have known this man for over twenty years and can vouch for both his character and his standing I give its substance here:

The attack on the barracks formed part of the IRA's overall objective of driving the RUC out of the countryside. A number of other Tyrone barracks had already been attacked, at Ballygawley, Carrickmore, Castlederg and elsewhere. Once destroyed, the IRA targeted, and sometimes killed, building contractors who attempted to rebuild them, regarding anyone who assisted the RUC or the British Army as collaborators. The object of the Loughall attack was to destroy the barracks, not to take life. That is why the operation commenced after the barracks' normal closure time, 7 p.m. Two vehicles were used, a mechanical digger and a van. The digger, holding two of the party, was intended to smash through the barracks' protective fence, after which it was planned to use a bomb, carried by the digger, to blow up the building.

Prior to the attack, the barracks, situated in a predominantly Loyalist town, had been extensively reconnoitred. However, the party – based across the border – which carried out the reconnoitring, used a car belonging to one of the raiding party's leaders. On one occasion it broke down, attracting Loyalist attention. The number was noted and the RUC computer did the rest. It was obvious that the only thing which would cause an IRA man of the calibre of the car's owner to come to Loughall was the barracks.

Heavy surveillance was instituted and by 8 May, the authorities were in possession of sufficient intelligence to enable them to ring the Loughall area with hundreds of hidden, armed police and soldiers. The actual killing was left to the SAS who were deployed in and around the barracks a few hours before the attack was scheduled to begin. Five of the IRA party from the van were killed in the opening fusillades. The two in the digger managed to detonate the bomb, destroying the barracks. Then they and the single survivor from the van were captured. All three were ordered to lie on the road and shot dead.

The IRA's view, said my contact, was that this was 'fair enough', the wiping out of an enemy unit. 'It was war. They'd have done the same.'

Loughall was a short term gain for the authorities. Each of the dead eight's funerals probably drew more than fifty replacements for the IRA and greatly increased support for Sinn Fein. It is difficult to overstress the potency of funerals in generating this kind of support for Republicanism. A month before Loughall, the television screens were filled with images from the delayed Lawrence Marley funeral in Belfast. Marley was a prominent IRA man who had been murdered by the UVF. In order to guard against military displays at his funeral, the RUC surrounded the Marley home. But the family refused to take the coffin through the cordons, and after three days the police compromised sufficiently for the funeral to go ahead – followed to the grave by thousands of sympathizers. Once again, the 'funeral factor' was back at work for the IRA, reversing another SAS inflicted defeat.

The phrase 'Death on the Rock' covers a triple series of killings, which like a three stage rocket, blasted the IRA on and on into the consciousness of the world's media during March 1988. The phrase had its origins in an IRA decision to extend its European campaign to Gibraltar in the spring of 1988 by car-bombing a changing of the guard ceremony. The intended bombers were three well-known IRA figures, Mairead Farrell, Daniel McCann and Sean Savage. McCann had served two years on explosive charges and though Savage had not been in jail, he was on RUC records as being an active IRA man. Farrell was the most prominent of the three. When I interviewed her in 1980, she was the leader of the Republican women prisoners on a Dirty Protest in Armagh Jail as part of the campaign for political status which eventually led to the Bobby Sands led hunger strikes of 1981. She was caked in filth and the walls of her cell were smeared with excrement and menstrual blood. Farrell had been destined for a medical career but her studies were interrupted by a ten-year sentence for attempting to blow up a Belfast hotel. She never resumed them.

The IRA unit's presence in Spain became known as early as November 1987, after the trio checked in their false passports at their hotel. The checking requirement had not been foreseen apparently. I am told that one of the documents did not contain a proper passport number, but the subject's social security number or some such. In any event, the Spanish authorities, thinking they might be involved in drug-running, notified Interpol, who informed the British. Farrell's presence in particular led the British to react initially by getting the Spanish to ensure that the trio were closely monitored. Subsequently, at Cabinet level in Mrs Thatcher's Government, a judicial murder was decided upon. On 2 March 1988, an SAS 'hit squad' was flown to Gibraltar with instructions to kill the IRA party.

On 6 March, the unarmed IRA unit carried out yet another reconnaissance mission into Gibraltar. They were shadowed to the border by Spanish security who were in radio contact with their British opposite numbers. As in Loughall they drove not into an arrest, but an ambush. They were shot dead on the streets of Gibraltar. This was the first stage of the fatal rocket. The second ignited at their funerals at Milltown Cemetery, Belfast, on 16 March. A Protestant gunman, Michael Stone, made a grenade and pistol attack on the huge attendance in revenge for an IRA atrocity (the Enniskillen bombing described below). Three people were killed and fifty injured. The third stage exploded three days later, on 19 March, at the funeral of one of Stone's victims, Kevin Brady. Two off-duty British corporals, Robert Howes and Derek Wood, were set upon by the crowd who mistakenly took them to be on another SAS/Stone mission. The men, who may have simply taken a wrong turning, were dragged out of their car by members of the crowd, stripped, beaten, and then shot dead.

The continuing controversy over the rocket's first stage, the Gibraltar killings, was heightened by the Thames TV documentary, *Death on the Rock*. The programme, for which Roger Bolton was responsible, was screened despite strenuous efforts by Mrs Thatcher's Government to have it stopped. It highlighted not only the circumstances of the shootings, but the British tabloid campaign, notably in Rupert Murdoch's *Sun*, against witnesses who had helped to discredit official attempts at a cover-up. Bolton later worked with me on the making of another, lengthier, drama-documentary on the Anglo-Irish Treaty of 1921, which explained how the entire Anglo-Irish problem had come about in the first place. He was at the editing stage of the programme in November 1991, when the final stage of the Gibraltar rocket crash-landed. The Conservatives announced that, in the review of broadcasting franchises which had been in progress for some months, Thames Television was to lose its licence.

Currently, Roger Bolton is an independent TV producer, Michael Stone is serving life imprisonment, as are some of the people who dragged the two corporals from their car, but the identity of those who shot them has not been established. Nor has it been made known who was responsible for the IRA's worst single atrocity of the period, the Enniskillen bombing on Remembrance Day, 8 November 1987, which ushered in the period during which the IRA campaign reached its nadir.

Enniskillen, and its aftermath, illustrates how, even for supporters of the IRA, the terrorist line of acceptable targets can be crossed into unacceptability. But it also demonstrates how the Northern Ireland situation generates circumstances that inevitably win back that support for the IRA. It serves too to encapsulate all the problems posed for a volunteer, underground army, depending largely on targets of opportunity, stemming from a recruitment of individuals whose emotions can outrun their educational or political attainments. The 'funeral factor' or, perhaps, hatred of the system, prejudice, whatever, may provide the courage and motivation for an attack, but not the foresight to gauge its political outcome.

At Enniskillen there was, as usual, a respectable turnout of Protestants for the annual commemoration of locals who had died in Britain's wars. To the attendance the fallen had given their lives to maintain a way of life, and a set of values symbolized by the Union. Suddenly, without warning, a bomb went off at the speakers' platform killing eleven civilian men and women, and injuring sixty-three others. The inexcusable slaughter caused the unit responsible to be disbanded, the IRA to apologize publicly, and Gerry Adams to declare at the subsequent Sinn Fein Ard Fheis (in January 1988) that the accidental killing of civilians would have to stop. Gordon Wilson, a Protestant shopkeeper whose daughter died in the blast, forgave her killers and aroused such widespread admiration that he was subsequently appointed a member of the Seanad, the Dail's Upper House.

But the toll of innocent civilians continued to grow. The following December an IRA bomb accidentally claimed the lives of two pensioners and over the ensuing months there was a series of equally ghastly events. The sister of a man wrongly thought to be in the UDR was shot in mistake for her brother. Two Catholics were killed by an IRA bomb set on the Falls Road, where it could hardly have failed to kill 'some of their own'. In July 1988, the entire Hannah family, apolitical Protestants, was wiped out by a bomb placed not for their car but that of a judge. In all, from Enniskillen to the Hannahs, there were seventeen grisly IRA mistakes, one of them a Dublin nun, Sister Catherine, accidentally caught in a blast that killed four RUC men. It was a time during which the IRA sustained an unprecedented barrage of criticism from London, Dublin and Belfast. A recurring theme both during and after this period was that the IRA were nothing more than an Irish version of the Mafia, Green Godfathers involved in racketeering.

If this were the simple truth about the IRA, the movement would have come to an end years ago through lack of popular support. But racketeers do not produce hunger strikers to the death from their ranks, nor volunteers willing to inflict and endure for stipends of often less than twenty pounds a week. The more complex truth about the IRA's finance is that both in the present era, and in the glory days which led to the setting up of an Irish Republic in twenty-six Irish counties, the IRA has always financed itself by a system of levies. Its theory of banking is based largely upon withdrawals. In the vast majority of cases these levies or subscriptions were and are given willingly. In a very small percentage of cases straightforward extortion has been known to occur, both in the previous and present IRA campaigns. Generally, however, when the IRA leadership has become aware of extortion or theft for individual gain, it has put an end to the practice; sometimes by the horrible punishment of kneecapping (crippling the victim with a bullet in the kneecap).

This is not to say that the IRA has not continued to derive funds from highly illegal and reprehensible activities such as bankrobberies, kidnapping and building site scams, but it does so to fund a war effort, not to enrich Godfathers. Of my own knowledge I can state that over the past quarter of a century I have carried out interviews in the homes and families of many of the top IRA leaders. Certainly these very often cramped 'kitchen houses' of back street Belfast showed no sign of affluence, nor did the lifestyle of their occupants. In dealing with the vexed question of the IRA's finance, one should perhaps keep in mind the axiom of a medical friend of mind who ran a hospital for the treatment of alcoholism. His rule of thumb about patients' consumption levels was to believe: 'Half what the wife says he drinks and twice what he says.'

The period of the IRA's 'mistakes' was horrific, but instructive; for despite the outrage generated by the IRA's blunders, that generated by the authorities' SAS-type response and the continuing bending of the rules of the judicial system enabled the IRA to survive. Indeed, not only to survive their mistakes, but to deliberately perpetrate fresh horrors: the introduction of the repulsive proxy bomber tactic. This, mercifully short-lived, initiative consisted of forcing people to drive bombs to targets by threatening their families. It reached its peak on 24 October 1990, when the IRA tied three alleged informers to the seats of trucks and compelled them to drive the lethal vehicles to British Army installations. One terrified, screaming, but inarticulate, driver failed to communicate his mission to puzzled soldiers and the resultant explosion claimed seven lives including his own.

However, coming against the background of all that had gone before, the continuing impact of Loughall and Gibraltar helped to level up the sympathy scales on the one hand, while on the other, episodes such as shooting down a helicopter at Crossmaglen, in June 1988, or blowing up a bus killing eight soldiers at Ballygawley, County Tyrone in August, showed the IRA to be engaged in a military campaign, not indiscriminate murder. One incident I know of may be cited as attesting to the depth of support for the IRA that exists in some areas of Northern Ireland.

Kevin Barry O'Donnell, aged 21, was one of four IRA men ambushed and killed by the SAS in a shoot-to-kill operation at St Patrick's Church near Coalisland, County Tyrone. (The others were Sean O'Farrell, 23, Peter Clancy, 19, and Daniel Patrick Vincent, 20.) They had driven to the Church, as part of their pre-arranged getaway plan, after shooting up Cookstown RUC barracks. A year earlier, O'Donnell had been cleared of arms charges at the Old Bailey in London. Somehow he convinced a jury that the rifles found in the boot of a car he was driving had been put there without his knowledge. During the period following his arrest, a source of mine in Tyrone, who has IRA contacts, was approached several times on O'Donnell's behalf by lads who knew him, either as a neighbour, or who had played football with him. None of them were in the IRA themselves, but they wanted my source to find out from the IRA what O'Donnell was doing with the rifles and to let it be known that they would complete the mission for him.

Of course on the Unionist side of the war, that admiration is paralleled by an equally intense detestation. The importance of Unionist outrage had been demonstrated the month before O'Donnell and the others were shot when the IRA blew up a van at Trebane, County

Tyrone, on 17 January 1992. It had been taking Protestant workers from an Army base. Seven were killed, seven more terribly injured.

The Northern Ireland Secretary, Peter Brooke, who had impressed most people, in the Republic at least, as a decent man, had earlier agreed to appear on Dublin's *Late Late Show*, the State's most popular TV programme. Once on he yielded to the urging of Gay Byrne, the show's star, to sing his party piece, 'My Darling Clementine'. Unionist politicians chose to regard the singing, a few hours after the blast, as a calculated insult and called for his sacking. Along with Clementine, another British political reputation had fallen into the foaming brine of Anglo-Irish relationships. For although initially backed by John Major, the British Prime Minister, who refused to accept his resignation, Brooke went in a Cabinet reshuffle which followed the Tory general election victory on 9 April 1992. He was replaced by Sir Patrick Mayhew, a plummy traditional Tory with a quiff and a pinstripe. As Attorney General he had alienated Nationalists by his refusal to prosecute RUC personnel alleged to have been involved in shoot-to-kill incidents. The man John Major wanted to send to Belfast, and who wanted the job, was the likeable, and intelligent, Chris Patten, who had experience in working in the Tories' Six County team. However, he lost his seat in Parliament in the general election. Appropriately enough, a place was found for him as Governor of Hong Kong, smoothing the path for eventual British withdrawal.

Mayhew's equally plummy and pinstriped colleague, who was awarded the Northern Ireland Defence portfolio, aroused Nationalists' sense of humour, but not their enthusiasm. Michael Mates, a former Colonel, had served with the Army in Northern Ireland. It was also noted that he shared a surname with that of the largest selling brand of condoms in the Six Counties, a new definition of a security posting! Mates' career was short and characterized by a series of bloopers. He was ultimately forced to resign in June 1993, not over matters Irish, but because of his involvement with Asil Nadir, a businessman who jumped bail in England while awaiting trial on fraud charges.

The comings and goings of British politicians made no impact on the IRA. A new type of bombing campaign was introduced in Northern Ireland and activities were not only stepped up on the UK mainland, but extended to take in British targets in Continental Europe. As stocks of Semtex were used up, the Provos reverted to making bombs out of fertilizer and sugar, and launched an economic war, not against personnel, but against commercial targets. A Press Association report, dated 6 July 1993, stated that it was estimated that the bill for 1990–93 would be £200 million. A Unionist MP, David Trimble, complained to the newspapers (*Irish Independent*, 20 January 1992) that there were fertilizer plants in the Republic manufacturing fertilizer with a higher potential explosive content than those in the North. He wanted the authorities to confirm that it was Republican fertilizer, not the Unionist variety which was causing the damage!

Wherever it came from, huge fertilizer bombs, sometimes weighing over a ton, were systematically employed to destroy whole commercial districts right across the province. The bombs caused havoc in Belfast, where targets included the Opera House and the much targeted Europa Hotel, both of which were regarded by the authorities as showpieces of the 'Normalization Policy'. But the bombers also caused devastation outside the city in a range of towns chosen to indicate that the IRA could strike at will across the Six Counties: Lurgan, Coleraine, Bangor, Portadown, Magherfelt and Newtownards. Sometimes the fertilizer bombs were alternated with firebombing devices which were used to destroy individual shops. Miraculously no lives were lost in the commercial blitz.

The same could not be claimed for the IRA campaign in England. An IRA man deliberately shot a prowler who broke into his car in London in 1988. The man, Patrick Sheehy, returned to Ireland, took to drink, became depressed and committed suicide three years later. Meanwhile, in 1989, ten Marine bandsmen were intentionally killed in a bomb attack on a Barracks in Deale Kent. Twenty-one were injured, one of them so badly that he died later. Although they could be considered soft targets, the view of IRA apologists was that they were Marines first and bandsmen second. Ian Gow, the notably pro-Unionist Conservative MP, was also deliberately blown up by a bomb placed under his car in July of the following year (1990). There were echoes of Gibraltar that September when Sir Peter Terry and his wife were attacked. Sir Peter, who was the more seriously wounded of the two, was a former Governor of Gibraltar. The following month the IRA were foiled in an attempt to give a practical demonstration of the subject at a conference on terrorism held in London at the Royal Overseas Club. A Semtex bomb was discovered under the speaker's lectern less than two hours before the Conference was due to open. The speakers included the Metropolitan Police Commissioner, Peter Imbert.

A more spectacular IRA attack was also foiled on 7 February 1991, by the branch of the tree in the garden of Downing Street which deflected the rocket intended for the War Cabinet (see below). But the bombing campaign continued against a variety of other targets: railway stations; that Tory citadel, the Carlton Club; the Stock Exchange. The railway campaign was especially widely felt. Beginning in the same month as the Downing Street onslaught with bombs at Paddington and Victoria stations in London, one (at Victoria) killed a man when police disregarded a phoned warning. This particular facet of the campaign played havoc with commuters' schedules when, after the Victoria fiasco, the authorities reacted promptly to every subsequent warning with the result that hoax calls frequently halted London's underground.

The 'prestige target' of the 1992 phase of the bombing campaign was the Baltic Exchange in the heart of London's financial nerve centre, the City of London. It seemed that the IRA's Irish strike-at-will commercial campaign had been successfully transported to England. But on a Saturday afternoon in March of the following year, 1993, it went terribly wrong. IRA bombs planted in a far from prestigious target, a shopping centre in Warrington, Cheshire, claimed the lives of two little boys. Again it was an occasion which created a situation in which one could measure accurately the depth of anti-IRA feeling in Ireland and England and the corresponding power of the IRA to ride out the storm.

I visited nearby Birmingham shortly after the Warrington bomb to take part in a TV programme involving a representative studio audience. Both the programme and the opportunity which the visit afforded of sampling opinion in the area were instructive. The audience were in a justifiable state of outrage at the atrocity. But they also showed how British public opinion viewed Northern Ireland. The audience erupted into spontaneous applause on three occasions. Once when a speaker suggested that Sinn Fein should be declared illegal. Again when someone else proposed re-introducing internment and the death penalty; and finally when someone, disagreeing with my proposal that the UN and the EC be invited to play a role, raised the cry: 'Ulster is British.' There was a stony, disapproving silence when I pointed out that, inexcusable as the outrage was, nevertheless, four Catholics in Northern Ireland had been murdered – allegedly by Loyalist death squads – by way of reprisal in the immediate aftermath of the bombing. Were not each set of deaths worthy of sympathy and analysis as to why they had occurred? There was booing and disagreement when I suggested that a political solution as opposed to a security one, was the desired objective. And yet, when I met the audience after the show, they thawed, grew friendly, and were disposed to discuss the problem rationally. But the bottom line was that Mr and Ms British Average do not think about Northern Ireland, or help to form any part of a political consensus on the subject, other than apathy and distaste, except in the wake of 'the atrocity nearby', when the reaction is likely to be of the knee-jerk variety: no giving in to terrorism. This was, of course, no surprise.

A more telling example of this attitude had come after Ian Gow's death. The Conservatives used his murder to the utmost in the subsequent by-election to elect his replacement. He had been a popular MP and the campaign invoked his fate and memory by every means imaginable. Yet, the Liberal Democratic Party obliterated his huge majority to take the seat. British politics are more concerned with bread and butter issues than with the side effects of the Irish involvement. But, for a time after the Warrington explosion, Irish nurses, taxi drivers, waiters and barmen told me they were keeping their heads down in Birmingham. The anonymous phone call in the small hours of the morning, and insulting comments about Ireland and the Irish gained a nasty, but fortunately short-lived currency. Shorter at any rate than the more deep-rooted anti-Irish prejudice that exists in some official circles.

In the Republic of Ireland the reaction to Warrington was one of guilt mingled with outrage. Again there was no empathy with the Catholics killed in the Six Counties, but there was an immediate, genuine outpouring of feeling for the stricken Warrington. Though selective, it was the same sort of decent national response to what one got, or gets, at moments like Bob Geldof's marathon rock concert for famine relief in Ethiopia, President Mary Robinson's visit to Somalia, or even the achievements of the Irish soccer team managed by an Englishman, Jack Charlton. The Irish have a keen perception of national pride. Warrington was not done in their name.

Two remarkable women spearheaded the response. One was a Dublin housewife, Susan McHugh, from the middle-class suburb of Clontarf. One day in the wake of the bombing, after dropping her children at school, McHugh decided that she had to do something. Without discussing it with anyone, she phoned Trinity College and secured a room. Then she got on to a live radio chat show, announced she wanted the killing stopped, invited people to meet at Trinity, and launched what turned out to be an enormous, but short-lived, peace movement, Peace Initiative '93. For a moment there was a re-run of the Peace Women Initiative. There were monster rallies in the centre of Dublin, cross-border meetings and much media attention. The mood of reparation and sympathy was heightened by President Mary Robinson, who supported McHugh's initiative and went to Warrington herself to attend a commemoration service for the dead children.

But the moment faded. The IRA's ability to maintain both its campaign and its support proved stronger than the public's capacity for sustained outrage. While the Peace Movement was at its height, the IRA detonated the most successful and devasting explosion of the entire British campaign. Just over a year after the Baltic Exchange bomb had caused damage to the tune of £350 million, another explosion, at Bishopsgate, on 24 April 1993, ripped the heart out of the financial district for a second time. This time the bomb, consisting of over a ton of fertilizer contained in a parked truck, claimed the life of a newspaper photographer who had been sent by the *News of the World* to cover the alert. It also caused an astronomical damage bill.

Initially there were efforts to minimize this. Insurance experts said that talk of £1.5 billion was exaggerated. Prime Minister John Major, the Chancellor of the Exchequer, Norman Lamont, and the Lord Mayor of London all made public statements saying that the bombers had failed to achieve a lasting effect, and that it would be business as usual for the City. But, as the days passed, and the full nature of the damage became known, it became evident that the final bill could well exceed the £2 billion mark. I visited the scene myself some weeks later and found that the TV and newspaper pictures had not conveyed a sense of the full extent of the devastation.

The confined nature of the city had ensured that the blast had burst along several narrow streets, ricocheting from one building to another. Over a million and a half square feet of office space was affected. Structures hundreds of yards apart had their windows blown out and their interiors damaged. The tallest building in the City, the 52-storey Nat West Tower, was badly damaged, and a number of other landmarks had suffered such irreparable harm that I was told they would have to be demolished. These included

St Ethelburga's, a medieval church which had survived the German blitz of World War II.

And the toll could have been far worse that Saturday morning, for two other IRA attacks did not come off when hijacked taxis exploded at Finsbury Park and King's Cross. The drivers had been ordered to make for Scotland Yard and Downing Street, but instead, they abandoned their vehicles and phoned the police. Not surprisingly, after visiting the City, I found webs of scaffolding in and around Downing Street; vast new, and expensive, bomb and bullet-proofing works were in progress. Clearly the British were not pinning all their hopes on Peace Initiative '93.

The IRA campaign in Britain has not been cost free to the movement. Several supporters have vanished into prison for terms of twenty years and more, for either aiding and abetting the campaign, or being found in possession of weapons or explosives. Nevertheless, it has been characterized by a high degree of success. Apart from individual actions such as the City of London bombings, the British campaign carries a special value to the IRA inasmuch as a bombing or shooting on the 'UK mainland' draws many times the attention of similar activities in the 'UK overseas', as one often hears Northern Ireland referred to in England.

The same is true of IRA activity on the Continental European mainland, where language and logistics barriers have not assisted the IRA in its long running attempts to extend the theatre of war to attack British bases and personnel in Europe. The British Ambassador to Holland, Sir Eric Sykes, was killed as far back as 1979. There was also a bomb attack that year on a British Army Band in Brussels, injuring seven bandsmen and nearly twice that many civilians. But, in IRA terms, the campaign was more costly than the results warranted. An effort to kill Christopher Tugendhat, a British EC Commissioner, failed. Then the Dutch police put an end to the European operation for a time with the arrests, in 1982, of two prominent IRA men, Brendan McFarlane and Gerry Kelly, both of whom had escaped from Long Kesh.

Five years later, in 1987, thirty people were injured by an IRA car bomb outside the British Army Headquarters at Rheindahlen, West Germany. This bombing ushered in a wave of approximately twenty gun and bomb attacks on British servicemen which petered out in

1990. Three members of the RAF were killed on the same day (1 May 1988) in separate incidents in Holland (at Roermond and at Nieuw Bergen), in which a machine gun and a car bomb were used. The campaign was characterized by a spate of IRA mistakes. In one case the wife of a British serviceman was shot in her car when gunmen mistook her for her husband. In another, two Australian tourists were gunned down in the belief that they were off-duty British servicemen.

Apart from bad publicity, the campaign cost the IRA about a dozen experienced personnel, who were captured by police, and a good deal of money and equipment. It probably also helped to heighten European reactions against terrorism generally and the IRA in particular. Yet, if the campaign did more to underline for the IRA the difficulty of operating away from Ireland, than to further its cause, it did mark a significant step in the movement's development. Also it increased British security costs and, of course, it underlined the fact that the IRA had come a long and bloody way from the five hand guns on the Falls Road at the outbreak of the troubles over twenty years earlier.

Even further away were America and Libya, both of which were important to the IRA in recent years. Two incidents, which serve to highlight that importance, also demonstrate how the IRA can expect to be treated differently by a legal system not susceptible to pressure from the British compared to one which is. By the mid-eighties Libya had come to present the IRA's best source of arms. Earlier assistance from the PLO had dried up as that organization came to forge stronger constitutional links with the Irish Government. I visited Libya in 1987 to interview Colonel Ghaddafi and was struck by the interest shown in the IRA by many people I met. One Army officer openly said: 'Tell them [the IRA] to come over here and we'll train them.' Ghaddafi himself quizzed me about the level of support for the movement in Ireland and made me promise to send him an edition of this book. I later discovered the reason for Tripoli's preoccupation with the IRA: the enemy of my enemy is my friend. As part of his general campaign against the West, and Britain in particular, Ghaddafi had turned again, as he had done in the *Claudia* affair, to supplying the IRA with weapons.

The story broke after what would have been the biggest

consignment ever, one hundred and fifty tons, was seized off the coast of France aboard the *Eksund* at the beginning of November 1987. At the end of the month, as information flowed from the seizure, the Gardai began what was probably the largest ever house-to-house and farm-to-farm search that had ever been mounted in Ireland. Tens of thousands of homes were visited. A small number of arms were found, and some amazingly large and well constructed bunkers, but that was all.

The most important seizure was that of two more participants in the Long Kesh escape, Joseph Clarke and Anthony Kelly. However, in the wake of the searches, and the subsequent trial of the *Eksund* crew in Paris, it emerged that at least four separate shipments had been landed on the Wicklow coast before the *Eksund* voyage. They constituted a remarkable breach in the invisible and, hitherto, supposedly impregnable screen against such arms shipments to Ireland from the Middle East. (Britain has reciprocal arrangements with various military alliances and intelligence networks, including the Israeli secret service, Mossad.)

The shipments would appear to have amounted to some one hundred tons of rockets, rifles, short arms, hand-grenades and ammunition. Above all they included large amounts of semtex. This light, easy to handle, and immensely powerful plastic explosive added enormously to the IRA's bomb- and rocket-making capability in subsequent years. The British were so angered by Ghadafi's lethal largesse to the IRA that he felt it necessary to attempt to assuage their wrath in the wake of the Lockerbie bombing of Pan Am Flight 103 on 21 December 1988, by turning informer on the IRA. During British/Libyan negotiations in Geneva in 1992, on the British demands that Libya hand over two Libyans suspected of the bombing, the Libyans instead handed over details of what they knew about the IRA. For once the British and the IRA agreed about something. 'Not a lot', was, I am told, the joint verdict of the worth of the information.

When the *Eksund* crew were eventually put on trial in Paris in January 1991, I was afforded an opportunity of witnessing a factor that adds even more capability to the IRA than semtex – family support. After appearing before the court as an expert witness, I was introduced to the daughter of one of the defendants. Following the arrests she had given up her job in Ireland, learned French, and got herself work in Paris, so that she could visit her father in Fresnes prison three times a week. In company with the families of some of the other accused she attended every day of the hearing.

In the case of the defendants whose case I was called in, the judges decided that the IRA were a politically as opposed to a criminally motivated organization and the men were freed a year later. Even allowing for the time they had already spent in prison, it was a slap-on-the-wrist sentence which would have been infinitely more severe had they been caught in Irish, English, or, it appears, American waters.

The most controversial American case involving the IRA was that of Crumlin Road jailbreaker, Joe Doherty, who had been an active IRA man since being interned in 1971. After the break-out, Doherty, who was accused of the murder of an SAS Captain,* fled to the US where, under an assumed name, he worked in a New York bar. Eventually the FBI caught up with him and a protracted trial began in 1984. Sean MacBride and I made lengthy appearances during the trial to explain the background to the Irish troubles. The prosecutor, who was instructed by officials from the British embassy, had the appropriate name of Ira H. Block! Judge Sprizzo apparently accepted our descriptions of the origins of the IRA and of the Northern state as indicating that the IRA was a historically based organization with a political goal, as opposed to a purely criminally motivated one, like the Mafia. The verdict, delivered in 1986, was that the British application for extradition should not be allowed on the grounds that he had been engaged in a legitimate conflict.

However, this did not prevent his continuing to be detained in prison while the battleground changed to a move by the US authorities to have him deported back to Belfast on charges of having entered America illegally. They were ultimately successful, and Doherty was extradited back to Belfast on 19 February 1992, to begin serving the life sentence imposed in his absence. His American incarceration was not taken into account. By contrast, the Irish Supreme Court had decided in the case of two of his fellow escapers that, as they had served ten year sentences in the Republic, they should not be extradited.

---

* Captain Richard Westmacott, during a shootout in Belfast in May 1980.

The Doherty case provided a focus for Irish-American concentration both because of the nature of the issues raised and because during his term in prison he manifestly matured and became a very different personality to the young revolutionary of the 1970s. The 'Republican University' had produced a well-read, reflective, analytical character who had developed into an independent-minded writer prepared to criticize IRA excesses such as the bombing of Musgrove hospital. A number of distinguished personages visited him in prison, including Cardinal O'Connor of New York and the Irish Cardinal, the late Cardinal O'Fiach. O'Connor publicly took issue with the prosecution's stated belief that Doherty's deportation was desired by the State Department as a matter of foreign policy. What business of the State Department's was it, the Cardinal asked, what went on in the courts? The interest taken in the case by Irish-American politicians – many of whom, as part of their campaign on his behalf also made a point of visiting Doherty – was reflected in the naming of a New York street corner in his honour.

Ironically, what cost Doherty his freedom in the end was an outburst of Republican independence of spirit on the part of Charles Haughey and the Dublin Government. Working behind the scenes, influential Irish-American lawyers like Paul O'Dwyer had succeeded in doing a deal with the authorities whereby Doherty would be sent out of America to a country which did not have an extradition treaty with any of the parties involved. Argentina agreed to take Doherty, but because Haughey had tilted towards Argentina and against Thatcher during the Argentinian-British conflict over the Falklands, which had resulted in an extradition treaty between Buenos Aires and Dublin, this proved unacceptable and Doherty stayed in jail. Accordingly, there was considerable resonance for Gerry Adams's comment to the *Irish Times* (20 February 1992) on Doherty's being sent back: 'The decision to extradite ... showed that the legal system in the United States had become a victim of British rule in Ireland.'

The British had earlier scored another notable legal victory in securing the extradition of a native born American, Michael Quinn. Quinn was born in San Francisco and was wanted for his part in the British mainland campaign. He had been in captivity in the US from 1981 to 1986, fighting charges which included the murder of a policeman, Constable Stephen Tibble. Unlike the Doherty affair, the courts held that the British campaign was not legitimate.

Quinn is currently serving a life sentence after an Old Bailey trial whose conduct has also been criticized because the jury were not allowed to hear evidence which would have undermined the prosecution's case.

A friend of Quinn's, Dr Frank Foster, of Santa Barbara, also figured in a case which became a cause célèbre in Irish-American circles. Foster was head of the local chapter of the Northern Irish Aid committee (NORAID) which is often accused of supporting the Provisionals. He refused to allow any demonstrations by NORAID against Queen Elizabeth's visit to Santa Barbara in 1983 on grounds of propriety. However, Foster, who was also a noted civil rights activist in the area, wrote to the Queen prior to the visit to suggest she meet him and some other Irish-Americans for a cup of tea. Dr Foster proposed a chat in which he said Her Majesty would hear views on Northern Ireland which would differ from those she might otherwise hear on her tour! Niall O'Dowd's *Irish America*, a glossy, prestigious magazine, described what happened next (in its March 1986 issue):

> Dr Foster was first arrested in January 1983, on the eve of Queen Elizabeth's visit to Southern California. The technical charge was for improperly prescribing medication and Dr Foster was to go through a Kafkaesque two years and four weeks in the courts system before being finally cleared.

However, though he won his case, Foster, an Assistant Clinical Professor of Medicine at the University of Southern California, lost both his house and his extensive private practice. Because of the publicity, he was forced to take a job 125 miles away from his home.

In another unusual case Gerry McGeough, a native of Tyrone, became the first Irishman to be extradited to the US from Germany, where he had been held for four years on arms charges. McGeough was sentenced to three years on 17 June 1993, in New York, on charges of trying to buy 'Red Eye' surface-to-air missiles for the IRA. The judge in the case, Federal Judge Sifton, after sentencing McGeough, then proceeded to grant him bail. He said that in twelve years of dealing with cases involving Irish Nationalists he had always been impressed with their honesty.

Irish-Americans are keen to point to several other examples of collusion between the FBI and the British. All are said to stem from the Reagan/Thatcher relationship which President Bush continued with. One of the most notable examples involved an admitted FBI 'sting' which put three supporters of the IRA behind bars in Florida in 1990. They are Kevin McKinley, Seamus Moley and Joe McColgan. The FBI approached them with an offer to sell a Stinger missile, 'the war winner', constantly dreamt of in some IRA circles, because it would make possible the shooting down of British helicopters. The men raised the money, handed it over, received the missile and were then arrested. The FBI then followed the money trail through several locations, including Arizona, Toronto, Palm Beach and New York, and, after widespread raids in New York and Arizona, more arrests followed on 11 November 1992. Those arrested were Patrick Moley, Tony Brannigan, Denis Leyne and Tommy Maguire, the owner of a popular pub in the Bronx, the Phoenix Bar. The indictment, read before a Grand Jury in Tucson, related to both the Stinger affair and the purchase of detonators.

An attorney prominent in Irish-American legal and political activities, Frank Durkan, told the New York *Irish Voice* (on 24 November 1992) that the arrests were part of 'a witch hunt against Irish-American businessmen.' He pointed out that it was common for members of the Irish-American community to regularly contribute money to defence funds and to various Irish political organizations. However, he said that: '... now decent and respectable business people are being subjected to harassment and are under threat at the direction of a pro-British State Department in Washington.' This sort of complaint would appear to have borne fruit under President Clinton's regime.

Good contact has been established between the Irish-Americans and the Clinton administration. To my knowledge the President has assured leaders of the Irish-American community that there would be 'no more Joe Doherty cases', and there is tangible evidence of the FBI being reined in. In the same month (November 1992) in which the four were indicted in Tucson, I had been asked to appear as an expert witness in a ludicrous case in Chicago which has evaporated since the Republicans exited the White House. It originated in a discussion between five men in the back bar of a run down bar on North Milwaukee Avenue, Chicago, The Irish Wolfhound. The group had a record of contributing to the relief of distress in Northern Ireland. The issue was whether or not it would now be politically correct to give money to a Republican fund-raiser who was expected in the city. During the discussion one member of the group, John Tuttle, was observed to be behaving oddly. He was a recent addition to the circle and the others thought that he was trying to pull a gun on them. They seized him – and found he was fiddling with a concealed microphone.

Within seconds the FBI had burst in and removed Tuttle, who later turned out to be a rather unstable young man. (He had also served a jail term after being dishonourably discharged from the army for selling LSD to his buddies.) A month before the Irish Wolfhound incident, the FBI had induced a state prosecutor to drop charges against him (for punching a woman), because he was a 'protected witness'. Following the Irish Wolfhound incident, the other four were all arrested. They were Chris Fogarty, his wife, Mary Sullivan, Tony McCormick and Frank O'Neill. They were charged with assault, of Tuttle, and damaging FBI property, a Nagra tape-recorder. If convicted they would have faced five years in jail.

The leading FBI man in the case, Ed Buckley, had already become an object of criticism in Irish circles in Chicago. Someone in law enforcement had floated a bizarre theory concerning the particularly savage murder, in the wealthy Chicago suburb of Winnetka, of husband and wife Richard and Nancy Langert. It was said that the murders were linked to the IRA, who were annoyed at Nancy's sister, Jeanne Bishop, a Chicago lawyer who had done *pro bono* work for a Protestant group interested in Northern Ireland called The Truth About Northern Ireland. After the murder story surfaced she suffered increased pressure, both from the authorities and the media. But then a local teenager, who was said to have been on drugs, was arrested and convicted of the Langert murders. It also emerged that the FBI had paid more money to Tuttle ($20,000) in the nine months prior to the Irish Wolfhound raid than the Fogarty group, The Friends of Irish Freedom, had been able to raise.

However, after Clinton entered the White House the FBI dropped the charges. Obviously the Chicago Four case is not typical of Irish-American collection activity on behalf of the IRA. The Four, in fact, had a history of donation to Irish relief funds, not the purchase of arms. But so long as there is trouble in Northern Ireland some Irish-Americans will support the Provisionals. The Libyan connection may have dried up but the Irish-American one will not be dammed. And to the ranks of first, second and third generation Irish-Americans one must add the constant stream of energetic, intelligent, pro-IRA activists who are constantly emigrating to the US. With or without a Green Card their sympathies are green. The guns, the money, the expertise and the political pressure will continue to be exerted.

Miscarriages of Justice

George Bernard Shaw once said that a Royal Commission reminded him of a man going to the lavatory. It sat for a long time, during which nothing was heard. Then there was a loud report – and the matter was dropped. He would have found nothing to make him revise his opinion in the Report of the Royal Commission on Criminal Justice. It had been set up in 1991 because of the publicity aroused by some appalling injustices perpetrated on Irish prisoners. One of the most respected journals in England said this of the Report's findings:

> When the Royal Commission on Criminal Justice was convened around two years ago, the phrase 'English justice' had become something of an oxymoron. A string of names and numbers – the Maguire Seven, the Guildford Four and, most poisonously – the Birmingham Six was humiliating shorthand for the manifest failure of what was once one of the world's most envied criminal systems.

The foregoing appeared in the staid economic journal, *The Economist* (on 10 July 1993). Writing in the better tradition of English journalism the magazine was acknowledging that the Birmingham Six, Guildford Four, Maguire Seven, Winchester Three and the unfortunate Judith Ward, were in the words of Michael Mansfield, the English barrister who defended many of them, subjected to 'unthinkable suffering handed down in the name of justice'.[*]

The outcome of the Maguire Seven case has been described earlier (Chapter 30). The innocence of the Birmingham Six, to which I have previously alluded also, was not admitted until they were freed in March 1991. Judith Ward was held until May 1992, before being let go. Hers was the worst case of injustice. A woman with psychiatric disorders, she had spent eighteen years in prison, two years longer

---

[*] The quotation and the others used to describe the Birmingham Six, and similar cases, are taken from Mansfield's book, *Presumed Guilty*, Heinemann, London, 1983, (p. viii).

than the Birmingham Six, for a crime of which she was totally innocent. The Guildford bombings took place in October 1974. It was
October 1989 before the wrongfully accused men were released. The
sort of evidence which moved the appeal judge to free them may be
judged from a file on the supposed ringleader of the group, Gerald
Conlon, who was in London when the bombs went off in Surrey. The
file contained a police interview with a witness who corroborated
Conlon's statement that he was in a London hostel on the day of the
explosions. Yet, the witness was never produced at the trial, and the
state prosecution marked the file, which would have acquitted Conlon
fourteen years earlier: 'Not to be disclosed to the Defence.'*

The Winchester Three were also set free during this period. They
were the luckiest of all. They had been found guilty of conspiring to
murder the then Northern Secretary of State, Tom King. Had they
received sentences of five years or so no one would have complained
unduly. The trio had been captured while apparently observing King's
movements at his Wiltshire estate. In fact, after a trial which at times
appeared to be conducted by the tabloids, they got twenty-five years
each. They had claimed the right to silence. But in the middle of the
trial King gave a press conference and using language which many felt
was in contempt of court, he announced that the Government was
withdrawing the right to silence in Northern Ireland. On appeal it was
accepted that the timing of the announcement must have prejudiced
the jury and the three were set free.

One could argue that these cases and many others grew out of a
combination of circumstances: the latent anti-Irish feeling I encountered in Birmingham; the need for the police to be seen to get
someone, anyone, for a series of horrifying bombings; the challenge
posed to a democratic society by a ruthless, undemocratic enemy. In
fact the cases, and their parallel activities in Northern Ireland, Diplock
Courts, the use of the SAS in undercover, shoot-to-kill operations,
and a whole panoply of other bendings of the law, illustrate that it is
not possible for Britain to remain in Northern Ireland without doing
severe damage to its democratic traditions.

The executive and the law are being drawn into the counter-
insurgency process. Even the Royal Commission referred to earlier,
while it has recommended some reforms – an independent authority
to review potentially unjust sentences and improvements in forensic

---

* Mansfield, p. 234.

testing, which, for instance, would have acquitted the Birmingham Six if in force – has reported with one eye on Northern Ireland. It proposed the ending of the right to trial by jury, and forcing defendants to disclose their defence in advance. As *The Economist* said: 'A royal commission designed to restore public faith in the courts has produced proposals that are more likely to erode it.'

In a nutshell, Britain is back where it was during the Anglo-Irish war of the 1916–21 period. Once more, because of public opinion, it cannot be seen to use its army in an all-out war of conquest. Therefore, once again, she has had to resort to the concept of a 'police war'. This time instead of Auxiliary Police Cadets and the Black and Tans, she makes use of the Special Air Services Unit, the SAS, and allows Protestant paramilitary death squads to operate on the principle of 'the enemy of my enemy is my friend'. Just as in the early Anglo-Irish war, the existence of such undercover dirty tricks was at first strenuously denied. But, inexorably, as in the first phase of warfare, revelations in the media (now augmented by the power of TV) have begun first to cast doubt upon and, increasingly, to seriously discredit official disclaimers. More and more, by 1993, the 'police' war was becoming revealed as being no more attractive, or effective, than its predecessor.

The Amnesty International Report for 1992 said flatly that the United Kingdom's behaviour in Northern Ireland had made it into one of the worst human rights violators in Europe. The report cited very disturbing court cases where bending of the rules occurred to secure convictions. Most notably, in the conduct of the trial of the seven men accused of charges arising out of the murder of the two British corporals seized at Milltown cemetery in 1988, the report stated 'Courts drew adverse inferences against defendants for having remained silent during police questioning or at trial'. Another Birmingham Six or Guildford saga appears to be under way. But, most damningly of all, the respected international organization said that there was evidence of collusion between the security forces in Northern Ireland and Loyalist paramilitary groups.

In his fine book *Big Boys' Rules*,* Mark Urban, a BBC correspondent and an ex-*London Independent* Defence Correspondent, was able to give chapter and verse of SAS shoot-to-kill ambushes which had

---

* *Big Boys' Rules: The SAS and the Secret Struggle against the IRA*, by Mark Urban, Faber, London, 1992, pp. 54–55.

claimed the lives of more than three dozen IRA men. However, he was less successful in establishing official collusion with outlawed Protestant paramilitaries. He states:

> ... in many interviews with people involved with undercover warfare, none has endorsed these allegations of widespread collaboration between intelligence officers and loyalist paramilitaries; on the contrary, they deny them with vigour.

Urban was commenting on separate claims made by two former British army officers, Fred Holroyd and Colin Wallace, and by a convicted Loyalist terrorist, Albert Baker. My experience is that getting corroboration depends on who the person 'involved with undercover warfare' is and how much he or she is in awe of the Official Secrets Act. I know at least one such figure who will not deny with 'vigour' the existence of 'widespread collaboration'. He has talked openly to me about what he knows, and, as a result, has written a book which will be published shortly.

This man, whom I will call 'Maxwell', is a former UDR officer and member of the UDA. In the UDA, Maxwell, who had been commissioned into the UDR at Sandhurst, worked with John McMichael, the number two man in the UDA leadership who was blown up as a result of collusion between a UDA racketeer called James Craig and elements in the Provisional IRA. McMichael had 'made his bones' by killing a number of Catholics and by arranging the killing of many others, including most of the leadership of the anti H Block campaign in 1980. He was responsible for the deaths of Miriam Daly, a Queen's University lecturer, John Turnley, a Protestant turned Republican, and Ronald Bunting whose father had once been one of Paisley's closest associates. However, in the flux of Six County revolutionary change, Bunting had become an INLA leader and was responsible for the assassination of Airey Neave, MP, Margaret Thatcher's close advisor who was blown up in a House of Commons car park. The one H Block leader McMichael failed with was Bernadette McAliskey, formerly Bernadette Devlin.

A respected writer, Martin Dillon, who worked in Belfast as a BBC correspondent, and is the author of a number of authoritative books on Loyalist terrorism, described what happened.[*]

[*] *Stone Cold*, p. 65, Arrow, London, 1992. Dillon's other books include *Rogue Warrior of the SAS*, *Political Murder in Northern Ireland* and *The Shankill Butchers*.

She lived with her husband in County Tyrone, near the town of Coalisand. On 16 January, an SAS team was in place in the grounds surrounding her house. She was unaware of their presence or the fact that they had cut the telephone wires to her home. A UDA active-service team arrived, entered the house and shot her several times; they were arrested as they left the scene. An Army officer rushed to Bernadette McAliskey's side and kept her alive until a medical team arrived. The presence of the SAS has never been explained. Some observers have concluded that their behaviour proved a connection between the UFF and Military Intelligence and ten years later, this belief hardened the suspicion that McMichael was an agent of British Intelligence.

McMichael always considered himself to be actually at war with the Provisional IRA, with justice as his fate indicates, and potentially, engaged in hostilities with the Republic. The fear that some day the Republic's army will cross the border is a deep-rooted one in Northern Ireland's Protestants. After the signing of the Anglo-Irish Agreement, McMichael began taking precautions against this 'Doomsday Day' situation as he termed it. A hit list of targets in the Republic was drawn up that included people, locations and national treasures. Teams of UDA men were sent southwards to scout the targets and their findings were collated on McMichael's computer.

Maxwell's targets included the Book of Kells, the Cuchulain statue in the Dublin GPO, and Peter Barry, then the Republic's Minister for Foreign Affairs, who had been one of the signatories to the Anglo-Irish Agreement. The first two had a symbolic value in UDA eyes. Cuchulain was a legendary hero who had defended Ulster against invaders from other parts of Ireland. The monastery in which the Book of Kells is thought to have been created was also in the North. Barry, owner of a flourishing tea business, lived in faraway County Cork. This did not deter Maxwell and his companion. They drove to Cork to monitor Barry's movements. Once, when they became afraid that their Northern car and accents might be attracting attention, they brazenly went up to a security man employed by Barry's company to say that they were becoming distracted by the Cork one way system. Would he mind if they used the company car park to compose themselves with the aid of their flasks and sandwiches? The obliging security man let them use the car park, where undisturbed, they observed departures and arrivals, videoing the proceedings to their hearts' content.

Readers have seen the sentence meted out to the Winchester Three when found guilty of taking part in a similar mission involving another signatory to the Anglo-Irish Agreement, Tom King. No such fate befell Maxwell. Instead he was employed by the RUC Special Branch to keep them informed on what was going on in the UDA. No meeting of the Anglo-Irish Conference, perennially preoccupied as they were by repeated British demands for closer Dublin co-operation with the RUC and UDR, was ever troubled with the information that both these organizations had *cezanne* of a plot to murder one of the Irish principals taking part in the discussions and much more besides. This, of course, need not surprise us in the light of what has since been revealed about British Army involvement in paramilitary atrocities. I am merely citing Maxwell's case to indicate that such collusion was a widely used tactic in the counter-insurgency effort. He was a trusted officer in the UDR, being one of those chosen to give Douglas Hurd, now the British Foreign Secretary, an unpublicized tour of his area. He also worked with Captain Robert Nairac, the British Intelligence officer whom the IRA captured and shot, after torture, in 1977.

McMichael himself once told me that the UDA effectively controlled the UDR. Maxwell confirmed this. In his experience, the sharing of information and the overlapping of membership were two of the givens of the situation. A third generation Orangeman – he once walked in a parade with his father and grandfather – he eventually became disillusioned with the entire paraphernalia of the Loyalist world: the Orange Order, RUC, UDA, UDR, and all the rest. For a while, he says, he fed the RUC 'duff' information about the UDA, then finally quit all four organizations. Along the way he suffered the almost inevitable Six County tension-induced crack-up, hitting the bottle and undergoing a short prison sentence for petty crime. He subsequently pulled himself together and is now happily remarried, building up a business and a staunch member of the Church of Ireland. His local vicar is one of those who supports his decision to write his memoirs, feeling that the ultimate message is that a man can go through such experiences and emerge a good Christian.

Maxwell says he thinks that the public should be made aware of how the British, through the security forces, are manipulating people and of the sort of incident to which this manipulation can lead. He cited the intelligence gathering units of the Army and the RUC Special Branch. He told me: 'If by writing the book I can help one other poor sod not to get involved it will be worth it.'

One of the people who worked in the UDA at the same time as Maxwell was its intelligence director, Brian Nelson, who was also a top British agent. On 3 February 1992, Nelson was sentenced to ten years' imprisonment by a Belfast court. He had pleaded guilty to five charges of conspiracy to murder and fifteen other offences. A British officer, identified only as Colonel 'J' of Military Intelligence, stated at the trial that he was Nelson's boss. The judge who sentenced him described him as a man who had 'shown the greatest courage', and the former Northern Ireland Secretary, Tom King, wrote a letter on his behalf. By way of illuminating the origin of this high level solicitude, it might be noted that Colonel 'J' told the court that he conducted regular briefings for the North's senior military figures at which Nelson's evidence was passed over. Furthermore he said: 'The Secretary of State for Northern Ireland might also be interested in such information.'

Nelson's arrest had followed an inquiry into allegations of collusion between the security forces and Loyalist death squads which had grown more persistent following the Stalker affair. The inquiry was conducted by John Stevens, a British police officer who, like Stalker, encountered sustained resistance by British Intelligence to the uncovering of evidence, including the fact that Nelson was supplied with over 1,000 photographs taken by the security forces.

Just before his trial the Crown prosecutors withdrew two charges of murder. This deal, which was sanctioned by the then Attorney General, Sir Patrick Mayhew, effectively closed off avenues of cross-examination which might have revealed highly explosive information about Nelson's links with British Military Intelligence. Nelson is a native of Belfast, but he was sent to England to serve his sentence. Nationalist lawyers say that he is likely to serve only some three to four years. Even if this does not prove to be the case, the leniency of his sentence in relation to the seriousness of the offences with which he was charged, compares very oddly with that handed down to the Winchester Three.

The fallout from the Nelson trial included leaks from those in the security forces who feel as Maxwell does about 'dirty tricks' operations, and some sustained investigative reporting by highly reputable sections of the media. These included *The Irish Times, The Irish News* and the BBC's *Panorama* programme. It became known that the British intelligence handlers who 'ran' Nelson knew that he had travelled to South Africa to purchase weapons in 1985. They allowed a South African shipment of arms to be landed on the County Down coast in January 1988, to protect his position within the UDA. In the three years prior to the shipment's landing the UDA and its hit squad, the UFF (Ulster Freedom Fighters), are reckoned to have killed three people. Between the landing and January 1993, the Loyalist death squads accounted for the murder of 160 people.

The dead, all of whom were killed with weapons from the South African consignment, included Michael Stone's victims at Milltown Cemetery, Patrick Finnucane, a Catholic solicitor famous in the Six Counties for defending Republican prisoners, and random targets such as taxi drivers, or punters who had the bad luck to wander into bookies' shops in Catholic areas. Throughout this spate of killing the British had Nelson and several other agents in the UDA. 'There would have been dozens of them in the UDR and the UDA,' Maxwell reckons. The information from these sources should have been sufficient to not only prevent the sectarian killings, but also the protection rackets which the UDA indulges in. But on top of this there is the British intelligence effort itself.

One intelligence officer quoted by Dillon said:[*] 'Files are kept on the whole population. In Northern Ireland which is not much larger than Yorkshire that is feasible. No one would believe the extent of phone tapping for other phone surveillance. It is very sophisticated.'

Why were the crimes allowed to continue? Mark Urban writes:[†]

> Despite evidence of Nelson's success as an agent, the case raised uncomfortable questions about the difference between the security forces' response to foreknowledge of republican and loyalist attacks. Clearly Nelson's intelligence and that of other loyalist informers has been used to thwart attacks, in the same way as information from republican groups. But it is clear that attempts to exploit this intelligence to ambush loyalists have rarely if ever been made.

That's one way of putting it. 'The enemy of my enemy is my friend,' is another. When a regular RUC report turns up information such as the present whereabouts of a targeted IRA man, or the name of the café where a Sinn Fein councillor is having lunch, an intelligence handler in the information chain has only to lift the phone to his agent. One

* *Stone Cold*, p. 136.
† Urban, *Big Boys' Rules*, p. 217.

more Loyalist killing will not only leave the security forces with one less opponent, but with clean hands into the bargain.

McMichael himself gave me an account of how one of the nastiest episodes of the entire period came to light. This was the Kincora Boys Home affair. The boys in this Belfast refuge were systematically preyed upon by the man responsible for running the hostel, William McGrath, who also ran a Loyalist murder gang called Tara. He abused the boys both for his own – and for his friends' – sexual gratification and hired them out to stag clubs and, as we shall see, other more highly placed customers. According to McMichael, two of the children who found they could no longer tolerate the abuse, made a suicide pact. On the ferry back to Belfast, after performing the duties for which McGrath had hired them to a stag club in Scotland, they would jump overboard. One child did jump, but the other's nerve failed and the affair came to light when the RUC questioned him about his companion's death. However, McGrath was protected as Martin Dillon has noted.[*]

> McGrath was shielded; he had been working for British intelligence . . . Tara to cloak his secret activities. He also monitored the life of his fellow Loyalists, but his other life included the provision of boys for homosexual colleagues within the British intelligence community in Northern Ireland and for several leading members of the British Establishment who visited Belfast regularly . . . In 1979 a Military Intelligence liaison officer sabotaged RUC attempts to trace the history of McGrath and his British intelligence connection.

Dillon says the cover-up was to prevent a scandal which would 'damage the reputation of well-known homosexuals within the British Military Intelligence community, and would also compromise others well-known in British public life.' McGrath received only a *two year* sentence for his Kincora crimes. His Tara activities were overlooked and journalists who attempted to follow up his story were intimidated into silence. A UDA leader who interrogated McGrath in jail was murdered not long after his release. His UDA colleagues say his death was connected with the McGrath investigation.

By 1993, the weight of evidence concerning British involvement in an underground dirty war was mounting. There were several books attesting to the fact. Apart from those I have mentioned by Dillon,

---

[*] *Stone Cold*, p. 57.

Holroyd, Urban and Wallace, there was also Fr Raymond Murray's, *The SAS in Ireland* and Peter Wright's *Spycatcher*. Television programmes were also being made, most notably the one in Channel Four's *Dispatches* series, which so enraged the RUC with its descriptions of Loyalist/RUC complicity in killings, that legal proceedings were instituted. Then came the most spectacular illustration of undercover British involvement in the dirtiest trick of all. Yorkshire TV's *First Tuesday* programme on 6 July 1993 reconstructed the events of the worst single day of the entire troubles, the Dublin and Monaghan bombings of 17 May 1974, which claimed thirty-four lives.

Shortly after the bombings, I had been informed by contacts in the Gardai that the Irish police suspected that the car bombs which exploded in rush-hour Dublin that day originated with Loyalist paramilitaries in Portadown operating under the tutelage of British Intelligence. Apparently the object of the slaughter was twofold. Firstly, Loyalist determination to bring home to the South, which they held partly culpable, the realities of the car-bombing they lived with. Secondly, British Intelligence wanted to lay a marker on the Dublin Government as to what might happen if they did not co-operate, as Britain desired, in the fight against the IRA. Later, as the jigsaw was pieced together by the police and Irish Military Intelligence, the names of those thought to have been involved became known.

However, two factors militated against any action being taken. Firstly, the RUC refused to assist the Gardai in making enquiries in the Six Counties. Therefore, hard evidence against the men suspected could not be obtained. Secondly, as we have seen, the Fine Gael/Labour Coalition Government of the time, which was particularly anti-IRA, believed in a policy of wooing the Unionists, and set a high premium on good relations with London. So much so that a 'Heavy Gang' within the Gardai was allowed off the leash in its treatment of IRA suspects to such an extent that it later became a factor in the Government's subsequent downfall.

In the circumstances, the Coalition decided that pursuing the matter might result only in the generation of publicity which would bring aid and comfort to the IRA. Accordingly, the Government tamely allowed the matter to drop. There is no evidence of any attempt being made by Dublin to bring pressure to bear on London to enjoin co-operation on the RUC. Over the years, as time took its toll, the bombers died or were killed, either in feuds amongst Loyalist factions, or by the IRA. Their names were well known to the security forces on both sides of the border. About a year before the showing of the programme I had a conversation with a friend of mine in the Special Branch who mentioned names quite casually, and for good measure threw in details of their identification. In one case, a farmer in County Monaghan had backed his tractor out of a field into the path of a green Avenger car being driven at such speed that a collision was barely averted. In the resultant altercation he got a good look at the occupants' faces and later identified them from photographs shown to him by the Gardai. The four men were the chief suspects in the Monaghan bombing. (They escaped across the border moments before the bomb went off.)

I also had had a meeting with Maxwell a week before the showing of the Yorkshire TV programme. There had been advance publicity which led us to a discussion about both the programme and the bombings. Of his knowledge, and quite unprompted by me, he mentioned the same names as had my Special Branch friend in Dublin. The only difference was that, in addition, he mentioned two British officers, Capt Tony Ball and his second-in-command, the then Lt Robert Nairac. In the subsequent programme, their names were amongst those cited as being involved in the preparation of the bombs. The operation was run by an SAS-trained unit known as the 'Fourth Field Survey Troop', which was then based at Castledillon, County Armagh. All the other suspects I had been told of by both the Special Branch man and the ex-Loyalist paramilitary, were squarely implicated. Most were members of the UDR as well as being in the UVF. Ex-British Intelligence officers appeared on the programme to state that at that time in Northern Ireland, British Intelligence controlled the UVF and that the UVF did not have the capability to manufacture the sophisticated timing devices needed to trigger the bombs. It was implied that these devices, and training in their use, were provided by the SAS.

The Gardai gave the programme makers access to material and granted interviews with former senior officers, as did the Irish Military Intelligence authorities, in a manner which could only have been sanctioned by the Government. Again it was a Coalition involving Labour, the difference was that this time it was with Fianna Fail. But it was a much different Labour party from that of the seventies. Gone, for example, was a figure whom many regard as a Unionist with a Southern accent, Dr Conor Cruise O'Brien. And its new leader, Dick Spring, who was both Deputy Prime Minister, and Minister for Foreign Affairs, was known to be increasingly frustrated by the lack of political initiative from London. The question of political progress, or lack of it, during the last few years will shortly be discussed, but two points concerning British/Loyalist paramilitary involvement should be made.

One, it has added to the possibilities for a Loyalist backlash in the event of London and Dublin concluding a political agreement away from the murky underworld of 'special ops'. I know from RUC sources that nowadays they sometimes find it hard to distinguish Loyalist suspects from Provisional IRA ones when they are brought in for questioning. 'They're just like Provos,' said one police officer. 'You get nothing out of them. They just sit there for days and say nothing. You have to let them go.' But along with anti-interrogation techniques, the new generation of Loyalists have also acquired more lethal skills, which constitute a problem for the future.

Part of this improved expertise, of course, came about simply because the conflict has gone on for so long. A new generation of Loyalist paramilitaries has grown up; younger, harder men, sons and nephews of the men who first founded the UDA. But part of it is also a result of undercover British training. Many a Loyalist paramilitary, like Brian Nelson, having served in the British Army or the UDR, came to the notice of agencies like the Field Research Unit and was then recruited for undercover work. Nelson, for example, was working in Germany when British intelligence contacted him to return to Belfast and join the UDA. The Field Research Unit is one of the British Army's most important agent recruiting operations. Colonel J, who gave evidence at Nelson's trial, was once the Commanding Officer of this unit. Its operations will assuredly leave Ireland with problems to solve in the future.

The final point I wish to make on this subject is that all the foregoing fully accepts the fact that the IRA has proved itself an implacable, ruthless foe. Apart from the list of its operations I have detailed, including proxy bombing, I could mention countless others, ranging from the killing of judges, to the placing of a bomb in Musgrove military hospital, a 'legitimate target' which claimed the lives of two army medical officers on 4 November 1991. When D Squadron of the SAS were sent into South Armagh in 1976, it was because the IRA had previously shot, or blown up, forty-nine soldiers.

Nevertheless, the basic instructions the SAS received would be illegal in England, the UK mainland. At the time the SAS were first dispatched to Ireland, a British Army spokesman writing anonymously in *The Times*, said their mission would be: 'what the Army has failed to do, kill terrorists.'* With no qualifications about a restrained use of force, the instructions, known as 'the yellow card', which govern an ordinary soldier's tour of duty, gave to the SAS a straightforward shoot-to-kill policy.

There are other factors which I have not gone into, which complicate the control of military operations; inter-security forces rivalry, for example. The 'police war' concept has resulted in the police and the army often being at loggerheads. This has led to confusion and ambushes where simple arrests would have been possible had the army really been acting 'in aid of the civil power'. None of this comes about through any inherent British brutality. It stems, like the My Lai massacre in Vietnam, from the fact of a normally disciplined army getting involved in a dirty, unwinnable war. A war which should be addressed by negotiation and political methods, not the force of arms and undercover murders. But British soldiers were as cruelly and as hopelessly entrapped by the ditches of South Armagh as were the Americans in the jungles of Vietnam.

Neither is the RUC to be thought of as an Irish *Stasi*, the notorious East German secret service. In fact, the force includes some of the best and certainly some of the bravest policemen in Europe. But the way the force was founded and operated for years meant that Protestants regarded it as being an instrument of 'their' law and 'their' order; the means of imposing a Unionist policy which, in plain language, came down to an Irish version of apartheid. The evils of that system generated the troubles and turned the Force into a counter-insurgency weapon, with the result that to the IRA the police became 'legitimate targets'. The absence of a political resolution of the conflict has kept them in the firing line.

Political Developments

During most of the period 1986–93, there was a great deal of political activity on both sides of the Irish Sea, but little movement. Naturally the resignation of the 'iron lady', Margaret Thatcher, as Prime Minister on 28 November 1990, gave rise to lively hopes in some circles that a change in British policy might follow. But an episode

* Quoted by Urban, p. 8.

which occurred less than three months later aptly symbolized the reality of the Irish situation for top British decision makers. It was deadly, but peripheral – an IRA rocket exploded in the garden of Number Ten Downing Street.

The man who succeeded Margaret Thatcher, John Major, was sitting in the Cabinet Room at the time of the explosion, 7 February 1991. With him were a group which included, amongst others, the Chancellor of the Exchequer, Norman Lamont, the Foreign Secretary, Douglas Hurd, and the Defence Secretary, Tom King. Both Hurd and King had been Secretaries of State for Northern Ireland. But it was not Northern Ireland which had brought them to the Cabinet Room. They formed part of the war cabinet assembled for Britain's priority war, the Gulf War. They were temporarily distracted by the rocket but that was all. The attack itself was a particularly daring piece of outrage. The rocket was one of three fired from a homemade rocket launcher based in a van with holes cut in its roof. The IRA had parked the vehicle a couple of hundred yards from the back of Number Ten. Those with a knowledge of history afterwards commented on the appropriateness of the parking site in Whitehall – alongside a statue commemorating the Duke of Devonshire who had led the opposition to Gladstone's Home Rule Bill in 1886.

Those around the table, however, were content to get on with bombing the Iraqis and leave the Northern Ireland Minister, Peter Brooke, to attempt to deal with the IRA bombers by holding a series of talks about talks with the Northern Ireland political parties. These were frustrated by a combination of Unionist stalling tactics and a fiercesome spate of sectarian killings which marred the spring of 1991. There was some internal dialogue within the Six Counties, but nothing meaningful occurred in the larger Dublin-London-Belfast context. The Unionists wanted the Anglo-Irish Agreement suspended before they would agree to talks with Dublin. Sinn Fein were to be excluded whether or not the Agreement went because of the party's backing for the IRA campaign. As neither condition offered a foundation for success, the talks, predictably, died without achieving anything tangible beyond preventing Irish-Americans from raising the profile of the Irish problem during the 1992 American Presidential election campaign. Nobody wanted to say anything that might get in the way of the mystical 'talks' that were said to contain a prospect of peace. In fact, after over a year of preliminary skirmishing, the 'Brooke initiative', as it was generally known, boiled down to a short-lived set of conversations. These began on 17 June 1991, after a seven week suspension of the Anglo-Irish Agreement, and petered out on 3 July, so as not to inflame the temperatures of those involved in the Six Counties' 'marching season'.

Charles Haughey ceased to be the Irish Prime Minister on 30 January 1992. He was succeeded by Albert Reynolds, about whom little was known beyond the fact that he was a wealthy dogfood manufacturer and former dancehall operator. Reynolds did not carry any of Haughey's ideological baggage stemming either from the arms trial era or the many political controversies which Haughey had been involved in subsequently. One of these had led to the creation of an Adam's rib party from the Fianna Fail body politic, the Progressive Democrats, led by Desmond O'Malley, a long standing critic of Haughey's. By one of the ironies of political life, the two men had been thrown together into a Coalition Government. But in January 1992, yet another scandal, over phone tapping, caused O'Malley to state that he would withdraw from the Coalition if Haughey did not resign. Haughey duly went but before doing so he had been helpful in the process that had led to the talks between John Hume and Gerry Adams and the more visible meetings between Reynolds and Major.

The two Prime Ministers discussed Northern Ireland on 27 April 1992. They got on well together socially, but politically were frustrated in their attempts to find common ground by the Unionists' continued 'not an inch' posture, and by Major's inability to manoeuvre while relying both on the Northern Ireland Unionist MPs, and the thirty or so 'Euro-sceptics' sitting in the Conservatives' back benches. (The term 'Euro-sceptic' in Tory circles being interchangeable with that of 'Thatcher supporter'.)

There was a further bout of 'talks about talks' that culminated in the opening of a set of formal, but inconclusive, meetings in London on 12 June 1992, between all the Northern Irish political parties, except Sinn Fein, under the Chairmanship of Sir Ninian Stephen, an Australian who was found to be acceptable to all concerned after much argument. One of the Unionist ploys used to abort the talks was a pre-condition set by Ian Paisley. Before agreeing to substantive discussion with Dublin he wanted the Republic to drop Articles 2 and 3 of its Constitution which can be interpreted as laying claim to the Six Counties. However, the notion that there was a 'talks process' still extant survived and was used to good effect in America by the British. Irish-

American support for Clinton did yield a return in a pre-election proposal to appoint a Peace Envoy to Northern Ireland. But adverse reaction from London helped to stall fulfilment of this promise. More importantly, Albert Reynolds, during a St Patrick's Day visit to Washington in March 1993, asked President Clinton to put the proposal on hold until the possibilities of talks resuming was more thoroughly teased out. However, both on the ground and in Westminster, the British guarantee to the Unionists, that they need not face change so long as they did not wish to, effectively froze the situation in a poisoned political aspic.

It soon became clear that Reynolds had no intention of allowing this situation to continue indefinitely. He had had some initial difficulties as leader of Fianna Fail. One of Haughey's legacies had been a long running judicial inquiry into alleged scandals in the meat industry. A clash of evidence between O'Malley and Reynolds at this Tribunal resulted in O'Malley departing the Coalition, a general election being held at the end of the year, and Reynolds returning as Taoiseach in the New Year (on 12 January 1993). However, he did so with a greatly reduced number of Fianna Fail deputies and in Coalition with Labour, which had gained substantially under the leadership of Dick Spring. It took him some time to work out an agreed programme with Spring and he was still proceeding cautiously in March when he saw Clinton. Nevertheless, when the dust settled, the political arithmetic in the Dail meant that Fianna Fail's sixty-eight seats, combined with Labour's thirty-three, gave the two parties an enormous advantage over the (fractured) opposition parties' combined total of sixty-five seats. If decided upon, new policies could be pursued from a position of strength.

Seemingly they were decided upon, for a new sound began to be heard in the political chorus emanating from Nationalist Ireland. Sinn Fein's Gerry Adams and the SDLP's John Hume had held inconclusive talks in 1988. The underground peace process involving the Roman Catholic clergy, which I mentioned earlier, resulted in talks between the pair resuming in April 1993. This elicited an outburst of disapproval from all shades of Unionist opinion and from the Dublin opposition parties, but not from Spring and Reynolds. Both of them made muted comments to the effect, summed up by Reynolds, that: 'Mr Hume is a very experienced politician. It is for Mr Hume to judge whether something useful can come out of those talks.' In Irish terms this lack of condemnation amounted to endorsement. That comment by Reynolds was carried in the Irish papers (26 April 1993) on the same day that Spring weighed in alongside Reynolds with a defence of Articles 2 and 3 of the Constitution. Spring said: 'I don't think any party should prejudice the talks by making pre-conditions and that is what we have been trying to explain over the last number of months.'

Reynolds, who was in America when he gave the interview, also said that he would be bringing up the matter of Northern Ireland when he met John Major in June. Pointedly he said that by then the local government elections (May) would be held in England, and consequently also in Northern Ireland, and 'the UK overseas' would be out of the way. This was code for stating that by June he would know whether the shared hope amongst Unionists, the Irish opposition parties, and most importantly the British Conservative Party would be realized. In a nutshell, that Sinn Fein would suffer a reverse. If they did, the British were hoping for results from yet another round of talks, based on an internal settlement within the existing structures. Sir Patrick Mayhew had signalled as much in a speech in Liverpool a few days earlier in which he had stated that he would be bringing forward British proposals for the future of Northern Ireland. Proposals it appeared, concerning which Dublin would have little input.

However, on that April weekend two other things occurred which underlined the impossibility of an internal settlement. One was very visibly external, the Bishopsgate bomb in the City of London. The other was a joint communique from Hume and Adams which expressly ruled out an internal settlement. It said:[*]

> ... we accept that the most pressing issue facing the people of Ireland and Britain today is the question of lasting peace and how it can best be achieved. Everyone has a solemn duty to change the political climate away from conflict and towards a process of national reconciliation which sees the peaceful accommodation of the differences between the people of Britain and Ireland and the Irish people themselves.
>
> In striving for that end we accept that an internal settlement is not a solution because it obviously does not deal with all the relationships at the heart of the problem. We accept that the Irish people as a whole have a right to national self-determination. This is a view shared by a majority of the people of this island though not by all its people.
>
> The exercise of self-determination is a matter of agreement between the people of Ireland. It is the search for that agreement and the means

[*] *Irish Times*, 26 April 1993.

of achieving it on which we will be concentrating . . . a new agreement is only achievable and viable if it can earn and enjoy the allegiance of the different traditions on this island, by accommodating diversity and providing for national reconciliation.

That statement represented a high water mark for Sinn Fein. The espousal of the right to self-determination marked a shift away from the largely middle-class supported viewpoint of the SDLP that reform was possible within the system, i.e., while retaining the British presence albeit with an 'Irish dimension'. The accommodation of diversity is also standard Republican dogma going back to the days of Wolfe Tone. The statement was a realistic acceptance of the position in Northern Ireland as it was before 'in 1969' in 1993 by the two shrewdest political brains in the area. Ironically, its importance was both underlined and overshadowed by the coverage of the Bishopsgate bombing. But the May by-elections duly came and went with no erosion of Sinn Fein's support.

Reynolds saw Major in June and found him impotent politically. The two men like each other, but Major was in fief to the forces of the ineluctable dialectic of history. Even though in the previous March a Gallup Poll had found that only 27 per cent of Britons wanted Northern Ireland to remain part of the United Kingdom; Britain, in irreversible decline, was facing the chill blasts of the late 20th century reality by clinging to the last rags of empire in Northern Ireland. If she divested herself of these, Scotland would be the next to depart the Union, and Scotland might take the North Sea oil revenues with her. In Dublin the Coalition was also concerned with revenues; the honouring by the EC of a promise, made at the Edinburgh summit, that, as the price of supporting the Maastricht Treaty, Ireland would get some £8 billion from the 'Convergence Fund' set up to help the poorer regions. Britain's bureaucrats were known to be amongst those in Brussels who wanted a cut in the Irish allocation.

But now the strength of the huge Coalition majority came into play. Throughout the latter part of June and the first week of July the Irish Government took a series of strong stands on various issues, including Northern Ireland. It was announced that the national airline was to be streamlined. This involved massive job losses, and the abandonment of the controversial Shannon stopover which prevented foreign airlines from flying into Dublin. If the EC's promise to Ireland were not honoured in full, Dublin said that she would veto the EC's budget.

On Northern Ireland the Government took no action to prevent President Mary Robinson attending a function in West Belfast at which the Sinn Fein President, Gerry Adams, was to be present, despite strong British pressure to do so. The President duly shook hands with Adams. It was a small but highly significant stepping stone on the way to the respectabilization of Sinn Fein. An opinion poll carried out for the Irish Independent Group showed a 77 per cent approval rating (*Sunday Independent*, 27 June 1993) for the gesture by Robinson, who was well recognized as a critic of violence. In the North, Unionist hackles were raised, but the Nationalist reaction was overwhelmingly favourable.

Then a curious incident occurred. In the House of Commons John Major visibly lost control of himself with Kevin McNamara, the Labour Party Opposition spokesman on Northern Ireland, in a discussion over a leaked Labour Party policy document.

The document suggested that if the Unionists continued to withhold their consent to an agreed solution, then London and Dublin would have to go it alone without them. The Labour Party's 'preferred option' was that of Joint Sovereignty, one of the three Irish Forum options ruled 'out' by Thatcher. Major denounced McNamara, a supporter of ultimate Irish unity. Uncharacteristically, he lost his temper, branding the Labour Party proposals as 'shameful'. Despite the fact that in earlier speeches Major had given assurances that all constitutional options were open to debate, he now said: 'The Union is vital for all parts of the United Kingdom . . . and we in the Conservative and Unionist Party stand four-square behind it.'

Was the beleaguered Major acting to abort a process stemming from the Hume-Adams talks which had led McNamara, or someone close to him, to leak the document? Did he attack McNamara in order to gain the support of the Unionist MPs in what was expected to be a very tight vote over the crunch issue of the Maastricht Treaty? Very likely so must be the answer. For Hume, who was sitting in the chamber, vainly tried to get into the discussion to call Major a 'liar', an unheard of performance for the normally controlled SDLP leader. He later told journalists that he regarded Major's performance as a 'cheap, destructive and ill-timed bit of partisanship, aimed mainly at winning a few parliamentary votes on issues quite separate from Ireland.'[*]

The reason for John Major's near hysteria became apparent when,

* *Economist*, 10 July 1993.

on 22 July 1993, the nine Official Unionist MPs supported the Conservatives on a crucial vote on ratification of a portion of the Maastricht Treaty. It was widely said, although strenuously denied, that the price of their support was a deal whereby a Select Committee on Northern Ireland was to be created, and the Unionists were somehow to be given more power in Northern Ireland.

Concurrent with this development, a leading member of the anti-Maastricht lobby, Norman Tebbit (now Lord Tebbit), said on his London-based television show, broadcast on Sky Television, that bombs in Dublin would be required to make the Irish Government abandon Articles 2 and 3 of the Constitution. Allowances could be made for the fact that both Tebbit and his wife were badly injured in the Brighton hotel bombing. Nevertheless, he is a former Tory Minister and member of Margaret Thatcher's Cabinet, a senior figure in the Conservative Party, and a member of the House of Lords. Inescapably, his words would have been taken as plain incitement to bomb Dublin by some factions of Loyalism.

Many people in Ireland began to uneasily remember the infamous remarks of another Conservative which had fatal results. Douglas Hogg, Under Secretary of State at the Home Office said, under privilege of the House of Commons (on 17 January 1989) that 'there are in Northern Ireland a number of solicitors who are unduly sympathetic to the IRA. I state this on the basis of advice ... I have been given by people who are dealing with these matters.' Less than a month later the Belfast solicitor Patrick Finnucane was murdered. The comment of Gregory Campbell, Paisley's party spokesman on security, on Tebbit's remarks, however, was: 'we would agree with this.'

Coming after Major's performance and the Yorkshire Television programme about British involvement in the 1974 bombings of Dublin and Managhan, Tebbit's utterances helped to further worsen the already rapidly deteriorating Dublin/London relationship. Privately the Dublin Government was known to be furious also about the role played by the British EC Commissioner, Bruce Millan, in attempting to cut the Irish EC funds in the same week as the Maastricht vote and the Tebbit affair. Too many coincidences seemed to be occurring all at once.

The components of the deal alleged to have been struck between the Conservatives and Unionists would, if true, have the effect of breaching both the spirit and the form of the Anglo-Irish Agreement.

It was apparent to all thoughtful observers that the football of Northern Ireland was once more bouncing around the division lobbies of Westminster.

Dublin clearly thought little of Major's performance either. The Department of Foreign Affairs has always been strongly responsive to SDLP policies on the North. So much so that critics have often charged that the Department has no policy other than that of Hume. It may be taken for granted that the Department and its Minister, Dick Spring, were fully briefed on the Adams-Hume talks and their long-term possibilities. Following Major's statement, Spring gave a highly significant interview to John Palmer of the *Guardian* newspaper (on 7 July 1993). In it he said flatly that the Unionists could no longer have a veto on progress. If they would not agree to talks, then London and Dublin must agree over their heads. The problem had gone on for too long and would have to be addressed. This was a very different Labour Party attitude from that which had obtained at the time of the Dublin bombings. It was an attitude, moreover, with which Reynolds agreed.

The Irish Government had deliberately chosen to throw down the gauntlet to the British and the Unionists five days before the 'twelfth', the annual 12 July celebration of the Orange high mass. But not only was the interview timed with an eye on the North, it was given on the eve of a scheduled meeting of the Anglo-Irish Conference. The media briefings from both sides which followed this meeting made no effort to disguise the fact that the encounter between Mayhew and Spring was stormy. Spring was also condemned from the Orange platforms a few days later, but unabashed, returned to his theme the day after the 'twelfth' in the Irish Seanad. He was speaking on the findings of the Opsahl Report.* This was a wide ranging inquiry, to which 3,000 people contributed, into every aspect of the Northern problem. It was financed by the Rowntree Trust, under the Chairmanship of the Norwegian academic, Torkel Opsahl. Significantly, amongst a range of other conclusions, it said:

> There was widespread agreement that any settlement that had entirely excluded Sinn Fein from the negotiating process would be neither lasting nor stable, and that some way had to be found to involve the party in future talks.

* *A Citizen's Inquiry: The Opsahl Report*, Liliput Press, Dublin, 1993.

The Commission also recommended that the broadcasting ban on Sinn Fein should be dropped by the Irish Republic.

Clearly, therefore, there are perceptible shifts of opinion occurring in Ireland. But old tendencies persist. Derry-born John Mathews was held in a maximum security prison for ten weeks on suspicion of being involved in the British bombing campaign. His case provides a good illustration of an attitude towards the Irish in Britain which is too frequently met with. At the end of the ten week interlude a magistrate directed that Mathews be discharged 'without a stain on his character', as he was clearly innocent. However, he was taken from the court after the hearing and brought to a police station where he was served with an exclusion order. The next day (7 July 1993) he was flown to Belfast accompanied by Home Office officials.

Unless the order is lifted he cannot pursue his higher education in England, or hope to succeed in getting a visa for the United States. Commenting on his treatment and that of other Irish suspects also released after being held for several weeks, he told RTE on the day he arrived home that: 'Being Irish meant you were treated like scum. We were innocent and had not even been brought to court, yet the warders, the police, everyone we came in contact with, treated us as if we were convicted terrorists. Every single thing was a hassle, whether you were trying to arrange a routine family visit, or looking for a pair of socks. It was all hassle.'

That British attitude, part ancestral prejudice, part a consequence of the IRA campaign, played its part in the spectacularly unjust miscarriage of justice cases I have already alluded to, those involving the Birmingham Six, the Guildford Four and Judith Ward. The Royal Commission has not altered attitudes. Three factors remain to be dealt with in England. One is the continuing tendency of the Tories – and when it suits them the Labour Party – to play for the Unionist MPs' support. On 17 July 1993, after all the furore caused by McNamara and Spring, Sir Patrick Mayhew gave a radio interview in which he publicly appealed to the Unionists to support the Tories over Maastricht. Decoded, his message was a blatant appeal to the Unionists to support the Conservatives, who would in turn support them, whereas Labour would sell them out to Dublin. Hume and Sinn Fein reacted to his comments with outrage, pointing out that they made a mockery of Tory protestations that the British had no strategic or political interest in remaining in Ireland. Contemporary British political exigencies had clearly tempted the Tories, yet again, to make a political football out of the Irish issue. However, the second factor, inertia, prevents any constituency arising in British politics to do anything about such opportunism. Only four Tory and two Labour back-benchers took part in the debate on Northern Ireland in the House of Commons, before the House rose for the summer. A third consideration is the *déjà vu* factor.

The situation, as the House yawned its way through the Irish issue in the summer of 1993, was in some ways strikingly similar to that which existed prior to the British declaration of a truce with the IRA in the summer of 1921. Then there was far more interest of course. But then too there was a hawks and doves split amongst British decision makers. On the one hand Lloyd George had unacknowledged civil servants in contact with Michael Collins. On the other the military men pressed for one more big push. In our day, the British military 'brass hats', as Lloyd George called them, also warned against any scaling down. Huge, unnecessary fortifications were set in train for Crossmaglen and Newtownhamilton, destined to achieve nothing more it seems than to moulder into the Irish landscape alongside Norman keep and Martello Tower. To decision-taking Dublin, which protested in vain against their erection, they served no more useful purpose than either. But to the IRS they provide a useful source of local discontent, more dragons' teeth. Meanwhile, secret talks continued between British civil servants and IRA negotiators, although the Tories' increasing dependence at Westminster on the Unionist representation rendered these ultimately nugatory.

Secret contacts also continued between the IRA and Loyalist paramilitary spokesmen. Orange bitters and Irish whiskey had by no means become a favourite Unionist drink but, while the latter did not like talking to the IRA, they could at least visualize a day dawning when the two sides would have to do business with each other. A little preliminary discussion, albeit of an often highly acrimonious nature, was thought to be not unhelpful in the circumstances. Accordingly, against this background, despite Dick Spring's remarks in the *Guardian*, the 1993 parades passed off peacefully. Criticism of him was widespread but not unremarkable. Some years earlier, there would have been riots.

36

Gerry Adams

Gerry Adams carried his weapons with him as he left his job in the famous Belfast pub, the Duke of York, on a fine August day in 1969. The regulars, many of them British TV and print journalists, were sorry to learn of his departure. He had been the most popular barman in the pub. They had not taken much note of his Republicanism. Nor would they have seen much to indicate it from what he was holding as he headed towards the rioting and petrol bombing which had erupted between the Catholic Falls Road area and the Protestant Shankill Road. Gerry Adams was going to war with a dozen large empty stout bottles.

His political evolution between August 1969 and 24 July 1994, when he and Sinn Fein delivered a verdict on the Downing St Declaration, at Letterkenny in Co. Donegal, which appeared to many outside observers to effectively kill off prospects for peace, is a mirror image of the growth in power and sophistication of the IRA and Sinn Fein in the intervening years. The power was evident in the size of the enormous media presence at the conference. The sophistication, not quite so apparent to outsiders, in the fact that the rejection was not simply what it seemed, but contained a signal to both the Dublin and London Governments that the peace process was still alive. This confirmed a message contained in an interview given by Adams the previous day (in Belfast, on the BBC's *Inside Politics* programme) on the eve of the conference to the effect that the conflict was ending its final phase.

The next day, in the wave of editorial and Unionist fury at Sinn Fein, most commentators overlooked the fact that the two prime ministers of the sovereign governments directly involved, London and Dublin, took a far more relaxed view of the proceedings than did the majority who rushed for microphones. In Dublin Albert Reynolds remarked on the 'positive' elements contained in the Sinn Fein reaction. From Downing St, as Unionists called for the ostracization of

Sinn Fein and a stepping up of the war against the IRA, there was no aversion to such calls, merely a reassurance that the peace process would continue. Also overlooked was the significance of an announcement – made public the morning after the Sinn Fein Conference –that Republican prisoners in the Maze prison were no longer to be locked into their cells at night. This extension of 'freedom of association', went far beyond what had been sought by the Republican prisoners who had starved themselves to death on hunger strike, for the principle. Unknown to the public it had been introduced several weeks earlier 'for the world cup'. Prisoners could, and did,* spend their nights in the TV room watching videos if they chose. The concession, which came about as a result of representations by Dublin through the inter-governmental conference, set up by the Anglo-Irish Agreement, was not the action of a government contemplating immediate and terrible war on the prisoners' outside associates. Nor, of course, was it the action of an administration which was out of contact with (or hope from) said associates.

Also unknown to the public was the fact that, while the Letterkenny Conference was in progress, Adams's speech and other relevant material, none of which was available to the media at that stage, was being dispatched to Washington from Dublin through American diplomatic sources. Part of the public's awareness of Adams stems from the furore over the granting of a visa to him to visit America. During the Presidential election campaign Irish-Americans succeeded in winning a pledge from Bill Clinton that if elected he would grant a visa to Adams. After his election he told Irish-American leaders (on 5 April 1993):

> I would support a visa for Gerry Adams or any other elected official from a government recognized by the United States. I understand the United States' historical policy towards Sinn Fein and on the advocacy of non-violence, but I honestly think that it would be totally harmless to let him [Adams] in.[†]

But a few months later the President caused widespread annoyance to the Irish-American community by reneging on his election pledge when Adams applied for a visa in order to publicize a book of his short

---

* The concession was also extended to Loyalist prisoners.
† *Irish Voice*, New York, 25 May 1993.

stories which was about to be published in the US. Clinton gave as his reason for the denial the fact that the British had furnished him with a dossier implicating Adams in terrorist activities. The Irish-Americans' anger was heightened by the fact that at around the same time that the British sent the Adams file to Clinton, Sir Patrick Mayhew had refused to accede to a request made by Judge Barbara Caulfield of the US District Court in San Francisco (on 11 June 1993), that she be sent a sensitive file to enable her to make a decision in the extradition case involving James Smith. She had wanted information concerning the Stalker-Samson inquiry into the RUC shoot-to-kill policy and the Kelly report which gave details of the disciplinary measures proposed against RUC officers in the case.

The British argued that the documents might prejudice British security operations in Northern Ireland. Judge Caulfield, who had guaranteed the documents' secrecy, replied: 'It is not whether there is terrorism in Northern Ireland, it's a matter of obeying American law.' But she did not get the documents. Whatever the British file contains, it is clearly not sufficient to bring charges against Adams because he is one of the most visible public figures in the Six Counties at liberty to come and go as he wishes – within the limits of his own security precautions. But to the British, he was clearly a dangerous apologist for his cause on American TV. How dangerous became apparent when, after a prodigious diplomatic battle, he was granted a mere 48-hour visa, early the following year. In that time he created a media storm, appearing on every TV networked show of consequence, and triggering off a storm of fruitless British protest. Long after he had returned to Belfast deputations of Unionist and British apologists were still toiling around American newspaper offices and TV stations in a vain attempt to roll back the publicity he generated. Bearded, good-looking, and disarmingly low-key in manner and speech, he has a sense of humour combined with formidable powers of analysis and logic in debate. He is also a first class writer and pamphleteer. Rightly or wrongly it is alleged that he has had a hand in the composition of every important policy change, and every significant document, ranging from writings attributed to Bobby Sands to the *Green Book*, which has emanated from Sinn Fein or the IRA in the past fifteen years.

He looks more like a tweedy, bespectacled academic than a revolutionary. But one can't help be aware that violence fringes his world. While we talked he casually mentioned the most recent attempt on his life. A few weeks before we met there had been a grenade attack on his home in which his wife and son had narrowly escaped – just as he had himself missed being killed, when fired upon, on a number of occasions. On 9 May 1991, his close associate, Danny Morrison, also a talented writer and more importantly, Sinn Fein's Publicity Director, began an eight year prison sentence for false imprisonment of an RUC informer. Soon after we talked, Adams's brother was arrested for IRA activities, and was then released due to lack of evidence. A cousin, Kevin Hannaway, was one of the 'hooded' men awarded compensation by the British Government because of his mistreatment during internment. Kevin Hannaway, an active Republican, survived an assassination attempt when a UVF gunman who had entered his home, panicked at his own reflection and emptied his gun into a wardrobe mirror which Hannaway flung open in front of him, before departing (rapidly) out the back door.

The Adams boys grew up in the Falls Road in a world of kitchen houses from which one was expected to progress upwards via 'the books'. Study, religion, 'having the crack', a Belfast expression for enjoying life, were the priorities of a lively family of ten brothers and sisters. Adams was the eldest. The Adamses are one of the spinal Republican families of Northern Ireland, though for years Gerry was not aware of the extent of the Republican backdrop. There was little or no discussion of things nationalistic that Adams can recall. He had not realized that his uncle, Dominic Adams, was in the IRA (he acted as Chief of Staff, during World War II) until he read the first UK edition of this book. The portcullis of years had come down and there was only a dim awareness amongst the children that two other uncles, Paddy Adams and Alfie Hannaway, had done time in the Curragh and in Belfast jail respectively.

The political figure in the family of whom he was most aware was his grandfather, William Hannaway, a remote, patriarchal figure who wore black laced boots. Along with the boots, Adams was impressed with the fact that Hannaway, a full-time labour official in Belfast, had been a friend of James Connolly, and was an agent for de Valera during the 1918 election. But political awareness bore in upon him sharply in 1964, during the Westminster election campaign. At that time it was illegal to display the Irish tricolour in the Six Counties under the Flags and Emblems Act. Ian Paisley, then a scarcely known preacher, discovered that the Republican candidate had a tricolour in his election headquarters window. The HQ was in Divis Street, an inconspicuous back street. Paisley, however, made himself conspicuous. Overnight, almost, he became a national figure, leading parades and demonstrations by Protestant Loyalists through the predominantly Catholic area. The resultant riots and petrol bombings saw the first car burnings to occur in Belfast. Television had not long come to Ireland and the public were shocked. After days of rioting the RUC forcibly removed the flag. The Divis Street incident had made Paisley a force to be reckoned with.

Divis Street also had the effect of making the young Gerry Adams join the Republican movement. It was then largely a ceremonial, symbolic organization. Although some 20,000 self-styled Republicans marched in the Easter Commemorations to honour the Anniversary of 1916, only about twenty would have been geared for actual fighting. The IRA was then dominated by the Marxist wing led by Roy Johnston. The thrust of the movement was towards working class solidarity with the Loyalists and the infiltration of trade unions. The folly of this approach in the sectarian climate of the Six Counties immediately became apparent to Adams. Catholics could not infiltrate anything that counted, except the ranks of the unskilled. For example, on the docks the casual workers were generally Catholic, the Protestants were the permanent workers. The craft unions in places like the shipyards, or the power plants, were overwhelmingly Protestant. (A fact which came home to roost during the workers' strike of 1974, when the Loyalists successfully defied the British Government, and wrecked the Sunningdale Agreement through their control of the electricity supply.)

Adams took less account of the IRA's Marxism than of the activities of the Dublin Housing Action Committee. He founded a similar organization in the New Barnsley and the Ballymurphy areas of the Falls Road. This was successful for a time, agitating over issues like the provision of railings for a pedestrian crossing after a Protestant child was knocked down. He saw how this homely initiative briefly united Protestant and Catholic. However, he also saw how the continuous Paisleyite agitation drove everyone back into their ancestral ghettos so that in the end, Protestant families had to be evacuated from New Barnsley after sectarian riots.

As the sixties progressed, he and the younger men in the IRA who thought like him came to believe that a campaign for civil rights alone would not bring democracy to Ulster. The then leadership of the IRA in Belfast, principally Jim Sullivan and Liam MacMillan, saw the growth of a civil rights movement, paralleling that in America, as leading to reform within the system. Adams argued that Unionism was not capable of democratization. He and his cohorts wanted to bring about a destabilization, out of which would grow a new and democratic state. He felt that the colonial relic of Unionist political culture was a decadent creation for which the British were responsible, manipulating the Unionists as they wished. He felt that the backlash factor could be orchestrated to suit British policies. The real backlash threat lay not with the Loyalist mobs, but with the well-armed RUC who had the motivation, equipment and local knowledge to run a successful pogrom against Catholics. Basically this is still his position.

The mid-1960s saw him leave school, and devote himself more and more to local agitation. To his parents' chagrin he did not proceed to university, but took a job in a bar and spearheaded a campaign against the building of Divis Flats on the Falls Road. However, the flats went ahead and duly became prey to all the problems associated with high rise complexes in ghettos everywhere, as Adams and his friends had forecast. The problems were compounded by the growth of paramilitarism. The Irish Republican Socialist Party (IRSP), the political wing of the Irish National Liberation Army (INLA) hung out there. But at the time of their building, they were welcomed by Catholic political and religious leaders as they prevented the Catholic vote being dispersed to other parts of the city. Because of sit-ins and other protests, Adams at one stage faced a grand total of fifty-four summonses for breach of the peace and for illegal entry. His first TV interview came about as a result of these activities.

His education progressed through street confrontations, the study of James Connolly, Irish history and literature. He became a member of the Wolfe Tone Society, the Republican-oriented literary and debating society. Curiously, neither he nor his friends read Marx; they were instinctive, working-class socialists. Ireland overall was experiencing the invigorating shock of the new which the sixties had brought everywhere in the West. There was an explosion in ballad singing and traditional music, always a particularly potent force in Ireland with its tradition of oral culture. Historically a nation on the run did not sculpt or paint portraits, but it could, and did, sing and recite poetry. Now all over the country there was a growth in Fleadhanna Ceol (Irish music festivals).

The Fleadhanna helped to spread the popularity of a Dublin group, the Dubliners, led by Ronnie Drew, who at the time were reviving a medley of Irish airs, old Ulster ballads like 'My Lagan Love', and political ballads like 'James Connolly' which told of his death by British firing squad. Even more potent, because closer to hand, was 'Sean South of Garryowen', who had lost his life only yesterday, in the 1956 IRA campaign. One would have to have witnessed a ballad session in a Republican pub or club to understand the sense of empathy these and similar songs brought, and bring, to young men and women of Adams's type. The drinking, the camaraderie, the shared sense of being 'us' against the hostile 'them' outside is a potent mixture. (The same formula works in Loyalist circles also of course.)

Adams's growing consciousness of being Irish was heightened by three factors: the 50th Anniversary Commemoration of the Easter Rising which took place in 1966, his move to a job in the Duke of York bar around this time, and his becoming involved, through the Wolfe Tone society, in the broad based Civil Rights Association which was founded in the International Hotel, Belfast, on 29 January 1967. The effect of the widespread commemoration events (lectures, concerts, Gaelic sporting events and so forth) for the anniversary of the Rising on an ardent young Nationalist can readily be imagined. The Duke of York had another effect, says Adams: 'The atmosphere was heady with ideas. There was a sort of effervescence in the air.' The clientele included actors, journalists, writers, politicians and the BBC and other international television crews being drawn to Northern Ireland by the clash between Unionists and the increasingly assertive civil rights groups.

A London correspondent who remembers Adams from the Duke of York interlude described him to me as: 'Your classic "favourite barman" type: efficient, friendly, intelligent. A great loss to the licensed trade!' The amalgamation of like-minded bodies into the Civil Rights Association broadened Adams's Duke of York contacts. 'You met all sorts of hues and views,' he recalled. There were British civil libertarians, communists, members of the Northern Ireland Labour Party, journalists, professionals like Dr Con McCluskey who first injected the concept of civil rights into the Six Counties, even some liberal Unionists. But as his contacts widened, so did two sets of conflict intensify. One, the internal, hidden, struggle between Adams and the other young tigers of the Republican movement with the older leadership over the wisdom of pursuing a purely civil rights campaign. Secondly, the increasingly visible tensions between the civil rights campaigners and the Unionists, amongst whom Paisley was becoming increasingly active.

Four sets of attacks in particular pushed the Six Counties into 'the troubles'. An RUC ban on a civil rights march in Derry on 5 October 1968 led to fierce rioting in which, under the eyes of the cameras, scores of people were injured. On 30 November, Paisley and a henchman, Major Ronald Bunting, intervened in a civil rights march at Armagh. The Paisleyites arrived in the city in the early hours of the morning in a cavalcade of cars containing stones, sharpened piping and cudgels with nails driven through them. They erected barricades and prevented the marchers traversing a route previously agreed with the RUC. The police made no effort to intervene. Nor did they interfere when at Burntollet, County Derry, similar mobs ambushed a People's Democracy march. The PDs, a student organization led by Bernadette Devlin and Michael Farrell, were driven into a river and beaten while scores of uniformed RUC stood idly by. Again the scenes were recorded on television.

The pot finally boiled over with the rioting in Derry and Belfast in August of 1969 during which Protestant mobs in both cities attempted to invade Catholic areas. In Belfast members of the RUC were observed looking at their watches and departing from their beats, shortly before the mobs arrived, led by their colleagues in the B-Specials. Since then the people of the Falls Road have fought to keep the police from re-entering their areas. Today they can only do so under British Army protection.

The Army arrived to protect the Catholics in Derry on 14 August, and in Belfast on 15 August. Gerry Adams had his own ideas as to how Nationalists should be protected. But on 13 August, after all the debate about force as opposed to constitutional action, the IRA's armament on the Falls Road had consisted of five handguns. There were no full-time guerrillas and no active service units. Outraged Nationalists altered the letters IRA on gable walls to read: 'Irish Ran Away'. Gerry Adams left his job in the Duke of York and walked not away, but towards the fighting.

Fighting in those early years involved home-grown expertise that was often more harmful to the Republicans than the authorities. Suitcases full of gelignite sometimes exploded prematurely taking with them the bombers, not the target. Nail-bombs claimed as many IRA fingers as British limbs. The 'Tipperary rifle', a hurling stick, was frequently employed, as was the 'kidney paver', that stock-in-trade of the Belfast rioter, a cobble-stone. Externally, the reaction to a Loyalist bombing of the Silent Valley reservoir caused the resignation of

Captain Terence O'Neill, the Six County Prime Minister. Within the IRA the arrest of the Commanding Officer of the Belfast Brigade, Billy McKee, led to a shake-up wherein new, and unknown (to the RUC) figures moved into positions of authority.

Ironically, McKee was a traditionalist who saw the IRA's role as defending the Catholics, not attacking the British. Adams, however, increasingly came to be identified with a belief formerly articulated by Michael Collins when he was urging the Sinn Fein of his day to go to war[*]:

> ... the sooner fighting was forced and a general state of disorder created throughout the country the better it would be throughout the country. Ireland was likely to get more out of the state of general disorder than from a continuance of the situation as it then was.

Adams's own immediate surroundings in the Ballymurphy district of the Falls Road were a scene of 'general disorder'. The inhabitants fought the British Army for a year without firing a shot. There was a plentiful supply of manpower available for the hostilities as male unemployment in the area commonly stands at 60 per cent. Homes were searched incessantly. Five or six searches a night was not uncommon. Gardens were more frequently occupied by Saracen armoured cars than by lawnmowers. But the citizens of Ballymurphy fought back fiercely, the women as much as the men. 'Bin Brigades' sounded the tocsin at the approach of troops by banging binlids on the pavements. Then the 'hurley brigades' attacked the intruders. Wet sacks were used to gather up the CS gas cylinders and hurl them back at the soldiers. Every home had basins filled with vinegar to counter the CS gas.

The vocabularies of the unfortunate troops was considerably added to, if not enriched, by the epithets hurled at them by amazonian women who perfected a technique of luring them into cul-de-sacs, where, amongst other things, the soldiers heard many original, and cacophonous, suggestions concerning their ancestry. The psychological injury inflicted must have been greater than anything done with a 'kidney-paver' or 'Tipperary rifle'.

The Adams family was not unscathed. One brother, Dominic, developed a stammer after a CS gas attack on their home. Gerry Adams himself was becoming a marked man as the situation escalated. Bloody turning points came and went: Falls Road curfew, July 1970; first British

---

[*] *The Man Who Made Ireland*, by Tim Pat Coogan, Roberts Rinehart, Colorado, 1992, p. 103.

soldier killed, February 1971; Internment, August 1971. Adams was married by Fr Des Murphy in a room behind the altar in St John's Chapel on the Falls Road during the height of the internment crisis. Adams's father was in Long Kesh. There was no wedding reception and the honeymoon was a few days in Dublin. On its last evening they heard Southern politicians address an anti-internment meeting in the fiery tones of verbal Republicanism outside the GPO. After the meeting ended, Gerry and Colette headed back to Belfast and the Republicanism of Reality.

In 1972 Adams himself was interned. He was interrogated and systematically beaten up. Other methods were also employed:

'You faced the wall for hours at a time, supporting yourself only with your finger tips. You'd be waiting all day for something to happen. Sometimes they came up behind you and dropped a tray with a crash. It would scare the living daylights out of you. Once they showed me a blood stained hatchet . . .'

In Castlereagh Barracks he remained silent for a week, using what he had taught himself of counter-interrogation techniques to defeat his captors. By way of example he indicated the room we were talking in. I had thought it rather spartan but he judged it a good place to be interrogated in: 'You see that curtain for example. It's made of tweed. You could think about how the tweed was made, where the materials came from, how they dyed it, what sort of people worked at making tweed, what their lives were like and so on.' One can certainly find echoes of that technique in the *Green Book*. After his interrogation, following which he lodged a formal complaint about his treatment, he was taken first to the Maidstone prison ship and then interned in Long Kesh prison.

He had no idea as to when he might be released and had gone on a thirteen day hunger strike with a group which included his uncle, Liam Hannaway, a prominent Belfast IRA man. The issue was the usual IRA demand for political status. Unexpectedly, it was conceded in extraordinary circumstances. Out of the blue Adams was freed. One day he heard his name being called for release. When, puzzled, he asked his uncle why his name was being called, all he received in return was a terse: 'Get out.' Outside the jail he discovered that a truce was to be negotiated with the British and that he and Daithi O'Connell were to do the negotiating. A truce was agreed on terms which eventually led to the great hunger strikes of the 1980s. On 20 June 1972, William Whitelaw, the Northern Ireland Secretary of State, announced the introduction of the new prison classification of Special Category Prisoner. This in effect conceded political status by another name to the IRA.

Another result of the Adams/O'Connell negotiation was that a group of IRA men, including Adams, were given a safe conduct to be flown to London aboard an RAF plane to meet Whitelaw to discuss a British withdrawal. The Irish and the British delegations met at the luxury home of Whitelaw's ministerial colleague, Paul Channon, in Chelsea, a far cry from Ballymurphy and Long Kesh. Too far, in more respects than one. Historically, it was a significant meeting; the first time representatives of the Irish 'physical force' tradition had met British statesmen since the time of Michael Collins and the Treaty negotiations. But the middle-class Catholics of the Six Counties were not with the Irish delegation because they supported the SDLP. Dublin had not been consulted and the Unionists were completely absent. Politically, therefore, there was no pressure on the British to seriously entertain the IRA demand for a withdrawal. Culturally, too, there was a yawning gulf between the Irish and the British. One of the Irish delegation, curiously the only man with a professional training on the Irish side, was so suspicious of the proceedings that his attitude towards the British was described to me, by an English civil servant, as being 'like a dog'. Not surprisingly all that emerged from the talks in concrete terms were agreements on an extension of the truce.

Adams actually took no formal part in the discussions. His role was that of 'listener'. Listening for the nuances of what the other side meant as opposed to what they said. During a break in the talks he had had a conversation with Whitelaw, whom he found surprisingly nervous, sweating profusely and obviously ill at ease. By contrast, the only time the Irishmen had felt any fear was when they were collected in an RAF helicopter, which circled for a time near the Glenshane Pass in the Sperrin Mountains, preparatory to setting course for their plane to London. They were uneasily conscious of the opportunities for marksmanship being afforded to their colleagues on the ground who had not been made aware of who was in the helicopter!

During his exchange with Whitelaw concerning their pact, Adams agreed that in the event of certain eventualities, 'all bets were off'. The truce only held for a matter of days and the next time Adams heard that phrase he was lying naked on the floor of a cell in the Springfield Road Barracks being kicked by a Special Branch interrogator who punctuated his kicks with the words: 'All bets are off now, Gerry.' He still has kidney problems stemming from that episode. He learned of the birth of his

son, Gearoid, from a warder in Long Kesh one September night in
1971. He and Colette were not reunited for another four years and even
then their relationship had to adapt to the fact of his being generally on
the run.

We have seen how, throughout the seventies, the IRA became
reorganized. More time will have to elapse before it can be said with
certainty what part, if any, Adams played in that reorganization. What is
undoubtedly true is that increasingly he emerged as the leading political
figure in the Republican movement. He deliberately sought to distance
himself, in the public mind, from the militant wing of Republicanism, as
I discovered accidentally one day when I got a phone call at the *Irish Press*
from my solicitor, Con Lehane. It turned out that he wanted to talk, not
about my business, but about another client of his, the well-known
politician, Mr Gerry Adams, whom the *Irish Press* had recently grossly
maligned by referring to him in a report as being a member of the IRA. A
lively, if not altogether courteous conversation ensued!

However, Adams went on to prove that he was indeed a politician of
rare skill and courage. He and the young tigers of Sinn Fein emerged
into national, and sometimes international, prominence in the crucible
of emotion generated by the hunger strikes which broke out in 1981 over
the British proposal to take away the Special Category status which he
had negotiated in 1972. As I had some peripheral dealing with the
situation myself, on behalf of Irish Government figures, I was able to
evaluate the performance of the new generation of Northern Irish Sinn
Fein leadership. It was unquestionably of high calibre. Danny
Morrison, Martin McGuinness, Tom Hartley, Jim Gibney, Joe Austin
and Richard McAuley all conducted themselves with restraint and
dignity. Moreover they showed themselves able to rise to the challenge
of the moment, whether it involved coping with political negotiation,
dealing with the media, or the distraught relatives of hunger strikers.

The hunger strikes lasted for 217 days, from 1 March to 3 October
1981. During that time ten men died: Bobby Sands, Francis Hughes,
Raymond McCreesh, Patsy O'Hara, Joe McDonnell, Martin Hurson,
Kevin Lynch, Kieran Doherty, Tom McElera and Michael Devine.
They have left an ineradicable imprint on Northern Irish politics. Bobby
Sands was elected to the British Parliament as MP for Fermanagh/
Tyrone as he lay dying. Over 100,000 people joined in his funeral
cortège. Adams regards that election as a crucial learning experience for
Sinn Fein. The young tigers learned how to conduct a campaign both in
nitty gritty detail, like finding out what a personation officer's function
is, to the more flamboyant aspects of electioneering.

He told me that it was: 'Exhilarating. Sometimes we'd come into a little town with Catholics corralled away up at the top as usual, the Loyalists living along the main street, with the businesses. We would come in with the tricolour flying and the bands playing and the Catholics would come down from the hills as if we were the relieving cavalry.' That cavalry charge took the young tigers to control of Sinn Fein and to a historic victory in the 1983 Westminster election when Adams defeated the SDLP leader, Gerry Fitt, for the West Belfast seat. Within Sinn Fein, Daithi O'Connell and Ruairi O'Bradaigh stood down as President and Vice President in recognition of the fact that Sinn Fein was now a Northern movement led by Northerners. Adams has been President of Sinn Fein since, and the movement has followed a hard Northern Republican line. No sops to Loyalism in the form of a federal arrangement as proposed in the Eire Nua document; a unitary state is Sinn Fein's preferred option for the future of Ireland.

However, Adams has not been MP for West Belfast since April 1992. His vote went up slightly but he was defeated by the SDLP candidate, Dr Joe Hendron. Hendron, a colourless, unimpressive figure, won not on his own merits but because some 3,000 Unionists voted tactically for him rather than support their own candidate, Fred Cobain, in order to defeat Sinn Fein. However, Hendron's popularity is not high, even with his own supporters. He won by less than six hundred votes (17,415 to 16,826) and a thousand new young voters have come on the register since the election. These are almost by definition sure to be Sinn Fein. The local government elections in May 1993, showed the Sinn Fein share of the vote, approximately 40 per cent of the total Nationalist poll, remains constant. Accordingly, Adams is generally expected to regain the seat at the next general election, whenever it may be.

During our interview, Adams and I talked – as inevitably we do when we have a serious discussion – about the possibility of a Loyalist backlash and the linked question of the existence of an RUC/Loyalist tie-up. 'I'll put it to you this way,' he replied, 'A few years ago the RUC were shooting Catholics in Tyrone. Catholics are still being shot in Tyrone, but the RUC's not doing it.' To illustrate his point Adams took as his theme the case of Declan 'Beano' Casey. Casey is yet another example of a paramilitary who worked for the security forces and then became a prey to homesickness and disgust both with himself and the set-up. He went public – at very great personal risk. Casey, though a Republican, has the same motive for speaking out as the

Loyalist 'Maxwell'. This former IRA quartermaster from Strabane, County Tyrone, genuinely wants other people to avoid the trap he fell into.

At the time Adams and I were conducting our interview, Casey had told a Belfast Court (on 22 June 1993) that he was: 'at all stages under the orders of the RUC Special Branch and everything I did had the prior and full knowledge of the Special Branch.' He had decided the week beforehand to blow his cover and tell the *Daily Mirror* that he had been allowed to go on killing for the IRA while working for the British Government. The British had set him up in a safe house in England, but Casey decided to come in from the cold. Even though he was under a death threat from the Provisional IRA, something I would rank ahead of that placed upon Salman Rushdie, he decided to confront his destiny. He came home and was arrested at the home of his father-in-law. Speaking in a calm voice he told the court that he regretted the traumas he had brought upon his wife, family, and the Republican movement then went on to say, echoing Maxwell:

'I appeal to anyone caught up in the same bizarre position as myself to come forward and make their position known to some public figure and not end up like me – soul-destroyed by the RUC Special Branch.' Casey was charged with possessing two rifles and with withholding information about the death of a UDR man. He said he found it a bit bizarre to be facing 'trumped up charges', having spent five years spying for the unit which had set him up in a safe house in England.

Adams made the point that any mother who had lost a son in the RUC to the IRA, or any widow, would feel 'sickened' on reading 'Beano's' evidence. 'Was this what they died for? They'll want to know was their son or husband set up? Even if he wasn't, what about the wee woman down the road?' It is a fair point that, along with the dawning sense of identity amongst Protestants, very obvious in Maxwell for example, who increasingly sees himself as Irish and wishes that the British would just go away. Such cases do pose a threat to Loyalism.

What else in the province do the authorities know about, say, concerning racketeering of both green and orange hue, and deliberately take no action on for their own purposes? More importantly, in the face of the manifest inability of the authorities to crush the IRA, the implications of the fact that only a half dozen Westminster MPs bother to turn up for a debate on Northern Ireland takes on an added significance in an era of governmental cutbacks and falling employment. There is a growing sense of betrayal amongst Unionists. In one part of their minds, for reasons of their own self-esteem, Maxwell and many like him would welcome a backlash. They can possibly stage one, albeit of a short-lived nature, but what then? The Loyalists still control a major proportion of the jobs and better class farms and homes in the Six Counties – precisely the sort of targets that would normally be attacked in a 'scorched earth' situation. But it would be the 'haves' earth which would be scorched, not the 'have-nots'. Where would the former 'haves' go after the scorching?

As essential component of Loyalism was supremacy. Quite obviously the Loyalists are no longer supreme over either the Provisional IRA in military terms or the Dublin Government in political ones. And on top of this, demographic changes are forcing the Protestants out of their traditional areas and out to the northern tips of the Six Counties: East Antrim and North Down. A bastion of Protestant supremacy, Mackie's Engineering Works, has left the Falls area. In the Queen's University, sixty-five per cent of the student body is now Catholic. Many well-off Protestant families, and their Catholic counterparts, are sending their children to English universities. The enrolment which does attend Queen's thus contains a high percentage of working class Catholics from the hardcore Republican areas. How many science and engineering graduates from this element are advising on the ever increasingly skilful use of technology by the Provos? The answer to that question is: 'No one knows but there is such a thing as the ineluctable dialectic of history.'

I asked Adams what was his guesstimate of the Provos' ability to continue. He declined to reply directly but recalled Mrs Thatcher's comment at the time of the hunger strikes, thirteen years earlier. She had said that the strikes represented the playing of 'the last card' by the IRA. Earlier we had talked about the devastation caused by the April 1993 bomb in the City of London. 'Draw your own conclusions,' he said.

For some years past, before Adams and I spoke, the IRA's Bodenstown statements had indicated a willingness to talk. The right of the Irish people to 'self-determination' has been a continuing theme. So too has that of asking those who would condemn the armed struggle to suggest another way. It was out of those evidences of willingness to listen to reason that the process which led to the Adams-Hume talks was born. Although Hume endured the public criticism, Adams was taking the greater risk. There are some personalities in the IRA for whom his life would not be worth a cent should it be thought that he was selling out the 'armed struggle'. The feeling stemmed not from blood-lust, but the same sense of the integrity of the fight which Sean, whom I mentioned in the prologue, displayed when I tried to talk him out of joining the IRA. Adams himself visibly has that same sense of the rightness of the struggle. His own experiences and his family background had taught him to regard many of the unceasing calls for truces, and the emergence and disappearance of sunburst peace movements, appear facile at best and, at worse, part of the counter-insurgency effort.

Too many have died to countenance a ceasefire without the possibility of a British withdrawal in sight. On one level 'self-determination' was a deceptively emollient phrase. It means, of course, excluding the British. But it also means including the Irish, all the Irish, and not just the Catholics of Northern Ireland. I found on this occasion, after the series of talks with Hume (who had also, of course, learned what the bottom line was for the Republicans), that Adams was prepared to enlarge the horizons insofar as Dublin was concerned. A combination of an elucidation of Dublin's position, which formed part of the discussions, plus Adams's own firsthand experience of the lack of support for Sinn Fein in Twenty-Six County elections, had injected a note of realism into the Republican position.

There was nothing of a once familiar refrain: 'To us a Garda is a British soldier in another uniform.' This time he spoke of the necessity to arrive at a solution based on agreement between Dublin and London. 'We would have to be included of course, but London and Dublin must get together in the first instance.' When his talks with Hume ended, Adams had said (on BBC Radio Ulster, 12 June 1993) that their discussions were the only initiative on the horizon and should be given the same encouragement as the talks Mayhew had been involved in. He said:

'It needs more than John Hume and me. Obviously it needs the Republicans, it needs Dublin, it needs the British, it needs the Unionists. Let us give, if not approval, the same sort of general encouragement to this process as was given to the nonsense that the British were involved in.' (The reason Adams spoke with such feeling on this occasion was because, unknown to the public, yet another series of underground, British-IRA talks, were grinding to a halt. Their existence was not acknowledged until the end of the year when

Downing St discovered that Unionists had become aware of what had taken place and were leaking the story to the *Observer* newspaper. The Downing St Declaration was unveiled a few days later. (Both developments are discussed on pp. 640 et seq.)

He repeated this sentiment to me, laying great stress on the Dublin-London relationship. 'That's where the settlement has to take place. As Republicans we would of course like to see the solution which eventuates being within a Republican framework. What we seek is a broad democratization of society: the right of the Irish people to national self-determination. In a post-British withdrawal Ireland we would see the rule of the ballot box as paramount. Contrary to propaganda, we see no role for the armed struggle in the Twenty-Six Counties. The end of Partition and the departure of the British should mean an end to the use of force. And look at the potential for investment, industry, tourism, and so on, that would follow.'

Adams used to be dismissive of a UN presence. But a discussion document* drawn up under his aegis in 1992 envisaged a UN conference on Ireland as a means to facilitate British withdrawal. The UN is thought of as being helpful in guaranteeing 'the economic and political rights of all the people of Ireland.' The document also called upon the UN Secretary General, under Article 73 of the Charter, to demand annual reports from the British government on its role in Ireland. 'But,' Adams says, 'not too many troops. We want less troops, not more in the province.' He is appreciative of such American initiatives as the MacBride Principles, the Clinton proposal for a Peace Envoy, and the support given by American lawyers to human rights cases. 'Basically the problem here is a human rights issue. The British are afraid of Irish-American influence. They are afraid of seeing me in the US. But since the hunger strikes, Sinn Fein is a valid and a vital force in Irish and Irish-American affairs. We are entitled to be listened to. We will not give up until we are heard. Thirteen members of Sinn Fein have been killed. To step into their shoes, another candidate has to publish his or her name and address and put their neck on the block. On top of that they have to get eight sponsors. They have to risk their lives too. Yet, every time one of our people is shot, another candidate comes forward. So do his sponsors. That's not Godfatherism.

'The British are going to go some day. We don't know when. At the

* Towards a lasting peace in Ireland, presented to the Sinn Fein Ard Fheis in 1992, by the Sinn Fein Ard Comfhairle (literally High Committee, or ruling body).

moment they're still operating on the belief that they can beat Sinn Fein and the IRA. Any more constructive approach is stalled by inertia, lack of vision, the past, everything. But they have nothing to offer. We've had Hillsborough and we're no further down the road. There's a vacuum. What we do know is that until they go we'll keep bothering them and poking at them until they leave.'

And how does young Sean feel about that prospect? He sent me a 'comm' which gives a fair indication of the state of his morale. It was five cigarette papers long. At the time he wrote it he was in the Punishment Unit 'on the boards' for thirty days for striking a Loyalist prisoner. As a result he was deprived of bedding and confined to his cell twenty-four hours a day. Some forty-six of his companions were in a similar situation because they had worn Easter lilies and conducted an illegal parade to commemorate 1916. He described conditions as follows:

> The fun continues. I don't think this place has changed from poor Tom Williams' time [Williams, as readers will recall, was hanged in the jail in 1942], a real dungeon . . . conditions here are very poor, lads haven't been getting out at all. Not even to empty piss pots, to wash, association etc. The results have been to empty the piss out of the cracks in the cell doors and shit into bags heaving them out the windows . . . I'm not used to this auld crack, the wing I came from was nice and peaceful . . .
>
> The present England campaign indicates that it's definitely winning the war at the moment. Hopefully it'll continue. The previous operations set us back greatly. [Warrington] I was shattered when I heard about it. It's sickening at times. But nothing's changed, I mean from '69 about young children dying. We've lost young ones too. That doesn't make any difference. But when I saw that shower of shit in Dublin I was boiling with anger [the peace demonstrations]. Where have they been for the last twenty years?

He went on to talk about his case and his hopes for the future. One of his fellow accused had 'broke bad'. As a result he expected to get a longer sentence. He told me not to worry about him. He said of Adams:

> Big Gerry is a Saint. May God protect him. He is one of our best.

When Sean's punishment term had ended, I visited him in the gloomy old Victorian jail. It is set in the Loyalist Crumlin Road amidst houses whose gable ends are decorated with murals showing battle-dressed, balaclavaed UVF men firing rifles at an unseen foe – Sean and his comrades. Despite the lowering surroundings, it was like visiting an eager young cadet in a Military Academy. Spotlessly clean, hair cut tightly, he wore jeans and an open necked shirt. He seemed to be taller, certainly leaner, but fit and full of cheer and energy. 'Ah sure they wouldn't let you get down in here. If they [the IRA jail structure] see you gettin' depressed they say "what are you on about" and put two men on you until you just have to get cheerful again.' He showed the same confidence in victory that he had expressed in his comm.

'Ah sure of course we'll win. And we'll get back that seat in West Belfast for Big Gerry. That's a certainty.' His only concern about his trial and sentence was that he wanted it to come quickly so that he could get started on a course of study. In the meantime he was reading everything he could and taking part in prison debates. In the short time which had elapsed since we had last shaken hands he had visibly matured and seemed to have a deeper grasp of affairs. He again mentioned Warrington saying: 'Ah sure that was shocking. You'd have to be against that.' When I suggested that fighting with Loyalist fellow prisoners was perhaps not the best way to secure a United Ireland he replied:

'Sure I know that . . . It was just one of those things, the screws won't allow segregation, and it leads to tensions. I was sorry I belted your man afterwards. We're all going to have to live together one day. You'd be sorry for them in here. They've no organization, and they feel the pressure. You see them cryin' for their mammies sometimes.' His mother, who had accompanied me on the visit, chided him for making fun of mothers and wagged her finger at him saying: 'Just because you're in here doesn't mean you don't have to show respect like the rest of the family, or I'll chastise you.'

He laughed at her and observed to me: 'Chastised! But isn't she lookin' well?' And indeed she was. The mini-skirted wonder who had opened the door to me so long ago was gone of course. But these days Sean's mother has lost weight, got her hair done and wears smart clothes. Her natural good looks are re-asserting themselves. Like her daughters, she is putting the best possible face on things for Sean. And not merely a face as his arrest has galvanized his sisters in their studies and helped to politicize the family. All are now active on behalf of Sinn Fein. They see their study and work as part of building a new society in which not only will Sean be free but the goals for which he went to prison will be realized. It's a common phenomenon in Northern

Ireland; the same support syndrome I mentioned in the case of Kevin Barry O'Rourke.

When the visit was up, Sean shook hands and waved goodbye like an athletic young freshman bidding friends adieu before returning to his studies. The idea that behind a locked door in the corner of the visiting room he was returning to a world which contained practices like 'shitting in bags' and 'pouring piss through door cracks' seemed incredible. His mother kept the tears at bay until he disappeared. We had planned to have a cup of tea. But when we emerged from the prison we discovered the Belfast traffic had been snarled by a rash of bomb scares. She had to leave immediately. We had to detour through a Loyalist area, which obviously terrified her, and made me wonder inwardly what our fate would have been had we been stopped or tailed from the jail by Loyalists. It was the sort of thought which occurs to her, and her family, every time any of them visit Sean or are stopped at a road-block, particularly at night. They know their car numbers are on a police computer. Can some UVF sympathizer, or member of some murky undercover squad, gain access to that computer? The possibility is not comforting. We parted without our tea. The bomb scares meant that she would be delayed on her way across the city to pick up a granddaughter as she always did in the afternoon, so as to enable the child's mother to work to earn money to pay for her studies. We had met because I had once wanted to encounter a typical Belfast Republican family. Now I was witnessing a typical day in the life of the same family in June 1993, twenty-five years later. Progress, Northern Ireland style.

37

Peace Comes Dropping Slow

Does the future hold any hope of creating a situation in which there will be no new Seans and he can look forward to an amnesty? While anything concerning the Six Counties has to be said more in hope than in confidence it is just possible that the answer could be 'yes'. The end of 1993 saw the publication (on 15 December) of the Downing St Declaration. The document was potentially the most important in Anglo-Irish relationships since the Treaty of 1921. Sinn Fein's initial attitude was described as 'à la carte', neither full acceptance, nor total rejection. The document underpinned the Unionists' position, which was obviously repugnant to the Republicans, but it also contained some of Gerry Adams' key ideas. How Sinn Fein policies came to be included in an official Dublin-London communiqué will be explained shortly. But first it is necessary to understand something of what the Document contains and the background to its publication.

Albert Reynolds and John Major bound themselves, while affirming the guarantee of the North's constitutional status, to:

> foster agreement and reconciliation, leading to a new political framework on consent and encompassing arrangements within Northern Ireland, for the whole island, and between these islands . . . the development of Europe will, of itself, require new approaches . . . The British Government agree that it is for the people of Ireland alone, by agreement between the two parts respectively, to exercise their right of self-determination on the basis of consent.

The document also reiterated a pledge originally given (on 9 November 1990) by Peter Brooke, as Secretary of State for Northern Ireland, that the British had:

> ... no selfish strategic or economic interest in Northern Ireland, their
> primary interest is to see peace, stability and reconciliation established
> by agreement among all the people who inhabit the island ...

Behind these emollient words there lay a far from easy diplomatic campaign by the Irish government, culminating in a successful attempt to enlist Bill Clinton's assistance in getting Major to agree to making the Declaration. I happened to be in Washington in the days prior to the President's making the decisive telephone call and I can testify that it was probably the biggest Irish diplomatic initiative since the tough sledging days of Irish neutrality in World War II. From Dublin also, the American ambassador, Jean Kennedy Smith, gave supportive advice to her brother, Ted Kennedy, who used his influence with the President. The pressure told, the White House came through and the Declaration was eventually signed.

Despite the initial difficulties, the British moved without delay to give effect to the provisions concerning the 'new political framework'. An Inter-governmental Liaison Committee, consisting of some of Dublin and London's top civil servants, was immediately set up to begin drafting work. In essence this meant providing a formula whereby Dublin and London, without seeming to advert either to the Unionists' pet-hate, the Anglo-Irish Agreement, or to the Forum Report, would build on these so as to create in effect a form of Joint Sovereignty over Northern Ireland. I saw some of the minutes of these meetings, and also some of the proposed drafts drawn up for negotiation. It did appear that both Articles 2 and 3 of the Irish Constitution, and the Government of Ireland Act were both on the table. Far reaching changes indeed.

What therefore were Sinn Fein's and the IRA's objections to all this? As an Irish diplomat, one of the architects of the Agreement, said to me: 'If we can get this much when the forest is green, from a Tory Government in a hung parliament, what can we not do when the forest is dry?'. The answer lay in two words: 'mistrust' and 'background'. Much of the reasons for the former can of course be deduced from these pages, but there was an additional reason in the immediate run up to the Declaration: Yet another set of British-IRA talks had ended inconclusively and with complaints about bad faith from the IRA's side. The IRA Sinn Fein response to the Downing St Declaration cannot be understood without reference to these talks.

Out of the welter of denials and revelations which accompanied this discovery in November 1993 it ultimately became clear that substantial contact between the Republicans and the British was renewed in 1990, at the instigation of the British. Sir Patrick Mayhew lodged a partial record of the communications between the two sides in the Library and Vote office at Westminster on 29 November. The lodgement referred only to contact between the two sides from 22 February 1993, which the British claim was initiated by Martin McGuinness on behalf of Sinn Fein in November 1992. On 1 December Mayhew admitted that there were errors in his version of what had transpired. The next day, 2 December, both Gerry Adams and Martin McGuinness made lengthy statements on the course of the talks. McGuinness and Gerrard Kelly had been the principal Sinn Fein representatives throughout the period. Subsequently Sinn Fein lodged a massive dossier,* containing a far fuller account of communications and statements than the British lodgement, in the Linenhall Library, Belfast and the National Library, Dublin. The following, necessarily abbreviated, account is based on these documents and on sources close to the talks.

The meetings began in October 1990 when a British official, since retired, contacted McGuinness and told him that the British were interested in reopening communication. As evidence of good intention an advance copy of a speech which the then Secretary of State, Peter Brooke, intended to deliver was furnished to Sinn Fein. The speech, which Brooke duly made on 9 November, contained a statement which later surfaced in the Downing St Declaration. Britain had no 'strategic or economic interest' in Northern Ireland and was prepared to accept the unification of Ireland by consent. The official duly retired and was replaced, but the contacts went on in the same pattern with Sinn Fein being supplied with assessments of British governmental thinking, urged to scale down violence, and being provided with advance copies of speeches, including on one occasion, a copy of a speech to be delivered by John Major in Scotland on 22 February 1992.

The tempo quickened in the early part of 1993. On 12 January the British official stressed the seriousness of the British approach. Talks were earnestly desired but could not begin without a noticeable decline in violence. He realized that an IRA ceasefire was a non-starter, but said that 'an easing-off would start the ball rolling in a significant way'. It appeared that events were to move onto a new plane of importance. On 26 February 1993, Sinn Fein was informed that:

---

* Copies in author's possession.

1. The British Government had agreed to hold talks with Sinn Fein, which if they went well, could speedily be announced publicly.
2. Suggested venues for the talks included the Scandinavian countries, Scotland and the Isle of Man.
3. It would be necessary that there be peace for the period of the talks which were expected to last between two and three weeks.
4. The British asserted that the outcome of the talks would be an acceptance by the Republicans that there was no further need for an armed struggle.

On 1 March the British proposed a meeting and a venue for 23 March, to discuss arrangements for what were referred to as 'delegation talks'. On 5 March Sinn Fein welcomed this proposal and named McGuinness and Kelly as their representatives to carry it forward.

Then things began to stall. The British response (on 11 March) spoke of preparing a 'considered and substantive response', but it said they were not yet able to send such a response because of the violence of the recent past. The IRA had exploded a number of massive bombs in the North at Bessborough, Bangor and Lurgan in the preceding days. And before that there had been the bombings at Warrington gas works and at Camden, London. However a British response was received by Sinn Fein on 19 March which said:

What is being sought at this stage is advice. The position of the British Government is that any dialogue could only follow a halt to violent activity . . . The British Government does not have, and will not adopt, any prior objective of 'ending partition'. The British Government cannot enter a talks process, or expect others to do so, with the purpose of achieving a predetermined outcome, whether the 'ending of partition' or anything else. It has accepted that the eventual outcome of such a process could be a united Ireland, but this can only be on the basis of the consent of the people of Northern Ireland. Should this be the outcome of a peaceful democratic process, the British Government would bring forward legislation to implement the will of the people. But until the people of Northern Ireland come to express such a view, the British Government will continue to uphold the union . . . within the totality of relationships in these islands.

On 23 March a British official told Sinn Fein that Mayhew was convinced that no settlement could be achieved without Sinn Fein.

He wanted a North–South settlement that would not frighten Unionists. The official's statements included one to the effect that the final solution was union. The Sinn Fein minute of the meeting with him reads: 'It is going to happen anyway [unity]. The historical train – Europe – determines that. We are committed to Europe. Unionists will have to change. This island will be one.'

The official stressed the sincerity of the British. Leading Sinn Feiners like Gerry Adams and Martin McGuinness owe their present ascendancy in the movement to the hunger strikes and what led up to them – a series of negotiations with the British in which the Republicans were out-manoeuvred. The official went out of his way to stress that the proposed talks would not be like those held with Republicans in 1975 under Merlyn Rees. The official quoted Rees, who said[*] of these; 'We set out to con them and we did.' In speaking thus frankly the official was implicitly acknowledging that not only had times changed, people had also. I once interviewed the official who had been in charge of the IRA negotiations in the Rees era and I found him inclined to be dismissive and contemptuous of the IRA personnel, regarding them as uneducated and unversed in the ways of politics, particularly British politics. Now the British were making the point that a qualitative shift had occurred within Sinn Fein in the meantime. Sinn Fein were informed that the top North of Ireland Civil Servant, Sir John Chilcott, who was also the Permanent Secretary at the Ministry of Defence, had promised that if Sinn Fein agreed to negotiate at six o'clock then the go ahead from the British side would be given 'at one minute past six'. However events soon had Sinn Fein wondering whether the Rees approach was still in operation.

Here it should be noted that there were other simultaneous sets of talks in progress involving Sinn Fein to a greater or lesser degree. One was the ongoing Dublin–London contact between both civil servants and politicians, especially that between Reynolds and Major. This last was to grow in importance and eventually dominate the picture. The other was the Hume–Adams exchange referred to earlier. The two Nationalist leaders released their communiqué, with its heavy emphasis on self-determination, and its ruling out of an internal settlement as we saw (p. 612) on 23 April. This was later advanced from the British

---

[*] In a letter to Harold Wilson, quoted on p. 28, 'Setting the Record Straight', the Sinn Fein record of the negotiations.

side as a reason for a diminution in British enthusiasm for the talks which now began to make itself felt.

On 4 May Sinn Fein sent a message to the British asking what was causing the delay in moving on to delegate meetings. In a series of communications concluding on 7 May the British replied that they were keen to proceed on the basis of their 19 March document, quoted above, but reiterated that it was essential that violence ceased first. In response to this Sinn Fein (on 10 May) informed the British that the IRA had agreed to a two week ceasefire, sought clarification as to the seniority of the British delegates proposed, told the British that the party had set up a secretariat to service the conference and furnished its own discussion document.

This pointed out that Sinn Fein had a democratic mandate to represent its electorate. The document repeated the point made in the Hume–Adams communiqué about self-determination:

> The route to peace in Ireland is to be found in the restoration to the Irish people of our right to national self-determination – in the free exercise of this right without impediment of any kind.

It sought an end to British jurisdiction, the cause of 'political instability and conflict' and went on to use the argument about Europe for its own purposes:

> The emerging political and economic imperatives both within Ireland and within the broader context of greater European political union support the logic of Irish unity. It is our view therefore that the British Government should play a crucial and constructive role in persuading the Unionist community to reach an accommodation with the Irish people.

Sinn Fein rejected the British claims that it had no prior objective in entering the talks. It pointed out that the upholding of the Unionist veto meant in effect the:

> maintenance of partition and the six-county statelet. And, consequently, the maintenance of the primary source of the conflict.

There was thus a wide gulf between the initial positions of the two sides. But, given the British assurances of seriousness of purpose, and the Sinn Fein delivery of a ceasefire which the British had thought a 'non-starter' only a few months earlier, there appeared to be a sound basis for the commencement of talks at least. After all, apart from the annual brief cessation of hostilities over Christmas there had not been an IRA ceasefire for some eighteen years since that in Merlyn Rees's time had proved a disaster for the IRA and a bonanza for the security forces. Moreover there was a reasonable expectation that the two weeks, once declared, could be stretched considerably. However, the internal party difficulties of the Tory party now began to bear upon the talks process.

It appears that Chilcott was pleased with the response. 'A sanguine man', as an Irish diplomat who deals with him described him to me, he advocated that John Major's approval be obtained for going ahead. Mayhew was less enthusiastic, afraid that an announcement about talks with Sinn Fein at that stage – local government elections were to be held on 19 May – would benefit Paisley's party at the expense of modern Unionism. However, after what the British government contact official told Sinn Fein was a 'hell of a battle' Mayhew yielded. Downing St personnel are credited with swaying him by arguing that the British could not defend the position historically if the 10 May position was not fully explored. A paper was accordingly prepared for the Prime Minister. The meeting with Major did not take place until two days before the elections, on 17 May. Amongst those present were Douglas Hurd, the Foreign Secretary, Mayhew, and Chilcott.

The meeting was not a success. Major either was not sufficiently well briefed, or pretended not to be, for a decision to be made. He wanted to know what guarantees were available that a ceasefire would either be forthcoming or would hold, and sought more 'evidence' that the IRA meant what they said. Hurd had to leave for a conference on Bosnia. Dublin's appreciation of Hurd was that he was at worst hostile, and at best, had no interest in the Irish question. Major adjourned the meeting until the following day, the eve of the local government elections. This time Kenneth Clarke, then the Home Secretary, was in attendance. He was described as being in a 'buoyant, bombastic mood.' His advice was that with the government in a state of siege the venture was too risky. In the present climate, if the IRA were sincere, such a departure from the publicly accepted policy of continuing with an anti-terrorist line simpliciter, should only be pursued slowly. Mayhew was undecided between seeking a longer ceasefire and arguing for acceptance.

In the event Major decided on a compromise proposal. He ordered his secretaries to draw up a new scheme, involving a longer ceasefire, which would be followed by secret, logistical talks, setting the agenda, location and so forth. After this he would inform the heads of the main political parties, the Irish cardinal, Dr Cathal Daly, and the head of the Church of Ireland, Archbishop Robin Eames, that he was instructing the North of Ireland Office to enter into talks. A day after doing this he would make a public announcement in parliament. This meeting effectively spelled the end of the talks idea.

The British response to the Sinn Fein position document and offer of a ceasefire did not arrive until 3 June, a long time after 'one minute past six'. It reflected the Clarke analysis saying that the government was working out a response which 'because it was radical, needed careful crafting. This meant deliberate (but not artificially slow) work at the highest levels.' The response had been halted, the message said, because 'renewed violence on a serious scale' had taken place in the interim. This could have been taken at its face value. In the days immediately following John Major's instruction to his staff to draw up a new plan for talks, IRA bombs caused sixteen million pounds' worth of damage in Northern Ireland. However, on the day this message was delivered, the Sinn Fein representatives who had met the British, also received a remarkable personal letter from the British official who had acted throughout as their main contact:

> There is depression and anger here over our failure to respond to your brave and straightforward offer. None feel it more than I do for obvious reasons. I appreciate – as do all most closely involved – the position this puts you in. It also contrasts with all that you have heard earlier. You have my word that all that was conveyed was done so honestly and accurately at the time. There would have been no quotation from 1975 [the Rees negotiations] if the intention was to copy that bad example and I for one would not be a party to it.
>
> The present position is that the local Chairman had accepted your offer, but such a vital economic issue had to go to the Board. We had miscalculated in assuming that the National Chairman would simply give it the nod of approval. Recent economic events have made him nervous of bold steps and your unfortunate headline events of April [the City of London bombings occurred on 24 April, the same day that the first Hume–Adams statement was issued; not the best of auguries for a peace process] have made acceptance of your offer much more risky for

him. You and I may think this should not matter, but the fact is that it does and it is that which is holding things up – if you like human characteristics rather than anything more sinister.

... there was a proposal worked out (the National Chairman's own and new idea of 18 May) which delayed us and was then put on one side after the events of 19 May. I know that you feel for our Bank 'the time is never right', but this time it will be. I cannot tell you when – our wheels turn far too slowly, but that is the way of the Bank, not any notion of stringing the other side along. If delay were a plot it is certainly taking up our attention just as much as yours!

I can only ask for patience for all our sakes. You will carry out your own financial policy and it would be impertinent for me to suggest anything otherwise (as well as being counter-productive); but in economic terms headline stuff knocks us back because the National Chairman is then wary of proceeding and it gives support to those who are against such a step.

I hope you will not mind me ending with a new meaning to Tiochfaidh ar la. [Tiochfaidh ar la is the Provisionals' slogan: Our day will come]

On 10 June Sinn Fein sent a message to London expressing concern at the delay and reiterating support for the Hume–Adams peace initiative on which the British had also been briefed. However, there was no response to either this message, or to others from Sinn Fein complaining about British inspired media leaks, until 17 July. By then the RUC had become so well informed that they were known to be briefing journalists about what was going on.

The British response stated that the delay had been caused by 'events on the ground', i.e. the IRA bombings. It further stated that talks could not be envisaged on the basis of a temporary ceasefire and asked Sinn Fein to confirm that: 'a lasting end to violence does not depend on your analysis being endorsed as the only way forward'. It concluded by stating that dialogue could only begin after the British had been assured that violence had been brought to an end and that in the meantime progress would be dictated by events on the ground.

Sinn Fein did not reply to this until 14 August when it pointed out that its tone and content had wandered far from the pre-10 May position. Expressing doubts about British commitment to a peace process the Sinn Fein response suggested that the alteration in tone may have been caused by 'expedient', internal and domestic party political reasons'. Very likely it was, as readers will recall (pp. 613–14) the

Unionists had voted with Major and against the so-called Maastricht rebels, on 23 July. Getting them on board while at the same time negotiating with the IRA would have been a difficult balancing act, even for the Tories. In its reply which continued to urge a resumption of the talks, Sinn Fein also referred to 'events on the ground', saying:

> The greatest number of fatalities for some time now in the conflict have resulted from the actions of loyalist groups acting both on their own agenda and as surrogates for British intelligence. South African guns supplied by the British agent Brian Nelson with the full knowledge of the British authorities are being used for attacks on the nationalist population, members of Sinn Fein and their families.

In a reply on 1 September the British made the not unreasonable assertion that: 'minds do not seem to be meeting at the moment.' The reply averred that the British had not stated that a two week ceasefire would have been sufficient to allow talks to begin. There had to be an end to violence before attempting the objectives of:

> an inclusive process . . . the pursuit of peace, stability and reconciliation on the widest possible basis.

Another oral message from the British on 6 September, however, said that Major was now 'a force for peace' and that the 10 May position had to be revived. It was suggested that Sinn Fein should comment on the PLO/Rabin terms in a very public fashion saying: 'If they can come to an agreement in Israel, why not here? We are standing at the altar why won't you come and join us?'

In its reply (on 10 September) Sinn Fein said it still believed that 'there exists a basis for progress which can be developed into a genuine, realistic and democratic peace process'. But said that it considered that the degree of political will needed to move forward had been 'singularly lacking on your part'. It indicated its political will by pointing to the on-going talks between Adams and John Hume and underlined its desire for a: 'new and imaginative initiative by the Dublin and London Governments, based on democratic principles to break the present deadlock.'

From this point on the Hume–Adams conversations began to dominate the headlines. A second Hume–Adams statement was published on 25 September. It said that their discussions had made considerable progress and that a report on them had been forwarded to the London and Dublin governments. The statement said:

> We are convinced from our discussions that a process can be designed to lead to agreement among the divided people of this island, which will provide a solid basis for peace. Such a process would obviously also be designed to ensure that any new agreement that might emerge respects the diversity of our different traditions and earns their allegiance and agreement.

The publication of this statement might be taken as ushering in one of the most cacophonous interludes in Anglo-Irish affairs. Television and newspapers were filled with speculation as to what the Hume–Adams initiative might contain [it has still not been published at the time of writing] and what the two governments proposed to do about it – if anything. There was a feeling abroad, that whatever it was, something serious was afoot. Symptomatic of the coverage was a decision by Channel Four to alter its scheduled programmes on a busy Saturday night (29 October) to stage a four-hour discussion programme embracing most shades of Irish and British opinion on the situation.

The British, and to a degree the Dublin Government, were keeping their lions in separate cages. London kept Dublin in the dark about the Sinn Fein talks. Hume was marginalized by both governments. He made a determined effort in the weeks prior to the Downing St Declaration to move the Hume–Adams document onto the agenda. But, despite a myriad of TV appearances, it was clear that his efforts were not welcomed at Downing St. Although he is a party leader at Westminster, and as such, would normally have automatic access to the Prime Minister, there were delays and rumours of snubbings before Hume was actually received at Number 10, but to little effect. Documents with a Sinn Fein imprint were not welcome. As we shall see, having gone as far in contact with the Republicans as it deemed safe, the talks were ended in circumstances of near farce. Under pressure from Albert Reynolds to do something about the North, Major decided that, difficult though movement was for an unpopular Government with a wobbly majority, dependent on Unionist support, Government to Government dialogue would fall within the acceptable norms of parliamentary nomenclature. Talks with Sinn Fein did not. Particularly as there had been strong reaction on the Tory backbenches at the newspaper pictures of Adams carrying the coffin of the IRA bomber who died (on 22 October 1993) in a premature explosion which claimed several innocent Protestant civilian lives in a fish shop on the Shankill Road.

Reynolds and Major met in Brussels and on 29 October issued a statement which effectively repudiated both the Hume–Adams approach and the Sinn Fein talks. It said:

> The Taoiseach gave the Prime Minister an account of the outcome of the Hume–Adams dialogue, in the light of the Irish Goverment's own assessment of these and other related matters. They acknowledge John Hume's courageous and imaginative efforts. The Prime Minister and Taoiseach agree that any initiative can only be taken by the two Governments, and that there could be no question of their adopting or endorsing the reports of the dialogue which was recently given to the Taoiseach and which had not been passed on to the British Government. They agreed that the two Governments must continue to work together in their own terms on a framework for peace, stability and reconciliation, consistent with their international obligations and their wider responsibilities to both communities.
>
> ... Negotiations on a political settlement could only take place between democratic governments and parties committed exclusively to constitutional methods ... there can be no talks between their Governments and those who use, threaten or support violence for political ends ... there could be no secret agreements between Governments and organizations supporting violence as a price for its cessation ...

Decoded this statement also made plain that Dublin policy on Northern Ireland was now firmly in Dublin hands. Hume became the target of an unprecedented bout of criticism. An article in the *Sunday Times* (31 October 1993) called on him to stand down as leader of the SDLP. The paper's editorial referred to him as being 'sadly discredited' by his talks with Adams and proposed internment as the solution to the North's problems. Fearing that the attacks on Hume could damage the SDLP to the benefit of Sinn Fein both Dublin and London went out of their way to praise him after a meeting of the Anglo-Irish Conference on 3 November. Mayhew and the Irish Deputy Prime Minister, Dick Spring, both acknowledged that he had helped the prospects of peace considerably. He saw Major subsequently, after a briefing from both Reynolds and Spring. But the strain told and he was admitted to hospital, in Derry, suffering from exhaustion on 8 November.

All the fuss over Hume's talking to the IRA began to look decidedly silly when, the day after he was admitted to hospital, it was disclosed that London had had secret talks with Sinn Fein.

The story was finally broken in Belfast by the knowledgable journalist and author, Eamon Mallie, of Downtown Radio, on 8 November. A variety of leaks and rumours from Unionist and security force sources had been in circulation for some weeks earlier. Mallie's standing made it impossible to ignore his disclosure. Nevertheless the first reaction of the British Government was to deny everything. Sir Patrick Mayhew went on BBC on 16 November to deny that there had been contact with Sinn Fein by anyone who could be regarded as acting for the Government. He made a number of subsequent statements to the same effect, notably in Derry on 19 November in which he said: 'Nobody has been authorized to talk or negotiate on behalf of the British government with Sinn Fein or any other terrorist organization.' John Major went further. After repeating the denials in the House of Commons the following day he copper-fastened his statement by declaring that the prospect of talks with Gerry Adams would 'turn my stomach'.

The next few weeks can hardly have been conducive to gastric peace. The DUP, which is traditionally regarded as having good links with the RUC, came into possession of one of the British communiqués sent to Sinn Fein, allegedly from an official in the North of Ireland office. The DUP MP, Willie McCrea, gave this to the *Observer* newspaper on 17 November 1993. The *Observer* sent it to the British Government on Friday, 26 November, asking for a comment. Faced with impending disaster Downing St reacted with an exercise in damage limitation. The leader of the Official Unionists, Jim Molyneaux, was called in for a briefing. After it he issued a coded statement advising his followers not to jump to conclusions over the weekend. The following day, Saturday, the Government admitted that contact with Sinn Fein had taken place. Mayhew attempted to put a spin on the facts by claiming that the contact had been in response to an overture from Martin McGuinness who asked how the conflict could be ended.

The following Monday (29 November) Gerry Adams added fuel to the fires of controversy by holding a press conference. During it he disclosed much of the substance of what had taken place between Sinn Fein and the British. Ironically however, because Sinn Fein had secreted the papers in hiding places where they could not be found by British security forces, he could not produce all the documentation. Mayhew got in first with a disclosure of documents that afternoon in

the House of Commons, which Sinn Fein challenged on the grounds
of both *suppresso veri* and forgery.

On 2 December Adams made a full disclosure of the bulk of the
documents involved, with the exception of a number which he alluded
to as being 'sensitive'. He described 'the recent phase of our history'
as being:

> . . . one of the most shameful in 25 years of conflict, or perhaps since the
> partition of this country. The British government's attitude to nationalist
> Ireland, whether represented by Albert Reynolds or John Hume or Sinn
> Fein has been despicable, devious and damnable. The British govern-
> ment knows, and has known for some long time now, that the Irish
> Peace Initiative presents a real opportunity for peace. John Hume has
> told them privately and publicly. We had told them this privately and
> publicly.

He also showed that the contact with the British stretched back to
1990, not to the beginning of the year (1993) as the British claimed.
But most startling of all was his demonstration of the fact that the
British presentation of documents included at least one forgery. A
communication alleged to have been sent by Sinn Fein to the British
on 2 November 1993 had in fact been concocted by the British. Adams
was able to produce a fax containing the written message. It showed
that the fax had been sent from London to Ireland, not the other way
round. And it was sent on 3 November, not 2nd.

The foregoing then provides the background to Sinn Fein's neither
'for', nor 'against' attitude to the Downing St Declaration. Apart from
feeling deeply mistrustful of the British there were fundamental incom-
patibilities between what appeared to be within sight on 10 May and
what was now on offer. For Sinn Fein, self-determination meant self-
determination by the people of the whole island, not merely within
the Six Counties. The party did not want to subscribe to a permanent
ceasefire, as called for by the Declaration, on the basis of a document
founded on a guarantee of the Unionists' veto. What Sinn Fein seeks
is a guarantee of a British withdrawal. Worse, from the Sinn Fein
point of view was the fact that that party was in a sense expected to
accept the crumbs that fell from the rich man's political table. Sinn
Fein was not to be allowed to enter talks until the ceasefire had demonstrably held for some months.

This was precisely what had happened to Michael Collins and the delegation who reluctantly signed the Treaty that accepted Partition in the first place. Negotiations only began several months after a truce was called. By that time, Collins's secret, underground, guerrilla army, the IRA of its day, was a secret no more. In Collins's own words, once a ceasefire was declared, the IRA men were: 'Like rabbits coming out of their holes.' Their main weapon, secrecy, was gone.

One result of the Treaty signing had been civil war. Now, anti-Declaration Republicans, fearing a sell-out, began referring to Sinn Fein Headquarters in Belfast, as 'Michael Collins House'. Adams and company fought a shrewd campaign to stave off a civil war amongst their supporters on the one hand, and on the other, to avoid being isolated from mainstream political opinion by seeming to give a knee jerk rejection to a widely popular initiative. Firstly the party let it be known that it had embarked on an exhaustive process of consultation within its own membership and that of the IRA. The IRA Army Council voted not to reject the document. This, without endorsing it in any way, allowed consultation to continue. Then Sinn Fein called on the British for 'clarification' of the Declaration. The British initially fought shy of responding to this call, despite Major's being urged to do so by John Hume at what appears to have been an edgy Downing St meeting on 14 January. Hume was still under pressure to explain his position when he visited the US for a St Patrick's Day dinner in Washington in March. Shortly before his visit the IRA had mortar bombed Heathrow Airport, on three successive days with dummy rockets. The joke in Dublin was that they were loaded with Gerry Adams's writings, but this did not appear funny to the American Congressmen and Senators who had supported Adams's visa application and could not understand the hang-up over clarification. A three day ceasefire called by the IRA at Easter, which in fact stretched for ten days, did little to help Hume, or quell the chorus of public criticism of Sinn Fien's delaying tactics. Eventually however the Major–Reynolds relationship told. London agreed to accept the clarification demands from the hands of the Dublin Government.

These were answered on 19 May 1994. Meanwhile Sinn Fein had enjoyed an almost undisturbed monopoly of media attention. Adams got his visa to the US and, more importantly, the Irish Government relaxed Section 31 of the Broadcasting Act which had banned Sinn Fein spokesmen from the airwaves. Though their appearances still had to be prerecorded, Gerry Adams, Martin McGuinness and the other spokesmen were able to appear on Irish TV screens commenting and debating, unlike the position in Britain where their faces could be screened, but their voices had to be dubbed by actors. All this created an expectation that peace was around the corner. Few people had any background knowledge of what had gone on before. The public at large looked to the Sinn Fein Ard Fheis at Letterkenny, Co. Donegal on 24 July 1994, in the expectation that a ceasefire was imminent.

In the event, the outcome was a crushing disappointment for the huge media presence. Gerry Adams said that: 'The Declaration did not deal adequately with some of the core issues and this is vital.' These issues included the Unionist veto, self-determination (a matter for all the people of Ireland), and getting Britain to join 'the persuaders' in getting the Unionists to accept that their future lay with the rest of the Irish people. While saying that the Declaration contained some 'negative and contradictory elements' the Ard Fheis did have some praise for the Document's acknowledgement that political and consti-tutional chance was necessary. Sinn Fein announced that it intended to pursue that change, on the basis of the Hume–Adams, Irish Peace Initiative.

But the trumpet call of history was sounding. Behind the scenes events were moving fast. Albert Reynolds had anticipated that within Sinn Fein and the IRA pressures of hawks against doves would result in Letterkenny being a disappointment, and had set out to reduce the fears of both the hawks and, incredibly enough, the loyalists. He had directed his North of Ireland expert, Dr Martin Mansergh, to enter into secret talks with Adams and Martin McGuinness. Simultaneously he had used this relationship with President Clinton and the Kennedys – Senator Edward, and Ambassador to Ireland, Jean – to elicit promises of American support in the event of a ceasefire. His existing friendship with John Major went into overdrive. Major was heard to remark wonderingly on more than one occasion that 'Reynolds has Voodoo. There's a problem. Reynolds goes off, does his voodoo and the problem goes away.' Both men had additional, extraneous reasons why an Irish settlement would benefit their careers. Major's officials grew visibly nervous whenever Reynolds disappeared into a tête à tête. The result inevitably tended to favour the Irish position, rather than the conven-tional wisdom of the Whitehall mandarins. But the British Prime Min-ister had a motive other than Reynolds' charisma for his growing interest in solving what had hitherto been perceived as the completely intractable Irish problem. Major was slumping so disastrously in the polls that only something of the magnitude of an Irish settlement could make the possibility of the Tories retaining power after the next general election appear even remotely possible. Reynolds had reason to fear that a report, expected in August 1994, of a lengthy, and very costly, public inquiry into the Irish meat industry might have severely damaged his government. One of the principal instigators of the tribunal was now his Deputy Prime Minister and Minister of Foreign Affairs, and his coalition partner, Dick Spring[1], the Labour Party leader. Accordingly the Liaison Committee of Irish officials which was set up after the Downing St Declaration was empowered to draft a framework document for an eventual Anglo-Irish settlement which envisaged very far-reaching changes indeed. Articles two and three of the Irish Constitution were to be re-worded in return for a revision of the Government of Ireland Act of 1920 which partitioned Ireland in the first place. New cross-border structures were envisaged and cast-iron guarantees for minorities were being worked on so that, in the event of demographic changes now in progress turning the existing minority, the Catholics, into a majority, the Protestants would have nothing to fear. By July 1994 it added up to a situation, if not of joint sovereignty, certainly of joint approach between London and Dublin.

However, sadly, the interaction of the nine Official Unionists at Westminster with the 'Maastricht rebel' element against the Tory back-benchers proved a serious retarding factor and, as time wore on, this cooperative approach began to wither noticably. It did not prove possible to produce an agreed framework document after a year of intensive discussions. Moreover the attitude of the minister most involved, the Secretary of State for Northern Ireland, Sir Patrick Mayhew, could fairly be described as grudgingly supportive, rather than wholeheartedly enthusiastic. However, from July through August the Reynolds–Major–Kennedy axis continued to yield dividends. The Church of Ireland Archbishop, Dr Robin Eames, had long since been pressed into service by Reynolds as a conduit to the Official Unionist party leader, James Molyneaux. The fruits of this contact were seen in the temperate, level-headed response of the Unionist leader to the ceasefire announcement. While Ian Paisley, the leader of the more extreme Democratic Unionist Party reacted with talk of a 'sell-out' by London to Dublin and spoke of civil war, Molyneaux advised his followers to remain calm and adopted a wait-and-see approach. In addition Dr Rory Magee, a Protestant clergyman with good contacts to the Loyalist paramilitaries, became an increasingly frequent visitor to the Taoiseach's office. Those visits helped to pave the way for the surprisingly generously worded ceasefire declaration which emanated from the Loyalist paramilitary leaders on 13 October 1994.

Happily there was also every indication that America intended to play a benign role in helping to resolve the Northern conflict. President Clinton is on record (*Irish Times*, 1 September 1994) as having told friends that he intended to be a friend to Ireland not merely on St Patrick's Day, but every day of the year. The reasons for this committment are twofold. One, the support which a group organized by Niall O'Dowd, Irish-Americans for Clinton–Gore, gave the President during his election campaign and in return secured a promise from Clinton that, if elected, he would appoint a peace envoy to Ireland and sanction the granting of a US visa to Gerry Adams. This group, headed by former Congressman Bruce Morrison, a former classmate of Clinton's, brought together a number of influential Irish-American businessmen, who remained committed to the Irish issue after the campaign was over. They included such respected figures as Bill Flynn, Chairman of Mutual of America, and Chuck Feeney, the founder of the world's largest duty-free shopping operation. The visits to Belfast and Dublin by these men, their assessment of Sinn Fein, and of Gerry Adams, were to prove crucial to the peace process. In his role as Chairman, of the prestigious Committee on American Foreign Policy, Bill Flynn extended the invitation to address a Conference on Northern Ireland (on 1 February 1994) which eventually brought Gerry Adams to New York.

The second reason for Clinton's strong pro-Irish stance was made up of a combination of factors. He was a student at Oxford when the Irish civil rights movement began, which left him with a lasting interest in the Irish situation. This made him predisposed towards reacting favourably to O'Dowd's campaign overtures. He had already formed an admiration for John Hume and subsequently developed a friendship with Albert Reynolds. He met Reynolds, sometimes rearranging his schedule at short notice, more than most other European leaders. He took time off in the white heat of the battle for NAFTA to see Dick Spring, the Irish Deputy Prime Minister, and subsequently he made the vital telephone call which induced John Major to 'go the extra mile' and sign on for the Downing St Declaration. He pledged financial aid to help the Northern Irish economy. Under Clinton, the National Security Council, headed by Anthony Lake, assumed ascendancy over the traditionally pro-British State Department, on the Irish issue.

Nancy Soderberg, a former aide to Senator Ted Kennedy, became both the staff director of the NSC and in charge of Irish strategy.

This ascendancy was both symbolized and furthered by the appointment of Senator Kennedy's sister, Jean Kennedy Smith, as the American Ambassador to Dublin. A slight, shy figure, she amazed decision-taking Dublin by her committment to, and grasp of, the Irish situation. In less than a year (she was appointed in 1993) she had belied her soft-spoken appearance by a demonstration of steely, Kennedy political skill. She succeeded in establishing Dublin as the undisputed centre of diplomatic influence on the Irish issue, over the pro-British, Bush-appointed, American Ambassador in London, Raymond Seitz, President Clinton replaced Seitz with Admiral Crowe, one of America's most distinguished military figures, after a notable Irish-American diplomatic victory had been achieved. Jean, with the assistance of her brother Ted, played a pivotal role in ending the isolation of Sinn Fein and securing a visa for Gerry Adams in the teeth of a concerted British counter-offensive in Washington.

Against the Kennedys and their allies Senators Chris Dodd and Patrick Moynihan, were lined up the State Department, the CIA, Speaker Tom Foley, Seitz and the influential British Ambassador to Washington, Sir Robin Renwick. After some ferocious behind the scenes infighting Clinton decided in favour of the Kennedys. Adams, to whom the President had earlier refused a visa, was allowed into New York for forty-eight hours. The result for Sinn Fein was one of the greatest media bonanzas in American history. Adams handled himself so well on television that Sinn Fein's image was transformed. The famous 'special relationship' between the British and the American governments was temporarily in tatters. For a month, the British media throbbed with rage. Kennedy Smith was dubbed the Jean Machine, but Seitz departed London. There were hiccups, notably the IRA mortaring of London Airport, but despite this, and disappointments such as Letterkenny, within the Republican movement Adams and those around him continued the drive towards a crossroads in Irish history where a signpost pointed away from war and towards a political route to peace.

There were several reasons impelling Adams along that route: his own, and his colleagues', growing and deepening political maturity; the influence, stretching back for more than a decade and a half, of the great unsung hero of the entire peace process, his close friend, Fr Alex Reid, a Redemptorist monk from the Clonard monastery situated in the IRA heartland off the Falls Road; Adams' experiences with Irish-Americans, both in Belfast and America; contacts with John Hume, and, through channels, with Reynolds. These things convinced him that physical force could effectively be replaced by political action. With his long-cherished ambition, of getting the Government of Ireland Act on to the table, now increasingly near to fulfilment, Adams could see other hopeful possibilities opening up. What he envisaged was arriving ultimately at a stage where negotiations on the future of Ireland would take place between everyone involved in the dispute, Unionists, the British and the Irish Nationalists. In this scenario the Irish would include not only Sinn Fein, but the SDLP, Fianna Fail, and the Irish Labour Party, all backed by the formidable Irish Civil Service, and standing benignly in the background, the White House, the Kennedys and the clout of Irish-America.

At the end of August the O'Dowd–Morrison group was invited to Belfast to meet Adams and the Sinn Fein leadership. There had been other such meetings. The Americans and the Dublin Government half expected that this one would consist of an exposition from the Sinn Fein perspective, of the difficulties still to be overcome before peace could be achieved. Indeed, in this expectation, O'Dowd and company had been briefed beforehand in government buildings as to what they should say to the Sinn Fein delegation. However, Adams caught everyone off balance by opening the discussion with a simple statement: the IRA had agreed to declare a ceasefire.

In the event the ceasefire was delayed by another wrangle over visas. Before the announcement Sinn Fein wanted the veteran Republican Joe Cahill, who in 1942 had been one of the group of young men in the Clonard area who had escaped the hangman's noose which claimed the life of Tom Williams (see pages 135 et seq), to go to America to explain the move to Noraid and Sinn Fein's supporters' in the US. The Provisionals' experience of splits and feuds made them acutely conscious of the danger of a breakaway group of Irish-American hardliners forming to arm some, as yet unknown, new faction of militants in Ireland. Cahill, regarded by many as one of the founding fathers of Noraid, was essential to the selling of the peace initiative. There would be no announcement of a ceasefire until Cahill, and a companion, Pat Treanor, were safely on American soil.

But Cahill's previous convictions for IRA offences made him technically ineligible for a visa. The US and the United Kingdom have signed an agreement on terrorism and security whose terms could be interpreted as excluding figures like him and, at British insistence, they were so interpreted. Reynolds was furious at what appeared to be short-sighted, bureaucratic nit-picking which could have derailed the peace process. He expressed his feelings forcefully to Jean Kennedy Smith, who went to bat once more. As often happens at moments of high human drama, an element of near-farce now entered the proceedings. Nancy Soderberg was on holiday but, once again, the Kennedy clout told. Days of hectic diplomatic activity culminated in a final round of telephone calls to Washington from the Irish Taoiseach and from Jean Kennedy Smith which, at five o'clock in the morning, Irish time, finally wrested agreement to a visa for the two Republicans from the American Justice Department. After Cahill and Treanor had taken off from Dublin Airport, an Irish television reporter, Charlie Bird, received an anonymous telephone call advising him to go to a location in north Dublin the following morning. He was handed two items. One appeared to be a 'comm'. The other a tape cassette. The 'comm', a tiny peace of paper, said that the contents of the tape would be announced 'at the sound of the Angelus'. In other words at twelve o'clock midday.

When he heard the contents of the tape Bird arranged for it to be played over the national airwaves immediately, at approximately 11.25 am on the morning of 31 August 1994. The tape contained the IRA ceasefire declaration[*]

> Recognizing the potential of the current situation and in order to enhance the democratic peace process and underline our definitive committment to its success the leadership of Oglaigh na hEireann have decided that as of midnight, Wednesday, 31 August, there will be a complete cessation of military operations. All our units have been instructed accordingly.
>
> At this historic crossroads, the leadership of Oglaigh na hEireann salutes and commends our volunteers; other activists; our supporters and the political prisoners who have sustained this struggle against all odds for the past twenty-five years. Your courage, determination and sacrifices have demonstrated that the spirit of freedom and the desire for peace based on a just and lasting settlement cannot be crushed. We remember all those who have died for Irish freedom, and we reiterate our committment to our Republican objectives.

[*] Copy in author's possession.

Our struggle has seen many gains and advances made by nationalists and for the democratic position. We believe that an opportunity to secure a just and lasting settlement has been created. We are therefore entering into a new situation in a spirit of determination and confidence: determined that the injustices which created this conflict will be removed and confident in the strength and justice of struggle to achieve this.

We note that the Downing St Declaration is not a solution nor was it presented as such by its authors. A solution will only be found as a result of inclusive negotiations. Others, not least the British Government, have a duty to face up to their responsibilities. It is our desire to significantly contribute to the creation of a climate which will encourage this. We urge everyone to approach this new situation with energy, determination and patience.

The prelude to the ceasefire had been an outbreak of slaughter. The Loyalist paramilitaries who had come together under an umbrella group styling itself 'the combined Loyalist Military Command' shot a total of nine Catholics dead in different parts of the Six Counties during April and May. An attempt to bomb a Dublin pub, the Widow Scallan's, during a concert, would have eclipsed all these events had it come off. An IRA volunteer, Martin Doherty, tackled the Loyalists and managed to prevent the detonation of the bomb, but was killed in the process. His death cost the life of the famous Dublin criminal Martin Cahill, about whom the film *The General* was made. On 18 August 1994, Cahill, whom the Gardai had been trying unsuccessfully to apprehend for years, was shot dead at the wheel of his car, by a Provisional IRA gunman. The Provisionals had intelligence to the effect that he had links with Loyalist paramilitaries, arising out of drug operations, and that he had provided the Loyalists with information on IRA activities in Dublin, which had guided them to the pub.

After Republicans shot two Loyalist paramilitary leaders on the Shankill Road (on 18 June) the UVF retaliated by spraying a pub in Loughinisland, Co. Down with gunfire as its Catholic patrons watched the Republic of Ireland play Italy in the World Cup. Six Catholics died in the massacre. On 11 July, the Provisionals shot Ray Smallwoods, a UDA leader. Accordingly the ceasefire was welcomed by a medley of reactions: joy, relief, disbelief, sceptism, euphoria, anger, nit-picking, and downright mulishness. Initially, the British, and in particular Sir Patrick Mayhew, quibbled over the fact that the statement did not speak of 'permanent' ceasefire as demanded by the Downing St Declaration. British intelligence, like Irish and American intelligence, was fully aware that, under IRA rules, such a decision could only be taken by a specially convened Army Convention. What Adams and his colleagues were doing was setting in train the conditions which could lead to the holding of such a Convention.

The people probably best placed to assess the Provisionals' sincerity, the Loyalist paramilitaries, also accepted the ceasefire as being genuine. On 13 October 1994, Gusty Spence, the UVF leader who had fired the first shots in anger of the entire conflict, back in 1966, was the fitting choice of the Combined Loyalist Paramilitary Council to read out the Loyalists' peace declaration. It was in many ways a remarkable document, imbued with better sentiments than much of what emanates from the constitutional Unionist politicians. It said:*

> After a widespread consultative process initiated by representations from the Ulster Democratic and Progressive Unionist parties, and having received confirmation and guarantees in relation to Northern Ireland's constitutional position within the United Kingdom, as well as other assurances, and, in the belief that the democratically expressed wishes of the greater number of people in Northern Ireland will be respected and upheld, the CLMC will universally cease all operational hostilities as from 12 midnight on Thursday, October 13, 1994.
>
> The permanence of our ceasefire will be completely dependent upon the continued cessation of all nationalist/republican violence, the sole responsibility for a return to war lies with them.
>
> In the genuine hope that his peace will be permanent we take this opportunity to pay homage to all our fighters, commandoes and volunteers who have paid the supreme sacrifice. They did not die in vain. The union is safe.
>
> To our physically and mentally wounded who have served Ulster so unselfishly, we wish a speedy recovery and to the relatives of these men and women we pledge our continued moral practical support.
>
> To our prisoners who have undergone so much depravation and degradation with great courage and forbearance, we solemnly promise to leave no stone unturned to secure their freedom.
>
> To our serving officer, NCOs and personnel, we extend our eternal gratitude for their obedience to orders, for their ingenuity, resilience

---

* Copy in author's possession.

and good humour in the most trying of circumstances, and, we commend them for their courageous fortitude and unshakeable faith over the long years of armed struggle.

In all sincerity we offer to the loved ones of all innocent victims over the past twenty-five years, abject and true remorse. No words of ours will compensate for the intolerable suffering they have undergone during the conflict.

Let us firmly resolve to respect our differing views of freedom, culture and aspiration and never again permit our political circumstances to degenerate into bloody warfare.

We are on the threshold of a new and exciting beginning with our battles in future being political battles, fought on the side of honesty, decency and democracy against the negativity of mistrust, misunderstanding and malevolence so that together we can bring forth a wholesome society in which our children and their children will know the meaning of true peace.

However the right-wing Tory–Unionist phalanx continued to dictate the pace of the British response. While Reynolds, and the Americans, did everything they could to advance the peace process to a point where it could not be derailed by wreckers either in the IRA or Loyalist camps, London continued to march only at the pace of the Orange drum. For example, Reynolds first publicly welcomed both Hume and Adams to Government Buildings and then on 28 October 1994 personally opened a Forum for Peace and Reconciliation at Dublin Castle attended by a Sinn Fein delegation led by Adams and Martin McGuinness. Neither the Democratic Unionist Party, nor the Official Unionists attended. The other most noticeable absentees were the British Ambassador and Peter Temple-Morris, the Conservative representative on the Dublin–London inter-parliamentary tier which is supposed to assist in bringing London and Dublin politicians together. The Forum's opening was an impressive (and homerically hospitable) moment in Ireland's history. A true sense of occasion marked this notable effort to bring those traditionally involved in Irish physical force into the mainstream of Irish political life, in the former citadel of British influence in Ireland. But it very soon became apparent that the British Government either could not, or would not, see the Forum as marking an important evolutionary stage in Anglo-Irish relationships. Unofficially, at a social occasion, I experienced the sort of reaction which the Liaison Committee encountered at official level in

London a few days later when the matter of the British Ambassador's non-attendance was raised by the Irish delegation.

Meeting the normally friendly Ambassador, David Bladerwick, at the Wexford Opera Festival a day or two after the Forum ceremonies, I ventured the opinion that it was a pity he had not made use of his invitation. His face clouded over. He stamped his foot and practically spat: 'That invitation. That was crass! Two days notice! It was crass! Crass!' At that he walked off, obviously fuming. I should point out, that because of the pace of events all those invited, including the rest of the diplomatic corps accredited to Dublin, got the same notice as did the British representatives. However, I later learned that the subsequent Liaison Committee meeting was held in the same ungenerous, suspicious spirit. Not surprisingly no agreement has either emerged, or shown signs of emerging from its deliberations. The shadow of the Ulster Unionist MPs hangs over the Conference table. John Major did stand up to Ian Paisley, causing him to be in effect ejected from Downing St when he refused to accept the Prime Minister's assurance that no deal had been done with the IRA. In a farcical incident, following the confrontation with Major, Paisley, and his two companions, Peter Robinson and the Reverend William McCrea, contrived to delay their departure, ostensibly by locking themselves into a Downing St lavatory to compose a statement for the media. This earned little reaction beyond causing the three to be dubbed the 'Pee Musketeers.'

There was little else to laugh about concerning Paisley's activities. At a party conference on the weekend of December 3–5 he announced that his party would wreck any Assembly that emerged from the talks process. With him to the right of the Official Unionist Party, ready to pounce on any sign, either real or imagined, of weakness on the Union, there was no incentive for James Molyneaux to come towards the centre with Major and Reynolds to further the Adams initiative. Indeed, developments elsewhere, emboldened the Official Unionists to be more than ordinarily obstructive. Following the vote on the Maastricht Treaty in July 1993, in which the nine Official Unionist MPs had proved crucial to Major's narrow victory, the Unionists had come to an unpublicized agreement with the Labour Party under John Smith. Under 'certain conditions', as one of the Unionist negotiators described it to me, the Unionists agreed that in a similar tight situation they would vote to keep Labour in power. The principal demand of the 'certain conditions' was the sacking of Kevin McNamara, the then

Labour spokesman of Northern Ireland, whom the Unionists regarded as being too pro-Nationalist. A few weeks after the declaration of the ceasefire, Mo Mowlam, who until then had not impressed decision-taking Dublin with either her enthusiasm for, or knowledge of, things Irish, was appointed in McNamara's stead by the new Labour leader, Tony Blair.

Following her appointment, she avoided contact with Sinn Fein and declared herself in favour of continuing with a bi-partisan approach to Northern Ireland, i.e. following the government line so as to keep the nine Unionist party MPs happy in their belief that they had nothing to fear from a Labour victory. Labour was so successful in this policy that the Unionist spokesman, John Taylor, made a series of statements at the end of November 1994 saying that since the sacking of Kevin McNamara, the Unionists no longer either feared a general election, or felt constrained to automatically vote Tory, the traditionally Conservative and Unionist Party. The fruits of this policy were seen when all the Unionists at Westminster, both Official Unionist grouping and Paisley's followers, voted against the Conservatives on 6 December, thus ensuring the defeat of an ill-conceived proposal to put VAT on fuel bills.

But many Nationalist observers were worried that the vote might also put an end to John Major's ability to further the peace process. For it is generally accepted in Dublin that it was his influence, rather than that of the Northern Ireland Secretary, Sir Patrick Mayhew, which delivered such concessions as the British made between the ceasefire declaration and the 6 December. These included a reduction in the Army presence on the streets of Northern Ireland. Also, after a good deal of foot-dragging, some border roads were reopened. In Long Kesh, the prisoners' regime was relaxed to a point where they were issued with keys to their cells. Sean, for example, could either opt for privacy, or spend the night visiting his cell mates, or watching videos in the TV room. The exclusion order which barred Adams from entering the UK (mainland) was lifted. But in other parts of the Six Counties these welcome gestures were spoiled by the Army's decision to go ahead with the building of huge forts at Crossmaglen and Newton Hamilton. Privately, Whitehall also fought issues like the Adams visa, or the proposals of the Irish officials at the Liaison Committee meetings, like rearguard actions in the field. Major personally phoned Clinton twice to urge him not to receive Adams at the White

House on his second visit to America during October. It took a determined counter-offensive by O'Dowd's lobby to arrange for a deflection of this snub, which would have been very damaging for Adams amongst Republican hard-liners. It was arranged instead that Adams would receive a telephone call from Vice-President Al Gore during a visit to the home of Ethel Kennedy, Robert Kennedy's widow. And the British ostentatiously hosted a diplomatic reception for Ken Maginnis, the Unionist MP. Maginnis, after considerable diplomatic pressure, was flown to New York as part of a spoiling operation to counter Adam's media appearances. Although the Unionists would not go on television with Sinn Fein representatives in Ireland or England, Maginnis appeared on the Larry King show in opposition to Adams on 4 October 1994, ostentatiously refusing to shake hands with him.

The British also tried to obstruct Adams' third visit to the US in December during which he was received at the White House on 6 December by the head of the National Security Council, Tony Lake, and had a meeting also with the Commerce Secretary, Ron Brown. This time they objected to his being allowed to collect money for Sinn Fein. A combination of this circumstance, combined with an effort to prevent Sinn Fein attending a major investment conference in Belfast, which was scheduled to attract some of the top decision-takers in the American and political and financial worlds, finally drew a public retaliation from Adams. London had at last agreed to stage a meeting between North of Ireland Office officials and a Sinn Fein delegation led, not by Adams, but by Martin McGuinness in the first week of December, 1994. However Adams announced that this would have to be postponed for two days ostensibly to allow him to return from the US. He followed up the laying of this marker by saying that unless Sinn Fein got the same sort of invitation as every other participant in the investment conference Sinn Fein might boycott the proceedings. As the main reason the American had accepted invitations to the conference in the first place was to satisfy themselves as to the calibre of Sinn Fein before committing themselves to investment, this threat caused the Americans to make it known that if Sinn Fein were not invited, they would not come either. The British changed their position on the Conference to admit Sinn Fein participation, although not at the same parity of esteem with other participants. For example, no Sinn Fein representatives were invited to the Conference's centrepiece dinner, hosted by John Major, to which Unionist and SDLP members were invited, as was US Commerce Secretary, Ron Brown. Adams raised the issue of parity of esteem when he visited the White House, arguing that it made no sense that a Conference, called because of discrimination, should then proceed to discriminate against participants. It was he said a symptom of the larger discrimination by the British against Sinn Fein.

The investment question was crucial to the lasting success of the peace initiative. Nothing weans young men away from paramilitarism like full employment. President Clinton recognized this by agreeing to chair personally a major conference to be held in Philadelphia in 1995 on the theme of attracting investment to Ireland, North and South. The Unionists objected to the principle of regarding the island as one economic unit lest it lead to political unity also. But the British and Unionist foot-dragging on the investment conference, and other issues, gave the Irish-American lobby an opportunity to score a notable success. Clinton was spurred into reactivating a version of his peace envoy idea. With so much talk of American investment in the air he appointed former Majority Leader Senator Mitchell to be his Economic Envoy to Northern Ireland on 2 December 1994. When Clinton was sworn in, the British had made the thwarting of the Peace Envoy proposal their first priority* of his presidency. Now, two years on, their own actions had served to bring forward a similar appointment, and a particularly heavyweight one into the bargain. Mitchell was a figure of considerable prestige in American politics and had access to, and influence on, the White House. Ireland was the one foreign policy success of the Clinton White House. Moreover it was an issue which aroused a reaction amongst some forty-three million Americans of Irish descent, whether they voted Democrat or Republican. For example, the new Chairman of the House of Representatives Foreign Affairs Committee, Ben Gilman, returned as a result of the mid-term elections in November 1994, was both a Republican and a long-term supporter of Irish causes.

But not all the obstructions on the path to peace were placed there by the Tories and the Unionists, the Nationalists also scored some

---

* On the day Clinton was sworn in at the White House, BBC news bulletins began their coverage with an announcement that Tory Party leaders would be seeking an early meeting with the President to 'dissuade him from pursuing the proposal to appoint a Peace Envoy to Northern Ireland.'

appalling own goals, which ominously recalled previous historic Irish failures of political and national character. Albert Reynolds was suddenly hurled from power. Historically minded Irish observers remembered the fall of Parnell, over a divorce scandal, when he was on the eve of securing Home rule (which would, of course, have prevented all the bloodshed that has ensued in Ireland since the nineteenth century). The root cause of Reynolds' fall did not involve Reynolds himself, and the issue was not divorce, but child abuse on the part of a Catholic priest.

Controversy erupted in mid-November 1994 when it was suggested that the Irish Attorney General's office had delayed the extradition of the priest, a Fr Smith. Despite the allegations, Reynolds pressed ahead with his decision to appoint the Attorney General, Harry Whelan, as President of the High Court. Whelan's successor as Attorney General, Eoghan Fitzsimmons, then revealed that this was not the first time there had been delay in processing such an extradition request and that Reynolds had known this when appointing Whelan to the High Court. Dick Spring, the Labour Party leader, refused to continue in coalition with Fianna Fail. After he and his party had withdrawn from the government, Reynolds was succeeded as leader of Fianna Fail on 19 November by the Minister for Finance, Bertie Ahern. Whelan also resigned his short-held judgeship. As provided for in the Constitution, Reynolds continued to act as Taoiseach while negotiations took place on the formation of a new government. Ahern and Spring had almost completed negotiations on the formation of another Cabinet, when, on 5 December, the *Irish Times* reported that not alone had Reynolds known of earlier delays in the Attorney General's office, he had, on being informed of them, first tried to induce Whelan not to go forward with being appointed to the High Court and then, having failed in this attempt, defended in the Dail Whelan's suitability for the post.

Unsubstantiated allegations of all sorts flew as to why Reynolds should have acted so. Gossip suggested motives ranging from the influence of Opus Dei, the clandestine lay Catholic elite sponsored by the Pope, on the Attorney General's office, to debts of gratitude owing because of the manner in which the State's legal machinery had been operated during the beef tribunal. All that can be said with certainty at this stage is that the affair caused a rupture in the Cabinet-building process. Once more Labour withdrew and Fianna Fail was cast into opposition. Sir Patrick Mayhew was quick to state *(Irish Times,* 7

December) that the political instability would cause a delay in bringing forward the framework document. Here again, only history will show what is the lasting impact of the Reynolds debacle on the peace process. One could either argue that it was holed below the waterline by the removal of one of its principal architects, in whom the Republicans reposed more confidence than in any replacement or, that having survived such a loss, the process could survive anything.

The Republicans, too, caused a nasty hiccup in the peace process. A robbery, at a post office in Newry, early in November 1994, in which a man was killed turned out to have been the work of the IRA. The incident was condemned by the Republican leadership when the facts were established. However it caused a hiatus in a planned release of IRA prisoners in the Republic. One of them, a man jailed for his part in the Mountbatten murder, had been the subject of controversy in Britain when the question of release became known. The Newry killing, therefore, came as a severe jolt to Dublin who immediately halted the planned releases, though these were expected to be proceeded with as expected when the dust settled. London, too, had a difficulty over the prisoners issue.

A Whitehall leak allowed it to be known that a group of prisoners being repatriated from Great Britain to Northern Ireland to serve their sentences, included one who had been jailed for bombing the Brighton Hotel in which the entire British Cabinet had almost been destroyed. Tory and British media anger, led by Norman Tebbit, whose wife was consigned to life in a wheelchair by the blast, was, not surprisingly, intense. However, the insensitivity, or attempt at sabotage, of the prisoners issue, and that of the other points of contention described above, did not prevent one most hopeful occurrence from taking place. On Friday, 9 December 1994, a Sinn Fein delegation passed by Carson's statue commanding the entrance to the former Stormont parliament, and commenced talks with British officials. Symbolically enough, the chamber in which the talks were conducted was afflicted by a burst of spontaneous combustion shortly afterwards. A wiring fault caused serious damage. It was hoped that the long-term outlook would be of a more constructive nature, for although long delayed, the mere fact that the talks began at all marked a profoundly important stage in the evolving Anglo-Irish relationship.

The next stage, which was awaited with bated breath by the participants, was the emergence of the 'framework document', as it had been known since it was first mooted in the Downing St Declaration discussions. This vitally important agreement was the blueprint for the future as perceived by Dublin and London.

The document as expected, contained proposals for changes in the Government of Ireland Act, which set up the Six County statelet in the first place, the Irish Constitution's claims to the area, and cross-border institutions. Not surprisingly, tough, bruising negotiations on its content continued without success from early 1994 to the end of January 1995. And there was widespread anger among Loyalists when a leaked version of the proposed document surfaced in the London *Times* on 1 February 1995. Several prominent Unionists greeted the leak with threats to end the peace process.

Nevertheless, despite all the false dawns over the previous quarter-century grounds for optimism continued. I wrote in an earlier edition of this book that: 'If John Major can be induced to hearken to the trumpet call of history and look beyond the narrow view of the Tory backbenches to the wider wishes of the British and Irish peoples, then we are at the most hopeful juncture in Anglo-Irish relationships for centuries. If not, this book could grow even thicker . . . If the Stormont talks lead to the two sovereign governments involved eventually coming together, the enormous influence of the Irish on corporate America could, clearly, provide economic assistance for Northern Ireland on something of the scale that Jewish-America assists Israel. Already there is talk amongst Irish-American investment circles of floating an Irish Bond Drive, similar to that already in existence for Israel. Visions of a Camp-David-style peace brokered by the Americans are no longer as unreal as they once appeared. It is still too soon to be able to forecast clearly what will really happen. But it does seem just possible that Bird's may be one of the last IRA 'comms', a consummation in itself devoutly to be wished. Perhaps Sean and I will have that pint, in Belfast and, for the first time in twenty-five years, not in circumstances of brutalization.'

I left the last words to a poet. I had been researching, and commenting on the IRA longer than most – for thirty years now. While nothing was certain, and nothing would be easy, I could say that at no stage in that period had I witnessed a better prospect of seeing an end to the physical-force tradition in Irish life. I had come to know and respect many of the major players, including Fr Al Reid, Gerry Adams, John Hume, Albert Reynolds, Ted and Jean Kennedy Smith, Dick Spring, Niall O'Dowd, and many others whose names and faces crowded into my memory. Some were dead, some wished to remain anonymous. But all of them gave me an insight into the emotions of William Butler Yeats when he wrote[2]:

> Think where men's glory most begins and ends,
> And say my glory was I had such friends.

---

[1] In the event a specially convened, three day Dail debate on the issue was completely overshadowed by the IRA ceasefire announcement which came on the day the debate began. By the time it ended Dick Spring was in America seeking President Clinton's assistance in copper-fastening the peace. (See p. 655.)

[2] 'In The Municipal Gallery Revisited'.

38

From Despair to Hope

There is a plaque on a wall in Edenappa, Co. Armagh close to the border with the Republic which reads: 'In loving memory of Margaret Moore, aged 12, Jonesboro, and Mary Connolly, aged 18, Jonesboro, shot dead by British soldiers near this spot on 23rd July, 1922.'

The shooting of the two girls, as they went to draw water, prompted an angry protest by Michael Collins to the British officer commanding, General Macready. The unsatisfactory reply he received from the General, coupled with the lack of any disciplinary reaction against the soldiers responsible, helped to make up Collins's mind that:*

> I am forced to the conclusion that we have yet to fight the British in the North-East. We must by forceful action make them understand that we will not tolerate this carelessness with the lives of our people . . . It is not individuals who are in charge of shooting parties or 'Hold-up' parties that are the guilty ones. The guilt lies with the high authorities, and we must face that.

However, a month after he wrote those words, Michael Collins was dead, killed in an ambush in his native County Cork by a fellow Irishman. What was the outcome of his resolve to engage the British on Northern Ireland? The earlier pages of this book indicate the answer. The 'high authorities' saw to it that the border was drawn so that, against their will, it enclosed this fiercely Nationalistic area of South Armagh into a Northern state which discriminated against them and as a consequence was repeatedly challenged by armed force.

One reminder of what transpired since Collins's death may be seen on the Edenappa wall a few feet from the plaque commemorating the

---

* Quoted in *Michael Collins* by Tim Pat Coogan, Hutchinson, London, 1990.

two girls. It reads: 'In proud and loving memory of Volunteer Frances (FRA) Johnston, aged 21. South Armagh Brigade Oglaigh na hEireann, murdered by Crown forces on 4th June 1975 while on active service in Bessbrook.' As I took down the wording in my notebook, a shadow fell on the page. It was a young British soldier, part of an armed patrol passing me by, walking backwards to guard against a shot in the back.

At that stage (30 January 2000) the interrupted IRA ceasefire was back in place. It had been reinstated after the break caused by the Canary Wharf bombing of 9 February 1996, following the installation of Tony Blair's Labour government in power in May 1997, independent of the Ulster Unionists.

As a result of the ceasefire the Good Friday Agreement had been signed, cross-border bodies had been set up, relationships between Dublin and London had improved, and, thanks to the alchemy of the former US Senate Majority leader, Senator George Mitchell, a new power-sharing executive had come into being at Stormont.

Less than two weeks after I took my note, however, the Parliament was suspended. The shadow of the young soldier and those of his comrades formed part of the complex reasons why. The stated issue was the decommissioning of IRA weapons. But Edenappa, its traditions, and those of a variety of little towns in the vicinity – Forkhill, Jonesboro, Camlough, Caledon and Crossmaglen – were also casting their shadows over the negotiating table.

Champagne corks had popped in Belfast (West Belfast, that is) when the ceasefire was declared. There were motorized cavalcades in the streets, tri-colours waved, and euphoria prevailed. But in South Armagh and Tyrone there was no euphoria. The ceasefire had been agreed to in these strongly Republican areas. It would be supported in them, but the border areas espoused a cautious 'wait and see' approach, very different to the attitudes which prevailed in Belfast Republican enclaves responsive to the charisma of the man who had made the ceasefire possible, Gerry Adams.

The collapse of the Stormont Executive occurred like bankruptcy in two ways, gradually and suddenly. The sudden part was seen by all the world: the passage through Westminster of legislation suspending the Northern Assembly, on Friday, 11 February 2000. The gradual takes us back to the declaration of the IRA ceasefire on 31 August 1994. As already indicated in the previous chapter, earlier in the year the focus of IRA, and indeed Irish political attention generally, was on the expected Framework Document. This emerged from Downing

Street and Government Buildings in Dublin on 22 February 1995.

The document said that it was aimed at assisting 'discussion and negotiation involving the Northern Ireland parties'. Its 'guiding principles' were:

> 'The principle of self determination, as set out in the Joint Declaration. That agreement must be pursued and established by exclusively democratic, peaceful means, without resort to violence or coercion.
> That any new political arrangements must be based on full respect for, and protection and expression of, the rights and identities of both traditions in Ireland and even-handedly afford both communities in Northern Ireland parity of esteem and treatment, including equality of opportunity and advantage.'

The document also envisaged changes in the relationships between the two parts of Ireland, within the North and South, and between Ireland and England. It proposed new North/South institutions which would 'enable representatives of democratic institutions, north and south, to enter into new, co-operative and constructive relationships'. The document presaged a new Northern Assembly, closer links between the Northern and Southern civil servants, and generally, in its own words, foresaw 'a new approach to the traditional constitutional doctrines on both sides'.

Nationalist Ireland welcomed the Framework Document and its 'new approach'. However, the Unionists greeted it with a very old approach, outright hostility. I have already indicated how Major's weakened position within his own party over the European issue affected progress in the peace process over issues like the Adams visas. The Unionists continued to take advantage of the leverage which this gave them in the House of Commons, which eventually crystallized around what became known as the decommissioning issue, the effort to force the IRA to give up its weapons before Sinn Fein would be allowed to take part in the Six Counties' Government. Before examining this crucial issue in some detail it should be noted that the irony of the decommissioning issue is that, left to itself, without duress, the IRA would want to get rid of its weapons voluntarily, lest they eventually fall into the hands either of criminals or dissident Republicans opposed to the ceasefire. It was only after the IRA guns fell silent that the demand was made that they should be given up.

Exactly how the issue came to be injected into the peace process has been hotly debated. But there can be no debate about the fact that the term 'injected' is sadly appropriate. It has been a toxic admixture to the body politic which has stuck both in the peace process and in Anglo-Irish relationships like a poisoned knitting needle in an elbow joint since shortly after the IRA ceasefire first came into effect in August 1994.

The IRA would not have agreed to a ceasefire had compulsory decommissioning been suggested during the background negotiations which preceded the 31 August declaration. Their position is that they were not defeated, and that for them to surrender their arms in advance of general demilitarization, on the part of all the belligerents involved in the conflict, including the British Army, would be both a surrender and an acceptance that as they held illegal weapons, their war too had been illegal, a criminal action. This would have been a denial of the traditional Republican view that the Irish have a moral right to wage war, equivalent if not superior to that claimed by the British to invade and occupy their land. It would also have been a negation of the reasons why Bobby Sands and his comrades died on hunger strike, in protest against criminalization. Other arguments advanced by the IRA against decommissioning in advance of clear evidence that the Stormont Executive was actually going to work, include the removal of the numerous British military installations, particularly in the border areas already mentioned, and the fear that unilateral decommissioning by the IRA would lead to an outbreak of sectarian assassinations by Loyalist paramilitaries.

The bedrock Republican position was articulated at Milltown Cemetery in May 1996 by the leading Provisional, Brian Keenan:* 'The IRA will not be defeated . . . Republicans will have our victory . . . Do not be confused about decommissioning. The only thing the Republican movement will accept is the decommissioning of the British state in this country.' Keenan, who was speaking at a ceremony in Milltown Cemetery in memory of Sean McCaughey, the IRA leader who died on hunger and thirst strike in Portlaoise Jail (see p. 199) and, as we shall see, would still be sticking to that position in the small hours of the frantic morning of 2 February 2000, as emissaries from the Dublin Government vainly sought to get him to change his mind in a bid to get David Trimble to withdraw the resignation threat which would yet again bring down a Stormont Parliament.

* *Irish News*, 5 May 1996.

Of course the traditional British military mind scoffed and was outraged at the thought of the IRA placing itself on the same footing as Her Majesty's Forces. But above and beyond any argument which might have been advanced against accepting the IRA ceasefire as genuine, there is the inescapable fact that the police on both sides of the border were in a position to test its bona fides and believed that the cessation was genuine. At a meeting of the British/Irish inter-governmental Conference, attended by Irish and British Ministers, their senior officials and security chiefs from both sides of the border, the merit of the issue was actively debunked, not by an Irish spokesperson as one might have imagined, but by a senior RUC officer who said frankly:

> This is not a military issue, it is a political issue. The major portion of the damage and death caused over the entire period of the troubles did not come from hand guns and rifles, from homemade mortars, or even from Semtex explosive. It was caused by the fertilizer bombs which can be made up by anyone with a schoolboy knowledge of chemistry. Two men with shovels can make up a thousand pound bomb in a Fermanagh cowshed and, if for some reason the operation has to be aborted, they can decommission it again, all within twelve hours. You can't decommission shovels. It's minds which have to be decommissioned.

I am printing that anecdote because I accept the word of the senior Irish civil servant who was present at the meeting that one day, under the thirty-year-rule system, his private note of that conversation will be proved accurate. Certainly the judgement that the matter is political, not military, is correct. It should be remembered that the entire modern Irish Republic grew out of the ceasefire and dump arms order issued by Frank Aiken (p. 35) which brought the Irish Civil War to an end. My father's side, which won the war, accepted the dump arms order at face value and allowed rust to become the decommissioning agent. Had it not done so, and attempted to enforce a surrender, the Civil War would probably still be continuing. As it was, the thrust of the Cumann na nGaedheal Executive was to force de Valera and his supporters into parliamentary activity, not to exclude them from it, as the Unionists have done. Some members of Fianna Fail found this so hard to believe that, far from decommissioning, they actually entered the Dail with revolvers in their pockets; one of them, who verified this to me, was Vivion de Valera, Eamon de Valera's eldest son. Despite the bitterness of the time, however, it soon became evident that the Cos-grave administration was serious about making the Parliament (the Dail) work and modern Ireland is the result.

A secondary, but most important, point, which underlines the fallacy of the decommissioning argument completely, is the very obvious one that if the IRA wished it could give up every piece of equipment it has and, given the availability of armaments in the world, replace them all almost immediately. I have seen several references, in various commentators' writings for TV programmes, to the IRA's stockpile largely consisting of weapons imported from Libya (see Chapter 35). But from my own knowledge I know of shipments that never surfaced in the media, which came from the ever-fertile procurement ground of America. One huge shipment, possibly the largest ever, may have contained a plastic explosive which was used in the attack on the Brighton hotel that nearly claimed Margaret Thatcher's life. But while America, and the ever-ready dollars of hard-core IRA supporters, is a constant potential source of supply, there are a myriad other areas in Europe, particularly since the fall of Communism, where arms can be purchased. Sweden is a country not normally associated with IRA arms trafficking, but it has a number of potential sources of supply because of the former threat from the Soviet Union. In remote areas all over Sweden, bunkers were prepared during the Cold War to which special units of Swedish guerrillas would have had access in the event of a Soviet invasion. These troops were issued with small wallet-like packs which, when their seal was broken, revealed the site of the nearest bunker. As the threat of the Cold War receded, many of these information packs became available to IRA sympathizers. As the dumps are all in remote parts of the country, it is a simple matter – for people of the IRA's calibre, that is – to drive trucks up to them under cover of darkness and make off with the lethal contents.

The IRA believe therefore that decommissioning was deliberately introduced into the equation, probably by someone high up in MI5, which the Irish police also regard as playing a dark hand of its own, as a wrecking device at a time when John Major felt it incumbent on him to go slow on the peace process. Unlike Scotland Yard, with which Dublin co-operates confidently, MI5 is regarded as a self-serving organization, keen to retain a role for itself, against other agencies, at a time when the Cold War's ending has lessened the justification for its presence. Its minor public schoolboy, gung-ho, defence of the realm attitude to Ireland is resented. Strange activities, including bugging

Garda HQ, can apparently be justified under the cloak of defending the realm. In any event, so far as I have been able to piece the jigsaw together, it seems that the decommissioning issue was deliberately introduced after the IRA ceasefire by John Major's administration.

Certainly that is the IRA view. Two years after the ceasefire was declared and had broken down, an anonymous IRA spokesman told the *Irish News*:*

> We want to make the talks work and if the IRA was satisfied that the talks would be a genuine way of moving the process forward, they would not stand in the way . . . But there is a real problem of mistrust between us and the British. People simply think Major is buying time to get through the autumn.

In the months after the August 1994 ceasefire, a meeting was scheduled between Martin McGuinness and Michael Ancram, the Minister for Political Development at Stormont. Major became concerned both at what the effect of this might be on his divided party and at the likely Unionist reaction. In Dublin, as we have seen, Albert Reynolds was forcing the pace with initiatives such as his handshakes with John Hume and Gerry Adams before the cameras on the steps of Government Buildings. But there were few handshakes in Downing St where, on the same day (6 September 1994) that Reynolds met Hume and Adams, John Major threw a DUP delegation, led by Ian Paisley, out of his office when Paisley refused to accept his word that a secret deal had not been done with the IRA. Paisley's subsequent press statement on the row was composed in the lavatories of Downing St to which, Republicans allege, he and his colleagues retreated in order to secure the correct ambience for its contents.

There was little else to laugh about emerging from Downing St. Major was in fief to forces which shared Paisley's viewpoint, a fact, as we saw, that was publicly highlighted in the House of Commons on 6 December 1994 when the Ulster Unionist Party MPs joined with Labour and Tory Party rebels to defeat the Conservatives 319 to 311 over the proposal to increase VAT on fuel bills.

Therefore, as Major's dependency on the Ulster Unionists grew and his parliamentary strength slipped away, the idea of introducing a retarding factor to the peace process must have appeared attractive to

* Ibid.

The IRA

him. Accordingly therefore it is said that, during the autumn of 1994, at a meeting in Chequers between British and Irish officials to review the situation and to set up the liaison committee of top Dublin and London civil servants to oversee the process, the British informally told the Irish that 'the boss' (Major) was concerned about the 'disposal of the arsenals', and intended raising this when he next met Reynolds under 'any other business'.

The Irish apparently did not realize the potential of the 'arsenals' issue, and it duly became a matter of discussion, and contention, first between the officials and then between the politicians. With a brazen disregard for his party's record in government, and his own background, the Unionist spokesperson on defence, Ken Maginnis, a former member of the B-Specials and of the UDR, both of which of course had to be 'decommissioned', became the first politician to enunciate the decommissioning argument, which he subsequently never tired of enunciating, i.e., that Sinn Fein could not be admitted 'to the table of democracy' without prior decommissioning.

The decommissioning demand was in clear breach of the commitment given in Article 10 of the Downing Street Declaration. This provided for the admission of democratically elected parties to talks 'once they proved that they intended to abide by the democratic process'.

Had, say, Martin McGuinness or Gerry Adams attempted either to secure decommissioning in advance of talks, or to go outside the commitments entered into in the Good Friday Agreement, they would have seriously jeopardized not only their own safety, but that of the peace process also, because their personal authority would have been destroyed.

At the time of writing there are 160,000 legally held weapons in Loyalist hands,* so many that at the time of the Dunblane massacre which caused handguns in the 'UK mainland' to be taken up, it was decided to secure similar handovers in Northern Ireland. In addition to these licensed weapons there are those that were not handed in when the B-Specials and the UDR were disbanded, and those smuggled into the country by British intelligence agents such as Brian Nelson.

---

* On 6 November 1994 the *Sunday Business Post* carried a major survey of the military situation in Northern Ireland, prepared with the help of the Queen's University sociologist, Mike Tomlinson.

Each of the 32,000 security force members also carries a personal weapon, as well as having access to others.

The combined British Army/RUC presence meant that in 1994/5, when the decommissioning demand was first enunciated, there was one security force person to every 3.7 Catholic males between the ages of sixteen and forty-four. In addition there were 600 MI5 personnel, all in an area the size of Yorkshire, and there were 135 fixed military installations. Where the RUC are concerned, to reduce the force to the policing levels obtaining in the Republic would entail a reduction of 12,000 members of the force (from 16,000 to 4,000) to arrive at the Republic's ratio of 1 Garda to 400 civilians.

One of the best books about the troubles is *The Irish War* by Tony Geraghty.* The British Government awarded it the supreme accolade of unsuccessfully attempting to prosecute the author, a former Chief Reporter of the *Sunday Times* and a historian of the SAS, under the Official Secrets Act. Ireland has traditionally been the laboratory in which Britain tried out experiments of both a military and constitutional nature and in the ceasefire era, which also coincided with Labour's introduction of devolution to Scotland and Wales as well as Ireland, both type of experiments were obviously carried out simultaneously, with massively harmful consequences for the constitutional effort. Geraghty writes:

> Throughout the ceasefires of 1995 and 1997–98, the British army energetically modernized its armoury of computers. The scale of cost of this programme reflected the army's belief that it would continue to fight an intelligence war in Northern Ireland for many years ahead and that the surveillance war would increasingly become part of normal life in England.

Geraghty notes that the computers give the British 'total cover of a largely innocent population'. He reveals that 'even as three governments placed their faith in peace talks' senior officers in Northern Ireland were informed that a standing army would be maintained 'comprising three brigades and headquarters; that is, a complete division of 10,000 troops or more, for the foreseeable future'.

The Army was so much more concerned with having a role in the future than with furthering the ceasefire that a secret report was

* *The Irish War* by Tony Geraghty, HarperCollins, London, 1999.

prepared on the necessity to safeguard military surveillance rights should the Prevention of Terrorism Act and the Emergency Powers Act be repealed.

Some commentators have argued that the British build up was put in train out of alarm, not at the IRA's activities, but at the Orangemen's, following the eruption of the Drumcree protests described below (pp. 686–90). But this thesis fails to explain why the vast bulk of new installations, and personnel, were all located in Nationalist areas. However, the sheer numbers involved give the military a strong say in what happens to them in any 'decommissioning' talks.

The Republic's leaders opposed the use of the decommissioning ploy to stall talks. While broadcasting a strong appeal* against getting hung up on the 'decommissioning' question, Albert Reynolds recalled how both his own party, Fianna Fail, and the Democratic Left had both emerged from the physical force tradition – by dumping their arms, not surrendering them – and so were able to carry their followers with them into the parliamentary arena. Dick Spring, the Deputy Prime Minister, said 'If we take the attitude that nothing will happen unless there is a surrender or decommissioning of arms, then I think that is a formula for disaster.'

Spring was speaking in Washington on 1 March 1995, at a particularly highly charged moment: the eve of the opening of a serious fissure in the much vaunted 'special relationship' between London and Washington over Ireland. Patrick Mayhew had successfully lobbied Washington not to allow Sinn Fein to collect funds in the US and not to invite Gerry Adams to the White House for the Clintons' gala on St Patrick's Day. However, his manner had offended Vice-President Al Gore, who had hitherto been unfavourably disposed towards the idea of Sinn Fein being allowed to collect funds. By contrast, Spring, visiting Washington during the same period, had made an excellent impression, and he was strongly in favour of Sinn Fein being allowed to collect. So far as decision-taking Dublin is concerned, the more dividends the peace process can be made to show for the Republicans, the less likely is a return to war.

Accordingly, the Irish-American lobby went into overdrive. The CIA, the State Department, the Justice Department, and, surprisingly, even the National Security Council, had all come out against fundraising permission being granted. However, at a White House election

---

* *The News at One*, RTE, 16 June 1995.

strategy meeting, Tony Lake and Nancy Soderberg were called into the Oval Office and told, in the words of the Framework Document, that a 'balanced constitutional arrangement' was needed. In other words they were to negotiate a mechanism with Sinn Fein whereby, in return for a statement moving the decommissioning issue forward, permission to fundraise in the USA would be granted. Niall O'Dowd acted as an intermediary between Adams and the NSC. A Sinn Fein statement was duly cobbled together which showed flexibility on the decommissioning issue. It then began to appear, to the Irish lobby at least, that the British agreed to begin talks at ministerial level provided that Sinn Fein agreed to discuss decommissioning as part of those talks.

As a result, St Patrick's Day in the White House was a night to remember. The roof almost lifted off to the sound of the cheers that greeted John Hume when he broke off singing 'The Town That I Loved So Well' to say, 'Come up here, Gerry, and join in'.

However, the Irish-Americans had not anticipated the virulence of the British reaction to the reversal on the fundraising decision and the extending to Gerry Adams of the invitation to the White House. John Major was so furious that for a whole week he refused to accept a phone call from Clinton. It was a moment unparalleled in recent Anglo-American relationships. Nearly three months later, on 14 June, the *Irish Times* Washington correspondent, Conor O'Clery, reported that London was making difficulties about Clinton's visit to Belfast at the end of 1995, as part of a trip to both Ireland and England. O'Clery reported that the British had told the White House that there were 'scheduling problems' over the dates proposed.

Clinton had intended to announce his Irish visit at the White House Economic Summit on Ireland which opened at the Sheraton Hotel, Washington on 25 May in the presence of most of *Fortune* Magazine's top 500 American corporate executives, the majority of them Irish-American. According to the *Irish Times* it 'represented the most significant engagement by the United States in the affairs of any European country since President Truman's Marshall Plan after the Second World War, which helped put Western Europe back on its feet'. Clinton himself presided over the three-day conference, which was also attended by Vice-President Al Gore, Commerce Secretary Ron Brown, Secretary of State Warren Christopher and Senator George Mitchell. The object of the conference was to generate American investment both in the Six Counties and in the adjoining counties of the Republic: Louth, Cavan, Monaghan, Sligo, Leitrim and Donegal.

However, London and the Unionists objected to the all-Ireland approach. Whitehall let it be known privately that there were objections to the idea of Ireland being regarded as one unit. The North of Ireland Office, heavily Unionist in outlook, was less concerned about revivifying the North's stagnant economy than preventing the Republic from gaining the lion's share of the hoped-for jobs, because of the Republic's attractive incentives for inward investment, which are superior to those in the Six Counties. More importantly, on top of this curmudgeonly approach, Sir Patrick Mayhew used the occasion of the conference to state that Sinn Fein would only be admitted to talks if the IRA passed a series of tests, proving that they had decommissioned. The tests became known as 'the Washington Three'. Irish-American lobbyists in Washington of the calibre of Bruce Morrison have told me that the decommissioning issue would have died before the conference had not new life been breathed into it by the man who succeeded Albert Reynolds as Taoiseach, John Bruton. The most charitable comment one can make about Bruton is that he possessed neither the grasp nor the empathy of Reynolds for the Northern Ireland issue. He became popularly known as 'John Unionist'.

Morrison told me: 'The Brits were reeling. They told us privately they knew it was all nonsense and would have to be dropped. Then this guy came along . . .' What Bruton did was to make a series of speeches, beginning in the traditional Irish political High Season in Washington, the run up to St Patrick's Day on 17 March, urging the IRA to decommission in advance of talks. Armed with this powerful ammunition provided by an Irish Taoiseach, Mayhew gleefully unleashed the 'Washington Three'. The respected *Irish Times* political correspondent, Geraldine Kennedy, described Bruton's intervention (on 17 February 1996) as an 'irreparable mistake':

. . . an irreparable mistake was made by Mr Bruton last March when he implicitly accepted the Washington 3 test . . . Bruton said he would be telling President Clinton that they had to see some movement on the arms question so that talks could begin between British Ministers and Sinn Fein. He made statement after statement implicitly supporting Sir Patrick's position in the US and at home . . . Either inadvertently – or worse knowingly – Mr Bruton underwrote the British demand for Washington 3, a decommissioning gesture prior to talks. He helped place it at the top of the Anglo-Irish agenda. It has dominated the agenda at heads of government, ministerial and official level ever since.

Thus aided by Bruton, Mayhew's approach began, in Whitehall's eyes at least, to show dividends. For, in order to fence-mend with London, the US administration also pressurized Sinn Fein on the decommissioning issue. The London *Times* reported (on 6 July 1995) that Gerry Adams had been told by the White House that it was: 'time for him to deliver on the issue of decommissioning the IRA's arsenal'. Days before the story appeared, Adams had in fact been presented with not one, but two documents containing what the *Times* correctly termed 'strongly worded demarches'. One came from Jean Kennedy Smith, the other from the American Ambassador in London, Admiral Crowe.

But the IRA were not impressed. Adams conveyed the Republican response on 27 July 1995 in an article in *An Phoblacht/Republican News* in which he said that a review of the peace process, 'even from the most neutral perspective', would find that:

The Unionist parties had not engaged at all and indeed that their leaderships are highly suspicious and hostile to the process . . . From an Irish Nationalist or Republican perspective the judgement would be much more damning. The British Government would be seen to have been minimalistic, begrudging and provocatively negative in its approach.

He firmly closed the door on the decommissioning issue:

The British Government and others may be miscalculating the IRA's position on decommissioning or the Sinn Fein leadership's room for manoeuvre on this issue. If this is so they do so with the benefit of having heard at first hand from Sinn Fein that the IRA will not decommission or surrender its weapons to anyone as a precondition for all-party talks. There is no room for manoeuvre . . . If a surrender of weapons had been imposed as a precondition to peace negotiations prior to the cessation there would have been no IRA ceasefire.

The Dublin Government conveyed its fears to London that the effect of the decommissioning debate was to enable the hawks in the IRA to make life difficult for the doves and warned that the issue was jeopardizing the peace process. The only tangible response from the British occurred in places like East Tyrone and South Armagh and elsewhere. The security forces harassed young men, as though peace had never come, although it was widely reported that these were the areas where opposition to the ceasefire was known to be strong. In addition, members of the RIR (formally the UDR) were quietly told to resume carrying their personal weapons in the anticipation of what Unionist spokesmen began referring to as a 'rolling return' to violence: in other words a planned, gradual return to full-scale hostilities throughout the Six Counties.

The IRA had no such plan, but whatever hand was manipulating the marionette's strings, the contagion of rumour spread. Some of the Loyalist paramilitary leaders who had been most prominent in the Catholic assassination campaign, but who had kept a low profile since the ceasefires, became highly visible again, particularly around Portadown, a seat of both Loyalist paramilitary activity, and of the Garvaghy Road agitation. There was a widespread belief amongst Republicans that a hidden intelligence hand was at work. The belief was strengthened when a group of Loyalists were arrested in Glasgow at the end of July on arms procurement charges. One of them, Lindsay Robb, had been conducting negotiations with Stormont ministers on behalf of the UVF.

The position of Irish prisoners in British jails also caused Republican tensions. The prisoners had to contend with a widespread prejudice in the British prison system against 'Irish terrorists'. In addition there were the difficulties experienced by relatives in finding the money and opportunity to travel to England to see prisoners, who were frequently switched from one jail to another at very short notice; particularly harsh sentences were imposed on the 'UK mainland', as compared even to the Six Counties with their Diplock Courts. One prisoner, Paul Norney, had served twenty-one years without review, for a life sentence imposed when he was seventeen years old. Beyond these factors there is the unacknowledged policy of using the Republican prisoners in British jails as hostages or bargaining counters in underground negotiations with the Republicans.

True to this tradition, as the Fianna Fail spokesperson on Foreign Affairs, Ray Burke, pointed out, these prisoners' conditions worsened from the declaration of the ceasefire, particularly in Belmarsh and Whitemoor. A dirty protest by a group of Irish prisoners broke out at Whitemoor. The British civil rights lawyer Garret Pierce, who defended the Guildford Four, described the conditions in an interview on RTE's *This Week* programme on 23 July 1995: 'Apart from contending with lack of exercise, and obstacles being placed in the way of their seeing their relatives and lawyers, the men were held in such cramped, unnatural conditions that they faced problems of arthritis and failing eyesight.'

Conditions were bad in the Conservative Party also. John Major decided that he had no option but to put his premiership on the line and hold a leadership contest, which he duly won, against the 'stalking horse' challenge of John Redwood, on 4 July. The day before his victory, while ignoring the plight of the Irish prisoners, he found it necessary to release the British paratrooper Private Lee Clegg, who had been jailed for shooting dead a Belfast teenaged girl joyrider and whose case had become a cause célèbre with the tabloid press. The release also occurred a few days before the pinnacle of the 'marching season' on 12 July. Timing apart, it was a highly provocative act, coming at a time when Protestant–Catholic relationships are traditionally at their worst in Northern Ireland.

The provocation was heightened rather than diminished by Tory spokespersons such as Lady Olga Maitland, who continuously made the point that Clegg's case was that of a man sent on a 'peacekeeping' mission to Northern Ireland, and could not be equated with that of Irish terrorists. The fact of the paratroopers, the most hated regiment in Ireland, being involved in major acts of violence quite apart from Bloody Sunday, was ignored. But not in Ireland – the country, North and South, was gripped by a sense of anger and injustice. The Tories' stated reasons for Clegg's release were both conflicting and an insult to the intelligence. The release had a) nothing to do with the leadership crisis, and b) was taken solely on legal grounds. The *Irish Times* commented that the British Government's attempts to 'justify the Clegg release on legal grounds had only exacerbated the feelings of anger surrounding the refusal to reconsider the position of Loyalist and Republican prisoners, since the main reason for action has been, in effect, "The law must follow its course".'

Trouble might have been avoided if Clegg's release had been accompanied by a display of similar clemency towards Loyalist and Republican prisoners. In the absence of such gestures, regrettably, albeit predictably, the hijacker and the petrol bomber returned to the streets of Northern Ireland. During the week of the leadership battle the Republicans orchestrated three days of multi-million-pound destruction, between 3 and 9 July, before Gerry Adams judged it opportune to make a successful appeal for calm. But had that destruction of property not occurred, there is every likelihood that guns could have come out and there would have been loss of life.

DRUMCREE

Widescale rioting broke out again a few days later because of the
12 July parades. This time the Orangemen were the source of the
disturbances. In Portadown they clashed with police, demanding to be
allowed to march through the Catholic Garvaghy Road area. The
Drumcree situation was to become a source of major disturbance all
through the period under review, and, I fear, is destined to extend
beyond it into the future as well, the reasons for which will become
apparent in the section on demographics (pp. 735–8). Strictly speaking,
the Garvaghy Road is not a 'traditional' march route, but is newly
built. Nevertheless Ian Paisley proclaimed that the right to march
through the area was a matter of 'Ulster or the Irish Republic, freedom
or slavery, light or darkness'.

His remarks fell on ears accustomed to a tradition of Portadown
Loyalists marching through Catholic areas at will, and being prepared
to beat up any Catholics who objected. The roots of these attitudes lie
in previous centuries of Protestant/Catholic rivalries which built up
over the linen industry. In the searches for arms, alleged to be held
in Catholic houses, Protestant militias frequently broke into Catholic
homes, with the approval of the local Justices of the Peace. Arms were
very seldom found in these searches, but in the consequent destruction
the Catholics' looms were always broken up. Echoes of this tradition
sounded loudly in Catholic ears around the Portadown district during
July 1995. Protestant paramilitaries were heard to make remarks along
the lines of 'Loyalism began in Portadown, and it'll finish here'.

There were three days of high anxiety, punctuated by outbursts of
violence in Portadown and its environs from 10 to 12 July, as various
intermediaries attempted to broker a compromise between the Nationalists' position of 'they shall not pass' and the Loyalists' 'traditional
right'. Unquestionably, the issue of marches through Catholic areas
was one seized upon by Sinn Fein. Gerry Adams was reported by
RTE (*Irish Times*, 5 March 1997) as telling Sinn Fein members at
Athboy:

> Ask any activist in the North did Drumcree happen by accident, and
> they will tell you, no ... Three years of work on the lower Ormeau
> Road, Portadown, and parts of Fermanagh and Newry, Armagh, and
> Bellaghy, and up in Derry ... Three years of work went into creating
> that situation, and fair play to those people who put the work in.

But Sinn Fein opportunism notwithstanding, as the Portadown back-drop explains, there was a long history of grievance to be seized upon. In other parts of the Six Counties, particularly in Belfast's Ormeau Road, there was trouble also. Orange provocations in the Ormeau district had included marchers holding up five fingers as they passed Graham's bookmaker shop in which five Catholics had been murdered in a sectarian attack. This area became particularly inflamed in the wake of the Lee Clegg decision, as did Derry, where an Apprentice Boys March was forced through, Martin McGuinness being one of the Sinn Fein protestors forcibly removed by the police.

Overall the entire scene was unhappily reminiscent of the Bombay Street and Derry rioting which ushered in the contemporary 'troubles'. But Garvaghy Road had a particular significance, because out of the disturbances there emerged the new leader of the Ulster Unionist Party, David Trimble. He helped to broker a compromise whereby the marchers were allowed to pass through the Catholic area silently, with no bands or provocative demonstrations. The atmosphere, not just in the Portadown area, but in Ireland as a whole, had been rendered electric by the Drumcree standoff. Province-wide rioting, road-blocking and hijackings grew out of the demonstrations. Tens of thousands of Orangemen occupied the fields around the Garvaghy Church. Orange drums throbbed through the night and the scene appeared set for an explosion which at the very least would destroy the ceasefire.

After Trimble's negotiations had helped to secure the Orangemen's right to march through the police cordons, which had hitherto kept them out of the Catholic area, he and Paisley clasped hands together in a triumphal arch as, with broad smiles on their faces, they led the brethren through the discomfited Catholics. The smiles on Trimble's face grew broader when, a little later (on 8 September), his playing of the Orange card proved strong enough to trump those of John Taylor, who had hitherto been the favourite to succeed James Molyneaux as leader of the Ulster Unionist Party.

Trimble, a law lecturer at Queen's University, had been prominent in the Vanguard movement which helped to bring down the power-sharing executive of 1974. He continued to be regarded in Dublin at least as a hardline Unionist, given to making hostile remarks about the Southern State. Nevertheless, as Republicans sourly observed after-wards, he was destined to become the first man to win a political horse race riding on the back of a rat – King Rat was the name of the notorious Portadown Loyalist paramilitary leader, Billy Wright, one of the principal figures involved in putting 'muscle' into the Garvaghy demonstration. During the Garvaghy confrontation, Trimble, who had a very public aversion to meeting Sinn Fein spokespersons on the grounds that they were associated with terrorism, met and talked with Wright.

Although powerful American sponsors of the peace process would later successfully lobby to secure a Nobel Peace Prize for Trimble (in the unfulfilled hope that the international recognition would cause him to act like an international statesman) because he signed the Good Friday Agreement, it is with the Garvaghy Road, rather than Stockholm, that Trimble remains associated in Republican minds. Garvaghy again became a source of national concern in 1996 and has continued so in subsequent years. The Orange Order refused to speak to the local residents to negotiate a compromise, because their leader, Brendan McCionnaith, was a Republican who had served a prison sentence for IRA activities. Nor would they accept the compromise proposed by Sir Hugh Annesley, the RUC Chief Constable, who announced that the Orangemen would not be allowed to march down the Garvaghy Road on their return to Portadown from Garvaghy Church, but were free to march back along the same uncontentious route they followed on the way to the church.

Annesley's decision became a source of rioting throughout the Six Counties. Orangemen held up traffic, burnt cars, and intimated Catholics out of their homes. On TV, crowds of Orangemen could be seen throwing stones and petrol bombs, and jeering the police. The taunts at the police were particularly menacing, as the names and addresses of serving officers were called out over loudspeakers and chanted by crowds through which moved known members of the local UVF. David Trimble, who for so long refused to speak with Sinn Fein because of their terrorist associations, was discovered (*Panorama*, 15 July 1996) to have gone to Drumcree to hold a meeting with Billy Wright.

The British Army could easily have contained the rioters. In fact, the paratroopers had conducted a survey of the Orangemen's strength, and concluded that a few deaths would soon prick the bubble of defiance. However, an Orange Bloody Sunday was not a cheerful prospect for Whitehall, which increasingly realized that it could not rely on the police. Although it was Orangemen who were taunting and intimidating them out of their homes as rioting spread, it was on the Catholic rioters that the RUC turned their batons and at whom they fired their plastic bullets. Of 6,000 baton rounds fired throughout the Six Counties, less than 500 were directed at Orange mobs. And at Drumcree, the Orangemen had in waiting a bulldozer which was intended for use to smash through the police barricades so that petrol tankers could follow afterwards – to be ignited in Catholic areas. The RUC finally brought the crisis to a head, by threatening that the force would call in sick if the stand-off continued.

Both in the Garvaghy Road and in the Ormeau Road, the batons accordingly fell on Catholic protestors and the Orangemen were forced through. Sir Hugh Annesley subsequently resigned. The Garvaghy Road has continued to be a major flashpoint in the period under review. A huge Orange demonstration throughout the Six Counties was called off before it spilled over into civil war, after a UVF petrol bomb had claimed the lives of the three Quinn children in their home at Bally-money in 1998, and in 1999 trouble was averted only because the Garvaghy residents arranged for squads of international observers drawn from various walks of life to monitor the procession under the eyes of the camera. Even though the media subsequently remarked on how 'peacefully' the procession passed off, I found the two days I spent in the Garvaghy area a particularly unnerving experience. The town of Portadown itself was shuttered and sullen, an air of menace hung over all, and no one thought to move out of their own area, or to venture beyond local GAA Club or their homes for a drink. The tradition of Nationalists exiting the Six Counties for the period of the 'twalfth' took a new twist. Even though Turkey had been hit by earthquakes and more shocks threatened, many Nationalists availed themselves of the cheap holidays which the Turks offered as a result, preferring the risks of Turkish upheavals to those at home.

A sunny day, and the presence of crowds of cheerful young people gave a superficial appearance of normalcy. But the menace was also evident. On the evening of the 11th, as worshippers gathered for evening mass a parade went by which marched in silence until it passed St John the Baptist Catholic Church, at which point the bands struck up booming Orange choruses, striking particular terror into the hearts of the elderly, the women and children in the church. One American woman observer, who had ventured to the edge of the churchyard to watch the parade pass, strayed a little too far from her colleagues and, being recognized because of her distinctive blue observer shirt, was set upon and was lucky to escape with only a fractured wrist and some bruises to the head and body. Marchers called out jokes concerning

the recent suicide of a local Catholic youth. To underscore the point
they also held up grisly drawings of a hanging man. The media cameras
did not record the fact that some of the most prominent local Loyalist
paramilitaries were also videoing the proceedings, targeting the Republicans and other prominent nationalist figures in the crowds.

At the time of writing, the forthcoming Garvaghy marches are being
viewed with dread, and no one can foresee their outcome. But one of
the ironies of these protests is that they help to strengthen the very
forces they are directed at: Sinn Fein and the IRA. As one young man
in the Garvaghy Road put it to me: 'I'm an SDLP supporter. I don't
approve of violence, but if they try to come down the Garvaghy Road,
I'll be there to stop them along with the IRA.' It was quite obvious
that the Orangemen were providing the IRA with recruits.

Let us now turn off the Garvaghy Road to return to the main
narrative. Alarmed at the drift of events, Bruton, Spring, Hume and
Adams issued a statement on 14 July 1995, directed at London, through
the Dublin Government's Information Bureau:

> We met today to review the peace process. We reiterate our total and
> absolute commitment to democratic and peaceful methods of resolving
> political problems and our objective of an equitable and lasting agreement
> that can command the consent and allegiance of all.
>
> The current impasse in the peace process is a cause for concern to
> all who share that objective. It must be overcome. Accordingly, we are
> seeking a commencement, as soon as possible, of the inclusive, all-party
> talks necessary to the achievement of our objective.

By a coincidence the statement was issued on the day the Forum
for Peace and Reconciliation ended its deliberations at Dublin Castle
for the summer. This, although boycotted by the Unionists, had proved
constructive. Several members of Sinn Fein afterwards commented to
me how useful it was. It gave them a first-hand exposure not merely
to the give-and-take, but also to the procedures of ordinary politics,
thus providing the fledgling parliamentarians with a valuable entrée to
Irish political life. But not sufficiently valuable as to enable them to
agree to a central element of the Forum's findings: 'The Democratic
right of self-determination by the people of Northern Ireland as a whole
must be achieved and exercised with and subject to the agreement and
consent of a majority of the people of Ireland.' Given the climate of
the time Sinn Fein feared, rightly as matters unfortunately proved

subsequently, that 'consent' meant that the Republicans would merely be signing up to a new form of Unionist veto.

The Irish-American group led by Morrison and O'Dowd returned to Dublin, and saw central players in the peace process. They returned to America convinced that Adams was still in firm control of his party, commanding wide support and still determined on peace, but that there was a dangerous groundswell of grassroots anger at the slow rate of progress in the peace process. After the Irish-Americans' visit, President Clinton gave an unusual interview to the *Irish Times* Washington correspondent, Conor O'Clery, on 3 August 1995, in which he clearly fired a shot across London's bows on the issue of both talks and prisoners. He said he would welcome movement on both the prisoner and talks issues and, despite the demarches, pointedly did not repeat London's demands for decommissioning as a precondition to talks. In Dublin, Jean Kennedy Smith said she was 'hopeful' that talks would start soon, increasing the speculation that Clinton visualized peace talks beginning in or around the time of his visit.

In addition to these hopeful developments, a few days before the Irish-Americans' visit, Gerry Adams had a secret meeting with Sir Patrick Mayhew in Derry. Republicans also met with British civil servants in Belfast to discuss the planned economic regeneration of the city. This was followed up after the Americans had left Belfast by a second meeting between Adams and Mayhew, at Stormont. Adams was accompanied by Martin McGuinness. The Republican leaders gave the British a detailed outline of how Sinn Fein saw a solution being found to the talks impasse.

On the day this took place (27 July 1995) it was announced that three prisoners on the dirty protest in Whitemoor were being sent back to the Six Counties to complete their sentences. Rumours that the British were planning to restore the 50 per cent remission of sentence which was withdrawn in 1989 also gained currency. To put these gestures in perspective it should be noted that the Irish Government released twelve Republicans from Portlaoise Jail on 29 July, making a total of thirty-two in all since the ceasefire. But the British, who held 1,000 prisoners, did not reciprocate by releasing anyone, either Republican or Loyalist. Moreover, they allowed the Apprentice Boys' March to go ahead in Derry on 12 August – the 25th Anniversary of the Battle of the Bogside.

Because of all this, and despite Bruton's known sympathies, Major's ever-growing 'tilt' towards Unionism badly strained relationships between Dublin and London. Dublin pulled out of a planned summit meeting between the Irish and British Prime Ministers at the eleventh hour. A bland Irish Government statement was issued (on 5 September 1995) saying: 'The Taoiseach, Mr John Bruton TD, has suggested the postponement of tomorrow's Anglo-Irish Summit and the British Prime Minister, Mr John Major, has agreed to this. The purpose for this is to allow some more time to attempt to resolve outstanding differences.'

Two days later at a dinner in Dublin Castle, Bruton made a statement which contained two vital elements:

1. The British and Irish Governments were working towards 'agreement on a target date for all-party talks' on a basis that included 'the maximum range of parties'.
2. The context of this agreement was that the Dail, that is Bruton's Government, and the opposition, Fianna Fail, and the Progressive Democrats, accepted 'that the cessation of violence by the IRA is irreversible'.

However, no agreement was reached with London over the successive months on either the decommissioning issue or that of all-party talks. Once more the initiative switched to Washington. President Clinton was due to visit Ireland at the end of November.

On the afternoon of 28 November, it was announced that a summit meeting would be held later that evening. A hasty dash to London by John Bruton and his officials did result in the issuing of a Joint Communiqué by the Irish and British Prime Ministers. It stated that, after 'intensive' efforts by both governments, a 'twin-track' process was being launched on both the decommissioning issue and that of all-party negotiations by the end of February 1996. Most importantly, the communiqué also announced the setting up of an International Commission under the chairmanship of Senator George Mitchell to 'identify and advise on a suitable and acceptable method for full and verifiable decommissioning'.

When Clinton heard the terms aboard Airforce One as he crossed the Atlantic, he broke open a bottle of champagne. He subsequently received a rapturous reception in both Dublin and Belfast. In the euphoria, few people studied the small print of the Joint Communiqué. Paragraph 3 contained a passage which stated that the matters to be considered in preparatory talks leading up to full-blown all-party negotiations 'could include', not 'would include', an examination of how all those involved could 'properly take account of democratic mandates and principles, including whether and how an elected body could play a part'.

The foregoing was related to a proposal which David Trimble made shortly after becoming the Ulster Unionist Party leader. Trimble was concerned, not to develop north–south links, that is between Belfast and Dublin, but between London and Belfast. As part of this approach, he suggested a new Assembly for the Six Counties.

A new Assembly, dominated by Trimble and his friends, was of course the last thing wanted by either Sinn Fein or the SDLP. However, the principal focus of attention switched to the Mitchell Commission. The International Body worked through Christmas and the New Year before issuing its report on 22 January 1996.

There had been some initial suspicions concerning the Commission in Nationalist circles. One of the members of the three-man body, the Canadian General John de Chastelain, was the son of a former member of MI6. Sinn Fein initially felt that Bruton should have balanced this appointment by getting 'his man' on the Commission. In the event, Chastelain, like the third man, Mr Hari Holkari, a former Finnish Prime Minister, proved to be a model of fair-mindedness and sagacity. Mitchell himself more than vindicated his already outstanding reputation.

His name will forever be remembered in Ireland as a synonym for patience. Initially he took torrents of abuse and vilification from Unionists at the prospects of his being introduced to talks – John Taylor presiding over talks as being like having a Serb presiding over Croatians. The British too betrayed him at a critical juncture: having agreed to install him and abide by his findings, they put up counter-proposals to his which as we shall see led to a breakdown of the IRA's ceasefire. But he remained involved, sequestered in Belfast for months on end, removed from his family, presiding over three different sets of crises in the process. Firstly, he devised the Mitchell principles which proved to be the springboard for the all-party talks process. Then he presided over the talks themselves for long, wearisome months, until the Good Friday Agreement eventuated. Finally, when this too stalled over Unionist insistence on a 'no guns, no government' policy, he again left his family and his business career to return to Belfast and preside over the acrimonious and tedious review process which finally led to the setting up of a short-lived executive.

By way of evaluating the overall situation it should be noted that while the Commission was sitting there was both a spate of punishment beatings throughout the Six Counties, and a return of the gun. An IRA front group styling itself 'Direct Action against Drugs' murdered some five Belfast and Derry Catholics accused in wall posters of being drug dealers. When Mitchell reported he condemned these killings and beatings, but judged that the continuance of the peace process was the most significant factor in the situation. More importantly, he found a formula for ensuring that the decommissioning argument did not bring the process to an end.

Paragraph 26 stated that 'we have concluded that the paramilitary organizations will not decommission any arms prior to all-party negoti-ations'. But the Report also noted that: 'However the decommissoning issue is resolved, that alone will not lead directly to all-party negoti-ations. Much work remains on the many issues involved in the political track. The parties should address those issues with urgency.'

Mitchell put forward the following six principles as a basis for talks. Participants were to commit themselves:

a. To democratic and exclusively peaceful means of resolving political issues;
b. To the total disarmament of all paramilitary organizations;
c. To agree that such disarmament must be verifiable to the satisfaction of an independent commission;
d. To renounce for themselves, and to oppose any effort by others, to use force or threaten to use force, to influence the course of the outcome of all-party negotiations;
e. To agree to abide by the terms of any agreement reached in all-party negotiations and to resort to democratic and exclusively peaceful methods in trying to alter any aspect of that outcome with which they may disagree; and
f. To urge that 'punishment' killings and beatings stop and to take effective steps to prevent such actions.

It appeared that Mitchell had found a way around the decom-missioning roadblock and that the next stop would be all-party talks by the end of November, as envisaged in the Downing Street Joint Communiqué of 28 November 1995. The consensus was that the light of lasting peace had finally dawned on a far horizon, no matter how agonizing the now seemingly inevitable all-party talks might prove to be. Alas, it was not to be. Paragraph 55 of the Mitchell Report (there were fifty-seven substantive paragraphs and five of 'concluding remarks') dealt with the vital issue of policing methods. It recommended that the RUC could 'contribute to the building of trust' by, among other steps, overhauling the use of plastic bullets, recruiting more Catholics into the police force and, significantly, reviewing the situation 'with respect to legally held weapons'.

Major ignored this – to Nationalists, a touch-stone recommendation – as of course he did the core Six Principles itemized above, and seized instead on Paragraph 56, the Report's penultimate substantive paragraph. This stated that 'several oral and written submissions raised the idea of an elected body if it were broadly acceptable within an appropriate mandate'.

Such an Assembly was, at that stage at least, far from being 'broadly acceptable'. But, against the background of the deteriorating situation outlined above, Major in effect rejected Mitchell's findings on decommissioning, and opted instead to pursue the question of an elected Assembly. This was to have a 'weighted majority' and would amount in practice to nothing more than a talking shop, going over ground already covered by the Republic's Peace and Reconciliation Forum and to even less effect because Sinn Fein were excluded. One of the most extraordinary aspects of Major's decision was that he and Bruton had a thirty-five-minute phone conversation the previous evening without Bruton being told what Major was planning. As soon as Major had finished speaking, John Hume rose to accuse the British Prime Minister of putting at risk the lives of women and children in Northern Ireland. However, the British immediately launched a prearranged publicity campaign built around the slogans which the Junior Minister for Northern Ireland, Michael Ancram, was sent to Washington to promulgate: 'Who can be afraid of elections? Who can be afraid of democracy?'

The fact that the Assembly would have almost no powers was not mentioned, nor was the fact that the 'weighted majority' principle would hit not only the Nationalists, but the emerging small Unionist groupings based on the Loyalist paramilitaries, whom the Ulster Unionist Party and the Paisleyites were equally anxious to stifle at birth. Instead the British and the Unionists argued (falsely as events proved) that such an Assembly would provide a forum for opening all-party talks.

Irish-American reaction was predictably hostile, as was that of the American media. Gerry Adams was quick to capitalize both on this reaction and on Clinton's remarkable empathy with the Irish issue.

After a lunch with Adams the White House issued a statement on 1 February 1996 saying that, during the meal:

> Mr Lake expressed his gratitude and appreciation to Senator George Mitchell and his colleagues and recommendations to advance the peace process. He found the Report's suggestions on the decommissioning issue helpful and believes other ideas should be urgently discussed in the political track of the twin-track process.

The President underscored the need for rapid progress to all-party talks. He encouraged all parties to remain committed to the search for peace and determined in its pursuit. Finally, the President discussed his visit to the United Kingdom and Ireland and the overwhelming support of the people to move beyond the violence and hatred of the past.

Decoded, the White House statement not only endorsed the Mitchell approach, but also rebuked Major for not 'urgently' discussing 'other ideas' with a view to meeting 'the need for rapid progress to all-party talks'. Major of course, along with the Dublin and Washington leaders, had co-sponsored Mitchell in appointing him to try to find a way out of the decommissioning bog. However, the IRA had a more severe form of rebuke than Clinton's in mind. Major's dithering incensed the militants: 'The only thing the Brits understand is the bomb and the bullet. We should go back to bombing London', was a commonly heard line of argument.

Visiting Belfast in mid-January, I found little enthusiasm for the peace process but a great deal of concern over the prisoner issue and a wide range of other grievances. These were principally the heavy presence of plain-clothes security-force operatives in Nationalist areas; the lack of progress on reforming the RUC; and, most tellingly in the decommissioning context, the fact that the British were building a huge new fortification in the Donegal Road area – the heartland of Republican West Belfast. Enjoining decommissioning on the IRA while building up its own military strength was seen as provocative and demanding of a response.

The IRA had attempted to learn the lessons of the 1975/6 ceasefire, which was used by the British to infiltrate the organization to such an extent that the IRA came close to being crushed. Secrecy was maintained, as to a degree was training, intelligence gathering and targeting. Contingency plans were also set in motion to mount a major bombing campaign in England should the political initiative break down. Senior IRA activists were warned at a gathering held at Fanad, Co. Donegal, in October 1995, that such a campaign was a possibility. Possibility became certainty on 9 February 1996. It would probably have done so months earlier had Clinton not been visiting Belfast.

A huge bomb was made up in a cowshed near the South Armagh/ Monaghan border. It was a literally devastating example of the fallacy of the arms decommissioning argument and entirely bore out the assessment that the decommissioning was a political, not a military, one. The bomb was made from ammonium nitrate fertilizer ground down in a barley crusher. Icing sugar was added and something approaching three tons of the lethal mixture was packed into a car transporter which was taken to England on a car ferry. It was driven to London's Canary Wharf and detonated by a timer, causing an estimated £150 million worth of damage to the City of London. The target area had been deliberately chosen. Not only did it contain financial centres such as banks, but it was also a communications hub containing some of the biggest newspapers in England, the *Mirror* and the *Telegraph*, and a number of advertising and TV companies. The bomb cost the lives of the owner of a newsagent shop Inam Bashir, and his assistant, John Jefferies, who had been warned by a policeman to clear out, but instead decided to stay back and close up the shop before leaving. It was a miracle that the bomb, which went off at 7 p.m., did not claim more lives, but it certainly served its purpose of claiming attention.

Gerry Adams phoned the White House before it went off to say that he had just been given some 'disturbing news' and would phone back. About the only person in Washington who did not feel that contact should be broken off with Sinn Fein was Clinton himself. He evaluated the bombing for what it was, a ruthlessly efficient method of cutting through the logjam of decommissioning and getting talks started. The IRA statement issued after the blast read as follows:

It is with great reluctance that the leadership of Oglaigh na hEireann announces that the complete cessation of military operations will end at 6 p.m. on 9 February, this evening. As we stated on 31 August 1994, the basis for the cessation was to enhance the democratic peace process and to underline our definitive commitment to its success. We also made it clear that we believed that an opportunity to create a just and lasting settlement had been created.

The cessation presented a historic challenge for everyone and Oglaigh na hEireann commends the leadership of Nationalist Ireland at home and abroad. They rose to the challenge.

The British Prime Minister did not. Instead of embracing the peace process the British Government acted in bad faith, with Mr Major and the Unionist leaders squandering this unprecedented opportunity to resolve the conflict.

Time and time again over the last eighteen months selfish party political and sectional interests in the London Parliament have been placed before the rights of the people of Ireland.

We take this opportunity to reiterate our total commitment to our Republican objectives. The resolution of the conflict in our country demands justice. It demands inclusive negotiated settlement. This is not possible unless and until the British Government faces up to its responsibilities. The blame for the failure thus far of the Irish peace process lies squarely with John Major and his Government.

A few days later another bomb went off in London, on a bus at Aldwych. It killed the IRA man who was carrying it, Edward O'Brien, from Gorey, Co. Wexford. His parents had been unaware that he was in the IRA. Some prominent Republicans attended the funeral, including Martin McGuinness's brother, William. Later that year another huge bomb went off at Manchester on 15 June. It too caused six-figure damage but no loss of life.

However, it soon became apparent that the intelligence gathering on both sides of the border had been assisted by the ceasefire. In the Republic, acting on information, Gardai closed down the IRA's principal bomb-making facility at Conaslee, Co. Laois. This in turn led to further arrests, and in July and September of 1996, the British police virtually cut the head off the IRA spear. Two teams of top IRA operators were arrested in London. In the second swoop, on 23 September, an unarmed volunteer, Diarmuid O'Neill, was shot dead in his London hotel room which had been pumped full of CS gas. Those arrested separately, as part of the operation, included Gerald Hanratty and John Crawley, a former US Marine. They were picked up before their plan to destroy the generating stations of south-eastern England could be put into effect.

However, much life was lost elsewhere. One of the most fatuous utterances of the entire course of the troubles was heard in the particularly unsettled month of July 1996, when Sir Patrick Mayhew told an interviewer to: 'Cheer up. No one has been killed yet.' In fact, in the absence of political movement after the IRA ceasefire of 31 August 1994 the litany of death and destruction (for the period from the ceasefire to the spring of the year 2000) was far worse than that contained in the list I drew up for a roughly similar period of time seventy years earlier (Chapter 2).

To it one must add the huge financial cost of incidents such as the Canary Wharf and Manchester bombings, the Drumcree stand-offs, the rioting following the release of Lee Clegg, and the suffering caused by incidents such as punishment beatings and the intimidation of families from their homes. The sufferings of families were not confined to incidents which occurred within the timespan covered by the chronology. Both as this was being written, and during a lengthy part of 1999, the families of the 'disappeared' also underwent severe trauma. The disappeared were those whom the IRA abducted, shot and secretly buried, for various offences against the movement. One particularly ghastly example was that of Mrs Jean McConville, the mother of ten children. Her 'crime', in the early days of the movement before discipline improved, was to try to comfort a dying British soldier whom the IRA had ambushed. In 1999, as part of the peace process the IRA gave information concerning the whereabouts of the graves of some of the victims. However, after fifty days of digging by Gardai, the search for six of the bodies, including that of Mrs McConville, was abandoned. After further negotiations, involving Fr Alex Reid, new information was provided by the IRA and digging resumed on 2 May 2000 but it too found nothing. The sufferings of the McConville family, and those of the relations of the other victims during the raising and dashing of hopes caused by the fruitless excavations can better be imagined than described.

All add to a powerful, but conflicting message that is in part a scream for peace and in part also the reason why the trust needed to find it by building on the IRA ceasefires has proved so difficult to obtain.

CHRONOLOGY OF DEATHS[*]

31 August 1994. Seran McDermott (37), Catholic.
Killed by: claimed by cover group Ulster Freedom Fighters (UFF), but believed to have been carried out by Ulster Defence Association (UDA).

1 September 1994. John O'Hanson (32), Catholic.
Killed by: IRA.

10 November 1994. Frank Kerr (54), Catholic.
Killed by: IRA.

22 December 1994. Noel Lyness (47), Catholic.
Thought to be a Loyalist sectarian killing.

2 March 1995. James Seymour (55), Protestant.
Killed by: IRA.

28 April 1995. Michael Mooney (34), Catholic.
Killed by: IRA.

5 September 1995. Tony Kane (29), Catholic.
Killed by: IRA.

28 September 1995. William Elliott (31), Protestant.
Killed by: Red Hand Commandos (RHC)

27 November 1995. Norman Harley (46), Catholic.
Thought to have been an unclaimed sectarian murder.

8 December 1995. Paul Devine (35), Catholic.
Killed by: IRA.

18 December 1995. Francis Collins, Catholic.
Killed by: Provisional IRA cover group, Direct Action against Drugs (DAAD).

19 December 1995. Chris Johnson (38), Catholic.
Killed by: DAAD.

27 December 1995. Martin McCrory (30), Catholic.
Killed by: DAAD.

2 January 1996. Ian Lyons (31), Catholic.
Killed by: DAAD.

---

[*] A more detailed chronology, giving the circumstances of deaths and other information is provided by Malcolm Sutton on the CAIN Web Service.

30 January 1996. Gino Gallagher (33), Catholic.
Killed by: Irish National Liberation Army (INLA).

9 February 1996. John Jefferies (31).
Killed by: IRA.

9 February 1996. Inam Bashir (29).
Killed by: IRA.

18 February 1996. Edward O'Brien (21), Catholic.
Killed by: Own bomb.

5 March 1996. John Fennell (40), Catholic.
Killed by: INLA.

15 March 1996. Barbara McAlorum (9), Catholic.
Killed by: INLA.

21 March 1996. Thomas Sheppard (41), Protestant.
Killed by: UVF.

25 May 1996. Dessie McCleery (37), Catholic.
Killed by: INLA.

7 June 1996. Gerard McCabe (52).
Killed by: IRA.

9 June 1996. Francis Shannon (21), Catholic.
Killed by: INLA.

8 July 1996. Michal McGoldrick (31), Catholic.
Killed by: UVF.

13 July 1996. Dermot McShane (35), Catholic.
Killed by: British Army.

3 September 1996. Hugh Torney (42), Catholic.
Killed by: INLA.

16 September 1996. John Devlin (30), Catholic.
Killed by: DAAD.

23 September 1996. Diarmuid O'Neill (27), Catholic.
Killed by: British police.

11 October 1996. James Bradell (43).
Killed by: IRA.

29 October 1996. Thomas Stewart (32), Protestant.
Loyalist, sectarian killing, unclaimed.

10 January 1998. Terry Enright (28), Catholic.

Killed by: LVF.

18 January 1998. Fergal McCusker (28), Catholic.
Killed by: LVF.

19 January 1998. Jim Guiney (38), Protestant.
Killed by: INLA.

19 January 1998. Larry Brennan (51), Catholic.
Killed by: UDA.

21 January 1998. Benedict Hughes (55), Catholic.
Killed by: UDA.

23 January 1998. Liam Conway (39), Catholic.
Killed by: LVF.

24 January 1998. John McColgan (33), Catholic.
Killed by: LVF.

9 February 1998. Brendan Cambell (30), Catholic.
Killed by: DAAD.

10 February 1998. Robert Dougan (38), Protestant.
Killed by: IRA.

17 February 1998. Kevin Conway (30), Catholic.
Loyalist sectarian killing, unclaimed.

3 March 1998. Damian Traynor (26), Catholic.
Killed by: LVF.

3 March 1998. Philip Allen (34), Protestant.
Killed by: LVF.

15 March 1998. David Keys (26), Protestant.
Killed by: LVF.

27 March 1998. Cyril Stewart (52), Protestant.
Killed by: INLA.

8 April 1998. Trevor Deeny (34), Protestant.
Killed by: INLA.

21 April 1998. Adrian Lamph (29), Catholic.
Killed by: LVF.

25 April 1998. Ciaran Heffron (22), Catholic.
Killed by: LVF.

1 May 1998. Ronan Maclochlain (28), Catholic.
Killed by: Garda Siochana.

3 July 1998. William Paul (49), Protestant.
Killed by: Loyalists, unclaimed.

12 July 1998. Three Quinn brothers, Richard (11), Mark (10) and
Jason (9).
Killed by: Loyalist petrol bomb attack on their home. Thought to
be UVF.

19 July 1998. Andrew Kearney (33), Catholic.
Killed by: Unclaimed, but thought to be internal IRA feud.

15 August 1998. Omagh bomb explosion.
James Barker (12), Fernando Blasco Bacelga (12), Geraldine Breslin
(43), Catholic, Deborah Cartwright (20), Protestant, Gareth Conway
(18), Catholic, Breda Devine (1), Catholic, Oran Doherty (8), nfNI,
Adrian Gallagher (21), Catholic, Esther Gibson (36), Protestant,
Mary Grimes (65), Catholic, Olive Hawkes (60), Protestant, Julia
Hughes (21), Protestant, Brenda Logue (17), Catholic, Anne
McCombe (48), Protestant, Brian McCrory (54), Catholic, Samantha
McFarland (17), Protestant, Sean McGrath (61), Catholic, Sean
McLaughlin (12), nfNI, Jolene Marlow (17), Catholic, Avril Mon-
aghan (30), Catholic, Maura Monaghan (1), Catholic, Alan Radford
(16), Protestant, Rocia Abad Ramos (23), nfNI, Elizabeth Rushe
(57), Catholic, Veda Short (56), Protestant, Philómena Skelton (49),
Catholic, Fred White (60), Protestant, Brian White (26), Protestant,
Lorraine Wilson (15), Protestant.
Killed by: Real Irish Republic Army (rIRA).

7 September 1998. Francis O'Reilly (30), Catholic.
Killed by: Red Hand Defenders (RHD).

2 November 1998. Brian Service (35), Catholic.
Killed by: RHD.

27 January 1999. Eamon Collins (44), Catholic.
Killed by: Unclaimed. Thought to be Provisional IRA.

15 March 1999. Rosemary Nelson (40), Catholic.
Killed by: RHD.

16 March 1999. Frankie Curry (45), Protestant.
Killed by: Unclaimed. Thought to be internal UVF feud.

9 May 1999. Brendan 'Speedy' Fegan (24), Catholic?
Killed by: Unclaimed, possibly Republican/drug-related.

5 June 1999. Elizabeth O'Neill (59), Protestant.

Killed by: Unclaimed.

13 June 1999. Paul Anthony Downey (37), Catholic.
Killed by: Unclaimed, possibly Republican/drug-related.

30 July 1999. Charles Bennett (22), Catholic.
Killed by: unclaimed, thought to be IRA.

In considering the foregoing one should also bear in mind the fact that the period saw the emergence of two highly dangerous Republican splinter groups and an equally lethal Loyalist offshoot of the UVF, which soon became involved in bloody feuding.

SPLINTER GROUPS:

Republicans

On 14 July 1996, the detonation of a 1200lb car bomb which destroyed the Killyhevlin Hotel near Enniskillen, Co. Fermanagh, announced that the Continuity IRA had come into being. The organization continued to let off bombs during the period under review, but intensive surveillance from the Gardai in particular resulted in several arrests which severely hampered the new grouping. The Provisional IRA tended to disparage its efforts and membership, and claimed that it did not have either number or calibre of membership to develop into a serious force. However, exactly the same thing was said about the Provisional movement itself when, with Ruairi O'Bradaigh as one of its principal leaders, it split from the then 'official' movement in 1970.

The emergence of the 'Real IRA' was a more serious matter. Again, this was a grouping of Republicans opposed to the ceasefire. Its political wing was known as the 32 County Sovereignty Committee which was formally launched in Dublin on 7 December 1997. A leading member of the Committee told me that the movement looked to the leadership of Michael McKevitt, a former leading Provisional, and, in the opinion of my informant, 'another Michael Collins'. McKevitt and his partner, Bernadette Sands, a sister of Bobby Sands, were particularly active in the South Armagh/Louth area, where they attracted a following. The settled belief of the 32 County Sovereignty Committee, according to their spokesman, was that the British had no right to have any say in an Irish settlement, that: 'If they stood aside, Republicans could easily come to an agreement with the Unionists. The Unionists would not fight seriously. Unionists could be swept aside by one Irish Infantry charge, as Parnell used to say.'

However, the key component of the Real IRA/32 County Sovereignty Committee doctrine concerned the Good Friday Agreement. At the time we spoke, there was considerable euphoria in the air, and election results and the general mood of the country pointed towards the Agreement being a success. However, my informant brushed the euphoria aside contemptuously: 'No way will it work. Gerry will fail, just as Rory (Ruairi O'Bradaigh) failed. The Unionists will never agree to anything when it comes to the crunch, and the British will never force them to. So there's only one way forward – physical force.'

It appeared that the Real IRA's 'way forward' was finally checked after a number of shootings and bombings when the Omagh bomb occurred on 15 August 1998. In the horror at the outrage – one of the victims was a pregnant woman carrying twins, others included visiting Spanish schoolchildren – both the Real IRA and the INLA declared ceasefires. The INLA's internal feuding had been causing nearly as much bloodshed as had its war on the security forces.

A causative factor in bringing about the cessations was a series of visits which Provisional IRA representatives paid to their former colleagues, warning them to desist. The warning was made public on 31 August, ironically the anniversary of the Provisionals' ceasefire, when an IRA spokesman was quoted in *An Phoblacht* saying that 'the Real IRA should disband and they should do so sooner rather than later'.

Both the British and Irish Governments passed tough legislation to deal with all groups not on ceasefire. Apart from the usual measures, such as restricting suspects' rights to silence, the Irish Government took the unusual step of warning that in future the land or property on which bomb-making equipment, weaponry and so on were discovered would be forfeit to the state. The Gardai took a hard line. At Ashford, Co. Wicklow, Ronan MacLochlain, a member of the Real IRA, was fatally wounded in controversial circumstances by Gardai who had advance notice of a robbery. It seemed that the pressure and the revulsion caused by Omagh had administered the coup de grâce to the Real IRA when the organization issued a statement on 29 August saying that it believed that it would be futile to continue its campaign 'in the circumstances of Omagh and the Mitchell [Good Friday] Agreement'. Provisional IRA sources continue to describe the Real IRA as being largely composed of drifters and malcontents who had been in not only the Provisionals but practically every other paramilitary organization around. Nevertheless, the fact that the Good Friday Agreement collapsed exactly as the 32 County Sovereignty Committee spokesperson quoted above said it would, has undoubtedly played into the hands of the organization. In one swoop on a training session in Stamullen, Co. Louth, the Gardai found that the organization was attracting not merely 'drifters' but recruits as young as fourteen years of age.

Loyalists

While at the time of writing the great question hanging over events is 'What will the provos do?', it is in fact the activities of the Loyalist paramilitaries which are causing the most immediate anxiety. There is a major feud going on within the now divided UVF which is causing fears that the UDA may become involved and that it may overspill to a familiar resumption of the killing of Catholics and almost certain Provisional reaction. The basis for the feuding is two-pronged: the peace process and drug money. The division in the UVF dates back to 1996 when Billy Wright, who opposed the peace process on the grounds that it was a sell-out to Dublin, broke from the Belfast-led UVF and founded his own, Portadown-based, Loyalist Volunteer Force whose first bombs appear to have gone off on 7 March 1997.

The Belfast UVF attempted to disband the new grouping and ordered Wright to leave the country on pain of death. Amongst those who came to his assistance was the prominent member of Ian Paisley's Democratic Unionist Party, the Rev. William McCrea, who appeared on a public platform with Wright (on 4 September 1996) without any apparent objection from Paisley. Wright, nicknamed King Rat, had the reputation of having killed more Catholics than anyone else, with the possible exception of 'The Jackal', Robin Jackson, who lived in nearby Lurgan. Prior to the ceasefires both men were thought to be working in collusion with the security forces, who employed them, on the principle that the enemy of my enemy is my friend. Jackson, who was dying of cancer, presented no threat to the peace process, but Wright, whose popularity in Loyalist circles, was so great that he was able to successfully defy the Belfast UVF leadership, most assuredly did.

Although he was credited with some thirty killings personally, and being responsible for many more, Wright, a born again Christian who saw himself as a soldier defending 'Ulster', was never picked up during the course of the troubles. However, he fetched up in Long Kesh on a relatively minor charge: issuing death threats, as opposed to actually dealing death, on 25 April 1997. By the end of the year he was dead, shot in the prison compound by members of the INLA who, by an inexplicable series of breaches of prison security, shared a wing with the notorious Loyalist, and were apparently able to proceed unimpeded through prison buildings and across roofs, all under the eyes of surveillance cameras, and a suspiciously unmanned watchtower, to carry out the murder. The wire separating the roofs had been cut previously, again under the eye of a surveillance camera and on a floodlit roof.

For a time after his killing (on 27 December 1997) the feud between the two wings of the UVF attracted less public attention than did the emergence of a new Loyalist grouping in Portadown called the Red Hand Defenders, whose first acknowledged victim died in a Portadown bomb explosion on 6 October 1998. Like much of the Loyalist paramilitary manifestation, this group also sought to give itself a religious patina. It took its text from Deuteronomy, Chapter 7, verse 2:* 'And the Lord thy God shall have delivered them to thee: thou shalt utterly destroy them. Thou shalt make no league with them, nor show mercy to them . . . neither shalt thou make marriages with them.'

The contemporary variant of this biblical injunction involved making pipe-bomb attacks on the latter day Canaanites, the Catholics of Northern Ireland, a number of whom went to their maker before their time courtesy of the Old Testament and Portadown Loyalism. The most prominent victim claimed by the Defenders was Rosemary Nelson, the Lurgan solicitor who had acted for the Garvaghy Road Residents Association and frequently complained about being threatened by the RUC. Ms Nelson was blown up by a bomb placed under her car on 15 March 1999. Since then there have been repeated allegations of RUC complicity in her death, but, ironically on the first anniversary of her murder, the British Government rejected a petition bearing over 100,000 signatures for a public inquiry into her death, and opted instead for a continuation of an inquiry conducted by a British police officer.

The Orange Volunteers first claimed bomb explosion occurred on 17 December 1998. Some observers feared that the organization might one day turn into the most dangerous of the loyalist groupings, because it seemingly originated during the peace process, on the heels of an appeal circulated secretly within the Orange Order for volunteers of particular merit from each Lodge. However, on 20 January 1999, David Ervine of the Progressive Unionist Party, which has links with the UVF, said on BBC Radio Ulster that the organization was nothing

---

* Red Hand Defenders statement in author's possession.

but an offshoot of the Loyalist Volunteer Force, and composed mainly of fundamentalist Protestants and drug dealers.

Perhaps the oddest grouping of all to emerge during this period was Caleb which, courtesy of the Internet, drew its ideological sustenance from the Ku Klux Klan, the Black Israelites, the fascist movement Combat Eighteen, called after Hitler's birthday (18 April 1889), and, from the Muslim world, the doctrine of the *jihad* or holy war. Mercifully, however, to the time of writing at least, Caleb has not shown itself capable of mounting either a holy or an unholy war. The war which has manifested itself, however, is the continuing struggle between the two wings of the UVF, the Loyalist Volunteer Force and the Belfast-led UVF. Apart from being a vicious struggle in itself, this feud is showing signs of involving the third major Loyalist grouping, the UDA, in the bloodletting.

Since the Good Friday Agreement resulted in the release of some very dangerous men on both sides of the Orange/Green divide, a combination of new alignments and old score settling has taken place. Normally the UDA would remain aloof from whatever was going on in the UVF and vice-versa, but since the Good Friday releases one of the most terrifying figures in the UDA has developed a relationship with the LVF. In January and February 2000, a series of very brutal murders occurred in Portadown and Tandragee as a result of the UVF split.

First, in January, the LVF shot dead the Portadown UVF leader, Richard Jameson. Then, in February, two Tandragee teenagers, Andrew Robb and David McIlwaine, both of whom were thought to have links with the LVF, were murdered in barbaric circumstances. Knives were used in a manner better imagined than described. Their parents seemed to have been in something of the same situation as those of Edward O'Brien, whose son, the young IRA volunteer accidentally killed in a bomb blast on a London bus, was in the IRA without their knowing it. There were repeated denials from the families of the two young men's involvement in any paramilitary activity. But, and this was a particularly worrying development for anyone concerned with reading the signs for the peace process, amongst those who turned up at the funeral were not only members of the LVF, but also some of the most feared figures in the Loyalist paramilitary world, known leaders of the most militant section of the UDA.

It is said that at the heart of the feud lies a combination of a turf war and drug money, between Wright's former supporters, known as the Rat Pack, and the UVF. Whatever the real motivations for the killings and threats of killings, the possibility of a renewed major feud involving elements of the UDA and the Rat Pack at the time of writing is not remote. The spillover from such a gang war into killing IRA men and thus triggering a civil war, is a dangerous but unfortunately not entirely remote possibility either.

GOOD FRIDAY AGREEMENT

The final stretch of the road to the Good Friday Agreement, as it is known to Nationalist Ireland (the Unionists and the British refer to it as the Belfast Agreement, a commentary in itself on differing perceptions), began to be laid down soon after the election on 10 June 1996. Initially it made very little progress. Although Sinn Fein had recorded the most significant vote of the election (15.5 per cent) the absence of an IRA ceasefire meant that the party was excluded from the talks. The IRA bomb which destroyed Manchester's Arndale Centre five days later underscored the futility of attempting to get peace in Northern Ireland without the IRA's representatives being involved. To further emphasize the intractability of the physical force tradition in Ireland, the Continuity IRA bomb exploded the following month, demolishing the Killyhevlin Hotel.

Events in London dictated the pace of events in Belfast until the following summer. In Ireland, the IRA, that is the Provisionals, did little beyond letting off a couple of bombs at the British Army headquarters in Thiepbal Barracks, Lisburn, Co. Antrim, on 7 October 1996, which were the IRA's first attack against security forces in the North since the 31 August ceasefire. The melancholy distinction of being the last British soldier to be killed in this phase of the troubles fell to Stephen Restorick, a lance bombardier who was talking to a woman in a car at an army checkpoint in Bessbrook, Co. Armagh, when he was shot dead by an IRA sniper on 12 February 1997.

The multi-party talks process sputtered on at Stormont, but the absence of Sinn Fein in Belfast and the growing presence of New Labour on London's political horizon made the proceedings increasingly irrelevant. The talks were finally adjourned on 5 March 1997 to allow the parties to contest the election scheduled for 1 May. The IRA in the interim registered its presence by disrupting British motorways with phoned bomb threats, and causing the Aintree Grand National to be postponed by the same means. But events were quickening.

I was travelling in the United Kingdom during the election campaign, and it was quite obvious that Britain wanted a change. Ireland was part of that change. Tony Blair's huge majority, greater than the total of Conservative MPs sitting opposite him at Westminster, coupled with his Irish background, generated a mood of near euphoria in Dublin, although there was some apprehension in Nationalist circles because the popular Kevin McNamara had been supplanted as Labour Party spokesperson by Mo Mowlam. As we saw, McNamara had been removed at the behest of the Unionists: after the Maastricht Treaty vote, which only passed because the Unionists supported John Major, the Labour Party under John Smith arrived at an understanding with the Unionists under James Molyneaux, the then Unionist Leader, that in a similar tight situation the Unionists would vote Labour. The Unionists' glee at getting rid of the hated 'Green' McNamara would later turn to an even greater hatred of Mowlam, but this lay in the future.

The departure of the Tories made for a sea change in Anglo-Irish relations. An Irish Government spokesperson told me, after attending a briefing on behalf of the new administration. 'If they deliver on what they say they'll deliver on, it will be revolutionary.' The early indications were that Labour did intend to deliver. Immediately on being elected, Blair sanctioned contact between British officials and Sinn Fein. These were temporarily suspended a month later when, on 16 June, the IRA shot dead two members of the RUC in Lurgan, Co. Armagh. However, the peace process continued, despite serious violence which followed the forcing through of the Orange march to the Garvaghy Road early in July.

As a result of the Blairite thaw Gerry Adams and Martin McGuinness had an important meeting with the IRA. Following it, the Provisionals announced that its ceasefire was being restored on 20 July. The following month, on 26 August, the Independent International Commission on Decommissioning was set up to oversee the decommissioning of all paramilitary weapons. The Commission was headed by General John de Chastelain, an alert, energetic figure whom the IRA eventually came to trust despite their initial suspicions of the fact that his mother had worked for MI6. In a set of choreographed moves, Mo Mowlam announced that the ceasefire provided a basis for Sinn Fein entering the multi-party talks and Sinn Fein duly signed up to the Mitchell principles and entered the multi-party talks at Stormont on 9 September. The Ulster Unionist Party (UUP) joined the talks as did the smaller Loyalist political parties, notably the Progressive Unionist Party, led by Billy Hutchinson and David Ervine. Ian Paisley's party boycotted the talks because of Sinn Fein's presence, as did the United Kingdom Unionist Party, led by Robert McCartney. A few weeks into the talks the choreography was completed when, on 13 October, Gerry Adams and Martin McGuinness met Tony Blair for the first time.

The choreography was brutally interrupted (on 27 December 1997) when members of the INLA shot and killed Billy Wright, the Loyalist leader, in Long Kesh, while he was being driven in a prison van to the visiting block. Later Billy Wright's father, David, was to provide disturbing evidence to confirm the widespread suspicions at the time that Wright was murdered with official connivance. But the immediate aftermath was an outbreak of sectarian murder which claimed the lives of several Catholics. The murder also helped to induce Loyalist prisoners to withdraw their support for the peace process. This was a serious setback as, in the Loyalist world, prisoners are as important as they are in the Republican one.

However, in a dramatic and courageous move, Mo Mowlam went into the prison and succeeded in persuading the prisoners to withdraw their opposition. For a time the talks followed an erratic course. Eventually, in an effort to induce momentum into the process, the venue was switched from Stormont in Belfast to Lancaster House in London on 26 January 1998. Immediately, another hitch developed because the Ulster Democratic Party (UDP), the political wing of the UDA and its sister organization, the Ulster Freedom Fighters (UFF), was expelled, because of the UFF's involvement in the killings of Catholics which followed the Wright murder. Nevertheless the removal from Belfast, and the nooks and crannies of the new venue, purpose-built for just such encounters, provided a fruitful context within which new contact, and confidence, flowered. Discussions took place between people who either would not, or could not, be seen in each other's company in Northern Ireland. A formula was found to readmit the UDP to the talks, on 23 February. However, this initiative almost immediately lost much of its significance when Sinn Fein was expelled from the talks because of IRA involvement in two killings: one, that of Brendan Campbell, carried out by DAAD, the other that of Robert Dougan, a member of the UDA.

But again the necessity of producing a prince if Hamlet were to be staged dictated Sinn Fein's return. Following another meeting between

Tony Blair and Gerry Adams, Sinn Fein rejoined the talks on 23 March and, a few days later, George Mitchell announced a seemingly impossible deadline of 9 April for the securing of an agreement. Nobody involved with the talks thought the deadline would be met. Gritty, exhausting, line-by-line examinations of a tide of documents that flowed across the participants' desks were carried out against a background of acrimony and suspicion. A Sinn Fein negotiator told me that his party returned a draft agreement to George Mitchell with seventy-seven amendments. And yet, somehow, agreement was ultimately reached in the small hours of Good Friday morning.

The Agreement is too long to reproduce in full; however an edited version of it in Annex B will enable readers to grasp the extent of what was lost when the power-sharing Assembly, and the cross-border and Anglo-Irish institutions for which it provided, were suspended, after flickering into brief but fruitful life nearly two years later. Suffice it to say here that it provided for a new vision of Irishness and of relationships both within Ireland and between Ireland and England. In short, it was the most significant treaty to be signed between Irishmen and Englishmen since the Anglo-Irish Treaty of 1921.

After the document was signed, Father Gerry Reynolds, a colleague of Father Reid's, who like him had given enormous service to the peace process, described the Agreement to me as being: 'Like a baby being born. Like with a baby, there is blood and torn tissues, but both will heal, and the baby will grow.' It was a wonderfully appropriate image. The only problem was that many on the Unionist side regarded the baby as a bastard. A prominent Ulster Unionist negotiator, Jeffrey Donaldson, a Westminster MP, objected to Sinn Fein's being admitted to government without decommissioning and stormed out of Stormont Castle without signing the Agreement.

But, for the moment, at least on the Nationalist side, all was euphoria. For Seamus Mallon and Mark Durkan of the SDLP there were congratulations for developing the 'parallel consent' doctrine. This meant in effect that neither side, Green or Orange could have a veto over the other's proposals unless a majority on either side agreed to the proposal. It looked on the face of it as though the Nationalists had in effect secured a Nationalist veto to replace, or at least match, the existing Unionists' veto. In fact, this provision was to prove the final nail in the coffin of the Agreement. Once David Trimble and his party pulled out, the ordinary democratic procedure of attempting to form a government based on the other parties – and perhaps some of those in Trimble's who supported the Agreement – could not be attempted.

On the Sinn Fein side, during the talks, Martin McGuinness was regarded as being the most relaxed. Martin Ferris as being 'very polite, but very tough'. Gerry Adams was tense, inclined to query detail. Even after documents were rewritten, he would say, 'I'm worried about this.' He was always particularly worried about securing recognition of the Irish language. When a Dublin civil servant complained that the Sinn Feiners were being unduly cautious, Gerry Kelly, once one of the Provisionals' most high profile members, explained patiently: 'You have to remember that paramilitaries are naturally suspicious.' The suspicions led to something in the order of thirty drafts of every single proposal being prepared before agreement was reached. The suspicions were not without foundation. TV viewers will probably have seen for themselves the pictures of Adams and McGuinness walking together, outside Stormont, during breaks in the negotiations. They were not doing this merely for fresh air. They knew that their rooms were bugged.

This background helps to explain why Sinn Fein were the more 'sticky' of the negotiators, more so even than the Unionists. Sometimes Monica McWilliams, and the members of the Women's Coalition, a cross-party grouping which came into politics to further women's issues, acted as brokers between Sinn Fein, the Unionists and the other parties. There were some issues which could not be brokered away. Outside the talks there were forces in the Republican community who would cheerfully have shot Adams for espousing the route of 'betrayal': recognizing the border, the British presence and, by accepting the principle of consent, presenting the Unionists with a gilt-edged opportunity to manipulate this into a restoration of their veto.

But, quite apart from any question of physical dangers, Sinn Fein had a deep psychological aversion to the notion of entering Stormont, and were only argued out of their suspicions of an Assembly in which, despite the checks and the balances, the Unionists would hold a majority by repeated small hours phone calls from Bill Clinton. Tony Blair performed a similar function for David Trimble. 'He let him rant and rave, and then politely took him through the hoops' was one participant's assessment. John Hume, who both philosophically and in terms of statesmanship, was an outstanding figure throughout the entire process, did not concern himself with detail but made interminable phone calls to Washington to ensure that figures like Chris Dodds and Ted Kennedy were kept on side.

The representatives of the fringe Loyalist parties, Billy Hutchinson of the PUP, and Davy Adams of the UDP, showed themselves to be the most flexible of the negotiators, and impressed the Dublin team for whom the talks were something of a baptism of fire in Northern attitudes. One official told me, 'the atmosphere was incredible. Everyone was forty-eight hours without sleep.' Bairbre de brun, a Sinn Fein negotiator, was observed to be 'nearly crying' with the tension. Liz O'Donnell, the Junior Minister for Foreign Affairs, whose good looks made her a particular favourite with the Republican inmates of Long Kesh whenever she came on television, was literally caught napping on camera in the closing stages of the negotiations.

At one stage, Paisley, who boycotted the talks – but subsequently accepted their benefits, i.e. well-paid seats in the Assembly – held a demonstration in the grounds of Stormont to protest at what was taking place, and over a hundred Red Hand Commandos, who supported the Billy Hutchinson/David Ervine participation, turned up to barrack him. Afterwards they continued into the building to see what was going on. Looking at the denimed horde of tattooed, shaven-headed, earringed toughies, mingling with ex-Provisionals, members of the UDA and UVF, a member of Dublin's legal team commented dazedly: 'There's more fucking murderers here in Stormont to the square inch than anywhere else in the world, including Death Row in San Quentin.' When it was all over, the parties assembled and, for the benefit of the camera, gave their assent to the agreement. The veteran Republican, Joe Cahill, stood behind Gerry Adams to show his appreciation and approval. It all appeared incredibly hopeful.

Sinn Fein were about to be in government. The war was over. But in the euphoria, no one thought to weigh up the significance of some of the incidents which seemed relatively insignificant at the time, but assumed a greater importance later. First, the fact that Trimble delivered a statement to the cameras immediately after the Agreement signing, to the effect that the Union was safe, and then pointedly left before Gerry Adams spoke. Then, the differences between Sinn Fein and the other Nationalist delegations; that between the SDLP and Sinn Fein was obvious, stemming from rivalry on the ground for the Six County Nationalist vote, but there were also more subtle differences in evaluation between Dublin and Sinn Fein. One Dubliner remarked on how well the Provos seemed to get on with Tim Dalton, the Secretary of the Irish Department of Justice, the man once most charged with suppressing the Provisional IRA. However, this was more due to

Sinn Fein politeness than political affinity. The Dublin civil servants felt, with justification, that they had been of considerable help to the Nationalist side, both to the SDLP and Sinn Fein, with advice and research back-up, and thus had established a rapport with Sinn Fein. But this was not so highly valued by Sinn Fein. 'They had their own agenda,' was how a Sinn Feiner put it to me. 'We did our own research,' he judged. Significantly, Sinn Fein did not stay for the celebratory drinks after the Agreement was signed. They headed back to West Belfast: Stormont was no place for Sinn Feiners to be seen celebrating.

But of all the differences the one which put the biggest stopper on celebration was decommissioning. The day after the Agreement was signed, a Dublin participant told me, 'Decommissioning was only a Unionist hobby horse, one party out of eight.' And then he laughed. 'We were complaining about the hang-up over decommissioning and a British civil servant rounded on us and said, "What are you talking about, blaming us for decommissioning? It was John Bruton brought that up." A fair debating point, I suppose,' mused my friend, 'but not a real issue.'

All concerned were shortly to find out how real the issue was, how much more than a debating point. Yet the Good Friday Agreement got off to a deceptively good start within the Ulster Unionist Party Executive. Fifty-five of its members voted for, and only twenty-three against. This vote undoubtedly represented the feeling amongst the party's grassroots support in favour of peace. But David Trimble's inadequacies as a leader were soon to be exposed, as month by month throughout the year, he allowed his opponents within the party to seize the initiative. He neither made a full-blooded attempt to rally his supporters, nor did anything of significance to check his enemies. Possibly, indeed probably, the only answer for Unionism at the time – the vote occurred on 11 April 1998 – was for Trimble without delay to set about creating contigency plans to create a new Unionist party, devoted to supporting the Agreement. Certainly in the event he failed to rise to the challenge.

However, the euphoria continued for some time. Privately, Sinn Fein put its reservations about Stormont to one side and went to bat for the Agreement amongst its membership in a big way. The arguments used included: 'Why should we be afraid of Stormont? It's our parliament too. We have to show the same courage in fighting the peace that was shown in fighting the war. We can, and we will, achieve the objectives we fought for physically by fighting and winning politically. We have the Dublin Government behind us, the Americans and Labour is supportive. Public opinion is with us. A return to war would lose this support and, after more violence and death, we would have to come back to the table anyhow.'

There were many long, bruising nights of argument and counter-argument as the familiar force *v.* constitutional action debate raged throughout the IRA. But little or nothing of the leadership's struggle to convince its followers showed publicly. In a series of speeches, Sinn Fein marked the Easter Rising commemoration rallies throughout the country by giving the Agreement a cautious welcome. But IRA watchers immediately saw the result of the private debate in the IRA's Easter message. In effect it contained a coded endorsement of Sinn Fein's efforts. The Army Council statement said that it would evaluate the Agreement 'against its potential to deliver a just and durable peace in our country'. The fact that the IRA did not reject the Agreement, despite its implications for a continuation of partition and the British presence, to say nothing of the potential it contained for an Orange veto, was interpreted by its supporters as meaning that the document could be accepted.

Although the Orange Order indicated that it would not support the Agreement, the Ulster Unionist Party continued to enjoy a fair wind of support and the Ulster Unionist Party's ruling Council committed itself a week after the executive had voted to an endorsement of 540 votes to 210, which, at 72 per cent, reflected opinion polls of the period in favour of the Agreement. When Gerry Adams, who was speaking that day (18 April 1998) at the Sinn Fein Ard Fheis in Dublin, received the news, he passed it on to the Assembly saying, 'Well done David', at which there was a burst of applause. Trimble did not receive Adams's support graciously. He described it as 'a poisoned chalice'. One of the forces weighing on Trimble was of course the influence of Paisley, who formed a focal point for dissident members of Trimble's party to rally around – as a number of them did at an Ulster Hall meeting on 23 April. Paisley set his sights on securing a 40 per cent No vote for his Party in the forthcoming referendum on the Agreement.

There was never any hope of his securing such a percentage – in the event he got approximately 28 per cent – but he and the other rejectionist Unionists were able to make capital out of one provision in the Good Friday Agreement. This was the undertaking to release political prisoners. There was consternation in Unionist ranks when some of the IRA prisoners, including members of the Balcombe Street unit, were allowed out on short-term release to attend the Sinn Fein Ard Fheis on 10 May. Their appearance was greeted with a huge spontaneous burst of applause. The cheering went on for at least ten minutes. Subsequently, when a week later Michael Stone, jailed for the Milltown cemetery attack, which claimed three lives, was allowed out to appear at a 'Yes vote' rally organized by the Ulster Democratic Party, which represented the UDA, Stone did not address the meeting as the Balcombe Street men had done. The element of fundamentalism, of the concept that transgressors should be punished in approved Old Testament style, was strong in the Protestant community, outside the ranks of Loyalism.

The ovations at the Sinn Fein Ard Fheis obscured the fact that the party had taken a significant step towards constitutionalism. Ninety-six per cent of the delegates voted to alter the party's Constitution to allow candidates to take their places in the new Northern Ireland Assembly envisaged in the Good Friday Agreement. This occurred after Adams had pointed out that, though the British and partition remained, the Sinn Fein negotiators had succeeded in removing the Government of Ireland Act from the British statute books. The cornerstone of the British position was gone and it was realistically possible to expect to see the remaining goals being achieved. This vital decision to drop abstentionism was, readers will remember, one of the reasons for the major split in the IRA in 1969–70, which led to the emergence of the Provisionals in the first place. However, it did not have the effect of impressing the Unionists that Republicanism was moving towards democracy, because the vote was overshadowed by the offence created by the ovations for released prisoners.

A U2 concert at Belfast's Waterfront Hall at which Bono, the lead singer, held aloft the hands of John Hume and David Trimble, set the seal on the Yes campaign. No one gave much thought to the significance of the fact that this was the first time in the campaign that David Trimble had been seen campaigning with the SDLP leader. Trimble was still looking over his shoulder at Paisley who, on the eve of the poll, told Trimble in an acrimonious TV debate (BBC Newsline, 20 May 1998) that he was about to 'break the Union'. In the event, the vote was as follows:

Northern Ireland	*Republic of Ireland*
Yes ... 71.12%	Yes ... 94.39%
No ... 28.88%	No ... 5.61%

The majority in the island overall for the 'Yeses' was 85.46 per cent. This was the first all-Ireland poll since 1918, and in the tide of optimism which engulfed the country, people forgot the significance of the fact that in the thirty years prior to and including 1918, the Irish had voted by similar percentages for Home Rule, but failed to achieve it in the face of a combination of Unionist obduracy, Tory connivance and British Army hostility towards Irish Nationalism. Events would show that these forces had not departed the Irish political landscape. However, despite some disturbing references in the Unionist camp to there being no place for Sinn Fein in the projected executive without prior decommissioning, the Assembly elections held on 25 June 1998 for the new Northern Ireland Assembly appeared to justify the general climate of hope.

One hundred and eight members were returned for eighteen constituencies. The Nationalist parties made a major breakthrough, the SDLP gained the largest share of the first preference vote, with 22 per cent, marginally ahead of the UUP on 21.3 per cent. Sinn Fein advanced to 17.6 per cent, significantly closing the gap on Paisley's Democratic Unionist Party, which only managed 18.1 per cent. The final tally of seats was as follows:

Ulster Unionist Party (UUP) . . . 28
Social Democratic & Labour Party (SDLP) . . . 24
Democratic Unionist Party (DUP) . . . 20
Sinn Fein (SF) . . . 18
Alliance Party of Northern Ireland (APNI) . . . 5
United Kingdom Unionist Party (UKUP) . . . 5
Progressive Unionist Party (PUP) . . . 2
Northern Ireland Women's Coalition (NIWC) . . . 2
Others . . . 3

The Sinn Fein gains were in marked contrast to the showing of the UDA's party, which failed to have any member elected. This meant that an important segment of Loyalism would subsequently have less input, or interest in, the political process, than was healthy, as subsequent UDA involvement in internal Loyalist feuding underlined.

The first business of the New Assembly when it met on 1 July was to elect a First Minister Designate and Deputy First Minister Designate, David Trimble and Seamus Mallon, Deputy Leader of the SDLP.

The deaths of the Quinn children a few days later were a stark reminder of how badly the region required political stability. But this stability was further threatened by a huge 'real IRA' bomb at Bambridge, Co. Down, a Loyalist stronghold, which injured thirty-five people, on 1 August 1998. The policy of letting off bombs in built-up areas had the inevitable result of turning injuries into deaths at Omagh two weeks later. One crumb of comfort from the bombing was the declaration by the Irish National Liberation Army (INLA) (on 22 August 1998) that it was declaring a ceasefire. As we have seen earlier, the Provisionals helped to pressurize the Real IRA into following suit on 29 August, although the Continuity IRA remained active.

President Clinton paid his second visit to Northern Ireland on 3 September 1998, and in the upbeat mood of the moment few people paid attention to the squabble over decommissioning which broke out on the eve of his visit. Gerry Adams had tried to sweeten the atmosphere with a statement which said (on 1 September 1998) that: 'Sinn Fein believes the violence we have seen must be for all of us now a thing of the past, over, done with and gone.' And in response to this, in an obviously choreographed sequence, Trimble and Adams met for the first time at a round table meeting with all the leaders of the Northern political parties on 7 September. However, the significance of this was rather undercut by statements made by the major Orange and Green protagonists before the meeting took place.

On 3 September, *An Phoblacht/Republican News* published an interview with an IRA spokesman who said that the IRA would not decommission its weapons and stated that the Unionists were merely using the issue in an attempt to renegotiate the Good Friday Agreement. Trimble countered this with an assertion that his party would not enter government in advance of decommissioning. Adams riposted by pointing out that there was nothing in the Good Friday Agreement to prevent the immediate establishment of an executive, including Sinn Fein. The relevant passages in the Good Friday Agreement are as follows:*

Those who hold office should use only democratic, non-violent means, and those who do not should be excluded or removed from office under these provisions:

---

* Strand One, Article 25, Good Friday Agreement.

And:*

> All participants accordingly reaffirm their commitment to the total dis-
> armament of all paramilitary organizations. They also confirm their
> intention to continue to work constructively and in good faith with the
> Independent Commission, and to use any influence they may have, to
> achieve the decommissioning of all paramilitary arms within two years
> following endorsement in referendums North and South of the agree-
> ment and in the context of the implementation of the overall settlement.

But the cannonading continued. There was more discussion about
the need to destroy IRA weapons after the guns fell silent than when
they were being used in full-scale guerrilla warfare. Trimble and Adams
held their first face-to-face meeting on 10 September 1998, and Adams
pronounced Trimble to be 'a man I can do business with'. As this was
the first time a Sinn Fein leader and a member of the Unionist Party
had met since the foundation of the North of Ireland state, optimism
flared. Prisoners began emerging from the jails, some British Army
installations and checkpoints were scheduled for demolition, patrols
were cut back and the public continued to whistle past the graveyard
which was being prepared for the Good Friday Agreement.

Sinn Fein attempted to quell the whistling in the run up to the
Labour Party Conference in Blackpool (on 30 September 1998) with
a number of statements. On the 19th, Gerry Kelly, one of the party's
most senior figures, warned of a looming crisis in the process if the
Unionists persisted with their decommissioning policy which he said
was 'generating unrealizable expectations' that decommissioning was
about to occur. Adams went to Blackpool to reiterate the message,
saying that decommissioning had the potential to wreck the Agreement.

However, Trimble repeated the Unionist demands at the UUP
Annual Conference on 24 October 1998, and a week later, the 31
October deadline for the formation of the Northern Ireland Assembly
Executive was missed. A promise by the SDLP at its Annual Confer-
ence on 14 November, that it would join with the Unionists in removing
Sinn Fein from the Executive if the IRA failed to decommission,
following the setting up of the institutions called for by the Good
Friday Agreement, failed to break the deadlock. In fact if anything it

---

* Decommissioning, Paragraph 3.

worsened, with the addition of a new element to the imbroglio, that of the Patten Commission.

One of the rather gilded offshoots of the troubles is the British and Irish Association, which attempts to bring together the great and the good, and sometimes the not so good, under Chatham House rules, at alternating venues in England, Oxford one year, Cambridge the next. The Association, also known as Toffs Against Terrorism, never asked me back after I disrupted its proceedings one year by saying that the Gardai did not trust the RUC because of the involvement of members of the force with Loyalist paramilitaries. The programme had to be rescheduled so that the Chief Constable of the RUC, Sir John Hermon, could be afforded an opportunity of denouncing me. One of those affected by my comments was the then Junior Northern Ireland Minister, Chris Patten, who remarked as he left the lecture hall: 'What a profoundly depressing afternoon'.

The unfortunate Patten had yet to discover how depressing, and controversial, the subject of the RUC could get. The Patten Commission was set up under the Good Friday Agreement, with Patten as chairman after he had completed the equally thankless task of being Governor of Hong Kong.

It should be understood that the RUC was never intended as an ordinary police force. It was set up in 1922 by Sir Henry Wilson, the military advisor to Sir James Craig, the first Prime Minister of Northern Ireland, with a counter-insurgency ethos. Wilson ordered that the existing Royal Irish Constabulary be disbanded, and placed another military figure, General Sir Arthur Solly-Flood in charge of the RUC. In tandem with the RUC he also organized various Special Constabulary corps, so that they subsumed members of organizations set up with the specific purpose of killing Catholics, such as the notorious murder gang the Cromwell Clubs. Flogging was one of the legal provisions introduced under the Wilson regime. The illegal activities of some of the early members of the force, notorious figures such as Inspectors Nixon and Harrison, whose names still resonate in Belfast folklore, included murder in the presence of witnesses, for which they were never prosecuted.*

Thus, from its inception the RUC was placed squarely in the cross-

---

* The documented history of Wilson's, and Nixon and Harrison's involvement in the early days of the RUC may be found in *Michael Collins*, Chapter 11, by Tim Pat Coogan, Hutchinson, London, 1990.

fire of that field of vision in which one man's terrorist is another man's freedom-fighter. It behaved badly towards the Nationalist community and was equally badly treated as a result, as the references throughout these pages to RUC officers being shot illustrate. Reform of the force therefore became an essential demand, not merely for Sinn Fein, but for any hopes of democratic evolution within the troubled area. There was initial controversy over the appointment of the members of the commission. Dublin did not succeed in having any of its nominees placed on the review body. Its members included Kathleen O'Toole, a legal expert on policing from Boston, the former Northern Ireland top civil servant, Dr Maurice Hayes, and Peter Smith, QC. Sir John Smith, a former Deputy Commissioner of London's Metropolitan Police, was also appointed.

Patten took evidence throughout the Province in painstaking fashion and eventually reported on 9 September 1999. It was a root and branch operation which proposed scaling down the size of the RUC, renaming the force the Northern Ireland Police Service, and scrapping its symbol, a badge with a British Crown on top of an Irish harp. The Commission also called for the Union Jack to be removed from outside police stations.

The Report stated that the reforms were aimed at creating a force acceptable to both traditions in the Province, and increasing Catholic recruitment. This was far from acceptable to one tradition. The reaction to the proposals to disband the force can well be imagined therefore. David Wright, Billy Wright's father, remarked to me even before Patten reported: 'When I was young we used to talk about the Orange Shamrock. We had the Orange Order, the Unionist Party and the RUC. Now they're all splitting up.' Apart from the fact that the Unionist community regard the laying of impious hands on the RUC as the ultimate obscenity, the destruction of their last bastion against the onrushing hordes of Nationalism, the inflated number of personnel in the ranks of the RUC itself constitutes a sizeable political lobby. Most families on the Unionist side of the divide would have a relation, or at least an acquaintance, in the force. Thus many would also have lost a friend or relation during the troubles.

Trimble expressed the sense of outrage of such people when he told a visibly shaken Tony Blair in the House of Commons that his espousal of the Patten Report had brought 'dishonour' on himself, the House, and on his party. Ironically, it would not be long, as we shall see, before opponents of the Good Friday Agreement would use the Patten

Report as their main battleground in the fight to get rid of Trimble himself.

However, during the period while Patten was conducting his hearings things temporarily took a hopeful turn. The growing improvement in Anglo-Irish relationships was highlighted by a felicitous speech from Tony Blair who, on 26 November 1998, became the first British Prime Minister to address both houses of the Oireachtas. More importantly, two days later, George Mitchell re-entered the picture, and began a series of meetings with the Northern political leaders.

Mitchell's soothing tones, however, were somewhat muted by the more raucous sounds emerging from Paisley's Annual Party Conference which was held the same day. At this, Paisley's Deputy, Peter Robinson, urged members of Trimble's party to 'topple' him. Robinson altered the traditional mantra of fundamental Unionism about Home Rule being Rome Rule by saying: 'Better by far that you topple Trimble now rather than give him time to drag this Province step by step to Dublin.' With this ringing in his ears, Trimble continued to stall on the setting up of the institutions called for by the Good Friday Agreement.

On 12 December he said that decommissioning would have to take place in front of the television cameras. Whether by accident or design, it became known the following day that a general Army Convention of the IRA had been held some time earlier, at which the Provisionals' traditional stand on decommissioning had been reaffirmed.

Nevertheless, things in Northern Ireland are never what they seem, and behind the scenes George Mitchell had been working his alchemy. What appeared to be a major breakthrough in the impasse over the Good Friday Agreement was announced on 18 December. There was to be an increase from six to ten ministries in Northern Ireland, and six new North/South administrative bodies. In the bruising, lengthy negotiations between the parties, which had preceded the announcement of the cross-border bodies, their functions were severely watered down. I spoke to one IRA activist shortly after he had read the text of their remits in the papers, and he was disgusted: 'What the hell was all the fuss about? These things don't amount to anything.'

The IRA man was both right and wrong. On the one hand, the six bodies did not appear to have a great deal of teeth. They covered inland waterways, agriculture, food safety, the Irish and Ulster Scots language, trade and European funding. But their headquarters were sited on both sides of the border. Their membership was drawn on an

all-Ireland basis and above all they held out the prospect of near
inevitable growth in scope and importance. The Unionists recognized
this and haggled over the Mitchell-brokered Agreement. The UUP
wanted the Northern Ireland Assembly to 'take note' of the Agreement,
whereas the SDLP, for example, wanted the two parties to approve
and formally accept what had been agreed. Ominously the IRA's New
Year message said that the Good Friday Agreement had failed in its
objective of delivering meaningful change, and that Unionists were
continuing on the path that had already led to the breakdown of the
1994 ceasefire.

By way of underlining the starkness of this message, Eamon Collins,
a former member of the IRA, who had given information to the RUC
under pressure, and subsequently embarked on a career as an author
and critic of the Provisionals, while, incredibly enough, continuing to
live in the border town of Newry, paid a brutal price for his temerity.
On the morning of 27 January 1999 he was found murdered, with his
eyes gouged out, on a road near his home.

A series of deadlines for the implementation of the 18 December
Agreement came and went, despite all the usual encouraging noises
from the White House at the St Patrick's Day celebration. Round table
discussions at Stormont a month later foundered on decommissioning;
indeed, it was agreed to scrap the Hillsborough Declaration, as it was
known. This had been agreed at the beginning of the month, when
Bertie Ahern and Tony Blair had set out a framework which, it was
hoped, would provide for progress towards the establishment of an
executive. Sinn Fein had seen this as an attempt to bypass the Good
Friday Agreement and create what Gerry Adams said in his Easter
Sunday message could have had merit, but could also have been
'counter-productive if it amounts to an ultimatum to armed groups'.

A hint of a potential new approach on the lines of joint authority
came on 15 June when an understandably exasperated Bertie Ahern
said that the decommissioning issue had been 'debated to death'. But
he also stated that if a breakthrough was not achieved by 30 June,
which Tony Blair a month earlier had announced was to be the 'absolute' deadline for the formation of an executive, then the British and
Irish Governments would 'set aside' the Good Friday Agreement and
seek alternative means to political progress.

The Blair deadline had been set after Trimble had once again failed
to deliver on what the other parties believed was a deal whereby the
so-called d'Hondt procedure would have been triggered by mid May.

(The d'Hondt system allows for the appointment of ministries on the basis of the number of seats won in an assembly.) The UUP, however, disappointed the Irish Government, the SDLP and Sinn Fein by failing to agree to proposals which Dublin at least believed that David Trimble had agreed to. However, the 'absolute' deadline brought no executive, even though Tony Blair pronounced that a 'seismic shift' had occurred in the Northern Irish political landscape. Unfortunately the only visible shift was in the focus of attention to Drumcree Five.

Blue water opened up between Dublin and London, not over Drumcree, but over differing interpretations of the role of Sinn Fein and the IRA. Blair said (on 8 July 1999) that the two organizations were 'inextricably linked', whereas Ahern said they were two separate entities. Who was telling the truth? The traditional Unionist attitude to Irish Nationalism is such that if good King William of Orange were to return to life to join the Pope, and the Dalai Lama, in delivering every weapon the IRA possessed to Ian Paisley's front door, the IRA's ceasefire would still be viewed with suspicion. But even if this visceral mistrust did not exist it would still be legitimate to examine the question of whether or not the IRA was sincere in declaring a ceasefire on 31 August 1994.

The question of the decision to resume the bombing in 1996 also raised issues about the involvement of Sinn Fein in IRA decision-taking and vice versa. Some writers and commentators, drawing on information proffered by British and Northern Ireland security sources, have from time to time confidently named the membership of the Army Council and included on it the names of such prominent Sinn Feiners as Gerry Adams, Martin McGuinness, Martin Ferris and the Vice-President, Pat Doherty. These assessments remind me of the curate's egg, good in parts. Quite obviously, figures like Adams, McGuinness and Doherty did not gain their ascendancy by moving upwards through the ranks of the Ballyfermot Boys Brass Band. Nor do names more ordinarily associated with militant Republicanism, such as Brian Keenan or Tom Murphy, come to mind because of their interest in, let us say, the Gaelic Athletic Association.

Are Sinn Fein spokespersons to be trusted, therefore, when they say the party does not speak for the IRA, and is entitled to be viewed as a democratic party acting solely in terms of the mandate it has received at the polls? 'Yes' is by and large an accurate answer, though it probably requires some amplification. Sometimes, for instance, a writer may be permitted a wry grimace when he sees, let us say, photographs of two prominent Sinn Fein women, and recalls how one was once described to him as being 'very good at the interrogations', and the other as being 'in charge of the punishment beatings'. But the truth is, in so far as I can judge from my own observation and contact, and the word of senior Irish security personnel, is that the IRA in the period under review was in a process of transition to democracy. Similar to that undergone by Fianna Fail in the 1920s, and subsequently by groupings such as Clann na Phoblachta, and Sinn Fein, the Workers Party. Some double membership, and some double-talk, inevitably occurred along the way. Nevertheless the transition was genuine.

The IRA and Sinn Fein are separate, if for no other reason than that the full-time nature of membership of one would make it impossible to function efficiently in the other. It is true that the most ferocious discussion and debate took place both before the ceasefire was declared and then after that, when it became apparent that John Major was not prepared to move. It is also true that in the autumn of 1995 the IRA took a decision arising out of this debate that 'bag stuff in London', i.e. fertilizer bombs, were the only thing to which the British would respond. The bomb had, of course, a catastrophic impact on Sinn Fein's credibility, particularly on Gerry Adams's. People who were aware of the IRA's 'bag stuff' decision found it very difficult to understand how Gerry Adams and the other Sinn Fein leaders either did not know of the decision or, if they did know, failed to prevent its implementation. It also had repercussions on the IRA itself as many of its members were caught unprepared by the explosion, and an angry debate along the lines of hawks versus doves ensued.

The commitment of the Adams/McGuinness/Doherty/Kelly/Ferris faction to the Peace strategy was to be seen, or more accurately, hidden from the general public in the debate which accompanied the restoration of the IRA ceasefire after Tony Blair came to power. The day before the ceasefire was announced (19 July), the Sinn Fein leadership managed to overturn a decision of the previous year's army convention, which had given the authority to call a ceasefire not to the Army Council, but to the twelve member Executive, on which the Hawks had a majority. However, the Sinn Fein, pro-peace process leadership, had a four-three majority on the Army Council. By successfully arguing that power should be exercised by the council, not the executive, the Doves in effect wrested control of the movement from the Hawks and forced through the ceasefire.

However, the calling of the ceasefire increased reservations about the Peace policy of Adams and company among the hardliners. The debate, out of which 'the real IRA', and Omagh, emerged, came to a head at a special IRA convention held in Falcarragh, near Gweedore, in Donegal on 10 October 1997. This secret meeting was attended by the top IRA men in the country, and a number of equally prominent Sinn Fein leaders. Hawks and Doves argued fiercely.

Again, a majority backed the Adams line. The Hawks weakened their case by personal attacks on Adams and by failing to produce any political strategy in support of their militaristic aims. In the resultant split some of the most prominent of the military wing went with the Real IRA. Around the same time, a public split developed in which some twenty Sinn Fein Councillors led by Francie Mackey and Rory Dougan resigned from Sinn Fein and pledged support to the 32 Country Sovereignty Committee. Throughout these upheavals and subsequently, the Adams faction argued successfully for a maintenance of the ceasefire, and were supported in America by the bulk of Irish American political and financial supporters.

However, Adams's position became increasingly dangerous. Until Omagh occurred, a series of Real IRA attacks undoubtedly won support in the ranks of the Provisionals. Fortunately for him though, apart from those who actually joined the Real IRA, no support either in bomb making, logistics or actually taking part in operations came from the Provisionals ranks. RUC and British Intelligence were of course well aware of Adams's policy and activities. But though this intelligence was available to senior Unionists, the Unionists made use of it not to advance the Peace Process, but to try to weaken Adams's position and force a more damaging split amongst the Republicans, by insisting both on decommissioning and a declaration that the war was over. To have done either would have invited political assassination, not for Adams alone, but for some of his closest supporters. In the event however, Omagh highlighted the folly of the Real IRA approach and Adams's position was strengthened, at least temporarily, because the decision by Peter Mandelson to bow to the Unionists by suspending the Northern Assembly (see pages 754–8) once again raised serious questions about both his strategy, and the future of the Peace Process.

But once 'normal' politics resumed – electioneering, constituency work and so forth – the two organizations could effectively be regarded as separate. An active IRA volunteer could efficiently canvass for a Sinn Fein candidate, but a fulltime Sinn Fein politician could not as easily respond to the dictates of the 'at-the-drop-of-a-hat' existence of an active guerrilla. He can, of course, if he is sufficiently respected, make his influence felt at meetings attended by the Army Council, the IRA Executive, or the more large-scale, and less frequently held IRA Conventions. The over-riding fact is that no matter what was done in the past, and some household names of today were admittedly responsible for some very frightening decisions, Adams and his circle, having striven for over twenty years, often at the risk of their lives, to bring the IRA into mainstream political life, are extremely unlikely, to put it mildly, to take any steps deliberately calculated to swing the movement back to violence.

However, as readers should by now have grasped from these pages, violence is never very far from the fringes of those who follow in the footsteps of the Irish physical force tradition. This was glaringly underlined in the month of June 1996. The two greatest question marks one could place against the sincerity of the ceasefire were the resumption of the British bombing campaign and the murder of Garda Gerry McCabe in County Limerick on 7 June 1996. He was shot in the course of a robbery initially thought to be the work of a dissident Republican group. But a third query also hangs over the real meaning of the acronym TUAS, of which more anon. The IRA appeared to be caught out in a massive lie over the shooting of Garda McCabe.

I have already adverted to the importance of Standing Order No. 8 of the IRA's 'Army Orders' (Chapter 12) which forbids any action 'against 26 County Forces under any circumstances whatsoever'. The Provisionals issued a statement in line with this policy after McCabe's death, and the public at large were disposed to accept this denial. However, the Gardai continued to insist that the shooting was the work of the IRA, and on 12 June another statement was issued which proved the Gardai were right. The IRA apologized both to the victims of the attack and to their relatives. I understand that the incident was not an indication of IRA duplicity, but of a slackness of discipline, brought about by the ceasefire. The unit involved had, prior to the shooting, had its funds cut off by a directive of the Army Council, because it had become increasingly out of control, and the IRA leadership simply did not know who was responsible.

The incident was clearly disquieting in itself, but later in that month, on 16 June, the *Sunday Tribune* newspaper published an IRA briefing paper which had been in existence since the previous April. It contained the following:

After prolonged discussion and assessment the leadership decided that if it could get agreement with the Dublin Government, the SDLP, and IA (Irish-American) lobby on basic Republican principles, which would be enough to create the dynamic that would considerably advance the struggle, then it would be prepared to use the TUAS.

The letters TUAS had been used in the IRA's internal debate as meaning 'total unarmed struggle' and in Irish-American circles it was translated as Tuas, the Irish word for origins. However, the *Sunday Tribune* correspondent, the respected Ed Moloney, revealed that TUAS had also been translated within the IRA ranks to reassure doubters, as meaning 'tactical use of armed strategy'.

There was a widespread feeling of shock at Moloney's disclosures. Was the renewed bombing campaign since Canary Wharf not merely a response to Major's procrastinations, but TUAS in action? Was the IRA still wedded to the pursuit of power with an 'Armalite in one hand and ballot box in the other'? Despite criticisms, however, Adams continued his negotiations with the IRA to secure a restoration of the ceasefire and actually rejected an offer of a 'tactical ceasefire', demanding instead the full restoration of the 1994 ceasefire. Labour's return to power eventually paved the way for the granting of his request. The most important figure to impose trust in Adams's bona fides throughout all this was President Clinton, who decreed that contact with Sinn Fein should not be broken off* after the Canary Wharf bombing. Privately Clinton's viewpoint was summed up in a colourful phrase retold to me by Niall O'Dowd: 'Shit happens'. And so, amidst doubt, cynicism and head-shakings, the peace process staggered on.

All the suspicions and differing interpretations, not merely of TUAS, but of the Good Friday Agreement, combined with the folly of attempting any rational political achievement during the height of the Unionists' marching season, came together on 15 July 1999. The balloon of the attempt to form an executive of the Northern Ireland Assembly collapsed when David Trimble and members of the UUP Assembly Party failed to turn up at Stormont. The SDLP and Sinn Fein went ahead and formed a temporary executive. It had to be disbanded almost immediately because under the terms of the Good Friday Agreement it did not have cross-community membership. However, Seamus Mallon, the SDLP Deputy Leader, and more importantly

* White House statement, 17 June 1996.

Deputy First Minister Designate, took a step which concentrated minds wonderfully. He resigned as First Minister Designate.

In panic, the two governments employed the now familiar formula for dealing with Northern Ireland crises, 'Send for Mitchell'. It was announced (on 20 July 1999) that the Senator would chair a review of the Good Friday Agreement. The following day the IRA gave the review a conditional green light by issuing a statement saying that while it would not propose to decommission 'in the current political context', it did confirm its 'definitive commitment' to the peace process. But the statement did not confirm support for a gesture made by Gerry Adams and Sinn Fein which agreed to further the review process by signing up to the principle that decommissioning should take place before the end of May 2000. However, neither did it rule out the prospect of decommissioning in the future if circumstances allowed.

Further signs of strain in the Republicans' maintenance of the peace process were revealed in the murder of a Belfast man, Charles Bennett, and the discovery of an attempt to import weapons through the post from Florida, both of which occurred in the last week of July. I understand that prior to the discovery of the Florida attempt, some weapons had got through, including a Barret sniper rifle, to augment those already in the possession of Crossmaglen marksmen. These were naturally worrying developments, but they did not vitiate Sinn Fein claims that the ceasefire remained intact. Even while he was negotiating the Anglo-Irish Treaty with the British, Michael Collins was engaged in arms importation efforts. If you want peace, prepare for war, is a maxim which the IRA at any stage in its history feels applies to it as much as to the British Army. Even if the weapons were not destined for use the fact that they were still being imported had a steadying effect on those IRA men who were wavering in their support for the ceasefire, thinking the movement was 'going soft'.

Both Mo Mowlam and Tony Blair accepted that, while there was no doubt that the IRA was involved in the Bennett murder and the Florida gun-running, nevertheless the ceasefire remained intact. Blair put this belief forcibly to Trimble when he met him in London (on 31 August 1999) and turned down Trimble's demands for the postponement of the Mitchell Review. The Review duly got underway (on 6 September 1999) but was almost immediately overshadowed by the publication of the Patten Report on the reform of the RUC (see p. 721–3), which created, in the words of Tony Blair, a seismic shift in Unionist opinion.

Although meetings between Trimble and Adams throughout October produced no meeting of minds over the UUP's refusal to allow Sinn Fein to take part in the executive in advance of decommissioning, Adams issued a statement, on Saturday 16 October 1999, saying that there was a requirement on the part of Republicans to address Unionist concerns in a spirit of 'respect and goodwill'. This followed the UUP Conference in Enniskillen, Co. Fermanagh, on 9/10 October 1999, at which for once Trimble had faced down his critics and strongly defended the Good Friday Agreement. But the Conference sentiment against admitting Sinn Fein to an executive in advance of decommissioning remained strong, and formed part of the reason for a unanimous decision of the Conference to reject the Patten Report and condemn it as a 'threat to security'.

The day after the Conference, another Unionist-perceived 'threat to security' was removed from the region. David Trimble, who the previous year had suggested Peter Mandelson as a replacement for Mo Mowlam, got his way. A Cabinet reshuffle recalled Mowlam to London, to the dismay of the Nationalists, and the glee of Unionists. For a brief moment, it appeared that hurling Mo Mowlam from the Stormont troika to the pursuing Unionist wolves had achieved its objective. The Stormont talks appeared to move on to safety and agreement. Adams spoke of the need to work with, not against, Unionists in the future; Trimble spoke of Nationalists' pursuit of a United Ireland being 'a legitimate aspiration' and declared himself in favour of inclusivity, equality and mutual respect. On 17 November 1999, the day after the issuing of the Unionist/Sinn Fein statements containing this unusual chorus of agreement, the IRA too issued a statement, which appeared to constitute a real breakthrough.

The statement said that the IRA was committed to peace, supported the Good Friday Agreement, backed the Sinn Fein leadership in its negotiation strategy, and most importantly, agreed to Dublin's pressure that it should appoint a representative to enter formal negotiations on decommissioning with General de Chastelain.

The familiar strains of the Lagan Four Step were sounding; Dublin, London, Belfast and Washington were on song. The day after the IRA statement was issued, George Mitchell announced that his Review led him to conclude that there was a basis for the formation of an executive and the triggering of devolution. Once more Mitchell appeared to have done the impossible, and he departed for America amid a chorus of praise as the Good Ship Peace Process once more floated off the rocks of decommissioning. However, the path of true mistrust never runs straight. In the chorus of universal delight at what appeared to be Mitchell's salvaging of the Good Friday Agreement, insufficient attention was paid to a crucial meeting of the Council of the Ulster Unionist Party in the Waterfront Hall, Belfast, on 27 November 1999.

The Council voted by 480 votes to 349 to support Mitchell's judgement and to allow Trimble and his party to form an executive containing Sinn Fein. But very little media attention was directed towards the price tag on this decision. Trimble wrote a letter of resignation and announced that he would step down as First Minister if decommissioning did not occur within a matter of months. In the euphoria of the moment, the media largely overlooked Adams's angry rejection of this strategy, which he pointed out was outside the terms of the Good Friday Agreement. But attention focused on the gladsome sight at Stormont on Monday, 29 November 1999, when the d'Hondt mechanism was triggered, Seamus Mallon was reinstated, and for the first time in twenty-five years, Northern Ireland once more had a power-sharing executive. The following day, Westminster approved devolution orders which transferred power from London to Belfast and ended direct rule.

UNIONIST PHILOSOPHY

Decision-taking Dublin, London, Washington and the wider media-watching public allowed themselves to be beguiled by the apparent spectacle of men of goodwill meeting at the centre in peace and goodwill, with David Trimble cast in the role of the de Klerk of Northern Ireland. In fact he proved to be a clerk. To be fair, he faced enormous psychological and political obstacles both within himself and in Unionism. Personally, Trimble faced the challenge of passing rapidly from his Vanguard and Garvaghy Road background to the role of reforming statesman. One of the reasons he failed the test was that whereas de Klerk's version of the Orange Order, the Broderbond, took a decision that change had to come, thus helping him bring it about, the Orange Order passed through no such sea change. Unionism contains within it a visceral anti-Catholicism, a mistrust of the British who will one day betray them and return to the metropole, leaving the hapless Loyalist settlers to confront the barbarians. The structures of Unionism are not geared to modern politics.

It would have appeared axiomatic, from reading the newspapers or watching television in the wake of the signing of the Good Friday Agreement, that as 85 per cent of the people of Ireland had voted in favour of the agreement, therefore it must succeed. Not so. Similar percentages had voted in favour of Home Rule for Ireland in the late nineteenth and early twentieth centuries, but the will of the ballot box was frustrated by the combination of Unionist intransigence and Conservative opportunism. Although Conservative influence was vastly diminished since those days, the old reluctance on the part of the British Army to uphold the wishes of the Green, as expressed in the ballot box, against those of the Orange, as expressed in lodge and caucus room, still persisted, notably in MI5. The securicrats, both by the spin they placed on their intelligence reports and by their stubborn refusal to scale down their presence in sensitive Republican areas, continued to be an irritant in the political oyster around which no pearl formed.

The old Conservative influence on Irish affairs continued to be exerted to a diminished, yet powerful degree through figures like Viscount Cranborne, a Cecil, and direct descendant of Lord Burleigh, the first Lord of the Plantation. After he supported John Major in the Redwood stalking horse challenge, Major gave him virtual control of Northern Ireland policy in the Cabinet Sub-committee on Northern Ireland. Figures like Cranborne and Tory backbench spokespersons on Northern Ireland also made their presence felt, both in Westminster and through a shadowy, but powerful grouping, the Friends of the Union, spear-headed by the North of Ireland Unionist, David Burnside. This London-based PR mogul attracted a good deal of publicity for his role in the 'dirty tricks war' conducted by British Airways against Richard Branson's Virgin Airways during their boardroom battle. He was to acquire more for his Irish activities. The advice, money and prestige which his influence could bring to bear on the narrow provincials of Belfast's ruling Unionist Council was considerable. Burnside sponsored, and carried, the motion on the RUC at the Unionist Council meeting which moved the goalposts of Unionist policy on 25 March 2000 and severely damaged David Trimble's leadership.

In its approach to the Good Friday Agreement the Unionist Party demonstrated that it is not principally motivated by economic, or contemporary issues. It has almost no women members to speak of, either amongst its elected representatives or its ruling Council. Its motor forces are preoccupations with the past, holding to a position, which has only evolved very slightly from the days of the Ulster crisis and the frustration of Home Rule pre-World War I to the present day. In the face of the obviously diminished role of the Catholic Church in Irish politics the slogan 'Home Rule is Rome Rule', though it obviously still possesses considerable resonance in Paisley's Democratic Unionist Party, does not have the same appeal within the official Unionist Party. Instead, as Peter Robinson declared, the focus has moved towards erecting roadblocks on the path towards Dublin. In fact, a large number of Protestants should be considered as being separate from Unionism. Though, to an outsider, this may appear as difficult as separating the IRA from Sinn Fein, such people would certainly vote for peace, better relations with Dublin, and an increased focus on issues such as education, jobs, health and their children's future. But the political structures of Protestant Northern Ireland are not primarily geared to such goals.

The Orange Order, which has over 100 delegates on the ruling Unionist Council of some 860 members, is an anti-Catholic, suprema-cist organization, for all the colour of the bands, the sashes and the picnics. The Ku Klux Klan also holds picnics and seemingly harmless rallies. Apart from the official representation of the Unionist Council, many members of that body are members of the Order, as is David Trimble and his deputy, John Taylor. Many respectable members of the party do not merely object to having a Fenian around the place, they detest Catholics also. The Young Unionist Council which, along with the Orange Order, also has a block vote on the ruling Council, is not, as its name suggests, a fount of youthful liberalism, but a fount of Unionist zealotry.

Probably the most telling moment for Unionism went largely ignored in the euphoria which greeted George Mitchell's apparently successful second attempt to kick-start the power-sharing executive. Nationalists commented on the fact that Trimble and the Unionists had apparently demonstrated their inability to 'do' real politics because of the compo-sition of the ten-man Ministry to which they had agreed. Trimble gave away the single most important portfolio, that of finance, to the SDLP's Mark Durkan. The North's biggest industry is agriculture, but this portfolio also went to the SDLP, to Brid Rogers. The North's two biggest spending departments are Education and Health, both of which went to Sinn Fein. (One result was that Martin McGuinness became known as the Minister for EducaSinn.)

The loss of these key portfolios was not brought about solely by

Trimble's inadequacies as a negotiator. The Unionist reasoning which governed the allocation of portfolios lay in the fact that these Ministries had an all-Ireland dimension. Agriculture, in particular, necessitates continuous contact, and was therefore, quite apart from the difficulties in the industry, regarded as a poisoned chalice.

DEMOGRAPHIC CHANGE

While in the short term these attitudes seemed to give the rejectionist Unionists a triumph in that they helped to get rid of the Ministries, they are in fact the policies of Canute. For we come now to the most important political fact underlying both constitutional and paramilitary developments in Northern Ireland: demography. This was the principal factor in the sustained strength of the IRA in the period of frustration and comparative inertia which followed the August 1994 ceasefire. The issue of demography has been a touchy one for all concerned in the troubles. The Unionists do not wish to admit that their hegemony is threatened and the Nationalists, in particular Dublin, neither wish to appear triumphalist nor to be committed to a policy of 'bonking for the border'. Nevertheless, demographic change holds the key to the entire problem, as was revealed after the 1991 census.

The census-taking for 1971 and 1981 was seriously interrupted by the IRA in Nationalist areas, partly because, being the years of internment and the hunger strikes, a general state of ebullition prevailed, and partly because the census-takers were regarded as spies, and some were shot as a result. Consequently there was a serious problem of under-enumeration in Catholic areas. However, though there was still a strong residual Republican distrust of co-operating with the census-taking, things had improved by 1991. Though there was some Nationalist abstention, there was no active IRA intereference and it is accepted that the census for that year is reliable, though probably still not fully representative of the Nationalist population.

At first glance, the 38.4 per cent of the population shown to be Catholic seemed to generally accord with the classical formulation of the North's population being roughly two-thirds Protestant to one-third Catholic. However, two of Ireland's most respected academics, Professors Dermot Walsh and Cormac O'Grada of University College, Dublin, decided to apply a test to the 'not stated' and 'none' categories of some 13.8 per cent. If the respondents appeared to have a combination of above average fertility and a knowledge of the Irish language, they were extrapolated as Catholics. When this was done the 38.4 per cent became 43.1 per cent. It is assumed that the reasons for answering 'none' or 'not stated' was that the respondents were living in Protestant areas.

The extrapolation set alarm bells ringing in the Unionist community, and the Stormont statistician, Dr E. Jardine, conducted his own examination of the figures. He could not seriously challenge the Dublin academics, however, placing the Catholic population at 42 per cent. Subsequently, Dr Paul Compton, a member of the Unionist think tank, the Cadogan Group, conducted a survey which placed the Catholic population at 41.3 per cent, but stated that present trends made a Catholic majority 'inevitable'. The inevitability is based on the fact that the census figures show that, even without extrapolation, Catholics were in a majority at age fifteen in 1991, so that the majority of new voters coming on the register from 1994 onwards have been Catholic. This statistic makes the rise in the Nationalist voting strength in recent Northern elections explicable. It also helps to explain why, while allegedly commanding two-thirds of the population, the Unionist vote had come down to 50 per cent in 1998. The Protestants have an older age profile. For example, the 1991 census showed that the Presbyterians, the largest denomination, had 30.3 per cent of its population in the over-75 bracket.

Another, particularly unwelcome factor is the continuing trend amongst younger Protestants to seek their education abroad, chiefly in the UK, principally in Scotland, and then to make their careers outside Northern Ireland. Anyone visiting Scottish universities, Aberdeen, Dundee or Stirling, will be struck by the number of Ulster Protestant young people who choose to study there. When I began researching the first edition of this book in 1965, the Catholic population of Queen's University, Belfast would have been something of the order of 10 to 15 per cent. Today it is around the 65 per cent mark, and the figure is larger in Magee College, Derry. A very disagreeable aspect of this situation is the fact that it is depriving the Protestant political culture of the bread of its future, an educated elite, which helps to explain, for example, the absence of women in Unionist parliamentary circles, or of new faces generally amongst the old warhorses who have trotted forth under Orange banners for close on half a century.

The brain drain, of course, has a direct relevance to the growth in strength of the IRA and Nationalist political culture. It can be measured in all sorts of ways. For example, readers can judge for themselves from the picture of what is happening to the Protestant/Catholic ratios in Tyrone painted below by Phelim Gildernew, or by the fact that booksellers will tell you that, apart from the Bible, the sales of books to the Unionist community is only a fraction of that to the Nationalists. In fiercely Republican West Belfast in the Falls Road area, the streets become almost impassable at school leaving and entering times because of the thousands of youngsters being transported to and from the area's numerous schools. In the nearly Shankill Road, however, the decline of the traditional shipbuilding and engineering industries and the collapse of the apprenticeship culture has resulted in such a picture of educational neglect on the part of Unionist politicians that as far back as 1992 the Church of Ireland Bishop of Connor, Dr Samuel Poyntz, told the Opsahl Commission that:

> Loyalists claim that when empty ground is found, it's always on their side of the peace wall. They are seeing their land disappear – for example, in Suffolk. And there are huge numbers of people leaving the Shankill. On the Shankill only 4 per cent passed the eleven plus in 1987. Only ten children passed in 1988. The number of schools on the Shankill has declined. There's only one secondary school for the whole area, while in the Falls there are plenty. The Shankill is not getting educated, but the Catholics have a good set-up.

Another contributor to the Commission, Mark Langhammer, said:

> The Catholic political culture is vibrant, active, with a dynamic civil society – they have, for example, a profusion of community groups. The Protestant community, by comparison, is apolitical. Outside the public life of its Churches, civil society barely exists.

The situation has worsened since the Opsahl Commission sat. In March 2000 the Harland & Wolff shipyard lost a vital tender, on which the future viability of the yard's 1,500 mainly Protestant jobs depended. The oft-prophesied closure of the yard seemed more likely to come true than ever before. In the wake of the collapse of the Good Friday Agreement the British Treasury pointedly refused to put up the credit facilities needed to match the winning French bid. However, subsequently, as a vital Unionist Council vote on the future of the Assembly neared, purse strings were loosened to allow for a three year continuation of the yard's operations. While the foregoing applies to the Loyalist areas of Belfast, similar factors are at work in rural parts of the province also. On the Protestant side, one encounters a sense of siege, of being on the losing end of a process of change. The Protestant middle class tend to retreat into ghettos of their middle-class fellows, just as do their working-class counterparts. The once confident dominant Protestant community is in retreat, apt to lash out angrily when circumstances permit. In their different ways, the protests over Drumcree and the Good Friday Agreement embody a sense of confused anger, both at their decline and at what is perceived as the reason for it: 'Violence pays. The British give in to the IRA at every step.'

A Protestant paramilitary, who once served simultaneously as an officer in the UDR, and as an agent for the RUC working alongside Brian Nelson, who was being 'run' by British Military Intelligence in the UDA headquarters, epitomizes the shared feelings of anger and betrayal which the self-proclaimed 'British' Protestant community feel at what they see as the spectacle of the British preparing to abandon them and making concessions to IRA violence. My friend, who has severed his links with paramilitarism, and is encouraging his children to visit the Republic and learn Irish, now feels that 'There'll be no peace until the British go, and then we'll sort it out amongst ourselves. I'm fed up with all this manipulation and under-cover stuff.' But then, almost in the same breath, he told me: 'I'm against the Good Friday Agreement. It's a sell-out to the IRA. I voted against it.' All these conflicting attitudes are being rapidly overtaken by events. As King Canute demonstrated, the tide cannot be kept back. This is being written in the year 2000. But in the light of the foregoing, it is significant to remember that next year, 2001, another census is due, and Dublin officials calculate that it will show a further fall in Protestant numbers, to approximately 800,000, while the Catholics, in this context the term 'cultural Catholics' would be more appropriate, will have advanced to some 45 to 47 per cent of the total population. Change is coming, no matter what either side wills.

THE BRANTRY

In the last week of the power-sharing executive's existence I revisited the border areas of South Armagh and Tyrone, which probably deserve to be regarded as the most fiercely Republican areas outside of Belfast to see how the process of change was affecting the IRA.

'The Brantry' is an area of Tyrone steeped in history. Not far from Dungannon, it was nearly wiped out during the Famine. But its tenacious survivors clung on with their memories of bygone Irish chieftains like Shane O'Neill, who recorded one of the few major Irish victories against the British, at nearby Benburb. It is a fertile breeding ground for the IRA. The little primary school at Derrylatinee is renowned for having produced some of the core IRA operators of the troubles. Gerry McGeough,* forty-one and now studying history at Trinity College, Dublin, is one of the more prominent Republicans produced in the area. His career in the IRA took him through three continents and several countries.

His international travels began when he escaped from hospital while being treated for a bullet wound which he later discovered took away his spleen. A party of friends came to visit him in his room, one of them wearing a wig. He was given the wig and clothes, and his moustache was dry-shaved off him. Then the man who had originally worn the wig got into his bed and, surrounded by his friends, McGeough walked down the long hospital corridor, keeping a smile on his face as his stitches tore at every step, past a number of unsuspecting detectives, and disappeared into the IRA network. Back in the hospital room, his substitute eventually became bored, got out of bed, and in his stockinged feet (McGeough had worn his shoes) and calling out 'goodbye now, Gerry' as he stepped through the door, strolled casually out of the hospital.

McGeough, who describes himself as 'ultra-Nationalist and patriotic' remembers that as a six-year-old, his interest in Irish history was stimulated by the series of programmes which RTE put out to commemorate the fiftieth anniversary of the 1916 Rising. He and his schoolboy friends, using stick rifles, played shooting Black & Tan games in the fields around his home. A few years later, as the Civil Rights movement gathered force, images of Dubček's 'Prague Spring' and Russian tanks vied on the television screen with those of Civil Rights marches.

Rumours spread that the RUC and the Loyalists would also be coming in tanks to quell the Civil Rights movement; that buses were coming to bring the men of the district to fight with the forces of 'the Free State'. Nearby Dungannon was a focal point for Civil Rights agitation. McGeough remembered one night persuading his father to

* Interviews by author, 28 March 2000.

allow him to stay up with him as his father patrolled their farm area at 3 a.m. The sky was lit up by the gunfire of the RUC and the B-Specials. They could hear shooting coming from Dungannon, and discovered the next day that nine Catholics had been shot and wounded by the RUC. The countryside was 'up'; Nationalists were taking to the streets to take the pressure off Belfast and Derry.

Both Orange and Green were looking to their defences. As he accompanied his father, McGeough carried a broomstick and a bin lid. But the wife of their Protestant neighbour was patrolling with a lighted torch and a .303 rifle. Her husband was away with the B-Specials. That was when McGeough says he realized that the real difference between his family and friends and those of the Orange tradition, with whom they normally got on extremely well, was not that a tri-colour floated from the barn of one, a Union Jack from the other, it was that he was carrying a broomstick, his neighbour a rifle.

McGeough moved to overcome this discrepancy in 1975, joining Sinn Fein at the age of sixteen. A year later, having reached the minimum age, he joined the IRA. He was first arrested in 1977, and had his first taste of interrogation in Cookstown RUC barracks. Four RUC officers stood around him, punching him and kicking him in shifts. He didn't talk, and was eventually released. It was the first of several such experiences in different barracks. The following year, 1978, he was on holiday in London, but the police, obviously knowing his reputation, regarded him as a potential bomber and arrested him.

He was again interrogated over a period of several days during exhausting seven-hour bouts of questioning, and was deported. Before deportation, he was solemnly warned that he could never again visit the Channel Islands, the Isle of Man, or the United Kingdom, and was then sent back to the Six Counties of Ireland, which were at war over the proposition that they should be regarded as part of the United Kingdom. The policeman, when reading his deportation order, obviously considered, from the solemnity with which he pronounced the sentence, that the worst part of the decision lay in the fact that McGeough would 'never be eligible to join the British Army'!

After recovering from his wounds following his hospital escape, McGeough acquired a deep religious faith – 'one tends to after receiving the Last Rights' – and a false passport which took him to America. He relied on himself, keeping away from Irish networks and districts like Queens, and survived in New York by digging tunnels. After some months living the brutal life of a sandhog, the IRA asked him to set up a gun-running network. He was doing this successfully when he was asked to take over for another Republican operative who was arranging a separate arms purchase.

McGeough was brought in a limousine to a wharfside meeting with 'arms dealers', which turned out to be an FBI sting. The armaments he had been procuring successfully up to the time of the meeting were captured. He went on the run, again keeping away from Irish contacts, and backpacked his way across America. He slept on the prairies 'petrified of the dark and the snakes'. Eventually he landed in California. The arrest of other IRA gun-runners made him realize that America was getting too hot for him – he subsequently learnt that he was on the FBI's 'Ten most Wanted' international list – and made for Hawaii: 'I reckoned that was the last place they would look for an IRA man'.

He worked at picking apples using a false ID supplied by a friend. (Many IRA men disguised their identities this way. A friend initially sacrifices his papers and, after a safe interval, reports them lost.) He managed to avoid arrest by cultivating an American accent and acquiring a tan. 'You let the sun bleach your hair and you watch what people are wearing, how they behave, and you become a sort of cultural chameleon. A lot of guys used to wonder how the Feds picked them up so easily – they'd come over from Belfast wearing their Belfast gear, denims and Doc Martens.'

Using a friend's ID, he got an American passport, and made his way to Sweden in 1983, where he applied for political asylum. This fell through because he became involved in setting up Irish support groups and picketing British functions, and 'landed up on page one'. With the aid of another false passport he made his way to Egypt, again 'not the sort of place they'd go looking for an IRA man', and then back to Ireland, where he was assigned, because of his languages, to Europe once more. Here he took part in the European campaign described in Chapter 35, which had the effect of confining some 70,000 British troops to barracks.

He and Gerald Hanratty were eventually caught by German police in a laneway between the Dutch and German border. Thatcher was delighted and graciously offered the Germans the services of her interrogators. The Germans politely declined. They had their own methods. For two years, McGeough was incarcertated in Frankepthal prison which had been built to house the Bader-Meinhoff gang and subjected to the treatment meted out to the Bader-Meinhoff. He lived for two years without stimuli of any sort, education, mass. His mail took three weeks to leave the prison and a further three weeks to get to its destination. He was allowed exercise for one hour each day with his arms handcuffed behind his back. If it had rained recently he was not allowed out. He was permitted three one-hour visits a month, with a stenographer present writing down every word.

He was then transferred to Wupperthal prison, where he was allowed more exercise. His trial began on 16 August 1990. It caught the attention of the public when he was seen on television replying to the question, 'Are you British?': 'If you were East German, would you say you were Russian?'.

The trial went on for two years during which he was transferred to Dusseldorf prison. 'It was a nightmare prison, dark at night and day. They had all sorts of electronic gear and the atmosphere was full of static. Your skin itched all the time. People died of cancer. Guards had to be replaced.' Then the US indictment for his gun-running came through. The meticulous German legal system meant that the court consulted every country with which McGeough had been involved and went all round Europe taking evidence, including Belfast. Danish, Dutch, German, British, and Northern Ireland police gave evidence, much of it fabricated. It all took time. In the midst of the proceedings, the Germans overlooked dealing with the indictment and so fell foul of a technicality whereby after a certain period in custody, someone sought under an extradition order had to be returned to the country seeking them.

The result was that McGeough wearing both German handcuffs and American arm and leg-irons which were chained together, was flown to Dover airforce base in Delaware from Frankfurt in May 1992. 'A girl on the flight tried explaining the safety drill to me. "Pull the life-jacket over your head so." With the chains on me! If that plane went down I was going straight to the bottom.' When he landed at Dover, 'The whole place was buzzing because they had just brought in Noriega from Panama.' He too speedily developed a buzz because he was released on bail for one million dollars – friends put their houses up as surety. He took to the road on the 'chicken and chips circuit' propagandizing for the Republican cause. The conditions of his bail stipulated that he check in with police in Brooklyn every day. He did so – by phone. The American authorities were not really interested in his case and would not have pursued it had it not been for the German enquiries. During this time, the Germans tried to have him returned to continue his trial, and actually sent a Lufthansa ticket made out in his name to Washington. Their request was turned down after his lawyer successfully argued that to return him meant conniving at the jumping of a one million dollar bail bond. He finally served two years in jail out of a three-year sentence, and returned to Ireland where he is now active in Sinn Fein politics. At the time of writing he was running the Trinity College branch of Sinn Fein and had just been elected to the Sinn Fein Ard Comhairle, the party's ruling body.

After all that, I asked him what he thought of the present position of the cause for which he inflicted and endured? He replied, 'A return to violence is a non-runner. We have passed now through the military phase to a period of conflict resolution.'

Is that a commonly met with sentiment in the border areas? In an effort to find out I conducted a series of interviews in the district at the end of January and the beginning of February 2000.

The significance of Crossmaglen I have already described (Chapter 21). The place looked more prosperous than it did then but the spirit of the district remains the same. I dropped into Paddy Short's pub where, as when I first met him a quarter of a century earlier, he was dispensing pints, observations on the human condition, and the pure unadulterated Republican gospel. With me was Conor Murphy, a Sinn Fein Assembly member from Camlough, South Armagh. Murphy is typical, both of the Republican tradition of the area and of the modern breed of young, university-trained Sinn Fein leader (that is both in the Republican university sense and the academic one, Conor having served a term in Long Kesh). One of his ancestors was Frank Aiken, whose Fourth Northern Division built up a terrifying reputation in the area, as we saw, and who signed the ceasefire and dump order which ended the Civil War in 1923 – without decommissioning.

It was dark when we drove into the village, yet as we left Paddy Short's, a couple of people hailed me on the street, saying things like, 'I thought it was yourself' or 'I saw you crossing the street'. To me it was pitch dark, and the street lighting was not all that bright, but in Crossmaglen they seemed to be equipped with human sensors. Inside Paddy Short's, the talk was of the Patten Commission Report on the RUC and its recommendations, the acid test of which Gerry Adams has said would be whether they would lead to young men from Crossmaglen considering the police as a career. Everyone agreed with Paddy when he said: 'I don't think anyone from around here will join the police force, no matter what they do. It's just not in their nature. You see, there was never employment around here. The people were never employed by a boss, or worked in factories. So they're not servile. They're very independent.'

Those present supported the ceasefire and wanted to see it hold. But they had the same muted caution with which they had greeted the ceasefire on day one back in August 1994: 'We'll see how it works out. We'll give it a chance. But there was no champagne or flags here when it was declared, and there are none now. We don't think the Unionists really want to do a deal, or that Trimble wants to in his heart. But even if the Assembly doesn't work, we won't go back to war that easy.' Even in the dark, one was reminded of the war. The car's headlights lit up what at first sight appeared to be ordinary road signs, but on closer inspection turned out to read: 'Sniper at work'. People pointed out the evidence of prosperity, new shop fronts, new homes, but in the same breath indicated buildings which had been blown up during the troubles and remembered where they were when the incidents occurred. Army helicopters still clatter overhead and no one gave any indication that they would be sorry to see the British Army barracks, which still dominates the town, join the vanished buildings.

A recent book, *Bandit Country* by Toby Harnden, a *Daily Telegraph* journalist, devotes a good deal of space to the smuggling and scam activities of South Armagh. Harnden's view, which is also that of his British Army sources, is accurate in so far as it goes, but it leaves out the obverse side of the coin. Side by side with the 'bandit country' image, there exists a strong cultural tradition. There is a love of music and of history. The environment and folklore of the area is treasured. People will drive long distances to hear a lecture or a debate. There are many such in the area nowadays on aspects of the political situation. They will generally be well attended, questioning will go on for at least as long as the talk, and the discussions afterwards only end when bartenders begin to complain of cruel and unusual punishment. Even then the departure of barmen or the closure of pubs only marks the ending of a stage in the hospitality.

After leaving a pub in Camlough, for instance, I was brought to Conor's in-laws' magnificent home, where fine wines and good food were produced. The girls of the house, some eight of them, returned from the disco to join us, and the festivities didn't break up until 5.30 in the morning. Obviously, the existence of the ceasefire added a dimension of gaiety, and security, to the gathering. But there was another factor at work. Though an outsider might have been forgiven for not seeing it. Like Conor's brothers and sisters, most of those girls live and work in the area, or at least in the nearby town of Newry. They share a love of travel common to both Catholic and Protestant, but unlike the Protestants they return from their travels. One of the sisters had only come home a few days earlier, from Australia and Vietnam. They see their future as lying at home, despite the uncertainties of the moment.

In Camlough, Conor Murphy's birthplace, one can see how the two traditions, not so much of lawlessness, but clan law, a pride in the area, and a disdain for the official system co-exist side by side. The area is prosperous looking. Many of the new houses have been built by mortgagees, who mysteriously develop a tendency to fall on hard times as soon as the house is built, with the result that the mortgage repayments on the tidy homes and their well-tended gardens have to be taken over by the State. Camlough takes its name from a small picturesque lake graced by the presence of flocks of swans, which has a reputation for being plentifully stocked with trout.

The lake owes its existence to a classic piece of South Armagh politics. The water in the lake fell year by year as the local council drained it off for various purposes. The trout were in danger of dying out, the swans disappearing. In vain did the local environmentalists protest. Then finally, one dark night, a couple of local eco-warriors, both prominent Republicans, dumped sacks of cement into the council outlet. The siphoning off of the water stopped, the lake regained its former level, trout and swans multiplied, and the place reverted to being the beauty spot it was in Conor Murphy's boyhood.

But his memory of the lake is not merely of fishing and swimming, Conor remarked: 'I remember I was getting out of the water and I heard these bangs. I didn't know what they were, but it turned out it was two policemen being shot.' The whole area is redolent of such memories: here two RUC police superintendents met their deaths, there is the Three Steps pub, where the British undercover agent, Captain Robert Nirac, passed into grisly legend, after being kidnapped in the pub's car park, tortured, shot, and ultimately turned into dog meat. Not far away is Edenappa, where I began this chapter.

Had I been writing prior to August 1994, I would have been describing events like the deaths of the superintendents and of Nirac, but now as the millennium dawns on a shaky peace, it is a different scene. Republicanism is as active as ever, but in a political and economic, rather than a military guise. The perfect place to see this in operation is Caledon, both a microcosm of the Six Counties and the place where in a very real sense the contemporary troubles began. This Tyrone village is one of the most beautiful in Ireland. It looks like an English village filled with stone gamekeepers' cottages, which was somehow set down in the Irish countryside. Around it lie three adjoining walled estates. One is owned by the Leslie family, whose ancestor Shane Leslie, Winston Churchill's cousin, was one of the sympathetic influences which helped to bring about the Irish Treaty. One by Lord Caledon, and one by the Stronge family. As I indicated in Chapter 33, Sir Norman Stronge and his son paid with their lives at the hands of Jim Lynagh's ASU for the discrimination and sectarianism which lay behind this outwardly idyllic vista of benevolent paternalism.

The reason for the killings was a UDA attack on Bernadette McAliskey (née Devlin) and her husband as they lay in bed a few days earlier. They survived their wounds, although one bullet caused Bernadette to walk with a limp thereafter. However, Jim Lynagh made a unilateral decision to, as he said, 'put an end to this shit'. Lynagh was a swashbuckling figure who often acted independently of GHQ discipline. His unorthodox skills as a guerrilla, which gave him virtual autonomy and cult status in the Republican community, also carried over into other aspects of life. Women fell for him in droves. Visiting a wounded colleague in hospital once, he discovered that his friend was worried that a bullet might have 'damaged his tackle'.

'Right,' said Lynagh, 'there's only one way to find out!' and left the room. He reappeared a little later with one of his girlfriends in tow. 'OK now,' he ordered, 'hop into bed there and test out your man's tackle.' He then departed, leaving the couple in bed to establish, with some difficulty, given the number of the stitches and tubes in the wounded man – to say nothing of the presence of a Special Branch police man sitting outside the door – that the 'tackle' was indeed functioning perfectly. The only threat of *coitus interruptus* came when a nurse unexpectedly entered the room, but left as speedily as she entered, remarking to no one in particular, 'Not too much wrong with your man.'

The Caledon raid demonstrated Lynagh's grimmer side. He took his unit on a search and destroy mission to the Stronge estate, because of the family's prominence in Unionist society, and after the Stronges were shot set fire to their mansion. Then in a manner reminiscent of a wild west shoot-out, he and his men shot their way through the armoured vehicles of the Stronges' RUC escort and made their escape. He and his unit died, as we have seen, at Loughall in an SAS ambush from which there was no escaping.

The superficiality of Caledon's benevolent paternalism became very clear to members of the Goodfellow, McKenna and Gildernew families in 1968. There was talk of civil rights in the air, the strains of 'We shall overcome' were to be heard in Caledon as elsewhere. It was the strain of living that weighed most heavily on Marie Theresa Goodfellow, who had married into a well-respected local Catholic family, the Gildernews. Marie Theresa had returned from England with her husband, determined to live in her native place. But, as explained earlier, housing was the keystone of Orange supremacy. Allocating houses to Protestants not only kept Catholics from settling in the area; the property franchise, long since abolished elsewhere in the United Kingdom, meant that ownership of a house entitled the owner to vote in Local Government elections. Marie Theresa had three children and they had to move in with her parents and their five children. Their circumstances were not particularly extraordinary. Some local Catholic families had as many as ten children, and had been on housing lists for fourteen years.

On a day in 1968, the Gildernews and the others learned that eighteen-year-old Emily Beattie, the secretary to a prominent local businessman, an Orangeman, had been awarded a house because she intended to get married. They decided to make an unheard of protest – stage a sit-in. On the morning the sit-in began, a Protestant neighbour of the Gildernews remarked that it was a fine day and asked Anne Marie Gildernew, the mother of eight children, 'was she not making hay?' 'No,' replied Anne Marie, 'we're making history.' They were. Numbers nine and eleven, Kinard Park, Caledon Housing Estate, became two of the most famous addresses in the Six Counties. The squat lasted for nine months in the teeth of the hostility of the outraged Protestant estate and district. The publicity created by a young Nationalist MP, Austin Currie, joining the protest, and the pictures of a pregnant woman and a grandmother being eventually evicted by the RUC caught the public's imagination. The nascent Civil Rights movement had received a huge impetus.

Shortly before I began to write this chapter, children in a Caledon school were given a project by their teacher: they were to research the history of the Caledon sit-in. One of the pupils put up her hand to ask for some information, and the shocked teacher suddenly realized that the teenager was a daughter of the former Emily Beattie. Accordingly, the teacher replied by telling the class that they should all consult their parents about the incident. So that evening, the former Miss Beattie sat her daughter down and explained to her the situation which had obtained in her area thirty-two years earlier. A little later, the mother met one of the Gildernew family in the local pub and burst into tears as she told him of the school project. The Green bought the Orange a drink, saying: 'Well, well. That's history for you. You're ashamed of it, and we're proud of it.' Gildernew could have been talking about the history of the Orange state and how the Republicans view their struggle to overthrow it.

I was driven around the area by two of the younger Gildernews. One, Michelle, is now a Sinn Fein Assembly member, the other, her brother Martin, was the child in the womb of the pregnant squatter, Geraldine Gildernew, during the sit-in. He too is an active Republican. As such, he was frequently stopped by the security forces and kept at the side of the road, sometimes for up to twenty hours while his car was checked and 'verification procedures conducted'. One day in 1993 at such a military checkpoint, a civilian photographer suddenly appeared and took several pictures of Martin. The pictures were passed on to a Loyalist paramilitary leader on the Shankill Road, who later served a prison sentence. Less than two months after the Gildernews told me of this incident Michelle was in the news* again because of a similar incident. She handed over to the Irish Government a list of twenty-three names found in a lost wallet, the contents of which Sinn Fein claimed identified the owner as a member of the Royal Irish Regiment. The names were those of Republicans living in a wide area of Tyrone and Armagh and were accompanied by the registration numbers of their cars, some bought only in the previous three weeks. The finding of the wallet occurred, of course, in peacetime. Martin Gildernew was particularly lucky: his photographs were taken during the war. This sort of frequently denied collusion between the security forces and Loyalist paramilitaries resulted in several deaths. The Army and the RUC were able to use the 'enemy of my enemy is my friend' policy to dispose of suspected Republicans (often many of the victims had nothing whatever to do with the IRA) without leaving any smoking guns lying around.

A friend of the Gildernews was not so lucky. On a wall near the border village of Aughnacloy, not far from Caledon, there is a plaque – the border area is full of such commemorative plaques – to Aiden MacAnaspie, a Gaelic football-playing friend of Martin's. Delays at the checkpoint were so notorious that on the day of a match, it was

* *Irish News*, 23 March 2000.

customary to allow an hour or more for the inevitable hold-up. One day, Martin and a group of friends were waved through with only a minimum delay. There was something different about the soldiers manning the checkpoint and the passengers in the car agreed 'there must be something up'. Ten minutes later, Aiden McAnaspie arrived at the post and was shot dead. That night the Army fired several shots around the area, and it was later claimed that McAnaspie had been accidentally killed by a ricochet.

As in Crossmaglen or Camlough, Caledon is dominated by a huge military fort, several floors of which are under ground level. As an aid to peacekeeping, the fort has the same effect on the people of the area as does a red rag on a bull. Caledon is so quiet that one could park a car across the middle of the main street on a Saturday afternoon without causing an obstruction. It doesn't look like the centre of an area where there could be any prosperity. But the prosperity exists. We have already described how the Brantry district and its traditions contributed to the military aspect of a prominent Republican from the area. At the Gildernew farm in the heart of Brantry, they will tell you how matters have fared in the economic and political spheres. Phelim Gildernew, Michelle's father, told me:

> When the squat took place there were twelve Catholics employed in this district. I could name them all for you still, mostly they were shop assistants. Now there are over 1,000 Catholics working around here. And the Protestants are moving out. They just won't stay. There's a fine 300 acre farm down the road, and the son of the place is living abroad. He's told the father, 'No. I'm not coming back.'

The Protestant exodus is not due, as some Unionist apologists would have it believed, simply to ethnic cleansing. Certainly, as both the Stronge killings indicate, and the subsequent wiping out of the IRA unit responsible, Jim Lynagh's ASU, at Loughgall, terrible deeds were done in Tyrone and in the border areas generally. Agrarian warfare traditionally possesses ghastly qualities of its own, a combination of the elemental, land hunger and sectarianism. It was inevitable that, as by tradition members of the Protestant community automatically joined either the RUC, the B-specials or the Ulster Defence Regiment which followed them, they would come into armed confict with their Catholic neighbours who either had, or were suspected of, joining or supporting the IRA. As a result, deeds were done of which neither side can feel proud.

But the differing traditions of the two sects played a large part in the growth of Catholic strength and the corresponding Protestant exodus. In vain did the Orange Order try to set up funds to buy Protestant farms to prevent them falling into Catholic hands. Nationalist auctioneers and solicitors could increasingly be heard employing rugby parlance to describe yet another sale by a Protestant to a Catholic: 'We took another one against the head today.' The sheer energy which created the Celtic Tiger, U2, Riverdance, and the rest of it on one side of the border, was at work on the other also. On top of this, whether in the area of the border or Belfast, they will tell you: 'The Catholics had to learn to beat the system. They had nothing. They had to hustle.'

The typical economic pattern which this produced around Caledon, for example, was explained by Phelim Gildernew: 'The Catholic would lay hands on a digger, or an old lorry, and he'd start working with that. Then maybe he'd set up a little engineering works, fixing tractors and so on. He'd buy a bit of land, and the first thing he'd do is he'd give a site to the son or the daughter who's getting married. Or maybe they'd do up the old house on the place and move in themselves and build a new house for the kids. So you'd have two, three, four families living in the one place.'

This was true of the Gildernews themselves, as it was of the Murphys. On either side of him Conor had a brother and a sister each living in comfortable bungalows, with a generous garden, all carved out of what was basically a small family farm. In addition, his in-laws lived only a short distance away. When I asked Michelle Gildernew if the fact of having parents and siblings living so close did not create a valley of the squinting windows syndrome, the military or clan aspect of the system immediately became apparent: 'No. It means that the family are there for you in times of trouble if the soldiers or the police come. If Loyalists are seen in the area.'

As the Protestants looked to the B-Specials, the RUC and the Army to protect them, they only thought of their holdings in conventional agricultural terms, with results which Phelim Gildernew described as follows: 'But if a Protestant farmer bought land, the first thing he'd do was level the old dwelling house and the garden so as to make more grazing. So that meant one less house. And then sheep and cattle prices went down. Whereas the Catholics, as they only had a small bit of land anyway, couldn't go in for grazing. They went for mushroom growing. And,' he remarked with unconscious irony, 'they made a bomb out of it.' He also told a story which, while funny in its way, illustrates the tragedy of the dwindling, and increasingly isolated Protestant community in the area, a microcosm of the position of the landed Protestants in the Six Counties as a whole. Along with the mushroom growing and the engineering, the great unstated method of making money in the area is smuggling diesel across the border from the Republic, where it is far cheaper than in the North. A certain Protestant farmer, driven by the exigencies of the agricultural situation, finally decided to go in for growing mushrooms. He did reasonably well, but the cost of diesel prevented him making a more comfortable living.

He finally pocketed his pride and called on a Catholic neighbour to ask for the address of the man who would supply him with the diesel in Co. Monaghan across the border. When I say across the border I mean the term literally. Not far from the Gildernews' home, Blackwater Bridge links Glaslough and Emyvale on either side of the border. It is in fact a symbol both of the proximity and divisions of the two parts of Ireland. Prior to the troubles, the farmers in the area used to use the bridge to access their land on either side of the river. But the Army have built barriers across the bridge so that traffic cannot pass and Stormont refuses either to remove the barriers or to tarmacadam the muddy approach road to the river. As a result of the ceasefire a myriad of other crossings within a couple of miles of this artificially divided rural area have been restored. However, the local people believe that because nearby Caledon Barracks has been attacked so often, the Army want to prevent this particular bridge being used to mount raids from the Republic. In fact, as we will see later, there is far more animosity towards the Army around Caledon itself than anywhere in the Republic.

But the Protestant farmer could only swallow his pride to the extent of obtaining the diesel supplier's address. He could not bring himself to admit to his neighbour that he did not know how to find the way to Monaghan. All his life had been spent facing east. The Republic, according to his mythology, was the Citadel of the Enemy. The unfortunate man had to ask three of his Protestant neighbours for directions before he finally found his way across the border to the neighbouring town. Once there, he easily obtained his diesel and was astounded at the bustle and life on the other side of the border, as compared to the stagnation around Caledon. At the time of writing, he and his wife are making regular trips to have Sunday lunch in one of the mushrooming, no pun intended, hotels in the Republic.

But not all reservations are as easily put to rest. As we drove through Caledon, we passed a platoon of paratroopers returning to their barracks

at the 'bomb burst'. Leaving and entering the barracks, it was customary during the troubles for the soldiers to burst into a run, each man
leaving several paces between himself and his comrade so as to minimize
the target open to a bomber. Now, after several years of ceasefire, the
most hated regiment in Ireland following Bloody Sunday were still
employing these tactics, loaded rifles at the ready, on the streets of
Caledon, where the Civil Rights movement took off, and led to the
Good Friday Agreement. Two days after seeing the paratroopers, from
our different vantage points in the building, Michelle Gildernew and
I witnessed the effects of the outworking of the paratroopers' presence
in Caledon on that process: the announcement by David Trimble that
as the IRA were not decommissioning, he would implement the threat
contained in his letter of resignation to the Unionist Council. The
Assembly swayed and was officially seen to fall a week later.

The atmosphere at Stormont was a combination of high drama and
farce. The outside of the building was ringed by satellite dishes beaming
the signals of the world's media around the globe. In the corridors of
the restaurant one bumped into famous actors in the drama of Ireland
– John Hume, Gerry Adams, Ian Paisley. Hume looks surprisingly
well on camera, but the composure was achieved with great effort. Close
up he showed the effects of four recent serious operations. Conversely,
Paisley in the flesh appeared ruddy-faced and powerful, belying the
shaky impression that he increasingly conveys on television. Adams,
Pat Doherty, Conor Murphy, Gerry Kelly, and the rest of the Sinn
Feiners bore smiling faces and attempted to convey an impression of
business as usual.

Journalists moved through the crowded lobby attempting to interview anything that moved. 'Is it true that senior Irish civil servants
met the Chief of Staff of the IRA this morning to get him to decommission? Why won't the IRA decommission? Why do they want to
hold on to a few secondhand guns and some mouldy explosive?' 'Will
the ceasefire break down?' 'I hear Clinton was on the phone . . . I hear
Blair was in touch with Dublin . . . Dublin has just been in touch with
Mandelson . . .' and so on. The overall atmosphere was cheerful, and
if one wasn't reading the papers or watching television, one could
simply get the impression of a busy provincial parliament at work.
Outside, there were delegations of farmers protesting agricultural
prices, and of schoolchildren seeking increased funding for education.
They were a paradigm of the Six Counties as a whole. The Assembly
would do nothing for them.

On the floor of the house, David Trimble rose to speak on a motion he had put down calling for a debate on decommissioning and the peace process. There was a rustle of expectation, followed by surprise as he announced that he was withdrawing his motion. The Assembly adjourned. Only Paisley and his son, Ian Junior (the pair are known in Loyalist circles as Papa Doc and Baby Doc) seemed annoyed. They had been preparing to deliver a broadside against Trimble for his handling of the peace process. Perhaps the crisis was over? Maybe Trimble had decided to get off the hook of decommissioning, abandon his threat to resign and try to make the Good Friday Agreement work? Not so. Half an hour later, Trimble called a press conference to announce that he had learnt that General de Chastelain's report would show that the IRA were not decommissioning, and therefore he intended to proceed with his resignation.

In the lobby, people were milling around. I met Billy Hutchinson, the Progressive Unionist Party leader, who had served a lengthy spell in Long Kesh for his UVF activities. He greeted me in friendly fashion and (correctly) diagnosed what was at the heart of what we had just witnessed both on the floor of the house and in the preceding months in the sparring over the decommissioning issue. 'This is all about Trimble looking over his shoulder at Paisley and his own 'no' men. It's all nonsense, everyone knows the Provos are not going back to war.'

That was the voice of enlightened working-class Loyalism. Roy Bradford, a Unionist Minister in the power-sharing executive of 1974, described to me once how, at the height of the crisis brought on by the Loyalist workers' strike, he was visited in his office by a predecessor of Hutchinson in the UVF leadership, Ken Gibson. After the visit Bradford withdrew his support from the executive and the Government fell. Leaving aside what the episode tells us about the relationship of paramilitaries to Unionist politicians – it would be unthinkable, for example, for an IRA Chief of Staff to be in a position to walk into a Cabinet Minister's office in Dail Eireann – Hutchinson wanted the Assembly to survive. Like his hero, Gusty Spence, the man who revivified the UVF in 1966, he was sick of the politics of sectarianism, of taking actions inspired by the wild and whirling words of others, which landed people like him in jail, and did nothing to further the interests of the Protestant working classes. Spence once famously remarked:* 'I

---

* At a Labour Party Conference in Bournemouth, 30 September 1985. Reported *Irish Times*, 1 October 1985.

am the founder of the UVF. I spent eighteen and a half years in prison and I am not proud of it. I am ashamed of it. I am against violence. I'd love to take Paisley by the scruff of the neck and rub his face in the blood and guts that have been spilled and make him smell them and taste them.'

But the day was not to be carried by the forces of progress or repentance. Now it was the Unionist Party politicians, Bradford's successors, who were intent on bringing down a power-sharing executive. The next Unionist figure I met was John Taylor, Trimble's second in command, the deputy leader of the Unionist Party. He and I have been debating on TV and radio programmes for some thirty-five years, and despite our differing views, I naturally walked over to him with my hand extended. He looked at me strangely and I took it that he had forgotten my name. So with my hand still extended I said, 'I'm Tim Pat Coogan, hello, John.' He replied, 'Who are you? Are you a farmer?', gave me a three-fingered handshake and disappeared. A week later, we were back on RTE radio (14 February 2000) discussing the collapse of the Assembly with Niall O'Dowd. In the intervening days, Taylor appeared to have transformed himself into a literary critic. He was able to criticize my writings, and those of Niall O'Dowd, for being 'Republican'.

More importantly, Taylor spelt out his party's sense of triumph at the outcome of events on the programme. He said: 'We have got rid of the Anglo-Irish Agreement. Articles 2 and 3 of the Irish Constitution have been removed, and the Maryfield secretariat has been abolished. Direct rule has been restored.' Later he would go further and, while ostensibly supporting Trimble in the leadership contest against Smith, voted against him on the Burnside motion on the RUC. This narrow view of what has befallen the peace process is unquestionably majority Ulster Unionist Party policy, as opposed to the studiedly moderate platitudes which party spokespersons utter to the media on their desire for inclusivity. In the face of the dangers posed by a breakdown of the peace process, of the inescapable logic of the demographic changes, Unionism remains impervious to reform.

Peter Mandelson in effect buttressed this intransigence when he announced the suspension of the Assembly in the House of Commons on 11 February 2000. No one knows why he did not attempt some sort of fudging stratagem to preserve both Trimble and the executive, as was done in the case of Seamus Mallon's resignation. He explained afterwards, during his background briefing trips to media citadels and to Washington, that he judged that if he did not act, Trimble would be replaced by someone more extreme. In the event, of course, his action meant that the policy of more 'extreme' Unionism prevailed. His decision has been explained in various ways. That he was quite simply out of his depth in life and death, blood and guts politics. A career in the world of the soundbite and the spin-doctor, amidst the colour supplement lives of opinion pollsters and focus group experts, was not a good preparation for negotiating the muddy by-ways of Fermanagh and Tyrone. That he was merely conforming to the traditional Labour policy in Ireland, of talking Green and acting Orange. The fact of his being suggested by Trimble as Mo Mowlam's successor was ruefully recalled in Dublin's Department of Foreign Affairs, as was the fact that he was a nephew of Herbert Samuel, who as Home Secretary first introduced the Unionist veto in 1949. On the actual issue of decommissioning, Mandelson would have been as aware from his intelligence reports, as was the Dublin Government from its sources, that the Provisionals had no intention of going back to war. The exact nature of the IRA's objection to giving up its weapons had been spelt out over and over again.

In the event, the hours prior to the suspension were filled with the most frenetic burst of meetings and negotiation of the entire peace process, greater even than those which secured the Good Friday Agreement itself. There was continuous contact not merely between Sinn Fein, Dublin, London and Washington, but directly between the IRA and Dublin officials. Finally, at 4.30 a.m. on Friday, 11 February, a formula of words which would be acceptable to both the de Chastelain Commission and the IRA was agreed upon. The IRA's concern was with the substance of decommissioning, not the style demanded by the Unionists, i.e. that there should be destruction of 'product' in the presence of military witnesses, before the television cameras.

The sort of settlement envisaged was described in the de Chastelain report* as follows: 'The representative [of the IRA] indicated to us today the context in which the IRA will initiate a comprehensive process to put arms beyond use, in a manner to ensure maximum public confidence.' De Chastelain said that his Commission believed that this commitment held out 'the real prospect of an agreement which would enable it to fulfil the substance of its mandate'. In other words, for the first time since the International Commission was set up, de

---

* Copy in author's possession.

Chastelain believed that he and his colleagues had a commitment from the IRA that decommissioning would happen. This was both a momentous development in itself and, as readers can judge for themselves, a significant advance on another report he had delivered shortly beforehand. (The text of the two de Chastelain reports are contained in Annex A.)

I am also reliably informed that the IRA were prepared, had matters gone other than they did, to issue a statement stating formally that the war was over. This was a demand which had frequently been made by both Conservatives and Unionists. By eleven o'clock on that fateful Friday, both the Dublin Government and Sinn Fein had told Tony Blair what was in the report. Bertie Ahern made it abundantly clear that he felt that it should be built on. However, Mandelson decided otherwise and Blair backed him.

After making his decision, late in the afternoon, Mandelson undercut any prospect there might have been for restoring Nationalists' trust in him by making a tour of Belfast's television studios, during which he at first gave the impression that he did not know what the IRA's offer was. Later in the evening he altered his presentation to suggest that from what he did know, it was so insubstantial as to leave him with no option but to forestall Trimble's resignation by suspending the Assembly. In fact, Mandelson had a copy of the de Chastelain report in his pocket as he made his rounds. This was pointed out on the BBC Northern Ireland *Spotlight* programme, which chronicled his tour of the studios that night, by the BBC's Belfast political correspondent, Stephen Grimerson, who saw him with the document.

On learning of Mandelson's decision the IRA announced that it was withdrawing from contact with the de Chastelain Commission and that its offer was no longer on the table. At a Sinn Fein briefing conference in Dublin two days later, Gerry Adams in effect told the British that if they wanted to talk to the IRA about decommissioning in the future, they would have to do so themselves without help from Sinn Fein. He received thunderous applause when he pointed out that the IRA had not been defeated, and that the Unionists and the British were relying on Sinn Fein to achieve something which they had not been able to do themselves. He accused Britain of 'attempting to gain by stealth what it could not achieve in twenty-five years of military conflict'.

In the wake of the débâcle, Bertie Ahern became so disgusted that he took the unusual step of writing an article in the *Irish Times* (14

February 2000) in which he gave a quotation from the de Chastelain report's reference to the IRA's proposal, an unheard of breach of confidentiality, and pointed out the immense difficulties the suspension caused for the Republic of Ireland, 'a State with a written Constitution'. The Republic's Constitution had been amended to include the terms of the British/Irish Agreement, which did not include provision for suspension. The amendments, made after a nationwide referendum, neutralized by a sweep of Mandelson's pen, had included the dropping of Articles 2 and 3 of the Irish Constitution which had laid claim to Northern Ireland. Other changes made by the Good Friday Agreement which subsequently provided headaches for the Dublin Government were the statutory provisions for setting up the cross-border bodies. Some existing Irish state boards, such as Bord na Gaelige, which promoted the spread of the Irish language, were subsumed into the new cross-border structures, and the destruction of the new creations raised questions about the legality of paying staffs for working in organizations which had technically disappeared.

Somebody in London apparently realized the extent of the débâcle and briefings to journalists commenced in a bid to square the circle of both acknowledging the merit in the IRA's statement and at the same time saving Peter Mandelson's reputation. On 19 February, the political correspondent of the *Irish Times* was informed, 'according to British Governmental sources', that the IRA statement given to de Chastelain would have been sufficient to avert both suspension of the political institutions and the resignation of David Trimble, if, and here lay an attempt to get Mandelson off the hook, 'it been delivered earlier'. The British Government's view was that the offer would have had to have been made formally, earlier, and without the conditions the IRA attached to it. The British position was that Mandelson would have needed another two weeks to persuade Trimble to go back to his Council and have his resignation withdrawn. It was alleged that, had the two weeks been available, the institutions could have continued.

However, this change of face did nothing to materially alter or improve the situation, particularly as Mandelson himself took off on a tour of Washington in which he moved the goalposts further. He told Niall O'Dowd, for example, that nobody except Gerry Adams had told him that the IRA would not decommission in the form demanded by the Unionists, and that he had been led to believe by Dublin that decommissioning was on. Therefore when the crunch came without certainty on any front, he had no option but to suspend the institutions.

In assessing where the Republican movement will go in the wake of the Assembly suspension, it is instructive, if depressing, to remember the importance which the movement attaches to the doctrine of continuity. There is an implicit message in the fact that someone like me, who has been researching Republicanism since the 1960s, finds that they are now interviewing the children, and in some cases the grandchildren, of men and women who had taken part in Republican activities not only during those years, but long before. It was no accident that the group of Republicans who now style themselves 'the Continuity IRA' chose that title. Ruairi O'Bradaigh, who denies that the Republican Sinn Fein Party which he leads is allied to the Continuity IRA, pointedly opened an office in Belfast a few days after the Assembly was suspended, saying:* 'In these days of betrayal, confusion and disillusion, it is surely a sign of hope and a return of morale to declare open this political office in the heart of West Belfast. Republican Sinn Fein,' he said, was 'no mere dissident organization. It was the authentic Republican grouping.' He reminded his listeners that the Party had been formed after Provisional Sinn Fein, i.e. the Adams faction, had voted to allow successful candidates to take seats in the Dail. He said, 'As we pointed out then, the road into the 26 County Parliament at Leinster House (the Dail) led on inevitably to Stormont and even to Westminster.' He condemned the demand for 'the shameful surrender of arms required to achieve the national independence of Ireland' and concluded: 'It is now abundantly clear to the world that the English Government is in charge in Ireland. What the Irish people want counts for nothing as Westminster once more upholds the Unionist veto, snubs the Dublin Government and Stormont collapses.' His recipe for rectifying this situation was to mobilize the people, 'not to bring back Stormont but to end English Imperialism in Ireland.'

Symbolically enough, the *Irish News* printed two large pictures of O'Bradaigh and Gerry Adams taken on the day the RSF office was opened. Adams was speaking at the Sinn Fein Ard Fheis in Dublin, admitting that the Good Friday Agreement was 'in tatters' and issuing a not very well received call to supporters to take to the streets. The caption under the pictures was 'Singing from different hymn sheets'. Which hymn will be listened to has to be a matter of speculation. The

---

* *Irish News*, 28 February 2000.

sheer durability of the Republican tradition came home to me forcibly several times as I researched this, that I fondly hoped to be last, revision of the IRA book. Readers will remember in Chapter 7 I described how a huge agitation built up to spare the lives of the six young men condemned to death for the murder of a policeman during the war years so that ultimately only one, Tommy Williams, was hanged. The last letter he wrote is reproduced on pages 181–2.

The original is now treasured by the family of Hugh McAteer, the late Chief of Staff of the IRA, and a contemporary of Williams, who loaned it to me. Today his son Fergus, a graduate of the Republican university, is one of the figures at the heart of the Republican movement, a policy-maker and central negotiator for Sinn Fein. I met him in Stormont on the day that David Trimble made his resignation announcement. His body language was not that of a happy man. At that stage Mandelson was still a few days away from formally suspending the Assembly. But it was becoming clear that the prospects for any agreement in Northern Ireland based on the consent of Unionists were decidedly slim. However, McAteer felt that for the forseeable future at least, the IRA ceasefire would hold, the policy of the Adams faction, which he had done much to help shape, would also continue, as would the continued growth of the party. However, it was quite clear to both of us that the future was highly dangerous. There were too many inponderables. One bullet could have a catastrophic effect on everything. So could a resumption of the sectarian assassinations, or a sudden eruption of violence during the marching season centred around particular flashpoints like Belfast's Ormeau Road or Portadown's Garvaghy Road.

We remarked on the huge turnout there had been on a Sunday shortly beforehand during which Tommy Williams's remains, which had finally been handed over to the relatives, were laid to rest in Belfast's Milltown Cemetery. The crowds had been of the order of those for the funerals of the hunger-strikers in 1981. Tri-colours flew from every lamppost on the not inconsiderable walk from the Clonard Monastery to the cemetery, evidence of the truth of the Sinn Fein saying, 'Our people come out when we're in trouble.' They didn't come out only for the Williams funeral. A few days after McAteer and I spoke, there was a by-election in Antrim and the Sinn Fein candidate won handsomely. Yet another indication of the difference in how grassroots Nationalism viewed the decommissioning issue compared, say, to the manner in which it was portrayed in the London right-wing press. The Sinn Fein vote mirrored the two dominant, seemingly contrasting attitudes in Republicanism: support for continued peaceful progress and equally strong support for a policy of no decommissioning.

But neither the by-election result, nor the Williams funeral attendance can be viewed merely in terms of Sinn Fein followers showing their support in bad times. After talking with McAteer, I met Sean, the young Republican who joined the IRA in protest at the rubber bullet killing. In the intervening years, he has matured into a most impressive, caring and good-looking young man. He attempted a university degree, but had to interrupt his studies, after a number of incidents made it clear that the journey between West Belfast and the university had made him a likely assassination target. We talked about the Williams funeral, and it was obvious that he was deeply stirred by the event. To him, and to young Republicans like him, Tommy Williams was a member of the Republican pantheon along with the men of 1916, Michael MacVerry, and Bobby Sands. On the day of the funeral, Sean might well have been witnessing the relics of the True Cross pass by. Any attempt to enforce decommissioning on Sean on the grounds that his arms were illegal and that he and his friends were engaged, not in following the footsteps of Williams and the others, but in holding on to criminal weaponry, would meet with a very stern response indeed. For him to countenance such a step the forts at Caledon and in West Belfast, past which they carried Williams's remains, would have to be decommissioned also, as would the weapons held by the Loyalist paramilitaries and the Unionist community generally.

I spent the night of the Trimble announcement in West Belfast. People were uneasy but not surprised. The general mood amongst the IRA members whom I met was that there'd be no going back to war, unless of course the Loyalists started to assassinate Republicans, or embarked on a renewed campaign against Catholics. The Republicans' comings and goings, their hurried leavings, their attendances at 'meetings' which seemingly took place in the small hours of the morning, certainly suggested a gearing up, the restoration of a state of preparedness. Nevertheless, I found no urge to resume hostilities or to make a pre-emptive strike, but there was a widespread sense of disillusionment and depression at the thought that matters should have come to this pass. The hopes that peaceful politics would bring about the result they sought, a United Ireland, a British withdrawal, had certainly been checked rudely, if not altogether dashed. Yet there was no recrimination against the leadership which had held out this vision of a promised land, except on one issue. There was a steely, almost angry, determination on one point. There would be no decommissioning.

> I don't know what Bertie [Bertie Ahern, the Irish Taoiseach] and those are going on about. The way they talk about decommissioning, you'd get the idea they think it is going to happen. There'll be no decommissioning, not one bullet. The IRA were not beaten, we're not going to surrender, we're not giving up our weapons. The war was not 'illegal'. This is a psychological thing, and if those people down at Stormont even attempt to force decommissioning, they're in for it . . .

I might have been back in the days of Michael Collins, listening to a young Republican opponent of the Treaty. That young IRA man had previously eulogized both Gerry Adams and Martin McGuinness to me for their leadership qualities and their integrity. Now, in the intensity of the moment, to him and his friends, Martin McGuinness, Adams, Gerry Kelly and all the other Sinn Fein icons were 'those people down at Stormont'. It was an authentic and valuable indication of how high feelings were running.

An already bleak political landscape turned darker when, against Trimble's wishes, at the Unionist Council meeting on 25 March 2000, David Burnside received overwhelming support from the delegates for his motion tying any re-entry to the Assembly to retaining the name and symbols of the RUC. Decoded, this meant that in addition to decommissioning the Unionists had succeeded in adding another, even more emotive, precondition to sharing power with Sinn Fein. Burnside's motion came in the wake of a poor showing by Trimble in a leadership challenge earlier in the day. The 68-year-old former Grand Master of the Orange Lodge, the Rev. Martin Smyth, secured 45 per cent of the vote to Trimble's 55 per cent. His supporters had been forecasting a 70 per cent plus poll for Trimble. The reduced vote may have been influenced by remarks Trimble made in Washington a few days earlier when, after a bout of arm-twisting by the Americans, he suggested that he might be prepared to see the Assembly restored before the IRA gave up their guns.

What then does the future hold for the IRA? Before attempting my own humble opinion let me quote two people who in a very real sense may have to pick up the pieces, one the Republic's Commissioner of the Gardai, Pat Byrne, the other, the mother of an IRA volunteer whom I asked how she felt in the wake of the Assembly's fall. She replied:

> I wonder will he be brought in to me in a coffin? Is it all going to start again? I think of the searches, the police and the army coming. Never knowing what the knock at the door means. Is it a Loyalist? It is bad news? Will the people start coming and going at all hours? Will I be back to wondering do the neighbours know? Can they be trusted? It's terrible to think of it all going wrong. But that's just the way it is up here. They're them and we're us.

Commissioner Byrne said publicly, obviously with the consent and knowledge of the Dublin Government*:

> The consensus we have come to is that unfortunately you will always have some type of 'IRA' while you have a British presence in Northern Ireland. I'm not making a case for them. As long as people realize that that's the way it's going to be.
>
> If we could turn the clock back I wonder would those wisest among us have insisted that this [decommissioning] is an issue that had to be dealt with before political progress could be continued or maintained or established.

I wish I could answer their questions with a firm guarantee that hostilities will not break out again. Obviously I cannot, but I feel entitled to express a cautious optimism, despite having to acknowledge the difference in the gloomy outlook which obtains at the time of writing, compared to the euphoria with which I ended the chapter completed in 1995. My optimism is based on the fact that the IRA remains tightly disciplined and its leadership, and the bulk of its membership, are committed to the ceasefire. The movement has entered a new phase of political maturity, and understands fully what the political fallout from a return to violence would be. Apart from being politically suicidal, resumption of hostilities by the Provisionals would be militarily so also. As one leading Republican said to me, it would cause 'unimaginable' losses. Unquestionably the security forces have used the ceasefire to vastly improve their intelligence on the IRA. This of course is not to deny that after a few years of attrition,

---

* *Irish News*, 31 March 2000, and quoted by *Irish Times*, 14 March 2000.

sufficient young blood could survive, and percolate through the ranks of the organization, so as to make the Provisionals a formidable – and double embittered – force, just as, seemingly impossibly weak, it emerged in the wake of the Official/Provisional split in 1970. Demonstrably the ceasefires have not ended the Irish physical force tradition as the emergence of the Continuity and Real IRAs illustrates. But the evolution of Sinn Fein into becoming the broad church Nationalist, working-class based, Fianna Fail of the Six Counties was given a considerable filip by their brief experience of power-sharing. Sinn Fein Assembly members hand over much of their pay to the party, retaining not a great deal more than they would receive on the dole, but the participants, many of them formerly active in the IRA, liked the feel of power and their followers liked the sight of their representatives taking decisions which actually benefited their lives. Whatever happens to the Assembly it is generally accepted that the next Belfast Lord Mayor will, for the first time in history, be a Sinn Fein representative. Derry already has a Sinn Fein Lord Mayor, Cathal Crumley, elected on 6 June 2000 by twenty-one votes to eight. Alex Maskie of Sinn Fein was only defeated in the June 2000 Belfast contest because two nationalist councillors fell ill.

It is also widely believed that the demographic and economic thrust of the Nationalists already referred to will be further highlighted, and accelerated, by the results of vital tests of strength scheduled for the early part of the year 2001. In April the census-taking and in May, the Local Government elections. A return to violence would damage the potential of the former for Sinn Fein and harm the vote in the latter, as it would do also in the approaching Westminster elections. Even while this was being written tangible evidence of an affirmative answer to Nationalist demands for justice was given in two important respects. Firstly, a proper enquiry into Bloody Sunday, not a whitewashing operation like that conducted by Lord Widgery, was opened under Lord Saville at the Guildhall in Derry on 27 March 2000. Secondly, wide-ranging reforms in the justice system, in line with proposals in the Good Friday Agreement were announced three days later. The system of appointing judges is to be changed and the Union flag will no longer fly in court buildings. Unlike the proposed RUC reforms these changes were received quite calmly by the majority of Trimble's party.

And over and beyond all these positive steps there was of course the remarkable outcome, on 6 May 2000 to a last-ditch effort to salvage the Good Friday Agreement spear-headed by the British and Irish governments in conjunction with Sinn Fein. The IRA issued a statement, containing the un-precedented concession that the organization would allow two distinguished international observers, to inspect some of their dumps, the former president of Finland, Marti Ahtisaari and Cyril Ramaphosa, the former secretary general of the ANC. The statement also committed the IRA returning to co-operation with the de Chastelain Commission and stating: 'There is no threat to the peace process from the IRA'. (The full text of the Statement is contained in Annex C.)

The statement was issued after weeks of intensive negotiation during which Adams and McGuinness spent long hours in Downing St., Bertie Ahern and Tony Blair spent even longer hours in contact with each other and Blair came to Belfast for the final push, even though, back in London, his demoralized party was reeling from the results of the Local Government elections, and the election of Ken Livingstone as Mayor of London that week. This time Blair sided with the Nationalists. A statement issued by the two governments promised to restore the Assembly by 22 May and carried a coded promise that neither Mandelson, nor any successor would be able to bring it down again with a stroke of a pro-consular pen.

The statement promised that if difficulties again arose over the arms issue that the two governments would consult with both the Assembly and the Executive and carry out an immediate formal review. In other words de Chastelain would not be over-ruled again and there would be no further precipitate suspension, as obviously the Assembly and Executive would have to remain in being so as to be consulted with. The much respected journalist Ann Cadwallader wrote (*Ireland on Sunday*, 7 May 2000) that Peter Mandelson was sidelined:

> when the horse trading was done in Downing St. and Hillsborough, just as Mo Mowlam was, for very different reasons, much earlier. Blair has learned that his Prince of Darkness doesn't walk on water.

In a historic joint letter to all the Northern party leaders the interest, and influence of Dublin on Belfast affairs was implicitly, but unmistakably conceded. Both David Trimble and Ian Paisley had the experience of receiving from the Irish Taoiseach and the British Prime Minister a document in which Ahern and Blair committed the British Government to take measures to safeguard human rights, further the spread of the Irish language and, significantly to: '... take all the necessary steps to secure as early a return as possible to normal security arrangements in Northern Ireland consistent with the level of threat.' As the IRA are committed to presenting no threat this was taken by Nationalists to indicate that the Border forts I described earlier might soon become a thing of the past.

The IRA concession on arms inspection stretched republicans to an extent none of them had ever imagined. Nevertheless, in the spirit that there's many a true word spoken in jest, I believe one IRA man may have summed up the Republican community's reaction accurately to all the foregoing when he said: 'Stormont has been up and down like a whore's knickers over the years, but this should put an end to the fucking around once and for all.'

Those with a taste for symbolism may gauge the reaction of the Unionist community from the result of the Unionist Council meeting at the Waterfront Hall in Belfast of 27 May 2000. The meeting took place against a background of Egyptian mummies arranged for a production of Verdi's Aida later that day. 'It all looked very strange – Trimble, the mummies and there, in the middle of it, the Union Jack,' a delegate commented to the *Irish Times* (29 May 2000). On the basis of the IRA statement, Trimble secured a majority of 53 per cent against 47 per cent in favour of going back into a power sharing Executive with Sinn Fein. Learning from the reaction of his party to his bringing down of the previous Executive – as we have seen a leadership challenge followed six weeks later – Trimble had campaigned for support, in a way he had not done for the Good Friday Agreement, in the week before the vote.

Nevertheless the anti-Agreement forces, led by Jeffrey Donaldson, responded to Donaldson's reminder that, as a member of the UDR, he had 'lain in ditches defending Ulster', by reducing Trimble's victory margin over Smith by 3 per cent and promising a further leadership challenge within months. Trimble himself indicated the degree of affection he held for his prospective Sinn Fein colleagues by telling a press conference after the vote that: 'As far as democracy is concerned these folk ain't house-trained yet'. If he felt it necessary to appeal to his 'moderate' supporters by the use of such language, the feelings of his opponents, especially over such issues as the reform of the RUC and the flying of the Union flag, can well be imagined. Clearly, in the words of the well-known song, 'There'll be trouble ahead.' However, within hours of the result being known Peter Mandelson signed the orders restoring the Executive and its institutions.

While one cannot make this last the basis for any prediction of an outburst of either magnanimity, or even common sense, amongst a majority of the Unionist political community, one can repose a certain faith in elements of what might be termed the unionist public. Amongst business men, in the Presbyterian Church leadership, and above all in the ordinary decent Protestant man and woman in the street the 6 May break-through was broadly, if privately welcomed.

However it emerged as this is being written that the Unionists had succeeded, with the conivance of Peter Mandelson, in getting the police reform Bill re-drafted so that Patten's proposed reforms for the RUC were virtually rendered meaningless. This not alone caused anger in the ranks of Sinn Fein, wherein Gerry Adams' standing was badly damaged as a result, but in the SDLP, to the Dublin Government and amongst Irish Americans. Trouble also looms over the flying of the Union flag on Government. The two Sinn Fein ministers in the Assembly have decreed that either it flies over their Departments, alongside the tricolour, or not at all. Accordingly, though it may yet prove better to have travelled hopefully towards the future than to arrive at it, I venture as much in hope as in confidence to conclude by re-echoing the judgement of Gerry McGeough: 'Return to violence is a non-runner. We have passed through the military phase and we're now into a period of conflict resolution.' Amen say I.

ANNEX A

1. The Full Text

The following is the full text of General John de Chastelain's report given to the British and Irish Governments on 31 January 2000.

1. In our report of 10 December, the commission undertook to report further on decommissioning in January. That is this report. Since December, the commission has held further discussions with representatives of the IRA, the UVF and the UFF.
2. Our previous report stated our belief that the results of the Mitchell review and the designation of IRA and UFF contacts, in addition to the UVF contact already in place, gave the basis for an assessment that decommissioning will happen. While we believe that conclusion was well founded we await further evidence to substantiate it.

3. The IRA contact has assured us of the unequivocal continuing support of his organization for the current political process. We have been made aware of, and recognize, the difficulties facing the IRA leadership in moving on decommissioning at this time. We are also conscious that the maintenance of the ceasefire, and of those of the UVF and UFF, have played and continue to play, an important part in the political advances that have been achieved to date and that are progressing.

4. Further, our contact has very recently emphasized that there is no threat to the peace process from the IRA. All of these factors are significant. But our sole task is decommissioning and to date we have received no information from the IRA as to when decommissioning will start.

5. In our most recent discussion with our UVF contact, he reminded us of the discussions he held with the commission over a long period, including the UVF's early engagement on the issues of modalities. He has also reiterated the UVF stance that while it is prepared to consider moving on decommissioning, it will not do so until it has received an unequivocal statement from the IRA that the war is over.

6. Similarly, our most recent discussion with the representatives of the UFF has confirmed their position stated during our earlier meeting, to the effect that while that group too is prepared to consider moving on decommissioning, it will not do so until it is clear that the IRA will decommission.

7. We will continue our efforts to continue the commission's role in the manner and within the time-frame approved by the political parties and the two governments. However, given our understanding of the quantity of arms held by the paramilitary groups, and the dispersed nature of their locations, we believe a time will soon be reached beyond which it will be logistically impossible for us to complete our task by 22 May. We remain prepared to state, at an appropriate date, when we believe decommissioning must start and how it must proceed if our mandate is to be fulfilled within the required period. But decommissioning is a voluntary act; any schedule we produce will only be of value if those who have the arms agree to follow it.

8. The foregoing noted intensive negotiations have taken place during the past few days. The commission will report further to the governments in the event that ongoing negotiations lead to concrete results.

9. If it becomes clear to us that decommissioning is not to happen the commission will recommend to the governments that it be disbanded.

Signed:

Tauno Nieminen

John de Chastelain

Andrew D. Sens

2. Report of the Independent International Commission on Decommissioning

1. In our report of 31 January 2000, the Commission stated that intense negotiations were continuing and we would report any concrete result that came from them. Since then, we have had several contacts with the IRA and Loyalist representatives.

2. The IRA declaration of support for the process leading to a permanent peace in Ireland, the contribution made by the ceasefires, and the statement that the IRA provides no threat to that process are recognized. We believe that these are important issues of considerable significance for peace and stability in Northern Ireland, and they were reflected in our 31 January report.

3. Since December 1999, the IRA has engaged frankly and helpfully with the Commission and we note their intention to continue to do so.

4. We also note the IRA assessment that the question of British forces and Loyalist paramilitaries in Northern Ireland must be addressed. While the future of British troops is outside our remit, the elimination of the threat posed by Loyalist paramilitary arms is clearly within the Commission's remit. We have been advised by Loyalist representatives of their commitment to address the issue of their arms in the context of similar action taken by the IRA. In our discussions this week with the UVF and UFF representatives, each confirmed their positions as stated in our 31 January report, and the UFF representatives further engaged with us on methods of decommissioning and related support issues.

5. We welcome the IRA's belief that the 'state of perpetual crisis' can be averted and that the issue of arms can be resolved. We find particularly significant, and view as valuable progress, the assertion made to us by the IRA representative that the IRA will consider how to put arms and explosives beyond use, in the context of the full implementation of the Good Friday Agreement, and in the context of the removal of the causes of conflict.

6. The Commission welcomes the IRA's recognition that the issue of

arms needs to be dealt with in an acceptable way and that this is a necessary objective of a genuine peace process and their statement that for those reasons they are engaged with us. The Commission further welcomes the IRA's commitment to sustain and enhance its contribution to a durable peace and their statement that they have supported and will continue to support efforts to secure the resolution of the arms issue.

7. The representative indicated to us today the context in which the IRA will initiate a comprehensive process to put arms beyond use, in a manner as to ensure maximum public confidence.

8. The Commission believes that this commitment, on the basis described above, holds out the real prospect of an agreement which would enable it to fulfil the substance of its mandate. We will make a further report to the two Governments as appropriate.

Tauno Nieminen
John de Chastelain
Andrew D. Sens
Belfast 11 February 2000

ANNEX B

The Good Friday (or Belfast) Agreement consisted of eleven sections:

A **Declaration of Support** in which the participants set out their commitment to a range of basic principles, including non-violence and partnership, equality and mutual respect. They promised to work in good faith to ensure the success of all the arrangements to be established. The interdependence of the various institutions was recognized.

In relation to **Constitutional Issues** the Governments set out their shared view, based on the principles of self-determination and consent as described in the Joint Declaration of 1993, in regard to the status of Northern Ireland as part of the United Kingdom and to how a united Ireland might be achieved with the consent of majorities in both parts of Ireland. Proposed changes to the Irish Constitution and to British constitutional legislation were included.

A new **Assembly** in Northern Ireland was to have devolved legislative powers over broad areas of social and economic policy (some matters, e.g. security, justice, taxation, foreign policy, remained with the British

Government) with executive authority being discharged by Ministers meeting in an Executive Committee, established in Northern Ireland. Appointments were proportionate to party strength and there were extensive safeguards and guarantees for both communities. All key decisions were to be taken only with cross-community support.

A **North/South Ministerial Council** was to have brought together the Irish Government and the Northern Ireland administration to develop consultation, cooperation and action on matters of mutual interest. The Agreement forecast that the Council would meet regularly and frequently and would be supported by a standing joint Secretariat. At least six all-Ireland or cross-border implementation bodies were agreed by the Irish Government and the Northern Ireland Executive, in its shadow, transitional phase, by 31 October 1998, and were scheduled to operate at the Agreement's entry into force.

A new **British–Irish Council**, comprising representatives of the two Governments and of devolved institutions in Northern Ireland, Scotland and Wales, together with the Isle of Man and the Channel Islands was created. Its goal was the harmonious and mutually beneficial development of the totality of relationships among the peoples of the islands. There was also to be a **British–Irish Intergovernmental Conference**, bringing together the British and Irish Governments to promote bilateral cooperation at all levels on all matters of mutual interest. It too had a Standing Joint Secretariat.

There were provisions in regard to **Rights, Safeguard and Equality of Opportunity**, with steps including the creation of Human Rights Commissions being taken both in Northern Ireland and in the South, and a range of commitments in regard to economic, social and cultural issues, in particular as concerned the position of the Irish language in Northern Ireland.

There was a commitment by all parties to work constructively and in good faith, and to use any influence, to achieve the **decommissioning** of paramilitary weapons within two years of approval of the Agreement.

In relation to **security**, it was noted that the development of a peaceful environment on the basis of the Agreement could and should mean a normalization of security arrangements and practices.

Terms of reference were agreed for an independent Commission on **policing**, which were to bring forward, 'no later than summer 1999', proposals to ensure that 'policing arrangements, including composition, recruitment, training, culture, ethos and symbols, are such that in a new approach Northern Ireland has a police service that can enjoy widespread support from, and is seen as an integral part of, the community as a whole'. There was also to be a parallel wide-ranging review of **criminal justice**.

There was an accelerated programme, which began at the end of June 1998, for the release of **prisoners** affiliated to organizations which have established and maintained complete and unequivocal ceasefires. The intention was that, should the circumstances allow it, any qualifying prisoners who remained in custody two years after the commencement of the scheme would be released at that point. The necessary legislation had been enacted in both jurisdictions and the first prisoners have been released.

A final section covered **validation, implementation and review**. It was agreed that referendums be held in both parts of Ireland on 22 May 1998. If there were public endorsement North and South, the two Governments would take all necessary legislative and other steps to bring all the new institutions into being, and to give effect to constitutional changes, at the same time. There were provisions for each institution to review its own operation; for the review of difficulties across two or more institutions, with the Governments acting in consultation with the parties in the Assembly; and for a review conference involving the two Governments and all parties in the Assembly after four years.

Sinn Fein moved further towards constitutionalism when, on 10 May, the party voted to alter its Constitution to allow candidates to take their places in the new Northern Ireland Assembly envisaged in the Good Friday Agreement. This vital decision to drop abstentionism was, readers will remember, one of the reasons for the major split in the IRA in 1969–70, which led to the emergence of the Provisionals in the first place.

IRA Statement, 6 May 2000.

The leadership of the IRA is committed to a just and lasting peace. We have sustained that committment despite the abuse of the peace process by those who persist with the aim of defeating the IRA and Irish republicans.

Republicans believe that the British Government claim to a part of Ireland, its denial of national self-determination to the people of Ireland, the partition of our country and the maintenance of social and economic inequality in the Six Counties are the root causes of conflict.

The maintenance of our cessation is our contribution to the peace process and to the creation of a future in which the causes of conflict are resolved by peaceful means. For our part the IRA leadership is committed to resolving the issue of arms.

The political responsibility for advancing the current situation rests with the two governments, especially with the two governments, especially the British government, and the leadership of the political parties.

The full implementation, on a progressive and irreversible basis by the two governments, especially the British government, of what they have agreed, will provide a political context, in an enduring political process, with the potential to remove the causes of conflict, and in which Irish Republicans and Unionists can, as equals, pursue our respective objectives peacefully.

In that context, the IRA leadership will initiate a process that will completely and verifiably put IRA guns beyond use. We will do it in such a way as to avoid risk to the pubilc and misappropriation by others and ensure maximum public confidence.

We will resume contact with the IICD and enter into further discussions with the commission on the basis of the IRA leadership's committment to resolving the issue of arms.

We look to the two governments, and especially the British government to fulfil their commitments under the GFA and the joint statement.

To facilitate the speedy and full implimentation of the GFA and the government's measures, our arms are silent and secure. There is no threat to the peace process from the IRA.

In this context the IRA leadership has agreed to put in place within weeks, a confidence-building measure to confirm that our weapons remain secure.

The contents of a number of our arms dumps will be inspected by agreed third parties who will report that they have done so to the IICD.

The dumps will be re-inspected regularly to ensure that the weapons remain secure.

APPENDIX I

1980–93: Violence in Northern Ireland

Statistics showing partial breakdown of violence

	1980	1981	1982	1983	1984	1985	1986	1987	1988	1989	1990	1991	1992	1993*
Shooting incidents	642	1142	547	424	334	237	392	674	537	566	559	499	506	211
Explosions	400	529	332	367	248	215	254	384	458	420	287	367	371	106
Armed robberies	467	689	693	718	710	542	839	955	742	604	492	608	738	251
Persons charged with terrorist offences	550	918	686	613	528	522	655	468	439	433	380	397	410	152
Deaths: civilians	50	57	57	44	36	25	37	66	54	39	49	75	76	24
Deaths: army	8	10	21	5	9	2	4	3	21	12	7	5	3	2
Deaths: UDR	9	13	7	10	10	4	8	8	12	2	8	8	3	2
Deaths: RUC/RUC(R)	9	21	12	18	9	23	12	16	6	9	12	6	3	3

*1993 statistics to 31 May.
Figures supplied by the Royal Ulster Constabulary.

APPENDIX II

The IRA Court Martial Procedure

1. A Court-martial is set up by the O/C of any Unit or by the C/S to try any Volunteer on a specific charge or charges.
2. The Court shall consist of three members of equal rank or higher than the accused.
3. The Convening Officer will appoint one member of the Court as President.
4. When a Court-martial is set up by a Unit O/C, the Adjutant of the Unit, or some member of the Unit delegated by the Adjutant to do so, will act as Prosecuting Counsel. When the Convening Authority is the C/S, he may appoint any officer other than the Adjutant General to act as Prosecution Counsel.
5. The accused may call on any Volunteer to act as his Defence Counsel, or, if he so desires, may defend the case himself.
6. A copy of the charges shall be supplied to the accused in reasonable time before the case is heard to enable him to prepare his defence. The Convening Authority may either supply the accused with a summary of the evidence it is proposed to place before the Court, or arrange for a preliminary hearing at which witnesses for the prosecution will give under oath, under a summary of their testimony. At such preliminary hearing, neither defence nor prosecution counsel will be present, but the accused may cross-examine the witnesses. The evidence shall be taken down in writing from each witness, shall be read over to him and shall be signed by him. If the accused wishes to make a statement or give evidence on oath he must be cautioned that anything he says may be taken down and used in evidence, at any subsequent hearing of the case.
7. If the accused objects to any of the three officers comprising the Court, his objection will be examined by the two remaining two members and, if upheld, the member objected to will be replaced.
8. The Convening Authority will ensure that the Prosecuting Counsel is in possession of all the facts relevant to the case and that all prosecution witnesses are present at the Court.
9. The Convening Authority will supply the Court with a copy of the charges and with copies of General Army Orders.
10. During the hearing of the case, all witnesses will be kept in a separate room as in the case of a Court of Inquiry. The only persons present in the Court shall be members of the Court, the accused, the Defence Counsel (if any) and the witness under examination.

11. The oath will be administered as in the case of a Court of Inquiry.
12. At the start of the case, the President will read each case to the accused and ask him if he pleads guilty to the charge.
13. Witnesses when called to testify will be cross-examined first by the Prosecuting Counsel and then by the Defence Counsel, or by the accused if conducting his own defence. Witnesses may be questioned by any member of the Court. Should either Counsel wish to recall a witness who has already testified, permission of the Court must first be obtained. The Court may recall any witness. Witnesses may not leave the precincts of the Court without permission from the Court.
14. At any time it so desires, the Court may go into private session to decide on points which may arise, such as the admissibility of evidence.
15. When all witnesses have testified, Defence Counsel will sum up and make closing address to the Court. This will be followed by summing up and closing address of the Prosecuting Counsel. The Court then goes into private session to consider its verdict and sentence.
16. For a breach of any General Army Order, the Court shall not have power to impose a lesser penalty than that laid down in such order.
17. The verdict and sentence of the Court shall be set down in writing and signed by the three members. This, together with a summary of the evidence, must be forwarded by the President to the Convening Authority. Sentence is subject to the ratification of the Convening Authority. Note: In the case of the death penalty, sentence must be ratified by the A/C.
18. The accused may forward an appeal against the verdict or sentence or both to the Adjutant-General who will place it before the Competent Authority. The appeal should be forwarded by accused through his O/C who in turn will forward it to the Adjutant-General with a signed copy of verdict and sentence and a summary of the evidence. The Competent Authority may order a new trial or reduce the penalty but may not increase the penalty imposed by the Court.

SELECTED REFERENCES

The principal source material for Part 1 of this book was, of course, the more than five hundred interviews I conducted with persons either in or connected with the IRA. I also made use of a wealth of Republican publications: IRA directives, regulations, proclamations, pamphlets, newspapers, records of courts-martial and of county brigade activities, letters and personal statements of various kinds. These, and other material not normally available to the public, such as the ritual (adopted 1931) and constitution (adopted 1946) of the Clann na Gael, were given to me through the kindness of individuals.

The principal Republican newspapers, such as *An Phoblacht*, the *Republican Congress*, *Republican File* and the contemporary *United Irishman* provided useful information, as did the national press, in particular the *Irish Press*, *Irish Times*, *Irish Independent*, *Irish News* and *Belfast Telegraph*. A series of articles in *The People* by Joseph Gallagher (commencing 10 December 1961) shed a good deal of light on Nazi–IRA activities.

These activities and other indications of German policy towards Ireland may be studied more formally in the captured documents on German foreign policy published by the Allies after the Second World War. (Some are in German.) Telegram 101410 dated 24 November 1941, is a lengthy assessment of the Irish position, the worth of Goertz's mission, the IRA's strength and an interpretation of the Hayes affair. It is particularly interesting and well worth translation. But the most comprehensive and easily available study of this aspect of Irish history is Enno Stephan's very fine work, *Spies in Ireland*.

Parts II through IV of this book are based largely on my own experiences, personal files and interviews, many of which must remain unattributable. However, the list of Commission reports published below indicates some of the other sources made use of, and I am appending a short bibliography for the reader whose interest in Northern Irish affairs may have been whetted by *The IRA*. Concerning these books I would make the following points. A. T. Q. Stewart's book and that of Robert Fisk should ideally be read together, Stewart's work (also mentioned in the references of Part 1) coming first. The two books deal with turning-point events in Northern Ireland in which the British army and government failed to confront Loyalists. David Boulton's *The UVF* should ideally be preceded by Bowen's, for the insight they give into Protestant thinking in the last century and in this. My own books I include for those stoic readers who may feel inclined to even more of my own writing, and Bowyer Bell's *The Secret Army* because it is a rival work to my own study of the IRA and, being written by an American, will afford readers an opportunity of seeing how a foreign academic sees the IRA. The depth and scope of Dr Bowyer Bell's earlier work is not matched by the chronology of events to which he has virtually reduced the most recent years of IRA activity. The Chronologies on *Northern Ireland Events*, published by Blackstaff Press, Belfast, and edited by Richard Deutsch and Vivien Magowan, are among the best things to appear over the whole period of the troubles and are an absolute must for any serious student of the period.

Agreed Communiqué of Conference on Northern Ireland between parties involved in setting up Northern Ireland Executive (Dublin, 1974).

Bennett Commission Report into charges of brutality against the RUC (London, 1978). (The Amnesty International Report which gave rise to the charges was published earlier in 1978.)

Cameron Commission on disturbances in Northern Ireland and Commentary on same by Northern Ireland Government (Belfast, 1969).

Compton Report into security forces behaviour arising from internment 9 August 1971 (London, 1971).

Diplock Report on terrorist activities in Northern Ireland (London, 1972).

Gardiner Report on workings of Emergency Power (London, 1976).

Green Paper on Northern Ireland (London, 1972).

Scarman Report, 2 vols. (London, 1972).

Hunt Report (Belfast, 1969).

MacRory Report on local government in Northern Ireland (Belfast, 1970).

Widgery Report into Bloody Sunday (London, 1972).

Boulton, David, *The UVF, 1966–1973* (Gill and Macmillan, Dublin, 1974).

Bell, Bowyer, *The Secret Army: The I.R.A., 1916–1979* (Academy Press, Dublin, 1979).

Bogdanor, Vernon, *Devolution* (Oxford University Press, Oxford, 1979).

Bowen, Desmond, *The Protestant Crusade in Ireland* (McGill-Queen's University Press, Belfast, 1978).

Coogan, Tim Pat, *Disillusioned Decades* (Gill and Macmillan, Dublin 1987).

Coogan, Tim Pat, *Ireland Since the Rising* (Pall Mall, London, 1966).

Coogan, Tim Pat, *The Irish: A Personal View* (Phaidon, London, 1975).

Coogan, Tim Pat, *The Man Who Made Ireland: The Life and Death of Michael Collins* (Roberts Rinehart, Niwot, Colorado, 1992).

Coogan, Tim Pat, *On the Blanket* (Ward River Press, Dublin, 1980).

Dillon, Martin, *Stone Cold* (Arrow, London, 1992).

Fisk, Robert, *The Point of No Return* (Andre Deutsch, London, 1975).

Feuchtwanger, E. J., *Gladstone* (Allen Lane, London, 1975).

Geraghty, Tony, *The Irish War* (HarperCollins, London, 1998).

Harnden, Toby, *Bandit Country* (Hodder & Stoughton, London, 1999).

Jones, Thomas, *Whitehall Diary*, vol. III (Oxford University Press, Oxford, 1971).

Mansfield, Michael, *Presumed Guilty* (Heinemann, London, 1983).

Miller, David, *Queen's Rebels* (Gill and Macmillan, Dublin, 1978).

McDonagh, Oliver, *Ireland: The Union and Aftermath* (Allen and Unwin, London, 1977).

Nairn, Tom, *The Break Up of Britain* (New Left Books, London, 1977).

O'Farrell, Patrick, *Ireland's English Question* (Batsford, London, 1971).

Opsahl, Torkel, ed., *A Citizen's Inquiry: The Opsahl Report* (Liliput Press, Dublin, 1993).

Stewart, A. T. Q., *The Ulster Crisis* (Faber, London, 1967).

Urban, Mark, *Big Boys' Rules: The SAS and the Secret Struggle Against the IRA* (Faber, London, 1992).

GLOSSARY

Ard Fheis Irish language term meaning 'high council' usually used in association with official conventions or conferences of Irish political parties.

Anglo–Irish Agreement A document agreed to by the Fine Gael/Labour Coalition Government of Ireland and Mrs Thatcher's Conservative Government in the United Kingdom in 1985. It stipulates that there shall be no change in the constitutional position of Northern Ireland for so long as the majority wishes to remain as part of the United Kingdom. However, there are provisions for some Dublin influence in Northern Irish affairs which makes in principle for a type of joint sovereignty. Rejected by the Unionists in the North and Fianna Fail in the South, mostly ignored by Sinn Fein and the IRA, it seems to have had very little effect on the current situation.

Articles Two and Three of the Irish Constitution These two provisions of the Irish Constitution lay claim to all thirty-two counties of Ireland, and are often cited by Unionists of the Six Counties as the major hurdle to their cooperation with the Dublin Government in any talks concerning the future of the Six Counties.

BBC British Broadcasting Corporation, the state owned media giant (TV, radio, and publication divisions) of Great Britain.

Black and Tans So nicknamed because of their khaki uniform and black and green belts and caps. These were mainly ex-servicemen sent over by the British as reinforcements for the Royal Irish Constabulary during the guerrilla War of Independence. Another related corps set up to assist the police at that time were the Auxiliary Cadets, the 'Auxies', consisting of ex-British officers. Like the IRA, they elected their own officers. Both corps are remembered in Nationalist folklore as having committed many atrocities.

B-Specials A Protestant state militia first formed in 1920 by Lord Brookeborough from former UVF and British Army members in the Six Counties as a back-up force for the police in helping maintain Protestant ascendancy. After the troubles broke out in late 1969, their activities so outraged British Prime Minister Harold Wilson, that they were disbanded and reconstituted as the Ulster Defence Regiment (UDR) in 1970.

Clann na Gael An Irish-American Nationalist organization founded in 1867 in the wake of the failed Fenian rising and later linked with the IRB. Its activities included fundraising, the heightening of awareness and the raising of support for Irish independence. It was the Clann under John Devoy that funded the 1916 Rising.

Conservative Party   One of Britain's two main political parties, the Conservatives are associated with right-of-centre politics. Also known as the Tory Party, they are allied with the Unionist parties in Northern Ireland.

Dail Eireann   Irish Parliament.

DUP   Democratic Unionist Party led by Rev. Ian Paisley.

EC   European Economic Community. Founded in 1957, this economic union now has fifteen member states. Ireland joined in 1973.

Fianna Fail   'Warriors of Fail' (a poetic symbol for Ireland). Founded in 1923 by Eamon de Valera when he split with Sinn Fein, this is the largest and most powerful of the Irish political parties.

Fine Gael   The second largest political party in the Irish Republic, formed in 1933 from the centre Party, the Blueshirts and Cumann na Gaedheal.

Gardai   Irish police force.

INLA   Irish National Liberation Army. A splinter group from the IRA.

IRA   Irish Republican Army.

IRB   Irish Republican Brotherhood, the Fenians, set up in 1858 as a revolutionary movement. It recognized itself as the provisional governing body of a free and independent Ireland. Reorganized by Michael Collins after the failed Easter Rising, it in effect became the leadership cadre of the Volunteers (IRA).

IRSP   Irish Republican Socialist Party. The political wing of the INLA.

Labour Party   (Irish Republic) The third largest political party in the Republic of Ireland.

Labour Party   (UK) One of Britain's two main political parties. It is usually associated with the labour unions and left-of-centre politics.

Loyalists   Loyal to the Union, these are Ulster Protestants opposed to a thirty-two county Ireland. (Same as Unionists.)

Maastricht Treaty   An agreement reached by the members of the EC in Maastricht, Netherlands in 1992, which lays out several important further steps in the transformation of the Community into a closer federation, and gives new powers to the European Parliament and government organizations.

NORAID   North American Aid. An American organization that raises money for Irish Republican causes.

Official Irish Republican Army   In 1970 the IRA split into the Official IRA and the Provisional IRA, which became the dominant grouping. The OIRA maintained the old line of the IRA, the wish for a socialist thirty-two county Ireland.

Orange Order   (Orangemen) Name taken from the victory of Protestant William of Orange over Catholic King James II. A powerful sectarian order of Protestants characterized by ritualistic pageantry and supremacist celebrations.

Provisionals   (Provos) Now the major IRA force.

Republicans   Supporting a thirty-two county Republic of Ireland.

RTE Radio Telefis Eireann. Irish radio and television network.

RUC Royal Ulster Constabulary. Police force in the Six Counties.

SAS Special Air Services. The special operations force of the British Army against whom most allegations of carrying out a shoot-to-kill policy are directed by Nationalists.

SDLP (Catholic) Social Democratic and Labour Party. Constitutional nationalist party of the Six Counties, founded in 1970 and believing in the necessity of majority consent for a united Ireland. It is largely supported by the middle class.

Seanad Translates as 'Senate'. Upper house of Parliament (the Dail) in Ireland.

Sinn Fein 'Ourselves Alone'. Political party and wing of the Provisional IRA. Mainly supported by working class Catholics.

Six Counties Six of the nine counties which make up the province of Ulster. The Six Counties are part of the United Kingdom.

Taoiseach Prime Minister of the Republic of Ireland.

Thirty-Two Counties The Republic of Ireland and the Six Counties – a united Ireland.

Twenty-Six Counties The Republic of Ireland.

UDA Ulster Defence Association. The major Protestant paramilitary group. UDA spokesmen have advocated that Ulster be independent of both Britain and Ireland. Now outlawed, it is alleged to have links with the DUP and UDR.

UDR Ulster Defence Regiment. Formed in 1970 to replace the old B-Special Corps. It too was heavily criticized and was placed under British Army control in 1992.

UFF Ulster Freedom Fighters. A UDA group which has claimed responsibility for several sectarian murders.

Ulster This should correspond to the ancient nine-county Irish province of Ulster. However, when the State was being set up the Unionists rejected the nine county unit because it contained too many Catholics, and settled for the six counties which they could control. The term is now commonly, but erroneously used by Unionists to refer to the Six Counties.

Unionists Those supporting the 1800 Act of Union when Ireland became part of the United Kingdom and totally opposed to any breaking of ties of the Six Counties with Britain. (Same as Loyalists.)

UVF Ulster Volunteer Force. Originally formed in 1912 with powerful British and Unionist support to oppose Home Rule. It is now a Protestant paramilitary group who have claimed responsibility for several sectarian killings.

INDEX OF NAMES

GENERAL INDEX

Saoirse Eire, 460

Saor Eire, 51, 58–60, 64, 68, 93, 234, 440, 460; Action Group, 331

Saor Uladh (Free Ulster), 283–4, 287, 317

SAS in Ireland, The, 605

S-Branch ('Broy Harriers'), 70

Scheduled offences, 484

Scotland Yard, 389, 461

Scott's Restaurant, Mayfair, 387, 389

SDLIP, *see* Social Democratic and Labour Party

Semtex, 583, 584, 590

Separatist, The, 234

'Setting the Record Straight', 644n

Shankill Butchers Gang, 379, 455, 655

Shergar, 523

Sheriffs office, Dublin, raid on, 47

Shoot-to-kill policy, 575–80, 582, 597–8, 608, 622

Shorts Brothers, 526

Sinn Fein, xv, xxii, 21–5, 37, 39–41, 48, 50–4, 255, 304, 307, 329, 330–1, 366, 367, 580, 585, 609, 610, 613, 617, 620–2, 631, 635, 636, 638, 639–56, 665; ceasefire wrangles, 658–9; new constitution and plans, 258–9; in North, 165–6, 358, 379, 410, 413, 417, 435, 440, 467, 502–4; not invited to Forum, 506; oath, Orange version of, 252, 342; peace talks, 668; resolution at 1925 Ard Fheis, 52; support following hunger strikes, 480, 497, 498, 502–3; Workers Party, 435, 459

Sinn Fein clubs, 44–5; *see also* Decommissioning issue; Good Friday Agreement; Mitchell Commission

Skylark Singing Her Lonely Song, The (Sands), 499

'Smashing of the Van' (ballad), 15

Social Democratic and Labour Party, 658, 729; in elections, 499, 505, 511, 611, 613, 630, 632; and Forum talks, 506; *Green Book* view of, 506, 662; origins of, 358; and Orange extremists, 358–9; at Sunningdale, 352; threat from Sinn Fein, 498; weakening influence, 359

Soloheadbeag, 24

South Africa, 602–3

Southern Volunteers, 17–18

Soviet Union, 435

Spanish Civil War, 41, 114, 122, 167, 209–10

Special Air Services (SAS), 405, 458, 460, 575–9, 582, 591, 597–600, 606–8, 658

Special Branch, 140, 146; relations with IRA, 148, 192, 275, 280; reorganized, 132

Special Category Status, 481, 485, 486–7, 630, 631

Special Constabulary, 721

Special Powers Act, 164

Special Powers Act (North), 306, 465n

Special Powers Tribunal (Dublin), 60

Splinter groups, 704–9

Spycatcher, 605

'Staff Report' (1977), 465–7

Stalker inquiry, 602, 605, 622

Standing Order Number Eight, 257, 478, 536, 545

Stirling Armament Co. Ltd, 432n

Stock Exchange, London, 585

Stone Cold, 599n, 603n

Stormont parliament, xxi, 5, 26, 39, 166, 280, 293, 287–8, 333; Executive, 672; Framework Document, 673; suspension of, 342, 345, 351, 356, 420, 445, 674

Strabane, 309, 405

Strikes, 79, 82; hunger strikes, 140–6, 343, 410–28, 480, 488–500, 631, 634; Loyalist strikes, 448, 450, 527; strip strikes, 187–90, 199, 200; Ulster Workers Council Strike (1974), 351, 448

Strip-searching, 517

Sullivan Principles, 478n

Sun, 579

Sunday Independent, The, 285, 376n, 614

Sunday Times, The, 438, 469n, 650, 679

Sunday Tribune, 729

Sunningdale Agreement, 350, 356, 361, 397, 399, 448, 461, 472, 473, 504, 511, 624

'Supergrass' methods, 518–21

Sweden, arms trafficking, 676

Tara Organization, 379, 604

Tenant Association, 89

Tenant Leagues, 81

Thames Television, 579

There will be Another Day, 62

Thiepbal Barracks bomb, 709

Times, The, 204, 288, 608

Tonight (BBC), 469n

Toronto, Canada, 594

Tower of London, 386

Tower Stream, 434

Tralee, 84

Treaty, the, *see* Anglo-Irish Treaty

Treaty ports, 149, 202–6

'Triangle', the, 15

Tribunal on Strip-Searching, 517

Trinity College, 9, 27, 31

Trace, the, 25–6

TUAS, 729

Tuberculosis campaign, 250

Tyrone, Co., 16, 133, 175

Ulster Army Council, 447

Ulster Clubs, 511

Ulster Covenant (1912), 9–10, 21, 23